S0-AXJ-560

Handbook of Federal Countries, 2002

Handbook of Federal Countries, 2002

Edited by
ANN L. GRIFFITHS

Coordinated by
KARL NERENBERG

Published for

by

McGill-Queen's University Press
Montreal & Kingston · London · Ithaca

ISBN 0-7735-2419-3

Legal deposit third quarter 2002
Bibliothèque nationale du Québec

Printed in Canada on acid-free paper

McGill-Queen's University Press acknowledges the financial support of the Government of Canada through the Book Publishing Industry Development Program (BPIDP) for its publishing activities. We also acknowledge the support of the Canada Council for the Arts for our publishing program.

This book is also available in French under the title *Guide des pays fédérés, 2002*.

National Library of Canada Cataloguing in Publication Data

Main entry under title:
Handbook of federal countries, 2002
Includes bibliographical references and index.
ISBN 0-7735-2419-3
1. Federal government – Handbooks, manuals, etc.
I. Griffiths, Ann L. (Ann Lynn), 1960– II. Nerenberg, Karl III. Forum of Federations.
JC355.H35 2002 321.02′02′02 C2001-904311-2

This book was typeset by Dynagram Inc.
in 10/12 Baskerville.

Contents

Tables

Preface

For more than two centuries federalism has provided an example of how people can live together even as they maintain their diversity. While the implosion of the former Yugoslavia illustrates that federalism does not, and cannot, provide a panacea to every political entity, the abiding success of federalism in other countries indicates that it is a system worth examining.

The Forum of Federations does exactly this. The Forum is an international non-profit organization that acts as a clearing house for information and resources on federalism. It is dedicated to the notion that the people who live and work in the various situations that we call "federal" – and others who may wish to adopt some or all of the principles of federalism – can benefit from talking to, and learning from, each other.

The work of the Forum of Federations is part of a broader effort worldwide to build and strengthen democracy. In the contemporary world, democracy often has to take root and grow in settings that are complex, diverse and vast. Just consider such countries as Brazil, Nigeria and Russia. For these and many other countries a healthy democracy almost seems to demand the adoption or maintenance of an effective federal system. This is the Forum's particular focus: working to enhance democracy through federalism. There is, of course, no simple prescription for achieving an "effective federal system," and it must be noted that whatever the value of sharing knowledge and expertise internationally, the experiences of one federation cannot automatically be applied to another.

The "practitioners" of federalism around the world, however, are discovering that they have something to gain from sharing experiences, lessons they have learned and practices that work best in a variety of situations. The idea of such a sharing process may be relatively new, but the Forum has discovered an eager appetite in many parts of the world for knowledge and expertise in the field of federal governance. And from what we have witnessed in our international activities thus far, it seems that learning how others deal with matters such as fiscal equalization, ethnic and linguistic diversity, and inter-governmental relations helps those involved in the delicate and complex enterprise of governance understand their own challenges more clearly.

It is for this reason that we have produced this book. We saw a need to put some basic information about all the federations of the world in one place for easy and convenient reference. There have been other extremely valuable books on comparative federalism published in the past – in particular, the late Daniel J. Elazar's *Federal Systems of the World: A Handbook of Federal, Confederal and Autonomy Arrangements* (2nd edition 1994), and Ronald L. Watts' *Comparing Federal Systems* (1999) – which have provided an inspiration to us as we worked on this project. We believe that this book provides an excellent companion to these earlier volumes.

This *Handbook of Federal Countries* includes articles about 25 countries that either classify themselves as federations, or incorporate enough elements to make it useful to include them in a study of federalism. In selecting countries to be included we tried to limit ourselves to those that can be reasonably described as federations, although there are borderline cases. Some countries call themselves federal even though they are extremely centralized. Others eschew the label even though they have many federal features, and yet others have constitutions outlining the principles and institutions of federalism which are currently in abeyance or completely ignored. The rule we have followed is if a country walks and talks like a federation (regardless of how it describes itself), we have included it in this volume. In the same way, if a country chooses to call itself federal even though many experts might dispute its right to that appellation, we, as a general rule, have included it here.

We cannot escape the fact that "federal," "federalist" and "federalism" are, in many parts of the world, controversial and emotionally-charged words. Political groups of all stripes have chosen to call themselves or their programs "federal/federalist," just as "progressive," "democratic" and "popular" have been appropriated over the years to the aims of every possible political program and ideology. Part of our purpose here is to take an examination and consideration of federalism out of the realm of ideology and polemic. The point of this book is to look dispassionately at how federal countries (broadly defined) actually function.

Each of the 25 country articles included herein – which were written by authors around the world – contains four sections in which the development, institutions and dynamics of federalism in that country are examined. These sections are: (1) History and Development of Federalism; (2) Constitutional Provisions Relating to Federalism; (3) Recent Political Dynamics; and (4) Sources for Further Information. As well, we have included maps of each of the 25 countries which give the borders of the constituent units and the location of the country. And, finally, each of the country chapters includes two statistical tables giving information on political and geographic indicators (Table I) and economic and social indicators (Table II).

It is clear that federal countries share not only many characteristics, but also similar problems and challenges at the beginning of the new millennium. It was with this thought in mind that we have also included four comparative papers in the book, each examining a theme that is of broad concern to practitioners and citizens of federal countries. The first comparative paper, "Federalism and Foreign Policy: Comparative Answers to Globalization," by Dr. Nelson Michaud, examines the conduct of foreign policy in an era of globalization which increasingly trenches on the jurisdiction of constituent units, and which, accordingly, increasingly involves the active participation of these units. The second comparative paper, "Federal Political Systems and the Accommodation of National Minorities" by Dr. John McGarry, examines an issue that is much in the minds of politicians and academics the world over – how federalism has been used, and can be used, to accommodate minorities. The third comparative paper, "The Distribution of Powers, Responsibilities and Resources in Federations" by Dr. Ronald L. Watts, examines an issue that is of concern to each federal country, and that is how resources and power are distributed. The final comparative paper, "Asymmetric Federalism as a Comprehensive Framework of Regional Autonomy" by Dr. Peter Pernthaler, uses the European context to examine issues relating to regional autonomy and federalism.

As with any information about the human species and its social and political organization, what you find between the covers of this volume started to become out-dated from the moment it was committed to paper (or to computer hard drive). Nonetheless, we have done our best to assure that all the information we provide is as current – and as accurate – as possible. The Forum will make updated information available on its website, www.forumfed.org.

We believe that this *Handbook* will be useful to students, researchers and "practitioners" of federalism and governance. It will also be of interest to anyone who has a fascination with learning how the world works. We at the Forum can already attest to the usefulness of the book – even before its publication Forum staff have been consulting selected chapters as they prepare for projects and missions.

We offer this book in the belief that we can all profit from each other's experiences. We hope it fills a gap in international knowledge about federal systems. We also hope that in some small way it advances basic human and democratic values – those values that federalism was, from the outset, designed to serve.

We cannot conclude this Preface without mentioning some of the people who have made this project a success. We have had help and encouragement from many quarters. We would like to acknowledge the assistance of the Forum's liaison organizations around the world – these contacts have provided valuable advice and suggestions for the country articles and the tables, as well as assistance in general for the project. We would like to thank Dr. John Kincaid who contributed the insightful "Introduction" to this book. We would also like to thank Mr. James Boxall, Head of the Map and Geospatial Information Collection at Dalhousie University, and his colleagues, particularly Jennifer Ashmore Smith, for producing the maps for this book, and Ms. Christine Arab, Mr. Graham Walker and Ms. Christie E. Dennison for their hard work in producing the statistical tables and tracking down the information to fill them. Without the assistance of these people, this book would not have been possible. Thank you.

Ann Griffiths
Editor

Karl Nerenberg
Project Coordinator

Handbook of Federal Countries, 2002

Introduction

JOHN KINCAID

Creation of the Forum of Federations in 1999 and publication of this handbook, as well as the growth of the International Association of Centers for Federal Studies in recent years, all reflect the increasing interest in federalism itself and the spread of federal ideas during the past decade.[1] In 1968, Carl J. Friedrich, a prominent Harvard political scientist, suggested that federalism was not, as many observers then believed, an anomaly in the modern era but rather a mode of governance that was moving to the forefront of political necessity and desirability in the second half of the twentieth century.[2] This was a prescient observation, especially at a time when federalism seemed to be retreating rather than advancing. In the United States of America, the archetype of the modern federal polity, federalism had become widely associated with the racism of southern states' rights. Elsewhere, several formally federal countries, such as the USSR, were actually highly centralized authoritarian or totalitarian regimes. A number of federal experiments had come to failure, while new federations, such as India, were experiencing centralization and developmental difficulties or,

1 See also, Daniel J. Elazar (ed.), *Federal Systems of the World: A Handbook of Federal, Confederal, and Autonomy Arrangements* (2nd ed., Essex, UK: Longman, 1994).

2 Carl J. Freidrich, *Trends of Federalism in Theory and Practice* (New York: Praeger, 1968).

more severely, civil war and corrupt military rule, as in Nigeria. Three older federal democracies – Australia, Canada and Switzerland – prospered contentedly but rather invisibly behind the dramatic conflicts of the Cold War. Germany had built a successful federal democracy on the rubble of the Nazi era, Austria had reconstituted federalism, and a small group of Western European countries was slowly building an economic union, but these, too, seemed like sideshows on a continent in which dictatorships still outnumbered democracies. The United Nations, a global federal experiment of sorts, was a hot-air balloon grounded by the deadweights of nationalism and superpower rivalry.

Yet, the publication of this handbook is a sign that the times have changed since 1968, so much so that as Carlos Fuentes wrote in 1990, "My hope is that we will witness a reevaluation of the federalist theme as a compromise between three equally real forces – the nation, the region and the world. To this end, *The Federalist Papers* should be distributed in the millions."[3] What happened between Friedrich's prescience and Fuentes' advocacy was the fall of the Berlin Wall in 1989. This was a monumental event that marked the collapse of an empire, ended the more than 40-year-old Cold War, unleashed democratic and nationalist forces worldwide, and discredited political theories and practices that had legitimized command-and-control centralization in the name of abstractions such as the people, democracy and nationhood.

THE FEDERALIST FERMENT

The painfully constructed union in Western Europe is now the European Union (EU), a body that is in the process of enlarging considerably.[4] The EU is a remarkable accomplishment in light of the centuries of war and terror that have plagued the continent. Federal Germany, now united, is a key leader in the European Union; Belgium has become formally federal; Spain's post-fascist state is quasi-federal; Austria sustains its federal system; and Switzerland, still outside the European Union, remains a robust federation with a newly revised constitution. These successes are countered partly, how-

3 Carlos Fuentes, "Federalism Is the Great Healer," *Los Angeles Times*, 16 December 1990, p. M1.

4 John Kincaid, "Confederal Federalism and Citizen Representation in the European Union," *West European Politics*, Vol. 22, No. 2 (April 1999), pp. 34–58.

ever, with the failure, or potential failure of several other European federations. Thus, Czechoslovakia is now two countries, Slovakia and the Czech Republic. Yugoslavia experienced traumatic disintegration into a shadow of its former self, and with a new federal arrangement, Bosnia-Herzegovina, having been carved out of former Yugoslav territory and now under Western military guarantees. Sprawling Russia, the largest geographic remnant of the USSR, with its 89 constituent units and thousands of nuclear weapons, is severely strained by centrifugal and centripetal forces, among other problems. These three cases – Czechoslovakia, Soviet Russia and Yugoslavia – however, were federal only in form, not in reality.

In Africa, the Middle East and Asia/Oceania, federalism has had mixed success. In Africa, Nigeria is again embarked on an effort to make democratic civilian government work; Ethiopia has established a federal democracy with a right of secession in its constitution; and post-apartheid South Africa established a quasi-federal democracy. However, the Federal Islamic Republic of the Comoros continues to be a fractious and troubled arrangement, and Senegambia was dissolved in 1989.

The Middle East is one region where federalism has not gained a firm foothold. The United Arab Emirates is the only entity in the region that has adopted federal principles. It consists of seven emirates in a federal-type alliance of chieftains. In Asia, India has sustained its federal "Union of States" for more than 50 years, but it is facing significant changes arising from the decline of the Congress Party and the end of the Cold War. Pakistan, again experiencing military rule, has had considerable difficulty building federalism and democracy. Malaysia, one of the few federations to expel a member (i.e., Singapore in 1965), remains highly centralized and troubled by ethnic conflict. The Federated States of Micronesia continues to be a federal country more as a result of its US trusteeship status than internal cohesion. Australia's federal system, however, has celebrated 100 years of democratic prosperity, and with the British Crown still in place.

In the Americas, the last decade witnessed the revival of more federal and democratic governments in Argentina, Brazil and Mexico, but oil-rich Venezuela, though nominally federal, is still held tightly by the centre. In the Caribbean, the Federation of St. Kitts and Nevis, the remnant of the short-lived British West Indies Federation, continues to be an uneasy marriage. Canada, however, remains one federation, with Quebec still in the fold, and carefully balanced mechanisms of accommodation and toleration sustain a prosperous, democratic federal polity. The United States, which became the world's only superpower in the 1990s, also experienced a revival of its more traditional federalist principles during the 1990s, especially in decisions emanating from the US Supreme Court – the umpire of the country's constitutional federal system. In so doing, the Court reiterated a more general point about the ends of federalism.

> The Constitution does not protect the sovereignty of States for the benefit of the States or state governments as abstract political entities, or even for the benefit of the public officials governing the States ... the Constitution divides authority between federal and state governments for the protection of individuals. State sovereignty is not just an end in itself: "Rather, federalism secures to citizens the liberties that derive from the diffusion of sovereign power."[5]

The federalist ferment afoot today is broader than ever because federalism is one of the key elements of debates and discussions about democratization, decentralization, marketization, individual rights protection, and minority community guarantees. The federalist ferment is very much a searching reaction against the era of highly centralized nation-states which so often proved to be internally oppressive and externally aggressive. As the case studies in this handbook clearly indicate, federalism can be an extraordinarily successful and democratic mode of governance; yet, it can also be a difficult mode of governance to bring into being and maintain over time.

The federalist ferment also reflects the necessity and desirability of federalism rather than statism in the twenty-first century.[6] The necessity for federalism lies in the need to develop modes of inter-governmental governance for our global village that can perform functions that progressively extend outside the competent reach of one's home, village, city, province, nation-state, region and continent. Such new modes of governance and orders of government cannot and should not be imposed by a central power but, rather, constructed by the coming together of all who live on the planet. The desirability of federalism lies in, among other things, its commitment to diversity rather than homogeneity and in its promise not to obliterate one's home, village, city, province, nation, region, or continent in the course of delegating powers to general and functional jurisdictions of larger territorial scope. This desirability is also a necessity insofar as the world's many diverse

---

5 *New York v. United States*, 505 U.S. 144 (1992).

6 Daniel J. Elazar, "From Statism to Federalism: A Paradigm Shift," *Publius: The Journal of Federalism*, Vol. 25, No. 2 (Winter 1995), pp. 5–18.

racial, ethnic, religious, linguistic and nationality communities seek to retain their identities. These identities must be accommodated if the world is to move away from statism toward federalism.

WHAT IS FEDERALISM?

Federalism is essentially a system of voluntary self-rule and shared rule.[7] This is implied in the derivation of the word "federal," which comes from the Latin *foedus*, meaning covenant.[8] A covenant signifies a binding partnership among co-equals in which the parties to the covenant retain their individual identity and integrity while creating a new entity, such as a family or a body politic, that has its own identity and integrity as well. A covenant also signifies a morally binding commitment in which the partners behave toward each other in accord with the spirit of the law rather than merely the letter of the law. Thus, the binding agreement is more than a contract. A covenant commits the parties to an enduring, even perpetual, relationship and to an obligation to cooperate to achieve the ends of the agreement and to resolve peacefully the conflicts that invariably arise in every relationship.

Federalism, then, can be said to be both a structure and a process of governance that establishes unity on the basis of consent while preserving diversity by constitutionally uniting separate political communities into a limited, but encompassing, polity. Powers are divided and shared between constituent governments and a general government having certain nation-wide, continent-wide, or world-wide responsibilities. This division of powers is combined with authoritative capacity to carry out those responsibilities on behalf of the people of the federal polity. Hence, the constituent governments also have broad local responsibilities and sufficiently autonomous self-government to carry out their responsibilities on behalf of their own people in concert with the whole people of the federal polity. The distribution of powers is intended to protect the integral authority of both the general and the constituent governments as well as the existence of their respective communities. A democratic federation is, in effect, a republic of republics, which emphasizes partnership and cooperation for the common good, while also allowing diversity and competition to foster liberty and efficiency.

7 Daniel J. Elazar, *Exploring Federalism* (Tuscaloosa, AL: University of Alabama Press, 1987), p. 5.

8 Daniel J. Elazar and John Kincaid (eds), *The Covenant Connection: From Federal Theology to Modern Federalism* (Lanham, MD: Lexington Books, 2000).

Advocates of federalism view it as a way to establish peace and security, and to construct common values and an overarching identity while still fostering pluralist democracy. They also view it as a way of protecting and also moderating human diversity, guarding against centralized tyranny by either a minority or a majority, and preserving both individual and communitarian liberty. As well, it can be seen as a way of promoting common-market prosperity, enhancing citizen participation and local self-government, giving citizens multiple points of access to public power, allowing citizens freedom to make choices among government jurisdictions, encouraging creative experimentation (e.g., the constituent units as laboratories of democracy and policy innovation), and improving public service efficiency by enabling governments to provide public goods that are economically appropriate to their territorial jurisdiction. Federalism can also be seen as a means to promote justice in a variety of ways, including matching the benefits of government closely to the burdens of paying for government, fostering mutual aid, and recognizing, within limits, diverse conceptions of justice held by the peoples of the constituent political communities.

Critics of federalism argue that it is a complex and complicated mode of governance that is slow to respond to change and challenges. They claim, as well, that it is inherently given to inequality and uneven development across jurisdictions, prone to wasteful duplication of functions and services, rife with recalcitrant veto points, cumbersome in implementing policy, and subject to decision-making paralysis.

STRUCTURAL VARIETIES AND PROCEDURAL FUNDAMENTALS OF FEDERALISM

In terms of constitutional design and government structure, federal arrangements can, and do, take many forms. Although there are some general guidelines for appropriately allocating functions in a federal system (e.g., equity, accountability, externalities and economies of scale), there is no one best, or ideal, federal constitution or structure of government, and no universal list of which functions or competences must be assigned to the general government and which to the constituent governments. As well, there is no one best way to mix delegated, enumerated, implied, inherent, exclusive, plenary, concurrent and reserved (or residual) powers in a federal democracy. In Canada, for example, the reserved powers lie with the federal government; in the United States, the reserved powers lie with the constituent states. A federal system can be parliamentary, presidential, or some hybrid. Ordinarily, a federal system has an umpire, usually a high court, that can resolve inter-governmental and inter-jurisdictional conflicts. High courts vary in their structures and powers, however, and recourse in some federations may be made to the people as the ultimate umpire. In these respects, there are varieties of federalism.[9]

In terms of process, there appear to be certain fundamentals characteristic of successful federal democracies. One is continual inter-governmental consultation and negotiation within and outside of the formal institutions of government, including diverse mechanisms for citizen participation and rules of public transparency. The outcomes of inter-governmental negotiations must ultimately be accepted by the people. Another is inter-governmental cooperation, especially a pragmatic approach to solving public problems. In the final analysis, all governments in a federal democracy serve all the people. Such cooperation is highly formalized and institutionalized in some federations; in others, it is fluid and informal. There is a need for federal loyalty as well, *Bundestreue* or *loyauté fédérale*. Federal loyalty is the moral commitment to work together to achieve the objectives and fulfill the needs of the federal polity. Federal comity is the willingness to compromise, exercise forbearance, and understand the point of view of others. At the same time, some inter-governmental and inter-jurisdictional competition is vital as well – to restrain power, promote efficiency, and foster innovation. Such competition is enhanced when there is freedom of mobility for citizens.

Generally, each government needs sufficient autonomous capacity – legislative, administrative, fiscal, and the like – to fulfill its duties rather than being dependent on, and thus potentially subservient to, another order of government. Most often, it is the allocation of revenues and especially of revenue-raising authority that is most contentious. For purposes of democratic accountability, it is best to keep spending and taxing authority tied together; that is, any politician who experiences the pleasure of spending tax money on constituents ought first to experience the pain of extracting it from his or her constituents. Inter-governmental transfers, or grants-in-aid, separate the acts of spending and taxing by giving one order of government the pleasure of spending while shifting the pain of taxation to another. However, for many historical and political reasons, all federations engage in inter-governmental transfers. Frequently, these transfers reflect a desire by the national government to maintain control over the constituent governments by decentralizing revenue expenditures while centralizing revenue-raising

---

9 Valeria Earle (ed.), *Federalism: Infinite Variety in Theory and Practice* (Itasca, IL: F.E. Peacock, 1968).

authority. Most federations engage in fiscal equalization, whereby the federal government (and sometimes wealthy constituent units too) supply revenue to poor constituent governments in order to lift their fiscal capacity for service provision up to the national average or to fulfill a constitutional command, such as the provision for "uniform living standards" in Germany's Basic Law.

FEDERALIZING OR DECENTRALIZING CENTRALIZED SYSTEMS

Historically, federalism has involved a coming together of separate, independent communities in classic covenantal fashion. In the late twentieth century, however, many efforts emerged to federalize previously centralized, dictatorial regimes by deconstructing the centre and deconcentrating powers so as to reconstitute the polity on a federal basis. Such efforts are novel and important experiments in federalism. However, even though the process is different from the classic pattern, the end requirement is the same; the constituent political communities that emerge from beneath the pall of suppression must still want to stay together. It is a process of coming apart and then voluntarily coming back together again. This process can be symmetrical, in which all the constituent units reach a federal bargain on an equal footing at about the same constitutional moment. Alternatively, it can be an asymmetrical process, in which the various constituent units obtain different levels of self-governing autonomy through bilateral constitutional agreements or treaties with the deconstructing centre or through a general constitutional provision that allows constituent political communities to assume more self-governing autonomy at variable speeds according to their preferences and capacities.

It is the coming apart stage of deconstruction, however, that often raises the most alarm about federalism, principally the fear that in coming apart, the constituent units will not unite again. Nationalist leaders, therefore, often decry federalism and reject it as a subterfuge for secession or a route to disintegration. At best, they express support for devolution or decentralization while assiduously avoiding the "F" word.[10] Although such resistance to federalism can itself be a subter-

10 John Kincaid, "Values and Value Tradeoffs in Federalism," *Publius: The Journal of Federalism*, Vol. 23, No. 1 (Spring 1995), pp. 29–44; Gabriele Ferrazzi, "Using the 'F' Word: Federalism in the Indonesian Decentralization Discourse," *Publius: The Journal of Federalism*, Vol. 30, No. 2 (Spring 2000), pp. 63–85.

fuge for resisting democratization, the possibility of disintegration of a formally centralized state is always present, especially where constituent racial, ethnic, religious and/or linguistic communities have experienced severe oppression or genocidal assaults. Even a minimum level of trust needed for federalization may not be present. However, efforts to hold onto centralized power and impose unity can exacerbate disintegration or else destroy both federalism and democracy.

Given that most nation-states are multi-national or multi-cultural, one of the leading appeals of federalism in recent decades has been its potential for accommodating racial, ethnic, religious and linguistic political communities within a single polity. Switzerland is the most venerable and successful model of this potential. Spain is a recent example of a deconstructing system thus far successfully accommodating such diversity. Canada is viewed by many citizens of Quebec as a compact between two peoples rather than as a federation of ten provinces, and India is a cacophony of multi-nationalism and multi-culturalism. Although such potential is clearly evident in federalism, it is also evident that federal accommodations of such diversity are difficult and delicate achievements. Yet, this points back to the seeming necessity of federalism; otherwise, what is the alternative? A centralized unitary system might hold a multi-national or multi-cultural society together, but the price of togetherness where the constituent communities do not really wish to be together may be the sacrifice of democracy and the burden of authoritarian rule. Such rule often fails as well, as indicated by the high levels of ethno-religious conflict and bloodshed in so many nation-states.

FEDERALISM VERSUS DECENTRALIZATION

There is, therefore, usually more interest in the decentralization of centralized systems than in federalism. The reason is simple. Federalism entails a level of political autonomy, even sovereignty, for constituent communities that rests uneasily, even threateningly, with traditional or elite conceptions of national unity. Federalism involves a polycentric non-centralized arrangement in which neither the constituent governments nor the general government can unilaterally alter the constitutional distribution of power. As Friedrich noted:

> A federal order typically preserves the institutional and behavioral features of a *foedus*, a compact between equals to act jointly on specific issues of general policy. Effective separate representation of the component units for the purpose of participating in legislation and the shaping of public policy, and, more espe-

cially, effective separate representation in the amending of the constitutional charter itself may be said to provide reasonably precise criteria for a federal as contrasted with a merely decentralized order of government.[11]

Decentralization involves a central power possessing authority to decentralize or devolve functional and administrative responsibilities to lower levels of government. The authority to decentralize, however, also includes the authority to *re*centralize power. Decentralization is concerned with administrative efficiency and functional efficacy in an otherwise unitary system.

This is not to say, however, that federal systems are not more or less centralized in terms of the balance of power between the general and constituent governments. In principle, a federal system can be more constitutionally and/or politically centralized than a decentralized unitary system. In turn, decentralization can occur in a federal system when the general government transfers shares of its own revenue, delegates implementation authority, and assigns administrative responsibilities to its constituent governments. In practice, moreover, the distinction between federalism and decentralization can be blurred where lower levels of government in decentralized unitary systems seek to enshrine autonomy guarantees of a federal nature in ordinary law or the constitution and where constituent governments in federal systems find their powers of self-government being eroded by the national government and replaced by mere administrative discretion.

CHALLENGES TO THE FUTURE OF FEDERALISM

The potential erosion of constituent self-government in federal systems has become of heightened concern in today's era of regional integration and globalization. In Western Europe, for example, regional and local governments, as well as national governments, have ceded considerable authority to the European Union. As well, global free-trade regimes, such as the World Trade Organization, pose threats to a wide range of constituent government powers that can generate non-tariff trade barriers. Meanwhile, global market competition places pressures on federal and unitary systems to deconcentrate or decentralize certain powers in order to give constituent governments more

11 Friedrich, *Trends of Federalism in Theory and Practice*, p. 6.

freedom and capacity to compete for investment and tourists, and to export local goods and services in the global marketplace.

The accommodation of human diversity, however, remains the leading challenge for federalism. It is also the leading challenge for the world. The flowering of cultural and national identities has created conflict worldwide. Equitable, democratic resolutions of these conflicts will require negotiated governance arrangements of a federal nature within and between nation-states.

At the same time, issues of environmental protection, global equity, and world peace all point to a need to employ federal principles and practices to help guarantee the future against catastrophe.

PART ONE

Country Articles

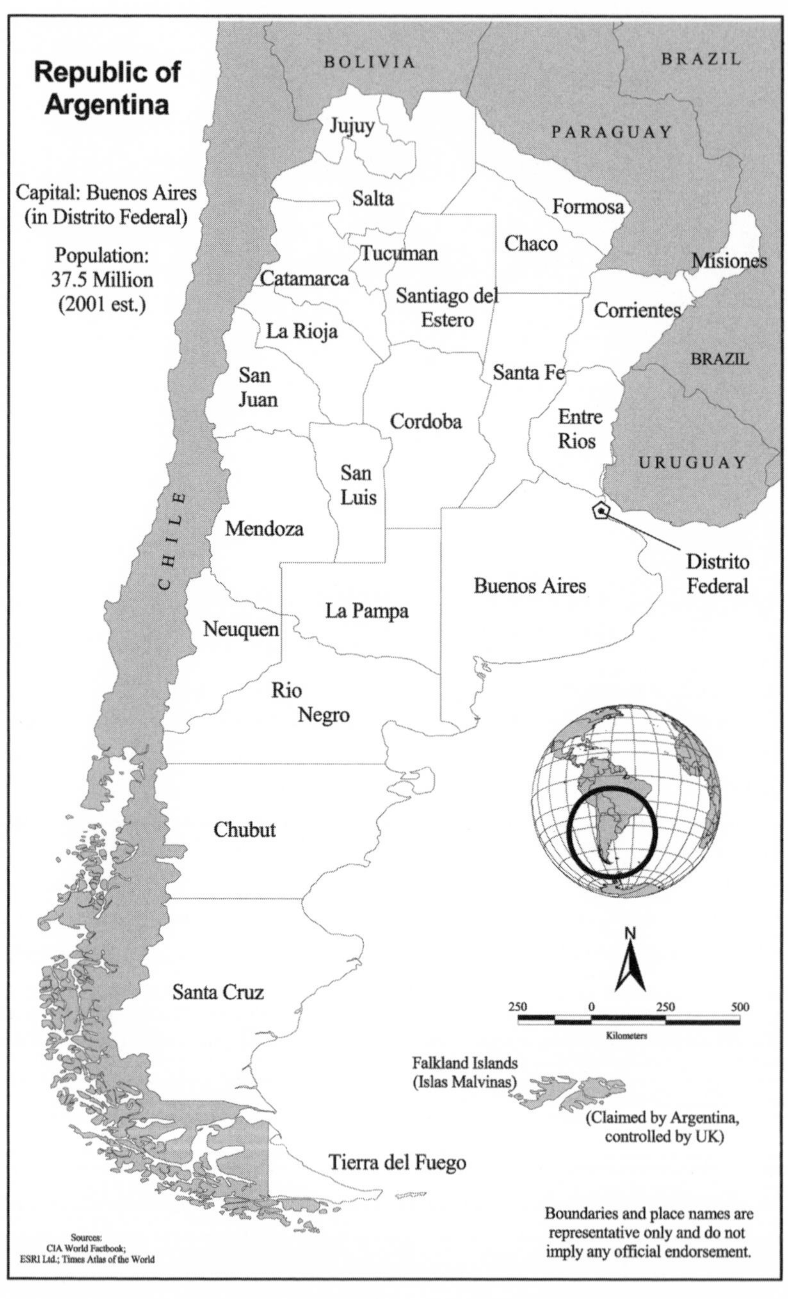

Republic of Argentina
Capital: Buenos Aires (in Distrito Federal)
Population: 37.5 Million (2001 est.)
BOLIVIA
BRAZIL
PARAGUAY
BRAZIL
URUGUAY
CHILE
Jujuy
Salta
Formosa
Chaco
Tucuman
Misiones
Catamarca
Santiago del Estero
Corrientes
La Rioja
San Juan
Santa Fe
Cordoba
Entre Rios
San Luis
Mendoza
Distrito Federal
Buenos Aires
La Pampa
Neuquen
Rio Negro
Chubut
Santa Cruz
N
250 0 250 500
Kilometers
Falkland Islands (Islas Malvinas)
(Claimed by Argentina, controlled by UK)
Tierra del Fuego
Boundaries and place names are representative only and do not imply any official endorsement.
Sources: CIA World Factbook; ESRI Ltd.; Times Atlas of the World

Argentina*
(*Argentine Republic*)

VIVIANA PATRONI

1 HISTORY AND DEVELOPMENT OF FEDERALISM

Argentina is located in the southern cone of South America, stretching over an area of almost 2.8 million square kilometres and encompassing several very diverse geographical regions. The population of the country is approximately 37 million (2000 estimate).

The first Spanish settlement in the territories that now encompass Argentina dates back to 1526. What was to become Argentina's main port and city, Buenos Aires, was founded in 1536 but was abandoned, due to repeated attacks by the native population, until 1580 when it was re-established. The colonization of the territory was mostly undertaken from neighbouring countries in the north.

The attempts to organize a national state began immediately after the first proclamation against Spanish rule and the overthrow of the Viceroy in May 1810. As with the rest of the continent, independence (which was declared at a congress of provincial representatives on 9 July 1816) was followed by a long period of civil wars, economic decline, the weakening of central authority, and the emergence of dictatorial regimes. In the particular case of Argentina, this was also accompanied by the loss of vast territories that until then had belonged

* The Forum of Federations would like to thank Jorge Horacio Lavopa for his comments on this article.

to the Viceroyalty. While independence was sought as a means to advance the commercial opportunities the elites longed for, the institutional means to provide for the political stability required to achieve this objective proved highly elusive.

The economic aspirations of regional leaders sometimes came into conflict with the interests of the Buenos Aires elites. Conflict over the nature of the relationship between the provinces and Buenos Aires and the particular way in which their diverse interests could come to constitute a nation acquired preeminence in the post-independence period. On one side of the conflict were those primarily, but not exclusively, represented by the Buenos Aires elite – the 'unitarians' – who believed that the most expedient form of organizing the country and guaranteeing political stability was through a strong central government and the elimination of provincial autonomy. The opposing forces were unified under the principle of federalism, maintaining that autonomy and self-government for the provinces was the only way of establishing political control in a country of such proportion and diversity.

The clash between these two forces characterized the first half-century of independence in the country. As unitarian forces in Buenos Aires pushed for the acceptance of legal reforms centralizing power, military leaders (*caudillos*) in the interior of the country fought to maintain their autonomy. As the struggle between unitarians and federalists intensified, any vestige of national authority vanished, and the attempts to unify the country under the aegis of Buenos Aires were not only unsuccessful but in many respects also generated deeper fractures. Nonetheless, several inter-provincial treaties signed during this period provided the basis for the eventual reconstruction of the country. Such was the case with the Federal Pact of 1831, which is considered to be the immediate legal antecedent to the constitution that eventually came to give institutional form to the state in Argentina. Nonetheless, the achievement of a general agreement on the possible political organization of the country was only reached in 1853, but at the cost of the secession of the province of Buenos Aires. This province sanctioned its own constitution in 1854 and retained its independence until the defeat of its army by the military forces of the Argentine confederation in 1859. Although defeated in battle, the need to preserve the interests of Buenos Aires explained the reforms introduced to the new constitution in 1860.

Notably, the unification of the country with the constitution of 1853 coincided with the accentuation of the economic imbalances between Buenos Aires and the rest of the country, as the fertile region surrounding the city – known as the *pampas* – gave rise to the cattle and cereal economies that propelled Argentina's insertion into the expanding world economy of the second half of the nineteenth century.

Growing economic opportunities for Argentine exports in international markets added, therefore, an extra premium in achieving the final consolidation of the country's territory and making the power of a national state effective. However, the basis for federalism was weak then and became even weaker as economic inequality among the regions grew. Power came to be increasingly centralized in Buenos Aires, and the dictatorial regimes that became a common feature in the political history of the country continued to centralize the power of the national government.

By the 1890s Argentina was a representative democracy. Politics, however, remained mostly an elite affair either because fraudulent practices restricted effective participation or because a large proportion of the electorate was foreign born. Early in the twentieth century, though, growing working class mobilization and middle class demands for political reform prompted changes in electoral laws that made the political process more inclusive. While these changes did not directly threaten the interests of the elite, the effect of the Depression of 1929 significantly altered the basis for the consensus that had allowed the opening up of the political arena. In 1930 conservative forces put an end to the democratic practices that had marked Argentina as a special case in the context of Latin America and initiated a period marked by authoritarian rule, limited democracy and political instability that lasted until 1983.

The period of 'oligarchic' rule initiated in 1930 was interrupted by the military coup of 1943 which provided the political platform from which Juan Domingo Perón was to emerge as the most powerful figure of the period. In the decade between his rise to power and the military coup that deposed him in 1955, Perón altered politics in the country in a radical way, particularly by transforming the working class and its organizations into key political players. Far from bringing back the order the military had sought, displacing Perón from power only contributed to further weakening the state's legitimacy and increasing polarization. Not only did Argentina experience recurring institutional crisis, but political conflict also became increasingly violent. Until 1983 political instability was one of the main features of the country and military regimes became a common feature of Argentine politics. Moreover, military regimes acquired new characteristics, growing increasingly detached from any kind of constitutional restriction in the exercise of power. Thus, while until the 1960s military regimes had temporarily suspended important aspects of the constitutional order of the country, for example by dissolving the Congress, the last two dictatorships (1966–1973 and 1976–1983) gave themselves their own legal framework, in effect replacing, and not simply suspending, the constitution. This reached catastrophic proportions during the last dictatorship and the use of state terror for the suppression of opposition and the curtailment of all civil and political rights were its most obvious manifestation. In 1983 the Argentinean military handed over power to civilian authorities. While this period has coincided with deep economic crises, it is evident that a new consensus exists today among all political actors in Argentina about the merits of democratic rule.

2 CONSTITUTIONAL PROVISIONS RELATING TO FEDERALISM

The constitution of 1853 plus changes made in 1866, 1880, 1898, 1957 and 1994 together form the body of the current constitution of the country. Other reforms to the constitutions have been shortlived, as was the case with the reform of 1949 under the presidency of Juan Domingo Perón (declared invalid in 1956), and the reform of 1972.

The constitution of Argentina establishes a republican, representative and federal form of government. As a republic, the constitution institutes a clear division of power among the Executive, Legislative, and Judicial branches of government. As a federation, the constitution creates the legal framework for the co-existence of a national federal government and the provincial governments and the city of Buenos Aries. According to the constitution, the provinces are autonomous bodies and as such are organized through their own provincial constitutions, which regulate the existence of local political institutions. To be valid, though, these constitutions must respect the representative and republican principles embedded within the national constitution (Article 5). Nonetheless, the provinces are not sovereign since they are bound by federal legislation (Article 31) and are subject to federal control (Article 6). Moreover, under certain conditions – for example, abrogation of republican forms of government within the province, foreign intervention, sedition, or aggression against another province – the federal government can intervene in the province, including the removal and replacement of provincial authorities. Provinces retain all the power not delegated by the national constitution to the federal government and select their provincial executive, legislative and other government functionaries.

Title II, Articles 121–128 of the constitution delimit the powers assigned to the federal and provincial governments. The former has explicit and exclusive power to declare a state of siege, conduct foreign affairs and defence, set custom duties, regulate navigation in domestic rivers and the establishments of ports, print money, regulate commercial relations among provinces and with other countries, enact Civil, Commercial and Penal Codes and regulations pertaining to mining, and legislate over immigration and nationalization (Article 126). It also possesses the implicit power to exercise exclusive authority in areas where provincial provisions could interfere with the prerogatives delegated to the federal government (Article 75(32)).

Article 123 of the national constitution specifies that provinces have the power to sanction their own constitutions, select provincial government officers, monitor the implementation of environmental legislation, and preserve the primary right over natural resources in their territories. Article 124 authorizes the provinces to create inter-provincial regions and, under strictly limited conditions, to conclude international agreements. The constitution explicitly prohibits provinces from declaring war or engaging in military conflict with one another (Article 127). There are also areas in which the federal and provincial governments share power, in particular on issues related to the extension of the railway system and navigation channels, and the design of economic policy (Articles 124(1) and 125).

The federal legislative power resides in the National Congress, located in the Federal District in Buenos Aires. The National Congress is a bicameral body composed of the Chamber of National Deputies (Diputados de la Nación) and the Senate which is comprised of representatives from the provinces and the city of Buenos Aires (Article 44). In some circumstances both chambers convene together, receiving in this case the name of Legislative Assembly. Senators are elected from the provinces and the city of Buenos Aires. The constitutional reform of 1994 established the autonomy of the city of Buenos Aires (Article 129), therefore it will retain the power to elect representatives to the legislative bodies even if it were no longer to be the capital of the federation.

National deputies are elected directly through simple plurality by voters in the provinces and in the city of Buenos Aires. If the Federal District were to change location, voters in it would also have the right to participate in the selection of National Deputies. Deputies are elected for a period of four years. Half the chamber must stand for election every two years. The constitution does not specify how the Chamber of Deputies should be organized but there are regulations within this chamber that establish the existence of a President, a first and second Deputy President, two secretaries and two assistant secretaries elected by members of the Chamber.

There are three Senators for each province and the city of Buenos Aires, two from the party with the largest number of votes and one from the party with the second largest number. Senators are elected directly by voters in these districts for a period of six years. One-third of the Senate must stand for election every two years. The constitution establishes that the Vice-President of the country is the President of the Senate. Deputies and Senators must have been born in the province they represent or have at least two years of residence, and both can serve more than one term in office.

Article 14 sets out Argentina's financial arrangements. This article states that the federal government will raise the necessary resources to finance national expenditures with the funds accruing to it from export and import duties, the sale or lease of federal public land, the revenue from postal services, the taxes approved by Congress, and loans contracted for the country and approved by Congress in case of national emergencies or when required by public enterprises. With respect to the power of taxation, the constitution stipulates in Article 75(2) that Congress shares with the provinces the power to set indirect taxes. Congress also has the power to impose direct levies for a specified period of time.

The reform of 1994 explicitly mentions that the taxes raised in accordance with these regulations are to be distributed among the federal government, the provinces and the city of Buenos Aires – except for those earmarked for specific purposes – in a fashion that protects the principles of equity and solidarity, and that promotes similar degrees of development. Also, the reform of 1994 establishes that the remittance of these funds will be carried out in agreement with the terms of legal accords between the national government and the provinces. The purpose of these accords is to guarantee the automatic remittance of funds to the provinces. Congress is also responsible for the approval of a national budget.

Article 116 of the constitution designates the Supreme Court of Justice and Lower Federal Tribunals as having the power to resolve any dispute concerning the interpretation of the constitution, the laws promulgated by Congress, and international treaties. The Supreme Court is also responsible for settling disputes among the provinces (Article 127).

Provisions for the "reform" (rather than amendment) of the constitution are outlined in Article 30. According to this article, it is Congress that proclaims the need for reform through an initiative that requires at least two-thirds of the votes of its members. The constitution does not clarify whether this initiative must take the form of a bill, but most constitutional reforms have been preceded by the enactment of a law promulgated by Congress. Although Congress then declares the need for a constitutional reform, the process itself can only be undertaken by a Constituent Assembly. Members of this Constituent Assembly are always elected by popular vote. Congress also sets the electoral system through which Assembly members are to be selected and their number.

The reform of 1994 introduced a number of provisions aimed at strengthening the federal system in Argentina in an attempt to reverse the "defederalization" of the country. Concern about this "defederalization" was the main motivation in the congressional debate leading to the promulgation of the law calling for the constitutional convention (Law 24.309). As a result of these provisions, the provinces have become the recipients of new powers with respect to the monitoring of the environment, participation in the institutions responsible for the control of public services, the capacity to create special regions with the goal of promoting economic and social development, and the possibility of participating in international agreements with the knowledge of Congress. The constitution also establishes the city of Buenos Aires as an autonomous institution, independent of its status as Federal District – that is, even if its status as capital of the federation were to change.

It is important to note that the relationship between the federal government and the provinces has suffered considerably as a result of the serious fiscal crisis that has affected Argentina since the early 1980s. Problems with transfer payments to the provinces have resulted in serious tensions between them and the federal government, and have produced situations of crisis in the provinces themselves.

3 RECENT POLITICAL DYNAMICS

With the return to democracy in Argentina in 1983 the country entered a period of constitutional stability virtually unprecedented in its history. Since then, there have been four consecutive democratic elections, and transitions of power from one party to another have been peaceful. However, the country has also experienced major economic dislocations over this period of time, and poverty and unemployment have become a major concern.

Federalism has become a key area of debate, not only for its significance in terms of consolidating democratic institutions, but also because of the changes implemented in the structure of the state and the delivery of public services. Moreover, the debate has encompassed a reexamination of the factors that led to a very weak federal structure of Argentina. In this sense, the 1994 constitutional reform represents an attempt to alter the political dynamic of the country and its federal structure by addressing the most important determinants of the lack of provincial autonomy and the centralization of power in the national government. While economic limitations might make impossible the resolution of the regional disparities that constitute one of the main sources of the unequal power of the provinces, some optimism has been expressed regarding other aspects of the reform.

One of the reforms introduced in 1994 (Article 36) stresses the prevalence of the constitution even when its rule might have been interrupted through an action against the institutional order – indeed, the constitution expressly mentions "acts of force" against the constitutional order. In addition, those acts are declared irrevocably void of any legality. The importance of this proviso is to state the legal incapacity of anyone to replace the constitution or place themselves above its rule. The article also states that those people working against the constitutional order are ineligible to occupy official positions in the future or to benefit from pardon or a reduction in their sentences. However, it might leave open the possibility of an amnesty. Given the political history of Argentina, it is clear that the intent of the article is to act as a deterrent, placing the constitution above any legal manipulation or claim to legitimacy from unelected governments.

In response to the profound political consequences of Argentina's recent history, the 1994 reforms invest with constitutional status a number of international treaties and accords on human rights that should therefore be considered as additions to the rights recognized by the constitution. Among them should be mentioned the Universal Declaration of Human Rights, the American Declaration of the Rights and Duties of Man, the Convention on the Prevention and Punishment of Genocide, the Convention against Torture and Other Cruel, Inhuman and Degrading Treatments or Punishments, and the Inter-American Convention on Forced Disappearances. Finally, Argentina places within the Senate the power to approve international agreements that delegate jurisdiction to supra-national bodies.

One of the most difficult political problems faced by the current government in Argentina has been the negotiation of the federal budget with the provinces. President Fernando de la Rúa, elected in 1999 and representing an alliance between the Radial Party and FREPASO (Frente País Solidario – Front for a Country in Solidarity) known simply as "Alianza," has encountered stiff opposition from the provinces in the implementation of measures aimed at curtailing the large fiscal deficit. But his problems have also been serious on other fronts. Allegations of corruption within the Senate – in particular the acceptance of bribes by Senators as pay-offs to pass labour legislation that the government considered key for its political and economic plans – resulted in a major scandal only a few months after his government took power. Moreover, the resignation of the Vice-President, Carlos Alvarez from FREPASO, raised some serious questions about the viability and the continuing unity of the alliance that was able to wrest power from the previous Peronist administration of Carlos Menem.

Relations between the national government and the provinces have been a delicate issue for all democratic regimes since 1983. The spirit of the reforms of 1994 is to strengthen the federal system in the expectation that this will also contribute to the promotion of democracy. The task has not been easy, however, and conflict has remained a key aspect of the relationship between the federal government and the provinces, particularly over financial and budgetary issues.

4 SOURCES FOR FURTHER INFORMATION

De Ruiz, Marta V., *Manual de la Constitución Nacional*, Buenos Aires: Editorial Heliasta, 1997.

López Rosas, José Rafael, *Historia constitucional argentina*, Buenos Aires: Editorial Astrea, 1996.

Mignone, Emilio Fermín, *Constitución de la Nación Argentina, 1994: manual de la reforma*, Buenos Aires: Editorial Ruy Díaz, 1994.

Rock, David, *Argentina, 1516–1987. From Spanish Colonization to Alfonsín*, Berkeley and Los Angeles: University of California Press, 1987.

Serrafero, Mario Daniel, *Momentos institucionales y modelos constitucionales: estudios sobre la constitución nacional*, Buenos Aires: Centro Editor de América Latina, 1993.

http://www.bartleby.com/65/ar/Argentin.html

http://www.msstate.edu/listarchives/latam/200001/msg00076.html

http://www.aceproject.org/main/english/es/esy_ar/default.htm

http://www.tau.ac.il/eial/IX_2/rock.html

Table I
Political and Geographic Indicators

Capital city	Buenos Aires
Number and type of constituent units	*22 Provinces*: Buenos Aires, Catamarca, Chaco, Chubut, Córdoba, Corrientes, Entre Ríos, Formosa, Jujuy, La Pampa, La Rioja, Mendoza, Misiones, Neuquén, Rió Negro, Salta, Santiago del Estero, San Juan, San Luis, Santa Cruz, Santa Fe, Tucumán; *1 Federal District:* autonomous city of Buenos Aires; *1 National Territory*: Tierra del Fuego; *5 Regions:* Andina, Centro, Litoral, Norte, Patagonia (Note: Argentina also claims sovereignty over the Falkland/Malvinas Islands, South Georgia, the South Sandwich Islands and part of Antarctica.)
Official language(s)	Spanish
Area	2 780 400 km^2
Area – Largest constituent unit	(province of) Buenos Aires (307 571 km^2)
Area – Smallest constituent unit	Federal District: autonomous city of Buenos Aires (200 km^2)
Total population	36 233 901
Population by constituent unit (% of total population)	Buenos Aires 38.4%, Santa Fe 8.4%, Córdoba 8.3%, Autonomous City of Buenos Aires (Federal District) 8.2%, Mendoza 4.3%, Tucumán 3.5%, Entre Ríos 3.0%, Salta 2.9%, Misiones 2.7%, Chaco 2.6%, Corrientes 2.5%, Santiago del Estero 2.0%, Río Negro 1.7%, Jujuy 1.6%, San Juan 1.6%, Neuquén 1.5%, Formosa 1.4%, Chubut 1.2%, San Luis 1.0%, Catamarca 0.9%, La Pampa 0.8%, La Rioja 0.8%, Santa Cruz 0.6%, Tierra del Fuego (National Territory) 0.3%
Political system – federal	Federal Republic
Head of state – federal	President Fernando de la Rúa (1999), Unión Cívica Radical (UCR) – elected to a 4-year term by universal suffrage.
Head of government – federal	President Fernando de la Rúa (URC) formed coalition government (Alliance). Cabinet appointed by President.

Table I (continued)

Government structure – federal	Bicameral: Congreso Nacional (National Congress): *Upper House* – Senado de la Nación (Senate of the Nation), 72 Seats. Formerly, 3 members were appointed by each of the provincial legislatures. Beginning in 2001, one-third of members will be directly elected every 2 years to 6-year terms. Vice-President presides over Senate. *Lower House* – Cámara de Diputados de la Nación (Chamber of Deputies of the Nation), 257 seats. One-half of the members directly elected every 2 years for 4-year term.
Number of representatives in lower house of federal government – Chamber of Deputies of the Nation	257 Seats: Alliance 130 (Unión Cívica Radical (UCR) 82, Frepaso 32, others 16), Justicialistas 99, Acción por la República (AR) 7, other 21
Number of representatives in lower house of federal government for most populated constituent unit	Buenos Aires: 70
Number of representatives in lower house of federal government for least populated constituent unit	Tierra del Fuego: 5
Number of representatives in upper house of federal government – Senate of the Nation	72 Seats: Justicialistas 30, UCR 20, other political parties 19
Distribution of representation in upper house of federal government – Senate of the Nation	Formerly, 3 members appointed by each of the provincial legislatures, 2 from the party with the largest number of votes and 1 from the party with the second largest number of votes. Beginning in 2001, one-third of the members will be directly elected every two years to 6-year term.
Constitutional court (highest court dealing with constitutional matters)	Corte Suprema (Supreme Court). The nine Supreme Court judges are appointed by the President with approval by the Senate.
Political system of constituent units	Approximately 2/3 of Provincial Legislatures are Unicameral and the rest are Bicameral. Each are directly elected to serve a 4-year term.
Head of state – constituent units	Governor – directly elected to serve a 4-year term
Head of government – constituent units	Governor

Table II
Economic and Social Indicators

GDP	US$476 billion
GDP per capita	US$12 900
Mechanisms for taxation	Two main forms of taxation: • Income Tax: Controlled by Central Government, with seven tax brackets ranging from 9% to 35 %; • Value Added Tax (VAT): Controlled by Central and Unit governments, ranging between 10.5% to 21.5%. There are also various types of excise taxes, corporate and property taxes.
National debt (external)	US$154 billion
National unemployment rate	16%
Constituent unit with highest unemployment rate	Entre Ríos: 17.5%
Constituent unit with lowest unemployment rate	Santa Cruz: 3.6%
Adult literacy rate	96.7%
National expenditures on education as a % of GDP	4.5%
Life expectancy in years	75.05
Doctors per population ratio (national)	268.4 per 100 000 inhabitants
Doctors per population ratio in constituent units (highest)	Buenos Aires (1 doctor per 113 inhabitants)
Doctors per population ratio in constituent units (lowest)	Formosa (1 doctor per 911 inhabitants)
National expenditures on health as a % of GDP	4.0%

Sources:

Central Intelligence Agency (CIA), *World Fact Book 2000*. CIA, www.cia.gov/cia/publications/factbook/index.html

Economic Commission for Latin America and the Caribbean (ECLAC), *Statistical Yearbook for Latin America and the Caribbean 1999*. ECLAC, www.eclac.org/estaditicas

Economist Intelligence Unit, "Country Commerce – Argentina," *The Economist Intelligence Unit 2000*. New York: EIU, 2000.

Elazar, Daniel J. (ed.) *Federal Systems of the World: A Handbook of Federal, Confederal and Autonomy Arrangements.* 2nd Edition. Jerusalem Institute for Federal Studies. London: Longman Group/Westgate House, 1994.

Honorable Cámara de Diputados de la Nación (Honourable Chamber of Deputies of the Nation). www.diputados.gov.ar

Instituto Nacional de Estadística y Censos (INDEC) (National Institute of Statistics and Census) – Department of Statistics, Government of Argentina. "Argentina by Province – Population and Area," "Financial Data," Ministry of the Economy. www.indec.mecon.gov.ar/

International Monetary Fund (IMF). *International Financial Statistics,* Vol. LIII, No. 12, December 2000. Washington, DC: the IMF Statistics Department, 2000.

Latin-Focus: The Leading Source for Latin American Economies. www.latin-focus.com/index.html

Ministry of Economy, Government of Argentina. "Summary," *Fiscal Bulletin 3rd Quarter of 2000.* www.mecon.gov.ar/gaspub/ingles/summary.htm

Pan-American Health Organization (PAHO/WHO). "Argentina: Demographic Indicators and Overview." www.paho.org/

Senate of the Nation (Senado de la nación). www.senado.gov.ar

United Nations. "Human Development Index," "Gender-Related Development Index," *Human Development Report, 2000.* Human Development Report Office. www.undp.org/hdro/report.html

World Bank. *World Development Report 2000/2001: Attacking Poverty.* www.worldbank.org/poverty/wdrpoverty/report/index.htm

World Health Organisation (WHO). "Estimates of Health Personnel." www-nt.who.int/whosis/statistics

World Health Organization (WHO). "Annex Table 8, Selected national health accounts indicators for all Member States, estimates for 1997." *World Health Report 2000.* Geneva, 2000. www-nt.who.int/whosis/statistics/menu.cfm.

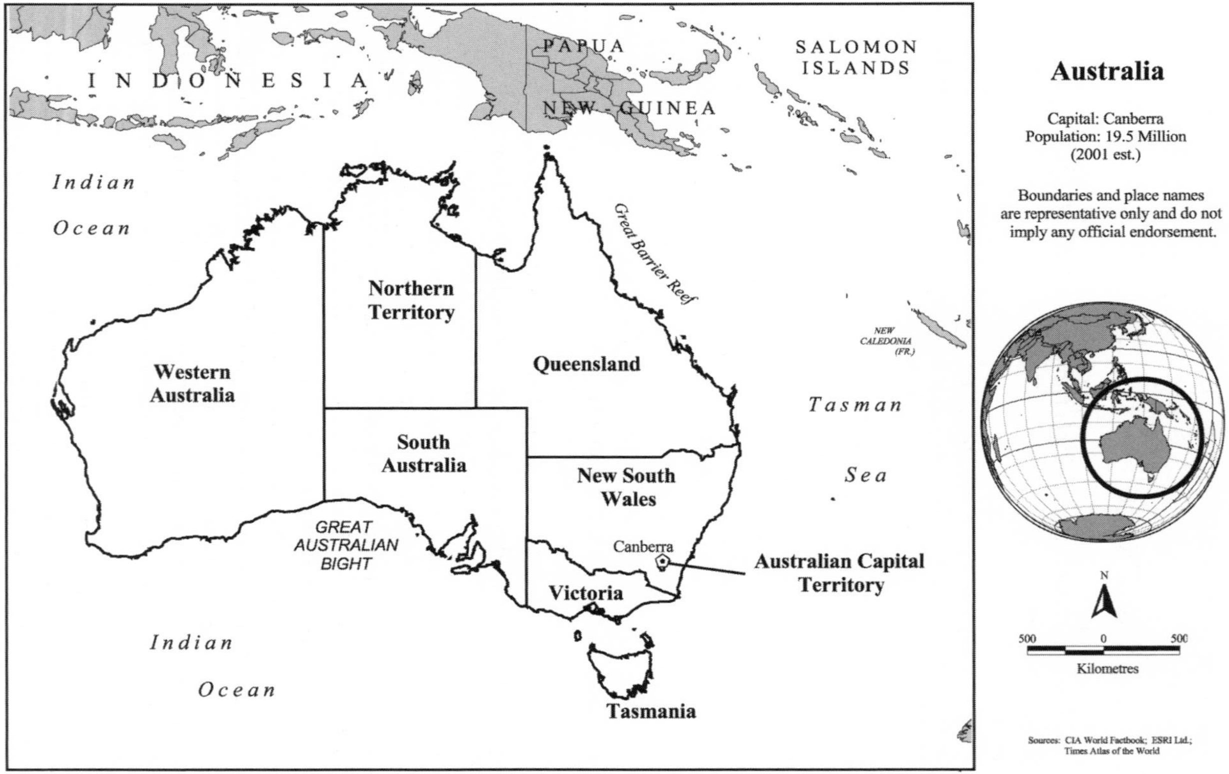

Australia

Capital: Canberra
Population: 19.5 Million
(2001 est.)

Boundaries and place names are representative only and do not imply any official endorsement.

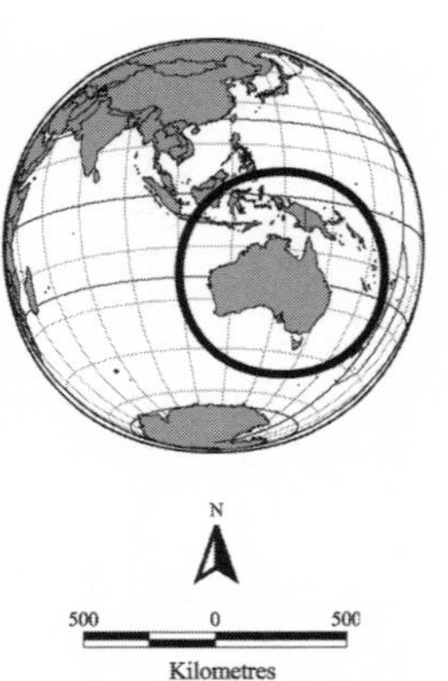

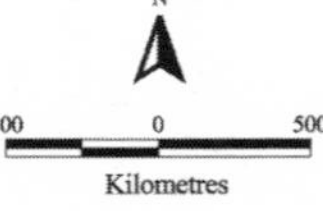

Sources: CIA World Factbook; ESRI Ltd.; Times Atlas of the World

INDONESIA
PAPUA NEW GUINEA
SALOMON ISLANDS
Indian Ocean
Great Barrier Reef
NEW CALEDONIA (FR.)
Northern Territory
Western Australia
Queensland
South Australia
New South Wales
Tasman Sea
GREAT AUSTRALIAN BIGHT
Canberra
Australian Capital Territory
Victoria
Indian Ocean
Tasmania

Australia
(*Commonwealth of Australia*)

CHERYL SAUNDERS

1 HISTORY AND DEVELOPMENT OF FEDERALISM

Australia was settled as a series of British colonies between 1788 and 1829. By that time, aboriginal peoples had inhabited the area for at least 50,000 years. Between 1850 and 1891 six separate self-governing colonies emerged, each with a constitution and institutions of government of its own. Throughout this period there also was some pressure for union, for economic, defence and other purposes. The final and most serious phase of the federation movement took place during the 1890s. The terms of federation and of the constitution on which it was based were negotiated in two major constitutional conventions in 1891 and 1897–98. The conventions were attended by delegations of Members of Parliament from each of the colonies. The constitution that emerged from this process was approved by referendum in each of the Australian colonies before it came into effect as an Act of the British Parliament.

In designing the constitution, the framers drew on the constitutional arrangements of both Britain and the United States. After some debate, they adopted the principles and institutions of responsible government – already in operation in the six colonies – for the new national government, the Commonwealth of Australia. Like Britain, they saw no need for constitutional protection of political rights. The federal system and the constitutional framework, however, were modelled on those of the United States.

The constituent parts of the Australian federation are the Commonwealth and the six Original States of New South Wales, Victoria, Queensland, Western Australia, South Australia and Tasmania. In addition, Australia has two self-governing mainland territories, the Northern Territory and the Australian Capital Territory. The territories are not full partners in the federation, but are treated as polities in their own right for many purposes.

2 CONSTITUTIONAL PROVISIONS RELATING TO FEDERALISM

Australia may be characterized as a dual federation. Each sphere of government has a complete set of institutions; legislature, executive and, with some qualifications, courts. Accordingly, the constitution provides for the federal division of executive and judicial as well as legislative power.

The Australian constitution assigns enumerated powers to the Commonwealth (Section 51), leaving the residue to the states. Forty listed Commonwealth powers cover essential national functions, including: defence and external affairs; major commercial functions, ranging from inter-state and overseas trade and commerce to the resolution of inter-state industrial disputes by conciliation and arbitration; and some social functions, including marriage and matrimonial causes. Most Commonwealth powers are concurrent, in the sense that the states also may exercise them. If a valid Commonwealth law and a state law are inconsistent, the Commonwealth law prevails.

In the 100 years since federation, Commonwealth powers have tended to expand, through usage and judicial interpretation. A turning point was a decision of the High Court in 1920 to give Commonwealth powers their literal meaning unconstrained by assumptions about the nature of the federation. These powers subsequently proved particularly adaptable, thus providing a broad base for Commonwealth action, include the powers relating to taxation, corporations and external affairs.

Despite the 1920 decision, judicial doctrine now recognizes some implied limits on the power of the Commonwealth and the states to legislate for each. In particular, the Commonwealth may not discriminate against or between states or threaten their existence or capacity to function. In recent years, the High Court has accepted that legislative power may be subject to other implied limitations, drawn from the system of representative and responsible government established by the constitution.

The Australian Senate is the principal means by which the states are represented in central institutions. The Senate is the upper house of the Commonwealth legislature. Under Section 7 of the constitution, Original States are entitled to equal Senate representation. Originally each state had six Senators, but the number gradually increased to 12 over the first century of federation.

The composition of the Senate ensures that the smaller states have greater representation in the Commonwealth Parliament than their proportion of the population would suggest. Otherwise, however, the Senate does little to represent the states, individually or collectively. Senators are directly elected, and vote on party lines. Since 1949, Senators have been elected under a system of proportional representation, using each state as a single electorate, which enables Senators to take account of the interests of the state as a whole if they wish to do so. More significantly, these arrangements tend to produce a Senate in which neither major party has a majority (since proportional representation facilitates the election of minor parties and independents) and on which the government cannot automatically rely for agreement and support. The effect has been to enhance the institutional role of the Commonwealth Parliament, at inevitable cost to the operation of responsible government.

The states are represented at the centre in other ways as well. First, Section 24 of the constitution guarantees each state a minimum of five members of the House of Representatives, irrespective of population. In practice, the federal Cabinet invariably includes at least one minister from each state, although this is not a constitutional requirement. Second, the Commonwealth is supposed to consult the states on the appointment of High Court judges. And, third, procedures for amending the constitution, discussed below, also ensure the representation of states as constituent entities.

Constitutionally, the Commonwealth and the states have full power to tax for their own purposes, with the following exceptions. First, the power to impose customs and excise duties is conferred exclusively on the Commonwealth. Second, Commonwealth tax laws cannot discriminate against states or parts of states. Third, neither sphere of government can tax the other's property. Fourth, neither level of government can tax to impose a discriminatory burden on inter-state trade. Finally, the states are extra-territorially limited in the imposition of taxation, as in other matters.

From the outset, the Australian federation was characterized by fiscal imbalance, which has worsened over time. Initially the cause was the inability of the states to impose customs and excise duties. Two factors in particular exacerbated the imbalance. The first was the expansion of the definition of duties of excise through judicial interpretation to preclude the states from imposing any taxes on goods. The second was the de facto transfer of income tax to the Commonwealth following World War II, when the wartime income tax scheme was extended indefinitely.

The mechanism for fiscal transfers from the Commonwealth to the states has become correspondingly more important. There is a vague constitutional requirement for the distribution of surplus revenue, which became a dead letter within the first decade of federation. Successive transfer arrangements have taken the form of both general and specific purpose grants and varied between formula-based arrangements and tax sharing. The distribution of general revenue funds between the states is calculated according to revenue-raising capacity and expenditure needs. In 1999, a Commonwealth commitment to entitle the states to receive all the revenues of the new goods and services tax ushered in yet another phase in the Australian history of revenue redistribution. The commitment is in place, but it is too early to tell whether it will last.

Australia has a three-way separation of powers at the federal level, but it is clear that the separation is significantly more marked in relation to judicial power than in relation to the other two arms of government. With one qualification, federal executive institutions in Australia are typical of those usually associated with responsible government in the British tradition. A Governor-General formally represents Queen Elizabeth II and in that capacity fulfils the function of a largely non-executive Head of State, acting on government advice. The government is drawn from the Parliament and relies on the confidence of the House of Representatives for its continuation in office. The qualification follows from the composition and powers of the Senate. The dismissal of a government by the Governor-General in 1975, after the Senate had rejected a supply bill, is a reminder that the Senate has the capacity to force from office a government with the confidence of the House.

Responsible government also operates in each of the states and in the self-governing territories. All states except Queensland have a bicameral Parliament, although not all upper houses are as powerful as the federal Senate. The coincidence of view between government and Parliament that characterizes responsible government facilitates inter-governmental arrangements in Australia. The operation of the Australian federation relies in part on an extensive network of ministerial councils and a rich diversity of cooperative schemes, designed to secure the uniformity or coordination of legislation and policy. Inevitably, these procedures distract from the authority of individual Parliaments and enhance the role of executive government.

Most disputes about the meaning and legal operation of the constitution are of a kind that can be resolved by the courts, which are the final mechanism for their resolution. As a general rule, disputes over inter-governmental arrangements are not resolved by the courts, unless an intention to establish legal relations can be derived from the terms of the arrangement. As a common law federation, Australia uses the ordinary court system for the purpose and has not established specialist courts.

The Australian constitution provides for a dual system of courts, except in two respects. First, the High Court of Australia, as Australia's highest court, is the final court of appeal in both federal and state jurisdiction (Section 73). It also has an extensive original jurisdiction in significant federal matters, including constitutional matters. Second, the constitution allows the Commonwealth Parliament to confer federal jurisdiction on state courts (Section 77(iii)). This power was used extensively during the first 70 years of federation, but towards the end of the twentieth century, its use decreased as the Commonwealth implemented a court hierarchy of its own. This departure from a dualist model, coupled with the appellate role of the High Court, has had significant effects. The High Court has held that the constitution provides some protection for the integrity of state courts, as potential recipients of federal jurisdiction. The court structure also has contributed to the conclusion that Australia has a unified common law, although statute law varies between states.

Only a small proportion of disputes between governments reaches the courts. Most are resolved through political means. Resolution is assisted when the same party is in government in the jurisdictions concerned. It is correspondingly more difficult when the protagonists come from different parties. Ministerial Council and other intergovernmental meetings of, for example, Solicitors-General also provide fora where disputes can be resolved.

From the outset, the Australian constitution provided a mechanism for its own amendment (Section 128). The mechanism reflects both the federal character of the constitution and the processes by which, initially, it was brought into force. Amendment involves two stages, initiation and approval. Proposals for change must be initiated by the Commonwealth Parliament, in the form of a Constitution Alteration bill. Generally, such a bill is passed through both Houses, with absolute majorities. A deadlock procedure enables a bill that has been rejected by one House to be passed by the other House twice. Bills passed in this way may be put to referendum. Double majorities are needed to approve them: a national majority and a majority in a majority of states. In exceptional cases, where alteration would affect the proportional representation of the state in the Commonwealth Parliament, or would affect state boundaries, majorities also are required in the state concerned.

The constitution has proved relatively resistant to change by this procedure. The Commonwealth Parliament is likely to initiate only proposals of interest to the Commonwealth government of the day. Only eight of the 44 proposals that have been put to referendum have been approved, and at least two of these were very minor. The rate of rejection has been attributed to the narrow procedure for initiation, lack of understanding of proposals, often fiercely partisan referendum campaigns, and the conservatism of the Australian electorate. The result has been to place increasing weight on judicial interpretation of the constitution and on inter-governmental cooperation.

Like most federations, Australia has a form of economic union that leaves some room for economic initiative at the state level. Key elements of the Australian economic union include the conferral of most economic powers on the Commonwealth, a requirement for the Commonwealth to act without preference in matters of tax and commerce, and exclusive Commonwealth powers over customs and excise, and currency and coinage. The centrepiece is Section 92, which provides that inter-state trade, commerce and intercourse are to be "absolutely free." For the first 90 years of federation, this was the most extensively litigated section of the constitution. In 1988, judicial review of the meaning of this section returned to what seems to have been the intention of the framers of the constitution. It is now established that Section 92 protects inter-state trade and commerce from discriminatory practices of a protectionist kind. It does not necessarily preclude the implementation of state policies that have an incidental impact on inter-state trade, as long as the impact is not disproportionate.

Most federations also seek to establish a degree of unity amongst their people through common citizenship and other means. The Australian constitution does relatively little in this regard. There was no legal category of Australian citizenship until 1949, and there is no reference to citizenship in the constitution. Some protection for inter-state mobility is, however, provided by Sections 92 and 117. The latter precludes discrimination against "subjects of the Queen" on the grounds of state residence. These two sections of the constitution were once grandly described by one High Court Justice as the "constitutional pillars of the legal and social unity of the Australian people."

3 RECENT POLITICAL DYNAMICS

Ongoing issues in most federations include the judicial interpretation of the federal division of powers and fiscal arrangements. Australia is no exception. A series of other more specific issues also has had a bearing on the division of powers, as well as being important in their own right.

One with implications for the Australian economy concerns the regulation of companies. While the Commonwealth has power to make laws with respect to corporations (Section 51 (xx)), it is not comprehensive. In particular, it does not allow the Commonwealth Parliament to make laws for the incorporation of companies. For many years, therefore, the Australian Corporation Law has been based on a complex cooperative scheme. Recently, High Court decisions have cast doubt on the validity of aspects of the scheme including the conferral of state jurisdiction on the federal court and state power on federal officials. New arrangements presently are being negotiated (March 2001). They are likely to involve extensive and sophisticated use of the constitutional power of the states to refer matter to the Commonwealth Parliament, coupled with an inter-governmental agreement.

Internationalization and globalization have had a substantial impact on the dynamics of the Australian federation. Most obviously, the proliferation of treaties associated with internationalization has placed strains on both the division of federal power and on executive legislative relations. In the face of internationalization, the High Court held that the federal "external affairs" power (Section 51 (xxix)) enables Parliament to legislate to implement any international legal obligations undertaken by Australia. In effect, this means that the Commonwealth can intervene in areas solely of state concern, the most sensitive of which include the environment and human rights. As this jurisprudence developed, relations between the Commonwealth and the states over international affairs were resolved through a series of agreed principles and procedures, recognizing the Commonwealth's final authority but providing mechanisms for prior consultation. The establishment of an inter-governmental Treaties Council subsequently reinforced these arrangements. In addition, new procedures were put in place in the Commonwealth Parliament to enable more timely and effective parliamentary involvement in the treaty-making process.

One other development, linked with globalization, might also be mentioned. Towards the end of the 1980s there was concern that, despite the constitutional requirement for freedom of inter-state trade, the Australian market was too small and too fragmented to meet the growing challenge of international economic competition. One response was reform of inter-governmental decision-making procedures and, in particular, the ministerial council system. Another was a series of measures to improve the effectiveness of the internal market. One such measure involved the introduction of a scheme for the mutual recognition by each jurisdiction of the standards of the others for goods and professional services. Mutual recognition has been quietly successful as a mechanism for increasing the mobility of goods and occupations without unduly inhibiting the regulatory capacity of the states. The scheme subsequently was extended to include New Zealand as well.

An issue of great national significance, which also affected the operation of the federation, was the decision of the High Court in *Mabo v Queensland No. 2* that Australian common law might, in some circumstances, recognize native title. *Mabo* directly affected the states because it applied new legal rules to the disposal of public lands – which is principally a state responsibility – and lands over which various interests falling short of freehold had been granted. The capacity of the states to avoid the effect of the decision was limited, however, by the overriding effect of the Commonwealth's Racial Discrimination Act, which precludes discrimination on racial grounds. State power was further limited by the Native Title legislation enacted by the Commonwealth to streamline the process of aboriginal lands claims. Both the design and the implementation of this legislation were contentious. Uncertainty about its meaning and operation has given rise to considerable litigation and continues to do so.

No new states have been established in Australia since federation. The most likely candidate for statehood is the large self-governing Northern Territory. Over the decade of the 1990s, debate took place about whether the Northern Territory would become a state. The debate exposed some uncertainties about the operation of the constitutional provisions in relation to new states. These included the extent to which, for example, the federal division of powers can be varied in relation to new states. In the event, the movement failed. A controversial process of designing a constitution for the new state culminated in a "no" vote by Northern Territorians. Statehood is still an issue but has been indefinitely postponed. The high proportion of indigenous Australians who live in the Northern Territory complicates the issue. Both the process for achieving statehood and the constitution on which it is based need to reflect this in an appropriate way.

One final recent political issue concerns the creation of an Australian republic. Over the decade of the 1990s, debate took place about whether and how to break Australia's links with the British Crown. Although a 1999 referendum on severing ties with the Crown was defeated, the issue is likely to be revived. It is relevant to federalism because, under the constitution, the Queen is directly represented not only at the national level but in each of the states, by Governors appointed on the advice of state Premiers. In order to become a republic, it is therefore necessary for Australia to agree on alternative arrangements at the state as well as the Commonwealth level. There is also a question of whether the Queen represents a unifying influence and, if so, the significance for the dynamics of Australian federalism of breaking the link with the Crown. This is one additional complication to be taken into account in designing a republican model if and when the republican issue revives.

4 SOURCES FOR FURTHER INFORMATION

Craven, G. (ed.), *Australian Federalism: Towards the Second Century*, Melbourne: Melbourne University Press, 1992.

Galligan, Brian, *A Federal Republic*, Cambridge: Cambridge University Press, 1995.

Hirst, John, *The Sentimental Nation: The Making of the Australian Commonwealth*, Oxford: Oxford University Press, 2000.

Irving, Helen, *To Constitute a Nation: A Cultural History of Australia's Constitution*, Cambridge: Cambridge University Press, 1997.

Irving, Helen (ed.), *The Centenary Companion to Australian Federation*, Cambridge: Cambridge University Press, 1999.

Saunders, Cheryl, "Federalism and Indigenous Australians," in Yash Ghai (ed.), *Autonomy and Ethnicity*, Cambridge: Cambridge University Press, 2000.

Saunders, Cheryl (ed.), *Courts of Final Jurisdiction*, Sydney: Federation Press, 1996.

Australian Treaty-Making Kit http://www.austlii.edu.au/au/other/dfat/reports/infokit.html

Table I
Political and Geographic Indicators

Capital city	Canberra
Number and type of constituent units	*6 States:* New South Wales, Queensland, South Australia, Tasmania, Victoria, and Western Australia; *1 Capital Territory:* Australian Capital Territory; *1 (mainland) Territory:* The Northern Territory (Note: Australia also has 7 external territories: Ashmore and Cartier Islands, Christmas Island, Cocos (Keeling) Islands, Coral Sea Islands, Herald Island, MacDonald Islands, and Norfolk Island.)
Official language(s)	English
Area	7 686 850 km^2
Area – Largest constituent unit	Western Australia: 2 525 500 km^2
Area – Smallest constituent unit	Australian Capital Territory: 2 400 km^2
Total population	18 886 000 (2000)
Population by constituent unit (% of total population)	New South Wales 34%, Victoria 25%, Queensland 16%, Western Australia 9%, South Australia 8.5%, Tasmania 3.5%, Australian Capital Territory 2%, The Northern Territory 1%.
Political system – federal	Federation – Parliamentary System
Head of state – federal	Queen Elizabeth II (1952), represented by Governor–General Peter Hollingsworth (2001), appointed by the Queen on the advice of the Prime Minister.
Head of government – federal	Prime Minister John Winston Howard (1996/1998), Liberal Party (Note: Leader of Coalition Government of Liberal Party and National Party). Prime Minister is an elected Member of Parliament and leader of the majority party directly elected into the House of Representatives or a leader of a majority coalition. Officially appointed by the Governor-General to serve a 3-year term. The Cabinet is appointed from among the MPs by the Governor-General on the advice of the Prime Minister.
Government structure – federal	Bicameral – Parliament *Upper House* – Senate, 76 Seats, elected through a system of proportional representation, with each state having 12 seats and the two self-governing territories having 2 seats each. The state Senators are elected for a 6-year term, with half of the seats renewed every three years. The territorial Senators serve 3-year terms. *Lower House* – House of Representatives, 148 seats, elected in single-seat constituencies on basis of preferential voting to serve for a 3-year term. No original state can have fewer than 5 representatives.

Table I (continued)

Number of representatives in lower house of federal government – House of Representatives	148 Seats: Australian Labour Party (ALP) 68, Liberal Party of Australia (LP) 63, National Party of Australia (NP) 15, non-partisans and others 3. (Note: General elections to be held 10 November, 2001.)
Number of representatives in lower house of federal government for most populated constituent unit	New South Wales: 50
Number of representatives in lower house of federal government for least populated constituent unit	The Northern Territory: 1
Number of representatives in upper house of federal government – Senate	76 Seats: Labour Party 29 Seats, LP/NP Alliance 35 Seats (Liberal Party of Australia (LP) 31, National Party of Australia (NP) 3, Northern Territory Country Liberal Party (CLP) 1), One Nation (ON) 1, Australian Democrats (AD) 9, Australian Greens (GREENS) 1, non-partisans and others 1. (Note: Half-Senate elections to be held in autumn 2001, timed to correspond with general elections 10 November, 2001.
Distribution of representation in upper house of federal government – Senate	The 6 states each have 12 seats. The 2 territories each have 2 seats.
Constitutional court (highest court dealing with constitutional matters)	High Court. The chief justice and six other justices are appointed by the Governor-General.
Political system of constituent units	Bicameral (with the exception of Queensland and the Northern Territory, which are unicameral): Legislative Assemblies, directly elected to serve for 3 or 4-year terms.
Head of state – constituent units	Queen's Representative: Governor. Appointed by the Queen on the advice of the Premier in the case of the States. No Head of State for the Australian Capital Territory. For the Northern Territory, the Head of State is an Administrator appointed by the Governor-General on the advice of the Chief Minister of the Northern Territory.
Head of government – constituent units	Premier (in the case of the States) – Leader of majority party in Legislature, appoints Cabinet, both serving for a 3 or 4-year term.

Table II
Economic and Social Indicators

GDP	US$445.8 billion
GDP per capita	US$23 200
Mechanisms for taxation	Federal Government Tax Agency levies and collects Personal Income and Corporate taxes and redistributes the revenue to the constituent units. • Personal Income Tax – four tax brackets, ranging from 17 to 47 % • Corporate Tax – 36 % • Medicare Tax is levied on income – 1.5 % • Goods and Services Tax – 10 % (replaced Wholesale Tax) • Excise taxes on tobacco and alcohol products, in addition to various luxury taxes.
National debt (external)	US$220.6 billion
National unemployment rate	6.9%
Constituent unit with highest unemployment rate	Tasmania: 9.2%
Constituent unit with lowest unemployment rate	New South Wales: 6.0%
Adult literacy rate	99 %
National expenditures on education as a % of GDP	6.1%
Life expectancy in years	78.3
Doctors per population ratio (national)	240 doctors per 100 000 inhabitants
Doctors per population ratio in constituent units (highest)	South Australia: 264 doctors per 100 000 inhabitants
Doctors per population ratio in constituent units (lowest)	Tasmania: 220 doctors per 100 000 inhabitants
National expenditures on health as a % of GDP	8.6 %

Sources

Australia Bureau for Statistics, August 2001. www.abs.gov.au

Central Intelligence Agency (CIA), *World Fact Book 2000*. CIA. www.cia.gov/cia/publications/factbook/index.html

Economist Intelligence Unit, "Country Commerce – Australia," *The Economist Intelligence Unit 2000*. New York: EIU, 2000.

Elazar, Daniel J. (ed.), *Federal Systems of the World: A Handbook of Federal, Confederal and Autonomy Arrangements*. 2nd Edition. Jerusalem Institute for Federal Studies. London: Longman Group/Westgate House, 1994.

International Monetary Fund (IMF). *International Financial Statistics*, Vol. LIII, No. 12, December 2000. Washington, DC: the IMF Statistics Department, 2000.

Organisation for Economic Co-operation and Development (OECD). www.oecd.org.
Parliament of Australia. www.aph.gov.au
United Nations Population Division. Department of Economic and Social Affairs, "Population in 1999 and 2000: All Countries." *World Population Prospects: The 1998 Revision, Vol. 1 comprehensive Tables.* www.un.org/Depts.htm
United Nations *Human Development Report, 2000.* www.undp.org/hdro/report.html
United Nations Statistics Division. "InfoNation." United Nations Statistical Database, 2000. www.un.org/
Watts, Ronald L. *Comparing Federal Systems.* 2nd edition. School of Policy Studies. Montreal/Kingston: McGill-Queen's University Press, 1999.
World Health Organisation (WHO). "Estimates of Health Personnel." www-nt.who.int/whosis/statistics
World Health Organisation (WHO). *World Health Report 2000.* Geneva, Switzerland 2000. www-nt.who.int/whosis/statistics/menu.cfm.

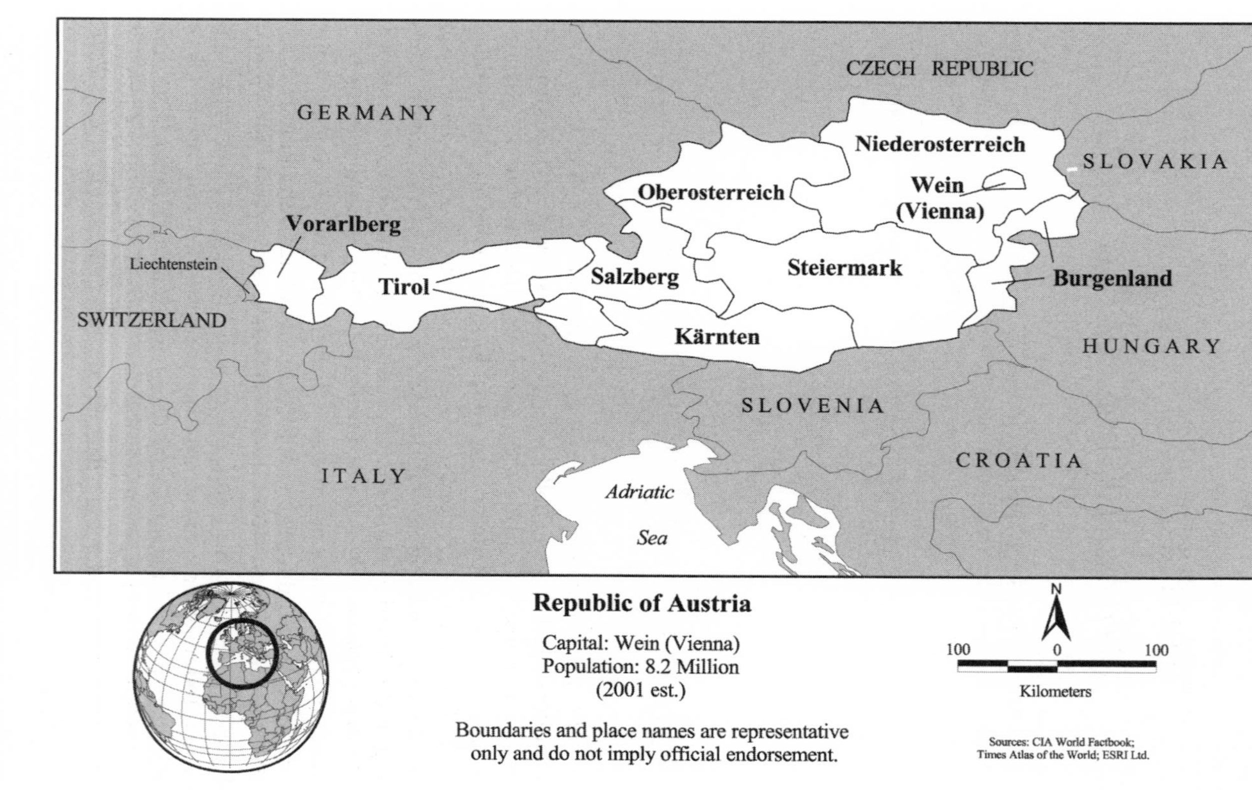
CZECH REPUBLIC
GERMANY
SLOVAKIA
Niederosterreich
Oberosterreich
Wein
(Vienna)
Vorarlberg
Liechtenstein
Tirol
Salzberg
Steiermark
Burgenland
SWITZERLAND
Kärnten
HUNGARY
SLOVENIA
CROATIA
ITALY
Adriatic
Sea
Republic of Austria
Capital: Wein (Vienna)
Population: 8.2 Million
(2001 est.)
Boundaries and place names are representative
only and do not imply official endorsement.
N
100
0
100
Kilometers
Sources: CIA World Factbook;
Times Atlas of the World; ESRI Ltd.

Austria*
(*Federal Republic of Austria*)

ROLAND STURM

1 HISTORY AND DEVELOPMENT OF FEDERALISM

The Austrian Republic is a central European state (83,858 km^2) with 8.1 million inhabitants (1998). It is the successor state of the Austrian-Hungarian Empire (1867–1918), which was a multinational empire, but had no federal structure. In 1918 Emperor Charles I, who ruled Austria from 1916–18, promised that he would introduce federalism in order to accommodate the diverse aspirations of the nationalities living in the Austrian-Hungarian Empire. His manifesto to the peoples of Austria (*Völkermanifest*) came, however, too late to have any practical consequences. It was not proclaimed until the last few weeks of the First World War and four days before the break-up of the Empire.

The first republic (1918–1933/34) which succeeded the Empire adopted a federal constitution. This constitution of 1920, which is still in force today, was a compromise between the political intentions of the conservative Christian Social Party and those of the Social Democrats. Whereas the latter wanted a strong central power, the Christian Social Party favoured a high degree of state (*Land*) autonomy. Early

* The Forum of Federations would like to thank Peter Bussjäger at the Institut für Föderalismus, Innsbruck, and Anna Gamper, Institut für Öffentliches Recht, Finanzrecht und Politikwissenschaft, Innsbruck, for their comments on this article.

Austrian federalism provided some disruptive effects on the unity of the country because it set the stage for bitter political conflict between the parties. It became a forum for the battle of conservative state governments against the Land of Vienna, the national capital, which was social democratic.

The constitution itself was revised several times and every revision contributed to a strengthening of the federal level of Austrian politics. An agreement on the division of competencies in financial affairs was reached in 1922 and came into effect in 1925. (It must be noted, however, that today's division of financial jurisdiction is based on the Financial Constitutional Act of 1925.) In 1925 a decision was made on the internal administration of the Länder and on their competency in the field of public education (revised in a 1962 act). In 1929 the role of the political centre in Austrian politics was strengthened even more by the introduction of a directly elected head of state, a federal President. It was even decided to reform the Bundesrat, the Second Chamber, and to add to the representatives of the states the representatives of the major social groups of society (*Stände*).

The latter reform was not implemented, but it indicated the growing influence of anti-democratic thought which culminated in the new Austro-fascist constitution of 1934. The government became the legislator and several appointed institutions, among them a Council of the States (Länderrat), were entitled to agree or disagree but not to change legislation. Even this limited control of the government was, however, irrelevant, because Austria was ruled simply by orders of government. In 1938 German troops occupied Austria, and the country was incorporated into Nazi Germany as the "Ostmark" of the Third Reich.

In 1945, after the defeat of Nazi Germany, the constitution (*Bundesverfassungsgesetz*) of 1920 with all its revisions and also the pre-1934 legislation were reinstated. Austria became once again a federal state. In the 1960s and 1970s the Austrian Länder tried to stop the trend towards ever greater centralization of power in Austrian politics. Although they succeeded in bringing about some constitutional change which strengthened their position vis-à-vis the federal government, Austria remains a country of "unitary" federalism – i.e., a country in which regional power is clearly subordinated to federal power.

In 1955 Austria regained its sovereignty in exchange for a constitutional guarantee of its permanent neutrality. In the same year the country became a member of the United Nations. Austria joined the Council of Europe in 1956, was co-founder of the European Free Trade Association (EFTA) in 1960, and became a member of the European Union (EU) in 1995.

2 CONSTITUTIONAL PROVISIONS RELATING TO FEDERALISM

The Austrian constitution is a long and detailed document which includes provisions not only on the tasks, but also on the institutional framework of the Länder (states) and on local government. Article 2 of the constitution stipulates that Austria is a federal state which consists of nine autonomous Länder, namely Burgenland, Carinthia, Lower Austria, Upper Austria, Salzburg, Styria, Tirol, Vorarlberg and Vienna. Special provisions are made for Vienna. In Vienna the county Parliament has the additional function of a state Parliament, the town Senate has the function of a state government and the Mayor the function of a Governor (Article 108).

The legislation of the states is carried out by the state Parliaments (Article 95). In theory the states could have wide-ranging powers, because Article 15 gives the states power over all matters not expressly assigned to the federation. Article 16 allows them even to engage in foreign policy. They are allowed to make treaties with neighbouring territories in matters which fall into their autonomous sphere of competence, although the federal government supervises the process and must consent to the treaty.

In practice constant revisions of the constitution strengthened the federation. This was facilitated by the fact that for most of its post-war history Austria was governed by grand coalitions which could easily muster the two-thirds majorities in both houses of Parliament necessary for constitutional change. Only a two-thirds majority of the members of the National Council, and a simple majority of the members of the Federal Council, has to consent in order to pass a federal constitutional bill. Since 1984 a two-thirds majority of the Federal Council has been required, but only if such bills restrict Länder jurisdiction. According to Article 98 of the constitution, the federal government may object to a bill passed by a state Parliament, but the bill can nevertheless come into force if the state Parliament passes it a second time with a vote of at least half of its membership.

The central government possesses many of the most important powers in the federation, including all judicial powers, responsibility for the police and the military, and control of public accounts and the administration of public funds on all levels of government (Articles 121–128). (Article 127(c), however, allows the Länder to establish their own Courts of Auditors.) Public administration is above all organized as "*mittelbare Bundesverwaltung*" (indirect federal administration, Articles 102 and 103). This means that, when he executes federal law, the state

Governor (*Landeshauptmann*) is bound by instructions from the federal government and individual federal ministers.

The states have also lost out financially. The constitution does not define tax-raising powers. This is left to federal legislation which cannot be vetoed by the states (Fiscal Adjustment Act). As a result the states have almost no tax income of their own and depend on tax income shared by the federation or transfer payments by the federation. Today's federalism is strongly centralized but, nonetheless, based on the cooperation of the federal government and the Länder.

This cooperation finds its expression above all in the administration of federal laws by the Länder. The constitution distinguishes four kinds of legislation: (1) federal legislation executed by the federal government, for example in the fields of foreign policy, banking, peace, order and security, and trade and industry (Article 10); (2) federal legislation executed by the Länder, for example in the fields of nationality and right of citizenship, national housing affairs, highway police, sanitation or some aspects of inland shipping (Article 11); (3) Federal Framework Legislation in which the Länder have to issue implementing laws and have to provide the administration, for example in the fields of social welfare policies, land reform or some aspects of labour legislation (Article 12); and (4) Land legislation executed by the Land.

The Länder have a role in federal legislation. With a few exceptions, no law can be made without the consent of the Second Chamber of Parliament, the Bundesrat (Article 42). In the Bundesrat all states are represented in proportion to the number of nationals in each of them (Article 34). The state with the largest number of citizens delegates 12 members, every other state receives as many as the ratio in which its nationals stand to those in the first-mentioned state. Each state is entitled to at least three representatives. The number of representatives of each state is determined by the federal President after every general census which is usually held at 10-year intervals.

The members of the Bundesrat are elected by the state Parliaments for the duration of their respective legislative periods in accordance with the principle of proportional representation, but at least one seat must fall to the party having the second largest number of seats in a state Parliament or, should several parties have the same number of seats, the second highest number of votes at the last election to the state Parliament. When the claims of several parties are equal, the issue is decided by lot. The members of the Bundesrat need not belong to the state Parliament which delegates them, but they must be eligible for that state Parliament (Article 35).

As the members of the Bundesrat are selected by political parties, their first loyalty is to the party and not to the government of the state from which they come. In the Bundesrat they do not form state caucuses, but join their respective party group. These party groups do not form parliamentary parties of their own, but belong to one party group together with the members of the First Chamber of Parliament, the Nationalrat, and follow the instructions they are given there. The political parties believe it would damage their political image if their representatives in the Second Chamber held views different from those of their colleagues in the First Chamber. This is further evidence of the low esteem in which Land identities are held in the Bundesrat and the subordinate role of the Bundesrat in federal politics.

A mild corrective which allows the expression of regional interests is the constitutional provision of Article 36(4). This provision gives the Governors the right to participate in the deliberations of the Bundesrat. They may even demand to be heard when topics are debated which concern their state. But they are not involved in the decision-making process.

A veto of the Bundesrat can only delay legislation. It cannot stop it. If the First Chamber of Parliament, the Nationalrat, in the presence of at least half its members once more carries its original resolution, this becomes law. In 1984 the constitution was revised and Article 44(2) was introduced which defines an exception to this rule. Constitutional changes which restrict Länder jurisdiction today need the consent of a two-thirds majority of the Bundesrat in the presence of at least half its members. The same majority is needed if the federal President follows the recommendation of the federal government and plans to dissolve a Land Parliament (Article 100). The representatives of the Land in question are not allowed to take part in this vote.

The Bundesrat is also involved in decisions which Parliament takes as a whole. The Bundesrat and the Nationalrat sit together as the Federal Assembly (Bundesversammlung) when the directly elected federal President is sworn in and for the adoption of a resolution on a declaration of war (Article 38).

The Constitutional Court is a joint institution of the federation and the Länder. It pronounces on conflicts of jurisdiction between the states as well as between the states and the federation (Article 138). Three of the 14 members of the Court and one of its six substitute members who the federal President appoints are nominated by the Bundesrat (Article 147). Other institutions also have the legal status of joint institutions. Among them are the Administrative Court (Article 130–136), the National Auditing Office (Articles 121–128), and the Ombudsmen Council (Article 148).

An important level of federalism in Austria is the self-coordination of the Länder. Although there are no constitutional provisions which provide a blueprint for the meetings of top civil servants of the Länder, Presidents of Land Parliaments or Governors, conferences of Länder representatives have become a device to coordinate and articulate Länder interests. Organizational support for these conferences is provided by a joint Länder office located with the government of Lower Austria.

3 RECENT POLITICAL DYNAMICS

In the 1960s and 1970s the Länder began to voice their discontent with the dominance of the federation in Austrian politics and demanded a strengthening of their position in order to strengthen federalism. As a consequence, some noteworthy corrections of the federal constitution were made in the years 1974, 1983, 1984, 1987 and 1988. But none of these constitutional changes was substantial.

At the end of the 1980s the Länder found themselves in a better bargaining position because their support for the planned membership in the European Union was needed. In 1989 an expert group (the so-called "Commission for Structural Reforms," Strukturreformkommission) was appointed. This commission had the task of identifying problems of the current division of jurisdiction between the federation and the Länder and to suggest new solutions. The recommendations of the expert group, which were published in 1991, provided the context for negotiations between the Länder and the federation. These negotiations were completed in 1992 with an agreement between the governments of the states and the federal government on the reform of Austrian federalism (*Perchtoldsdorfer Paktum*). State Parliaments as well as the federal Parliament were ignored, a strategy which had negative political consequences.

It turned out that once the necessary legislation was introduced into Parliament, the agreement was not the end of political controversy. It took until 7 June 1994 before the federal government was able to present a constitutional reform bill. The decision on the bill was not made before the federal elections of 1994. In these elections the grand coalition of the Social Democrats (SPÖ) and the Conservatives (ÖVP) lost its two-thirds majority in the Nationalrat, which it needed for the planned reform. A new round of negotiations began, this time including the opposition parties. The new consensus found was in a number of aspects, however, watering down the concessions already made to the Länder. For this reason the state Governors' conference rejected the new compromise.

What followed was one year of absolute standstill. The general election which was held at the end of 1995 gave the grand coalition again a two-thirds majority of seats in the Nationalrat. The constitutional reform bill was re-introduced in its original form. But at the same time it was planned that this bill should be revised by the "Reform of Federalism" Task Force. This task force was made up of representatives of the states and the federation and was installed by the Governors' conference. Although the Governors tried time and again to make progress with the reform of federalism, the federal government was not responsive.

After the general election in 1999 the grand coalition broke apart. The new Conservative-Freedom Party (FPÖ) coalition does not have the necessary two-thirds majority for constitutional reform in Parliament and has also not made constitutional reform one of its priorities. Austria's federalism remains in its constitutional design strongly centralized and unitary in character.

What can be counted as a recent success of the Länder is, however, that they were able to force the federal government to give them a role in the political decision-making process concerning the European Union (Article 23). The Länder argued that they would use Article 50(1) of the constitution, which stipulates that they need to agree to international treaties affecting their autonomous sphere of competence, and that they were willing to use their influence in the referendum campaign on the country's membership of the EU to strengthen the "No"-camp if the government was not prepared to make concessions and to amend the constitution in their favour.

The federal government is now obliged to inform the Länder without delay about all EU initiatives which affect their jurisdiction or could be of interest to them. They have a right to comment on such proposals. If the Länder agree on a certain position concerning their autonomous sphere of competency, the federal government has to accept this position and has to vote accordingly on the European level. An exception can be made, however, for reasons which have to do with foreign policy or the European interests of Austria. The federal government needs to inform the Länder about such reasons without delay. Common views of the states are, however, not always the rule. Disagreement on policies among the Länder tends to undermine their position vis-à-vis the federal government in European politics.

If an EU initiative affects the competence of Austria's Länder, it is now possible that a politician nominated by the Länder can become the representative of Austria in negotiations between Austria and the EU. It is important to note that this is only a possibility, not a fixed rule. The federal government must agree to the handing over of its responsibility for foreign policy to the Länder. The Länder also have the right to nominate the Austrian members of the EU Committee of the Regions. One representative of each of the Länder is present at the office of the

Permanent Representative of Austria in Brussels. Every state (except for Vorarlberg) also has its own quasi-embassy to the EU there.

Austrian federalism today has its greatest dynamic in the states themselves. An important factor which has sustained federalism is the federal structure of interest groups and political parties, as well as the strong historical roots of the Länder (except for the Burgenland which became a part of Austria as a result of the Treaty of Trianon of 1921). It is telling that the Governors, who have no constitutional role in the Second Chamber and are outside the process of federal legislation, have become the engines of change. This reflects also the growing acceptance of federal diversity among the people in the states. The states use private company law to engage in activities, such as regional economic policy, labour market policies, health and culture policies. This is a way to become active in fields which the constitution reserves to the federal government.

What remains of the constitutional autonomy of the Länder has, however, also gained additional importance. State constitutions were reformed. They now guarantee some basic rights which are wider than the rights guaranteed by the federal constitution or not part of the federal constitution. Many states not only introduced new forms of direct democracy, but also strengthened the powers of the Land Parliaments and Land audit offices vis-à-vis Land governments.

Another important factor for the new political dynamic on the state level has been the differences in party political majorities and coalition arrangements between the states and between the states and the federation. It used to be the case that in all states – with the exception of Vienna and Vorarlberg – the constitution demanded that the relative strength of the parties in Parliament had to be mirrored in government. This gave the Governor a strong role as moderator. We now observe growing criticism against state Parliaments without opposition parties and initiatives, such as the constitutional reforms in Salzburg and Tirol in 1998, to introduce majority government.

Last but not least, membership in the European Union has redefined the aims of the Land governments. Now, not only are they confronted with the example of federal states such as Germany and Belgium which give their federal sub-units a much greater role in national politics, they also have to come to grips with the economic challenge of regional competition in the Single European Market.

5 SOURCES FOR FURTHER INFORMATION

Bischof, Günther and Anton Pelinka (eds), *Contemporary Austrian Studies, 4 volumes*, New Brunswick, NJ: Transaction Publishers, 1993–1996.

Institut für Föderalismusforschung, *Annual Reports*, Wien: Braumüller, since 1977.
Pelinka, Anton, Fritz Plasser and Wolfgang Meixner (eds), *Die Zukunft der österreichischen Demokratie*, Wien: Signum Verlag, 2000.
Pernthaler, Peter, *Kompetenzverteilung in der Krise*, Wien: Braumüller, 1989.
http://www.austria.gv.at/oesterreich/landeskunde.htm
http://www.ris.austria.gv.at

Table I
Political and Geographic Indicators

Capital city	Vienna
Number and type of constituent units	9 States (Bundesland/Bundesländer): Burgenland, Kaernten (Carinthia), Niederoesterreich (Lower Austria), Oberoesterreich (Upper Austria), Salzburg, Steiermark (Styria), Tirol, Vorarlberg, Wien (Vienna).
Official language(s)	German
Area	83 858 km^2
Area – Largest constituent unit	Lower Austria: 19 174 km^2
Area – Smallest constituent unit	Vienna: 415 km^2
Total population	8 131 111
Population by constituent unit (% of total population)	Vienna 19.5%, Lower Austria 19%, Upper Austria 17%, Styria 15.5%, Tirol 8%, Carinthia 7%, Salzberg 6%, Vorlberg 4%, Burgenland 3.5%
Political system – federal	Federal Republic
Head of state – federal	President Dr. Thomas Klestil, Österreichische Volkspartei (ÖVP), (1992/98) – The President is directly elected to serve a 6-year term.
Head of government – federal	Chancellor Wolfgang Schüssel, OVP, 2000 – The President appoints the Chancellor from the largest party or a coalition in the Nationalrat and the Chancellor nominates the Cabinet.
Government structure – federal	Bicameral: Federal Assembly (Bundesversammlung) *First Chamber* – The Nationalrat (National Council) has 183 members elected by proportional representation to serve for a 4-year term. *Second Chamber* – Bundesrat (Federal Council) has 64 members representing the constituent units, and they are indirectly elected by party list vote of provincial parliaments from 9 multi-seat provinces (with a minimum of 3 and a maximum of 12 representatives per province), to serve a 5- to 6-year term.
Number of representatives in lower house of federal government – Nationalrat	183 Seats: Sozialdemokratische Partei Österreichs (Social-Democratic Party of Austria) SPÖ 65, Freiheitliche Partei Österreichs (Freedom Party of Austria) FPÖ 52, Österreichische Volkspartei (Austrian People's Party) ÖVP 52 and Die Grünen (The Greens) Grüne 14.
Number of representatives in lower house of federal government for most populated constituent unit	Lower Austria – 31 seats (Vienna 28 seats)

Table I (continued)

Number of representatives in lower house of federal government for least populated constituent unit	Burgenland – 5 seats
Number of representatives in upper house of federal government – Bundesrat	64 Seats: ÖVP 26, SPÖ 24, and FPÖ 14
Distribution of representation in upper house of federal government – Bundesrat	Distribution of Seats: Lower Austria 12, Vienna 11, Upper Austria 11, Styria 10, Tyrol 5, Carinthia 5, Salzburg 4, Vorarlberg 3, and Burengland 3
Constitutional court (highest court dealing with constitutional matters)	Constitutional Court (Verfassungsgerichtshof). The Constitutional Court is composed of a President, a Vice-President, 12 further members, and six substitutes. All members are appointed by the Bundespraesident. The appointments of the President, the Vice-President, six further members and three substitutes are based on recommendations by the Bundesregierung (federal cabinet). The appointment of the remaining six members and three substitutes are based on the recommendation of the National Council (for three members and two substitutes) and of the Federal Council (for three members and one substitute).
Political system of constituent units	Unicameral: Each Land operates on its own constitution and has an elected Assembly (Landtag or Diet). Membership ranges between 36-56 members, and all elect a government consisting of a Governor and Councilors. In the case of Vienna, the City Council fulfils the functions of a State Diet or Landtag. The Landtag is directly elected and is governed by the constitutions of each state.
Head of state – constituent units	Governor, elected by the Diet.
Head of government – constituent units	Governor – Both Governor and Councilors are elected by the Diet, and are responsible to this body.

Table II
Economic and Social Indicators

GDP	US$203 billion
GDP per capita	US$25 000
Mechanisms for taxation	Taxation is primarily controlled by the Central Government, and is shared with the states or disbursed through transfer payments. • Income Tax: five tax brackets ranging from 10 to 50%. • Value Added Tax (VAT): On all goods and services, with an average rate of 20%. In addition to these, there are corporate taxes (approximately 35%), real estate taxes (approximately 7.15%) and various excise taxes.
National debt (external)	US$16 billion
National unemployment rate	5.4%
Constituent unit with highest unemployment rate	Vienna – 5.8%
Constituent unit with lowest unemployment rate	Oberoesterreich – 2.6%
Adult literacy rate	99%
National expenditures on education as a % of GDP	5%
Life expectancy in years	77.1
Doctors per population ratio (national)	290 doctors per 100 000 inhabitants
Doctors per population ratio in constituent units (highest)	Vienna – 560 doctors per 100 000 inhabitants
Doctors per population ratio in constituent units (lowest)	Upper Austria and Burgenland both have 230 doctors per 100 000 inhabitants
National expenditures on health as a % of GDP	8.0%

Sources

Austrian Institute of Economic Research (WIFO). "Table 17.4–Table 17.12." *WIFO Economic Data Service.* www.wifo.ac.at

Austrian National Bank. "Chapter Five." *Focus on Statistics 2000.* www.oenb.co.ag

Central Intelligence Agency (CIA), *World Fact Book 2000.* CIA, www.cia.gov/cia/publications/factbook/index.html

Constitutional Court of Austria. www.vfgh.gv.at

Economist Intelligence Unit. "Country Commerce." *The Economist Intelligence Unit Database 2000.* New York, 2000. www.eiu.com

Elazar, Daniel J. (ed.), *Federal Systems of the World: A Handbook of Federal, Confederal and Autonomy Arrangements.* 2nd Edition. Jerusalem Institute for Federal Studies. London: Longman Group/Westgate House, 1994.

Eurostat. "Table IV.I Expenditures 1992" and "Table VII.I Health Personnel and Equipment," *Regions: Statistical Yearbook 1996*. Luxembourg: Office of Statistics for the European Community (Eurostat), 1996.

International Monetary Fund (IMF). *International Financial Statistics*, Vol. LIII, No. 12, December 2000. Washington, DC: the IMF Statistics Department, 2000.

Republic of Austria Website. "Political System – The Parliament." www.austria.gv.at/e/

United Nations. "Human Development Index," "Gender-Related Development Index," *Human Development Report, 2000*. Human Development Report Office. www.undp.org/hdro/report.html

United Nations Statistics Division. "InfoNation." www.un.org/

World Health Organisation (WHO). "Estimates of Health Personnel." www-nt.who.int/whosis/statistics

World Health Organisation (WHO), *World Health Report 2000*, Geneva, Switzerland, 2000, www-nt.who.int/whosis/statistics/menu.cfm

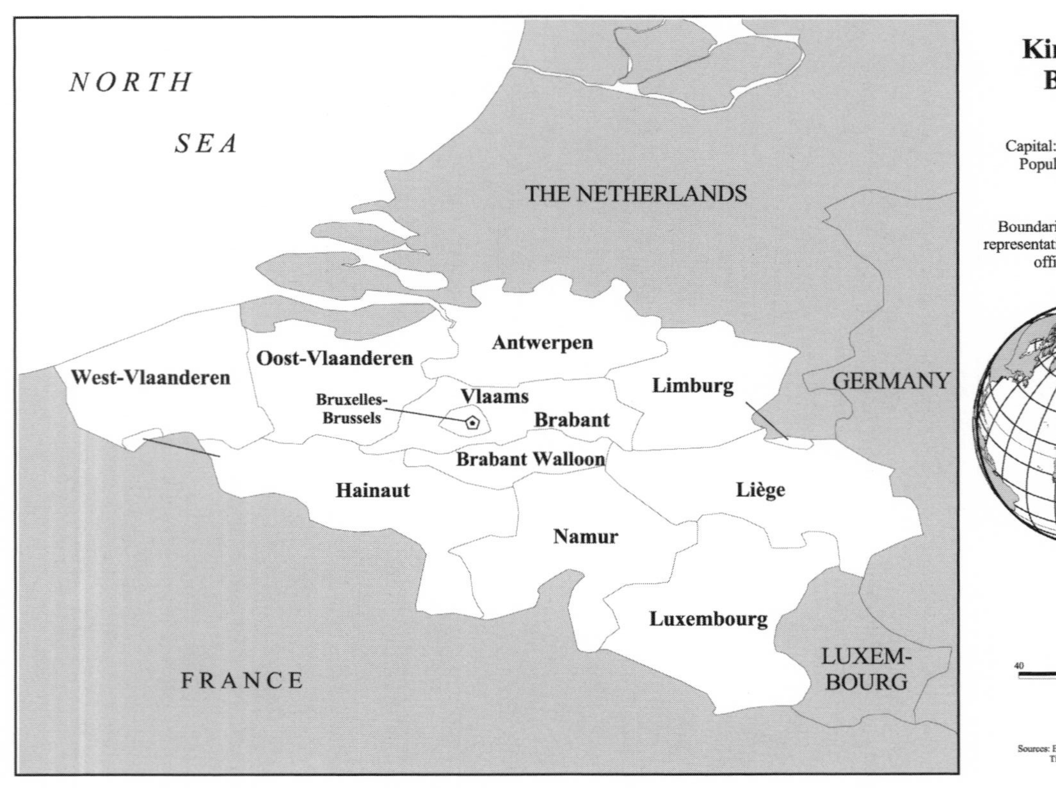

Kingdom of Belgium

Capital: Bruxelles (Brussels)
Population: 10.3 Million
(2001 est.)

Boundaries and place names are representative only and do not imply official endorsement.

N

40 0 40
Kilometers

Sources: ESRI Ltd.; CIA World Factbook; Times Atlas of the World

Belgium*
(*Kingdom of Belgium*)

ANDRÉ LECOURS

1 HISTORY AND DEVELOPMENT OF FEDERALISM

Belgium is a small – 32,547 km² – West European democracy with a population of just over 10 million. The country's defining political feature is its multilingual character. Belgium's northern half, Flanders, is home to the bulk of the country's Dutch-speakers (almost 6 million; referred to as "Flemish") while the south, Wallonia (3.3 million), is French-speaking. This linguistic picture is complicated by the presence of a tiny German-speaking population in the southeast (70,000 people) and by Brussels (1 million), which is located north of the linguistic frontier but is predominantly French. Tensions between linguistic groups have been a central feature of Belgian politics since the late nineteenth century but they are superimposed on and intersect with two other fundamental divisions in this complex state – religion and class. The perennial *problème communautaire*, as expressed through nationalist/regionalist politics, was the motor for the recent federalization of the Belgian state.

The territories of present-day Belgium were detached from the Dutch kingdom and made into an independent state in 1830 by a French-speaking bourgeoisie who opposed the linguistic and religious

* The Forum of Federations and the author would like to thank Johanne Poirier for her helpful comments on this article.

policies of King William I of Orange. Belgium was created as a strongly centralized unitary state which operated, despite the absence of any formal constitutional provision specifying language use, almost completely in French. This situation proved unacceptable to a Flemish traditional lower-bourgeoisie who saw Belgium as a bilingual and bicultural nation. It is in this context that the Flemish Movement emerged and struggled to achieve Dutch equality with French. Despite opposition from French-speaking elites, formal-legal equality was achieved in 1898 with the De Vriendt-Coremans law, although French remained the dominant language.

The Flemish Movement then proceeded to seek official bilingual status for Flemish-speaking provinces, but these claims, especially those pertaining to the south, met with staunch opposition from French-speakers. In this context, the Flemish Movement re-directed its activism away from the larger Belgian framework to the northern part of the country for which it now sought monolingual status. This goal was largely accomplished in the 1930s with language laws that instituted territorial monolingualism. French-speaking elites formed the Walloon Movement to counter the claims of the Flemish Movement. Their first reaction was to call for a return to the Belgium of 1830 but as the Flemish Movement became increasingly powerful, they switched strategy, abandoning French-speakers in Flanders, and later in Brussels, to focus on Wallonia where French was dominant.

The *problème communautaire* became increasingly acute after World War II when a series of issues, ranging from the status of King Leopold III to school funding, pitted the two linguistic communities against one another. Politicians attempted to defuse this tension by strengthening territorial monolingualism through new linguistic legislation. Laws passed in 1962–63 created four linguistic regions: monolingual Flanders, monolingual Wallonia, bilingual Brussels, and a German-speaking area. A series of censuses determined linguistic borders and the *communes* (municipalities) were fitted into their 'proper' language region. The border was then 'frozen' in 1963 by abandoning the census as an adjusting tool and enforcing administrative unilingualism, all in the hope of increasing homogenization.

This strategy proved a failure as tension continued to mount in the 1960s with the newly formed community parties Volksunie (Flemish nationalist), Rassemblement Wallon (Walloon regionalist) and Front Démocratique des Francophones (Brussels-based) applying considerable political-electoral pressure on the traditional parties (Christian-Democrat, Socialist, Liberal). Forced to become more militant on community issues, the traditional political parties developed linguistic wings and, in the 1970s, split upon linguistic grounds. Indeed, a peculiarity of the Belgian political system is its party system: there are no national parties in Belgium; they are all language-specific. As a consequence of Belgium's consociational arrangements, this transformation led to a further dichotomization of political *and* social life. For example, trade unions, although officially unified and presenting a common front to public authorities, have developed different language working groups. Voluntary associations and many other civil society organizations have also adopted bipolar structures.

The federalization of Belgium occurred step by step – there were constitutional-institutional reforms in 1970, 1980, 1988 and 1993. The main reason for the incremental nature of the process was that Flemish and Francophone parties favoured different federal models. The Flemish side advocated a bipartite federalism structured around the two major linguistic/cultural communities. Francophone leaders argued for tripartite federalism in which both Wallonia and Brussels would be, along with Flanders, constituent units. It should be noted that these constitutional changes also arose from the negotiations that are a necessary element of coalition governments, which are characteristic of Belgian federal politics.

Crises in relations between linguistic groups were crucial in jump-starting the federalization process when it appeared to be stalled. In the mid-1980s, the trigger came when the Mayor of Voeren (Fourons in French), a small municipality of 4,000 people which had been moved from Wallonia to Flanders in 1963, refused to use Dutch in formal proceedings as the law prescribed. The Voeren episode led to the constitutional revision of 1988 and a compromise over Brussels which was made into a federated unit as Francophone parties wished. In exchange, Flemish parties obtained protection of the minority Flemish population of Brussels and agreement that the city's borders would be limited to the existing 19 *communes*. In the early 1990s, it was the decision by left-wing Flemish parties to oppose an arms sale to Saudi Arabia, which would have benefitted Walloon industries, that triggered a community crisis. This conflict led to the 1993 reform and the formal transformation of Belgium into a federal state.

2 CONSTITUTIONAL PROVISIONS RELATING TO FEDERALISM

The peculiarity of Belgian federalism is that it involves two different types of constituent units: Communities and Regions (Articles 2 and 3). There are three Communities (Flemish, French and German) and three Regions (Flanders, Wallonia and Brussels). This intriguing feature has to be understood in the context of the Flemish Movement's historical struggle for cultural/linguistic preservation and the more recent fight of the Walloon Movement for economic autonomy. The Communities were created in 1970 and immediately provided with institutions (except for the German-speaking Community which was fully institutionalized in 1983). They have power over language, culture, education and *matières personnalisables,* Belgian constitutional jargon for social services such as health care (but not health care insurance which is part of federal jurisdiction) which involve direct contact between state-provider and citizen.

Although the Regions are clearly territorial units, the Communities are linked to individuals and language more than territory, which makes them one of the most complicated elements of Belgian federalism. Their membership is determined in reference to the constitutional distinction between the language regions (Article 4), and their existence stems from the Flemish objective to acquire cultural autonomy. Consequently, Dutch-speakers in Brussels belong to the Flemish Community as do those living in Flanders. Similarly, French-speaking residents of Brussels are members of the French Community just like Walloons. There are, however, exceptions to the idea of language-based Communities. Indeed, the substantial francophone minority in Flanders does not belong to the French Community, and the same is true for the (rare) Dutch-speakers of Wallonia. In other words, the "person-bound" Communities have not introduced sub-nationalities among the Belgian population.

Regions are territorial units that were formed in response to Walloon concerns over their region's economy. Flanders and Wallonia established institutions in 1980 – more than 10 years after the 1970 constitutional reform outlined the intention to create Regions – and Brussels did so in 1988. The Regions have power over regional economic development, urban planning, the administration of provinces and *communes,* housing, public works, water, energy, transportation, the environment, and job training. (As well, an agreement has just been signed to transfer power over international trade and agricultural policy to the Regions.) In 1980, the Flemish Region and Community merged their institutions. This means that the two entities still exist from a constitutional point of view in Flanders, but there is a common Flemish government and Parliament (with certain exceptions relating to Brussels), thereby further accentuating the asymmetry of Belgian federalism.

The federal government retains power over financial and monetary policy, justice, social security (employment insurance, pensions, and so on), some aspects of health care (eg., insurance, which represents approximately 90 per cent of the health budget), some public corporations, national defence and the direction of international relations (although the Regions and Communities can conclude international treaties, with some limitations). Overall, decentralization was quite substantial; in fact, Regions and Communities administer over 40 per cent of the national budget, although these financial resources are allocated by the central state.

The 1993 reform instituted two fundamental changes to central institutions and their relationships with Communities and Regions. The first change was the re-definition of the composition and role of the Senate. The new Belgian Senate includes different categories of Senators: 40 are directly elected; 21 are drawn from the Community Councils (10 from both the Flemish and French Community Councils and one from the Council of the German-speaking Community); and 10 more are appointed by Senators from the two previous categories. In most cases *(lois ordinaires),* the Senate can examine a bill and suggest modifications which may or may not be accepted by the House of Representatives. The Senate also has the power to initiate legislation but the House has final say. For issues relating to international relations and the structure of the state *(lois bicamérales),* bills have to be approved by both the House and the Senate on equal footing. For community questions *(lois votées à majorité spéciale),* the legislative process involves a special procedure that necessitates majority support within each parliamentary linguistic group (Flemish and French) both in the House and in the Senate as well as a two-thirds majority in each of the two chambers. Membership in a parliamentary linguistic group is decided by the linguistic regime of the constituency where a parliamentarian has been elected. The formal existence of these groups stems from Article 43 of the constitution.

The second change brought by the 1993 reform was the introduction of direct elections in the Flemish and Walloon Parliaments where members were previously drawn from the House of Representatives. The Flemish Parliament now has 118 directly elected members and six other members drawn from the Flemish group in the Brussels Parliament. The Capital Region's Parliament, which has had directly elected representatives since 1988, has 75 representatives – 65 French-speakers and 10 Dutch-speakers. The French Community Council is composed of all members of the Walloon Parliament plus 19 French-speaking members of the Brussels Parliament. The German-speaking Community has directly elected its 25 members since 1983. As a consequence of this change, the number of federal House members was lowered to 150;

they remain directly elected using a proportional representation system (Article 62).

Sensitivity to the protection of the French-speaking minority is reflected in the federal executive where there must be an equal number of Dutch- and French-speaking ministers (Article 99). The Prime Minister is exempt from that rule and is most often Flemish. The other component of Belgium's dual federal executive, the monarch (currently Albert II), does not have a linguistic personality *per se*; his symbolic significance lies in his embodiment of a Belgian nation irrespective of cultural/linguistic differences.

Belgian politicians have always been reluctant to give substantial power to the judiciary in the political system. However, the federalization of the state left them no choice but to create a court (Cour d'arbitrage) that would control the constitutionality of laws with respect to the division of power among the federal government, Regions and Communities. The scope of the *Cour* remains quite narrow in other matters: it can rule only on the principles of equality (Article 10), non-discrimination (Article 11), and freedom in the area of education (Article 24). Its composition is guided by the idea of linguistic parity and resistance to the "government of judges." Thus, the *Cour* includes 12 judges, half of whom are Dutch-speakers and the other half French-speakers, and also half are professional judges and half are ex-politicians who are not necessarily trained in the law. There are two Presidents, one from each linguistic group, working on the basis of an alternating effective presidency.

The procedure for amending the Belgian constitution is complex. The federal Parliament must be dissolved, an election held, and only then can the newly constituted Parliament hold a vote on the proposed constitutional revision. In order to pass, the proposal must receive support of a two-thirds majority in each chamber. This procedure is somewhat antiquated; it was devised when Belgium was a unitary state and, as a consequence, does not involve the constituent units or even include references to linguistic groups. Ironically, the legislative process, as it relates to community issues (*lois votées à majorité spéciale*), offers more protection for the minority linguistic group than the amending formula of the constitution.

Two constitutional provisions deserve mention for their significance to political accommodation in multilingual (or multi-ethnic) societies and federalism in Belgium. The first provision is the 'alarm-bell' procedure designed further to protect French-speakers. This procedure allows a federal parliamentary linguistic group, if it can present a list with the signatures of three-quarters of its members, temporarily to stop a legislative initiative it fears threatens its Community or endangers Community relations (Article 54). The legislative text is then sent back to the Cabinet (where there is linguistic parity) which can amend it, accept it as is (in this case it needs to show how the legislation would not have the negative consequences foreseen by the motion's backers), or simply resign. The alarm-bell procedure complements the legislative mechanism of 'special laws' and the principle of executive parity. It is also used in the bilingual Region of Brussels where it protects the Flemish minority.

The second provision gives Regions and Communities power in the area of international cooperation, including treaty-making power on matters falling within their respective jurisdictions (Article 167). The units must keep the federal government informed of their international activity; in fact, if the national Cabinet has any objections to a specific treaty, it can send the matter to a conciliation body made up of members from all governments (*la conférence interministérielle de la politique étrangère*) which gives a consensual decision either to stop the treaty or let it go ahead. If a consensus cannot be reached, the federal government can suspend the treaty-making process, although only if it clashes with Belgium's international obligations or involves foreign countries with which Belgium has bad or no diplomatic relations. Despite these control mechanisms, Belgium's constituent units have great power in international relations which can perhaps be seen as either pushing the federal logic to its ultimate conclusion, or as presaging a more decentralized, compartmentalized form of political organization.

Another important institution in this context is the "Concertation Committee," a multilateral body composed of the federal Prime Minister, five federal ministers, and six members of the federated governments (1980 Ordinary Act of Institutional Reforms, Article 31). This body is equally divided between French- and Dutch-speakers. Its role is to solve so-called "conflicts of interest," that is, actions by one order of government in the federation that can have an adverse impact on another order. It does not review the legality but the actual advisability (*opportunité*) of an executive or legislative measure. The potentially "injured" executive can refer the matter to the Committee, which freezes the proposed measure for up to 60 days while it attempts to find a compromise. Legislative assemblies can also, upon a vote of three-quarters of their members, submit the legislative bill of another assembly to the Concertation Committee. If no solution emerges within the 60 days, the challenged legislative measure can be adopted.

3 RECENT POLITICAL DYNAMICS

The Belgian political scene was greatly transformed following the 1999 elections. For the first time in nearly 40 years, the Christian parties (Flemish and French) were left out of the federal government. The big winners were the Liberals, who now lead a governing coalition (the Prime Minster is Flemish Liberal Guy Verhofstadt) involving the Socialists and the Greens. These elections further confirmed a now well-established convention of Belgian politics: despite the split of the traditional parties along linguistic lines, parties from the same ideological family are part of, or left out of, the federal government together. Indeed, the politicization of linguistic divisions in Belgium has added to, rather than superseded, ideological differences.

The key issues facing Belgian federalism, however, stem from the 'community question'. One continuing controversy involves the 120,000 or so francophones living in Flanders, close to the linguistic border or on the periphery of the Brussels Region. These French-speakers enjoy "linguistic facilities" – which means access to municipal services, a very important issue in Belgium because the municipality is often the point of contact between citizens and federal services – the exact status of which has already been at the centre of several other controversies. For Flemish parties, the facilities are temporary and transitional measures, and the ultimate fate of these francophone populations is assimilation into the dominant Flemish culture. Francophone parties denounce this position and view linguistic facilities as permanent fixtures. These polarized positions give the issue of the French-speaking minority in Flanders the potential to cause acute conflict in present-day Belgian politics.

Not too far behind is the larger question of Belgium's political future. Flemish leaders view the 1993 reform as just another step towards increased autonomy, the creation of a confederal model, or perhaps even the dissolution of the Belgian state into a new continental political order such as the "Europe of Regions." This vision is opposed by francophones who tend to see the last constitutional revision as the final one, and resist any further decentralization. The contrast in positions is exemplified by the recent debate over social security: many Dutch-speakers seek its 'federalization' while francophones want to see it remain in the domain of the central government. Francophone parties in the governing coalition recently accepted a proposal to 'federalize' agriculture and foreign trade in exchange for a 're-financing' of the Communities. This newest package of constitutional reforms known as the Saint-Polycarpe Accord, which also features certain fiscal autonomy for the Regions, underwent formal ratification in the summer of 2001.

There are two other sources of tension worth mentioning in Belgium federalism. The first is the uncertainty relating to the future of the Walloon Region and French Community. Unlike in Flanders, the two units have not merged; Walloon regionalists oppose, and indeed fear, the dissolution of Wallonia within the French Community. As a consequence, the relative importance of these two units remains an open-ended question, although the Walloon Region has, because of greater financial resources, a decided advantage.

The second source of tension comes from the Vlaams Blok, a far-right Flemish nationalist party which espouses neo-fascist positions on such issues as immigration and rejects the Belgian political framework. The Vlaams Blok's goal of creating an independent Flemish state is, however, an unlikely outcome for a number of reasons: (1) Brussels, with its large francophone majority, would be too hard to swallow but impossible to forgo for historical and symbolic reasons; (2) secession would most likely be unwelcome by Belgium's European partners; (3) the Flemish fully control their regional institutions and can wield much power at the national level as a result of their numerical majority; and (4) attachment to Belgium, among both Flemish- and French-speakers, remains substantial, despite, or perhaps because of, the massive decentralization process engineered by its elites.

4 SOURCES FOR FURTHER INFORMATION

Alen, André, *Belgium: Bipolar and Centrifugal Federalism*, Brussels: Minister of Foreign Affairs, External Trade and Development Cooperation, 1990.

Alen, André and Rusen Ergec, *Federal Belgium after the Fourth State Reform of 1993*, 2nd ed., Brussels: Ministry of Foreign Affairs, External Trade and Cooperation for Development, 1998.

Craenen, G. (ed.), *The Institutions of Federal Belgium: An Introduction to Belgian Public Law*, Leuven: Acco, 1996.

Deprez, Kas and Louis Vos (eds), *Nationalism in Belgium. Shifting Identities, 1780–1995*, New York: St. Martin's Press, 1998.

Mabille, Xavier, *Histoire politique de la Belgique. Facteurs et acteurs de changement*, 2nd ed., Bruxelles: CRISP, 1997.

Martiniello, Marco and Marc Swyngedouw (eds), *Où va la Belgique? Les soubresauts d'une petite démocratie européenne*, Paris: L'Harmattan, 1998.

McRae, Kenneth D., *Conflict and Compromise in Multilingual Societies. Belgium*, Waterloo: Wilfrid Laurier University Press, 1986.

www.belgium.be
www.cfwb.be
www.vlaanderen.be
www.dglive.be
www.wallonie.be
www.bruxelles.irisnet.be

Table I
Political and Geographic Indicators

Capital city	Brussels
Number and type of constituent units	*10 provinces:* Antwerpen, Brabant Wallon, Hainaut, Liege, Limburg, Luxembourg, Namur, Oost-Vlaanderen, Vlaams Brabant, West-Vlaanderen (Note: the Brussels Capital Region is not included within the 10 provinces.) In addition, these provinces are divided into: *3 Regions* (Flemish, Walloon and Brussels) which have authority over socio-economic matters such as urban planning, housing, environment, economic development, employment, energy, public works and transport as well as the administrative supervision of the provinces and the communities; and *3 Communities* (Flemish, French and German) which deal with cultural matters, education, use of languages and "person-related matters", such as health policy, policy of the disabled and protection of youth.
Official language(s)	Dutch/Flemish, French, German
Area	32 547 km^2 (Note: To reach this figure, the area of Brussels (162 km^2), 2 017 km^2 of sea territories (as of July 1999), and a 2 000 km^2 piece of land in Zelzate along the Ghent-Terneuzen Canal (granted to Belgium by the Netherlands in May 2000) were included in the measurement.)
Area – Largest constituent unit	Luxembourg (4 440 km^2)
Area – Smallest constituent unit	Brabant Wallon (1 091 km^2)
Total population	10 239 085
Population by constituent unit (% of total population)	Antwerpen 16%, Oost-Vlaanderen 13.3%, Hainaut 12.5%, West-Vlaanderen 11%, Liege 10%, Vlaams Brabant 9.9%, Limburg 7.7%, Namur 4.3%, Brabant Wallon 3.4%, Luxembourg 2.4%
Political system – federal	Constitutional Monarchy – Parliamentary System
Head of state – federal	King Albert II
Head of government – federal	Prime Minister Guy Verhofstadt, Vlaamse Liberalen en Democraten – VLD (Flemish Liberals and Democrats). The VLD is a coalition government comprising members from the VLD, PRL, PS, SP, Agalev and Ecolo. The Prime Minister and Council of Ministers (Cabinet) are appointed by Monarch and then approved by Parliament, to serve a maximum 4-year term.

Table I (continued)

Government structure – federal	Bicameral Parliament: *Upper House* – Senate, 71 seats. 40 members are directly elected by popular vote, 31 are indirectly elected, all serve 4-year terms. *Lower House* – Chamber of Deputies, 150 seats. Members are directly elected by popular vote on the basis of proportional representation to serve maximum 4-year terms.
Number of representatives in lower house of federal government – Chamber of Deputies	150 Seats: Vlaamse Liberalen en Democraten – VLD (Flemish Liberals and Democrats) 23, Christelijke Volkspartij VLP (Christian People's Party) 22, Parti Socialiste – PS (Socialist Party) 19, PRL-FDF-MCC (Parti Réformateur Libéral /Liberal Reformist Party, Front Démocratique des Francophones/Democratic Front of Francophones, Mouvement des Citoyens pour le Changement/Citizens' Movement for Change) 18, Vlaams Blok –VB (Flemish Block) 15, Socialistische Partij – SP (Socialist Party) 14, Ecolo 11, Agalev 9, Parti Social Chrétien – PSC (Christian Social Party) 10, Volksunie-ID21 (People's Union-ID21) (Volksunie-Vlaamse Vrije Democraten – ID21, VU-ID21 (People's Union-Flemish Free Democrats) 8, Front National/ Front voor de Natie – FN (National Front/Front for the Nation) 1.
Number of representatives in lower house of federal government for most populated constituent unit	Antwerpen: 24 (14 for Anvers, 10 for Malines-Turnhout)
Number of representatives in lower house of federal government for least populated constituent unit	Luxembourg: 3
Number of representatives in upper house of federal government – Senate	71 seats: VLD 6, CVP 6, PRL-FDF-MCC 5, PS 4, VB 4, Socialistische Partij (14) 4, Ecolo 3, Agalev 3, PSC 3, VU-ID21 2; indirectly elected senators 31.
Distribution of representation in upper house of federal government – Senate	40 members (of which 25 are Dutch and 15 are French) are elected through popular vote, 31 are indirectly elected in the following manner – 10 each are drawn from the French and Flemish Community Council and 1 from the German Community Council, and 10 (of which 6 are Dutch and 4 are French) are appointed by Senators from the 2 previous categories.
Constitutional court (highest court dealing with constitutional matters)	Supreme Court of Justice (Hof van Cassatie – Dutch, Cour de Cassation – French). Judges are appointed for life by the monarch.

Table I (continued)

Political system of constituent units	Due to the 1993 constitutional revision that lead to the federal state, there are now three levels of government (federal, regional and linguistic community) with a complex division of responsibilities. Dutch-, French- and German-speaking Communities and the Flemish, Walloon and Brussels Regions each have a directly elected Parliament/Legislative Council and an executive body elected by and from the Councils. The Councils deal mostly with regional economic matters. The 3 Linguistic Communities have their own Councils that are responsible for cultural and educational matters.
Head of state – constituent units	Representative of King Albert II: Provincial Governor. The Provincial Governor is named by the monarch. He/she is also the first representative of the federal government at the provincial level, and the representative, more precisely of the Ministry of the Interior. In recent years, the Provincial Governor has also become the representative at the provincial level of Regional and Community governments.
Head of government – constituent units	Regional Legislative Councils and Linguistic Community Legislative Councils. There are also Communal Commissions. The makeup of the executive body is dependent upon the region/community in questions. All are directly elected from the councils.

Table II
Economic and Social Indicators

GDP	US$259.2 billion
GDP per capita	US$25 300
Mechanisms for taxation	The Central, Communal and Municipal Governments impose taxes. • Income Tax – ranges from 25% to 55% • Municipal Tax – approximately 8% • Crisis Tax (or surcharge) of 4% on income (to be abolished). Various real estate, excise and corporate taxes are also imposed at all three levels of government.
National debt (external)	$28.3 billion
National unemployment rate	8.4%
Constituent unit with highest unemployment rate	Hainaut – 16.6% (1999)
Constituent unit with lowest unemployment rate	Vlaams Brabant – 3.9% (1999)
Adult literacy rate	99%
National expenditures on education as a % of GDP	6.1%
Life expectancy in years	77.3
Doctors per population ratio (national)	403.7 doctors per 100 000 inhabitants
Doctors per population ratio in constituent units (highest)	Bruxelles and Brabant Wallon (combined): 680.9 doctors per 100 000 inhabitants
Doctors per population ratio in constituent units (lowest)	Limburg: 273.5 doctors per 100 000 inhabitants
National expenditures on health as a % of GDP	8.6%

Sources

Behrens, Axel. "Regional Gross Domestic Product in the European Union 1998." *Statistics in Focus.* Theme 1–3/2001. Produced by Eurostat. www.europa.eu.int/comm/eurostat/

Behrens, Axel. "Unemployment in the Regions of the European Union 1999." *Statistics in Focus.* Theme 1–3/2000. Produced by Eurostat www.europa.eu.int/comm/eurostat/

Belgium Federal Government National Website. www.belgium.fgov.be/en_index.htm

Central Intelligence Agency (CIA), *World Fact Book 2000.* CIA, www.cia.gov/cia/publications/factbook/index.html

Economist Intelligence Unit, "Country Commerce – Belgium," *The Economist Intelligence Unit 2000.* New York: EIU, 2000.

Elazar, Daniel J. (ed.), *Federal Systems of the World: A Handbook of Federal, Confederal and Autonomy Arrangements.* 2nd Edition. Jerusalem Institute for Federal Studies. London: Longman Group/Westgate House, 1994.

International Labour Office. "Indicators on Unemployment." UNSD. www.un.org/Depts/unsd/social/unempl.htm

International Monetary Fund (IMF). *International Financial Statistics,* Vol. LIII, No. 12, December 2000. Washington, DC: the IMF Statistics Department, 2000.

Organisation for Economic Co-operation and Development (OECD). 2000. www.oecd.org/std/gdp.htm

Scientific Institute of Public Health. Ministry of Social Affairs, Public Health and Environment (Belgium). "Tableau 10: Densité médicale par 10 000 hab au 1/1/2000." www.iph.fgov.be

United Nations/ECE. *Trends in Europe and North America 1999: Country Profiles from the* UN/ECE *Statistical Yearbook,* UN/ECE Statistical Division www.unece.org/

United Nations. "Human Development Index," "Gender-Related Development Index," *Human*

Development Report, 2000. Human Development Report Office. www.undp.org/hdro/report.html

United Nations Statistics Division, "InfoNation," UNSD On-line database, www.un.org/

Watts, Ronald L. *Comparing Federal Systems.* 2nd edition. School of Policy Studies. Montreal/Kingston: McGill-Queen's University Press, 1999.

Watts, Ronald L., *The Spending Power in Federal Systems: A Comparative Study,* Institute of Intergovernmental Relations, School of Policy Studies, Queen's University, Montreal/Kingston, 1999.

World Bank. *World Development Report 2000/2001: Attacking Poverty.* www.worldbank.org/poverty/wdrpoverty/report/index.htm

World Health Organisation (WHO). "Estimates of Health Personnel." www-nt.who.int/whosis/statistics

World Health Organisation (WHO). *World Health Report 2000.* Geneva, Switzerland, 2000. www-nt.who.int/whosis/statistics/menu.cfm

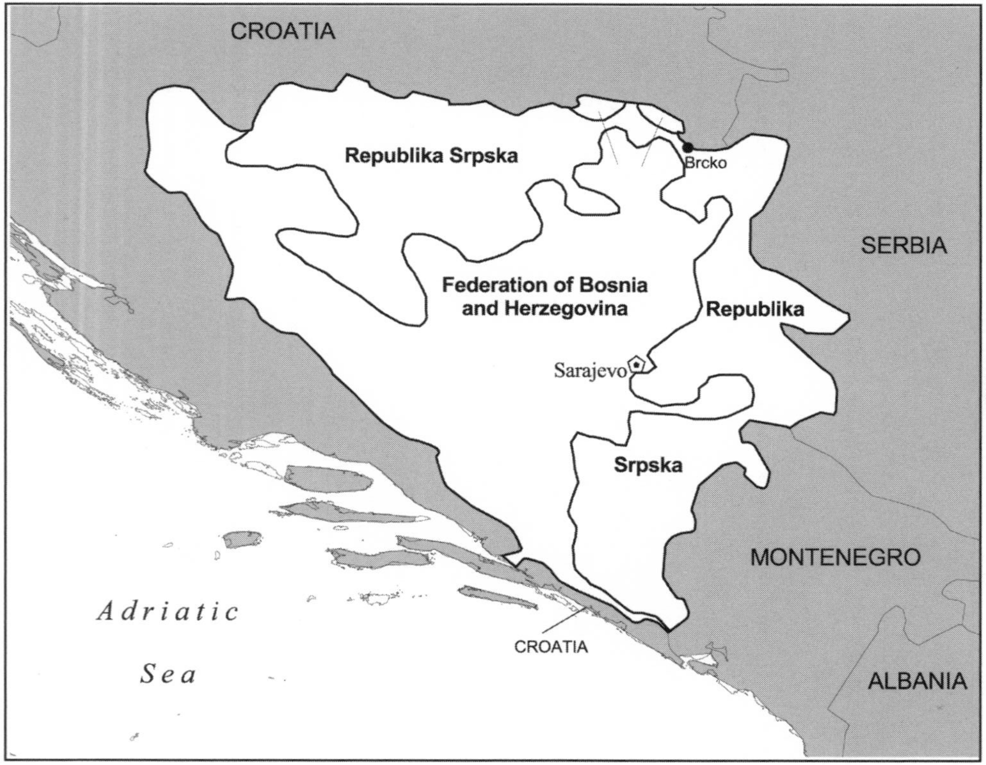

CROATIA

Republika Srpska

Brcko

SERBIA

Federation of Bosnia and Herzegovina

Republika

Sarajevo

Srpska

MONTENEGRO

Adriatic Sea

CROATIA

ALBANIA

Republic of Bosnia and Herzegovina

Capital: Sarajevo
Population: 4.3 Million
(2000 Est.)

The Brcko District is a self-governing unit under the sovereignty of Bosnia and Herzegovina, and is neither part of the Federation of Bosnia and Herzegovina nor the Republika Srpska.

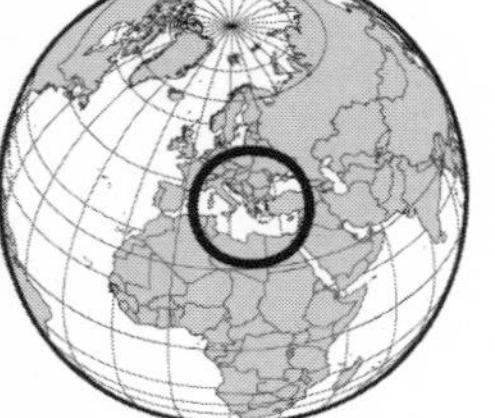

Internal boundaries are approximate,and are based upon the "Dayton Agreement" (1995); names and locations do not imply endorsement.

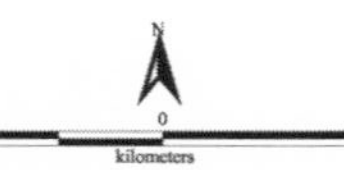

Sources: UN Cartographic Department; CIA World Factbook, ESRI Ltd. (2002); Office of the High Representative for Bosnia and Herzegovina.

Bosnia and Herzegovina (*Republic of Bosnia and Herzegovina*)

MARIE-JOËLLE ZAHAR

1 HISTORY AND DEVELOPMENT OF FEDERALISM

The Republic of Bosnia and Herzegovina (51,129 km^2) is located in southeastern Europe. It borders Croatia, Serbia and Montenegro and has a very narrow (20 km) access to the Adriatic Sea. The territory of Bosnia and Herzegovina was the site of many conquests – Roman, Goth, Slav, Hungarian and Ottoman, among others. In the twelfth century, Bosnia became a Hungarian *banat* (province). In 1376 Ban Stephen Tvrtko proclaimed himself King of Serbia and Bosnia. After his death, the kingdom disintegrated and by 1463, the Ottoman Empire had conquered most of Bosnia. It would remain an Ottoman province for the next 400 years.

In 1878, the Congress of Berlin gave Austria-Hungary administrative rights over the area. By 1908, the Austro-Hungarian Empire had annexed Bosnia and Croatia. On 1 December 1918, following the overthrow of the dual monarchy, Bosnia and Herzegovina became part of the Kingdom of the Serbs, Croats and Slovenes under the rule of Prince Aleksandar I (1921–1934). In 1929, Aleksandar renamed the kingdom Yugoslavia (i.e., "Land of the South Slavs").

During World War II, the Axis powers invaded and dismembered Yugoslavia. With their support, a pro-fascist Croat puppet state was established on the territory of Croatia and Bosnia. At the end of the war, Josip Broz Tito, a Croatian communist and leader of the resistance movement known as the Partisans, created the Federal Socialist Republic of Yugoslavia. Bosnia and Herzegovina was one of the six republics that composed the federation.

Since Ottoman times, Bosnia has been home to a Slav Muslim population. The geographic and ethnic origins of the Muslim Slavs are the subject of scholarly disagreement. The Muslims of Bosnia-Herzegovina, who speak Serbo-Croatian as their mother tongue, have consistently emphasized their unique identity. Since World War II, however, both Serbs and Croats have claimed ethnic ties with the Muslim Slavs in an attempt to gain political advantage. In 1971, Tito promoted the Slavic Muslims (also referred to as Bosniacs) to a fully-fledged constituent Yugoslav people.

The original constitution of Bosnia and Herzegovina was written in 1974 and modelled on the Yugoslav federal constitution of the same year, a charter that weakened federal institutions and decentralized Communist controls to the republican level. Under the 1974 constitution, Bosnia was endowed with a bicameral legislature: a 130-seat Chamber of Citizens and a 110-seat Chamber of Communes. The collective nine-member Presidency and the Prime Minister were to be selected from among members of the legislature. Government officials served a standard four-year term, except the President of the Presidency, who was to be elected from among the nine members for a one-year term. This rotating Presidency and the proportional representation electoral system were designed to reflect the republic's ethnic diversity.

In January 1990, the League of Communists of Yugoslavia agreed to surrender its monopoly on political power. Bosnia held its first multiparty elections that same year. Three major nationalist parties dominated the political scene: the SDA (Stranka Demokratska Akcija led by Alija Izetbegovic), the HDZ (Hrvatska Demokratska Zajednice Bosne-i-Hercegovine led by Mate Boban) and the SDS (Srpska Demokratska Stranka led by Radovan Karadzic). Temporarily united against the Communist Party, a coalition of the three parties held the collective Bosnian Presidency. Strains would soon tear the coalition apart.

The dismemberment of the former Yugoslavia had already begun. In 1991, a ten-day war failed to prevent the secession of Slovenia. In September of the same year, Macedonia declared its independence. The war in Croatia lasted seven months (July 1991 to January 1992). Upon recognition of Croatia's independence by the European Community, Bosnia faced a stark choice: either remain in Serb-dominated Yugoslavia or declare independence too. In October 1991, Muslim and Croat members of Parliament – but not Serb members –

approved the holding of a referendum on sovereignty. The referendum, held in February 1992, was boycotted by Serbs but 64.4% of eligible voters cast their votes and 99.7% of those votes favoured independence. In March 1992, Bosnia proclaimed independence and descended into war.

In March 1994, under international pressure, Bosnia's Muslim and Croatian leaders signed an agreement in Washington, DC, that ended the conflict between the two groups and established a Muslim-Croat federation, officially called the Federation of Bosnia and Herzegovina. The federation became one of the two "entities" of Bosnia and Herzegovina.

On 21 November 1995, Serb, Croat and Muslim leaders initialled a peace agreement at Wright-Patterson Airbase in Dayton, Ohio. This ended almost four years of conflict in which 250,000 people were killed, two million became refugees, and terrible atrocities were committed. The General Framework Agreement for Peace (GFAP, also known as the Dayton Peace Agreement or DPA) was signed by all the parties in Paris (14 December 1995) and became the basis for peace in Bosnia and Herzegovina.

2 CONSTITUTIONAL PROVISIONS RELATING TO FEDERALISM

In Annex 4 of the Dayton Peace Agreement, the mediators and negotiating parties outlined a new national constitution for Bosnia and Herzegovina. Under its terms, Bosnia is a democracy consisting of two constituent entities: the Federation of Bosnia and Herzegovina, which is also known as the Bosniac-Croat Federation (thus establishing a federation within a federation), and the Republika Srpska (hereafter "the entities").

The federal structures reflect the complexity of the ethno-territorial arrangement reached at Dayton. The entities share a central legislature, the Parliamentary Assembly of Bosnia and Herzegovina (Article IV) – consisting of a House of Representatives and a House of Peoples (note that there is a "House of Representatives" and a "House of Peoples" at the federal level *and* in the Bosniac-Croat Federation) – and a three-member collective Presidency (Article V). This central government is two-thirds Muslim and Croat and one-third Serb.

The federal House of Peoples is comprised of 15 delegates – two-thirds come from the Bosniac-Croat Federation (five Croats and five Bosniacs), while the other third (five Serbs) comes from Republika Srpska (RS). Croat and Bosniac delegates are elected respectively by the Croat and Bosniac delegates to the federal House of Peoples. The National Assembly of Republika Srpska selects the Serb delegates to the federal House of Peoples.

The federal House of Representatives comprises 42 members, two-thirds elected from the Bosniac-Croat Federation and one-third from the Republika Srpska. The constitution does not specify how representatives are to be elected, only that they "shall be directly elected from their Entity in accordance with an election law to be adopted by the Parliamentary Assembly" (IV-2(a)). However, the two entities have adopted a proportional party list system according to which voters vote for a party rather than an individual.

All legislation requires the approval of both chambers and decisions are made by a majority of those present and voting (IV-3(c), IV-3(d)). However, the constitution also stipulates that members attempt to ensure that the majority includes at least one-third of votes of members from each entity.

Members of the Presidency (one representative from each group – Bosniac, Croat and Serb) are directly elected from the Bosniac-Croat Federation (Bosniac and Croat members) and from the RS (Serb member).

The constitution delineates the rights and duties of both entities. The division of power is as follows. The federal institutions are responsible for: foreign policy and trade; customs; monetary policy; finances of the institutions and international obligations of Bosnia and Herzegovina; immigration, refugee, and asylum policy and regulation; international and inter-entity criminal law enforcement; the establishment and operation of common and international communications facilities; regulation of inter-entity transportation; and air traffic control (III-1). Additionally, the constitution allows the central institutions to take measures and create additional institutions as necessary in order to preserve the sovereignty, territorial integrity, political independence, and international personality of the country (III-5). The same provision opens the door for the eventual transfer of responsibilities temporarily entrusted to the institutions created under Annexes 5–8 of the General Framework Agreement for Peace (GFAP) back to the central authorities.

All governmental functions and powers not expressly assigned in the constitution to the central institutions fall immediately within the preserve of the entities (III-3-a). The most important of these functions and powers must certainly be the power of taxation. The two entities are also responsible for civilian law enforcement, health care, agriculture and local affairs. However, in some cases, the entities may appear to intrude into the jurisdiction of the central government. Thus, although foreign policy is in the purview of the central government, the entities can establish relationships with neighbouring states, and enter agreements with foreign states and international organizations with the consent of the federal Parliamentary Assembly. The entity and central governments are jointly entrusted with the regulation of citizenship (I-5), the protection of the human rights enshrined in the European Convention on Human Rights and 15 other similar international instruments listed in Annex 1 of the constitution (II).

The constitution does not specifically outline federal financial arrangements. It does, however, give the power of taxation to the entities, and provide general guidelines regarding the financial responsibilities of the entities vis-à-vis the federal institutions. Article IV-4(b) states that the federal Parliamentary Assembly has responsibility for "deciding upon the sources and amounts of revenues for the operations of the institutions ... and international obligations of Bosnia and Herzegovina." Under Article VIII-1, each year the Parliamentary Assembly adopts a budget covering these expenditures. The Bosniac-Croat Federation provides two-thirds and the RS one-third of the revenues required by the federal budget, "except insofar as revenues are raised as specified by the Parliamentary Assembly" (VIII-3). Under Article III-2(b) the entities are also expected to provide "all necessary assistance" to the central government in order to enable it to honour its international obligations.

Article VI sets out procedures for the resolution of constitutional disputes. This article provides for the establishment of a Constitutional Court consisting of nine members. The Court has exclusive jurisdiction to resolve disputes between the entities, between Bosnia and Herzegovina and an entity or entities, or between institutions of the central government (VI-3(a)). The Court also has appellate jurisdiction over issues under the constitution arising out of the judgement of any other Bosnian court. The Bosniac-Croat House of Representatives selects four members of the Constitutional Court and the Assembly of the Republika Srpska selects two members. The remaining three members are non-Bosnians selected by the President of the European Court of Human Rights after consultation with the Presidency (VI-1). The unusual appointment of foreigners to the Constitutional Court reflects international concerns about the fragility of the Dayton scheme and the heavy international involvement to bring about its implementation.

Article X provides for amendments to the constitution to be based on a decision of the Parliamentary Assembly, including a two-thirds majority of those present and voting in the federal House of Representatives. It is important to note, however, that Article X specifically states that no amendment may eliminate or diminish any of the rights and freedoms listed in Article II of the constitution. This refers to the fact that the constitution includes a number of special provisions relating to human rights, refugee rights and the "vital interests" of the three constituent peoples of the country. These special provisions are a function of the circumstances surrounding the drafting of the constitution and its inclusion in the General Framework Agreement that ended the war in Bosnia.

Article II-1 provides for the establishment of a Human Rights Commission for the country. This commission is comprised of an ombudsman appointed by the chairman of the Organization for Security and Cooperation in Europe (OSCE) and 14 members – six Bosnians (four members from the Bosniac-Croat Federation and two members from Republika Srpska) and eight non-Bosnians appointed by the Committee of Ministers of the Council of Europe, after consultation with the parties. Article II also states that the rights and freedoms set forth in the European Convention for the Protection of Human Rights and Fundamental Freedoms and its Protocols have priority over all other law (II-2), and contains a lengthy statement about the rights of refugees and displaced persons to return to their places of origin and have property lost in the hostilities restored to them (II-5).

The constitution also requires that all competent authorities in Bosnia cooperate with and provide unrestricted access to international human rights monitoring mechanisms, the supervisory bodies established by the international agreements listed in Annex I to the constitution, the International Criminal Tribunal for the Former Yugoslavia, as well as any other organization authorized by the UN Security Council with a mandate concerning human rights and humanitarian law (II-8).

Finally, a proposed decision of the Parliamentary Assembly may be declared "destructive to a vital interest of the Bosniac, Croat, or Serb people" (IV-3(e)). This provision allows members of the ethnic groups to block the enactment of contested legislation (IV-3(e)). In such instances, a joint committee including three members of each ethnic group reviews the legislation; if it fails to reach agreement, the matter is forwarded to the Constitutional Court (IV-3(f)). A similar veto exists within the Presidency (V-2(d)).

It is important to note that, although symmetrical in their relation to one another and to the federal institutions, the two entities are organized according to different principles. As its name indicates, the

Federation of Bosnia and Herzegovina, or Bosniac-Croat Federation, is organized according to federal principles. It consists of eight cantons (territorial subdivisions) ruled by a strong central government. The Presidency, Vice-Presidency, and the office of the Prime Minister rotate between the two ethnic groups. The Bosniac-Croat Federation has a bicameral legislature comprised of the House of Representatives and the House of Peoples (also referred to as the House of Nations), in addition to canton-level assemblies. Federation voters directly elect the 140 members of the entity's House of Representatives. The 74 members of the entity's House of Peoples (30 Bosniac, 30 Croat, and 14 Other) are elected from members of the cantonal legislatures – themselves elected directly by the voters in the entity.

The Republika Srpska (RS) is a highly centralized structure. The entity government directly oversees the municipalities, and cantons do not exist. The RS has a single legislative chamber or National Assembly (sometimes referred to as the House of Representatives), and a President. Members of the RS National Assembly are elected for a four-year term by simple proportional representation.

3 RECENT POLITICAL DYNAMICS

As the previous section will have illustrated, the government structure established at Dayton is extremely complex. Given this, it would be unwieldy even under optimal political conditions. The threat of paralysis is a major concern as nationalist parties have taken advantage of the complex structure to entrench themselves at the entity level.

Cooperation between the entities is minimal. Even within the Bosniac-Croat Federation, Bosniacs and Croats have maintained separate lines of authority.[1] Power sharing is premised on the willingness of the parties to compromise, but federal representatives of the three Bosnian ethnic groups have not demonstrated such willingness. Instead, the Office of the United Nations High Representative has gained a reputation for imposing solutions on the Bosnian parties whenever they reach a deadlock. Under Annex 10 of the GFAP, the High Representative is mandated to "facilitate, as [he/she] judges necessary, the resolution of any difficulties arising in connection with civilian implementation" (Article II-1(d)). In 1997, the Peace Implementation Council, which represents all the donor countries,

1 See Jon Western and Daniel Serwer, *Bosnia's Next Five Years: Dayton and Beyond*, USIP Special Report (Washington, DC: USIP, 2000), p. 2.

endowed the High Representative with the authority to make binding decisions including the right to remove "obstructionist" officials.

The powers of the High Representative are only symptomatic of a larger trend. The Dayton Peace Agreement gives the Commander of the NATO-led Stabilization Forces (SFOR) analogous powers in terms of military implementation. Annex 3 of the GFAP provides the OSCE with a mandate to administer elections for all levels of government, a mandate that has been repeatedly extended beyond its original scope. Annex 6 established the Human Rights Commission for Bosnia, the highest judicial resort in human rights cases. As discussed earlier, the OSCE and the Committee of Ministers of the Council of Europe respectively nominate the commission's ombudsman and human rights chamber, with a foreign majority.

In recent years a number of major regional changes have occurred, including NATO's Kosovo campaign, the death of Croat President Franjo Tudjman, and the overthrow of Slobodan Milosevic in Yugoslavia. These regional changes have spurred calls for accelerating Bosnia and Herzegovina's post-conflict transition. However, opinions are divided on the means of achieving such an objective.

Centrifugal forces include the growing strength of the multi-ethnic Alliance for Change, a coalition of 10 moderate parties, which won a slight majority in the November 2000 elections to the Bosniac-Croat Federation Parliament thus marginalizing the nationalist Bosniac SDP and Croat HDZ. Many observed, however, that despite years of effort and expense by the international community, the electorate still generally voted along ethnic lines. Before the elections, the OSCE's Provisional Electoral Commission (PEC) changed the electoral procedures for the Bosniac-Croat Federation's Parliament. Initially Croat and Bosniac members of the cantonal assemblies elected their respective deputies to the entity's House of Peoples. Under the new rules, members of the cantonal assemblies can vote for a deputy in Parliament irrespective of their nationality. In Republika Srpska, the nationalist SDS party managed to wrest 30 per cent of votes but failed to win the necessary support among other parties to form the government.

The federal Constitutional Court has also issued a number of landmark decisions. The Court struck down the consociational arrangement enshrined in the Law on the Council of Ministers of 1996, thus effectively leaving the country without a government. The law, adopted when the federal House of Representatives failed in 1996 to achieve agreement on a single candidate, stated that the chair of the Council consists of two co-chairs and a vice-chair who occupy the positions on a rotating basis. This contradicts Article IV of the constitution according to which the chair of the Council is a single individual. Parliament enacted a law providing that Council chairmanship rotate among the three constituent peoples every eight months.

Sidelining extremists continues to require the active involvement of the international community. In November 1999, High Representative Wolfgang Petritsch used his special powers to dismiss 22 officials from elected positions, targeting hard-line Serb, Croat and Bosniac nationalist politicians. Earlier that same year, the OSCE refused to register the Serb Radical Party and the Serb Party of Krajina and Posavina for the April municipal elections. The lists of both parties included persons accused of violating the Dayton Agreement. These elections – certified by the OSCE as fair and free – indicated that Croat and Serb nationalist parties continue to dominate at the municipal level while the Bosniac Party for Democratic Action (SDA) suffered significant losses in major urban areas at the hands of the multi-ethnic Social Democratic Party (SDP).

More recently, the Croat National Democratic Union Party (HDZ) and the Croatian Democratic Union of Bosnia and Herzegovina (CDUBH) reacted strongly to the changes introduced by the Office of the High Representative (OHR) to the legislative procedures of the Bosniac-Croat Federation. In conjunction with the November 2000 general elections, the CDUBH organized a referendum of the Croat people asking whether they thought the Croat part of the Bosniac-Croat Federation should be given greater autonomy. In March 2001, the CDUBH held a Croat National Assembly, declared the Federation of Bosnia and Herzegovina (the entity) dead and proclaimed so-called Croat self-government. The Assembly stated that it would no longer recognize the authority of the entity government on the territory under Croat self-government. Relations between the CDUBH and the OHR continue to be tense.

4 SOURCES FOR FURTHER INFORMATION

Constitutional Watch–Bosnia, *East European Constitutional Review.* All volumes.

Hayden, Robert M., "Bosnia: The Contradictions of "Democracy" Without Consent," *East European Constitutional Review,* Vol. 7, No. 2 (Spring 1998).

O'Hanlon, Michael, "Turning the Bosnia Ceasefire into Peace," *The Brookings Review,* Vol. 16, No. 1 (Winter 1998).

Western, Jon and Daniel Serwer, *Bosnia's Next Five Years: Dayton and Beyond,* USIP Special Report (Washington, DC: USIP, 2000).

http://www.bosnianembassy.org
http://www.ohr.int
http://www.odci.gov/cia/publications/factbook/geos/bk.html
http://www.intl-crisis-group.org
http://www.bosnia.org.uk
http://www.nytimes.com/specials/bosnia/
http://www.washingtonpost.com/wp-srv/inatl/longterm/worldref/country/bosniahz.htm

Table I
Political and Geographic Indicators

Capital city	Sarajevo
Number and type of constituent units	*2 Administrative Divisions/Entities*: Bosniac-Croat Federation, Republika Srpska (Note: Brcko in northeastern Bosnia is a self-governing administrative unit under the sovereignty of Bosnia and Herzegovina, but is not part of either the Bosniac-Croat Federation or the Republika Srpska.)
Official language(s)	Bosnian, Serbian and Croatian
Area	51 129 km^2
Area – Largest constituent unit	Bosniac-Croat Federation (26 076 km^2)
Area – Smallest constituent unit	Republika Srpska (25 053 km^2)
Total population	3 972 000 (Note: The population is difficult to estimate due to large displacement of persons during the war in 1999).
Population by constituent unit (% of total population)	Bosniac-Croat Federation 66%, Republika Srpska 34%
Political system – federal	Emerging Democracy – Federation
Head of state – federal	The presidency is a three-member rotating position, each member serving for 1 year. Presidency: Živko Radišić, Beriz Belkic. (Note: Ante Jelavić, the third member, was dismissed from his post by the United Nations High Representative in March 2001). The three members of the Presidency (1 Bosniac, 1 Croat and 1 Serb) are elected by popular vote to serve a 4-year term. The member with the most votes becomes the Chair of the Council unless he or she was the incumbent at the time of the election. Chair: Jozo Krizanovi (since 14 June 2001).
Head of government – federal	Chairman of the Council of Ministers: Zlatko Lagumdzija (since 18 July 2001). The chairman of the Council of Ministers is appointed by the presidency and confirmed by the National House of Representatives. The Council of Ministers (cabinet) is nominated by the council chairman. The Council of Ministers must be approved by the National House of Representatives.

Table I (continued)

Government structure – federal	Bicameral – Skupstina (Parliament): *First Chamber* – Zastupnički dom/Predstavnički dom (House of Representatives), 42 seats. Members are elected through proportional representation to serve 2-year terms. Of these 42 seats, 28 members are elected from the Bosniac-Croat Federation (14 Bosniacs and 14 Croats) and 14 members (Serbs) are elected from the Republika Srpska. *Second Chamber* – Dom Narodu (House of Peoples), 15 Seats (5 Bosniac, 5 Croat and 5 Serb), of these seats, 10 are elected by the National Assembly of the Bosniac-Croat Federation and 5 members by the Parliament of the Republika Srpska through party lists.
Number of representatives in lower house of federal government – House of Representatives	42 Seats: Socijaldemokratska Partija Bosne I Hercegovine-Socijaldemokrati – SDP (Social Democratic Party) 9, Stranka Demokratski Akcije – SDA (Party of Democratic Action) 8, Srpska Demokratska Stranka – SDS (Serb Democratic Party) 6, Hrvatska Demokratska Zajednica – HDZ-BiH (Croatian Democratic Community) 5, Stranka za Bosnu i Hercegovinu – SBH (Party for Bosnia and Herzegovina) 4, PDP 2, Nova Hrvatska Inicijativa – NHI (New Croatian Initiative) 1, Democratska Stranka Penzionera – DSP (Democratic Party of Pensioners) 1, Srpski Narodni Savez RS – Biljana Plavšić – SNS (Serbian People's Union – Biljana Plavsic) 1, Stranka Nezavisnih Socijaldemokrata (Party of Independent Social Democrats) and Demokratska Socialisticka Partija (Democratic Socialist Party) – SNSD-DSP 1, Democratska Narodna Zajednica – DNZ (Democratic Peoples Union) 1, Socialisticka Partija Republika Srpska – SPRS (Socialist Party RS) 1.
Number of representatives in lower house of federal government for most populated constituent unit	Bosniac-Croat Federation: 28 members (14 Bosniac and 14 Croats)
Number of representatives in lower house of federal government for least populated constituent unit	Republika Srpska: 14 members (Serbs)
Number of representatives in upper house of federal government – House of Peoples	15 seats
Distribution of representation in upper house of federal government – House of Peoples	15 seats: 10 Bosniac-Croat Federation (5 Croats, 5 Bosniacs) 5 Republika Srpska

Table I (continued)

Constitutional court (highest court dealing with constitutional matters)	Constitutional Court. Consists of nine members. Four members are selected by the Bosniac/Croat Federation's House of Representatives, two members are selected by the Republika Srpska's National Assembly, and three non-Bosnian members are selected by the President of the European Court of Human Rights.
Political system of constituent units	The Parliament of the Bosniac-Croat Federation is Bicameral: Zastupnički dom Federacije (House of Representatives) has 140 members, elected for 4-year terms by proportional representation. Dom Narodu (House of Peoples) has 74 members (30 Bosniac, 30 Croat and 14 others). The National Assembly of the Republika Srpska is Unicameral and has 83 members elected by popular vote to serve 4-year terms.
Head of government – constituent units	Bosniac-Croat Federation: President Karlo Filipvic (since February 2001), Vice-President Safet Halilovic (since February 2001). Note: The President and Vice-President rotate every year. Republika Srpska: President Mirko Sarovic (since November 2001)

Table II
Economic and Social Indicators

GDP	US$6.5 billion
GDP per capita	US$1 700
Mechanisms for taxation	The Constituent Units are autonomous in their taxation mechanisms, sharing the taxation powers among the cantons (in the case of the Bosniac-Croat Federation) and the municipalities (in the case of the Republika Srpska). Bosniac-Croat Federation levies the following taxes: • Corporate Tax: 30% • Personal Income Tax: 2 brackets 15% and 25%. • Sales tax: 20%, however a sales tax on services is also levied on the value of goods sold at the retail stage, so that the actual total sales tax on goods is 32%. • Wage Withholding Tax – 15% and a cantonal personal income tax rate of up to 50% also being deducted. • Various excise taxes on tobacco and alcohol. Republika Srpska: • Corporate Tax – 4 rates ranging from 10-20% • Personal Income Tax – 3 rates ranging from 15-25% • Sales tax – on average 20% but may vary from 5 to 20% • Wage Withholding Tax – 15% with a municipal personal income tax rate of up to 45% also being deducted. • Various excise taxes on tobacco and alcohol.
National debt (external)	US$3.4 billion
National unemployment rate	35-40%
Constituent unit with highest unemployment rate	Republika Srpska: 38.6%
Constituent unit with lowest unemployment rate	Bosniac-Croat Federation: 35%
Adult literacy rate	92.7%
National expenditures on education as a % of GDP	N/A
Life expectancy in years	71.75
Doctors per population ratio (national)	143 doctors per 100,000 inhabitants
Doctors per population ratio in constituent units (highest)	N/A
Doctors per population ratio in constituent units (lowest)	N/A
National expenditures on health as a % of GDP	7.6%

Sources

Bosnia-Herzegovina Ministry of Foreign Affairs Official Website. www.mvp.gov.ba

Central Bank of Bosnia and Herzegovina. *Annual Report 1999*. Released March 2000. www.cbbh.gov.ba/annualreport99_eng

Central Intelligence Agency (CIA), *World Fact Book 2000*. CIA, www.cia.gov/cia/publications/factbook/index.html

Derbyshire, J. Denis. *Encyclopedia of World Political Systems*. Volumes I and II, New York: Sharpe Reference, M.E. Sharpe, Inc, 2000.

International Monetary Fund (IMF). "Basic Economic Indicators." *Bosnia and Herzegovina: Selected Issues and Statistical Appendix*." IMF Staff Country Report No. 00/77. www.imf.org

Official Website of the Embassy of Bosnia and Herzegovina to the Kingdom of the Netherlands. www.xs4all.nl/~bih/

Serbian Unity Congress. "Reconstruction and Development, 1997." www.suc.org/Republic_of_Srpska/development/emp.htm

United Nations Population Division. Department of Economic and Social Affairs. "Population in 1999 and 2000: All Countries." *World Population Prospects: The 1998 Revision, Vol. 1 comprehensive Tables*. www.un.org/Depts.htm

United Nations. "Human Development Index," "Gender-Related Development Index," *Human Development Report, 2000*. Human Development Report Office. www.undp.org/hdro/report.html

World Bank. *World Development Report 2000/2001: Attacking Poverty*. www.worldbank.org/poverty/wdrpoverty/report/index.htm

World Health Organisation (WHO). "Estimates of Health Personnel." www-nt.who.int/whosis/statistics

World Health Organisation (WHO). "Annex Table 8, Selected national health accounts indicators for all Member States, estimates for 1997." *World Health Report 2000*. Geneva, 2000. www-nt.who.int/whosis/statistics/menu.cfm

Federative Republic of Brazil

Capital: Brasilia
Population: 175 Million
(Jul. 2001 est.)

Brasilia, the Capital, is situated within the Distrito Federal.

Boundaries and place names are representative only and do not imply official endorsement.

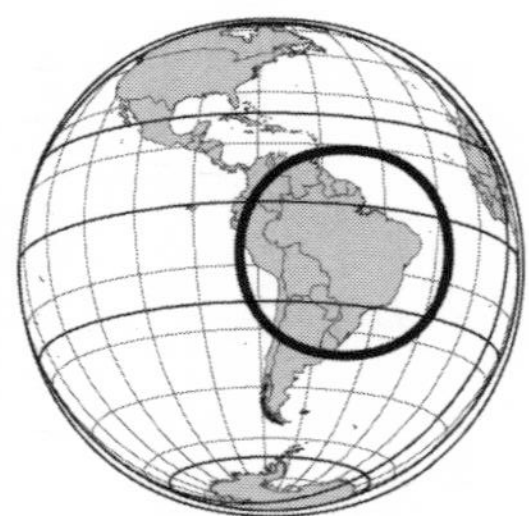

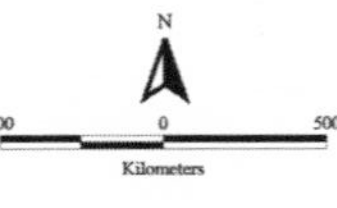

Sources: ESRI Ltd.; CIA World Factbook; Times Atlas of the World

Brazil
(*Federative Republic of Brazil*)

VALERIANO MENDES FERREIRA COSTA

1 HISTORY AND DEVELOPMENT OF FEDERALISM

With a total area of over 8,500,000 km^2, the Federative Republic of Brazil is the fifth largest country in the world. Its population is more than 170 million inhabitants (census 2000), and it has a Gross Domestic Product (GDP) of around US$500 billion. Brazil has historically been characterized by major social and economic disparities and its pattern of inter-governmental relations, even before the institution of federalism, has evolved through alternating phases of centralization and decentralization. The Brazilian federation encompasses three levels of government: the Union; 26 states plus the Federal District; and over 5,500 municipalities.

Although its formal discovery by Pedro Alvares Cabral took place only in 1500, the Treaty of Tordesillas (1494) had already legally settled the question of division and possession of the new lands between Spain and Portugal. As the settlement of the land evolved, an integrated system of administration was deemed necessary and the Portuguese Crown divided the territory into 14 hereditary fiefs, or captaincies (*Capitanias Hereditárias*), "ceded" to Portuguese nobles, who became responsible for their defence and development. The captaincy system has influenced the territorial and political pattern of the country.

The first three centuries of European occupation were marked by the presence of scattered population in fortified coastal settlements and, occasionally, military and commercial expeditions, called *bandeiras*, that expanded Portuguese possessions in the seventeenth century. The boundaries of the country were established by the Treaty of Madrid (1777), leaving only secondary conflicts of delimitation that were settled after independence.

From independence, proclaimed in 1822, to the end of nineteenth century, Brazil adopted a monarchical regime (headed by two descendants of the deposed Portuguese monarch) as the only political regime that could preserve the two basic elements of the colonial system deemed necessary to the maintenance of the dominant landed aristocracy – slavery and a unitary political administration. Although this period was characterized by political and administrative centralization, it was also a time of consolidation of the power of regional elites whose economic success was not matched by political participation.

Immediately after the military coup d'état that ended the monarchy in 1889, the republican alliance adopted a federal system in which the provinces of the empire were transformed into states. The parliamentary system was replaced with a presidential one, a bicameral Congress (Chamber of Deputies and Senate) was created, and a completely independent Supreme Court was created. The federal regime, incorporated by the constitution of 1891, accorded great political autonomy to the already economically powerful state elites.

The federation, however, was only consolidated during the presidency of Campos Sales (1898–1902). Known as the "Governors's Politics" (*Política dos Governadores*), the Brazilian oligarchic version of federalism meant, in fact, a pact between state elites and the President of the Republic. According to this pact, in exchange for the non-intervention of the Union government in the states' internal affairs, the members of National Congress would approve all presidential initiatives. As the system evolved, it resulted in a peculiar federative party system in which there was only one political party in each state (all called "republican"). The system was supported by systematic electoral fraud.

Contested presidential elections in 1929, led to revolution in 1930. Revolutionary forces installed a Provisional Government (1930–1937) that reduced the autonomy of the states through the imposition of *interventores*. These *interventores* were politico-administrative managers of the states who were appointed by Getúlio Vargas, a defeated presidential candidate and leader of the movement. In November 1937 Vargas led another military coup that centralized political power in the President's hands. During this dictatorial regime, known as *Estado Novo*, the autonomy of the states was officially abolished.

The overthrow of the *Estado Novo* by military officials in 1945 reinstalled a federal regime associated, for the first time in the Republic's history, with a competitive national party system. During this period, state governorships became highly disputed political assets because of their importance for the presidential elections. This peculiar federative dynamic is one of the reasons for the easy political success of the 1964 military coup. The heated dispute of the Governors of the greater states (São Paulo, Minas Gerais, Guanabara e Rio Grande do Sul) around the coming 1965 presidential election played an important role in the institutional weakening of President João Goulart's authority.

The distinguishing characteristic of the military regime installed in 1964 was that it maintained several representative constitutional provisions, including the federal provisions and the regular election of the Governors (albeit indirectly by the state assemblies) and state assemblies. At the national level, the military Presidents were confined to fixed mandates, with no right to seek re-election. Although the armed forces had a decisive influence in their choice of President, their choice had to be formally ratified by an Electoral College composed by the members of the National Congress and representatives of state assemblies.

In 1982, the first direct elections for state governments since 1965 were held, and the first elections for Congress under a multi-party system. The election of the state Governors before the presidential election influenced the pattern of re-democratization. Between 1982 and 1994 the state Governors were the most powerful elected officials occupying executive posts. From 1990, when Fernando Collor became the first directly elected President of the Republic in 30 years, to 1994 when Fernando Henrique Cardoso became President, the Governors played a major role in national politics, influencing the behaviour of federal deputies especially through the exercise of patronage or manipulating their chances of re-election.

The increased predominance of state interests in the federal regime culminated in the creation of the Constitutional Assembly (1987–88) in which the state and municipal governments consolidated the process of fiscal decentralization initiated in the late 1970s. However, this process of political and fiscal decentralization coincided with the crisis of the "Developmental State," based on import substitution and industrial protectionism. The 1980s, and the first half of 1990s, were largely characterized by inflationary surges, debt and economic stagnation. The economic crisis, that affected first and most the national government, combined with the decentralization of revenues contributed to it, severely reduced the capacity of the Union to coordinate the intergovernmental relations in Brazil.

The centralization of power in the federal government that had been the most important instrument of management of Brazilian federalism since the 1930s, has given way to a disorganized process of decentralization in which the states and municipalities behave like "predators" of a politically and fiscally wounded federal government.

2 CONSTITUTIONAL PROVISIONS RELATING TO FEDERALISM

The republican regime in Brazil – except during the authoritarian periods – has been marked by two general characteristics:

1 a plebiscitary presidentialism in which a strong President is sided by a symmetric, bicameral, multi-party and regionalist, legislative power and an independent judiciary; and
2 a federative system which reproduces the presidential division of powers at the state level (except that there are no state senates) and accords considerable constitutional autonomy to states and municipalities.

As we can see, the Brazilian federalism is marked by the complex combination of these majoritarian and consociative institutional arrangements.

The 1988 constitution has detailed provisions about the political, administrative and fiscal organization of the federation. Article 18 defines the Federative Republic of Brazil as composed of the Union, the States (26), one Federal District (Brasília) and the Municipalities (approximately 5,500). All of them are autonomous in their own jurisdiction. The constitution also provides (paragraphs 3 and 4) for the possibility of the creation of states and municipalities, subject to the approval of the concerned population, by means of plebiscites, and of the National Congress (or the state assemblies in the case of municipalities), by means of specific laws. However, these legal constraints have not impeded the creation of over 1,300 new municipalities between 1988 and 1997.

Articles 20 to 25 establish the division of powers between the members of the federation. The constitution (Article 25, paragraph 1) provides the states with residuary power – i.e., all the powers which are not specifically reserved for the federal government or assigned to the municipalities. However, the detailed and extensive definition of the Union's constitutional powers (Articles 20 to 22) has limited the exercise of this power by the states.

Article 23 is one of the constitutional provisions that could be crucial to the configuration of a cooperative pattern in inter-governmental relations as it lists the several powers that should be exercised *in common* by the Union, the states and the municipalities. The supplementary law that should establish the rules for inter-governmental co-operation, however, has not up to now been approved by Congress.

Article 24 defines the powers that should be concurrently legislated by the Union, the states and the Federal District. These powers include, *inter alia*, education, health, social assistance and environmental protection. However, as the Union's legislation over-rides state and municipal legislative powers, there have not been substantial opportunities to exercise concurrent legislation by sub-national governments without federal consent.

Unlike most other federations, the Brazilian constitution provides detailed rules for the management of the over 5,500 municipalities that are autonomous in strictly local affairs. Each municipality operates under its own constitutional provisions, called Organic (Basic) Law, which must be approved by a qualified majority in the Municipal Council (Article 29).

The federal executive is headed by the President of the Republic. A constitutional amendment (1997) permits the President and the Vice-President to seek re-election, but they cannot serve more than two consecutive terms. The President appoints the State Ministers who are directly responsible to him and who he may dismiss at any time. Unlike most presidential regimes, members of the National Congress may be appointed as Ministers (or to any other political position in the federal administration).

The President of the Republic has important powers in the legislative process. Thus, for example, Article 61(1) defines the cases in which the President has exclusive initiative to introduce laws in financial and budgetary matters, and Article 64(1) provides that the President may request urgency in the examination of bills of his own initiative. Article 66(1) authorizes the President to veto a bill that was approved by the Congress, and Article 66(4) states that a presidential veto may only be rejected by an absolute majority of Deputies and Senators by secret voting.

The representation of the population is provided by the election of the members of the Chamber of Deputies for a four-year term through a system of proportional representation. The representation of the constituent units in the central government is guaranteed by the election of three Senators from each state and the Federal District. Senators are elected for a term of eight years. Both Deputies and Senators can stand for re-election without restriction. The current legislature (51st) has 513 members and 81 Senators.

One aspect of the political system that affects the actual configuration of Brazilian federalism is the over-representation of the less populated (and less developed) regions of the country in the Chamber of

Deputies. This unequal distribution of parliamentary seats results from the constitutional provision (Article 44) which establishes that the states must have a minimum of eight and a maximum of 70 deputies. This provision favours especially the north, the least populated region, in detriment to the southeast, the most populated. The extreme case is the state of São Paulo, the richest (35% GDP) and most populated (21%), which should have 111 deputies rather than the current 70.

Another important political feature that affects Brazilian federalism is the configuration of the federal Senate. Senatorial representation of the northern, northeastern and centre-western states – which represent 43% of the population – controls 74% of the seats. This fact acquires importance when one takes into account that the Senate has symmetric legislative powers to the Chamber and, most of all, that it has exclusive power to approve presidential nominations and authorize debt margins for the states and municipalities.

The Federal Supreme Court is the apex of the judicial system (Articles 101–103). It is composed of 11 Justices who are appointed by the President, and subjected to the approval of the Senate. The Federal Supreme Court is vested with the power to make decisions about constitutional conflicts that involve the members of the federation. The state judiciary follows the federal pattern and has its jurisdiction defined so as to avoid any conflict with the federal courts.

Constitutional amendments (Article 60) can only be proposed by: (1) at least one-third of the members of the Chamber of Deputies or of the federal Senate; (2) the President of the Republic; or (3) more than one-half of the Legislative Assemblies of the units of the federation, each by a relative majority of its members. Constitutional amendments (Paragraph 2) must be discussed and voted upon in each House of the National Congress, in two readings, and will only be approved if they obtain in both readings, three-fifths of the votes of the respective members. Four constitutional matters are excluded from amendments: the federal form of state; the direct, secret, universal and periodic vote; the separation of government powers; and individual rights and guarantees.

The definitions in the constitution about the national tax system – in contrast to the ones relating to the expenditure responsibilities – are detailed and precise. In fact, the constitutional fiscal provisions resulted in a transfer of tributary revenues from the federal government to the states and municipalities without precedent in the country's history. Moreover, the 1988 constitution strengthened the already significant tax base of the states and municipal governments.

The provisions relating to fiscal federalism are in Title VI (Taxation and Budget). Articles 153 to 159 define the taxes that are exclusive of each member of federation and the procedures for the sharing of tax revenues between the Union and the states and municipalities. The most important taxes pertaining to the states (Article155) are the ICMS, a kind of a state's VAT, accounting for about 25% of the total amount of taxes levied in Brazil, and the IPVA, a tax on the ownership of automotive vehicles licensed in each jurisdiction. The municipalities can levy two taxes, which has considerable impact on the revenues of the major ones (Article156). They can levy the IPTU, levied on urban buildings and urban land property, and the ISS, which is levied on services of any nature not included in Article 155. In fact, the level of fiscal autonomy of each sub-national government varies greatly with the level of economic development which is highly concentrated in the southeast and south regions.

The sharing of revenues among the Union and the states and the municipalities is accomplished through two funds composed of about half the net revenues of the three main federal taxes: the personal (IRPF) and corporate (IRPJ) income taxes and the selective VAT (IPI). The Revenue Sharing Fund of the States is constituted with 21.5%, and the Revenue Sharing Fund of the Municipalities with 22.5% of these net revenues. The distribution of the funds among the states and municipalities is mainly based on redistributive criteria.

The trend toward fiscal decentralization can be best seen by examining the distribution of the expenditures by level of government. Subnational governments account for 62% of payrolls for active civil servants, 71% of other current expenditures and 78% of fixed investments. On the other hand, the central government concentrates its outlays on transfers to persons (basically, social security benefits) and interest on the public debt (respectively, 80% and 90% of the total).

3 RECENT POLITICAL DYNAMICS

The political event in recent years that has had great impact on the configuration of Brazilian federalism was the election (and re-election) of Fernando Henrique Cardoso. Leading a heterogenous coalition of centre-rightist forces, President Cardoso won the 1994 presidential election against Luis Inacio Lula da Silva, a popular leftist leader.

The political mandate of the new President was strongly associated with the adjustment of the chaotic situation of the national economy, particularly the lack of fiscal balance in the public sector. In fact, his greatest political asset as candidate was the successful implementation of a monetary stabilization program, known as *Plano Real,* while in charge of the Ministry of Finance in the last months of President Itamar Franco's administration (1992–1994).

During his first administration (1995–1998), President Cardoso approved in the National Congress an extensive set of legislative measures, such as economic deregulation, privatization, downsizing of the public administration, and reform of the social security system, that radically transformed the relationship between state and society.

The effects of the monetary stabilization, particularly the interruption of the inflationary spiral, hit with particular virulence the finances of the highly indebted sub-national governments. The federal government took this opportunity to reverse the adverse balance in intergovernmental relations. The first action in this regard, issued as a Provisional Measure (1.514/96) in 1996, was a program aiming at the reduction of the involvement of the states in financial and banking activity. In fact, since then, all of the banks belonging to the large states have been privatized, liquidated or transferred to the management of the Central Bank.

As a compensation, the federal government proposed to the states the "federalization" of their debts – i.e., the consolidation, refinancing and transference of most of the state debts to the National Treasury. In addition, restrictive clauses were included in refinancing contracts that suspended all issues of new state or municipal security debt. These measures, which complemented the program of macro-economic stabilization, severely constrained the fiscal and financial autonomy of the states. Up to this time, the states had exercised a "quasi-monetary authority" through the uncontrolled issue of papers in the financial market, and were systematically bailed-out by the federal monetary authorities.

Another important law in the same area (Supplementary Law No. 96, 1999) established ceilings on the expenditures on the personnel of federal and sub-national governments, and the ceilings are different for each level of government. Finally, the federal government sent to Congress, and got approved in the middle of 2000, the Fiscal Responsibility Law, inspired by the Fiscal Responsibility Act in New Zealand. This law imposed maximum limits on the debts and personnel outlays of the federal government, states and municipalities. Among other provisions, the new law requires that all levels of government formulate and publicize three year targets, prohibits the federal government from formalizing new operations that bail out state and municipal debts and applies hard sanctions (including criminal ones) to those responsible for the misuse of government monies.

Besides the fiscal adjustment program, two others reforms have had some impact in the inter-governmental relations. First, a constitutional amendment (14/96) created a fiscal fund – composed of state and municipal revenues – to finance, in redistributive (per capita) terms, the basic public educational systems (called FUNDEF). And second, in the health sector, the federal government has recently instituted a fund that provides direct monetary transfers for basic municipal health programs based on per capita criteria.

In sum, the reforms implemented during the two Cardoso administrations have transformed the pattern of inter-governmental relations and increased the coordinative capacity of the federal government, without recourse to authoritarian centralization practices. Yet, several problems persist that will challenge Brazilian federation in the next years. The most important of all is the protracted tax reform that was designed to reduce distortions like cumulative charge and regressivity, and curb incentives for fiscal war among sub-national governments.

4 SOURCES FOR FURTHER INFORMATION

Valeriano Mendes Ferreira Costa, with Fernando Abrucio and Konrad Adenauer, *Reforma do Estado e o Contexto Federativo Brasileiro,* Sao Paulo: Stiftung, 1998.

http://www.brazil.gov.br
http://www.mre.gov.br/cdbrasil/itamaraty/web/ingles/index.htm
http://www.bndes.gov.br/english/
http://www.federativo.bndes.gov.br
http://www.senado.gov.br
http://www.camara.gov.br
http://www.fazenda.gov.br
http://www.georgetown.edu/pdba/Constitutions/constudies.html
http://www.ipea.gov.br/pub/td/td.html
http://www.ibge.gov.br/english/default.php

Table I
Political and Geographic Indicators

Capital city	Brasilia
Number and type of constituent units	*26 States* (Estados, singular Estado): Acre, Alagoas, Amapá, Amazonas, Bahia, Ceará, Espírito Santo, Goiás, Maranhão, Mato Grosso, Mato Grosso do Sul, Minas Gerais, Pará, Paraíba, Paraná, Pernambuco, Piauí, Rio de Janeiro, Rio Grande do Norte, Rio Grande do Sul, Rondônia, Roraima, Santa Catarina, São Paulo, Sergipe, Tocantins. *1 Federal District (Distrito Federal)*: Brasilia (Note: Formally the 5 561 municipalities are considered constituent units since the constitutional reform of 1988, but in practice the 26 states and the Federal District are the constituent units.)
Official language(s)	Portuguese
Area	8 511 965 km^2 (Note: This figure includes Arquipelago de Fernando de Noronha, Atol das Rocas, Ilha da Trindade, Ilhas Martin Vaz, and Penedos de ao Pedro e São Paulo.)
Area – Largest constituent unit	Amazonas (1 564 445 km^2)
Area – Smallest constituent unit	Federal District of Brasilia (5 814 km^2)
Total population	169 544 443
Population by constituent unit (% of total population)	São Paulo 22.0%, Minas Gerais 10.5%, Rio de Janeiro 8.4%, Bahia 8.0%, Rio Grande do Sul 6.0%, Paraná 5.6%, Pernambuco 5.0%, Ceará 4.4%, Pará 4.0%, Maranhão 3.3%, Santa Catarina 3.1%, Goiás 3.0%, Paraíba 2.1%, Espírito Santo 2.0%, Alagoas 1.9%, Amazonas 1.7%, Piauí 1.7%, Rio Grande do Norte 1.6%, Mato Grosso 1.5%, Mato Grosso do Sul 1.2%, Federal District of Brasilia 1.1%, Sergipe 1.0%, Rondônia 0.08%, Tocantins 0.07%, Acre 0.04%, Amapá 0.03%, and Roraima 0.02%
Political system – federal	Federal Republic
Head of state – federal	President Fernando Henrique Cardoso (1994/1998), Partido da Social Democracia Brasileiro (PSDB). Directly elected by popular vote for 4-year term. Next election to be held October 2002.
Head of government – federal	President Fernando Henrique Cardoso (1994/1998). President appoints Cabinet.

Table I (continued)

Government structure – federal	Bicameral: Congresso Nacional (National Congress): *Upper House* – Senado Federal (Federal Senate). Members are elected by majority vote from the 27 constituent units (26 States, 1 Federal District), with each unit receiving 3 seats; Senators serve 8-year terms. *Lower House* – Camara dos Deputados (Chamber of Deputies). Members are elected by proportional representation to serve 4-year terms with a fixed maximum number of representatives allowed to each constituent unit, with all states being guaranteed a minimum and maximum number of Deputies.
Number of representatives in lower house of federal government – Chamber of Deputies	513 Seats: Partido da Social Democracia Brasileiro – PSDB (Party of the Brazil Social-Democracy) 100, Partido da Frente Liberal – PFL (Party of the Liberal Front) 94 + Partido Social Trabalhista – PST (Social Labour Party) 5 = 99, Partido do Movimento Democrático Brasileiro – PMDB (Party of the Brazil Democratic Movement) 93, Partido dos Trabalhadores – PT (Workers' Party) 56, Partido Progressista Brasileiro – PPB (Brazilian Progressive Party) 51, Partido Democrático Trabalhista – PDT (Democratic Labour Party) 17 + Partido Popular Socialista – PPS (Socialist People's Party) 13 = 30, Partido Trabalhista Brasileiro – PTB (Brazilian Labour Party) 27, Partido Socialista Brasileiro – PSB (Brazilian Socialist Party) 16 + Partido Comunista do Brasil – PCdoB (Communist Party of Brazil) 10 = 26, Partido Liberal – PL (Liberal Party) 20 + Partido Social Liberal – PSL (Social Liberal Party) 5 = 25, Partido Verde – PV (Green Party) 1, Partido da Mobilização Nacional – PMN (Party of National Mobilization) 2, Sem Partido – S.PART (No current party affiliation) 2, Partido Trabalhista Nacional – PTN (National Workers' Party) 1, Partido Humanista da Solidariedade – PHS (Humanist Solidarity Party) 1, Partido Social Democrata Christão – PSDC (Christian Social Democratic Party) 1.
Number of representatives in lower house of federal government for most populated constituent unit	São Paulo State: 70
Number of representatives in lower house of federal government for least populated constituent unit	Roraima State: 8

Table I (continued)

Number of representatives in upper house of federal government – Federal Senate	81 Seats: Partido do Movimento Democrático Brasileiro – PMDB (Party of the Brazil Democratic Movement) 25, Partido da Frente Liberal – PFL (Party of the Liberal Front) 20, Partido da Social Democracia Brasileiro – PSDB (Party of Brazil Social-Democracy) 12, Partido dos Trabalhadores – PT (Workers' Party) 7, Sem.Partido – S.PART (No current party affiliation) 4, Partido Socialista Brasileiro – PSB (Brazilian Socialist Party) 3, Partido Democrático Trabalhista – PDT (Workers' Democratic Party) 3, Partido Trabalhista Brasileiro – PTB (National Workers' Party) 3, Partido Progressista Brasileiro – PPB (Brazilian Progressive Party) 2, Partido Popular Socialista – PPS (Popular Socialist Party) 2.
Distribution of representation in upper house of federal government – Federal Senate	3 seats for each of the 26 states and Federal District.
Constitutional court (highest court dealing with constitutional matters)	Supreme Federal Tribunal. Eleven ministers are appointed by the President and confirmed by the Senate.
Political system of constituent units	Unicameral: 40 representatives on average. Elected on basis of proportional representation, serve 4-year terms.
Head of state – constituent units	Governor – directly elected by popular vote for 4-year term.
Head of government – constituent units	Governor

Table II
Economic and Social Indicators

GDP	US$1.13 trillion
GDP per capita	US$6 500
Mechanisms for taxation	Five main forms of taxation: • Income Tax (IRPF/IRPJ) – imposed by central government: 3 tax brackets ranging from 15-28%. • Value-Added Tax (IPI) on select goods – imposed by central government. • Social Security Taxes – imposed by central government. • Value-Added Tax (ICMS) on goods and services, inheritance and gifts and a vehicle tax (IPVA) – both are imposed by constituent units: rate varies, but accounts for 25% of total taxes levied in Brazil. • Rural property tax (IPTU) and a tax on services (ISS) – imposed by municipalities.
National debt (external)	US$232 billion
National unemployment rate	7.1%
Constituent unit with highest unemployment rate	Bahia – 9.9%
Constituent unit with lowest unemployment rate	Rio de Janeiro – 5.4%
Adult literacy rate	84.5%
National expenditures on education as a % of GDP	5.1%
Life expectancy in years	67
Doctors per population ratio (national)	127.2 doctors per 100 000 inhabitants
Doctors per population ratio in constituent units (highest)	southeast region – 181.3 doctors per 100 000 inhabitants
Doctors per population ratio in constituent units (lowest)	northern areas – 60.2 doctors per 100 000 inhabitants
National expenditures on health as a % of GDP	6.5%

Sources

Cámara dos Deputados (Chamber of Deputies). *Lideranças na Câmara dos Deputados.* www.camara.gov.br

Central Intelligence Agency (CIA), *World Fact Book 2000.* CIA, www.cia.gov/cia/publications/factbook/index.html

Serra, José and José Roberto Afonso. "Fiscal Federalism Brazilian Style: Reflections." Paper presented at the Forum of Federations International Conference on Federalism. Mont-Tremblant, Quebec, Canada, 1999.

Economic Commission for Latin America and the Caribbean (ECLAC), *Statistical Yearbook for Latin America and the Caribbean 1999.* ECLAC, www.eclac.org/estaditicas

ECLAC/UN. « Decentralizaçao fiscal na América Latina : Estudo de Caso do Brasil. » José Roberto Rodrigues Afonso. *Quadros estatisticos e boxes do relatório.* Série Politica Fiscal, no. 61, 1994. www.federativo.bndes.gov.br

Economist Intelligence Unit, "Country Commerce – Brazil," *The Economist Intelligence Unit 2000.* New York: EIU, 2000.

Elazar, Daniel J. (ed.), *Federal Systems of the World: A Handbook of Federal, Confederal and Autonomy Arrangements.* 2nd Edition. Jerusalem Institute for Federal Studies. London: Longman Group/Westgate House, 1994.

International Labour Office. "Indicators on Unemployment." www.un.org/Depts/unsd/social/unempl.htm

Instituto Brasileiro de Geografia e Estatistica (IBGE) (Department of Geography and Statistics). Federal Republic of Brazil. www.ibge.gov/br/english/estatistica/

Latin-Focus: The Leading Source for Latin American Economies. www.latin-focus.com/index.html

Pan-American Health Organization (PAHO/WHO). On-line country demographic indicators and "Profiles of the Health Services System" of respective countries. www.paho.org

United Nations. "Human Development Index." *Human Development Report, 2000.* www.undp.org/hdro/report.html.

World Bank. *World Development Report 2000/2001: Attacking Poverty.* www.worldbank.org/poverty/wdrpoverty/report/index.htm

World Health Organisation (WHO). "Estimates of Health Personnel." www-nt.who.int/whosis/statistics

World Health Organisation (WHO). "Annex Table 8, Selected national health accounts indicators for all Member States, estimates for 1997." *World Health Report 2000.* Geneva, 2000. www-nt.who.int/whosis/statistics/menu.cfm

Canada

Capital: Ottawa
Population: 31.5 Million

Boundaries and place names are representative only and do not imply official endorsement.

The three northern territories, while adminstrative divisions, are not provinces.

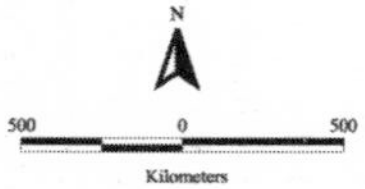

N

500 0 500
Kilometers

Sources: ESRI Ltd.; National Atlas of Canada; Times Atlas of the World

Canada

DAVID R. CAMERON

1 HISTORY AND DEVELOPMENT OF FEDERALISM

Canada is a parliamentary democracy. The head of state is Her Majesty Queen Elizabeth II, represented in Canada by the Governor-General at the federal level, and Lieutenant-Governors provincially. The country has a land mass of more than 9 million km^2, spanning six time zones. Its population is almost 31 million people, most of whom live in cities and towns stretched along a narrow band just north of the US border.

Canada is the product of the 1867 union of three British colonies in 'British North America': Nova Scotia, New Brunswick, Quebec and Ontario (which were united in one colony and were called Canada East and Canada West). Six other provinces have joined Canada: Manitoba (1870); British Columbia (1871); Prince Edward Island (1873); Saskatchewan and Alberta (1905); and Newfoundland (1949). In addition, there are three northern territories: Yukon; the Northwest Territories; and Nunavut, which was carved out of the Northwest Territories in 1999.

Canadian federalism has been affected by the country's linguistic diversity, centred on the French-English relationship, its regional diversity, and its ethno-cultural diversity. Reflecting the historical presence of two language communities, Canada has two official languages, French and English. English is the mother tongue of more than 60% of Canadians and French of about 24%, mostly concentrated in Quebec.

Since Canada's settlement and growth have depended heavily on immigration, approximately 14% of Canadians have other mother tongues. In 1991, almost 1 million people in Canada reported having aboriginal origins, in whole or in part.

Canada's economy is the seventh largest among Western industrialized countries and Canada is a member of the Group of Seven industrial countries. Barriers to international trade between Canada and other countries have been steadily lowered since World War II. Exports represent about 40% of Gross Domestic Product (GDP) (one of the highest rates in the world), and approximately 80% of those exports go to the United States. The Canadian economy is tightly integrated into the US economy and, in fact, the two countries are each other's largest trading partners. The integration of the North American economy has been furthered with the Canada-US Free Trade Agreement (implemented in 1989), and the North America Free Trade Agreement (NAFTA), involving Canada, the United States and Mexico (December 1992).

Canada's wealth, historically, was generated largely from the exploitation of its abundant natural resources. Today, industrial and high technology sectors also play an important role in an economy which is highly regionalized. More than half of Canada's economic output is produced in the central provinces of Ontario and Quebec, which together house more than 80% of Canada's manufacturing capacity.

Economic development aside, Canadian federal experience since World War II has been shaped by four great forces. The first is the construction, consolidation and then constraining of the Canadian welfare state. The second is the emergence in the 1960s of a form of liberal nationalism in Quebec, the province in which a majority of the population is French-speaking. Parallel to that is the third factor, the 'province building' enterprises of several Canadian provinces. The fourth is the aspiration for self-determination of Canada's aboriginal peoples. Clearly, these are not the only forces one might identify, but they are the ones most relevant to this account of Canadian federalism.

2 CONSTITUTIONAL PROVISIONS RELATING TO FEDERALISM

Canada was the first country to establish itself as a parliamentary federation – i.e., a federal system in which sovereignty is divided between central and regional governments, both constituted according to the principles of British parliamentary democracy. The Canadian system expresses a divided rather than a shared model of federalism, including: watertight compartments for the division of powers; independent taxing authority for both orders of governments; and weak provincial representation at the centre. Canada's parliamentary federation has produced strong executive-led government in Ottawa and in the provincial capitals, which – combined with a weak Senate – has led to executive domination of relations between and among the federal partners.

Canada was founded in 1867 as a centralized federation, with the key powers of the day vested in Ottawa and a strong, paternalistic oversight role assigned to Ottawa vis-à-vis the provinces. Despite its origins, however, Canada has become highly decentralized. This has occurred due to a a number of factors. First, judicial interpretation of the division of powers broadly favoured provincial governments over the federal government. Second, the country's central institutions have been unable to represent adequately Canada's regional diversity, and there has consequently been popular support for the assertion of provincial power, especially in the stronger provinces. Third, provincial areas of responsibility, such as health, welfare and education, which were of little governmental consequence in the nineteenth century, mushroomed in the twentieth, thus greatly enhancing the role of the provinces. Finally, post-World War II nationalism in Quebec has helped to force a process of decentralization from which other provinces have benefitted.

The result is that Canada has powerful and sophisticated governments both in Ottawa and in the provinces, engaged in competitive processes of community building, and social and economic development at both levels. Managing this system requires elaborate forms of inter-governmental coordination, and at times dissolves into bitter inter-governmental conflict.

Canada's two principal constitutional documents are the Constitution Act, 1867, and the Constitution Act, 1982. The Constitution Act, 1867, formerly known as the British North America Act, was an Act of the British Parliament that created Canada out of the three original colonies and provided the federal and parliamentary structure. It is in this document that one finds the general provisions for the distribution of powers, and the establishment of Parliament, the provincial legislatures and the courts. The Constitution Act, 1982, patriated the constitution from the last vestiges of British authority by introducing a Canadian amending formula, affirmed aboriginal and treaty rights of the aboriginal peoples of Canada, and introduced an entrenched Charter of Rights and Freedoms which applies to all citizens and to which all governments and legislatures are subject.

Sections 91–95 of the Constitution Act, 1867, allocate powers between the federal and provincial governments. The broader and more comprehensive assignment of authority was to the Parliament of

Canada (Section 91), and any power not specifically allocated by the constitution was deemed to fall to the federal Parliament (the residual power). The powers exclusively assigned to the provinces (Section 92) were meant to be specific and limited. Broad judicial interpretation, however, has turned the "property and civil rights" power of the provinces (Section 92(13)) into a kind of residual power of its own.

Federal legislative powers are found chiefly in Section 91 of the Constitution Act, 1867, which opens with a sweeping grant of authority, stating that Parliament may "make laws for the peace, order and good government of Canada" in relation to all fields not explicitly assigned to provincial legislatures. The drafters of the constitution then listed 29 heads of power that form part of the general grant of authority to Parliament. In the years since 1867, however, the courts have declined to confirm this broad understanding of the Peace, Order and Good Government or POGG power. Instead, they have relied heavily on the 29 enumerated heads of power and have restricted POGG to three principal situations: where the distribution of authority leaves a legislative gap (e.g., offshore mineral resources or federal language policies); where the matter is of 'national concern', but not caught within any of the enumerated federal powers (e.g., marine pollution or aeronautics); and where there is a national emergency (e.g., apparent civil disorder or acute inflation in the economy).

Some of the important enumerated powers are:

- regulation of trade and commerce (Section 91(2)), which now covers inter-provincial and international trade and commerce, and the general regulation of trade affecting the whole country;
- unemployment insurance (Section 91(2a)), added by the Constitution Act, 1940;
- taxation (Section 91(3)) which allows the federal government to raise revenue "by any mode or system of taxation";
- Indians and lands reserved for the Indians (Section 91(24));
- treaty power (Section 132), which gives the government of Canada the power to negotiate and sign binding international treaties – however, when a treaty involves matters within provincial jurisdiction, the treaty will not be operative until enacted by the provinces; and
- authority for money and banking, and for inter-provincial transportation.

Sixteen specific heads of power are assigned to the provinces in Section 92 of the Constitution Act, 1867. The most important of these are:

- direct taxation (Section 92(2)) which gives provinces the right to "direct taxation within the province in order to the raising of revenues for provincial purposes";
- management and sale of public lands (Section 92(5)), which means that public or crown lands, including natural resources, within a province are the property of that province, thus providing provinces with a significant source of revenue and a substantial capacity to manage the provincial economy;
- health and welfare (Section 92(7)), a responsibility which has gained importance in the twentieth century, and health care now typically is the largest single expenditure field for provincial governments;
- municipal institutions (Section 92(8)), which means that municipal governments can be made and un-made by the provincial government;
- local works and undertakings (Section 92(10));
- property and civil rights within the province (Section 92(13)), which is generally thought to be the most important provincial head of power because, through it, for example, the provinces gain the right to legislate within their territory in relation to real property, personal and intellectual property and proprietary civil rights; and
- matters of a local or private nature (Section 92(16)) which has been seen as another important source of provincial authority because it relates to matters not specifically falling under any other enumerated provincial powers which are of a local or private nature.

There are four specified concurrent powers. The first concurrent power relates to agriculture and immigration (Section 95). Section 95 authorizes both the federal Parliament and the provincial legislatures to legislate in relation to these matters with federal legislation being paramount in cases of conflict. The second power relates to natural resources (Section 92(a)). This section was added as a result of the constitutional discussions of 1980–82. It enables provinces to control the export of their non-renewable, forestry and electricity resources to other provinces (although not to another country), reversing the restrictions formerly imposed on them. In the case of conflict, federal legislation has paramountcy. The third area of concurrent jurisdiction is education (Section 93). Education is listed here although the federal entitlement to act is not general, but arises only out of specific situations. Education is the responsibility of the provinces, subject to: a number of limitations designed to protect minority groups and denominational schools; and a federal power to pass 'remedial' legislation which in fact has never been used. Like the health and welfare fields, education grew into a central responsibility of the modern democratic state in the twentieth century. Canada is unusual, even among federations, in vesting so little authority for this matter in the federal government. And the fourth area of concurrent jurisdiction relates to pensions (Section 94(a)). Originally added to the constitution in 1951 and amended in 1964, this section provides for concurrent legislative powers with respect to old age pensions and supplementary benefits. Atypically, it provides for *provincial* paramountcy in cases of conflict between provincial and federal legislation.

In addition to the relatively few concurrent powers, there are three areas in which federal and provincial authority overlap. The first area is criminal law. Section 91(27) gives Parliament the power to make laws in relation to criminal law, including procedure in criminal matters, but Section 92(14) gives the provinces responsibility for the administration of justice. Thus, the Criminal Code is a federal statute, but policing and prosecution under its provisions are executed by the provinces.

The second area is the courts. Canada has an integrated judicial system in which the federal government is responsible for the nomination, salaries, allowances and pensions of superior court judges, and the provinces are responsible for the establishment of courts and their administration, as well as having full responsibility for the junior courts in each province.

The third area is the federal spending power and shared cost programs. One of the most important and controversial areas of Canadian federalism is the field of shared cost programs in which the federal government transfers funds to provincial governments to assist them in fulfilling certain of their constitutional responsibilities. By far the largest programs relate to health care, social assistance and post-secondary education, which are now combined in the Canada Health and Social Transfer Program. It involves cash and tax transfers in the order of $25 (Cdn) billion annually. The federal government's authority to do this – its 'spending power' – derives not from an explicit head of power in Section 91, but is inferred from several provisions of the Constitution Act, 1867, relating to the authority to tax and spend.

The second or upper house of the Canadian Parliament is the Senate. There are 105 members who are appointed by the Governor-General based on the recommendation of the Prime Minister according to a system of rough regional representation and political considerations (often reward for loyal service to the party in power). Legislation must be passed both by the House of Commons and the Senate, which in effect gives the Senate a veto. In practice it has rarely exercised its power, and is unlikely to do so. As an appointed, rather than an elected chamber, it has become chiefly a house of prime ministerial patronage, and as such lacks democratic legitimacy. There have been numerous proposals to reform the Senate – in particular to elect it and to make it a more effective voice for the provinces in the federal government – but no reform has yet been accomplished.

Until 1949, the British Judicial Committee of the Privy Council (JCPC), a part of the British House of Lords, was the supreme authority interpreting Canadian constitutional law and practice and settling disputes between the two orders of government. Appeals to the JCPC were abolished in 1949. Since that time, the ultimate judicial authority has been the Supreme Court of Canada. Its existence, curiously enough, is based simply on federal legislation, not on a constitutional provision, and its judges are appointed solely by the government of Canada with no formal provincial role, although judges are generally appointed based on regional criteria.

In addition to patriating the constitution, the Constitution Act, 1982, added the means of amending it. Thus, the amendment of the constitution became possible without resort to the British Parliament. There are five methods of amending the constitution, depending on the matter concerned, but the general amending formula requires the approval of the Parliament of Canada and the approval of seven of the 10 provincial legislatures together having at least 50% of the population.

3 RECENT POLITICAL DYNAMICS

The defining moment for the Canadian federation in the last decade was the referendum on sovereignty held by the province of Quebec in October 1995. The secessionists lost by a hair's breadth – those opposing the secession of the province from Canada won by 50.6% of the votes cast. The referendum detonated a series of political explosions, large and small, in Canada's political system. As an immediate consequence, Quebec Premier Jacques Parizeau resigned and was replaced by Lucien Bouchard. Bouchard had been until then the party leader of the Bloc Québécois, the sister party to the Parti Québécois at the federal level. Another consequence was that Prime Minister Chrétien arranged for the passage of two parliamentary resolutions, one acknowledging Quebec as a distinct society and the other promising to recognize de facto a veto for Quebec over future, general constitutional amendments. As well, the federal government transferred responsibility for several policy fields to the provinces chiefly in recognition of these as longstanding concerns of successive Quebec governments.

To dissipate public confusion in Quebec about the consequences of any future positive referendum vote, the federal government asked the Supreme Court of Canada to clarify whether Quebec had the right to secede unilaterally under either domestic or international law. Unsurprisingly, the Court said in its opinion in August 1998 that Quebec had no such right, and that the secession of a province would have to be negotiated using the existing provisions for the amendment of the Canadian constitution. More surprisingly, however, it declared that a strong positive vote on a 'clear' question in a future Quebec referendum would oblige the federal government and the other provinces to negotiate this matter with Quebec. Building on the Court's emphasis on the need for there to be a clear vote and a clear question (which the judges declined to define), the federal government had the 'Clarity Bill' passed through the Parliament of Canada. This bill sets out the processes by which Ottawa would judge whether a future referendum question and a possible majority vote were 'clear'. Quebec, for its part, responded with a piece of legislation contesting the federal position.

Strangely, while these post-referendum events were occurring, the people of Quebec were shifting their attention away from the question of secession and toward other matters. The positive federal gestures had very little impact on Quebec opinion, and the potential 'provocations' – the Supreme Court Reference and the Clarity Bill – seemed to awaken little reaction or interest. True, the Parti Québécois, under the leadership of Lucien Bouchard, won re-election provincially, but so did the federal Liberals under Jean Chrétien in 1997. As evidence that nationalist fervour remains in abeyance for the time being, one need look no further than the fall 2000 federal election, which brought Jean Chrétien and the Liberal Party back to power for a third time. Significantly, they gained seats in Quebec and took a higher proportion of the popular vote than the secessionist Bloc Québécois, despite being led by Chrétien, a politician held in relatively low esteem by many francophone Quebecers. Partly in recognition of this current ebbing of the sovereignist tide, Lucien Bouchard resigned as Premier of Quebec in early 2001.

It is almost as if Quebecers, like other Canadians, decided that the last half of the 1990s would be devoted to getting federal and provincial finances under control. Both the federal and provincial governments undertook programs of severe fiscal restraint in the effort to eliminate their deficits, to reduce the accumulated debt, and to put the country and its regions into a more competitive position internationally. Inter-governmental relations during this period of financial reform have been less fraught than one would have expected, given the cutbacks in federal transfers to the provinces, and the downloading of costly program responsibilities. With the federal government and many of the provincial governments now in a surplus position, it remains to be seen whether the inter-governmental mood will shift.

At any rate, Quebec nationalism appears to have been put on hold, at least for now. The validity of this hypothesis will be tested in all likelihood in the next year or so, given that Lucien Bouchard has been replaced by a more militant successor, Bernard Landry, who hopes to reignite the fires of sovereignist aspiration.

The re-emergence of intense regional alienation in Western Canada is another matter that may well require the attention of the national government and central Canada over the coming years. Effectively locked out of national power since the Progressive Conservative Party collapsed in the 1993 federal election, people in the western Canadian provinces are showing increasing signs of frustration and discontent with the operation of the federation, which appears to neglect their interests and aspirations. The incessant focus on Quebec and its status in Canada has not helped matters, any more than the fact that all notions of constitutional reform (for example, the reform of the Senate) have been held hostage to the constraints the country is facing vis-à-vis Quebec.

Finally, the place of aboriginal people within the Canadian community has proven to be a painful and intractable issue with significant potential to shape the evolution of Canadian federalism in the future. Negotiations over land claims and treaty rights, together with significant court decisions relating to these matters, have already begun to affect the way in which Canadians conceive of their constitutional and political system, and the aspirations of aboriginal peoples for self-government has raised the possibility of the emergence of a third order of government in Canadian federalism.

The country currently appears to be in a holding pattern the character and duration of which is very hard to read. Beneath the surface calm, many would argue that significant, permanent shifts of attitude are underway which will reshape the politics of this country in the years to come.

4 SOURCES FOR FURTHER INFORMATION

Canadian Network for Federalism Studies (in development) – www.cnfs-rcef.net

Funston, Bernard and Eugene Meehan, *Canada's Constitutional Law in a Nutshell,* Toronto: Carswell, 1994.

Hogg, Peter, *Constitutional Law of Canada,* 2nd ed., Toronto: Carswell, 1985.

Queen's University, Institute of Intergovernmental Relations – www.qsilver.queensu.ca/iigr

Statistics Canada, *Canada Year Book,* Ottawa, *www.statcan.gc.ca*

www.gc.ca

www.forumoffederations.org

Table I
Political and Geographic Indicators

Capital city	Ottawa
Number and type of constituent units	*10 Provinces*: Alberta, British Columbia, Manitoba, New Brunswick, Newfoundland and Labrador, Nova Scotia, Ontario, Prince Edward Island, Quebec, Saskatchewan. *3 Territories*: Northwest Territories, Nunavut, Yukon.
Official language(s)	English and French
Area	9 984 670 km^2
Area – Largest constituent unit	Quebec (1 542 056 km^2)
Area – Smallest constituent unit	Prince Edward Island (5 660 km^2)
Total population	30 750 100
Population by constituent unit (% of total population)	Ontario 38%, Quebec 24%, British Columbia 13.%, Alberta 10%, Manitoba 4%, Saskatchewan 3.3%, Nova Scotia 3.1%, New Brunswick 2.5%, Newfoundland and Labrador 2%, Prince Edward Island 0.5%,Northwest Territories 0.13%, Yukon 0.10%, Nunavut 0.09%
Political system – federal	Federation – Parliamentary System
Head of state – federal	Queen Elizabeth II. Queen's Representative in Canada: Governor-General Adrienne Clarkson (1999), appointed by Queen based on the Prime Minister's recommendation.
Head of government – federal	Prime Minister Jean Chrétien (1993/1997/2000), Liberal Party of Canada, leader of majority party elected through popular vote for maximum 5-year, renewable term. Prime Minister names the members of the Cabinet, who are, in most cases, Members of Parliament.
Government structure – federal	Bicameral – Parliament: *Upper House* – Senate, 105 seats. Members appointed on a regional basis by Governor-General, based on the Prime Minister's recommendation, to serve until 75 years of age. *Lower House* – House of Commons, 301 seats. Members are elected on a single-member constituency basis with seats apportioned based on population, to serve for a maximum 5-year term.
Number of representatives in lower house of federal government – House of Commons	301 Seats: Liberal Party of Canada 172, Canadian Alliance (CA) 58, Bloc Quebecois (BQ) 38, Progressive Conservative/Democratic Representative Coalition (PC/DR) 20, New Democratic Party (NDP) 13.

Table I (continued)

Number of representatives in lower house of federal government for most populated constituent unit	Ontario: 103
Number of representatives in lower house of federal government for least populated constituent unit	Province – Prince Edward Island: 4 Territory – Nunavut: 1
Number of representatives in upper house of federal government – Senate	105 Seats: Liberal 57, PC 30, Independent 5, CA 1, Vacant 12. (Note: The 12 vacant seats are to be allotted, according to constitutional provisions regarding the distribution of representation in the Senate, to: New Brunswick 3, Nova Scotia 2, Quebec 2, Manitoba 1, Newfoundland and Labrador 1, Ontario 1, Prince Edward Island 1, Saskatchewan 1.)
Distribution of representation in upper house of federal government – Senate	105 Seats: Ontario and Quebec – 24 seats each Nova Scotia and New Brunswick – 10 seats each Newfoundland and Labrador, British Columbia, Manitoba, Alberta, Saskatchewan – 6 seats each Prince Edward Island – 4 seats Territories – 1 seat each
Constitutional court (highest court dealing with constitutional matters)	Supreme Court of Canada. 9 judges are appointed by the Governor-General, on the recommendation of the Prime Minister.
Political system of constituent units	Unicameral – Provincial Legislature. Members are directly elected to serve for maximum 5-year term.
Head of state – constituent units	Queen's Representative: Lieutenant-Governor. Appointed by Governor-General, based on recommendation of head of government of constituent unit (Premier).
Head of government – constituent units	Premier – Leader of majority party in Legislature. Appoints Cabinet, each serving for a maximum 5-year term.

Table II
Economic and Social Indicators

GDP	US$774.7 billion
GDP per capita	US$24 800
Mechanisms for taxation	Both the federal government and provincial governments have the right to levy taxes, however for the most part, it is the central government that collects personal income taxes and then re-distributes these taxes to the provinces (the exception to this general practice is the province of Quebec). • Personal Income Tax: Tax brackets range from 16%-29%, with a 5% surtax on all income above CD$85 000 • Federal Goods and Services Tax (GST): 7% • Provincial Sales Tax (PST), ranging from 0%-15%, depending on the province (no provincial sales tax in Alberta). • Corporate Tax – 28%
National debt (external)	US$1.9 billion
National unemployment rate	6.8%
Constituent unit with highest unemployment rate	Newfoundland – 16.6%
Constituent unit with lowest unemployment rate	Manitoba – 4.6%
Adult literacy rate	99%
National expenditures on education as a % of GDP	7.3%
Life expectancy in years	79.1
Doctors per population ratio (national)	185 doctors per 100 000 inhabitants
Doctors per population ratio in constituent units (highest)	Quebec: 212 doctors per 100 000 inhabitants
Doctors per population ratio in constituent units (lowest)	Province – Prince Edward Island: 128 doctors per 100 000 inhabitants Territory – Northwest Territories: 92 doctors per 100 000 inhabitants
National expenditures on health as a % of GDP	9.3%

Sources

Canadian Council of Ministers of Education. "Figure 3.26: Educational Expenditures from Public and Private Sources for Educational Institutions as a % of GDP by level of Education, Canada and Jurisdictions, 1995." *Education Indicators in Canada (PCEIP) 1999*. Produced by Statistics Canada, 2000. www.cmec.ca/stats/pceip/1999/Indicatorsite/index.html

Canadian Institute of Health Information (CIHI). "Health Expenditures, Provincial and Territorial Indicators 1997" and "Provincial and Territorial Indicators – Total of

Physicians for 1998 per 100,000 population." *Canadian Institute of Health Information.* www.cihi.com

Canadian Parliamentary Guide. www.laurentian.ca/library/govdocs/govguide.parlgd.html

Canadian Parliamentary Website. "Standings in the Senate, 2001" & "Standings in the House of Commons, 2001." www.parl.gc.ca

Central Intelligence Agency (CIA), *World Fact Book 2000.* CIA, www.cia.gov/cia/publications/factbook/index.html

Economist Intelligence Unit, "Country Commerce – Canada," *The Economist Intelligence Unit 2000.* New York: EIU, 2000.

Elazar, Daniel J. (ed.), *Federal Systems of the World: A Handbook of Federal, Confederal and Autonomy Arrangements.* 2nd Edition. Jerusalem Institute for Federal Studies. London: Longman Group/Westgate House, 1994.

International Monetary Fund (IMF). *International Financial Statistics,* Vol. LIII, No. 12, December 2000. Washington, DC: the IMF Statistics Department, 2000.

Organization for Economic Co-operation and Development (OECD). www.oecd.org/std/gdp.htm

Statistics Canada. "Canada – Land Area" and "Population by Year." (Matrices 6367–6378 & 6408–6409). www.statcan.ca

Statistics Canada, "Economic Indicators," *Statistics Canada On-line Database,* www.statcan.ca.

Statistics Canada, "Economic Indicators as of October 2000: Labour force, employment and unemployment." (CANSIM Matrix 3472 and Catalogue number 71-529-XPB). www.statcan.ca.

Statistics Canada "Expenditure on education at all levels, 1997–1998". www.statcan.ca.

Statistics Canada. "Non-health indicators Table 2.8 Average Personal Income, 1995." *Health Indicators – December 2000,* 82-221-XIE. www.statcan.ca.

Statistics Canada. "Provincial and Territorial Government Finance: Assets and Liabilities, March 31/1999." *The Daily.* www.statcan.ca/English/day-quo.htm

United Nations. *Human Development Report, 2000* www.undp.org/hdro/report.html

World Bank. *World Development Report 2000/2001: Attacking Poverty.* www.worldbank.org/poverty/wdrpoverty/report/index.htm

World Health Organisation (WHO). "Estimates of Health Personnel." www-nt.who.int/whosis/statistics

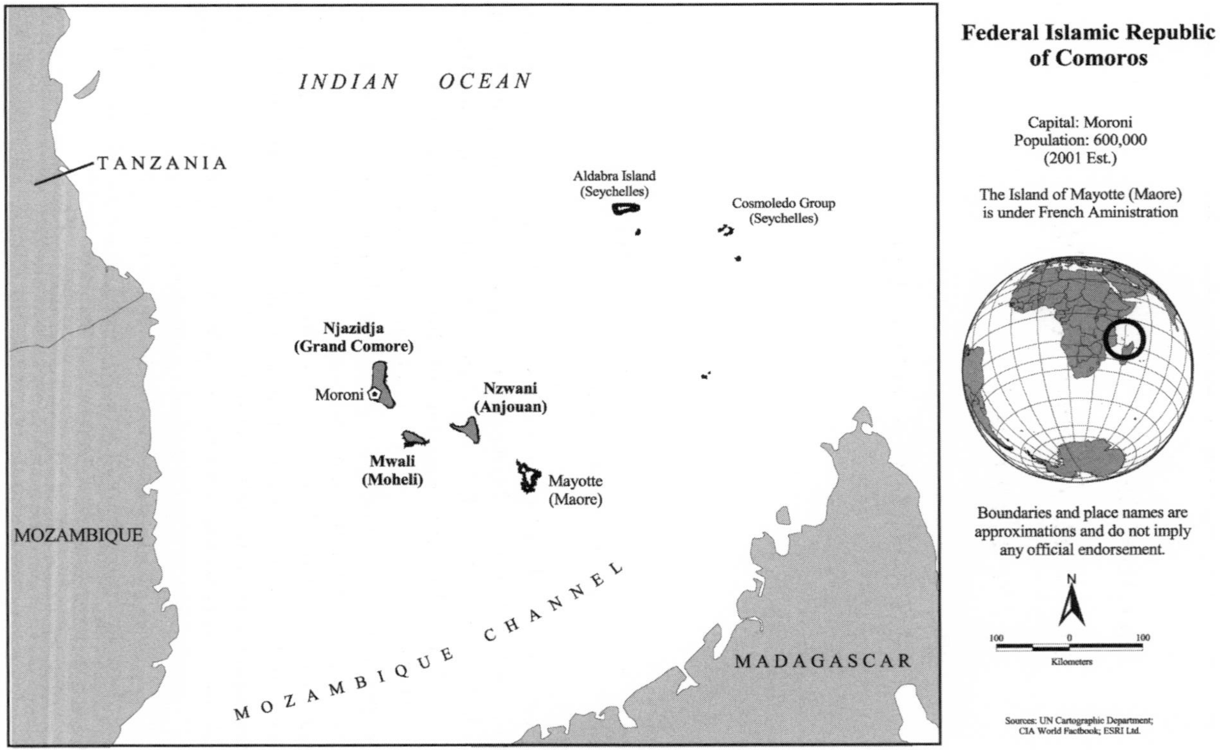

Federal Islamic Republic of Comoros

Capital: Moroni
Population: 600,000
(2001 Est.)

The Island of Mayotte (Maore) is under French Aministration

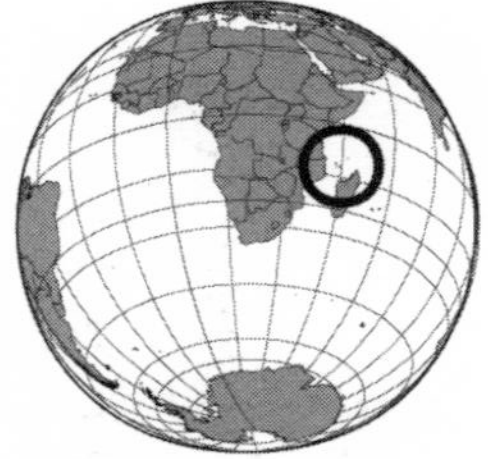

Boundaries and place names are approximations and do not imply any official endorsement.

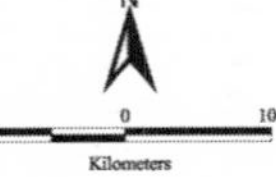

Sources: UN Cartographic Department; CIA World Factbook; ESRI Ltd.

Comoros*
(*Federal Islamic Republic of the Comoros*)

FAISSOILI BEN MOHADJI

1 HISTORY AND DEVELOPMENT OF FEDERALISM

The Comoros archipelago includes four islands in the southwest Indian Ocean between Madagascar and the east coast of Africa. Grande Comoros (Njazidja), Anjouan (Nzwani) and Moheli (Mwali) form the Federal Islamic Republic of the Comoros (FIRC). A fourth island, Mayotte, remains under French administration.

The population of Comoros is approximately 500,000, with an average density of 300 inhabitants/km^2, 80 per cent of whom live in rural areas. Migration and intermarriage have mixed Malaysians, Persians, Arabs and Cafres, and the original Swahili civilization of the western Indian Ocean. Demographic growth is high – between 2.7% and 3% per year – and the population is very young, with nearly 50% of inhabitants below the age of 15. The population is poor and often malnourished.

The economy of the Comoros is closely tied to agriculture. Eighty per cent of the population earns its livelihood through agriculture which is the main source of exports and brings in 97% of foreign currency. The country has little industry and no valuable minerals. Foreign debt represented 90% of the GDP in 1990, compared with 8% in 1970, and the state does not have the means to deal with this debt.

* The Forum of Federations would like to express its appreciation to Abdourahim Said Bakar for his helpful comments on this article.

Europeans first discovered the Comoros Islands in the sixteenth century but they were not united under a single authority until French colonization in the nineteenth century. Before that numerous sovereign sultanates co-existed on the territory. The French managed to unify the Comoros Islands using a highly centralized structure. Yet, despite the many years of French administration and centralized political authority, the sultanates have persisted in collective memory and behaviour. Comorans identify first and foremost with their family, their village or their region and rarely, if ever, with the central government.

The independence movement in Africa provoked a burst of nationalism in the Comoros. Prince Saïd Ibrahim, from Grande Comoros, took power in 1970 at the peak of this period of nationalism. He made overtures to Mayotte and Moheli in an attempt to calm the tension that characterized relations between these islands and the government in Moroni (Grande Comoros). Nonetheless, it was not his destiny to orchestrate sovereignty for the Comoros Islands. He was forced out of politics democratically on 12 July 1972, following a vote of non-confidence. Ahmed Abdallah, a former Senator in the French National Assembly, took over.

The Parliament of the Comoros expressed the people's desire for independence with a resolution on 23 December 1972. Following this, Ahmed Abdallah travelled to Paris and on 15 June 1973, he signed a joint declaration with the French government on the independence of the Comoros Islands. As stipulated in the French constitution, a referendum on accession to international sovereignty was held in Comoros on 22 December 1974. The results showed a vast majority of the population favoured independence, except in Mayotte where the opposite was true. Once the results of the referendum were announced, the Comoran Parliament instituted a complex process for accession to independence, taking into account Mayotte's refusal to leave the French Republic. President Abdallah, with the support of all Members of Parliament except those from Mayotte, opted for a unilateral declaration of independence on 6 July 1975.

Ali Soilihi (from Grande Comoros) seized power from Ahmed Abdallah (who was from Anjouan) with a coup on 3 August 1975. In addition to soured relations with France, the new regime had to cope with simmering inter-island rivalries and the fact that the previous government had eliminated neither the authority of the sultans nor that of the centralized colonial administration. Ali Soilihi neutralized the Anjouan resistance but an attempt to muster support on the rebel island of Mayotte ended in failure.

Representatives from Mayotte and Moheli perceived the disparate development of the islands as a consequence of centralized power, which was either in the hands of Grande Comoros or Anjouan. A federal solution therefore became attractive to Mayotte's dissidents on the eve of independence. Federation offered the possibility of each island preserving its identity by managing its own affairs and assets. But the Comoran authorities staunchly opposed federalism because they viewed it, in light of Mayotte's dissent, as incorporating the seeds of partition.

With President Ahmed Abdallah's return to power in 1978, federalism re-surfaced as a last recourse for bringing Mayotte into the fold. Although previously Abdallah had rejected federalism as a divisive manoeuvre by the colonizers, in October 1978 he had a federal constitution adopted. The arrangement provided him with strong executive powers and techniques for keeping the federated islands under control.

Unfortunately, during Ahmed Abdallah's leadership, from 13 March 1978 to 27 November 1989 (the date on which he was assassinated), economic problems proliferated. Regionalized investments accentuated the disparities in development and the inequality of opportunity among the different islands. While some enjoyed fortunes amassed under dubious circumstances, poverty was widespread. This led to rebellious behaviour and divisive movements that undermined national unity. Each island had a tendency to defend its interests by opposing those of the overall group.

It was this defiant society that Said Mohamed Djohar inherited when he was elected President. In his constant quest for political balance, Djohar governed with contradictory decrees, which resulted in the Supreme Court's unsuccessful attempt to have him removed from office for incompetence in August 1991. The island of Moheli suffered particularly from this dysfunctional situation. Distanced from an increasingly centralized power and its attendant privileges, Moheli demanded equality for the islands. This demand, coupled with opposition demands, led to the first national conference, which met from January to April 1992, to develop a constitution for the Federal Islamic Republic of the Comoros.

2 CONSTITUTIONAL PROVISIONS RELATING TO FEDERALISM

From independence to the present day, the Comoros Islands have had four constitutions, two of which were federal in nature. The first was the Constitution of the Federal Islamic Republic of the Comoros, 1978 to 1989. This constitution was developed with no parliamentary intervention. The constitution was built around the need for national cohesion and outlined a central organization to promote economic growth – two tendencies which indicated that it was a centralized federation.

As a result of the 1978 constitution, each island was recognized as an autonomous entity free to administer itself. These entities were known as governorates. Each governorate had an Island Council elected for a four-year term by universal suffrage. The Council was a deliberative assembly that voted on the island's laws and adopted the local budget. Each island managed its own budget, along with almost all social matters – including, health, education, training, community facilities, etc. A Governor was elected for a five-year term by direct universal suffrage. The Governor administered federal laws and those of the Island Council. He was assisted by commissioners that he appointed himself, who were responsible individually and collectively to him and the Island Council.

On a national level, the main offices of the federal state (presidency of the republic, presidency of the Federal Assembly and presidency of the Supreme Court) were divided among the three islands. This same formula applied to the make-up of the central government, where each island had one or more ministers. The government was unicameral and therefore the islands were not represented in a chamber of the central government. The constitution divided jurisdictions among the Governors and the federal government, reserving for the latter and its leader an impressive list of powers and trusts.

This seemed to be an attractive arrangement, but the highly uneven distribution of scarce resources between the governorates and the federal state limited the autonomy of the islands. The federal government collected all tax and non-tax resources, as well as international public funding for development. The jurisdiction allocated to the governorates did not include sufficient means for the independent management of each island, and the constitution denied them the possibility of benefiting from foreign aid without the approval of the federal executive, which capitalized on this opportunity for control. Eighty per cent of the governorates' budgets came from the federal state. The funds were allotted each month, in principle, at the discretion of the Finance Minister. The redistribution of national resources and foreign aid in the form of federal grants was accompanied by central guidelines on how the funds were to be used. This situation gave the central government in Moroni legal authority that penetrated deep into each island's internal affairs.

The increased federal interference by President Ahmed Abdallah reduced autonomy on the islands and stripped the federation of its substance, leaving only the legal entity. In this context, the President met with the 90 members and councillors from the islands in Mrodjou (Grande Comoros) on 24 October 1983, to revise the constitution. The constitution was also revised in 1984 and again in 1989, when the position of Prime Minister was eliminated, and Article 16, which limited the head of state to two successive terms, was also amended.

For 11 years, Abdallah's authority proved invincible. He crushed not only individuals but also the constitutional institutions that could have balanced the ambitions of an authoritarian President with vast powers. The Assembly and the Supreme Court were the trustees of his personal power. Their role was one of consultation – they provided opinions that neither bound the government nor ratified its decisions.

The second federal constitution was developed after Abdallah's assassination – the 1992 Constitution of the Federal Islamic Republic of the Comoros. This constitution, for once in the history of the Comoros, was developed by a national conference that met in early 1992, and brought together all the political parties and representatives from civil society.

Under the 1992 constitution each island was an autonomous territorial entity, governed by a Governor and an Island Council. The Governor was elected for a five-year term by direct universal suffrage, and was eligible to run for one additional term. He ensured that the island's laws and regulations were respected, represented the island government, and exercised regulatory powers in areas not defined in the constitution as part of the federal domain. The Island Council determined the island's resources and spending. These included: the proceeds of direct taxation collected on the island; a share of indirect taxes collected throughout the republic; external resources allotted to the island; and a share of external resources allotted to the republic and not specifically designated to one island. Federal law set the share of indirect taxes destined for the federal budget at between 30% and 40%. The remainder was proportionately divided among the islands according to population size. The islands were eligible for grants or other external assistance, with the government's consent. Each Island Council was elected for five years by direct universal suffrage. It had to be consulted on matters relating to the preparation and application of multi-year economic, cultural and social development programs, and federal public concessions located on the island.

The 1992 constitution outlines that the President is to be elected for five years by direct universal suffrage, and gives him a number of roles. The President is to ensure that the constitution is respected and to oversee the regular functioning of public powers and the continuity of the state. He is the guarantor of national independence, the unity of the republic, the autonomy of the islands, and respect for international commitments. The President's role includes the determination and conduct of foreign policy. Governmental appointments made by the President are to be made with regard for equity and balance among the islands.

According to the constitution, the government determines and implements the nation's policies and controls the federal administration and the armed forces. The government's actions are directed by a minister appointed by the President from the party with the majority in the Federal Assembly. The government is collectively terminated if the Federal Assembly questions it in a vote of non-confidence by at least one-quarter of the members and an absolute majority vote by the members of the Assembly.

The constitution states that the Federal Assembly is elected for four years by direct universal suffrage. In each electoral riding, voters are to elect one member. Ridings are determined by federal law and there can be no fewer than five per island. The right of constitutional amendment is the joint prerogative of both the government and the Federal Assembly.

Unlike the earlier constitution, the 1992 constitution provides for a Senate in which the islands have equal representation. Five Senators per island are to be elected for six years by an electoral college consisting of municipal and island councillors. The 1992 constitution gives the Senate some power to change legislation. Thus, laws and other acts which are voted on by the Federal Assembly but contested by all Senators of an island are withdrawn if, upon second reading in the Federal Assembly, they are also contested by a majority of members from the same island.

The constitution also created The Council of the Ulema which is an Islamic institution that promotes and protects Islam. Judicial power is independent of executive and legislative power, and justice is rendered on the entire territory in the name of Allah. The High Court of Justice, which includes one-quarter of Assembly members, one-fifth of Senators and high-ranking magistrates, is responsible for trying the President of the Republic, Presidents of the Federal Assembly and the Senate, the Constitutional Council, members of the government, ambassadors and island Governors accused of high treason, crimes or misdemeanours in carrying out their duties. There are a number of other courts outlined in the constitution. Thus there is also a Supreme Court, a Court of Cassation/Appeal, a State Council, a Court of Auditors and a Court of Conflicts. Decisions made by these bodies cannot be appealed.

The Constitutional Council was designed to oversee the constitutionality of laws, rulings, regulatory texts, proceedings on the islands and international commitments. It has also been given the responsibility of monitoring elections for President of the Republic, Assembly members, Governors, island councillors, Senators and municipal councillors. The members of the Constitutional Council are to be appointed for a seven-year term as follows: three by the President of the Republic; three by the President of the Federal Assembly; and one by each Island Council.

3 RECENT POLITICAL DYNAMICS

A coup on 28 September 1995 ended the rule of President Djohar, who had not succeeded in setting up the democratic institutions set forth in the 1992 constitution and had changed the make-up of his government 17 times.

Mohamed Taki Abdulkarim was elected President on 16 March 1996, with a 64 per cent majority. His election sparked great hope for change. In a few months, however, he had amended the constitution to increase his powers and scheduled a ratification referendum in October 1996. The opposition refused to participate, and also ignored the legislative elections in late 1996. Like his predecessors, Taki faced huge social protests rooted in worsening youth unemployment, the growing gap between the ruling class and the poorer classes, and the anger of civil servants who were forced to wait months before getting paid. In the summer of 1997, Anjouan and Moheli were engulfed by rebellion.

Taki appealed to the Organization of African Unity (OAU), the League of Arab Nations, the European Union and the United Nations to help settle the crisis. With the OAU's mediation, an inter-Comoran conference was held in Addis Ababa, Ethiopia, in December 1997. The sole result was the adoption of the principle of an inter-island conference to be held as soon as possible, under the auspices of the OAU. Its goal would be to define a new institutional framework.

President Mohamed Taki died suddenly in November 1998, and finding a successor proved difficult. According to the constitution, interim President Tadjidine Saïd Ben Massounde, a 70-year-old Anjouan, was not eligible to run in the election, which had to take place within 30 to 90 days. But the prospect of finding another candidate with sufficient support within the given time-frame was unrealistic, given the separatist crises on Anjouan and Moheli.

By March 1999, the situation was increasingly confusing: Anjouan was split into two factions, and Grande Comoros itself had succumbed to the virus of separatism. Before the divisiveness could spread even further, the OAU announced that a conference on Comoran reconciliation would take place in Antananarivo, Madagascar from 19–23 April 1999. An agreement-in-principle took shape, in favour of maintaining the territorial integrity of the Comoros Islands. Even the Anjouan and

Moheli delegations recognized the principle, with a number of conditions, including a rotating federal presidency and a Federal Assembly designated by the island assemblies. The Anjouan delegation members, however, refused to sign the final declaration, although they agreed in principle, claiming that they needed time to consult the population.

On the night of 29–30 April 1999 another coup took place, perpetrated by the Chief of Staff of the Comoran Army, Colonel Assoumani Azzali. This coup meant the removal of the interim President, Prime Minister, the Council of Ministers (appointed by the President), and the dissolution of the Federal Assembly. On 6 May Colonel Azzali made himself leader of a state committee with 12 commissioners. He promised he would apply the Antananarivo agreement, but this has not occurred.

The governments of the Comoros have been constantly plagued by the endless rivalries on and between the islands. Despite efforts by the international community, political parties and island movements, the integrity of the country remains threatened. Separatists in both Anjouan and Moheli declared independence in 1997, although these declarations are still unacceptable to the central government. Today there are demands for self-determination coming from all three islands.

A tripartite committee is working on a new constitution which will regulate the "Nouvel Ensemble Comorien." Representatives of the OAU and Francophonie continue to work with the Comoran authorities and civil society in an attempt to reach a reconciliation agreement. Although the country is currently ruled by a constitutional charter developed and custom-tailored by the military leaders who took power in April 1999, a schedule has been established for presidential elections and the establishment of new decentralized institutions to give more autonomy to the islands, and the tripartite committee continues to negotiate a new legal and constitutional framework for the country.

4 SOURCES FOR FURTHER INFORMATION

Abdou Djabir, *Les Comoros: un état en construction*, Harmattan, 1993.

Deval, Raymond, *L'islam aux Comoros*, Monde et Culture, 1980.

Hervé, Chagnou and Ali Haribou,. *Les Comores. Que sais-je?* Paris: PUF, 1980.

Maurice, Pierre, *Communication sur un séminaire international annuel du 26 novembre 1999: la position de la France et la Communauté internationale à l'égard des îles Comoros*, La Réunion: Saint-Denis.

Wadahane. *Mayotte et le contentieux entre la France et les Comores*, 1994.

Constitution of the Federal Islamic Republic of Comoros, 1978.

Constitution of the Federal Islamic Republic of Comoros, 1992.

Table I
Political and Geographic Indicators

Capital city	Moroni (Njazidja)
Number and type of constituent units	*3 Islands:* Moheli (Mwali), Grande Comore (Njazidja), Anjouan (Nzwani)
Official language(s)	Arabic and French
Area	2 170 km^2
Area – Largest constituent unit	Grande Comore/Njazidja (1 148 km^2)
Area – Smallest constituent unit	Moheli/Mwali (290 km^2)
Total population	578 400
Population by constituent unit (% of total population)	Grande Comore/Njazidja 55%, Anjouan/Nzwani 40%, and Moheli/Mwali 5%
Political system – federal	Republic
Head of state – federal	President Assoumani Azzali (1999) (Note: the interim government of President Tajiddine Said Ben Massounde was overthrown in a coup by Colonel Azzoumani Azzali in April 1999.) According to the constitution, the President is directly elected to serve a 6-year term.
Head of government – federal	President Assoumani Azzali. Prime Minister Boléro Hamada Madi (2000), Prime Minister and Council of Ministers (Cabinet) are appointed by the President.
Government structure – federal	Bicameral – Parliament: *Upper House* – The Senate, 15 seats. 5 Senators elected from each island. Members are selected by Island Councils to serve for 6-year terms. *Lower House* – Assemblée Fédérale (Federal Assembly), 42 members, elected by popular vote for a 5-year term in single-seat electoral wards, with each island having at least 10 wards
Number of representatives in lower house of federal government – Federal Assembly	42 seats. Parliament has been dissolved (1999).
Number of representatives in lower house of federal government for most populated constituent unit	Each island has at least 10 seats in the Federal Assembly.
Number of representatives in lower house of federal government for least populated constituent unit	Each island has at least 10 seats in the Federal Assembly.

Table I (continued)

Number of representatives in upper house of federal government – Senate	15 seats; parliament has been dissolved (1999).
Distribution of representation in upper house of federal government – Senate	15 seats; each Island is allocated 5 seats.
Constitutional court (highest court dealing with constitutional matters)	Supreme Court (Cour Suprême). Two members are appointed by the President, two members are elected by the Federal Assembly, one is elected by the Council of each island, and the remaining seats are filled by former Presidents of the republic.
Political system of constituent units	Unicameral – Island Councils
Head of state – constituent units	Governors. According to 1992 constitution, Governors are elected for a 5-year term.
Head of government – constituent units	Governor. Appoints up to 4 commissioners to assist in administration of the island. Each island has its own directly elected Island Council, to serve a 4-year term.

Table II
Economic and Social Indicators

GDP	US$419 million
GDP per capita	US$720
Mechanisms for taxation	N/A
National debt (external)	US$197 million
National unemployment rate	20%
Constituent unit with highest unemployment rate	N/A
Constituent unit with lowest unemployment rate	N/A
Adult literacy rate	58.5%
National expenditures on education as a % of GDP	3.9%
Life expectancy in years	60.03
Doctors per population ratio (national)	7.4 doctors per 100 000 inhabitants
Doctors per population ratio in constituent units (highest)	N/A
Doctors per population ratio in constituent units (lowest)	N/A
National expenditures on health as a % of GDP	4.5%

Sources

Central Intelligence Agency (CIA). "Comoros." *Chiefs of State and Cabinet Members of Foreign Governments.* www.odci.gov/cia/publications/chiefs/chiefs40.html

Central Intelligence Agency (CIA), *World Fact Book 2000.* CIA, www.cia.gov/cia/publications/factbook/index.html

Elazar, Daniel J. (ed.), *Federal Systems of the World: A Handbook of Federal, Confederal and Autonomy Arrangements.* 2nd Edition. Jerusalem Institute for Federal Studies. London: Longman Group/Westgate House, 1994.

United Nations Population Division. Department of Economic and Social Affairs. "Population in 1999 and 2000: All Countries." *World Population Prospects: The 1998 Revision, Vol. 1 comprehensive Tables.* www.un.org/Depts.htm

United Nations. *Human Development Report, 2000.* www.undp.org/hdro/report.html

United Nations Statistics Division. "InfoNation." United Nations Statistical Database, 2000. www.un.org/

UNESCO. *World Education Report 1998: Teachers and Teaching in a Changing World.* Paris: UNESCO, 1998.

World Health Organisation (WHO). "Estimates of Health Personnel." www-nt.who.int/whosis/statistics

World Health Organisation (WHO). *World Health Report 2000.* Geneva, Switzerland, 2000. www-nt.who.int/whosis/statistics/menu.cfm

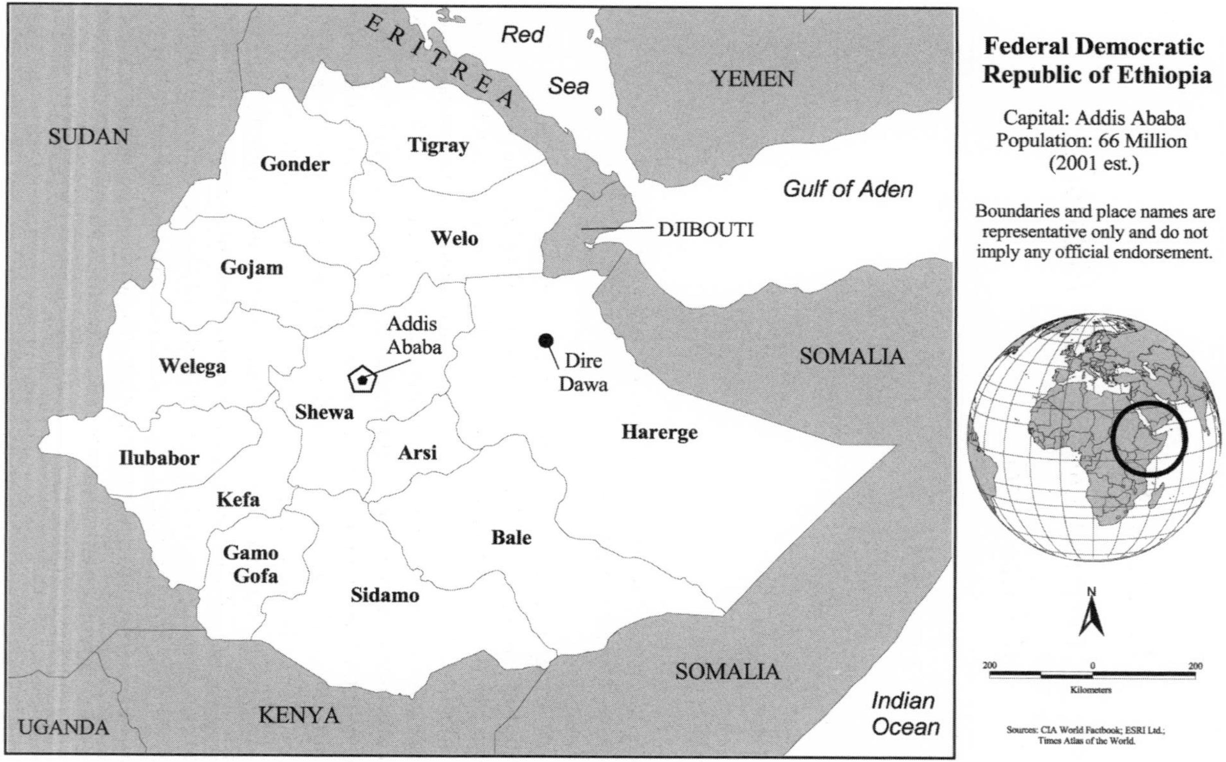

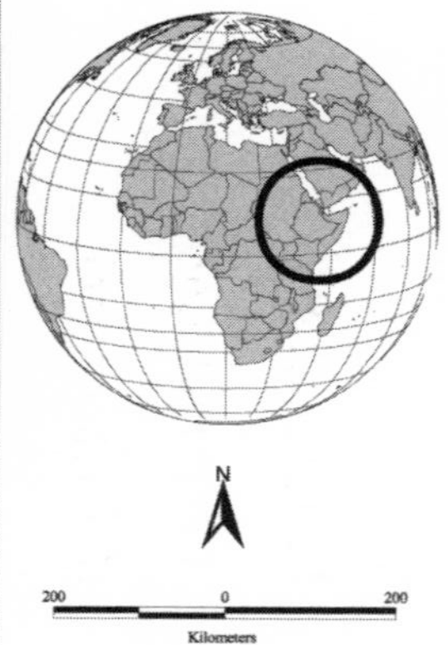

Federal Democratic Republic of Ethiopia

Capital: Addis Ababa
Population: 66 Million
(2001 est.)

Boundaries and place names are representative only and do not imply any official endorsement.

Sources: CIA World Factbook; ESRI Ltd.; Times Atlas of the World.

Ethiopia
(*Federal Democratic Republic of Ethiopia*)

TOM PÄTZ

1 HISTORY AND DEVELOPMENT OF FEDERALISM

The Federal Democratic Republic of Ethiopia (1,112 million km^2) is located at the Horn of Africa. It is bordered by Sudan on the west, Kenya on the south, Somalia and Djibouti on the east, and Eritrea on the north. It has a population of some 63 million inhabitants, about 90 per cent of whom earn their living from the land, mainly as subsistence farmers. Agriculture is the backbone of the national economy. The country has a GNP per capita of just 100 US$, making it the poorest country in the world in 2000, according to the World Bank.[1] Life expectancy at birth is 42 years for males and 44 years for females.

Due to its 3,000 year history, Ethiopia is seen as the oldest "state" in Africa and one of the oldest in the world. Starting from the Da'amat State (ca. 500 BC-100 AD), followed by the advanced civilization of the Axumite Empire and finally the Era of the Princes, Ethiopia has existed within different patrimonial empires. Modern Ethiopia was created by Christian highland rulers largely through twin processes of political subjugation and economic exploitation in the late nineteenth and early twentieth centuries. The Imperial Crown Prince and Regent,

1 This dismal standard of living can in part be attributed to diversion of government resources to the recent conflict with Eritrea. With the end of the conflict, the situation may improve.

Haile Selassie, established ascendancy over regional feudal lords from 1916 to 1930, when he became Emperor. Haile Selassie was driven into exile during the Italian occupation of Ethiopia between 1936 and 1941. Following the country's liberation by Allied forces in 1941, he returned from Britain and ruled until his overthrow in 1974.

Eritrea, created at the end of the nineteenth century through Italian colonialism, was federated with Ethiopia in 1952 after 10 years under a British mandate. The United Nations General Assembly passed a resolution, the Federal Act, by which Eritrea came under the sovereignty of the Ethiopian Crown. The UN resolution – Resolution 390(v)(a) of 2 December 1950 – contained 15 articles, the first seven of which regulated the relations between Eritrea and Ethiopia. According to the first article of this UN document, Eritrea was to constitute "an autonomous unit federated with Ethiopia."

Growing contradictions between an emerging capitalist system and feudalism, and questions about the value of the monarchy, fuelled unrest. In 1961 the royal body guard attempted a coup d'état which revealed popular dissatisfaction with the pace of modernization and development. In recognition of this, in 1962 the government moved to increase centralization.

In 1974, the Provisional Military Council (Derg in Amharic) toppled the Haile Selassie's regime and proclaimed Ethiopia a socialist state. In the early years of the regime – a time referred to as the "red terror" – struggles for power and the establishment of a socialist state resulted in, at a conservative estimate, 100,000 people killed and several hundred thousand more fleeing the country.

Following the Soviet model, a Workers' Party of Ethiopia was created in 1984, and in 1987, the People's Democratic Republic of Ethiopia was promulgated under a new constitution. The constitution conferred ultimate state power on the so-called national Shengo and its standing organ, the Council of State. However, like other socialist/ communist countries, the ruling political party – through the Central Committee and the Politburo of the Workers' Party – maintained power through informal 'parallel' channels of communications and decision making, and in reality, had ultimate decision-making power in the country.

At the end of the Cold War, Soviet support wavered and the integrity of the centralized state was challenged. Two years of military defeats in Eritrea and Tigray, in addition to the gradual desertion of his Soviet allies, fatally weakened the regime of Colonel Mengistu.

In 1991 the Ethiopian Peoples' Revolutionary Democratic Front (EPRDF), a newly created coalition, launched a decisive military assault through central and western provinces, while in the east, Eritrean forces closed in on the cities of Assab and Asmara. Colonel Mengistu fled to Zimbabwe. In July 1991, EPRDF forces took control of Addis Ababa. A conference was convened to endorse a transitional charter. The charter became the legal basis of four years of interim rule under an EPRDF-dominated legislature with an executive headed by the leader of the Tigray People's Liberation Front (TPLF), Meles Zenawi. The transitional government implemented extensive economic reforms and a radical form of federal devolution to nine of the new regional states along predominantly ethnic lines. On 8 December 1994, the 538-member Constituent Assembly approved a draft constitution prepared by the Constitution Drafting Commission. During the drafting process, the public was consulted, mainly at meetings held at the local level. Voters accepted the constitution in a referendum, and the Federal Democratic Republic of Ethiopia was proclaimed in August 1995.

After the fall of the Provisional Military Council, the different liberation forces transformed themselves into political parties. They were not, however, able to convert in this short time from fighting forces into democratic players, and they continued to try to *overcome* others rather than democratically cooperating with them. In May and June 1995, Ethiopia held national parliamentary and regional legislative elections. Most opposition parties boycotted these elections – led by the Oromo Liberation Front which, seeing itself trailing the Tigray People's Liberation Front (TPLF), went underground – thus ensuring a landslide victory for the TPLF. International and non-governmental observers concluded, however, that opposition parties would have been able to participate had they chosen to do so.

In May 1991, the Eritrean People's Liberation Front (EPLF), led by Isaias Afwerki, assumed control of Eritrea and established a provisional government. This provisional government independently administered Eritrea until, on 23–25 April 1993, Eritreans voted overwhelmingly for independence in a UN-monitored free and fair referendum. Eritrea was declared independent on 27 April 1993.

In May 1998 rising tensions between Eritrea and Ethiopia led to an offensive military operation launched by Eritrea. Trench warfare turned into an intensive military operation by Ethiopia which eventually led to an Agreement on the Cessation of Hostilities, signed on 18 June 2000. Finally, on 12 December 2000 Ethiopia and Eritrea signed a peace agreement in Algiers. Currently, 4,200 UN troops are deployed along the border between Eritrea and Ethiopia. The reason for the outbreak of hostilities – a border dispute – will now be settled under the auspices of the Organization of African Unity (OAU) and the UN.

2 CONSTITUTIONAL PROVISIONS RELATING TO FEDERALISM

The Federal Democratic Republic of Ethiopia (FDRE) is a parliamentary democracy. Its head of state is the President, who is nominated by the House of Peoples' Representatives and then elected for a six-year term by a two-thirds majority vote of a joint session of Parliament (Article 70).

The federal Parliament is bicameral. The legislative institutions of the federal government are the House of Peoples' Representatives and the House of Federation. Members of the House of Peoples' Representatives are elected for a five-year term in a "first-past-the-post" electoral system. According to the constitution, this House cannot have more than 550 members, and at least 20 seats are reserved for minority nationalities. Its functions consist of legislative, financial, deliberative, informative, and representative subjects (Article 54). It is also provided with questioning power (Article 55(17)).

The composition of the House of Federation is surprisingly very open. The election of members can be direct or indirect – the decision is left to the state councils. Thus, state councils can decide whether they elect the members themselves or whether elections are held. Additionally, each nation or nationality gets one additional member for each one million of its population (Article 61). At present there are 112 members. Of this number, 71 are appointed by the states, and the other 41 seats are apportioned based on population (Article 61).

Ethiopian federalism has ethnicity as its underlying organizing principle. Ethiopian citizens are categorized into their different ethnolinguistic groupings. Member units of the federation are moulded by "settlement patterns, language, identity and consent of the people concerned" (Article 46(2)). Ethnic federalism is expressed by the formulation of "We the Nations, Nationalities and Peoples of Ethiopia" (Preamble of the Constitution). Whether minorities are specially acknowledged in the federal Parliament, or self-governed administrative units at the local level, the Nationality Right is a main constructional feature of the constitution and also a factor in the determination of the division of power.

The House of Federation is the sole custodian of the constitution. It has the exclusive right (Article 62(1)) and ultimate authority (Article 83) to interpret the constitution and this is its main function. The Council of Constitutional Inquiry was established in Article 62(2) to examine constitutional issues and to submit findings to the House of Federation. The Chief Justice of the Federal Supreme Court heads the Council. The House of Federation is not bound by the advisory opinion of the Council of Constitutional Inquiry.

The FDRE is comprised of the federal government and nine member states (also referred to as "regional states") (Article 50). Member/regional states are Tigray, Afar, Amhara, Oromia, Somali, Benishangul/Gumaz, Southern Nations, Nationalities and Peoples, Gambela, and Harar (Article 47). The head of each member/regional state is called the President of the Region. He is head of the administration and Chairman of the Executive Committee of the state. The President of the Region is accountable to the Council of the Region (the name of each state legislature) and to the Executive Committee of the state. The Executive Committee is made up of the President, the Vice-President, the Secretary and other sector heads – for example, of Planning and Finance, Economy, Administration, and Social Affairs. All members of the Executive Committee are elected by the Council from within its members to serve a five-year term.

Chapter Five of the constitution – Articles 50–52 – deals with the structure and division of powers. A very detailed description of the powers and functions of the federal government is given in Article 51(1–21). All of the federal powers are directed towards issues of national concern. These are, *inter alia,* overall economic and social development, national standards and basic policy criteria for health and education, defence, federal police, foreign policy, foreign commerce, declaration of a state of emergency, immigration and granting of passports, copyright, standards for measurement and calendar, and possession and bearing of arms. The exhaustive description of federal powers is followed by a general provision regarding the powers and functions of the states. Article 52(1) indicates that "all powers not given to the Federal Government alone, or concurrently to the Federal Government and the States are reserved to the States." According to Article 52(2), the states can establish their state administration, enact and execute state constitutions, formulate policies, strategies and plans, administer land, levy and collect taxes and duties, enact and enforce laws relating to the state civil service, and establish and administer a state police force.

Article 49 of the constitution gives special status to the capital city, Addis Ababa. According to Article 49(2), Addis Ababa has a "full measure of self-government." Addis Ababa is generally seen as the country's tenth entity. The Governor of Addis Ababa – the administrative head of the city – is elected by the city Council. But, because the Governor is accountable both to the Council *and* to the Prime Minister (Proclamation 87/1997, Article 12), and the administration of the city is responsible to the federal government (Article 49(3)), Addis Ababa is not as independent as the states.

The constitution deals at great lengths with fiscal and financial arrangements of the state and the federal governments (Articles 62,

94–100). In general, in carrying out their responsibilities and functions the federal government and states each have to raise the necessary revenues. The constitution enumerates powers of taxation (Articles 96, 97) of both levels. The federal power of taxation (under Article 96) includes, *inter alia,* duties, taxes and other charges on imports and exports, air, rail and sea transport services, and income tax on employees of the federal government. The federal government levies and collects income, profit, sales and excise taxes on enterprises owned by the federal government. The state power of taxation includes, *inter alia,* income tax on employees of the state and of private enterprises as well as of enterprises owned by the state, fees for land usufructuary rights, income from transport services rendered on waters within its territory, incomes derived from private house and other properties, and royalty for the use of forest resources (Article 97). Concurrent powers of taxation are outlined in Article 98 and include, *inter alia,* profit, sales, excise and personal income taxes on enterprises the federal government and states jointly establish, taxes on the profits and companies and dividends due to shareholders, and taxes on incomes derived from large-scale mining, petroleum and gas operations, and royalties on such operations.

A joint session of Parliament has to vote by a two-thirds majority on tax powers not specifically given separately or jointly to one or both of the two levels (Article 99). The House of Federation decides upon the formula for subsidies which states may be entitled to receive from the federal government. Revenues from *joint* federal and state tax sources and subsidies provided by the federal government to the states are also determined by the House of Federation based on recommendations made by the Committee of Revenue Sharing (Article 62(7)).

Constitutional amendments involve state and federal legislative organs (Article 105) and can be initiated by both levels (Article 104). A two-thirds majority of state councils or federal Houses is needed so that the proposal can be further processed. There are two possible procedures based on the importance of the amendment. If amendments refer to fundamental rights and freedoms, both Houses of Parliament must accept the proposal by a two-thirds majority and all state councils must agree by a majority vote. In all other cases, a joint meeting of Parliament must agree by a two-thirds majority vote and two-thirds of the states must approve the proposed amendment by a majority vote.

An exceptional provision contained in the constitution is the right to secession (Article 39). It is part of the broader right of self-determination outlined in the Preamble. Self-determination is the most important constitutional, legislative and policy instrument upon which Ethiopia has drawn to affect the positive development of federalism. The constitution includes the right to develop one's languages, promote one's culture and preserve one's history, and it gives to states the opportunity of leaving the FDRE. Detailed procedures are provided for constitutional exercise of the right of secession in Article 39(4). The procedures includes as steps a two-thirds majority vote of the council of the respective state, a referendum organized by the federal government, and a majority vote in the referendum. It was through this process that Eritrea gained de jure independence in May 1993. No other member state has ever attempted to secede.

Following the notion of the right of self-determination, Article 47(2) of the constitution states that "Nations, Nationalities and Peoples within the States … have the right to establish, at any time, their own States." A "Nation, Nationality or People" has to establish a "Council," its own representative body, to start the process of establishing its own state. This "Council" is the chief negotiator for the process, although it is nowhere specified exactly how the Council should be established, or who should serve on it. As in the case of secession, precise procedures are given in the constitution about how to establish new states within the FDRE, (Article 47(3)), including a two-thirds majority vote of the members of the Council of the Nation, Nationality or People concerned and a referendum.

Ethiopia is a multi-ethnic state with more than 80 different ethnic groups. A great variety of languages are spoken in the country – there are approximately 80 languages with some 200 dialects. Although Amharic is the working language of the federal government (Article 5(2)), all Ethiopian languages enjoy equal state recognition under Article 5(1). States determine their respective working language by law (Article 5(3)). Language is not the only difference among Ethiopians – religious practices differ as well. Ethiopians are members of a number of different religions (approximately 40% are Muslim, approximately 40% are Christians, and the remaining 20% are animists and others), yet conflicts because of religious membership are not known.

3 RECENT POLITICAL DYNAMICS

Elections for the House of Peoples' Representatives took place on 14 May 2000. (The election in the member state of Somali was postponed to 2 September 2000 because famine in the first half of 2000 made it impossible to organize the election properly.) The total number of parties participating in the elections was 49, and of these, 31 won seats. The government – led by Prime Minister Meles Zenawi of the TPLF – has a comfortable two-thirds majority in the House of Peoples' Representatives.

Ethiopian federalism faces several serious challenges, including restructuring and political devolution. Political restructuring involves incremental steps to improve the process of governance. Federalism demands political maturity which means that awareness has to grow so that citizens realize they have an interest in joining to fashion a common approach to the problems of federalism. The problem for Ethiopia is, in its long history, the country has never known either a democratic political system or an administrative culture. The peoples of the Abyssinian 'heartland' and of the more traditional societies of the south and the east are used only to strictly hierarchical and highly patriarchal systems. The normative principles of the federal system and their adaptation to Ethiopia's cultural and historical context is the prominent challenge faced by the federal and state governments.

The formal constitutional solution that Ethiopia has offered to deal with the problem of governance in general, and ethnicity in particular, is highly affected by the degree of political maturity and administrative capacity of the states, which varies greatly. This may be related to the vast differences in state populations. Some states have relatively small populations – for example, approximately 200,000 in Gambela and approximately 500,000 in Benishangul/Gumaz – while others have extremely large populations – for example, over 14 million in Amhara and over 19 million in Oromia.

Some states are able to take ownership of the given opportunities while others – particularly at the *Woreda* (district) and *Kebele* (local) level – have little capacity even to run the daily governmental and administrative routine. Even if one assumes good intentions by the governments on the different levels, due to extraordinarily low administrative capacity a lot is left undone or is not properly done. In some years, the so-called Emerging-Regions (Afar, Somali, Benishangul/Gumaz, Gambela) which have extremely low capacity, were not even able to spend the allocated financial resources facilitated through the financial equalization scheme. They "refunded" in some years up to 60 per cent of what was allocated to them. Therefore, building administrative capacity for the public sector is a major feature of the Five Year Development Plans of both the federal and the state governments.

States have adopted their own constitutions as a blueprint. State leaders have become increasingly aware of their specific situation and are adjusting their constitutional setting accordingly. Adjustments are necessary in regions dominated by traditional clan rule, as is the case in nomadic societies. In Afar and Somali, clan rule plays a more dominant role in many areas of public life than the formal political structure. In the Southern Nations, Nationalities and Peoples Region, where no one knows precisely how many ethnic groups exist and how many languages are spoken, the levels of the administration are adjusted frequently and new jurisdictions are founded now and then to meet the demands of the people.

4 SOURCES FOR FURTHER INFORMATION

Fasil Nahum, *Constitution for a Nation of Nations: The Ethiopian Prospect*, Lawrenceville, NJ: Red Sea Press. Inc., 1997.
http://www.cyberethiopia.com
http://www.electionworld.org/election/ethiopia.htm
http://www.telecom.net.et
http://www.ethiopar.net/English/Contents.htm
http://www.politicalresources.net/ethiopia.htm
http://www.gksoft.com/govt/en/et.html

Table I
Political and Geographic Indicators

Capital city	Addis Ababa
Number and type of constituent units	*9 Member States/Regional States* (Astedader Akakabiwach/Astedader Akabibi): Afar, Amhara, Benishangul/Gumaz, Gambela, Harar, Oromia, Somali, Southern Nations/Nationalities and Peoples' Region, Tigray. *2 Chartered Cities:* Addis Ababa, Dire Dawa.
Official language(s)	Amharic
Area	1 127 127 km^2
Area – Largest constituent unit	Oromia: 353 690 km^2
Area – Smallest constituent unit	Gambela: 25 274 km^2
Total population	62 565 000
Population by constituent unit (% of total population)	Oromia 29.9%, Amhara 22.1%, Southern Nations/Nationalities and Peoples's Region 16.6%, Somali 5.5%, Tigray 5.0%, Chartered City of Addis Ababa 3.7%, Afar 1.8%, Benishangul/Gumaz 0.7%, Gambela 0.3%, Harar 0.2%, Chartered City of Dire Dawa 0.2%
Political system – federal	Federal Republic – Parliamentary System
Head of state – federal	President Girma Woldegiorgis (2001). According to a law passed 8 October, 2001, the President must be nonpartisan and independent. The President is elected by the House of Peoples' Representatives to serve for a 6-year term.
Head of government – federal	Prime Minister Meles Zenawi (1995/2000), heads a coalition of 24 parties (Ethiopia Peoples' Revolutionary Democratic Front (EPRDF)). The Council of Ministers is selected by the Prime Minister and approved by the House of Peoples' Representatives.
Government structure – federal	Bicameral – Parliament/Federal Parliamentary Assembly *Upper House* – The Yefedereshn Mekir Bet (House of Federation), 112 seats. 71 members are appointed by regional bodies and 41 are apportioned based on population. In the case of the members selected from the regions, it is up to the region to determine if the representative is directly or indirectly elected (by the Council of the State) to this seat, to serve a 5-year term. *Lower House* – Yehizbtewekayoch Mekir Bet (House of Peoples' Representatives), 548 seats. Members are elected for a maximum 5-year term in single-member constituencies, using the first-past-the-post system. At least 20 seats are reserved for minority nationalities.

Table I (continued)

Number of representatives in lower house of federal government – House of Peoples' Representatives	548 Seats (elected): Ethiopian Peoples' Revolutionary Democratic Front (coalition of 24 parties) (EPRDF) 481, Oromo Peoples' Democratic Organization (OPDO) 183, Amhara National Democratic Movement (ANDM) 146, Southern Ethiopia Peoples' Democratic Front (SEPDF) 112, Tigray Peoples' Liberation Front (TPLF) 40, Afar National Democratic Party (ANDP) 8, Benishangul/Gumaz Peoples' Democratic Unity Front (BGPDUF) 6, Council of Alternative Forces for Peace and Democracy in Ethiopia 4, Gambela Peoples' Democratic Front (GPDF) 3, Hadiya National Democratic Organization (HNDO) 3, Southern Ethiopia Peoples' Democratic Coalition (SEPDC) 2, Ethiopian Democratic Party (EDP) 2, Oromo Liberation United Front (OLUF) 1, All Amhara Peoples' Organization (AAPO) 1, Oromo National Congress (ONC) 1, Sidama Hadicho Peoples' Democratic Organization (SHPDO) 1, Siltie Peoples' Democratic United Party (SPDUP) 1, Harari National League (HNL) 1, non-affiliated members 13.
Number of representatives in lower house of federal government for most populated constituent unit	Oromia: 178
Number of representatives in lower house of federal government for least populated constituent unit	Harar: 2
Number of representatives in upper house of federal government – House of Federation	112 seats
Distribution of representation in upper house of federal government – House of Federation	N/A
Constitutional court (highest court dealing with constitutional matters)	The House of Federation is the sole custodian of the constitution. A Council of Constitutional Inquiry advises the House of Federation but the House is not bound by the Council's advisory opinions.

Table I (continued)

Political system of constituent units	The administrative regions are quite autonomous and are headed by an elected regional council, Council of the Region. Additionally, within each region different "nationalities" are recognized and most have the right to elect "national local administrations" for self-government or to join with neighbouring nationalities for this purpose. Addis Ababa has special status and fully autonomous self-government.
Head of state – constituent units	President of the Region
Head of government – constituent units	President of the Region

Table II
Economic and Social Indicators

GDP	US$39.2 billion
GDP per capita	US$600
Mechanisms for taxation	Ethiopia has a complex tax system whereby federal and constituent unit governments share in the levy and collection of taxes on jointly established enterprises, large-scale mining, all petroleum and gas operations, and royalties on these. Taxation jurisdiction assigned to the federal government includes: custom duties, imports and exports, income for federal employees, state-owned enterprise revenues, and other areas of federal jurisdiction such as lotteries, property ownership, licensing, monopolies, and stamp duties. Taxation jurisdiction assigned to constituent unit governments includes: income for constituent unit employees, constituent unit-owned land or enterprise, transportation within constituent units, mining operations, royalties on mining operations, land rentals for such operations, and forest resources. Residual taxation jurisdiction is to be decided by a 2/3rds majority vote in the House of Peoples' Representatives. • Sales Tax: 12% (goods produced in Ethiopia for export are exempt) • Capital Gains Tax: 30% • Corporate Income Tax: 35% (45% for companies engaged in mining under large-scale mining licenses) • Sales and Excise Tax on specified goods manufactured in Ethiopia: 10%-200% (10% on textiles, 200% on pure alcohol). Percentage is based on cost, insurance and freight value.
National debt	US$10 billion
National unemployment rate	Urban: approximately 10% Rural: approximately 0.1%
Constituent unit with highest unemployment rate	Oromia
Constituent unit with lowest unemployment rate	N/A
Adult literacy rate	36.3%
National expenditures on education as a % of GDP	2.7%
Life expectancy in years	43.4
Doctors per population ratio (national)	6.1 doctors per 100 000 inhabitants
Doctors per population ratio in constituent units (highest)	N/A

Table II (continued)

Doctors per population ratio in constituent units (lowest)	N/A
National expenditures on health as a % of GDP	3.8%

Sources

Central Intelligence Agency (CIA), *World Fact Book 2000*. CIA, www.cia.gov/cia/publications/factbook/index.html

Elazar, Daniel J. (ed.), *Federal Systems of the World: A Handbook of Federal, Confederal and Autonomy Arrangements.* 2nd Edition. Jerusalem Institute for Federal Studies. London: Longman Group/Westgate House, 1994.

UNESCO. *World Education Report 1998: Teachers and Teaching in a Changing World.* Paris: UNESCO, 1998.

United Nations Population Division. Department of Economic and Social Affairs. "Population in 1999 and 2000: All Countries." *World Population Prospects: 1998 Revision, Vol. 1 comprehensive tables.* www.un.org/Depts

United Nations. *Human Development Report, 2000.* www.undp.org/hdro/report.html

United Nations Statistics Division. "InfoNation." United Nations Statistical Database, 2000. www.un.org/

World Bank. *World Development Report 2000/2001: Attacking Poverty.* www.worldbank.org/poverty/wdrpoverty/report/index.htm

World Health Organisation (WHO). *World Health Report 2000.* Geneva, Switzerland, 2000. www-nt.who.int/whosis/statistics/menu.cfm

NORTH SEA
DENMARK
SWEDEN
BALTIC SEA
Schleswig-Holstein
Mecklenburg-Vorpommern
Bremen
Hamburg
Niedersachsen
Brandenburg
Berlin
Sachsen-Anhalt
POLAND
THE NETHERLANDS
Nordrhein-Westfalen
Sachsen
BELGIUM
Hessen
Thuringen
CZECH REPUBLIC
Rheinland-Pfalz
Luxemburg
Saarland
Baden-Wurttemberg
Bayern
FRANCE
AUSTRIA
SWITZERLAND
ITALY

Federal Republic of Germany

Capital: Berlin
Population: 83.2 Million
(2001 est.)

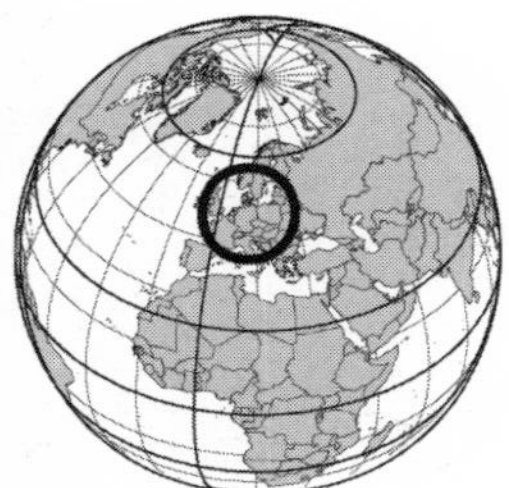

Boundaries and place names are representative only and do not imply official endorsement.

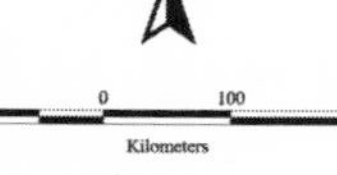

100 0 100 200
Kilometers

Sources: ESRI Ltd.; CIA World Factbook; Times Atlas of the World

Germany
(*Federal Republic of Germany*)

RUDOLF HRBEK

1 HISTORY AND DEVELOPMENT OF FEDERALISM

Federalism is one of the key features of the political system of Germany. This is based on historical foundations and was re-established in the post-World War II situation. Before political unification in 1871 (at which time the German Empire under Prussian leadership was established) "Germany" consisted of a patchwork of states composed of territorial units differing in size (from large Prussia to city-states such as Hamburg), character (dynasties or republican authorities) and power. The Empire was a federation of 25 states of which Prussia was the dominant entity. The states continued to possess considerable internal autonomy and formed the Bundesrat as the supreme sovereign institution representing the governments of the states. Federalism was characterized by the dominance of executives and public administrations, by the preservation of special features in the participating states, and by the lack of a single national centre.

After World War I, under the constitution of the Weimar Republic, the federal elements in Germany were weakened by strengthening the Reich authorities (President, government and Reichstag as Parliament) at the expense of the states, which were now called Länder. Towards its end (1932–33), the Weimar Republic had, in fact, adopted features of a centralized state. The totalitarian Nazi regime following thereafter (1933–45) abolished all remaining federal elements and established a highly centralized system.

World War II ended with the unconditional surrender of Germany. At this time, there were no German authorities, not even at the local level. The USA, UK, Soviet Union and France took over all powers and responsibilities in the country. They agreed to divide German territory into four occupational zones and to dissolve Prussia. From 1946 Länder were established in all four zones under the supervision of the respective occupational power. These decisions, although not designed to prescribe the future territorial structure of post-war Germany in all details, had a major impact on its future development.

The Cold War deepened the gap between the Soviet and the three Western zones and made an agreement among all four powers on the future of Germany impossible. The three Western allies, after having merged their occupational zones for practical purposes, decided in summer 1948 to further stabilize the situation by establishing a German state in the area of the three zones they administered. In the *Frankfurter Dokumente* (June 1948) the three Western allies called upon the German authorities to prepare a constitution. They demanded that the provisions of the new constitution should protect basic individual rights, be based on democratic principles, and introduce a federal structure. These requirements could be understood as a reaction to the centralized and undemocratic Nazi regime but also to some shortcomings of the Weimar Republic. They were fully accepted by the German representatives. The federal structure was primarily expected to provide for a system of checks and balances and, thereby, contribute to the principle of separation of powers, and strengthen democracy.

The body to formulate the new constitution was not a directly elected constituent assembly but rather was composed of representatives of the Länder Parliaments in the three Western zones (reflecting the strength of political parties in these Parliaments). This body was designated the Parliamentary Council (Parlamentarischer Rat). Although the Germans agreed on the establishment of a federal structure, the deputies in the Parliamentary Council disagreed on how to define the relations between the federal government and the Länder in terms of distribution of competences and allocation of powers. The solution laid down in the Basic Law (*Grundgesetz*) – this was the name of the new constitution which entered into force in May 1949 – can be regarded as a compromise, according to which the strength of the central authority was modified by the establishment of the Bundesrat. According to the Basic Law, the Bundesrat is composed of representatives of the Länder governments (in line with the historic tradition of its "predecessor" in the 1871 Empire), with considerable powers in the legislative process at the federal level. These provisions, however, did not determine ultimately and comprehensively the balance between the two levels. This was to emerge, to develop and to change in the course of the political development of the new West German state (Bundesrepublik Deutschland/Federal Republic of Germany (FRG)) in the following years.

The Soviet Zone was transformed into the German Democratic Republic (GDR/Deutsche Demokratische Republik), the second German state, with all the features of a communist regime. As early as 1952 the GDR adopted a centralist territorial structure by abolishing the five Länder which had been established after 1945 and replacing them with 15 administrative districts (Bezirke). This centralist territorial structure was in accordance with the dominance of the Communist Party – a real federal structure would have been incompatible with such a regime.

Although the federal structure of the FRG is protected against abolition by a special constitutional provision (Article 79.3) – the so-called "eternity clause" – territorial reform should be possible, since with the exception of Bavaria and the two city-states (Bremen and Hamburg) which have historic continuity, all other Länder were artificial creations. On the basis of a special constitutional provision (Article 118) three newly established Länder in the southwest of Germany merged to become Baden-Württemberg in 1952. However, all subsequent efforts towards territorial reform – aiming at the formation of a smaller number of larger and more efficient Länder – failed. In 1957 the Saarland joined the FRG to become the eleventh Land, following the rejection (by two-thirds of the electorate) of a proposal to give this territory, under French control since 1945, a "European Statute" (which would have meant that it would adopt the special status of a "europeanized" area rather than joining either Germany or France).

Following the collapse of the Communist regime in the GDR, and in the context of the reunification process in 1990, the five original Länder were re-established and the reunified Germany now consists of 16 Länder. An attempt to bring about a merger of Berlin and Brandenburg failed in a referendum held in these two Länder in May 1996, much to the disappointment of those who had hoped that a positive decision would increase the possibility of territorial reform throughout Germany.

Since 1949 the federal system in the FRG has developed towards a pattern of united policy making and problem solving due to the following factors:

- the reduction of the legislative powers of the Länder since the provisions on concurrent powers made the Federation the primary actor in terms of the uniformity of living conditions as key criteria;

- the provisions of the "financial constitution" according to which the most important revenues are shared between the Federation and the Länder and which has, in addition, mechanisms of financial equalization between the two levels and among the Länder themselves;
- the role of the Bundesrat which enables the Länder governments to participate in federal legislation; and
- the tendency amongst the citizens to want to have uniform living conditions (e.g., all aspects of the infrastructure) and not to accept disparities; an attitude understandable after the situation in post-war Germany when there were large disparities between individual Länder.

The united pattern of German federalism has emerged for a number of reasons: (1) the Federation has exploited the provisions on concurrent powers; (2) cooperation between the Federation and Länder and amongst the Länder themselves has increased, accompanied by shared financial responsibilities; and (3) the institution of Joint Tasks (*Gemeinschaftsaufgaben*) was introduced in the constitution by a whole set of amendments in 1969. In the 1980s there were attempts to strengthen the Länder by reducing the fields for Joint Tasks, by self-restraint on the part of the Federation in its legislative activity, and by improving the financial basis of the Länder. These attempts did not succeed, however. Both the overall economic situation and, since 1990, the challenge of reunification, have negatively affected the financial freedom of manoeuvre of all the entities in the federal system. The reform of German federalism has been on the political agenda since the mid-1980s, and will remain an issue of vital concern.

2 CONSTITUTIONAL PROVISIONS RELATING TO FEDERALISM

The Länder as constituent units of the FRG have the quality of states, with their own institutions. The constitutional order of the Länder has to conform to basic principles, such as basic human rights, democracy, rule of law, and it has to provide for directly elected political representation of the citizens (Article 28). Each of the Länder has a parliamentary system of government, with a directly elected Parliament (with a four or five year legislative term) and a government accountable to it. The Länder constitutions differ, however, in terms of provisions on special aspects of the governmental system, such as referendums, government formation procedures, provisions on motions of no-confidence or votes of confidence, individual accountability of ministers, etc. There are also differences concerning rights; in the constitutions of the five new Länder we find, for example, provisions on both basic human rights and social rights (including employment, environment, housing, education, etc.).

According to the "eternity clause" in Article 79.3 the federal system as such must not be abolished. Territorial reform is, however, possible which means that there is no guarantee of the existence or territorial integrity of individual Länder. The Basic Law envisages two procedural routes for territorial reform: a very complicated procedure (Article 29) which is seen as a barrier to reform; and a clause (following the model of Article 118 for reform in the German southwest, as mentioned earlier) relating to the special case of Berlin and Brandenburg (Article 118(a)), allowing territorial reform via bilateral agreement, including a referendum in both Länder.

The constitution sets out the division of legislative powers between the Federation and the Länder. Matters falling into the exclusive jurisdiction of the Federation are listed in Article 73, matters falling into concurrent jurisdiction are listed in Article 74, and matters for which the Federation has the right for framework legislation are in Article 75 (a framework law gives only a general outline and requires subsequent Länder legislation, thus allowing the Länder to decide on details). Article 78 sets out conditions under which the Federation may legislate, namely "if and to the extent that the creation of equal living conditions throughout the country or the maintenance of legal and economic unity makes federal legislation necessary in the national interest." Article 70 stipulates that "the Länder have the right to legislate insofar as this Basic Law does not confer legislative powers on the Federation." Their exclusive competencies are, however, restricted to issues in connection with their own constitutions and related to the local level, to the organization of the administration, and to matters relating to police and public order, culture, the media and education.

It is a feature of German federalism that the Länder are responsible for implementing federal legislation in their own right (Article 83). There are very few examples of direct federal administration, such as foreign service, army, border control, air traffic, waterways, inland navigation and federal finances including customs.

The Länder participate in federal legislation via the Bundesrat. It is composed of members of the Land governments, and the number of votes varies as follows: each Land has at least three votes; Länder with more than two million inhabitants have four, Länder with more than six million inhabitants five, and Länder with more than seven million inhabitants six votes (Article 51.2). The votes of each Land have to be cast uniformly (in practice as a block vote by one Land government member) and cannot be split. Participation in federal legislation applies, first, to the right of the Bundesrat to initiate federal legislation and submit a bill, as the Bundestag and the federal government. Second, each bill, after having been adopted by the Bundestag, has then to be submitted to the Bundesrat. There are two categories of laws: those which require the explicit consent of the Bundesrat, with a majority of its votes; and those which do not. This second category gives the Bundesrat a suspensive veto, which, after a limited period of time, can be overruled by the Bundestag with an absolute majority (or two-thirds majority if two-thirds of the Bundesrat votes have been cast against). The major criteria for laws requiring approval in the Bundesrat are that the law would affect administrative powers of the Länder (they have to implement federal legislation) or have financial implications for the Länder. More than half of all federal legislation at present falls into this category.

The constitution provides, in this context, for a special mediation procedure – the "Mediation Committee" (Vermittlungsauschuβ), which is composed of an equal number of members from the Bundesrat (16, one for each Land Government) and the Bundestag (16, selected according to party strength). The function of the committee is to find a consensus which is submitted to both Houses for approval. This Mediation Committee can be called upon by the Bundesrat, the Bundestag and the federal government. Amendments to the constitution require the explicit approval of two-thirds of members in both houses.

In terms of financial arrangements, the constitution provides that the most important tax revenues are shared between the Federation and the Länder. Thus income and corporation tax are shared half and half, and the Value-Added Tax (VAT) is shared in a ratio which has to be adjusted every three years by federal legislation requiring Bundesrat approval. Other tax revenues are apportioned either to the Federation (e.g., excise duties) or the Länder (e.g., property, inheritance, motor vehicle and beer taxes). Of particular importance are mechanisms and measures of financial equalization between the Federation and Länder and, horizontally, amongst the Länder themselves.

Constitutional disputes, amongst them those related to the federal system, are resolved by the Federal Constitutional Court (Bundesverfassungsgericht), upon appeal by one of the disputing parties. The Court consists of 16 members elected by an electoral body composed jointly of members of the Bundestag and Bundesrat.

In its decisions, the Federal Constitutional Court has repeatedly formulated and confirmed the principle of federal comity (*Bundestreue*) which is seen as representing a basic feature of the German federal system, even if there is no explicit clause in the constitution. This principle obliges the Federation and Länder, mutually, to consider, when conducting their affairs, the concerns of the other side.

3 RECENT POLITICAL DYNAMICS

There are three issues which have substantial implications for German federalism: the consequences of reunification; the challenge of European integration; and initiatives towards a comprehensive reform of the federal system.

Reunification has increased the disparities, amongst them economic and financial, between the Länder. This has had the result that weaker Länder are more dependent on the Federation and thus the Federation could win additional weight, which could have consequences for the overall federal balance. Furthermore, the system of horizontal financial equalization (*horizontaler Finanzausgleich*) has been affected by the widening gap. All five new Länder – Hessen, Baden-Württemberg, Bayern, Nordrhein-Westfalen and Hamburg – belong to the group of net-receivers, with consequences for previous net-receivers (they may become net-payers or, at least, suffer some losses) and the "traditional" net-payers (their burden, transfer payments, may grow). And, finally, the party system in the five new Länder differs from the pattern in the "old" Länder, with the Partei des demokratischen Sozialmus (PDS) – the successor of the Communist Party in the former GDR – becoming a third force beside the Christian Democratic Union (Christlich demokratische Union, CDU) and Social Democrat Party (Sozialdemokratische Partei Deutschlands, SPD), and the fact that the liberals (Free Democratic Party, Freie demokratische Partei, FDP) and the Greens are not represented in the respective Land Parliaments. This has had consequences for coalition patterns (SPD with PDS, or grand coalitions, if one party cannot form a majority on its own) which may have an impact on political developments in German politics as a whole.

The deepening process of European integration has posed a persistent challenge to the legal status of the Länder and therefore to the federal structure of the FRG. The first challenge arises from the fact that the European Union (EU) has extended its functional scope considerably which means that EU activities fall into areas which have been reserved to the Länder in the internal allocation of competencies. The second challenge has arisen from the modalities of EU decision making. In the EU, the Council of Ministers is the most important decision-making and legislative body, and Germany is represented in the Council by the federal government. This means participation of the federal government in decisions in fields belonging to the exclusive competence of the Länder. The third challenge lies in the field of implementation of

European legislation in Germany; this is primarily the responsibility of the Länder which until recently had no opportunity to influence the legislation and thus saw themselves under a strong degree of control by the federal government.

The Länder have reacted to this challenge successfully. First, they established in 1992–93 (in the new Article 23, supplemented by the "Law on the Cooperation of Federation and Länder in Affairs of the EU") rights of participation in dealing with EU matters at the domestic level. The federal government now has to consider Länder concerns, formulated by the Bundesrat, and in matters which fall under the exclusive competence of the Länder, is even obliged to hold to the Bundesrat view. A further transfer of sovereign powers when this would alter the content of the Basic Law requires a two-thirds majority in support of the measure in the Bundesrat. Second, the Länder have established and developed autonomous EU activities (e.g., setting up liaison offices in Brussels and lobbying directly). Finally, they have acquired the right to participate formally and directly in the decision-making process at the EU level. They are represented in the Committee of the Regions established in 1993, and they can represent Germany in the Council when matters falling under their jurisdiction are on the agenda. In addition, the new Article 24.1(a) allows the Länder to transfer (subject to federal government consent) sovereign powers to cross-border institutions insofar as the Länder have the competence in the policy fields concerned. On the whole, the position of the Länder has been strengthened. In their relations with the federal level they have managed to increase their weight in the overall federal balance.

The thorough and substantial reform of federalism has been on the political agenda since the 1980s with the Länder – amongst them primarily the stronger ones – pushing towards "competitive federalism" (*Wettbewerbsföderalismus*) instead of "participatory federalism" (*Beteiligungsföderalismus*). They demand an increase in their autonomous competencies, combined with the reduction of federal level activities (e.g., in the areas of concurrent legislative powers). Second, they are interested in extending their freedom of manoeuvre in cross-border activities and "external" relations. Here they refer to functional needs in connection with the EU "Internal Market" policy (i.e., abolish internal economic borders and create a unified market for all EU member countries) and the new geographical centrality of Germany with a larger number of neighbouring countries in an enlarging EU. The third topic, which is very controversial amongst the Länder themselves but vis-à-vis the Federation as well, has to do with the financial system. The stronger Länder (as net-payers) are trying hard (by appealing to the Federal Constitutional Court and through political negotiations aiming towards a consensual new equalization system) to reduce their burden. Since all changes would affect vested interests, one can only expect modest reform steps.

4 SOURCES FOR FURTHER INFORMATION

Jeffery, Charlie (ed.), *Recasting German Federalism. The Legacies of Unification*, London/New York: Cassell, 1999.

Laufer, Heinz and Ursula Münch, *Das federative System der Bundesrepublik Deutschland*, Opladen: 1998.

Wehling, Hans-Georg (ed.), *Die deutschen Länder. Geschichte, Politik, Wirtschaft*, Opladen: 2000.

http://www.gksoft.com/govt/en/de.html

http://www.bundesrat.de

Table I
Political and Geographic Indicators

Capital city	Berlin
Number and type of constituent units	*16 States (Länder)*: Baden-Wuerttemberg, Bavaria, Berlin, Brandenburg, Bremen, Hamburg, Hessen, Mecklenburg-Vorpommern, Niedersachsen, Nordrhein-Westfalen, Rheinland-Pfalz, Saarland, Sachsen, Sachsen-Anhalt, Schleswig-Holstein, Thueringen
Official language(s)	German
Area	357 021 km^2
Area – Largest constituent unit	Bavaria (70 553 km^2)
Area – Smallest constituent unit	Bremen (404 km^2)
Total population	82 220 000
Population by constituent unit (% of total population)	Nordrhein-Westfalen 22%, Bavaria 15%, Baden-Wuerttemberg 13%, Niedersachsen 9.5%, Hessen 7.3%, Sachsen 6%, Rheinland-Pfalz 5%, Berlin 4%, Sachsen-Anhalt 3.2%, Schleswig-Holstein 3.2%, Brandenburg 3%, Thueringen 3%, Mecklenburg-Vorpommern 2.4%, Hamburg 2.1%, Saarland 1.3%, Bremen 0.08%
Political system – federal	Federal Republic
Head of state – federal	President (Bundespraesident) Johannes Rau (1999), Social Democratic Party (SPD), elected to serve a 5-year term by an electoral college comprised of all Federal Assembly representatives and an equal number of representatives selected by the Länder Parliaments.
Head of government – federal	Chancellor (Bundeskanzler) Gerhard Schröder (1998), Social Democratic Party (SPD), elected by the Federal Assembly and is appointed by the President for a 4-year term. Cabinet is appointed by the President on the advice of the Chancellor.
Government structure – federal	Bicameral – Parliament: *First Chamber* – Bundestag (Federal Assembly), usually consists of 656 seats (Note: for the 1998 term there are 669 members because of the so-called surplus mandate or *Uberhangmandate*). Members are elected through a "mixed-member proportional system," which combines 328 single-member constituencies with 328 seats allotted through proportional representation. Members are elected for a 4-year term. *Second Chamber* – Bundesrat (Federal Council), 69 seats. Members are elected indirectly by state councils from 16 multi-seat states (with a range of 3-6 per state, depending upon Land size).

Table I (continued)

Number of representatives in lower house of federal government – Bundestag	669 Seats: Social Democratic Party (SPD) 298, Christian Democratic Union (CDU) 198, Christian Social Union (CSU) 47, Alliance '90/Greens 47, Free Democratic Party (FDP) 43, Party of Democratic Socialism (PDS) 36
Number of representatives in lower house of federal government for most populated constituent unit	Nordrhein-Westfalen: 148
Number of representatives in lower house of federal government for least populated constituent unit	Bremen: 5
Number of representatives in upper house of federal government – Bundesrat	69 seats: Baden-Württemberg 6 (CDU/FDP), Bavaria 6 (CSU), Lower Saxony 6 (SPD), Hesse 5 (SPD/CDU), North Rhine-Westphalia 6 (SPD/B90/Grüne), Berlin 4 (SPD/B90/Grüne), Brandenburg 4 (SPD/CDU), Rhineland-Palatinate 4 (SPD/FDP), Saxony 4 (CDU), Saxony-Anhalt 4 (SPD), Schleswig-Holstein 4 (SPD/B90/Grüne), Thuringia 4 (CDU), Bremen 3 (SPD/CDU), Hamburg 3 (SPD/CDU), Mecklengurg-Western Pomerania 3 (SPD/PDS), Saarland 3 (CDU)
Distribution of representation in upper house of federal government – Bundesrat	69 seats: Members are elected indirectly by Land councils from 16 multi-seat Länder with a range of 3-6 per Land, depending upon Land size. Länder with less than 2 million inhabitants have 3 representatives, Länder with more than this have 4 representatives, those with more than 6 million inhabitants have 5 representatives and Länder that have more than 7 million inhabitants have 6 representatives. These votes must be cast as a block. Composition and term are dependent upon the composition of the Länder governments and may change at any time.
Constitutional court (highest court dealing with constitutional matters)	Federal Constitutional Court (Bundesverfassungsgericht). Half of the judges are elected by the lower house (Bundestag) and half by the upper house (Bundesrat).
Political system of constituent units	Unicameral – Legislatures (Landtag). Composition varies from Land to Land.
Head of state – constituent units	Prime Minister (in case of city-state, the Head of State is the Mayor)
Head of government – constituent units	Prime Minister or Mayor

Table II
Economic and Social Indicators

GDP	US$1.936 trillion
GDP per capita	US$23 400
Mechanisms for taxation	Most of the tax revenues (Income tax, Corporate taxes and VAT) are shared equally between the Federation and the Länder: • Income Tax – brackets range from 22.9% to 48.5% (after Tax Reforms of 2000/2001) • Solidarity Tax: a surcharge levied on personal income tax – 5.5% • Value-added Tax (MWSt): varies according to application, but is usually around 16%.
National debt (external)	N/A
National unemployment rate	9.9%
Constituent unit with highest unemployment rate	Sachsen-Anhalt – 19.9%
Constituent unit with lowest unemployment rate	Bayern – 5.0%
Adult literacy rate	99%
National expenditures on education as a % of GDP	5.9%
Life expectancy in years	77.44
Doctors per population ratio (national)	350 doctors per 100 000 inhabitants
Doctors per population ratio in constituent units (highest)	Hamburg – 470 per 100 000 inhabitants
Doctors per population ratio in constituent units (lowest)	Brandenburg – 240 per 100 000 inhabitants
National expenditures on health as a % of GDP	10.3%

Sources

Central Intelligence Agency (CIA), *World Fact Book 2000*. CIA, www.cia.gov/cia/publications/factbook/index.html

Economist Intelligence Unit, "Country Commerce – Germany," *The Economist Intelligence Unit 2000*. New York: EIU, 2000.

Elazar, Daniel J. (ed.), *Federal Systems of the World: A Handbook of Federal, Confederal and Autonomy Arrangements*. 2nd Edition. Jerusalem Institute for Federal Studies. London: Longman Group/Westgate House, 1994.

European Observatory on Health Care Systems. *Health Care Systems in Transition – Germany*. www.bundesbank.de

Euro Regions Web (FEDRE). www.fedre.org

Eurostat. "Table VII.I Health Personnel and Equipment." *Regions: Statistical Yearbook 1996*. Luxembourg: Office of Statistics for the European Community (Eurostat), 1996.

Federal Statistics Office, Germany. "Electoral Returns." www.statistik-bund.de

Federal Statistical Office Germany. "Public Finance – Debt 1999." www.statistik-bund.de/basis/e/fist/fisttab024.htm

International Monetary Fund (IMF). *International Financial Statistics*, Vol. LIII, No. 12, December 2000. Washington, DC: the IMF Statistics Department, 2000.

IMF. "Table A2: Germany – Aggregated Demand," *IMF Staff Country Report – Statistical Appendix*. No. 99/130. www.imf.org

IMF. *IMF Staff Country Report – Germany*. No. 00/142. www.imf.org/external/index.htm

United Nations. "Human Development Index," "Gender-Related Development Index," *Human Development Report, 2000*. Human Development Report Office. www.undp.org/hdro/report.html

World Health Organisation (WHO). "Estimates of Health Personnel." www-nt.who.int/whosis/statistics

World Health Organisation (WHO). "Annex Table 8, Selected national health accounts indicators for all Member States, estimates for 1997." *World Health Report 2000*. Geneva, 2000. www-nt.who.int/whosis/statistics/menu.cfm

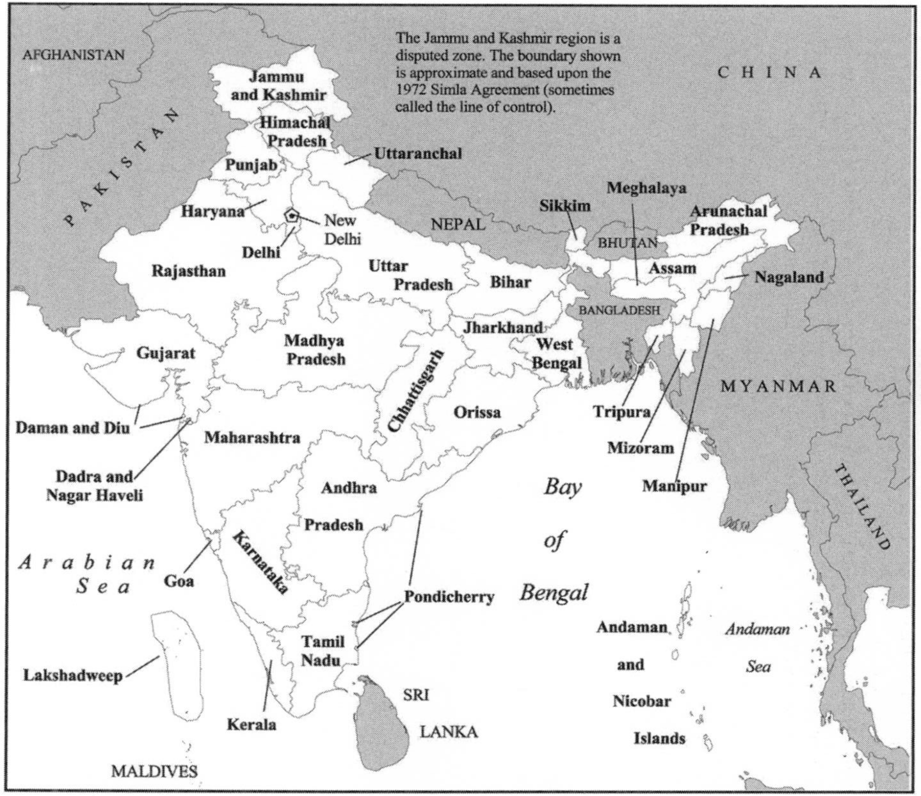

AFGHANISTAN
PAKISTAN
Jammu and Kashmir
Himachal Pradesh
Punjab
Haryana
Delhi
New Delhi
Uttaranchal
The Jammu and Kashmir region is a disputed zone. The boundary shown is approximate and based upon the 1972 Simla Agreement (sometimes called the line of control).
CHINA
NEPAL
Sikkim
Meghalaya
Arunachal Pradesh
BHUTAN
Assam
Nagaland
BANGLADESH
Rajasthan
Uttar Pradesh
Bihar
Gujarat
Madhya Pradesh
Jharkhand
West Bengal
Chhattisgarh
Orissa
Tripura
Mizoram
Manipur
MYANMAR
THAILAND
Daman and Diu
Maharashtra
Dadra and Nagar Haveli
Andhra Pradesh
Karnataka
Goa
Arabian Sea
Bay of Bengal
Pondicherry
Tamil Nadu
Kerala
Lakshadweep
SRI LANKA
MALDIVES
Andaman and Nicobar Islands
Andaman Sea

Republic of India

Capital: New Delhi
Population: 1 Billion (2001 est.)

Boundaries and place names are representative only and do not imply any official endorsement.

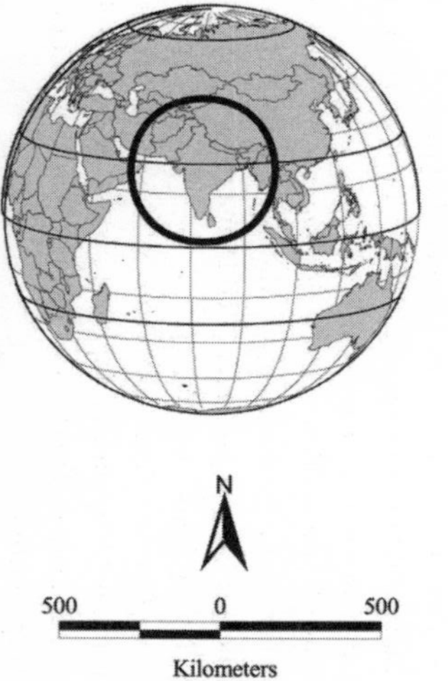

N

500 0 500

Kilometers

Sources: Times Atlas of the World; ESRI Ltd.; CIA World Factbook

India
(*Republic of India*)

GEORGE MATHEW

1 HISTORY AND DEVELOPMENT OF FEDERALISM

India covers an area of 3.28 million square kilometres. With a population of about 1 billion, India is a country of a wide range of ethnic backgrounds, languages and cultures. It has 28 states and seven union territories (UTS) (including Delhi, the National Capital Territory), which differ greatly in terms of their natural resources, administrative capacity and economic performance. The country continues to have a high concentration of poverty. According to estimates in 1993, 320 million people (36 per cent of the total population) lived below the poverty line. In 2000–01, however, India was able to achieve a GDP growth rate of six per cent.

In 1858 the British Crown took over administration of India after a century of colonial rule by the British East India Company. A highly centralized form of government was established in which legislative, executive and financial powers rested with the Governor-General who functioned as the agent of the British government. Difficulty in exercising centralized rule led to a devolution of powers, which was accomplished via the Councils Act of 1861 and later by the Minto-Morley Act of 1909. Provincial autonomy came into being with the Montagu-Chelmsford Act of 1919 which provided for the introduction of the principle of responsible government in the provinces, although only for certain subjects.

During this period, the British government was mainly interested in containing Indian nationalism and affirming British suzerainty. The Simon Commission Report of 1930, Round Table Conferences and finally the Government of India Act, 1935 were all attempts to do this. The Government of India Act was a watershed in the present federal structure. It provided for a federation by taking the provinces of British India and the Indian states ruled by kings (known as princely states) as units. It was left to the princely states whether to join the federation or not, and when their consent was not forthcoming, the federation did not take effect as planned.

The 1935 Act divided legislative powers between the provincial and central legislatures and, within their defined sphere, the provinces were autonomous units of administration with restricted powers. To this extent, the government of India assumed the role of a federal government vis-à-vis the provincial governments, although without the princely states. The arrangement came to an end with the Second World War.

India achieved independence on 15 August 1947. The constitution was adopted by the Constituent Assembly on 26 November 1949 and came into force on 26 January 1950. The constitution envisaged a strong centre. The 14 states and six union territories were divided according to the historical context in which they were governed and administered.

In 1955 a "States Reorganisation Commission" was established. It was proposed that there be a territorial re-organization based on the following principles: preservation and strengthening of the unity and security of India; linguistic and cultural homogeneity; and financial, economic and administration considerations. The linguistic factor – because language corresponds with socio-cultural identity – was uppermost in determining the re-organization of the constituent units. It was thought that the resulting 1956 States Reorganisation Act, which re-organized the states primarily on the basis of the languages spoken in the area, might provide the solution to multifarious problems like economic inequalities, lopsided development, and the domination of certain castes or classes. Since 1956, there have been several further adjustments to the states, the most recent being the creation in November 2000 in the northeast of three new small states – Chhatisgarh, Jharkhand and Uttaranchal – carved out of existing states.

At the time the constitution was written the predominant concern of the founding fathers was the preservation of the unity and integrity of India, which had more than 600 varied princely states plus the provinces of British India at the time of independence. Nowhere in the constitution is the word "federal" mentioned – indeed, the constitution says India is a "Union of States" and it envisaged a strong centre. B.R. Ambedkar, the architect of the Indian constitution, has said that the use of the word "Union" was deliberate. The drafting committee wanted to make it clear that although India was to be a federation, it was not the result of an agreement initiated by the constituent states. During normal times India functions as a federation but it can be – and has been – transformed into a unitary state during extraordinary circumstances.

2 CONSTITUTIONAL PROVISIONS RELATING TO FEDERALISM

India is a federal republic with a parliamentary system. It consists of 28 constituent units – three of which, as mentioned above, have only recently been created. The federal Parliament is bicameral, consisting of the Rajya Sabha, or House of States (upper house), and the Lok Sabha, or House of the People (lower house).

Scholars studying India over the last 50 years have described the Indian political system as a federation without federalism, and variously referred to its federalism as cooperative, executive, emergent, responsible, parliamentary, populist, legislative, competitive, fiscal, restructured, reluctant, or "quasi." Whatever it may be, the federal element has been an underlying principle of the Indian polity, despite several attempts by the centre to usurp the powers and jurisdiction of the states by parliamentary legislation.

There are several provisions of the constitution that permit the centre to infringe on state rights. First, under Article 249, if the Rajya Sabha (the upper house of Parliament) declares, by a resolution supported by two-thirds of members present and voting, for the sake of expediency and national interest, that Parliament should make laws with respect to any matter enumerated in the State List, it could do so. Such a resolution remains valid for a year and can be extended for another year by a subsequent resolution.

The Seventh Schedule of the constitution outlines the duties and division of powers between the Union government and governments of the states. There is a Union List consisting of 97 items, and State and Concurrent Lists with 66 and 47 items respectively. Some of the important items on the Union List pertain to defence, atomic energy, diplomatic-consular and trade representation, citizenship, extradition, inter-state trade and commerce, audits, currency-coinage and legal tender, and foreign exchange. The State List includes, among other things, public order, local government, public health and sanitation, communications, agriculture, fisheries, trade and commerce within the state, taxation and police. Criminal law, forests, economic and social planning, trade unions, education, and preventive detention are some of the important items in the Concurrent List. Over the years, the lists have been subjected to constitutional amendments in favour of the federal government.

The second constitutional provision that allows the centre to infringe on state rights is Article 250. According to this article, Parliament is empowered to make laws on any item included in the State List for the whole or any part of India while an "emergency" has been proclaimed. (According to Article 352, the central government also has the power to determine when an emergency exists. An emergency under Article 352 was declared in: October 1962 (Sino-Indian conflict), revoked in 1968; December 1971 (war with Pakistan); and June 1975 (internal disturbances), revoked March 1977.) Making use of Article 250, Parliament has taken away five items from the State List, added five to the Concurrent List and added three to the Union List. Thus, for example, the Constitution (Third Amendment) Act, 1954, amended the Seventh Schedule, and the scope of items in the Concurrent List was widened. This related to trade and commerce, production, supply and distribution of industrial products, foodstuffs, cattle-fodder and cotton. With the Constitution (Sixth Amendment) Act, 1956, the Union government was authorized to tax a broader range of inter-state trade in goods. The Constitution (Forty-sixth Amendment) Act, 1982, gave the Union the power to tax consignments in inter-state trade and commerce. The Constitution (Forty-second Amendment) Act, 1976, made far-reaching changes in the Seventh Schedule, moving items pertaining to education, forests, protection of wildlife, weights, measures and standards from the State List to the Concurrent List. Most importantly, the amendment gave the Union the power to deploy its forces in any of the states, while at the same time retaining control over the armed forces. This reduced the control of the concerned state governments over the armed forces which are deployed.

The third provision which allows the centre to intervene in state jurisdiction is Article 356. Under this article, "President's rule" (by which the central government can directly take over the government of a state) has been imposed over states more than 100 times since 1950. This has given rise to severe criticism as it violates the federal character of India, and in 1994 the Supreme Court of India ruled that the power of the central government, under Article 356, to remove a state government from office was not an absolute but a conditional power.

An amendment to the Indian constitution can be initiated only by the introduction of a bill in Parliament. The bill, which can be introduced in either House of Parliament, has to be passed in each House by a majority of the total membership of that House and by a majority of not less than two-thirds of the members of that House present and voting. The amendment procedure also requires ratification by the legislatures of the states (not less than one-half of the states) after which it is presented to the President of India for his assent.

Relations between the central government and the states have often been problematic, so a statutory body to deal with inter-state relations was created – the Inter-State Council. Article 263 of the constitution states that if at any time it appears to the President that the public interest would be served, he can establish a Council and define the nature of its duties. In general, the Council is charged with: (a) inquiring into and advising upon disputes which may have arisen between states; (b) investigating and discussing subjects in which some or all of the states, or the Union and one or more of the states, have a common interest; and (c) making recommendations, in particular, recommendations for the better coordination of policy and action with respect to the subject under dispute.

The Supreme Court of India is the guardian of the Indian constitution (Article 124). Presently, the Supreme Court consists of a Chief Justice and 25 judges who are appointed by the President. It is the final arbiter in disputes between the states, and between the Union and the states. It has been observed that the jurisdiction and powers of the Supreme Court of India are wider in their nature and extent than those exercised by the highest court in other countries.

The taxation powers of the Union and the states have been separated. The Union List contains 12 items of taxation, and the State List contains 19 items. The urban and rural local bodies also have some powers of taxation. In financial matters, it may be said that the general tendency has been in favour of centralization, thus making the central government more powerful. Developments of the last 40 years show that economic institutions and trends have tended to encourage systems of administration which have not entirely been in tune with true federal concepts.

Article 280 of the constitution provides for the creation of a Central Finance Commission by the President every five years. It consists of a Chairman and four other members appointed by the President. The Commission gives recommendations relating to centre-state fiscal relations. Its recommendations are based on a detailed assessment of the financial position of the central and state governments and extensive consultations with all stakeholders. A prescribed percentage of the net proceeds of all central taxes and duties is assigned to the states. While working out the share of central taxes/duties and grants-in-aid to distribute to states, the Commission considers the trends in total transfers from the centre to the states, and gives its recommendations on the basis of the premise that tax devolution and grants from the centre to the states should not exceed 37.5 per cent of total centre revenues, both tax and non-tax.

The Planning Commission at the centre and the Autonomous Councils in the states (which will be discussed in Section 3) are important tools of centre-state relations. When India became independent, planning was essential to tackle the problems of poverty, illiteracy, food deficits and industrial backwardness. The Planning Commission was constituted in March 1951 to carry out the planning process and, after this, five-year plans and annual plans were drawn up and implemented within an economy where a large role was assigned to the public sector and a lesser role to a state-regulated private sector. Major projects and programs have to be approved by the Planning Commission before any budget provisions for financing them are made. The determination and allocation of plan assistance is its main task. As the aggregate plan resources are limited, and given the unequal distribution of resources among the states, sharing of resources remains a cause of friction in federal relations.

3 RECENT POLITICAL DYNAMICS

The major failure of the constitution has been that it has not been able to provide an integrated administration which works under the elected bodies from villages/towns to the centre. The reality was that by seeking justification in the need to keep India united, several provisions of the constitution were turned on their head. As a result, in the 1980s India began to face problems of violence, threats of secession, autonomy, self-determination and radical devolution of powers to the states. Given the manifold dimensions of India's pluralistic society, the federal principle offers the only viable basis for the maintenance of a strong and united Indian state. Only in a federal polity could the unique socio-cultural diversities of the country as a whole and the states in particular be held together. India had reached a point at which the Union could not survive without recognizing the socio-political realities at different levels. Therefore, the search for institutional arrangements for improving the federal system moved to the top of the agenda of concerned intellectuals, jurists and political parties.

By the late 1980s it was acknowledged that extension of the federal idea hinged on decentralization at the sub-state level. It was in this context that the Union government set up a Commission in June 1983 (Sarkaria Commission) to review the arrangements between the Union and the states with regard to powers, functions and responsibilities in all spheres, and to recommend such measures as may be appropriate. The report submitted in January 1988 did not advocate any radical change in relations, and stayed within the two-level federal frame. The Commission criticized the trend towards concentration of powers at the centre and recommended, among other things, the curtailment of centrally-sponsored schemes in the exclusive sphere of the states and restraint on the part of the Union with respect to subjects in the Concurrent List. The report made useful comments about the need to decentralize power below the state level to local elected bodies, but these fell short of multi-level federalism.

The move towards multi-level federalism in the mid-1980s is perhaps the most significant trend in Indian federalism in recent years. There had been historic attempts to create lower tiers of government, but the recent trends have been more comprehensive, democratic and sustainable.

The fact that village councils (*panchayats*) and municipalities had no constitutional status hampered not only their growth and development but also the decentralization of power. The constitution recognizes only the Union and states but, by the early 1980s, discussion about giving the local bodies constitutional status had begun. Experiments in West Bengal (1978), Karnataka (1987) and Andhra Pradesh (1987) evoked extraordinary response from the people.

On 15 May 1989 a bill (64th Amendment) was introduced in Parliament by then Prime Minister Rajiv Gandhi to bring the *panchayats* under the purview of the constitution. This was a welcome step, but there was serious opposition to it on two grounds: (1) the bill overlooked the states and was seen as an instrument of the centre to deal directly with *panchayats*; and (2) it was imposing a uniform pattern throughout the country instead of permitting individual states to legislate the details according to local circumstances. There was an outcry against this bill from political parties, intellectuals and concerned citizens. Although it received a two-thirds majority in the Lok Sabha, in the Rajya Sabha on 15 October 1989, the bill failed to meet the mandatory requirement by two votes.

At another level, perhaps with wider implications for multi-level federalism, several councils have been created, including: Darjeeling Gorkha Hill Council (1988), Bodoland Autonomous Council (1993), Jharkhand Area Autonomous Council (1994), Autonomous Hill District Council for Ladakh (1995). They are new decentralizing units, which give further impetus and meaning to a multi-level federal system and a boost to the multi-layered institutional arrangement within the Indian federal framework.

In September 1991, the Congress government under Prime Minister Narasimha Rao introduced two bills – one for rural local bodies (*panchayats*) and another for urban local bodies (municipalities) – extending participatory democracy to the villages and municipalities. These bills were passed by Parliament on 23 December 1992 and came into force in 1993 as the 73rd and 74th Amendments after almost 10 years of discussion, debates and legislative moves at various levels. With these amendments 47 subjects were to be transferred by the states to the *panchayats* and municipalities. The amendments were extended to the tribal areas (Fifth Schedule areas in the constitution) in December 1996.

These historic constitutional amendments meant a number of changes. First, the *panchayats* and municipalities became "institutions of self-government" and not just development agencies. Second, *gram sabhas* (village assemblies) and ward committees in municipalities became the basic units of the democratic system. Third, the amendments introduced new levels in the system – the *panchayat* system was made up of three tiers or levels: at the lowest level was the village, at the intermediate level was the block and at the top was the district. Fourth, the amendments broadened the democratic base of the country – seats in the *panchayats* and municipalities at all three levels are now to be filled by direct elections for a five-year term, and seats are reserved for hitherto excluded groups like lower castes and tribes, and women. Fifth, an independent Election Commission was created in each state for supervision, direction and control of the electoral process and preparation of electoral rolls and State Finance Commissions. And, sixth, the amendments determined the principles upon which adequate financial resources are transferred to the *panchayats* and municipalities, and created District Planning Committees. Grants from central and state governments constitute an important source of funding but state governments are also expected to assign the revenue of certain taxes to the *panchayats*. In some cases, the *panchayats* are permitted to collect local taxes and retain the revenue.

With the constitutional amendments, a de facto third tier of governance with a wide democratic base has come into existence. Before this India had about 4,963 elected members in Parliament and the state assemblies, but today every five years three million representatives are elected. Out of this, one million are women. A large number of excluded groups and communities are now included in decision-making bodies. India is moving from a two-level federation (Union and states) towards multi-level federalism with local bodies (*panchayats* and municipalities) at the district level and below becoming the third level. This has made the country, as two contemporary writers on

Indian federalism, Nirmal Mukarji and Balveer Arora, put it, "a cascading federalism; a federation of federations."

Some analysts claim that this process is merely strengthening "administrative federalism," in order to facilitate and encourage delegation of administrative and financial powers from the states to local bodies. The administrative powers and the financial resources of the local bodies to exercise these powers are entirely derived from legislation that has to be passed by the state. They have no definite executive, legislative, financial or judicial power and, according to this school, constitutional status and elections do not mean they are a third tier of governance. This, however, is a limited view of the scope of the democratic and political changes that have taken place.

Others believe that this trend heralds a qualitative change in the federal character of the Indian polity. Each state has become a federating unit with three layers below it – district, block and village. This is a unique federal feature and India must struggle to find a proper balance, and to create links in a democratic process from Gram Sabha (village assembly) to Lok Sabha. Multi-level arrangements in India represent the new and ongoing search for new modes of adaptation to the pressure created by democratic development.

In order to make the multi-level federalism effective, the centre must develop a willingness to share powers with the states on an equal measure. Institutional innovations are necessary conditions for strengthening the federal framework. India's federal polity is not static. As Rasheeduddin Khan, an expert on Indian federalism, puts it, "India is an evolving federal nation. India has crossed the half century mark as a nation and along with it has *de facto* entered the multi-level federal era – a change from being just a Union of States."

It is important to note one other trend in Indian federalism – the changing political party system. Until the 1977 parliamentary elections, the Congress Party dominated the political scene in India. Since then, however, coalition parties have come to stay, not only at the centre but also in the states. Thus, today even the Congress Party cannot hold power on its own and must find support from other regional parties to stay in power. (The present government of India is made up of a coalition of 24 parties.) In India there are currently over 550 registered political parties, out of which only six are recognized as national, 40 are state-level and 504 have only a local base. The regional or state-level parties wield considerable influence at the centre and thus the accountability of the centre has increased substantially. When a significant party (or parties) forming a governing coalition withdraws support – on policy matters or regional/state interests – the central government cannot survive.

4 SOURCES FOR FURTHER INFORMATION

Arora, Balveer. "Adapting Federalism to India: Multi-level and Asymmetrical Innovations," in Balveer Arora and Douglas V. Verney (eds), *Multiple Identities in a Single State: Indian Federalism in Comparative Perspective*, New Delhi: Konark Publishers.

Government of India, "Report of the Eleventh Finance Commission," Ministry of Finance, Department of Economic Affairs, June 2000.

Khan, Rasheeduddin, *Rethinking Indian Federalism,* Shimla: Indian Institute of Advanced Studies.

– *Federal India: A Design for Change,* Delhi: Vikas Publishing House Pvt Ltd.

Mathew, George, "Federalism, Local Government, and Economic Policy" in C. Steven LaRue (ed.), *The India Handbook,* Chicago: Fitzroy Dearborn Publishers, 1997.

– "Institutions of Self-Government in India: Towards Multi-level Federalism," in *Review of Development and Change,* Vol. II. No. 2 (July-December 1997), Chennai: Madras Institute of Development Studies.

Mukarji, Nirmal and Balveer Arora (eds), *Federalism in India: Origins and Development,* New Delhi: Centre for Policy Research and Vikas Publishing House Pvt. Ltd., 1972.

Mukarji, Nirmal, "The Third Stratum," *Bombay: Economic and Political Weekly,* 1 May 1993.

Santhanam, K., *Union-State Relations in India,* New Delhi: Indian Institute of Public Administration and Asia Publishing House, 1960.

Table I
Political and Geographic Indicators

Capital city	New Delhi
Number and type of constituent units	*28 States:* Andhra Pradesh, Arunachal Pradesh, Assam, Bihar, Goa, Gujarat, Haryana, Himachal Pradesh, Jammu and Kashmir, Karnataka, Kerala, Madhya Pradesh, Maharashtra, Manipur, Meghalaya, Mizoram, Nagaland, Orissa, Punjab, Rajasthan, Sikkim, Tamil Nadu, Tripura, Uttar Pradesh, West Bengal; Note: In November 2000, 3 new states were created by the central government: Chatisgarh (carved out of Madhya Pradesh), Jharkhand (carved out of Bihar), and Uttaranchal (carved out of Uttar Pradesh). Statistical information for these new states is not included in these tables. 6 *Union Territories:* Andaman and Nicobar Islands, Chandigarh, Dadra and Nagar Haveli, Daman and Diu, Lakshadweep, Pondicherry *1 National Capital Territory*: Delhi
Official language(s)	Hindu, Bengali, Telugu, Marathi, Tamil, Urdu, Gujarati, Malayalam, Kannada, Oriya, Punjabi, Assamese, Kashmiri, Sindhi, and Sanskrit, Konkani, Manipuri and Nepali (the last three were added in 1992) Note: English has associate status
Area	3 287 590 km^2
Area – Largest constituent unit	Madhya Pradesh (443 946 km^2)
Area – Smallest constituent unit	Lakshadweep (32 km^2)
Total population	1 029 991 145 (July 2001 estimate)
Population by constituent unit (% of total population)	Uttar Pradesh 16%, Bihar 10%, Maharashtra 9.1%, Andhra Pradesh 8%, West Bengal 8%, Madhya Pradesh 7.6%, Tamil Nadu 7.1%, Karnataka 5.4%, Gujarat 5%, Rajasthan 5%, Kerala 4%, Orissa 4%, Assam 3%, Punjab 2.5%, Haryana 2%, Delhi 0.9%, Jammu and Kashmir 0.9%, Himachal Pradesh 0.6%, Tripura 0.03%, Manipur 0.02%, Goa 0.14%, Nagaland 0.11%, Arunachal Pradesh 0.1%, Mizoram 0.09%, Chandigarh 0.07%, Meghalaya 0.3%, Sikkim 0.05%, Andaman and Nicobar Islands 0.03%, Dadra and Nagar Haveli 0.015%, Daman and Diu 0.009%, Pondicherry 0.09%, Lakshadweep 0.005%
Political system – federal	Federal Republic – Parliamentary System

Table I (continued)

Head of state – federal	President Kocheril Raman Narayanan (1997), elected to serve a 5-year term by an Electoral College comprised of Members of the Parliament and the legislatures of the states.
Head of government – federal	Prime Minister Atal Behari Vajpayee (1998/1999), Bharatiya Janata Party – BJP (Indian People's Party), elected by Electoral College formed by members of both houses of Parliament and the legislatures of the states. Serve maximum 5-year term. Council of Ministers (Cabinet) is appointed by the President on the recommendation of the Prime Minister.
Government structure – federal	Bicameral – Sansad (Parliament): *Upper House* – Rajya Sabha (House of States), not more than 250 seats. 12 members are appointed by the President and the remaining members are elected by proportional representation (single transferable vote) for a 6-year term, one-third every 2 years, by the members of the legislatures of the states and territories. *Lower House* – Lok Sabha (House of the People), 545 seats. 543 members are elected for a 5-year term in single-seat constituencies and 2 members are appointed by the President to represent the Anglo-Indian community.

Table I (continued)

Number of representatives in lower house of federal government – Lok Sabha	545 seats: Bharatiya Janata Party – BJP (Indian People's Party) 180, Indian National Congress – INC 112, Communist Party of India-Marxist – CPI-M 32, Telugu Desam – TDP (Telugu Land) 29, Samajwadi Party – SP (Socialist Party) 26, Shiva Sena – SS 15, Bahujan Samaj Party – BSP (Majority Society Party) 14, Dravida Munnetra Kazhagam – DMK (Dravida Progressive Federation) 12, Janata Dal (Samata) – JD(S) (People's Party – Samata) 12, All India Anna Diravida Munnetra Kazhagam – AIADMK (All-India Anna Diravida Progressive Federation) 11, Biju Janata Dal – BJD 10, All India Trinamool Congress – AITC 9, Nationalist Congress Party – NCP 8, Rashtriya Janata Dal – RJD (National People's Party) 7, Janata Dal (United) – JD(U) 6, India National Lok Dal – INLD 5, Pattali Makkal Katchi – PMK 5, Jammu & Kashmir National Conference – JKN 4, Lok Jan Shakti Party – LJSP 4, Marumalarchi Dravida Munnetra Kazhhagam – MDMK 4, Communist Party of India – CPI 3, Revolutionary Socialist Party – RSP 3, Akhil Bharatiya Lok Tantrik Congress – ABLTC 2, All-India Forward Bloc – FBL 2, Muslim League Kerala State Committee – MLKSC 2, Rashtriya Lok Dal – RLD (National People's Party) 2, Shiromani Akali Dal – SAD (Akali Religious Party) 2, All-India Majlis-e-Ittehadul Muslimmen – AIMIM (All-India Muslim Federal Assembly) 1, Bharipa Bahujan Mahasangha – BBM 1, Communist Party of India (Marxist-Leninist Liberation) – CPI(ML)(L) 1, Himachal Vikas Congress – HVC 1, Janata Dal (Secular) – JD(S) 1, Kerala Congress – KEC 1, Kerala Congress (Mani) – KEC(M) 1, M.G.R. Anna D.M. Kazhagam – MADMK 1, Manipur State Congress Party – MSCP 1, Peasants' and Workers' Party of India – PAWPI 1, Shiromani Akali Dal (Simranjit Singh Mann) – SAD(M) 1, Sikkim Democratic Front (SDF) 1, Samajwadi Janata Party (Rashtriya) – SJP(R) (Socialist People's Party-National) 1; Independent 6, Vacancies 5
Number of representatives in lower house of federal government for most populated constituent unit	Uttar Pradesh: 85
Number of representatives in lower house of federal government for least populated constituent unit	Lakshadweep: 1

Table I (continued)

Number of representatives in upper house of federal government – Rajya Sabha/House of States	245 seats: Indian National Congress (INC) 62, Bharatiya Janata Party – BJP 43, Communist Party of India-Marxist – CPI(M) 16, Telugu Desam (TDP) 10, Dravida Munnetra Kazhagam (DMK) 9, Rashtriya Janata Dal (RJD) 9, Samajwadi Party (SP) 7, Communist Party of India (CPI) 7, All-India Anna Diravida Munnetra Kazhagam (AIADMK) 5, Shiva Sena (SHS) 5, Shiromani Akali Dal (SAD) 5, Bahujan Samaj Party (BSP) 4, Biju Janta Dal (BJD) 3, Tamil Manila Congress (Moopanar) (TMC) 3, Jammu & Kashmir National Conference (JKN) 2, Muslim League Kerala State Committee (MLKSC) 2, All-India Forward Block (FBL) 2, Asom Gana Parishad (Assam People's Council (AGP)) 2, Sikkim Sangram Parishad (SSP) 1, Autonomous State Demand Committee (ASDC) 1, Revolutionary Socialist Party (RSP) 1, Himachal Vikas Congress (HVC) 1, Kerala Congress (KEC) 1, Jharkhand Mukti Morcha JMM 1, India National Lok Dal (INLD) 1, Haryana Vikas Party (HVP) 1; others 5 Independents 14, nominated members 12.
Distribution of representation in upper house of federal government – Rajya Sabha/ House of States	Distribution is according to constitutional provision "Fourth Schedule, Annexure I:" Allocation of seats in the House of States (245 seats): Uttar Pradhesh 34, Bihar 22, Maharashtra 19, Andhra Pradesh 18, Tamil Nadu 18, Madhya Pradesh 16, West Bengal 16, Karnataka 12, Gujarat 11, Orissa 10, Rajasthan 10, Kerala 9, Assam 7, Punjab 7, Haryana 5, Jammu & Kashmir 4, Himachal Pradesh 3, Delhi 3, Nagaland 1, Manipur 1, Tripura 1, Meghalaya 1, Sikkim 1, Pondicherry 1, Mizoram 1, Arunachal Pradesh 1, Goa 1 + 12 Nominated.
Constitutional court (highest court dealing with constitutional matters)	Supreme Court. Judges are appointed by the President and remain in office until they reach the age of 65.
Political system of constituent units	Legislative Assemblies (Vidhan Sabha) composed of between 32 and 425 members, popularly elected for a 5-year term. Some of the larger states have a second smaller legislative chamber called a Legislative Council (Vidhan Prishad).
Head of state – constituent units	Governor, appointed by the President, under the recommendation of the Prime Minister, to serve for a 5-year term.
Head of government – constituent units	Chief Minister heads Council of Ministers, who are drawn from the Legislative Assembly.

Table II
Economic and Social Indicators

GDP	US$2.2 trillion
GDP per capita	US$2 200
Mechanisms for taxation	The taxation system in India is very complex. Federal and constituent governments share taxation powers. • Corporate Taxes: 0–35% (0% for foreign companies, 35% for domestic companies.) • Personal Income Taxes: 4 brackets, ranging from 0–30%. • Value-added Tax (VAT): 16% • Wealth Tax: 0–2% • Sales and Excise Taxes: 8–24% • Extensive customs and import taxes • Municipal Sales taxes
National debt (external)	US$99.6 billion
National unemployment rate	4%
Constituent unit with highest unemployment rate	N/A
Constituent unit with lowest unemployment rate	N/A
Adult literacy rate	55.7%
National expenditures on education as a % of GDP	3.3%
Life expectancy in years	62.9
Doctors per population ratio (national)	48 doctors per 100 000 inhabitants
Doctors per population ratio in constituent units (highest)	N/A
Doctors per population ratio in constituent units (lowest)	N/A
National expenditures on health as a % of GDP	N/A

Sources

Central Intelligence Agency (CIA), *World Factbook 2000*, CIA, Washington, DC, 2000, On-line source, Central Intelligence Agency (CIA), *World Fact Book 2000*. CIA, www.cia.gov/cia/publications/factbook/index.html

Derbyshire, J. Denis. *Encyclopedia of World Political Systems*. Volumes I and II. New York: Sharpe Reference, M.E. Sharpe, Inc., 2000.

Economist Intelligence Unit. "Country Commerce -India" Released November 2000. *The Economist Intelligence Unit Database 2000*. New York, 2000.

Elazar, Daniel J. (ed.), *Federal Systems of the World: A Handbook of Federal, Confederal and Autonomy Arrangements*. 2nd Edition. Jerusalem Institute for Federal Studies. London: Longman Group/Westgate House, 1994.

Income Tax Department Delhi. www.incometaxdelhi.nic.in
International Monetary Fund (IMF). *International Financial Statistics*, Vol. LIII, No. 12, December 2000. Washington, DC: the IMF Statistics Department, 2000.
Statistics Division of the United Nations Secretariat and International Labour Office. "Indicators on income and economic activity." www.un.org/Depts/unsd/social/inc-eco.htm
UNESCO. *World Education Report 1998: Teachers and Teaching in a Changing World.* Paris: UNESCO, 1998.
United Nations. *Human Development Report, 2000.* www.undp.org/hdro/report.html
United Nations Statistics Division. "InfoNation." United Nations Statistical Database, 2000.
United Nations Population Division. Department of Economic and Social Affairs. "Population in 1999 and 2000: All Countries." *World Population Prospects: 1998 Revision, Vol. 1 comprehensive tables.* www.un.org/Depts
World Bank. *World Development Report 2000/2001: Attacking Poverty.* www.worldbank.org/poverty/wdrpoverty/report/index.htm
World Health Organisation (WHO). "Estimates of Health Personnel." www-nt.who.int/whosis/statistics
World Health Organisation (WHO). "Annex Table 8, Selected national health accounts indicators for all Member States, estimates for 1997." *World Health Report 2000.* Geneva, 2000. www-nt.who.int/whosis/statistics/menu.cfm

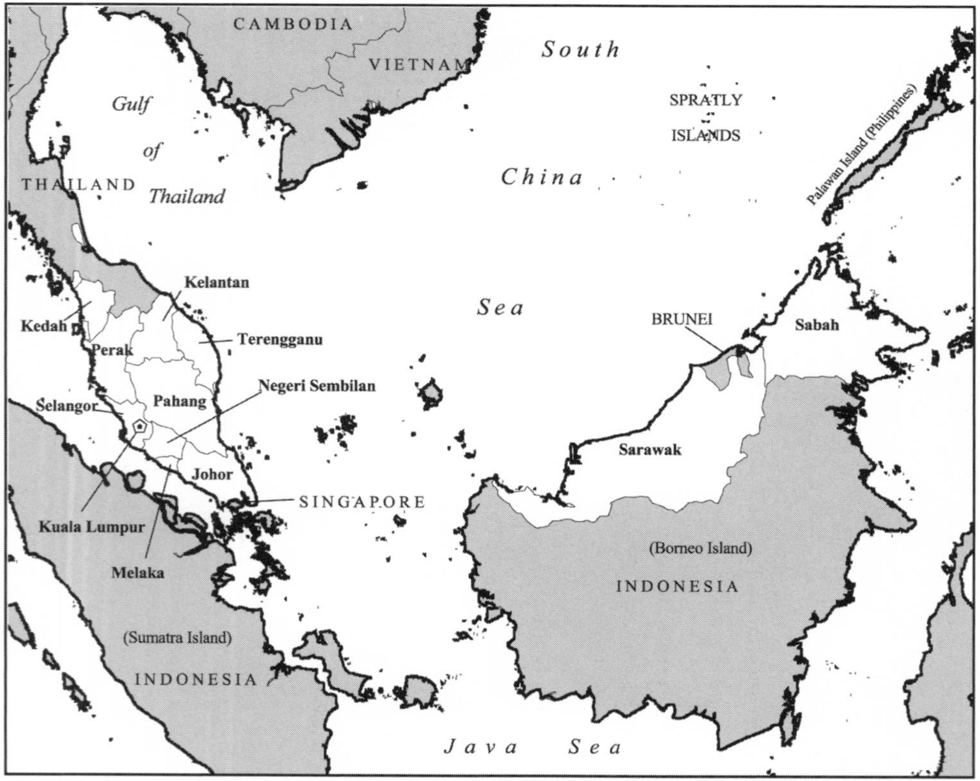

Federation of Malaysia

Capital: Kuala Lumpur
Population: 22.5 Million
(2001 est.)

Boundaries and place names are representative and do not imply any official endorsement.

Sources: ESRI Ltd.; CIA World Factbook; Times Atlas of the World

Malaysia
(*Federation of Malaysia*)

GORDON P. MEANS

1 HISTORY AND DEVELOPMENT OF FEDERALISM

The Federation of Malaysia is composed of 13 states and one federal territory. It is located on the Malay Peninsula at the southeastern tip of continental Asia and along the northern part of the island of Borneo. The federation evolved from the pattern of British rule, which was based on treaties with Malay sultanate states. Four of the Malay states joined in a federation in 1896, while five states remained "unfederated." In the colonial period the British also directly ruled three colonies – Singapore, Malacca and Penang – and exercised indirect colonial rule over the states of Sarawak and North Borneo on the island of Borneo.

After the Second World War, various efforts were made to unify these states and territories. A proposal to form a Malayan Union had to be abandoned due to the combined opposition of the Malay sultans and the Malays, who feared loss of political power if immigrant communities of Chinese, Indians and others were fully represented in the proposed democratic institutions. Instead, in 1948 a Federation of Malaya was created, with special provisions to protect the powers of the Malay Rulers and the interests of their Malay subjects. The federal system was designed to assure the political dominance of the Malays and provide a bulwark against pressures from immigrant communities for full representation and democratic reforms. The 1948 federation included nine Malay states and the former colonies of Malacca and

Penang, but not Singapore. The system centralized legislative powers but decentralized administrative responsibility to the states.

British rule over the Federation of Malaya continued until 1957 when Malaya was granted independence. A new constitution in 1957 providing for independence revised the federal system, and gave each level of government prime responsibility for the administration of subjects within its legislative competence. Both the states and the federal government were given power to delegate their powers to the other through agreements made by executive action. This feature has made the federal system flexible over time and amenable to the enhancement of federal authority.

During the years from 1948 to 1960, the government was preoccupied with a communist guerrilla insurrection, which was gradually suppressed. The guerrillas attempted to recruit support primarily from Chinese labouring and rural communities. In response, government counter-insurgency policies attempted to address the threat by vigorous military measures and by meeting some of the demands of the immigrant communities, thus slightly tempering the overt ethnic bias (in favour of the Malay population) of the federal system.

In 1963 the Federation of Malaya expanded to include the states of Singapore, Sarawak and Sabah (formerly North Borneo), which had been under British rule and were now facing independence. An agreement was worked out for the creation of an expanded Federation of Malaysia. The proposal was vigorously opposed by some minorities in the joining states and by both Indonesia and the Philippines. Despite the opposition, however, the Federation of Malaysia came into being in 1963. The new Malaysia Agreement further modified the federal system in a complex set of special arrangements to placate the concerns both of joining states and of the federal leaders in Malaya.

Shortly after the formation of the Federation of Malaysia, a disagreement developed between the leaders of Singapore and the federal government over the terms of the Federation Agreement defining the relative autonomy of Singapore and the exercise of federal powers over security and political activity. At issue was whether the ruling party in Singapore had the right to mobilize political support in the remainder of Malaysia and whether the political supporters of the federal government, backed by sympathetic federally-controlled security forces, could mobilize opposition to the government in Singapore. Political demonstrations rapidly escalated over ethnic issues, since the population of Singapore was 75% Chinese and only 14% Malay, while the rest of Malaysia, excluding Singapore, was 45.9% Malay and 36% Chinese. Furthermore, the federal government was committed to asserting the primacy of the Malays as the indigenous people through an elaborate system of special rights. Thus, the contest between the federal authorities and Singapore raised fundamental issues of ethnic political supremacy, rights of minorities, and the equality of citizenship. Demonstrations and counter-demonstrations, egged on by politicians on both sides, inflamed ethnic passions. Finally, Malaysia's Prime Minister, Tunku Abdul Rahman, decided Singapore should be expelled from the federation. Confronted with an ultimatum, Singapore's leaders agreed and in August 1965, with great secrecy and haste, Malaysia's Parliament ratified the Constitution Amendment Bill which expelled Singapore.

This dramatic event demonstrated the superior political and legal powers of the federal government and had a profound effect on the subsequent development of federal-state relations within the revised Malaysian federation. Singapore's exit from the federation also changed the political calculus since Malaysia without Singapore reinforced the political dominance of the Malays and assured that federal policies would remain unchallenged. This was especially true for the formula of inter-ethnic relations – based on a system of Malay rights and privileges – that was being promoted by the Malay leaders in the federal government. There were differences in the ethnic mix between the peninsular states and those in Borneo, yet, after Singapore's exit, there was steady pressure from federal authorities to bring the Borneo states into conformity with federal policies and integrate their party structures into the system of ethnic party alliances that sustained the federal government.

Great effort has been taken by federal authorities to intervene in Borneo state politics to maintain in power political coalitions that would collaborate with the federal leadership and be harmonious with federal objectives and policies. Extensive federal patronage, combined with federal police and other coercive powers, have been used to reward supporters and isolate and defeat those state leaders who defend all the conditions of state autonomy for Sarawak and Sabah that were incorporated into the original Malaysia Agreement.

A constitutional crisis developed in May 1969 which dramatically shifted the balance of the federal system. Following an inconclusive election, racial riots broke out and the government declared a national emergency which suspended both the constitution and Parliament. For over 15 months a government-appointed National Operations Council ruled the country by decree. State governments continued to function but under the restrictions of emergency rule. When constitutional rule was finally restored, the Sedition Act was amended to make it unlawful for anyone, including Members of Parliament, to discuss or criticize the powers or status of Malay Rulers, citizenship rights, Malay special rights, the status of Islam as the official religion, and Malay as the national language. Since some of these issues were included in the federal-state distribution of powers, this ordinance made it a crime to have public discussion of any of these issues even in Parliament or in state legislative assemblies. Conviction under the Sedition Act is an automatic disqualification for holding elected office. On ethnic issues, it became clear that the states had to conform to the direction of federal leaders.

2 CONSTITUTIONAL PROVISIONS RELATING TO FEDERALISM

Malaysia is a parliamentary democracy. The head of state is a constitutional monarch known as *Yang Di-Pertuan Agong* (Paramount Ruler). He is elected on the basis of seniority for a five-year term by the Conference of Rulers from among their own members who are the nine Malay Rulers (Sultans) of the original Malay States in the earlier Federation of Malaya (Articles 32–38). This system creates a rotation of office among the Malay Rulers. The Malay Rulers are important defenders of federalism, since they exercise substantial power at the state level and they provide political continuity with a traditional political system that predates British colonial rule.

After Singapore's expulsion from Malaysia in May 1965, the federal system was composed of 13 constituent units which included nine Malay States plus Penang and Malacca (both former British colonies) in Peninsular Malaysia, plus the two East Malaysian (Borneo) states of Sarawak and Sabah. The nine Malay States are headed by a hereditary ruler (Sultan) and the other four states are headed by a Governor appointed by the Paramount Ruler (on the advice of the federal Prime Minister). Each constituent state is governed by an elected Legislative Assembly, with effective power given to a Chief Minister who is elected by majority support in the Assembly.

Each state has a constitution which must include "essential provisions" set out in the Eighth Schedule of the federal constitution, thereby imposing a degree of uniformity on all the states. Parliament has legislative power to remove constitutional provisions in the states that are inconsistent with the Eighth Schedule. Both the federal government and the states are given the power to delegate their powers to the other through executive agreements.

The formal division of powers in the constitution allocates to the federal government the most important powers thus giving the federation a very strong central government. Federal powers include, inter alia, external affairs, defence, civil and criminal law, citizenship, state and federal elections, finance, trade, commerce and industry, taxation, education, health, labour, and social security (Article 74, Ninth Schedule). Federal laws take precedence over state laws in matters of incompatibility. Although residual powers are assigned to the states, the extensive list of functions defined in the constitution has left virtually no unassigned residual powers for the states to claim. The states have primary responsibility for land and agriculture, local government and services, plus administration of Islam and Malay customary law (Article 95B, Ninth Schedule). Because the latter issues are less relevant to the non-Malay states, additional powers were given to the states of Sarawak and Sabah at the time they joined the federation, thus creating a federal system with unequal powers among the constituent states.

At the federal level, the upper house of Parliament, the Senate (Dewan Negara), was designed to represent the states and to be a bulwark against federal encroachment of state rights. The Senate consists of 69 members, two elected from each state by the Legislative Assembly, and the rest appointed by the Paramount Ruler on the advice of the Prime Minister. Because the ruling Alliance Party has usually won controlling majorities in at least nine or more of the state assemblies, Senators have been appointed for their loyalty and service to the ruling party, thus making the Senate an important source of patronage for the ruling party. In practice the Senate has not defended state interests but has become primarily a rubber stamp for government-sponsored legislation coming from the popularly elected lower house of Parliament (Dewan Rakyat).

A constitutional amendment requires the support of a two-thirds majority in Parliament without any participation by the states (Article 15). In practice, because the federal government has always commanded greater than a two-thirds majority, constitutional amendments have been passed at a rapid pace, some of them with retroactive effect to make legal those federal actions which might otherwise have been challenged in court. A number of constitutional amendments were introduced, passed both houses of Parliament and received royal assent in a matter of hours with no prior public announcement and virtually no public debate. From 1957 to 1977, the constitution was amended 23 times, and since then the pace of new amendments has continued with a cumulative effect of creating overwhelming superiority of federal power and federal control over state policy and administration.

Fiscal arrangements outlined in the constitution favour the central government. All major tax powers are assigned to the federal government, but states are guaranteed a share of federal revenues calculated primarily on the basis of population and road mileage (Tenth Schedule). There have also been revenue-sharing agreements involving oil revenues for the littoral states for offshore production. A National

Finance Council composed of federal and state representatives was supposed to provide coordination but, because it had only consultative authority, it never developed into an effective coordinating institution. Instead the Economic Planning Unit in the Prime Minister's Department and the Ministry of Finance produce the annual economic reports and the national five-year economic plans that shape public revenue distributions and set economic goals. With strong federal direction and scrutiny, a series of national, state and district development committees oversee and coordinate the implementation of those national economic plans.

Because all major taxing powers reside with the federal government, all levels of government rely on a system of transfers from federal to state authorities and from state authorities to local authorities. In 1995, about 13% of federal revenues were transferred to state governments, and state governments in turn transferred about 40% of their revenues to local authorities. This system has created a persistent financial deficit for state and local authorities, making them reliant on federal bailouts or special grants, which give federal authorities leverage over policy and politics at both state and local levels.

The largest sources of federal revenues are derived from direct tax on companies, petroleum tax and individual income tax, which together accounted for over 40% of revenue in 1995. Other federal sources include property tax, capital gains tax and estate duties. In addition, export and import duties on a wide variety of products and commodities, plus excise duties on products, petroleum and motor vehicles, combined with indirect taxes give the federal government a very extensive tax base. The major sources of revenue for the states are derived from license fees and royalties from forests, lands and mines. The limited base of state revenues has tended to generate excessively rapid resource depletion policies by state authorities both to generate needed state revenues and also to provide lucrative opportunities for high levels of corruption by state authorities controlling the allocation of resource extraction licenses. Rapid resource depletion is particularly rampant in states with large stands of tropical rain forest, despite sustained protests by many of the inhabitants living in the areas affected.

The constitution assigned resolution of constitutional disputes to the courts. However, the power of the courts is limited under Article 150 of the constitution which gives the federal government authority to declare an "Emergency." When invoked, emergency legislation cannot be challenged in the courts on grounds of constitutionality, except as relating to religion, citizenship, language, Malay custom and native law. Preventive detention laws and the Sedition Act, which prohibits any "seditious tendency," have given virtually unbridled powers to the Prime Minister to restrict individual rights and freedoms, and these acts also over-ride the balance of powers in the federal system. The role of the courts was further compromised in 1988 when Prime Minister Mahathir objected to several Supreme Court decisions relating to individual rights and to the legal status of the ruling party. First a constitutional amendment was passed limiting the power of the courts, leaving ultimate jurisdiction for the federation as a whole to Parliamentary enactments. Then, Prime Minister Mahathir appointed an impeachment tribunal which removed the Lord President and two other Supreme Court judges from the High Court. Finally, the Prime Minister appointed judges who were less confrontational. Following that crisis, a constitutional amendment transferred the power of judicial review from the courts to Parliament. Thereafter, subject to increased executive control, the courts now give extraordinary deference to federal authorities in the interpretation of laws and the constitution.

In addition to their preeminent financial powers and their capacity to influence the judiciary, federal authorities have consistently relied upon Parliament's power to amend the constitution to enforce their view on any matters of dispute in the federal system.

3 RECENT POLITICAL DYNAMICS

The traditional Sultans in the nine Malay States symbolized Malay political dominance and were given prerogative powers to protect Malay rights. Because they were also made part of democratic institutions, their role was somewhat ambiguous, especially on matters requiring "royal assent." In several states, the Sultan refused to cooperate with a Chief Minister in disputes over timber concessions, patronage, legislation, or alleged lack of deference. Prime Minister Mahathir decided to reduce the scope of royal powers by a constitutional amendment that would allow 15 days for royal assent to bills, after which assent was deemed to have been given. A crisis ensued when the Paramount Ruler refused to assent to the amendment passed by Parliament. Despite the Sedition Act which prohibits any public discussion of the status and prerogatives of the Malay Rulers, in 1983 the government launched a campaign to build public support for the disputed amendments. Eventually, agreement was reached with the Sultans that royal assent could only be delayed for 30 days. This did not end the erosion of their powers. In 1993 constitutional amendments revoked the Rulers' power of delay in conferring royal assent, eliminated their immunities for personal actions, and terminated their power to grant pardons.

In 1997 the countries of Asia experienced devastating economic problems, with stock markets plunging, high corporate debts, bankruptcies and falling currency values. In Malaysia a dispute arose between Prime Minister Mahathir and Deputy Prime Minister Anwar

Ibrahim, who was also Finance Minister, over how best to deal with the problems. Mahathir favoured implementing economic controls by imposing fixed currency rates, limiting currency transfers, providing government bailouts combined with forced mergers of debt-ridden enterprises. Anwar Ibrahim favoured the program of free market economic reforms promoted by the International Monetary Fund, including reduction of government spending, and elimination of waste and patronage. Mahathir blamed the economic crisis on "globalization," international currency traders and share-market speculators. Anwar blamed cronyism, nepotism and corruption.

When these policy differences became public, faced with a potential succession challenge, Mahathir first removed Anwar from office, then removed his supporters from government, party posts and party-owned enterprises. After public rallies in support of Anwar, Mahathir had him arrested and charged with corruption and sodomy. The trial opened a major fracture in the government's political support base, amid charges of violations of human rights, forced confessions, coercion of witnesses, and manipulation of the justice system. After 14 months of legal proceedings and massive public protests, Anwar was sentenced to 15 years in prison and also barred from participating in politics for five years after his release. A number of Mahathir's critics and journalists were convicted of sedition or other offences, including Anwar's defence lawyer for his efforts to prove the innocence of his client during the trial. In the wake of this prolonged crisis, the issues of federalism and the balance between federal, state and local government have received no serious public attention.

The federal system in Malaysia is dominated by the central government. Yet, for political and cultural reasons, the states continue to be viable because of citizen loyalties to their states and political leaders, especially to the Malay Rulers in the Malay States. The federal government relies on the states for administration of many of its programs, and the political system at all levels is based on state representation. Proposals have been made for reforms which would balance revenue sources in the federal system and revive the powers and autonomy of local government. If and when a more open and democratic political system becomes established at the federal level, it may then be possible to address the accumulating issues of reform and renewal at both state and local levels of government.

4 SOURCES FOR FURTHER INFORMATION

Amnesty International, *Malaysia Human Rights Undermined: Restrictive Laws in a Parliamentary Democracy*, London: Amnesty International, 1999.

Crouch, Harold, *Government and Society in Malaysia*, Ithaca, NY: Cornell University Press, 1996.

Lau, Albert, *A Moment of Anguish: Singapore in Malaysia and the Politics of Disengagement*, Singapore: Times Academic Press, 1998.

Lee, H.P., *Constitutional Conflicts in Contemporary Malaysia*, Kuala Lumpur: Oxford University Press, 1995.

Means, Gordon P., "Federalism in Malaya and Malaysia" in Roman Serbyn (ed.), *Fédéralisme et Nations*, Montréal: Les Presses du l'Université du Québec, 1971.

– *Malaysian Politics*, 2nd ed., London: Hodder and Stoughton, 1976.

– *Malaysian Politics: The Second Generation*, Singapore: Oxford University Press, 1991.

Milne, R.S. and Diane K. Mauzy, *Malaysian Politics Under Mahathir*, London: Routledge, 1999.

Muhammad Kamil Awang, *The Sultan and the Constitution*, Kuala Lumpur: Dewan Bahasa dan Pustaka, 1998.

Sheridan, L.A. and Harry E. Groves, *The Constitution of Malaysia*, Dobbs Ferry, NY: Oceana Publications, 1967.

http://www.malaysianews.net/

http://www.emedia.com.my/

http://www.asia1.com.sg/

Table I
Political and Geographic Indicators

Capital city	Kuala Lumpur
Number and type of constituent units	*13 States* (*Negeri-Negeri*): Johor, Kedah, Kelantan, Melaka, Negeri Sembilan, Pahang, Perak, Perlis, Pulau Pinang, Sabah, Sarawak, Selangor, Terengganu; *2 Federal Territories (Wilayah-wilayah Persekutuan):* Labuan, and Wilayah Persekutuan Note: the city of Kuala Lumpur is located within the federal territory of Wilayah Persekutuan.
Official language(s)	Bahasa Melayu (Malay)
Area	329 750 km^2
Area – Largest constituent unit	Sarawak (124 449 km^2)
Area – Smallest constituent unit	Federal Territory of Wilayah Persekutuan (243 km^2)
Total population	23 800 000
Population by constituent unit (% of total population)	Perak 13%, Johor 12%, Selangor 11.1%, Sarawak 9.3%, Sabah (includes Federal Territory of Labuan) 8%, Kedah 8%, Kelantan 7%, Wilayah Persekutuan 7%, Pulau Pinang 6.5%, Pahang 6%, Negeri Sembilan 4.1%, Terengganu 4.1% Melaka 3.3%, Perlis 1.1%
Political system – federal	Constitutional Monarchy – Parliamentary System
Head of state – federal	Paramount Ruler (Yang Di-Pertuan Agong) Sultan Salehuddin Abdul Aziz of Selangor (1999), elected for a 5-year term by and from among the Conference of Rulers, who are the nine Malay Rulers (Sultans) of the original Malay States in the earlier Federation of Malaya.
Head of government – federal	Prime Minister Datuk Seri Mahathir Mohammad (1981/1999) Pertubuhan Kebangsaan Melayu Bersatu (United Malays National Organization – UMNO), leader of the party that wins a plurality of seats in the House of Representatives, to serve a 5-year term. Cabinet is appointed by the Prime Minister from among the MPs with the consent of the Paramount Ruler.
Government structure – federal	Bicameral – Parliament: *Upper House* – Dewan Negara (Senate) 69 seats. Members serve for a 6-year term, with 43 members nominated by the Paramount Ruler on the advice of the Prime Minister, and 2 elected by each of the 13 state Legislative Assemblies (26). *Lower House* – Dewan Rakyat (House of Representatives), 193 seats. Members elected by popular vote in single-seat constituencies to serve for a 5-year term.

Table I (continued)

Number of representatives in lower house of federal government – House of Representatives	193 seats: Barisan Nasional (National Front (BN): Pertubuhan Kebangsaan Melayu Bersatu – UMNO (United Malays National Organization) 71, Persatuan China Malaysia – MCA (Malaysian Chinese Organization) 29, Parti Pesaka Bumiputra Bersatu – PBB (United Traditional Bumiputera Party) 10, Parti Rakyat Bersatu Sarawak/Sarawak United People's Party – SUPP 8, Kongres India Se-Malaysia/Malaysian Indian Congress – MIC 7, Parti Gerakan Rakyat Malaysia/Malaysian People's Movement Party Gerakan 6, Parti Bansa Dayak Sarawak – PBDS (Sarawak Native People's Party) 6, Parti Kebangsaan Sarawak/Sarawak National Party – SNAP 4, UPKO 3, Parti Majuh Sabah/Sabah Progressive Party – SPP 2, Parti Liberal Demokratik/Liberal Democratic Party – LDP 1, Parti Angkatan Keadilan Rakyat (Peoples Justice Movement) 1 Barisan Alternatif (Alternative Front (BA)): Parti Islam se Malaysia – PAS (Islamic Party of Malaysia) 27, Parti Tindakan Demokratik/Democratic Action Party – DAP 10, and Parti Keadilan Nasional (National Justice Party (Keadilan)) 5 Parti Bersatu Sabah – PBS (United Sabah Party) 3
Number of representatives in lower house of federal government for most populated constituent unit	Perak: 23
Number of representatives in lower house of federal government for least populated constituent unit	Perlis: 3
Number of representatives in upper house of federal government – Senate	69 seats. 26 elected
Distribution of representation in upper house of federal government – Senate	69 seats: 43 members are nominated by the Paramount Ruler, and each of the 13 states elects 2 members (26).
Constitutional court (highest court dealing with constitutional matters)	Federal Court. Judges are appointed by the Paramount Ruler on the advice of the Prime Minister.
Political system of constituent units	Unicameral Legislative Assembly
Head of state – constituent units	Each of the 9 Malay States is headed by a hereditary ruler (Sultan) and the other 4 states (Melaka, Penang, Sabah, Sarawak) are headed by a Governor who is appointed by the Paramount Ruler (on the advice of the federal Prime Minister).
Head of government – constituent units	Chief Minister, who is elected by majority support in the Assembly.

Table II
Economic and Social Indicators

GDP	US$223.7 billion
GDP per capita	US$10 300
Mechanisms for taxation	All major taxation power resides with the central government: • Corporate Taxes: 28% • Petroleum Income Tax (Corporate): 38% • Personal Income Taxes: 5 brackets ranging from 15–29% • Sales taxes ranging from 5–15% on local products and imports. • Service tax (on certain services): 5%
National debt (external)	US$41.8 billion
National unemployment rate	2.8%
Constituent unit with highest unemployment rate	N/A
Constituent unit with lowest unemployment rate	N/A
Adult literacy rate	93.7%
National expenditures on education as a % of GDP	4.1%
Life expectancy in years	72.5
Doctors per population ratio (national)	65.8 doctors per 100 000 inhabitants
Doctors per population ratio in constituent units (highest)	N/A
Doctors per population ratio in constituent units (lowest)	N/A
National expenditures on health as a % of GDP	2.4%

Sources

Central Intelligence Agency (CIA), *World Fact Book 2000*. CIA, www.cia.gov/cia/publications/factbook/index.html

Derbyshire, J. Denis. *Encyclopedia of World Political Systems*. Volumes I and II, New York: Sharpe Reference, M.E. Sharpe, Inc., 2000.

Economist Intelligence Unit. "Country Commerce – Malaysia." *The Economist Intelligence Unit 2000*. New York: EIU, 2000.

Elazar, Daniel J. (ed.), *Federal Systems of the World: A Handbook of Federal, Confederal and Autonomy Arrangements*. 2nd Edition. Jerusalem Institute for Federal Studies. London: Longman Group/Westgate House, 1994.

Government of Malaysia. Referral Information System. www.smpke.jpm.my

International Monetary Fund (IMF). *International Financial Statistics*, Vol. LIII, No. 12, December 2000. Washington, DC: the IMF Statistics Department, 2000.

Parliamentary Website of Malaysia. www.parlimen.gov.my

UNESCO. *World Education Report 1998: Teachers and Teaching in a Changing World.* Paris: UNESCO, 1998.

United Nations. "Human Development Index," "Gender-Related Development Index," *Human Development Report, 2000.* Human Development Report Office. www.undp.org/hdro/report.html

United Nations Population Division. Department of Economic and Social Affairs. "Population in 1999 and 2000: All Countries." *World Population Prospects: The 1998 Revision, Vol. 1 Comprehensive Tables.* www.un.org/Depts

United Nations Statistics Division. "InfoNation." United Nations Statistical Database, 2000. www.un.org/

Watts, Ronald L. *Comparing Federal Systems,* 2nd Edition. School of Policy Studies. Montreal/Kingston: McGill-Queen's University Press, 1999.

World Bank. *World Development Report 2000/2001: Attacking Poverty.* www.worldbank.org/poverty/wdrpoverty/report/index.htm

World Health Organisation (WHO). *World Health Report 2000.* Geneva, Switzerland, 2000. www-nt.who.int/whosis/statistics/menu.cfm

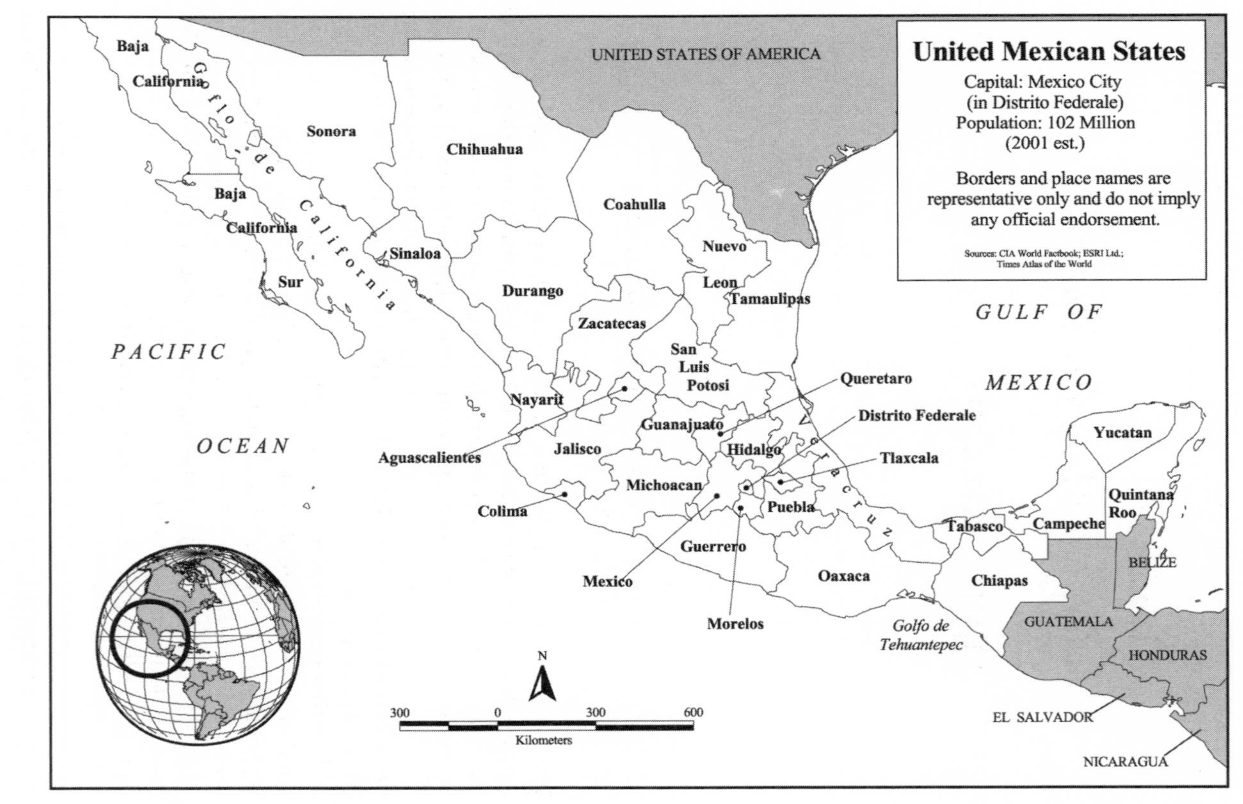
United Mexican States
Capital: Mexico City
(in Distrito Federale)
Population: 102 Million
(2001 est.)
Borders and place names are representative only and do not imply any official endorsement.
Sources: CIA World Factbook; ESRI Ltd.; Times Atlas of the World
UNITED STATES OF AMERICA
GULF OF MEXICO
PACIFIC OCEAN
Golfo de California
Golfo de Tehuantepec
Baja California
Baja California Sur
Sonora
Chihuahua
Coahulla
Nuevo Leon
Tamaulipas
Sinaloa
Durango
Zacatecas
San Luis Potosi
Nayarit
Aguascalientes
Jalisco
Guanajuato
Queretaro
Hidalgo
Distrito Federale
Tlaxcala
Veracruz
Colima
Michoacan
Mexico
Morelos
Puebla
Guerrero
Oaxaca
Tabasco
Chiapas
Campeche
Yucatan
Quintana Roo
BELIZE
GUATEMALA
HONDURAS
EL SALVADOR
NICARAGUA
N
300
0
300
600
Kilometers

Mexico*
(*United Mexican States*)

YEMILE MIZRAHI

1 HISTORY AND DEVELOPMENT OF FEDERALISM

Ever since 1810, when Mexico became an independent country, tensions between the states and the centre have dominated the political landscape. Indeed, the war of independence started in the states as a reaction to the excesses of a powerful central government. The precarious equilibrium between the centre and the periphery in Mexico has been crystallized in the different constitutions that have been drafted since independence.

The first constitution, the Constitución de Cádiz of 1812, was modelled after the Spanish system and defined two institutions at the regional level: municipal and state governments. Municipal governments were elected, but the state governments were appointed by the central government. This constitutional arrangement allowed the first independent government of Mexico, the short-lived monarchy of Agustín de Iturbide, to centralize power in the capital.

In 1824 an insurrection led by General Santa Anna forced Iturbide to resign, and he was later assassinated. With the downfall of the monarchy, the states reacted by establishing their own governments. In the

* The author would like to thank Juan Espindola for his valuable assistance in the preparation of this article.

new Constituent Assembly (1823–24), representatives of the state governments were able to exert a considerable influence in the drafting of the new constitution. It was in the 1824 constitution that federalism was first introduced. It was conceived by the Constituent Assembly as an institutional mechanism to preserve the union and prevent the secession of several states and, thus, what it reveals most is a fear of national disintegration. This is why its drafters sought to create a strong executive while at the same time recognizing some form of state autonomy and the separation of powers among the executive, legislative and judicial branches of government.

The tensions between the states and the centre made the 1824 constitution inoperable. The desire for independence on the part of some states could not be contained, and thus, in 1836 Texas declared its independence from Mexico. More importantly, the tensions between the Liberals (federalists) and the Conservatives (centralists) seriously divided the country. Political instability was so high that no government was able to rule effectively. By 1835, a new Constituent Assembly had amended the constitution and eliminated federalism as a form of government. The centralization of power became more explicit during the dictatorships that followed.

In 1857 a new constitution was drafted after dictator Antonio López Santa Anna was removed during an armed insurrection. In reaction to the strong powers granted to the executive in the 1824 constitution, the 1857 constitution sought to limit the power of the executive by strengthening Congress. As a mechanism to do this, the constitution eliminated the Senate. It was thought that a single legislative chamber would be more powerful and more effective in checking the power of the executive. Although this constitution recognized federalism as a system of government, it granted the central government great economic and political powers vis-à-vis the states. Moreover, by eliminating the Senate, the states lost their representation in the federal government.

In practice, this constitution also proved unmanageable, particularly given the political instability that was still prevalent in the country, and given that it did not create the institutional mechanisms to allow the executive to govern effectively. As Marván argues, this constitutional design granted Congress enormous power without accountability or appropriate checks and balances, and at the same time, granted the executive enormous responsibilities without sufficient autonomy.[1]

---

1 Ignacio Marván, *¿Y después del presidencialismo qué? Reflexiones para un nuevo régimen constitucional?*, México: Océano, 1998, p. 54.

The 1857 constitution was drafted by the Liberals, and the Conservatives' opposition to it culminated in a civil war. The war between Conservatives and Liberals ended with the victory of the Liberals in 1867. In order to strengthen the executive, President Benito Juárez sought to reform the constitution and, although he died in 1872, a constitutional amendment was passed which re-installed the Senate in 1875. Juárez promoted the Senate as a means of strengthening the central government which he thought was necessary in order to reconstruct the country. The fact that the Senate was re-established did not mean that it was empowered, as many prerogatives remained with Congress – for example, the ratification of all Cabinet members and Supreme Court justices, the suppression of Presidential veto power, and the right to subject the President to a political trial with a simple majority. Also, the Senate was excluded from participating in the discussion and approval of the budget. With this limitation, federalism was impaired, for the states were excluded from taking part in the budgetary decision-making process. This limitation continues to the present.

Porfiro Díaz took power in 1876. This began a period of prolonged and repressive dictatorship. Although during his time in power Juárez used extraordinary provisions to govern and suspended individual rights, the regime of Porfiro Diaz took this to greater extremes. Díaz gained control over the press, the Church, Congress, Governors and local elites. He also managed to amend the constitution to allow for his indefinite re-election.

A severe economic crisis, combined with popular disenchantment with a repressive regime that rested on a highly unequal distribution of wealth, and the emergence of a new generation of leaders who reacted against the entrenchment of a political elite who obstructed their political ambitions, made the conditions ripe for revolution and indeed that is what happened. In 1910, the start of the Mexican Revolution forced Porfirio Díaz to leave the country. As in the past, the revolution originated in the periphery, but was won in the centre. It ended when two moderate northern generals (Venustiano Carranza and Alvaro Obregón) defeated the more radical faction. Carranza and Obregón consolidated their victory when they took control of the centre and were able to dominate the periphery.

After the civil war, a Constitutional Assembly was convened to draft a new constitution. The constitution of 1917 was modelled after the 1857 constitution and the 1875 amendments, but it granted the executive greater discretionary powers and it included a series of "social rights" (education, labour, health) that institutionalized the ideals of the Revolution. This constitution, which is still valid today, became one of the most important institutional pillars of Mexico's political regime.

The other major pillar of the regime was the official party, the Partido Revolucionario Institucional (PRI), which maintained virtually hegemonic control of power from its creation in 1929 to 2000. With the victory of an opposition candidate in the 2000 presidential elections, a significant number of politicians, academics and journalist have started to talk about the need to draft a new constitution.

2 CONSTITUTIONAL PROVISIONS RELATING TO FEDERALISM

According to the 1917 constitution, Mexico is a "federal, democratic, and representative republic, composed of free and sovereign states in regard to their internal regime" (Article 40). It is divided into 31 states and one Federal District (Mexico City). Although the constitution declares that Mexico is federal, in practice however, the country has been extremely centralized, both politically and economically, and until recently, it was neither democratic nor representative. Centralization of power became part and parcel of the construction of the national state after the Revolution. The constitution grants the federal government, and particularly the President, vast discretionary powers. An authentic federal system, as was formally stipulated in the constitution, would have undermined the pacification of the country in 1917, for there were regional chiefs hoping to impose their rule in their territories.

The President has substantial powers. According to the constitution, the President can appoint all members of his Cabinet without the ratification of Congress, with the exception of the Attorney-General, the head of the armed forces, and ambassadors (Article 89(II)). The President can introduce legislation to Congress (Article 71(I)), and also names the 21 Justices of the Supreme Court (Articles 94–107) with Senate approval (Article 89(III)). From 1928 (when a constitutional amendment eliminated local government in the Federal District) to 1997, the President also appointed local officials in the Federal District. This provision was changed in 1997 when people in the Federal District were able to choose their mayor for the first time.

The division of power is heavily weighted in favour of the central government. Until the introduction of reforms to decentralize health and education in the 1990s, the federal government had exclusive responsibility in a host of policy areas like commerce, education, health, labour, agriculture, energy, natural resources and food policy. The federal government also possesses enormous financial and economic power. According to the constitution, the powers not explicitly defined for the federal government are reserved for the states. However, virtually all articles in the constitution contain restrictions that limit the power of the states.

In terms of fiscal power, the federal government collects all income tax and, since 1980, it also collects all consumption taxes. While states and municipalities receive a share of tax collection, the criteria for distributing financial resources to sub-national governments have been a matter of controversy, particularly after opposition parties started to win elections at the local and state level. The federal government can also invest in the states with a high degree of discretion. There are no formulae or rules to determine how much the federal government invests in each state.

The Senate provides for the representation of states in the central government. It is made up of 128 members. Each of the 31 states, and the Federal District, elects two members through a majority principle. As well, one seat per state and the Federal District is assigned to the person who came second in the Senate election in that state. (This was a concession granted by the government – at a time when the PRI was still in power everywhere – to allow the opposition to obtain seats in the Senate without much of a sacrifice to the power of the PRI.) The remaining 32 Senators are elected through proportional representation, not on a state basis but using the country as a whole as a constituency (Article 56). This means that these 32 Senators are not elected to represent a constituent unit.

A term in the Senate is six years. In addition to ratifying the selection of Supreme Court justices, ambassadors, the Attorney-General and the head of the Mexican National Bank, the Senate approves all international treaties, and participates in the legislative process. As mentioned earlier, however, the Senate cannot participate in the approval of the budget, so Senators are excluded from taking part in deciding how much is spent in their states, and how it is spent.

Despite the centralizing tendencies of the constitution, Article 135 provides a role for Congress and the states to play in the amendment process. Thus, amendments to the constitution must be approved by two-thirds of the members of Congress and by a majority of state legislatures.

One of the most interesting and influential elements in the constitution is its prohibition on re-election. To prevent the perpetuation of the executive in power, the constitution forbids re-election of *all* elected officials. Originally, Municipal Presidents and Deputies could be re-elected, but in 1933, the PRI introduced a constitutional amendment banning re-election of all officials. This was in large part designed by the PRI to permit the circulation of elites – for, lacking effective competition for office, the PRI became the central mechanism to gain access to power. Thus, a great number of elected positions regularly became available for the PRI to distribute to its supporters and followers.

In 1983 the government introduced a constitutional reform proposal that sought to strengthen the authority and institutional capacity of local/municipal governments in Mexico. The proposal explicitly defined the powers and responsibilities of municipal governments. Among other things, municipal governments were granted authority over the collection of property taxes and were given responsibility for investing and administering a host of public services. However, these changes benefitted mainly urban municipalities – those that could collect property tax and could provide urban services. For the majority of the country, which is rural and poor, these reforms were much less relevant. More importantly, without the possibility of re-election, institution-building is impaired because successful innovations in government do not have sufficient time to be institutionalized. Every three years new municipal authorities have to start from scratch.

Although the constitution certainly centralizes power in the hands of the executive, the centralization of power in Mexico would not have been possible without the long hegemony exerted by the ruling PRI. From its creation in 1929 to the elections in 2000, the "official party" controlled the presidency without interruption. Until the mid-1980s, the PRI also controlled all the states and the majority of the municipalities in the country. And until 1997, the PRI had a majority in Congress. Without a functioning political opposition, federalism could not exist in Mexico.

Through the hegemony of the PRI, which was maintained through a combination of legitimate popular support, skewed electoral rules and fraud, the President was able to subordinate state and local governments, both in political and economic matters. The President became the virtual leader of the party during his term in office (usurping the authority of the President of the party and the National Executive Committee), and not only decided who could run for all governorships, he also had enormous discretionary power to spend resources in the states and municipalities. Even though some resources were transferred to states and municipalities according to a well-established formula, the federal government still had ample room of manoeuvre to transfer resources to the states following political criteria.

The lack of political alternatives outside the PRI fostered strong discipline inside the party. Lapses in discipline were severely punished by means that ranged from fiscal strangulation to political demotion. Governors became, in effect, representatives of the executive in the states. This state of affairs started to change during the 1980s when opposition parties gained strength and managed to win elections first at the local level and, after 1989, at the state level.

One other element of the Mexican system deserves mention here – the Supreme Court. Although a Supreme Court has existed in Mexico for many years, it has not played a major role in Mexican federalism. During the rule of Porfirio Diaz (which ended in 1910), the court was discouraged from intervening in political and electoral conflicts. This pattern remained until 1997 when the Court ruled that it had the authority to resolve these matters.

3 RECENT POLITICAL DYNAMICS

For many years, the centralization of Mexico's political and economic life was not a matter of concern to the government. Until the late 1960s the economy was growing at a steady rate of six per cent per year with low levels of inflation. But once the economy started to decelerate during the 1970s, centralization began to be perceived as a problem and a major obstacle to equitable and sustainable economic development.

The legacies of centralization in Mexico have been extremely negative. These legacies include: a severe regional disequilibrium, with relatively rich and industrialized states in the north and extremely poor and undeveloped states in the south; a highly uneven distribution of income (among the most uneven in Latin America); and decreasing quality and efficiency in the services provided by the government, particularly education and health. With a slowing economy, the federal government became overloaded with many responsibilities and functions it could not meet.

During the 1970s the federal government recognized that decentralization was a tool that could be used to promote more equitable regional development and to divest itself of excessive responsibilities. At first, decentralization was more a rhetorical than a concrete policy project, but during the 1980s, and particularly during the 1990s, the government introduced serious decentralization efforts. Thus, health and education were transferred to the state governments, sub-national governments received greater resources, and the allocations of funds to states and municipal governments became less discretionary. However, in many respects, decentralization has been haphazard, for the federal government has retained the control over critical areas of decision making. For example, in education the federal government still fixes teacher wages and has control over educational materials. As well, states and municipal governments continue to be financially dependent on the federal government. Although the federal government has transferred more resources to sub-national governments, most of these resources are earmarked for specific projects. State and local governments complain that these conditions severely limit their capacity to plan their own development strategies.

After the election of President Zedillo (1994–2000), federalism became a central issue in public debate. The eruption of the guerrilla insurgency in the southern state of Chiapas, the strengthening of the opposition in several states, and the severe economic crisis the country experienced in 1995, significantly reduced the federal government's room for manoeuvre. Although the federal government still holds vast discretionary powers, President Zedillo believed that the excessive centralization of Mexico's political and economic life was becoming a serious obstacle to addressing the extreme regional inequalities and the impoverishment of thousands of Mexicans. To strengthen state and local governments, and to reform financial inter-governmental relations, the government launched a new program, entitled "New Federalism." This program sought to transfer more resources to states and municipalities, to reduce the discretionary power of the federal government in the allocation of funds, and to simplify and clarify the process of resource distribution to states and municipalities.

Although during the Zedillo administration states and municipalities received greater resources and were granted more responsibilities, many of the patterns of the past persisted. Mexico continued to be a highly centralized country, particularly compared to other Latin American countries. The federal government still continued to control most public spending – by 1996, the federal government was responsible for 75% of total expenditures, and in 1998, the federal government controlled 70.9% of total income, distributing 24.4% of total income to the states, and 4.7% to municipal governments. Perhaps more importantly, states and local governments became more dependent on transfers from the federal government. The increase of transfers had the perverse effect of reducing their efforts to raise their own income. And, most of the transfers are still earmarked for specific projects, which seriously restricts the capacity of states and local governments to plan their spending and decide on their priorities.

These are the dilemmas that confront the administration of President Vicente Fox. For him, federalism is not only a matter of transferring more resources to the states and municipalities. Having been Governor of the state of Guanajuato, President Fox believes that inter-governmental relations need to change and that states and municipalities need not only greater resources, but more decision-making power. This, however, has become quite problematic for the new administration, since at the state level some Governors still rule in a traditional authoritarian fashion. Granting more decision-making authority and resources to these Governors would strengthen these authoritarian islands in the new democratic ocean.

The conflict between the federal government and the state of Yucatán illustrates this clearly. In August 2000 the Governor of Yucatán, Víctor Cervera Pacheco, an old-time member of the PRI and a typical *cacique* (authoritarian local chief) manipulated the process for selecting the new Electoral Council, a body in charge of organizing and supervising the gubernatorial elections in the state which were scheduled for May 2001. The opposition complained, claiming that the Electoral Council was not impartial and, therefore, could not guarantee a fair electoral process.

The case was taken to the Federal Electoral Tribunal, which ruled in favour of the opposition in October 2000. The Governor and the PRI local deputies, however, defied this ruling, claiming that the Tribunal violated the autonomy of the state. The PRI and the Governor defended their case using federalism as their banner. The federal government refused to use the police to force the Governor to comply with the Federal Electoral Tribunal's decision because the President believes that using public force will only complicate matters. Instead, the opposition resorted to the Supreme Court. The conflict finally ended in April 2001 when the Supreme Court ruled against the Governor, and the Electoral Council was forced to dissolve. This is the first time in the history of contemporary Mexico that the Supreme Court has resolved a conflict between a state and the federal government.

4 SOURCES FOR FURTHER INFORMATION

Carmagnani, Marcelo (coord.), *Federalismos latinoamericanos: México/Brasil/Argentina*, Mexico: El Colegio de México-FCE, 1993.

Giugale, Marcelo and Steven Webb (eds), *Achievements and Challenges of Fiscal Decentralization. Lessons from Mexico*, Washington, DC: The World Bank, 2000.

Martinez, Carlos and Alicia Ziccardi, 2000. "Límites y posibilidades para la descentralización de las políticas sociales," in Rolando Cordera y Alicia Ziccardi (eds), *Las políticas sociales de México a fin del milenio. Descentralización, diseño y gestión*, México: Miguel Angel Porrúa-UNAM.

Marván, Ignacio, *¿Y después del presidencialismo qué? Reflexiones para un nuevo régimen constitucional?*, México: Océano, 1998.
Merino, Mauricio, *Fuera del centro*, México: Universidad Veracruzana, 1992.
www.eclac.org/estadisticas
www.inegi.gob.mx
www.shcp.gob.mx

Table I
Political and Geographic Indicators

Capital city	Mexico City
Number and type of constituent units	*31 States (Estados)*: Aguascalientes, Baja California Norte, Baja California Sur, Campeche, Chiapas, Chihuahua, Coahuila de Zaragoza, Colima, Durango, Guanajuato, Guerrero, Hidalgo, Jalisco, México, Michoacán de Ocampo, Morelos, Nayarit, Nuevo León, Oaxaca, Puebla, Querétaro de Arteaga, Quintana Roo, San Luís Potosí, Sinaloa, Sonora, Tabasco, Tamaulipas, Tlaxcala, Veracruz-Llave, Yucatán, Zacatecas; *1 Federal District (Distrito Federal):* Mexico City
Official language(s)	Spanish
Area	1 958 201 km^2
Area – Largest constituent unit	Chihuahua (244 938 km^2)
Area – Smallest constituent unit	Federal District (1 479 km^2)
Total population	97 361 711
Population by constituent unit (% of total population)	México 13.3%, Federal District 8.8%, Veracruz-Llave 7.1%, Jalisco 6.5%, Puebla 5.2%, Guanajuato 4.8%, Michoacán de Ocampo 4.1%, Chiapas 4.0%, Nuevo León 3.9%, Oaxaca 3.5%, Guerrero 3.2%, Chihuahua 3.1%, Tamaulipas 2.8%, Sinaloa 2.6%, Baja California Norte 2.5%, San Luís Potosí 2.4%, Coahuila de Zaragoza 2.4%, Hidalgo 2.3%, Sonora 2.2%, Tabasco 2.0%, Yucatán 1.7%, Morelos 1.6%, Durango 1.5%, Queretaro de Arteaga 1.4%, Zacatecas 1.3%, Tlaxcala 0.11%, Aguascalientes 0.10%, Quintana Roo 0.10%, Nayarit 0.09%, Campeche 0.07%, Colima 0.06%, Baja California Sur 0.04%
Political system – federal	Federal Republic
Head of state – federal	President Vicente Fox Quesada (2000), AC-PAN; Includes the Alianza por cambio (Alliance for Change), which is comprised of the Partido Acción Nacional – PAN (National Action Party), and the Partido Verde Ecologista de México – PVEM (Ecologist Green Party of Mexico). The President is elected by popular vote for a 6-year term, and cannot serve a second term.
Head of government – federal	President Vicente Fox Quesada (AC-PAN). President can appoint Cabinet without ratification of Congress, except Attorney-General, head of armed forces and ambassadors.

Table I (continued)

Government structure – federal	Bicameral: Congreso de la Unión (National Congress): *Upper House* – Cámara de Senadores (Senate), 128 seats. Senators are elected for a 6-year term, and cannot seek re-election. *Lower House* – Cámara Federal de Diputados (Federal Chamber of Deputies), 500 seats. 300 members are elected from single-seat constituencies. The remaining 200 are elected from multi-member constituencies on the basis of proportional representation. Deputies are elected for a 3-year term. Deputies cannot seek re-election.
Number of representatives in lower house of federal government – Chamber of Deputies	500 Seats: *Alianza por Cambio (Alliance for Change):* Partido Acción Nacional – PAN (National Action Party) 218 and Partido Verde Ecologista de México – PVEM (Ecologist Green Party of Mexico) 5; Partido Revolucionario Institucional – PRI (Institutional Revolutionary Party) 209; Alianza por México – AM (Alliance for Mexico): Partido de la Revolución Democrática – PRD (Party of the Democratic Revolution) 53, Partido del Trabajo – PT (Labour Party) 9; Convergencia por la Democracia – CD (Convergence for Democracy) 2, Partido Alianza Social – PAS (Social Alliance Party) 2, Partido de la Sociedad Nacionalista – PSN (Nationalist Society Party) 2
Number of representatives in lower house of federal government for most populated constituent unit	México: 57
Number of representatives in lower house of federal government for least populated constituent unit	Baja California Sur: 2
Number of representatives in upper house of federal government – Senate	128 seats: *Alianza por Cambio (Alliance for Change):* Partido Acción Nacional – PAN (National Action Party) 46 and Partido Verde Ecologista de México – PVEM (Ecologist Green Party of Mexico) 5; Partido Revolucionario Institucional – PRI (Institutional Revolutionary Party) 60; *Alianza por México – AM (Alliance for Mexico)*: Partido de la Revolución Democrática – PRD (Party of the Democratic Revolution) 15, Partido del Trabajo – PT (Labour Party) 1, Convergencia por la Democracia – CD (Convergence for Democracy) 1

Table I (continued)

Distribution of representation in upper house of federal government – Senate	96 Senators are elected from three-seat constituencies per state and the Federal District and 32 Senators are elected through proportional representation in the country as a whole. In the constituencies, two seats are awarded to the party winning a plurality and one seat to the first runner-up.
Constitutional court (highest court dealing with constitutional matters)	Supreme Court of Justice (Corte Suprema de Justicia). Judges are appointed by the President with consent of the Senate.
Political system of constituent units	Unicameral: Chamber of Deputies directly elected with Deputies serving 3-year terms. Deputies cannot seek re-election.
Head of state – constituent units	Governor – directly elected for a 6-year term (appoints a Cabinet and set of advisors). Governors cannot seek re-election.
Head of government – constituent units	Governor Note: In the case of the Federal District, until 1997, a Mayor was appointed by the President of the central government. Since 1997, municipal elections have been held.

Table II
Economic and Social Indicators

GDP	US$915 billion
GDP per capita	US$9 100
Mechanisms for taxation	Main forms of taxation: • Income Tax – controlled by Central Government. There are 10 tax brackets that range from 3–35%. • Value-added Tax (IVA) – controlled by Central Government and Constituent Units. Taxes goods and services, with basic exemptions. Rate is 15%. • Excise tax on new vehicles (ISAN): Controlled by Central Government and Constituent Units: rate is between 2–17%, depending on the value of the car. • Corporate Tax: 34%
National debt (external)	US$162 billion
National unemployment rate	2.2% (urban)
Constituent unit with highest unemployment rate (urban areas only)	Coatzacoalcos (urban area within Veracruz): 3.2%
Constituent unit with lowest unemployment rate (urban areas only)	Ciudad Juárez (urban area within Chihuahua): 0.8%
Adult literacy rate	90.8%
National expenditures on education as a % of GDP	5.1%
Life expectancy in years	71.5
Doctors per population ratio (national)	186.4 doctors per 100 000 inhabitants
Doctors per population ratio in constituent units (highest)	N/A
Doctors per population ratio in constituent units (lowest)	N/A
National expenditures on health as a % of GDP	5.3%

Sources

Bank of Mexico, *Annual Report, 1999*. Report released April/2000.

Central Intelligence Agency (CIA), *World Fact Book 2000*. CIA, www.cia.gov/cia/publications/factbook/index.html

Economic Commission for Latin America and the Caribbean (ECLAC), *Statistical Yearbook for Latin America and the Caribbean 1999*. ECLAC. www.eclac.org/estaditicas

Economist Intelligence Unit. "Country Commerce – Mexico." *The Economist Intelligence Unit 2000*. New York: EIU, 2000.

Elazar, Daniel J. (ed.) *Federal Systems of the World: A Handbook of Federal, Confederal and Autonomy Arrangements*. 2nd Edition. Jerusalem Institute for Federal Studies. London: Longman Group/Westgate House, 1994.

Instituto nacional de estadística geográfica e informática (INEGI) (National Institute of Statistical Geography and Information). www.inegi.gob.mx/difusion/ingles/portadai.html

International Labour Office. "Indicators on Unemployment." www.un.org/Depts/unsd/social/unempl.htm

Latin-Focus: The Leading Source for Latin American Economies. www.latin-focus.com/index.html

Ministry of Finance, Mexico. www.shcp.gob.mx

Pan-American Health Organization (PAHO/WHO). On-line country demographic indicators and "Profiles of the Health Services System." www.paho.org

United Nations Statistics Division. "InfoNation." United Nations Statistical Database, 2000. www.un.org/cgi-bin/pubs/infonatn.html

United Nations. "Human Development Index," "Gender-Related Development Index," *Human Development Report, 2000.* Human Development Report Office. www.undp.org/hdro/report.html

World Bank. *World Development Report 2000/2001: Attacking Poverty.* www.worldbank.org/poverty/wdrpoverty/report/index.htm

World Health Organisation (WHO). "Estimates of Health Personnel." www-nt.who.int/whosis/statistics

World Health Organisation (WHO). "Annex Table 8, Selected national health accounts indicators for all Member States, estimates for 1997." *World Health Report 2000.* Geneva, 2000. www-nt.who.int/whosis/statistics/menu.cfm.

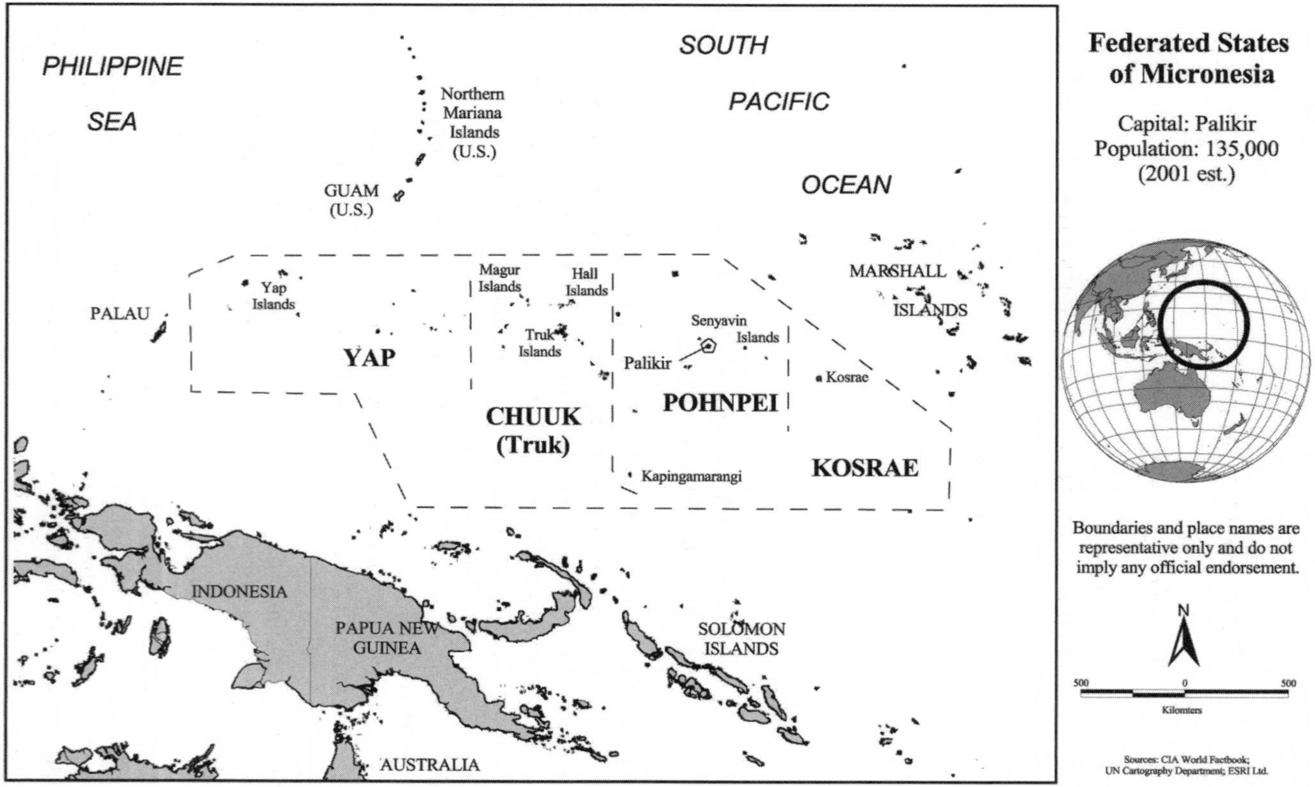

Federated States of Micronesia

Capital: Palikir
Population: 135,000
(2001 est.)

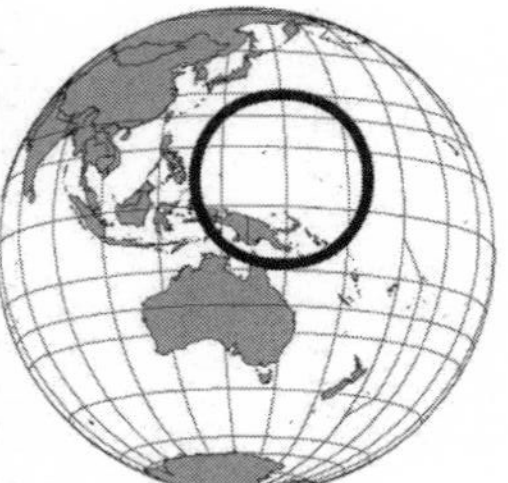

Boundaries and place names are representative only and do not imply any official endorsement.

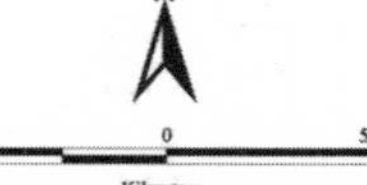

Sources: CIA World Factbook;
UN Cartography Department; ESRI Ltd.

The Federated States of Micronesia

DIRK ANTHONY BALLENDORF

1 HISTORY AND DEVELOPMENT OF FEDERALISM

Micronesia is a collection of island groups in the Pacific Ocean comprised of four major clusters: the Marianas, Carolines, Marshalls and Gilberts (now known as Kiribati). The Federated States of Micronesia (FSM) is part of the Caroline island archipelago. The FSM consists of the island groups of Chuuk, Yap, Pohnpei (formerly Ponape) and Kosrae. The total land area of the FSM is approximately 700 km^2, but the islands are spread over 2.5 million km^2. It has a population of 144,000 people.

The history of Micronesia is one of almost continuous exploitation since Ferdinand Magellan first landed briefly in the region in 1521. Four successive colonial administrations – Spanish, 1521 to 1898; German, 1899 to 1914; Japanese, 1914 to 1944; and American, 1944 to independence in 1986 – have controlled the many small islands of Micronesia.

In 1947, the United States was assigned administration of Micronesia under a United Nations Trusteeship Agreement. Like previous colonial administrations, the American administration was centralized, with Saipan in the northern Marianas as the capital. The Micronesian peoples were divided into six separate administrative districts: Marianas, Yap, Palau, Truk (now Chuuk), Ponape (now Pohnpei), and the Marshalls, and they remained largely self-sufficient and isolated from the rest of the world. In 1977, a seventh district, Kosrae, was created from a division of the Ponape district.

Minimal attention was paid by both the United States and the United Nations to US obligations under the UN Charter until a UN mission to the area during the Kennedy administration drew attention to an extensive list of local complaints. These complaints included: poor transportation; failure to settle the war damage claims; failure to compensate adequately for land taken for military purposes; poor living conditions at the American missile range in the Marshalls; and, almost non-existent medical care. Micronesia proved to be an embarrassment to the American policy against colonialism in the world community. With a cash income of $90 per capita, Micronesia ranked with the poorest countries of the Third World.

The United States responded by doubling the appropriations for Micronesia from $6.8 million in 1962 to $15 million in 1963. The money created a Western-style education system, increased medical services, undertook some basic infrastructure development, improved transportation and communication facilities, and provided wages for personnel working in the Trusteeship administration. There was little attempt, however, to establish projects to promote economic self-sufficiency.

A large portion of US funding was invested in an "accelerated" education program for Micronesian children. English instruction was expanded and increased and became a more standard classroom language. College scholarships were offered to Micronesian youth to pursue education at American universities. Some of this resulted in Micronesians being trained for diversified white collar jobs that did not exist in sufficient quantity in the islands, and so instead of promoting development, and greater self-reliance, it caused migration and unemployment or under-employment.

Under the Trusteeship administration, government employment provided the main source of jobs for an increasing number of Micronesians. The monetary appropriations from the United States became the primary supplier of income for well over half of Micronesia's working population. The degree of US influence on the social, political and economic aspects of Micronesian life has been overwhelming in comparison to previous colonizers.

The concept of federalism in Micronesia can be traced to 1946 when the United States saw complete annexation, with Guam as the capital, as the best option for the political status of the region. However, during the closing weeks of World War II, the Soviet Union occupied a few of the Japanese northern islands, and held them as war spoils. The United States wanted the Soviet Union eventually to return the islands to Japan, and so quickly abandoned its plan for the total annexation of Micronesia, realizing that the Soviets could easily use such annexation as a precedent against the United States. These islands, however, continue to be held by Russia.

The Nixon administration commenced negotiations on Micronesia's future political status in 1969. The American position was that the Micronesians would come together as one political entity that would be known as the Federated States of Micronesia. This federation would be comprised of the political districts that existed at the time: the Marianas, Yap, Palau, Truk (Chuuk), Ponape (Pohnpei), Kosrae (Kusei), and the Marshall Islands. President Nixon's Ambassador to the Micronesian Status Negotiations placed the federal concept on the table very early in the negotiations. However, during the period 1969 to 1972 serious philosophical differences emerged among the Micronesians. The Chamorros of the northern Marianas preferred a close, permanent relation with the United States, and had been petitioning for this status since their first elected legislature came into existence in 1963. Accordingly, the United States agreed to abandon its preference for political unity in Micronesia, and in December 1972, opened separate negotiations with the Northern Mariana Islands.

Palau and the Marshall Islands, with the other Caroline districts, wanted the identical but separate status of "free association." This status would maximize internal self-government, and ensure autonomy sufficient to enable them to establish their own international legal personality while forming the basis for a close and enduring political relationship with the United States. Palauan and Marshallese separation from the other Micronesia districts was motivated essentially by economic considerations. They saw political unity as a drain of their resources to the more populous and less well-endowed central districts of Yap, Ponape, Truk and Kosrae. While the United States continued to urge political unity (excluding the Northern Mariana Islands), the elected Palauan and Marshallese representatives steadfastly maintained that the proposed constitution for a single constitution of the "Federated States of Micronesia" would be defeated in their districts when put to a vote.

Thus, in 1977 the United States was confronted squarely with the fact that, after 30 years of administrative unity, an all-Micronesia state which was strong enough to unite the culturally disparate island groups had not developed. By recognizing the right of each legislature to select its own negotiators, the Carter administration bowed to the inevitable and recognized the right of Palau and the Marshall

Islands to determine their own future, independent of the four remaining districts.

On 12 July 1978, a referendum was held on the proposed Federated States of Micronesia Constitution. As predicted, the constitution was rejected in Palau and in the Marshalls, but ratified in the four central districts of Yap, Ponape, Chuuk, and Kosrae. The Marshall Islands subsequently approved their own constitution in a referendum on 1 March 1979. The Palauan draft constitution was approved on 9 July 1980 and the government of Palau inaugurated on 1 January 1981. Thus, four new political entities emerged out of the former Trust Territories of the Pacific Islands: (1) The Commonwealth of the Northern Mariana Islands (CNMI); (2) The Federated States of Micronesia (FSM); (3) The Republic of the Marshall Islands (RMI); and, (4) The Republic of Palau (ROP). The FSM received independence from the United States in 1986.

2 CONSTITUTIONAL PROVISIONS RELATING TO FEDERALISM

The constitution of The Federated States of Micronesia declares that the territory is comprised of the island groups that ratified the constitution: Chuuk, Yap, Pohnpei (formerly Ponape) and Kosrae. The constitution provides for democratic governance, with universal suffrage for all citizens 18 years of age and older. The rights of citizens are protected by Article IV(1–13).

According to Article VII of the constitution there are three levels of government in the FSM: national, state and local. Article IX outlines the structure and functions of the national legislature (Congress), and provides that each state has one at-large delegate, and the rest are allocated by apportionment according to population. It is important to note that the national legislature is unicameral. Thus, there is no second chamber which provides representation for the states in the central government. The President and Vice-President are elected by Congress and serve four-year terms with the possibility of one re-election (Article X). They cannot serve more than two consecutive terms.

Article IX(2) lists the powers of Congress. These powers include, inter alia, national defence, treaty ratification (with state agreement), citizenship, taxes on income and imports, currency, banking, navigation and shipping, regulations relating to the exploration and exploitation of natural resources in marine areas (beyond 19 km from the islands), and criminal law. While these powers may seem extensive, in reality the national government is not sovereign in many of these areas. For example, defence and banking/currency are among the national government's powers, yet Micronesia exists within the US defence framework and it is important to note that in Micronesia the US banking system operates – there is no bank of issue in the country and US currency is used.

There is no specific list of state powers in the constitution. Article VIII(1) indicates that a power expressly delegated to the national government, or a power of such an indisputably national character as to be beyond the power of a state to control, is a national power. A power not expressly delegated to the national government, nor prohibited to the states, is a state power (s. 2). Thus, all powers not assigned expressly to the national government, are left to the states. There are a number of powers which the national government and states hold concurrently (Article IX(3)). These include appropriation of public funds, borrowing money on the public credit, education, health, and security and public welfare.

The constitution outlines the structure and function of the judiciary in Article XI. It provides for a Supreme Court in which there is one Chief Justice and not more than five associate justices (XI(2)). The justices are appointed by the President and must be approved by two-thirds of the Congress. Justices serve while on good behaviour (XI(3)) – they may be removed for reasons of treason or corruption by a two-thirds vote in Congress (IX(7)). The Supreme Court can hear cases relating to interpretation of the constitution (XI(7)), and has played a role in matters relating to the division of powers and jurisdictional disputes.

Article XII "Finance" outlines the financial arrangements in the federation. All taxes that are levied and collected are assigned to a general fund. There is also a "foreign assistance fund" in which is deposited all foreign aid monies given by non-FSM countries. The President submits an annual budget to the Congress, and the Congress must appropriate funds for all bills passed. According to Article IX(5), national taxes must be imposed equally and each state must receive at least 50 per cent of the taxes collected in that state.

The constitution provides for amendments in Article XIV. Amendments can be proposed by a constitutional convention, popular initiative or Congress. As well, at least every 10 years Congress must ask voters, "Shall there be a convention to revise or amend the constitution?." If a majority answers in the affirmative a constitutional convention must be convened. An amendment becomes part of the constitution "when approved by 3/4 of the votes cast on that amendment in each of 3/4 of the states" (Article XIV(1)). There will be a constitutional convention held in the summer of 2001 to consider amendments to the constitution.

An interesting provision in the constitution of the FSM is the protection of "traditional rights" and "traditional leaders." Article V states that the constitution cannot take away a role or function of traditional leaders, or prevent them from being recognized and given a role in any level of government. Traditional Chiefs hold such titles in each of the four constituent states of the country. Councils of Chiefs are provided for in an on-going way by the governments of the states. Article V(3) states: "The Congress may establish, when needed, a Chamber of Chiefs, consisting of traditional leaders from each state having such leaders, and elected representatives from states having no traditional leaders. The constitution of a state having traditional leaders may provide for an active, functional role for them." States may also set aside one of their congressional seats for traditional leaders (Article IX(11)).

3 RECENT POLITICAL DYNAMICS

Over the past 15 years these arrangements have worked very well for the United States. But for the people of The Federated States of Micronesia, federalism has not fared very well. Indeed, the centrifugal tendencies in the country are very strong.

The current President is Leo Falcam, who is from Pohnpei State. He was elected by Congress in 1999 to a four-year term. It is apparent in Micronesia that the office of the President is not necessarily a coveted position. Several years ago, a poll taken among Micronesian students at the University of Guam indicated that if given the hypothetical choice of being the Governor of their home state, or being the President of the FSM, some 78 per cent chose the former. Most Micronesians today tend to look at their central government as simply another colonial administration!

Tensions have arisen recently in The Federated States of Micronesia over the issue of land purchases. Naturally, in a country made up of islands, land is a valuable resource. Article XIII(4) of the constitution prohibits the purchase of land by non-citizens or corporations that are not wholly owned by citizens, but every citizen of the FSM may purchase land anywhere in the country. However, many Micronesians do not approve of this, and when this in fact began to happen, there were loud protests. They do not want outsiders – and anyone not from that island is considered an outsider – to buy land in their individual states. This will be a major issue in the upcoming constitutional conference.

As in other federations the division of resources is a contentious issue. Some states of the FSM require a greater share of national finances. Chuuk, for example, always needs extra appropriations from the general fund to meet its payroll and provide for public services each year. A further point of contention is the up-keep and maintenance of the new facilities, and the salaries of the staff, of the national government in the capital located in Palikir, Pohnpei State. These expenses are all paid for with FSM taxes, which many people complain are too high. There is also some dissatisfaction with the apportionment of federal taxes to the four states.

Problems associated with the re-negotiation of the Compact of Free Association – a "treaty" which has been negotiated with the United States and governs Micronesia's relations with the United States – have begun to appear on the political agenda. Under the Compact, the United States provides block grants to each state each year, and also provides certain umbrella services such as postal services, federal aeronautical administration, and a weather bureau. The Compacts have to be re-negotiated every 15 years. As preparations for the next re-negotiation begin, there is discontent in the FSM. There is some talk about breaking up the FSM and negotiating separate Compacts. In the upcoming negotiations, therefore, we may see the fragmentation of the FSM.

4 SOURCES FOR FURTHER INFORMATION

Gale, Roger W., *The Americanization of Micronesia: A Study of the Consolidation of U.S. Rule in the Pacific*, Washington, DC: University Press of America, 1979.

Hills, Howard L., "Compacts of Free Association for Micronesia," *The International Lawyer*, Vol. 18, No. 3 (1984), pp. 583–609.

McHenry, Donald F., *Micronesia: Trust Betrayed?* New York: Carnegie Endowment for International Peace, 1975.

Micronesian Support Committee and Pacific Concerns Resource Center, *From Trusteeship to ... .?*, Honolulu, Hawaii, 1985. Copy available at the University of Hawaii, Hamilton Library, Pacific Collections.

Nevin, David, *The American Touch in Micronesia*, New York: W.W. Norton, 1977.

Peoples, J.A., *Island in Trust; Culture Change and Dependence in a Micronesian Economy*, Boulder, Colorado: Westview Press, 1985.

Statham, E. Robert, Jr., "The Freely Associated States of Micronesia: Pragmatism vs. Principle in U.S. Foreign Policy," *Asian Culture Quarterly*, Vol. 27, No. 3/4 (Autumn/Winter, 1999), pp. 27–42.

The Trusteeship Agreement, 61 Stat. 3301, T.I.A.S. no. 1665, 8 U.N.T.S. 189, 18 July 1947, Washington, DC.

Trust Territory of the Pacific Islands, *Annual Reports, 1961–1964*, Washington, DC: US Department of the Interior.

Table I
Political and Geographic Indicators

Capital city	Palikir
Number and type of constituent units	4 states: Chuuk (Truk), Kosrae, Pohnpei, Yap
Official language(s)	English
Area	702 km^2
Area – Largest constituent unit	Pohnpei (344.5km^2)
Area – Smallest constituent unit	Kosrae (111.4km^2)
Total population	134 597
Population by constituent unit (% of total population)	Chuuk (Truk) 50%, Pohnpei 31%, Yap 12% and Kosrae 7%
Political system – federal	Constitutional Government in Free Association with the United States of America
Head of state – federal	President Leo Amy Falcam (1999), elected by the Congress to serve a 4-year term
Head of government – federal	President Leo Amy Falcam
Government structure – federal	Unicameral – Congress: Congress, 14 non-partisan members (Senators), 10 members elected by popular vote in single-seat constituencies, to serve 2-year terms. Additionally, each state elects, through proportional representation, 1 "Senator at Large" to serve a 4-year term. Note: No political parties exist.
Number and distribution of representatives in federal government – Congress	14 seats; 6 representatives from Chuuk/Truk, 4 representatives from Pohnpei, 2 representatives (each) from Yap and Kosrae
Constitutional court (highest court dealing with constitutional matters)	Supreme Court. 1 Chief Justice and not more than 5 associate Justices. Justices are appointed for life by the President, with confirmation from the Congress.
Political system of constituent units	Unicameral legislatures, directly elected to serve 4-year terms (except in the case of Chuuk/Truk, where there is a bicameral legislature comprised of a 10-member Senate and a 28-member House of Representatives).
Head of state – constituent units	Governor, elected from and by the state legislature to serve 4-year term.
Head of government – constituent units	Governor, elected from and by the state legislature to serve 4-year term.

Table II
Economic and Social Indicators

GDP	US$263 million
GDP per capita	US$2 000
Mechanisms for taxation	N/A
National debt	US$111 million
National unemployment rate	16%
Constituent unit with highest unemployment rate	N/A
Constituent unit with lowest unemployment rate	N/A
Adult literacy rate	89%
National expenditures on education as a % of GDP	N/A
Life expectancy in years	67
Doctors per population ratio (national)	57.3 doctors per 100 000 inhabitants
Doctors per population ratio in constituent units (highest)	N/A
Doctors per population ratio in constituent units (lowest)	N/A
National expenditures on health as a % of GDP	N/A

Sources

Central Intelligence Agency (CIA), *World Fact Book 2000.* CIA, www.cia.gov/cia/publications/factbook/index.html

Derbyshire, J. Denis. *Encyclopedia of World Political Systems.* Volumes I and II, New York: Sharpe Reference, M.E. Sharpe, Inc., 2000.

Elazar, Daniel J. (ed.) *Federal Systems of the World: A Handbook of Federal, Confederal and Autonomy Arrangements.* 2nd Edition. Jerusalem Institute for Federal Studies. London: Longman Group/Westgate House, 1994.

MSN Encarta Reference, "Federated States of Micronesia" www.encarta.msn.com

United Nations Population Division. Department of Economic and Social Affairs. "Population in 1999 and 2000: All Countries." *World Population Prospects: 1998 Revision, Vol. 1 comprehensive tables.* www.un.org/Depts

United Nations, *Human Development Report, 2000,* UNDP and the Human Development Report Office (HDRO), On-line source, United Nations. *Human Development Report, 2000.* www.undp.org/hdro/report.html

United Nations Statistics Division. "InfoNation." United Nations Statistical Database, 2000. www.un.org/

World Bank. *World Development Report 2000/2001: Attacking Poverty.* www.worldbank.org/poverty/wdrpoverty/report/index.htm

World Health Organisation (WHO). "Estimates of Health Personnel." www-nt.who.int/whosis/statistics

World Health Organisation (WHO). "Annex Table 8, Selected national health accounts indicators for all Member States, estimates for 1997." *World Health Report 2000.* Geneva, 2000. www-nt.who.int/whosis/statistics/menu.cfm.

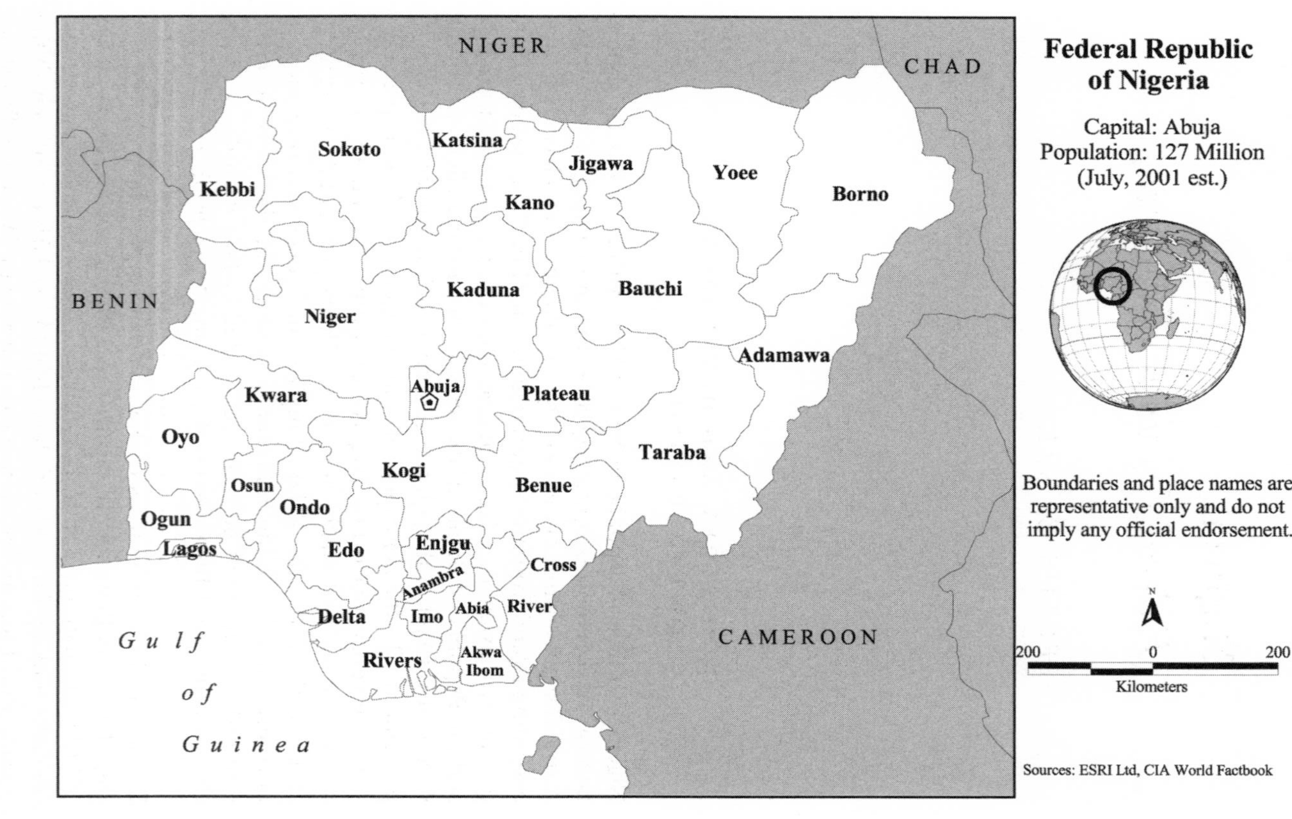
Federal Republic of Nigeria
Capital: Abuja
Population: 127 Million
(July, 2001 est.)
NIGER
CHAD
BENIN
CAMEROON
Gulf of Guinea
Sokoto
Katsina
Jigawa
Kebbi
Kano
Yoee
Borno
Kaduna
Bauchi
Niger
Adamawa
Abuja
Kwara
Plateau
Oyo
Taraba
Kogi
Osun
Benue
Ondo
Ogun
Lagos
Edo
Enjgu
Cross
Anambra
Delta
Imo
Abia
River
Rivers
Akwa Ibom
Boundaries and place names are representative only and do not imply any official endorsement.
N
200
0
200
Kilometers
Sources: ESRI Ltd, CIA World Factbook

Nigeria
(*Federal Republic of Nigeria*)

FESTUS C. NZE

1 HISTORY AND DEVELOPMENT OF FEDERALISM

Nigeria is a federal republic in West Africa. With an estimated population of 123,000,000 people, Nigeria is the most populous country in Africa. It spans an area of 925,000 square kilometres and has a landmass extending inland from the eastern end of the Gulf of Guinea deep into the western savannah. Nigeria lies between the Cameroon on the east and the Republic of Benin on the west; to the north is Niger and to the northeast is Chad. Although the country is rich in mineral resources – particularly oil – the per capita income in Nigeria is only $300 per year.

The territory that is now Nigeria was formerly made up of various states, empires, and smaller territories. The largest and the most influential of these was the Fulani Empire which extended over most of northern Nigeria in the nineteenth century. In the more forested south which could not be easily penetrated by Fulani cavalry were the Oyo (Yoruba) and Benin states. East of the Niger lived the Igbo and Ibibio communities. The earliest authentic records date European influence in the coastal areas of Nigeria from 1472, when Portuguese ships landed in Benin. Until the arrival of the Europeans, the coast was of little international political significance. Before the Portuguese sailors came looking for gold and slaves from West Africa, contact with the outside world was undertaken across the Sahara. When the British arrived in the area a century later, it marked the beginning of a new period in Nigerian history.

At the Berlin Conference of 1885 British interest along the River Niger was given official recognition. In 1900, the British Crown took over the administration of the territory from the Royal Niger Company and declared protectorates over Northern and Southern Nigeria. In 1914 a Nigerian Council of 30 Europeans and six Nigerians was inaugurated. This Council was not given any legislative or executive powers – its function was advisory in character. The constitution of 1922 (known as the Sir Hugh Clifford Constitution) expanded and reconstituted the Legislative Council. It now had 46 members, 10 of whom were elected, and made laws for the colony and the Southern Provinces. The Governor continued to legislate for the Northern Provinces.

The constitution of 1946, called the Richards Constitution after Sir Arthur Richards who masterminded it, set up a Legislative Council for the entire country and divided the country into three regions – north, west and east. The Council had 45 members, 28 of whom were Nigerians (four of the 28 were elected and the remaining 24 were nominated). The constitution also established three regional legislatures. The regional legislative bodies considered matters referred to them by the Governor and advised him accordingly.

In 1951, the constitution was changed to make necessary provisions for a Council of Ministers of 18 members (12 Nigerians and six other members who were ex-officio members from the colonial bureaucracy). The Council of Ministers was made up of equal representation from each of the three regions and the nomination of regional representatives was by the Regional Legislature. A House of Representatives was created consisting of 142 members, of this number 136 were Nigerians. The regional legislative bodies had powers to legislate on a limited number of local matters, but the laws made by them were subject to reference to the Governor. In a fundamental sense, the 'regional' concept introduced by the Richards Constitution provided the building-blocks for a federal system of government in Nigeria.

In 1954 another constitution was adopted. This constitution strengthened the federal character of Nigeria even further. It declared Nigeria a federation, recognized the limited autonomy of the regions, and continued the regional representation on the Council of Ministers. While the centre presided over foreign relations, defence, the police, etc., the regions were responsible for primary and secondary education, agriculture, public health and local government. The judiciary, the Public Service Commission and the Marketing Boards were regionalized. Responsibility for economic development, labour matters and higher education was shared between the centre and the regions. Thus, Nigeria achieved federation by disaggregation. Between 1954 and 1960, the three regions achieved self-government. On 1 October 1960, the Nigerian federation was granted full independence by Britain. Three years later, on 1 October 1963, Nigeria became a federal republic (the "First Republic"), with a republican constitution.

The Republican Constitution of 1963 gave exclusive powers to the federal government in areas such as defence, external affairs, immigration, passports, currency, railways, post and telecommunications, aviation and meteorology. In addition, the federal government could legislate on any matter outside its exclusive legislative list during any period of national emergency. The Concurrent List in the 1963 constitution contained subjects on which the federal and regional legislatures could initiate legislation, including undertaking a census, industrial development and antiques. The residual powers left to the regional legislatures contained matters such as primary and secondary school education. Regional legislatures could legislate on these items as deemed appropriate.

Nigeria is a multi-ethnic country and by the 1960s the various ethnic groups were in constant competition for control of the central government and power within their own regions. This led to demands for more regional units, and in 1963 in response to this, the Western Region was split, creating the Mid-Western Region. This marked the beginning of a process which has increased the number of constituent units in the country from three to 36.

In January 1966 there was a military coup led by Major Chukwuma Nzeogwu, an Igbo. Killed in the coup were the Prime Minister of the federation, the Premier of the Northern Region, the Premier of the Western Region, and a number of senior military officers. The plotters of the coup failed to secure Lagos and eventually Major-General Aguiyi-Ironsi, the most senior officer in the Nigerian Army, and an Igbo, took control and ordered the arrest of the coup perpetrators. Most of those involved in the coup were Igbos and because of this, it was wrongly described as an Igbo coup, even though one of the main participants was a Yoruba major. After taking control of the federal government Ironsi abolished the federal system and opted for a unitary system. This action abolished the regions.

Northern civil servants felt threatened by the highly trained and educated southerners. The north reacted. Igbos in the north were attacked and thousands were killed. In July 1967 there was a second coup staged by junior northern military officers. Many Igbo officers were killed in this coup. This redressed the balance of power in favour of the north and brought Lieutenant-Colonel Yakubu Gowon to power. From this time the Igbo leaders wanted secession, and this demand was further fuelled by a second wave of massacres of the Igbos in September 1967. Having lost confidence in the Nigerian political system, more than one million Igbos from all parts of the country fled to their homeland. Attempts at striking a compromise with the Igbos failed and on 30 May 1967, the former Eastern Region was declared an independent sovereign state of Biafra by Lieutenant-Colonel Odumegwu Ojukwu. Civil war broke out between Nigerian and Biafran forces and ended only in January 1970 with Biafra's surrender.

Despite the massive wealth generated by Nigeria's oil industry in the 1970s, political unrest continued. In 1975 General Gowon was overthrown. His successor, General Murtala Mohammed, initiated a number of political reforms, but was killed in an unsuccessful coup attempt in 1976. Lieutenant-General Olusegun Obasanjo succeeded him. In mid-1976 the military government appointed the Aguda Panel to look at alternatives for reform. The panel recommended that the federal capital be moved from Lagos to Abuja and that seven new states be created. In 1979 a general election was held. Shehu Shagari, leader of the National Party of Nigeria (NPN), won the presidential elections in 1979 (and again in 1983). General Obasanjo handed over power to Shehu Shagari and he became President of the Second Republic, inaugurated in October 1979.

The inauguration of the Second Republic was preceded by the adoption a new constitution entitled "The 1979 Constitution of the Federal Republic of Nigeria." The 1979 constitution introduced the presidential system of government, and stated that "Nigeria shall be a Federation consisting of states and Federal Capital Territory" (Section 2(2)). The 1979 constitution recognized local governments as constituting the third tier of government within the Nigerian federation, with defined functions (Schedule 4).

In December 1983, citing corruption and economic inefficiency, the military overthrew the civilian government. Another coup by military leaders occurred in 1985 and Major General Ibrahim Badamosi Babangida took over. Babangida announced that he would allow the country to return to civilian rule but then annulled the results of the June 1993 presidential elections. An interim national government (ING) was implemented by the military. (This is usually referred to in official circles in Nigeria as the "Third Republic.") The suspended 1979 constitution was to be reviewed during this period. During this time the National Assembly was revived with limited powers and there were some elections for government officials. Babingida's government was overthrown in November 1993 by General Sani Abacha who then dissolved the National Assembly and dismissed all elected officials. Abacha died suddenly in June 1998 and General Abdulsalam Abubakar became President. Abubakar announced that elections would be held, and in 1999 Nigeria elected a civilian government, headed by Olusegun Obasanjo (now a civilian). A new constitution, "Constitution of the Federal Republic of Nigeria 1999," ushered in the Fourth Republic in May 1999.

2 CONSTITUTIONAL PROVISIONS RELATING TO FEDERALISM

The 1999 constitution retained the provisions of the 1979 constitution of the Federal Republic of Nigeria, with some amendments. The constitution made specific provisions relative to the constituent units of the federation and the representation of these units in the central government.

Section 2(2) of the constitution states that Nigeria is a federation now consisting of 36 states and a Federal Capital Territory. Section 4(1) vests the legislative powers of the Federal Republic of Nigeria in a National Assembly, consisting of the Senate and the House of Representatives. The Senate consists of three Senators from each state and one from the Federal Capital Territory, Abuja. Section 49 stipulates that the House of Representatives will consist of 360 members representing constituencies of nearly equal population as far as possible, provided that no constituency falls within more than one state.

The constitution empowers the National Assembly to make laws for the peace, order and good government of the federation or any matter included in the Exclusive Legislative List. This list includes 68 items on which the federal government can legislate, including, for example: the accounts of the federal government and of the offices, courts and authorities thereof; aviation, including airports; bankruptcy and insolvency; banks, banking, bills of exchange; defence; and nuclear energy. The National Assembly can also legislate on any of the 12 items on the Concurrent Legislative List, such as the allocation of revenue, antiquities and monuments, archives, collection of taxes, electoral laws and electoral powers.

Section 6 vests state legislative powers in the House of Assembly of that state. The House of Assembly of a state has powers according to Section 7(a-b) of the constitution to make laws for the peace, order and good government of the state. Each state can make laws on any matter not included in the Exclusive Legislative List. States can also legislate on matters included in the Concurrent List as set out in the second schedule of the constitution.

Regarding fiscal arrangements, Section 162(1) of the constitution states that the federation shall maintain a special account to be called the "Federation Account" into which are paid all revenues collected by the government of the federation. The only exceptions according to the constitution, are proceeds from the personal income tax of members of the armed forces, the Nigerian Police Force and the External Affairs Ministry. One other exception is the proceeds from the personal income tax of the residents of the Federal Capital Territory, Abuja. Subject to the approval of the National Assembly, amounts standing to the credit of the Federation Account can be disbursed among the federal, state and local government councils in each state. In allocating monies from the Federation Account, certain allocation principles are used, namely population (and population density), equality of states, internal revenue generation, and land-mass. In applying these principles, Section 2 of the 1999 constitution stipulates that the "principle of derivation shall constantly be reflected" and this should be "no less than 13 per cent of the revenue accruing to the Federation Account directly from any natural resources."

The constitution makes provisions for the executive offices of President and Vice-President (Section 130(1)). All executive powers of the federation, subject to the provisions of the 1999 constitution, are vested in the President. The President is the Head of State, the Chief Executive of the Federation and Commander-in-Chief of the armed forces of the federation. In addition, Section 153(1) provides for the establishment of 14 "federal executive bodies," like the Code of Conduct Bureau, the Council of State, and the Federal Character Commission, to name a few. Section 5(2) of the constitution vests executive powers of a state in the Governor of that state.

Like most federations, Nigeria's constitution sets out procedures for the resolution of constitutional disputes. Sections 230(1) and 237(1) provide the constitutional basis for a Supreme Court and a Court of Appeal. The Supreme Court, to the exclusion of any other court, has original jurisdiction in any dispute between the federation and a state, or between states. The Supreme Court has jurisdiction, to the exclusion of any other court, to hear and determine appeals from the Court of Appeal.

The Court of Appeal has wide powers, including original and appellate jurisdiction, and it can hear appeals from the lower courts on all matters. In addition, it has, to the exclusion of any other court of law in Nigeria, original jurisdiction in matters touching on the validity of an election of any person to the office of President or Vice-President. It has jurisdiction to hear and determine any question as to whether the "term of office of the President or Vice President has ceased; or the office of the President or Vice President has become vacant."

Section 9(2) of the constitution states that an act of the National Assembly for the alteration of the constitution "not being an Act to which Section 8 of this Constitution applies shall not be passed in either House of the National Assembly unless the proposal is supported by the votes of not less than two-thirds majority of all the members of that House and approved by resolution of the Houses of Assembly of not less than two-thirds of all the states." To alter Section 8 of the constitution, which deals with fundamental human rights, the proposal must be approved by the votes of not less than a four-fifths majority of all the members of each House. It must also be approved by resolution of the Houses of Assembly of not less than two-thirds of all the states.

The "federal character" of the country is entrenched in the 1999 constitution. Thus, Section 14(3) states that the composition of the government of the federation or any of its agencies and the conduct of its affairs shall be carried out in such a manner as to reflect the federal character of Nigeria and the need to promote national unity.

3 RECENT POLITICAL DYNAMICS

An important principle of federalism is that power in a federal arrangement "should be so weighted as to maintain a fair balance between the national and regional governments."[1] Stated differently, federalism "presupposes that the national and regional governments should stand to each other in a relation of meaningful independence resting upon a balanced division of powers and resources."[2] For a long time in Nigeria these principles were breached. As a result, Nigeria masqueraded as a federation when in reality it operated as a unitary system of government. The return to civil rule, after many years of military dictatorship, has provided the right atmosphere for an unrestrained discussion of Nigerian federalism by Nigerians.

Recently, the introduction of Sharia law (the law of Islam), in the northern parts of Nigeria sparked off riots. During the riots, many people from the southeastern zone of the federation were killed and their

1 B.O. Nwabueze, *Federalism in Nigeria Under the Presidential Constitution* (London: Sweet and Maxwell, 1983), p. 2.

2 Ibid.

property destroyed. Following the crisis, the Governors of the states in this region held a summit during which the attacks on people from the southeastern states living in the north was extensively discussed. A communiqué was issued at the end of the summit in which the Governors stated that if the "persecution" continued, they would "subscribe to a future of a loose confederacy with a weak lean centre for purely administrative purposes where the various zones can pursue their individual destinies within the whole confederacy."

A similar summit was held by the Governors of the South-South zone (one of six geopolitical zones in Nigeria, consisting of Akwa Ibom, Bayelsa, Cross River, Delta, Edo and Rivers States) made up of states which produce most of the petroleum in Nigeria. The Governors pressed for a restructuring of the Nigerian federation to make the system "equitable," with greater powers given to the states. This way, in the words of the Governors, "true federalism" in Nigeria could be guaranteed. The summit concluded that non-compliance with the "tenets of true federalism" was responsible for the many problems facing the Nigerian federation today.

On 10 October 2000, the Governors of all the states in the southern part of Nigeria (i.e., South-East and South-South zones) met for the first time at an historic summit in Lagos. One of the issues discussed during the summit was the state of Nigerian federalism. The summit called for the entrenchment of "true federalism" in Nigeria, in which "the component parts should control their resources." This kind of federalism in the view of one of the southern Governors would ensure "value-added federalism" in Nigeria. At the time of writing, phrases like "true federalism," "cooperative federalism," "principled federalism," "economic federalism" and "value-added federalism," have become part of the vocabulary for discussing Nigerian federalism. Whether Nigeria will, after the constitutional review which is pending, achieve these brands of federalism remains a matter for conjecture.

4 SOURCES FOR FURTHER INFORMATION

Blitz, Franklin L., *The Politics and Administration of Nigerian Government*, London: Sweet and Maxwell, 1965.

Ekeh, P.P, P. Dele-Cole and Gebriel O. Olusanya,, *Nigeria Since Independence: The First 25 Years: Politics and Constitutions*, Volume 5, Ibadan: Heinemann Educational Book (Nigeria) Ltd., 1989.

Elaigwu, J.I., *The Nigerian Federation: Its Foundations and Future Prospects*, Abuja, Nigeria: National Council on Inter-Relations, 1994.

Federal Republic of Nigeria, *Constitution of the Federal Republic of Nigeria 1999*, Lagos, Nigeria: Federal Government Press, 1999.
Forrest, T.G., *Politics and Economic Development In Nigeria*, Boulder, Colorado: Westview Press, 1993.
Nwabueze, B.O., *Federalism in Nigeria Under the Presidential Constitution*, London: Sweet and Maxwell, 1983.
Ola R.F., *Introduction to Nigerian Public Administration*, Benin City, Edo State Nigeria: Ambik Press, n.d.

Table I
Political and Geographic Indicators

Capital city	Abuja
Number and type of constituent units	*36 States:* Abia, Adamawa, Akwa Ibom, Anambra, Bauchi, Bayelsa, Benue, Borno, Cross River, Delta, Ebonyi, Edo, Ekiti, Enugu, Gombe, Imo, Jigawa, Kaduna, Kano, Katsina, Kebbi, Kogi, Kwara, Lagos, Nassarawa, Niger, Ogun, Ondo, Osun, Oyo, Plateau, Rivers, Sokoto, Taraba, Yobe, Zamfara; *1 Territory:* Abuja Federal Capital Territory
Official language(s)	English
Area	923 768 km^2
Area – Largest constituent unit	Borno (70 898 km^2)
Area – Smallest constituent unit	Lagos (3 345 km^2)
Total population	126 635 626
Population by constituent unit (% of total population)	Lagos 6.5%, Kano 6.5%, Oyo 4.3%, Kaduna 4.3%, Katsina 4.2%, Rivers 3.5%, Benue 3.4%, Jigawa 3.2%, Akwa Ibom 3.1%, Anambra 3.0%, Bauchi 3.0%, Borno 3.0%, Imo 2.9%, Sokoto 2.7%, Abia 2.7%, Osun 2.6%, Delta 2.6%, Ogun 2.6%, Ondo 2.6%, Niger 2.6%, Adamawa 2.4%, Kebbi 2.3%, Zamfara 2.3%, Enugu 2.3%, Plateau 2.3%, Kogi 2.3%, Edo 2.2%, Cross River 2.0%, Ekiti 1.8%, Taraba 1.7%, Yobe 1.6%, Kwara 1.6%, Gombe 1.5%, Nassarawa 1.3%, Bayelsa 1.2%, Ebonyi 1.1%, Abuja Federal Capital Territory 0.4%.
Political system – federal	Republic in transition from Military to Civilian Rule
Head of state – federal	President Matthew Olusegun Fajinmi Aremu Obasanjo (1999) People's Democratic Party (PDP), directly elected to serve 4-year term.
Head of government – federal	President Matthew Olusegun Fajinmi Aremu Obasanjo, Federal Executive Council (Cabinet). The Executive Council is comprised in part with the input of the State Governors.
Government structure – federal	Bicameral – Parliament/National Assembly: *Upper House* – Senate, 109 seats. Senators are elected for a 4-year term in 36, 3-seat constituencies, and 1 in a single-seat constituency (the Federal Capital). *Lower House* – House of Representatives, 360 seats. Members are elected for a 4-year term in single-seat constituencies

Table I (continued)

Number of representatives in lower house of federal government – House of Representatives	360 seats: People's Democratic Party (PDP) 221, All People's Party (APP) 70, Alliance for Democracy (AD) 69.
Number of representatives in lower house of federal government for most populated constituent unit	Lagos: 24
Number of representatives in lower house of federal government for least populated constituent unit	Abuja Federal Capital Territory: 2
Number of representatives in upper house of federal government – Senate	109 seats: People's Democratic Party (PDP) 67, All People's Party (APP) 23, Alliance for Democracy (AD) 19
Distribution of representation in upper house of federal government – Senate	109 seats: 3 Senators from each state, 1 Senator from the Federal Capital Territory.
Constitutional court (highest court dealing with constitutional matters)	Supreme Court.
Political system of constituent units	Both Unicameral and Bicameral Legislatures.
Head of state – constituent units	Governors, appointed by the AFRC/PRC.
Head of government – constituent units	Governors and the State Executive Council. Local government is to return to a system of freely elected councilors serving on local assemblies.

Table II
Economic and Social Indicators

GDP	US$117 billion
GDP per capita	US$950
Mechanisms for taxation	The central and constituent unit governments are in the process of defining who may levy which tax, and the mechanisms that are to be used. • Corporate Taxes: levied by the central government. The general rate is 30%, however for petroleum producing companies the rate is 85%. Companies must pay an education tax of 2%. • Personal Income Tax: levied at the constituent unit level. 5 tax brackets ranging from 5%-25%, with a .05% tax bracket for low-income families. • Value-added Tax (VAT): levied at the federal level to be re-distributed at the constituent-unit level – 5%
National debt (external)	US$32 billion
National unemployment rate	28%
Constituent unit with highest unemployment rate	N/A
Constituent unit with lowest unemployment rate	N/A
Adult literacy rate	57.1%
National expenditures on education as a % of GDP	0.7%
Life expectancy in years	56
Doctors per population ratio (national)	18.5 doctors per 100 000 inhabitants
Doctors per population ratio in constituent units (highest)	N/A
Doctors per population ratio in constituent units (lowest)	N/A
National expenditures on health as a % of GDP	0.2%

Sources

Central Intelligence Agency (CIA), *World Fact Book 2000*. CIA, www.cia.gov/cia/publications/factbook/index.html

Derbyshire, J. Denis. *Encyclopedia of World Political Systems*, Volumes I and II, New York: Sharpe Reference, M.E. Sharpe, Inc, 2000.

Economist Intelligence Unit. "Country Commerce – Nigeria." *The Economist Intelligence Unit 2000*. New York: EIU, 2000.

Elazar, Daniel J. (ed.) *Federal Systems of the World: A Handbook of Federal, Confederal and Autonomy Arrangements*. 2nd Edition. Jerusalem Institute for Federal Studies. London: Longman Group/Westgate House, 1994.

International Labour Organization. “Indicators on Unemployment.” www.un.org/Depts/unsd/social/unempl.htm

International Monetary Fund (IMF). *International Financial Statistics,* Vol. LIII, No. 12, December 2000. Washington, DC: the IMF Statistics Department, 2000.

UNESCO. *World Education Report 1998: Teachers and Teaching in a Changing World,* Paris: UNESCO, 1998.

United Nations. “Deterioration in Education and Health Services.” *Africa Recovery Online.* www.un.org/ecosocdev/geninfo/afrec/vol13no1/health.htm

United Nations Statistics Division. “InfoNation.” United Nations Statistical Database, 2000. www.un.org/cgi-bin/pubs/infonatn.html

United Nations. *Human Development Report, 2000.* www.undp.org/hdro/report.html

United Nations Population Division, Department of Economic and Social Affairs, “Population in 1999 and 2000: All Countries,” *World Population Prospects: The 1998 Revision, Vol. 1 Comprehensive Tables,* UNSD On-line database, www.un.org/Depts.htm

World Bank. *World Development Report 2000/2001: Attacking Poverty.* www.worldbank.org/poverty/wdrpoverty/report/index.htm

World Health Organisation (WHO). “Estimates of Health Personnel.” www-nt.who.int/whosis/statistics

World Health Organisation (WHO). “Annex Table 8, Selected national health accounts indicators for all Member States, estimates for 1997.” *World Health Report 2000.* Geneva, 2000. www-nt.who.int/whosis/statistics/menu.cfm

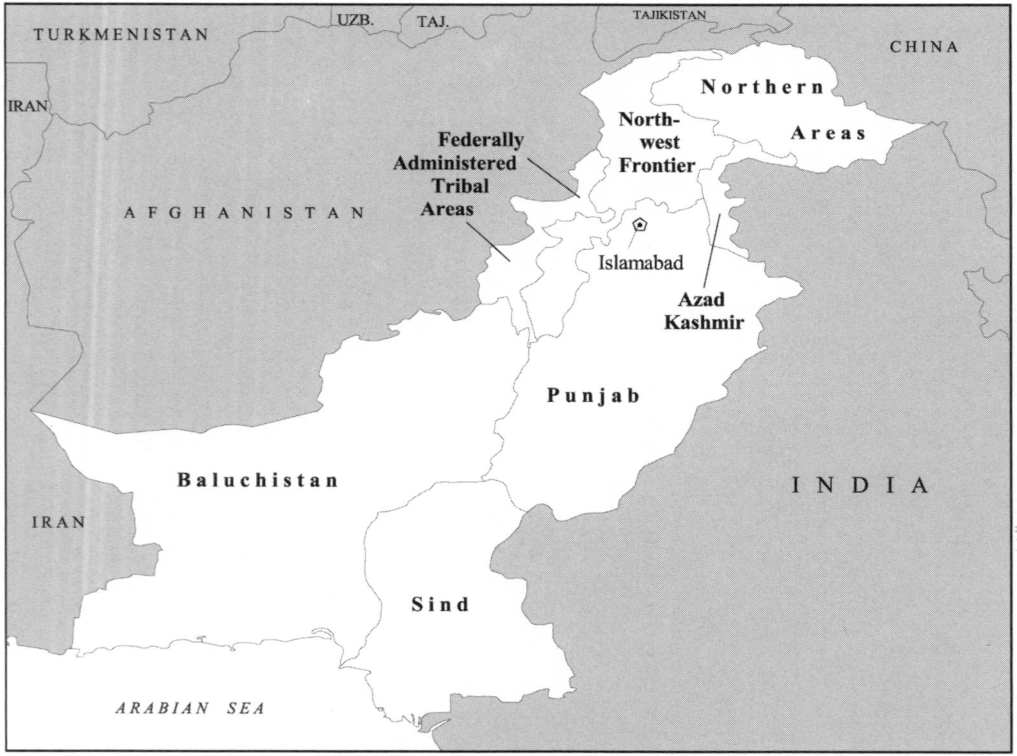

TURKMENISTAN
UZB.
TAJ.
TAJIKISTAN
CHINA
IRAN
Northern Areas
North-west Frontier
Federally Administered Tribal Areas
AFGHANISTAN
Islamabad
Azad Kashmir
Punjab
Baluchistan
IRAN
INDIA
Sind
ARABIAN SEA

Islamic Republic of Pakistan

Capital: Islamabad
Population: 145 Million (2001 est.)

Boundaries and place names are representative only and do not imply any official endorsement.

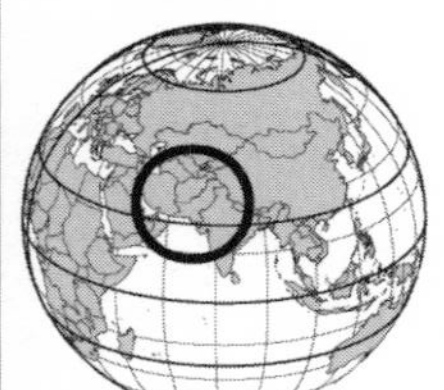

The Northern Areas and Azad Boundaries are disputed among India and China. Boundaries are shown as approximating the 1972 Line of Control defined under the Simla Agreement.

N
100 0 100 200
Kilometers

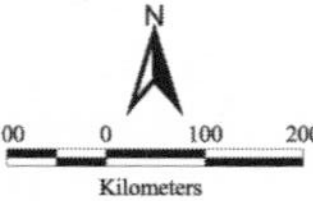

Sources: CIA World Factbook; ESRI Ltd.;Times Atlas of the World; National Geographic Society

Pakistan*

(*Islamic Republic of Pakistan*)

AISHA GHAUS-PASHA
AND KAISER BENGALI

1 HISTORY AND DEVELOPMENT OF FEDERALISM

Pakistan sits at a strategic location, situated as it is at the conjuncture between the Middle East and Asia. Its neighbours are India to the east, the central Asian republics and China to the north, Afghanistan and Iran to the West, and the Persian Gulf and the Indian Ocean to the south. The country has an area of 879,902 km^2 and a population of over 140 million people.

The territory comprising Pakistan today encompasses the Indus Valley civilization and, thus, is an entity with ancient roots. For most of the past 4,000–5,000 years the Indus Valley has remained a distinct socio-political entity, but it has interacted closely with central Asia to the west and the Gangetic valley to the east. For three periods, amounting to only about 500 years – during the Mauryan (323–180 BC), the Mughal (1526–1857) and the British (1857–1947) reigns – the region was brought under a single centralized rule.

While 1857 represents the formal end of the Mughal Empire, it had been in decline for some years and had already lost control over several states, which acquired an independent or quasi-independent status for between 50 and 100 years before being incorporated into

* The authors are grateful for the excellent research assistance provided by Ms Zainab Dossa in preparing this paper.

British rule. British rule was extended to these territories with the occupation of Sindh in 1843 and Punjab in 1849. Most of what is now the North West Frontier Province (NWFP) was part of Punjab and fell to the British in 1849. British control over the mountain tribes, however, was secured only after the Third Afghan War in 1878, and northern Balochistan was brought under British rule as late as 1876.

Pakistan emerged as an independent state on 14 August 1947. It was comprised of two wings, separated by over 1,500 kilometres of Indian territory. The western wing consisted of the Muslim majority provinces NWFP and Sindh, the Muslim majority western part of Punjab province, and the territories comprising Balochistan. The eastern wing consisted of the Muslim majority eastern part of Bengal province and the Muslim majority district of Sylhet in Assam province. It included all princely states falling into the jurisdiction of the new country. The states of Hyderabad and Junagadh were populated largely by Hindus, but were ruled by Muslim kings. They acceded to Pakistan, but were occupied and annexed by India. The accession of the Muslim majority state of Jammu and Kashmir is a matter of dispute between Pakistan and India.[1]

The nature of the struggle to create Pakistan plus its geography and demographic composition have always demanded and continue to demand a federal solution. This, unfortunately, has not been the case. The failure to adhere to federal principles of organization and governance has caused a great amount of instability and strife, including a civil war which resulted in the separation of its eastern wing.

The creation of Pakistan was the culmination of the political struggle of the Muslims of British India. The movement proceeded in two phases. The first phase revolved around ensuring Muslim rights in a united India through separate electorates, provincial autonomy and adequate representation at the centre. The phase ended with the Government of India Act of 1935. The attitude of the Indian National Congress set in motion the second phase of the struggle and Muslims began to question the very nature of federalism as a solution to India's

---

1 The state of Jammu and Kashmir had a Muslim majority, but was ruled by a Hindu king. At the time Pakistan and India were moving towards independence, the people of Jammu and Kashmir were engaged in a revolt against the tyrannical king. They sought Pakistan's support in their struggle, while the king sought Indian support. Within days of achieving independence, India and Pakistan sent their forces and a war ensued. India took the matter to the United Nations, which ruled that the matter of accession to Pakistan or India should be decided by a plebiscite to ascertain the views of the people.

chronic inter-communal problems. Muslims began to see themselves as a separate nation in order to determine their own cultural, social, legal and political system. It was against this background that the Lahore Resolution of 1940, now known as the Pakistan Resolution, called for a separate state of the Muslim majority provinces of British India. The failure of federalism led to the partition of British India and was accompanied by civil strife on a vast scale.

The essence of federalism was embedded in the Lahore Resolution. In the elections of 1946, the provinces of Punjab and Bengal voted the Muslim League – the party leading the struggle for Pakistan – to power by a landslide. The Sindh Provincial Assembly voted to join Pakistan and NWFP and Sylhet voted for Pakistan through a referendum. All princely states within these territories acceded to Pakistan. The Kalat State Assembly initially voted for independence, but was subsequently persuaded to become part of Pakistan. Pakistan, thus, represents a case where the regional units set about establishing a federation, rather than a central authority granting provincial autonomy to its various components.

Pakistan was made up of two parts separated by over 1,500 kilometres. Federalism was, thus, ordained by the very nature of the country's geography. The separation of the eastern wing (now Bangladesh) in 1970 left Pakistan as a linguistically and ethnically diverse, but geographically homogenous, entity. Today, the country is comprised of four provinces – Punjab, Sindh, NWFP and Balochistan. The demographic composition of the country is skewed, with Punjab comprising about 56 per cent of the population and the rest of the provinces *combined* comprising about 44 per cent. In a democracy based on majoritarian rule, this means that in any issue where the country is polarized along provincial lines, three provinces combined will comprise the minority and the one majority province will carry the vote. The interprovincial demographic composition, thus, rules out a unitary state or even a quasi-federal state.

2 CONSTITUTIONAL PROVISIONS RELATING TO FEDERALISM

The first steps towards federalism were initiated by the British government with a package of constitutional reforms embodied in the Government of India Act of 1935. The Act established a highly centralized federal – or quasi-federal – system, controlled and managed by the colonial bureaucracy and with sovereignty resting in the British Crown. The "federal" structure was constructed for an India that was neither free nor independent and was administered by a colonial power which was compelled to give some autonomy to its subjects but was extremely suspicious of them.

Through the Independence Act of 1947, Pakistan adopted the Government of India Act of 1935, along with certain amendments, as its interim constitution. Pakistan, thus, inherited its constitutional provisions from the British. Despite the federal structure and provisions enshrined in the constitution, however, Pakistan is basically a unitary and centralized state.

Post-independence Pakistan has effectively retained the quasi-federal character of the state. The central bureaucracy continues to be in control. According to the Preamble (paragraph 2) of the constitution of the Islamic Republic of Pakistan, sovereignty rests with Allah, to be exercised by the representatives of the people. *De facto,* however, sovereignty has come to rest with the military establishment. The repeated abrogation or suspension of constitutional rule and the imposition of direct military rule, the fact that the 1962 constitution was imposed by the military, and the fact that the amendments in the 1973 constitution[2] were dictated by the military bear testimony to this fact.

There are four elements in the constitution which relate to federal provisions and deal with the division of powers and functions between the centre and the provinces. They are: (1) the Upper House of Parliament (the Senate) (Article 59); (2) the legislative lists (Federal and Concurrent Lists) (Article 70(4)); (3) the Council of Common Interests (Article 153); and (4) the National Finance Commission (Article 160).

The constitution provides for a bicameral federal Parliament, comprised of two Houses (Articles 50, 51, 59). The National Assembly is the Lower House and represents the country as a whole. The Senate is the Upper House and represents the constituent units. National Assembly members are directly elected by adult franchise in a first-

2 The military regime of General Zia ul Haq agreed to transfer power to Parliament (elected under military supervision and control and on a non-party basis) on the condition that it enact the Eighth Amendment to the constitution. The amendment procedures specified in Part XI, Articles 238–239, were duly followed, albeit under duress. The Constitution (Eighth Amendment) Act, 1985, altered over 65 clauses of the constitution and provided immunity to all executive actions of the military regime over 1977–1985, validated all laws promulgated during this period, and granted the President the power to dissolve Parliament and dismiss elected governments at will. The laws validated include some of the most retrogressive religious laws, with adverse impacts on women and religious minorities. The power to dismiss ensured that no elected government managed to complete its term.

past-the-post electoral system. Seats in the National Assembly are allocated on the basis of population to each province, the Federally Administered Tribal Areas (FATA), and the Federal Capital. The Senate consists of 63 members who are elected by the provincial Assemblies. All provinces are equally represented in the Senate. The four provincial Assemblies elect 14 members each, the National Assembly members from FATA elect five members, and two members are selected to represent the Federal Capital. The entire National Assembly acts as an electoral college for electing the members of the Senate from the Islamabad capital territory.

The constitution divides power amongst the executive, legislature and the judiciary. But, as in most federal states, it is the principle of division of powers among the constituent units that has remained a significant issue in the constitutional development of Pakistan. The division of powers between the federation and the provinces is largely determined by two legislative lists: the Federal List and the Concurrent List. The federal Parliament can enact laws on the 67 subjects in the Federal Legislative List, and both the federal Parliament and the provincial Assemblies can enact laws on the 47 subjects in the Concurrent Legislative List. Subjects outside of these two lists are considered residuary subjects and comprise the exclusive domain of the provinces. Aside from the provisions which grant residuary power to the provinces, and allow each province to have its own legislature, virtually all other clauses ensure the hegemony of the government at the centre over the governments in the provinces.

The functions of the federal government extend deep into the workings of the provincial governments (Articles 128, 145–152). The federal government can appoint the Governor for each province, approve the dissolution of the provincial Assembly by the Governor, approve the appointment of a caretaker provincial government by the Governor, confer functions on a province with respect to any matter to which the executive authority of the central government extends, and give directions to a province. Furthermore, the federal government can appoint and transfer the judges of the High Court, the highest provincial court and second to the Supreme Court at the federal level (Article 193). The federal government is entitled to appoint the provincial chief secretary and the provincial police chief, thus ensuring control of the provincial civil service and the provincial police. Federal governments have routinely used the powers outlined in Article 112(2) to dissolve provincial assemblies and dismiss provincial governments.

Although the composition of the Senate means that the provinces are represented in the federal government, the Senate's role is undermined by Article 73, which denies it any role pertaining to money bills, including the federal budget. It is excluded from any role in decisions relating to the borrowing of money, or the giving of any guarantee, by the federal government, even though one or more of the provincial governments may be incurring the liability of any such loan. The Senate is also excluded from any role relating to the audit of the accounts of the federal as well provincial governments.

With reference to the legislative lists, although the provinces have no jurisdiction over the Federal List, the federal Parliament has power in terms of provincial jurisdiction (Article 142(b)). Where there is a conflict between the federal Parliament and a provincial Assembly on a subject relating to the Concurrent List, the writ of the former prevails (Article 143). Thus, the Concurrent List has in actual fact become part of the Federal List. The centre has appropriated even a subject like local government, which is on neither the Federal nor Concurrent Lists and which, according to Article 142(c), lies within the exclusive jurisdiction of provincial governments. In effect, this means that the provincial governments have merely promulgated the relevant Local Bodies Ordinances as per the draft received from the federal government. Functionally, thus, the country is a federation in name but centralized in substance.

There are two important institutions which are outlined in the constitution and should be mentioned here. The first, the Council of Common Interests (CCI), is outlined in Article 153. It is a quasi-executive body comprising of the chief executives of the centre and the provinces or their designated representatives. It is charged with the duty of formulating and regulating policies in relation to the subjects enumerated in Part II of the Federal Legislative List (railways, mineral oil – as opposed to palm, castor seed or sunflower oil, which are used to prepare cooking oil – and natural gas) and one item of the Concurrent List (electricity). The Council has been given the mandate to take up matters of dispute between the provinces, and between the centre and any one or more provinces. However, the measure of the potency of the Council can be gauged from the fact that it met only once during a whole decade of constitutional rule from 1988 to 1999.

The second institution is the National Finance Commission (NFC) (Article 160), which is a joint federal-provincial body with the mandate to deal with the distribution of federal tax receipts. This is an important provision, given that the taxation structure shows a clear federal bias and federal taxes account for more than 90 per cent of all taxes put together. This feature has remained more or less the same since the constitutional reforms of 1935. The fact that the centre holds a virtual monopoly over the purse strings imposes a major constraint on the operation of the already weak and feeble federal provisions.

Article 70 (4(43–53)) of the constitution entitles the federal government to collect nine categories of taxes, duties and fees. They include taxes on: non-agricultural income; corporate income; sales and purchase of imported, exported, produced and manufactured goods consumed within the country; capital value of assets; mineral oil, natural gas and materials used in the generation of nuclear energy; and transportation of goods and passengers carried by railway, sea or air, and their fares and freights. The federal jurisdiction also includes duties on imports and exports, excise, estate and property, and succession to property, as well as fees in respect of any of the above.

The major tax revenue sources of the provinces are a stamp duty and a motor vehicle tax. A few years ago, the federal government abolished the district export tax and the municipal *octroi* (an entry tax on goods). The federal government did not have constitutional jurisdiction to impose a decision relating to the residuary domain of the provinces, but such blatant interference is a common feature of Pakistan's federal-provincial relations. In practical terms, local bodies now have virtually no source of income and have to rely almost exclusively on federal and provincial grants to meet their expenses, including payment of salaries.

Transfers from the federal divisible pool account for the major share of the revenues of provincial governments. These transfers are made according to the award given by the National Finance Commission every five years, with the last award having been given in 1996. The federal divisible pool consists of all taxes levied by the federal government, federal excise duties, and export duty on cotton. The federal government retains 62.5% of the net proceeds, arrived at after deducting 5% as collection charge, and the remaining 37.5% is distributed among the four provinces. The basis of distribution continues to be a one-point criterion: population. Thus, according to the population census of 1991, the provincial shares were arrived at as follows: Punjab 57.88%, Sindh 23.28%, NWFP 13.54% and Balochistan 5.30%.

In addition to the federal divisible pool, provinces also receive net profits, royalty, excise duty and a development surcharge, as the case may be, on account of generation/extraction of hydro power, crude oil, and natural gas on the basis of location of production. Two provinces – NWFP and Balochistan – also receive special grants on account of their relative underdevelopment.

3 RECENT POLITICAL DYNAMICS

Pakistan has made several attempts since independence to construct a federal model suited to the various components of Pakistani society.

The first constitution was enacted in 1956, but was abrogated by the military in 1958. The military imposed a constitution in 1962, which was again abrogated by yet another military general in 1969. Finally, the first directly elected Parliament enacted a constitution in 1973 which has continued to command the writ of the people, despite its suspension by the military, first in 1977 and again in 1999, and despite the distorting amendments incorporated by military rulers. A common feature of all the constitutions is that they embed the quasi-federal model of governance promulgated in the Government of India Act of 1935.

Currently, Pakistan is under military rule and the constitution remains suspended.[3] This is not an unknown occurrence in Pakistan. The country was also under military rule from 1958 to 1962, from 1969 to 1973, and from 1977 to 1988. For the intervening periods – 1947 to 1958, 1962 to 1969, 1973 to 1977, and from 1988 to 1999 – the country was under some sort of constitutional rule. All the constitutions provided for a federal form of government, at least in name. Military rule, however, amounts to a de facto reversion to a unitary form of government. This is the state of affairs today.

In addition to the issues relating to military rule, revenue and finance have also been a contentious issue in recent years. In 1997 federal transfers to the provinces declined by about 5 per cent, causing severe difficulties for the provincial financial managers. This decline is related to lower federal tax receipts on account of lower tax collection and a decline in the level of economic activity. This is indicated by the fact that in the fiscal year 1998–99, actual tax revenues were lower by one-third relative to the revenues projected by the National Finance Commission.

The reason for the lower than anticipated revenue receipts is thought to be the wide-ranging series of reforms introduced by the federal government according to the terms of the structural adjustment program recommended by the International Monetary Fund (IMF) beginning in 1997. The reforms included massive tax and tariff rate cuts, which caused a decline in sales tax and import duty receipts. The anticipated supply-side stimulus to the economy and the expected increase in the level of economic activity did not materialize and depressed revenue receipts further. Lower federal tax revenue receipts

3 At face value, the military took over because the Prime Minister dismissed the Army Chief of Staff and the military took an affront at this act of civilian impudence. The underlying reason was the growing rift between civilian and military powers over the sharing of the shrinking economic and fiscal resource base.

translated into a smaller size of the federal divisible pool and, consequently, into lower transfers to the provinces.

The important point here is that the provinces have born the brunt of the economic reforms and the resulting decline in federal revenue receipts, given the substantial reliance of the provinces on federal transfers. Yet they had little say in decisions regarding the implementation of the economic reforms by the federal government. The Senate remains excluded from any economic policy-making because of the constitutional provision excluding its involvement in financial matters.

The continued violation of federal principles has severely strained the national political fabric of the country.[4] The failure in 1970 to arrive at an entente between Islamabad and Dhaka – the federal and the eastern wing capitals, respectively – caused the latter to break away[5] in a 21-month civil war, costing thousands of lives, and leading to an invasion by India. In today's Pakistan too, there are equally serious strains, reflected in the chronic disputes with respect to the allocation of federal revenues and development funds, the composition of federal jobs in the civil service and the military, and the distribution of water from the Indus River system.

Ensuring that Pakistan is a truly federal state will require three major amendments to the constitution. One, it would require the abolition of the Concurrent List so as to substantially enhance the residuary jurisdiction of the provinces. Two, it would require the granting of equal

---

4 As early as 1955, the central government forced the merger of all the provinces in the western wing to form the province of West Pakistan. There were now only two provinces of West Pakistan and East Pakistan, each comprising 44 and 56 percent of the population, respectively. However, the constitution enacted in 1956 forced East Pakistan to accept parity with West Pakistan with regard to representation in the unicameral Parliament, thereby destroying the essence of federalism.

5 In 1969, the West Pakistan province was dissolved under pressure from East Pakistan and the erstwhile provinces in the western wing were restored. General elections were held in 1970 on the basis of one-man-one-vote; thereby acknowledging the 56 per cent majority of the province of East Pakistan. The leader of the Awami League of East Pakistan, Shaikh Mujib ur Rahman, won all but two seats in East Pakistan and, consequently, a majority in the new Parliament. However, the military refused to hand over power, cancelled the scheduled parliamentary session, and launched a brutal crackdown on the Awami League. The crackdown in March 1970 led to a civil war, which ended in December 1970 with the Indian invasion and declaration of the independent state of Bangladesh.

legislative powers, including jurisdiction over money bills, to the Senate and the National Assembly. And three, it would require a redistribution of fiscal powers and the provincialization of certain tax bases. Above all, however, it is imperative for the constitution to remain in force as the Basic Law of the land and for the military to remain subservient to the constitutional government.

4 SOURCES FOR FURTHER INFORMATION

Ahmed, Syed Jaffer, *Federalism in Pakistan: A Constitutional Study*, Karachi: Pakistan Study Centre, University of Karachi, 1990.

Ahsan, Aitzaz, *The Indus Saga and the Making of Pakistan*, Karachi: Oxford University Press, 1996

Constitution of the Islamic Republic of Pakistan, Islamabad: Government of Pakistan, 1973.

Imtiazi, I.A., "Organization Structure and Working of the Federal and Provincial Government in Pakistan," in Jameelur Rahman Khan (ed.), *Government and Administration in Pakistan*, Islamabad: O & M Division, Government of Pakistan, 1987.

Social Democratic Movement, *Charter of Reforms*, Islamabad, 1997.

Table I
Political and Geographic Indicators

Capital city	Islamabad
Number and type of constituent units	*4 Provinces:* Balochistan, North-West Frontier, Punjab, and Sindh *1 Territory:* Federally Administered Tribal Areas (broken down into 6 areas) *1 Capital Territory:* Federal Capital Territory of Islamabad
Official language(s)	Urdu
Area	803 940 km^2 (Note: The Pakistani-administered portion of the disputed Jammu and Kashmir region includes Azad Kashmir and the Northern Areas.)
Area – Largest constituent unit	Balochistan (347 190 km^2)
Area – Smallest constituent unit	North-West Frontier (74 521 km^2) (smallest province), Federal Capital Territory of Islamabad (907 km^2)
Total population	144, 616, 639 (2001 est.)
Population by constituent unit (% of total population)	Punjab 56%, Sindh 23%, North-West Frontier 13%, Balochistan 5%, Federally Administered Tribal Areas 3%, Islamabad Capital Territory 0.04%
Political system – federal	Federal Republic
Head of state – federal	President Mohammad Rafiq Tarar (1997). Elected for a 5-year term by an electoral college. The President must be a Muslim. Note: The President has been allowed to remain in office since the 1999 military coup, but plays a ceremonial role only.
Head of government – federal	Following a military coup 12 October 1999, General Pervez Musharraf suspended Parliament and the constitution and assumed the title of Chief Executive. He appointed an 8-member National Security Council to function as Pakistan's governing body. In May 2000 the Supreme Court validated the 1999 coup and set a 3-year limit to Chief Executive Musharraf's term. According to the constitution (now in suspension) following legislative elections, the leader of the majority party or majority coalition is elected Prime Minister by the National Assembly to serve a 5-year term.

Table I (continued)

Government structure – federal	Bicameral – Majlis-e-Shoora (Parliament): *Upper House* – Senate, 63 seats. Senators are indirectly elected by the Provincial Assemblies to serve 6-year terms. One-third of Senators are up for election every 2 years. *Lower House* – National Assembly, 217 seats. 207 members are directly elected for 5-year terms, and 10 seats are reserved for non-Muslim minorities. Note: Parliament was dissolved in 1999.
Number of representatives in lower house of federal government – National Assembly	Parliament was dissolved in 1999.
Number of representatives in lower house of federal government for most populated constituent unit	See above.
Number of representatives in lower house of federal government for least populated constituent unit	See above.
Number of representatives in upper house of federal government – Senate	63 seats
Distribution of representation in upper house of federal government – Senate	63 seats: 14 Senators are elected by each Provincial Assembly, 5 from the Federally Administered Tribal Areas and 2 from the Federal Capital Territory of Islamabad. Note: Parliament was dissolved in 1999.
Constitutional court (highest court dealing with constitutional matters)	Supreme Court. Justices are appointed by the President.
Political system of constituent units	Provincial Assemblies
Head of state – constituent units	Governors and Councils of Ministers (Cabinet), drawn from elected Provincial Assemblies.
Head of government – constituent units	Governor and Councils of Ministers (Cabinet). Provincial Assemblies are directly elected. There are separate seats designated for Muslims and Non-Muslims in each Provincial Assembly and each community elects their own representatives. The Tribal areas are administered directly by the federal government.

Table II
Economic and Social Indicators

GDP	US$282 billion
GDP per capita	US$2 000
Mechanisms for taxation	Constituent units are increasingly gaining revenue through the levying of taxes. In 2000, the federal government introduced the National Tax Number (NTN) System to integrate all federal taxes. • Corporate Income Taxes: Public Companies 30%, Private Companies 35%, Banks 55%. • Personal Income Taxes: 7 tax brackets ranging from 5% to 35%. • Zakat (Wealth) Tax 7.6%. • Capital Value Tax (CVT) 8.5%. Applies to transactions for real estate, cars and the purchase of international airline tickets. • Goods and Services Tax (GST): 15% broadly applied. • Zila Taxes: charged on the movement of goods throughout the country. • General excise taxes on beverages, tobacco, petroleum, etc.
National debt (external)	US$38 billion
National unemployment rate	5.9%
Constituent unit with highest unemployment rate	North-West Frontier: 11.89%
Constituent unit with lowest unemployment rate	Sindh: 3.19%
Adult literacy rate	42.7%
National expenditures on education as a % of GDP	2.3%
Life expectancy in years	63.1
Doctors per population ratio (national)	57 doctors per 100,000 inhabitants
Doctors per population ratio in constituent units (highest)	Sindh: 121.8 doctors per 100 000 inhabitants
Doctors per population ratio in constituent units (lowest)	Balochistan: 43.7 doctors per 100 000 inhabitants
National expenditures on health as a % of GDP	4.0%

Sources

Central Intelligence Agency (CIA), *World Fact Book 2000*. CIA, www.cia.gov/cia/publications/factbook/index.html

Derbyshire, J. Denis. *Encyclopedia of World Political Systems*, Volumes I and II, New York: Sharpe Reference, M.E. Sharpe, Inc., 2000.

Economist Intelligence Unit. *"Country Commerce – Pakistan." The Economist Intelligence Unit 2000*. New York: EIU, 2000.

Elazar, Daniel J. (ed.) *Federal Systems of the World: A Handbook of Federal, Confederal and Autonomy Arrangements.* 2nd Edition. Jerusalem Institute for Federal Studies. London: Longman Group/Westgate House, 1994.

Federal Bureau of Statistics. *Labour Force Survey 1999–2000.* Ministry of Finance and Economic Affairs Division. Government of Pakistan.

Government of Pakistan. Statistical Division. www.statpak.gov.pk

International Monetary Fund (IMF). *International Financial Statistics,* Vol. LIII, No. 12, December 2000. Washington, DC: the IMF Statistics Department, 2000.

UNESCO. *World Education Report 1998: Teachers and Teaching in a Changing World.* Paris: UNESCO, 1998.

United Nations. *Human Development Report, 2000.* www.undp.org/hdro/report.html

United Nations Population Division. Department of Economic and Social Affairs. "Population in 1999 and 2000: All Countries." *World Population Prospects: 1998 Revision, Vol. 1 comprehensive tables.* www.un.org/Depts

United Nations Statistics Division. "InfoNation." United Nations Statistical Database, 2000. www.un.org/

Watts, Ronald L, *Comparing Federal Systems,* 2nd Edition, School of Policy Studies, Queen's University, Montreal/Kingston: McGill-Queen's University Press, 1999.

World Bank. *World Development Report 2000/2001: Attacking Poverty.* www.worldbank.org/poverty/wdrpoverty/report/index.htm

World Health Organisation (WHO). *World Health Report 2000.* Geneva, Switzerland, 2000. www-nt.who.int/whosis/statistics/menu.cfm

Russian Federation
(Overview)
Capital: Moscow
Population: 146 Million
(2001 est.)
Boundaries and place names are
representative only and do not
imply any official endorsement.
N
1000 0 1000 2000 3000
kilometers
Sources: ESRI Ltd.; CIA World Factbook;
Times Atlas of the World
ARCTIC OCEAN
BARENTS SEA
BERING SEA
NORTH PACIFIC OCEAN
EASTERN RUSSIA
NORTH-CENTRAL RUSSIA
WESTERN RUSSIA
Moscow
FINLAND
UKRAINE
KAZAKHSTAN
MONGOLIA
CHINA
N.KOREA
S.KOREA
JAPAN
TURKEY
IRAQ
IRAN
PAKISTAN
INDIA
EGYPT
SAUDI ARABIA
SUDAN

Russian Federation (North-Central)

Russian Federation (Eastern)
ARCTIC OCEAN
Zemlya Frantsa-Iosifa
Novaya Zemlya
Kara Sea
Severnaya Zemlya
Laptev Sea
Novosibirskiye O-Va
East Siberian Sea
Vrangelya
U. S. A.
Bering Sea
CENTRAL RUSSIA
Taymyrskiy (Dolgano-Nenetskiy) AOk.
Evenkiyskiy AOk.
R. Sakha (Yakutiya)
Chukotskiy AOk.
Koryakskiy AOk.
Magadanskaya o.
Kamchatskaya o.
Sea of Okhotsk
Kuril Islands
Krasnoyarskiy k.
Irkutskaya o.
Khabarovskiy k.
Sakhalinskaya o.
R. Tyva
R. Buryatiya
Chitinskaya o.
Amurskaya o.
MONGOLIA
CHINA
JAPAN
PACIFIC OCEAN
R. - Republic
A.Ok. - Autonomous Okrug
O. - Oblast
K. - kray
1. Ust'-Ordynskiy Buryatskiy AOk.
2. Aginskiy Buryatskiy AOk.
3. Yevreyskaya A.Oblast
4. Primorskiy k.
5. R. Khakasiya
N
500 0 500
kilometers
Sources: ESRI Ltd.; CIA World Factbook

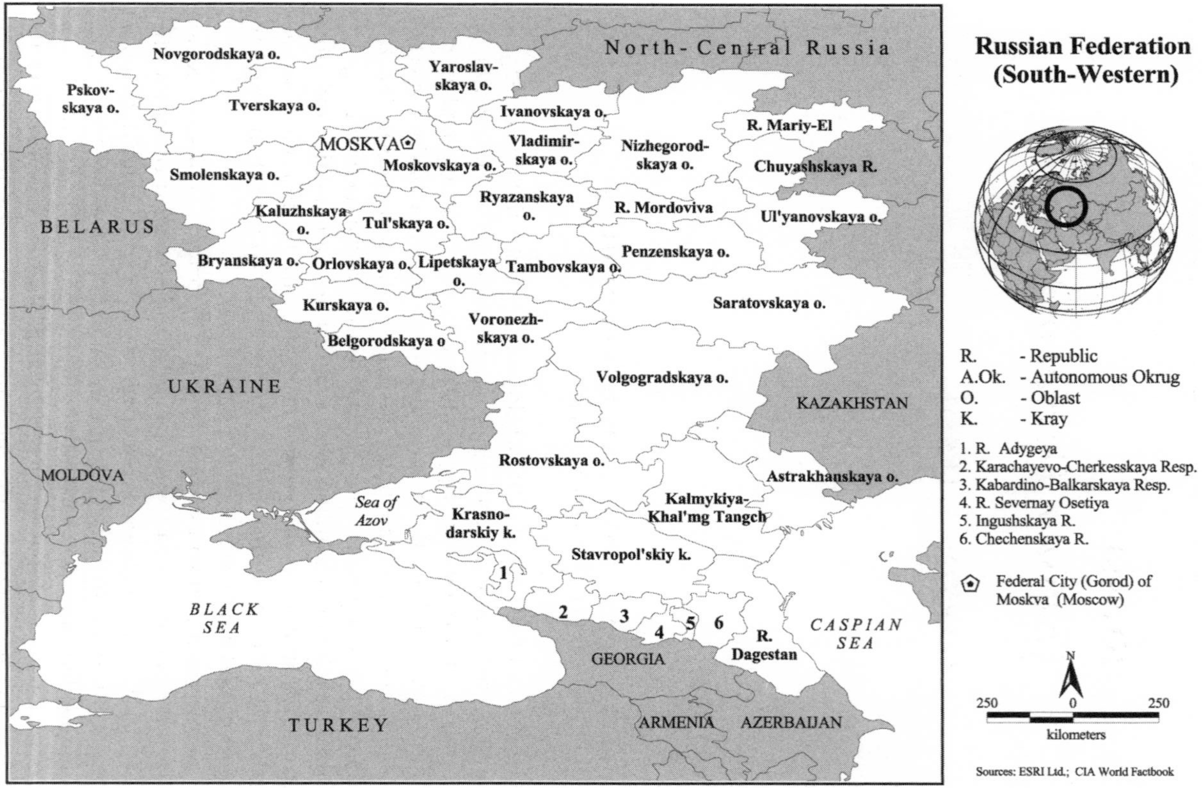

North-Central Russia
Novgorodskaya o.
Pskov-skaya o.
Tverskaya o.
Yaroslav-skaya o.
Ivanovskaya o.
R. Mariy-El
MOSKVA
Moskovskaya o.
Vladimir-skaya o.
Nizhegorod-skaya o.
Chuyashskaya R.
Smolenskaya o.
Kaluzhskaya o.
Tul'skaya o.
Ryazanskaya o.
R. Mordoviva
Ul'yanovskaya o.
BELARUS
Bryanskaya o.
Orlovskaya o.
Lipetskaya o.
Tambovskaya o.
Penzenskaya o.
Kurskaya o.
Voronezh-skaya o.
Saratovskaya o.
Belgorodskaya o
UKRAINE
Volgogradskaya o.
KAZAKHSTAN
Rostovskaya o.
MOLDOVA
Astrakhanskaya o.
Sea of Azov
Krasno-darskiy k.
Kalmykiya-Khal'mg Tangch
Stavropol'skiy k.
1
2
3
4
5
6
R. Dagestan
BLACK SEA
CASPIAN SEA
GEORGIA
TURKEY
ARMENIA
AZERBAIJAN

Russian Federation (South-Western)

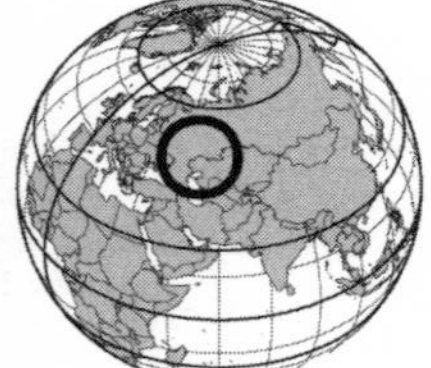

R. - Republic
A.Ok. - Autonomous Okrug
O. - Oblast
K. - Kray

1. R. Adygeya
2. Karachayevo-Cherkesskaya Resp.
3. Kabardino-Balkarskaya Resp.
4. R. Severnay Osetiya
5. Ingushskaya R.
6. Chechenskaya R.

Federal City (Gorod) of Moskva (Moscow)

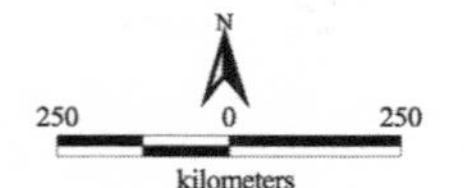

Sources: ESRI Ltd.; CIA World Factbook

Russia
(*Russian Federation*)

GARY N. WILSON

1 HISTORY AND DEVELOPMENT OF FEDERALISM

The Russian Federation is the world's largest federal state (17,075,000 km^2). A vast country, spanning two continents and 11 time zones, it is home to approximately 145 million people. With a population of more than 8 million, Russia's capital, Moscow, is one of the largest cities in Europe. Although ethnic Russians constitute a majority (80%) of the country's population and Russian is the official state language, the Russian Federation contains over 100 distinct nationalities and ethnic groups. A number of these national groups are territorially based and have the political authority to preserve and promote their respective cultures and languages.

Russia has a rich and storied history. The origins of modern Russia, however, can be traced to the fifteenth and sixteenth centuries when the various principalities of European Russia came under the domination of Moscow. In the centuries to follow, the Russian tsars (kings) spearheaded the eastern and southern expansion of the Russian Empire. The development of the modern Russian state structure (bureaucracy, military) began in the late seventeenth century, during the reign of Peter the Great, and continued under subsequent members of the Romanov dynasty. By the early nineteenth century, Russia was considered a major European power and one of several empires that dominated the global political scene.

During the second half of the nineteenth century, however, Russia experienced a series of radical political and societal transformations, and military setbacks. The cumulative pressures of modernization, industrialization and urbanization, coupled with popular demands for a relaxation of the autocratic system of government and the harsh conditions of World War I would ultimately lead to the overthrow of the tsarist regime and the creation of the Soviet Union.

Under the leadership of Vladimir Lenin, the Bolshevik (majority) faction of the Russian Social Democratic Labour Party seized power in October 1917 and proceeded to consolidate its hold over the vast territory that comprised the former Russian Empire. Following the civil war of 1917–1921, Bolshevik-inspired communist factions came to power in many of the regions of the former empire and joined to form the Union of Soviet Socialist Republics (USSR).

The Soviet Union's federal status was theoretically enshrined in the 1936 constitution. In practice, however, the federal model that existed during the Soviet period was a façade that veiled the highly centralized political and economic system. Although the various republics that comprised the federation had limited autonomy over cultural and some administrative matters, the overwhelming dominance of centralized structures such as the Communist Party of the Soviet Union (CPSU) and the systems of economic planning and administration effectively nullified the country's federal character.

In the late 1980s and early 1990s, nationalist tensions, emanating from the constituent members of the federation (the Union-Republics), initiated the downfall and disintegration of the Soviet Union. Soviet leader Mikhail Gorbachev's policy of *glasnost* (openness) encouraged nationalist groups and politicians in the republics to press for greater autonomy and even independence from Moscow. At the same time, the rigid, centralized institutional apparatus began to give way under the weight of reforms (*perestroika*/reconstruction) that exposed the structural weaknesses of the Soviet regime. The Soviet Union eventually disintegrated in the wake of a failed hard-line coup attempt against Gorbachev in August of 1991.

Russia's first post-Soviet President, Boris Yeltsin, was actually elected President of the Soviet Union's largest Union-Republic, the Russian Soviet Federated Socialist Republic (RSFSR), in June 1991, prior to the collapse of the Soviet Union. Yeltsin was instrumental in opposing the above-mentioned coup attempt and became President of the independent Russian Federation on 25 December 1991 when the Soviet Union ceased to exist.

Over the past decade, one of the most pressing issues facing the Russian Federation's democratically elected leaders has been the task of constructing a stable and integrated federal state. In many respects, the choice of a federal system of government was the only acceptable option at the outset of the transition. The Russian Federation inherited the complicated regional structure of former RSFSR. In the late 1980s, many of the RSFSR's regions had become involved in the broader struggle for autonomy taking place at the Union-Republic level and both Gorbachev and Yeltsin offered concessions of autonomy to the RSFSR's diverse regions in an attempt to bolster their own respective authority. In the early post-Soviet period, many feared that the Russian Federation would suffer the same fate as its Soviet predecessor. The territorial integrity of the Russian Federation, however, was preserved when all but two of the former constituent units of the RSFSR signed the Federation Treaty in March 1992. Only the republics of Tatarstan and Chechnya refused to sign this treaty. Tatarstan later negotiated its formal entry into the Russian Federation on the basis of a bilateral treaty in 1994. The Chechen government, on the other hand, has never fully recognized its incorporation into the Russian Federation and remains a painful thorn in the side of this emerging federal state.

Since the collapse of the Soviet Union, the Russian Federation has undergone a period of intense political, economic and social transition. Steps have been taken to reform the economy and create a viable civil society and party system, but the legacies of 75 years of communist rule and the negative impact of transition on society remain major impediments to the construction of viable democratic and market institutions. In many respects, the uncontrolled decentralization of power to the federal units that has occurred during the post-Soviet period has contributed to the political and economic confusion facing the country by weakening the federal government and undermining its ability to coordinate the national reform program.

The Soviet Union played a major role in world politics for much of the twentieth century. After the forced agricultural collectivization and industrialization of the country in the 1930s and its major role in the defeat of Nazi Germany in World War II – events that exacted an enormous human toll on the country's population – the Soviet Union became a feared and respected global superpower, and was granted one of five permanent seats on the United Nations Security Council (which Russia retains). In recent years, however, Russia's international status has eroded. Thus, according to the latest United Nations' Human Development Index (2001), the Russian Federation ranks 62nd out of 174 countries surveyed. Its GDP per capita is US$7,473 and life expectancy (at birth) is 66.1 years. Despite these setbacks, Russia has tremendous potential, especially in terms of its highly literate population and its enormous natural resource wealth (oil, gas, minerals, precious metals and timber).

2 CONSTITUTIONAL PROVISIONS RELATING TO FEDERALISM

The political system outlined in the Russian constitution (adopted on 12 December 1993 in a national referendum) is a unique hybrid of a presidential and parliamentary republic. The President appoints the Cabinet ministers, including the Prime Minister (formally referred to as the Chairman of the Government), but these ministers must also retain the confidence of the Parliament to govern. Cabinet ministers, however, do not have to be elected members of the legislature, as in the Westminster parliamentary model.

As the head of state, the President plays a very important role in the exercise of power. He or she has the authority to issue presidential decrees. These decrees have the force of law, but may not violate existing laws and can be superseded by laws passed by the Parliament. Under certain conditions, the President can also dissolve Parliament.

The organization of the federation is outlined in Chapter 3, Articles 65 to 79 of the constitution and in earlier articles on the principles of the constitutional system (Chapter 1). The federation is comprised of 89 constituent units: 21 republics, 49 *oblasts* (regions), six *krais* (territories), 10 autonomous *okrugs* (districts), one autonomous *oblast* and 2 federal cities (Moscow and St. Petersburg (Article 65)). The republics are situated at the top of the federal hierarchy. Their status is based on the fact that they contain significant non-Russian ethnic populations (Tatars in Tatarstan, Bashkirs in Bashkortostan, etc.). Oblasts and krais are non-ethnically-based regions and generally have less autonomy than republics. Autonomous okrugs have a rather ambiguous position within the federal hierarchy. These ethnically-based districts are the homelands of Russia's indigenous aboriginal populations. Constitutionally speaking, they are considered both separate members of the federation and parts of the oblasts and krais in which they are located; a situation that has led to numerous jurisdictional disputes over the past decade.

These constituent units are represented at the federal level of government in the Federation Council, the upper chamber of Russia's bicameral Parliament. Each constituent unit has two representatives in the Federation Council. Territorial representation also exists in the State Duma, the lower chamber of the Parliament. Half of the 450 Duma deputies are elected from constituencies across Russia, while the other half are elected on the basis of proportional representation.

The constitution contains both symmetrical and asymmetrical federal features. Article 5(1) of the constitution states that all the constituent units are equal members of the federation. Similarly, Article 5(4) says that all the constituent units are equal in their relations with federal bodies of state authority. Article 5(2), on the other hand, states that only republics shall have their own *constitutions* and laws. The other constituent units are entitled to their own *statutes* and laws. Article 68(2) gives the republics the right to establish their own state languages, in addition to Russian (usually the language of the titular, non-Russian nationality).

It is important to note that there are a number of non-constitutional treaties and agreements that strengthen the asymmetrical character of the federal framework. The above-mentioned Federation Treaty, for example, is actually a series of three different treaties between the federal government and the republics, the oblasts and krais, and the autonomous okrugs, oblast and federal cities. The republican version, for example, gives the republics greater autonomy than the other regions. Since 1994, many individual constituent units have signed special bilateral treaties with the federal government. In many cases such treaties provide the members in question with more autonomy in relation to the federal government than members that have not signed bilateral treaties. The constitutional status of the bilateral treaties, however, is still unclear. Although Article 11(3) of the constitution does state that the demarcation of authority between the Russian Federation and the constituent units can be realized through the constitution and other agreements on the demarcation of subjects of jurisdiction and authority, the provisions of the bilateral treaties (and the Federation Treaty, for that matter) are not included in the constitution. As such, the federal government has consistently viewed these treaties as sub-constitutional documents.

According to Article 15 of the constitution, laws passed by the constituent units are not allowed to contravene the federal constitution. While such a provision may exist in theory, one of the most controversial disputes of the post-Soviet period has been the "war of laws" between the federal government and the constituent members. The Russian Ministry of Justice recently revealed that upwards of 50,000 regional legislative acts do not comply with the federal constitution or federal laws.

The division of powers between the federal government and the constituent units is outlined in Articles 71 to 73 of the constitution. Article 71 lists the federal areas of jurisdiction. These include such matters as the regulation and protection of human rights and freedoms, the financial and banking system, federal energy systems, foreign policy, international relations and external economic relations, defence and security, and the organization of the court system. Areas of concurrent or joint jurisdiction between the federal government and the constituent units are outlined in Section 72. Among the more important matters of concurrent jurisdiction are questions relating to the possession, use and disposal of lands, minerals, water and other natural resources, education, science and public health. Article 73 states that any areas of government not outlined in Articles 71 and 72 fall under the jurisdiction of the constituent units.

The most controversial aspect of this division of powers is the ambiguous nature of the concept of concurrent jurisdiction. As a result of frequent political stalemates at the federal level, many regions have acted unilaterally in areas of concurrent jurisdiction. Consequently, their legislation often contradicts the federal constitution or subsequently adopted federal laws. The constitution itself is very unclear about how the federal government and the constituent units are supposed to coordinate their legislative activities.

The constitution, however, does outline two particular mechanisms for resolving disputes between the federal government and the constituent units or between the constituent units. Article 85 states that the President may use reconciliatory procedures to settle such disputes. If no agreement is reached, the President may send the case to the appropriate court. The President also has the power to suspend executive acts of the constituent units if they contradict the federal constitution, federal laws, the international obligations of the Russian Federation or constitute a breach of human or civil rights and freedoms.

The 1993 constitution makes provision for a Constitutional Court. The main responsibilities of the Court are to rule on the constitutionality of the laws and other normative acts that are adopted by the legislative and executive branches of government. Another important function is to delineate and interpret the division of powers between the federal government and the constituent unit governments. The constitution states that the 19 judges that sit on the Court must be nominated by the President and confirmed by the Federation Council. As a result of political infighting following the ratification of the constitution in December 1993, the Court was suspended until March 1995.[1] Since its re-instatement, it has worked to establish its autonomy and authority in relation to the other branches of government

1 A Russian Constitutional Court was initially established in July 1991, prior to the breakup of the Soviet Union. At that time, the Soviet Parliament – the Congress of People's Deputies – elected the Court's 15 judges. In the period between 1991 and 1993, the Court was involved in a number of political disputes, culminating in the conflict between President Yeltsin and the Russian Parliament in 1993. After proposing a resolution to the crisis that was accepted by both sides, the head of the Court, Valerii Zorkin, sided with the parliamentary cause and later condemned Yeltsin's decision to suspend the Parliament. Yeltsin responded by suspending the Court until a new constitution could be ratified.

and the constituent units. The Court has made a number of important decisions on the constitutionality of regional laws, but at times has met stiff opposition from the governments of the constituent units.

Proposals for amending the federal constitution may be submitted by a variety of institutions including the President, the Federation Council, the State Duma, the government of the Russian Federation, and the legislative bodies of the constituent units. Proposals for amending Chapters 1, 2 and 9 of the federal constitution (Principles of the Constitutional System, Human and Civil Rights and Freedoms, Constitutional Amendments and Revision of the Constitution) must first receive the support of three-fifths of the Federation Council and the State Duma. The proposal is then submitted to a specially convened constitutional assembly, which confirms the existing constitution or drafts a new document. The new document passes if it receives two-thirds support of the constitutional assembly or more than one-half of eligible voters in a nationwide referendum. Changes to Chapters 3 to 8 of the federal constitution, on the other hand, require the approval of at least two-thirds of the constituent units.

Russia's system of fiscal federalism is a complicated web of established and negotiated taxes, revenue sources and regional assistance funds. Since 1991 considerable revenues and expenditures have been transferred from the federal government to the constituent units, and at present, their share of tax revenues is about 50 per cent of total revenues. In theory, the units are supposed to remit a negotiated portion of their tax revenues to the federal government. Value added (VAT) and corporate profit taxes and excises are shared between the federal government and the constituent units at negotiated rates, while personal income tax is given entirely to the constituent units. The State Tax Service, which is responsible for collecting taxes, has been administratively subordinated to the federal government since 1991. In reality, however, tax collectors are often loyal to and dependent on the administrations of the constituent units.

Of the 89 federal units that comprise the Russian Federation, less than 10 can be classified as donor or "have" regions (meaning they remit more revenues to the federal government than they receive in subsidies). The importance of negotiation as a tool for determining revenue flows means that politics plays a critical role in the fiscal system. In the past, the federal government has used fiscal federalism to shore up support for the regime or provide incentives for accepting political deals. Often, politically powerful constituent units pay less taxes than they are supposed to, while the weaker units bear the brunt of the taxation burden. More importantly, the financial difficulties experienced by the Russian state during the turbulent economic transition period has meant that many constituent units have not received the fiscal subsidies to which they are entitled.

3 RECENT POLITICAL DYNAMICS

Buoyed by rising world resource prices and a devaluation of the rouble following the financial crisis of August 1998, the Russian economy has recently enjoyed a healthy rate of growth. A tremendous amount of work needs to be done, however, before Russia completes its transition to a market economy. Most importantly, the government must put in place a stable legal environment for business activities and foreign investment. Without such a framework, the Russian economy will struggle to compete, combat corruption and maintain growth.

Russia's fledgling democratic system has also undergone some serious challenges in recent years. Despite the fact that the country's democratic institutional framework has a constitutional foundation and elections at all levels of government have been held on a regular basis, Russia's civil society remains weak, and electoral contests, especially at the regional level, continue to be tainted by irregularities. The mass media are still largely controlled by the state or by individuals with close links to the current government and independent journalists who are critical of the government and its policies have faced prosecution, persecution and harassment.

On 31 December 1999, Boris Yeltsin stepped down as President of the Russian Federation, setting in motion a new phase in the country's post-Soviet political history. Vladimir Putin, a relatively unknown former member of the security services from St. Petersburg, became Acting President. Putin, who had been appointed Prime Minister by Yeltsin in 1999, was elected President in March 2000.

Since coming to power, Putin has embarked on an ambitious series of reforms to Russia's federal structure. His primary goals are to strengthen the authority of the federal government in relation to the constituent units and harmonize federal and regional legislation. First, he authorized the creation of seven federal *okrugy* (districts) – Central, North Caucasus, Northwest, Volga, Urals, Siberia and Far East. Each district encompasses approximately 10 to 12 geographically concentrated constituent units. The districts are headed by federally-appointed presidential representatives who are primarily responsible for overseeing the activities of the constituent units and making sure that regional laws comply with their federal counterparts and the federal constitution.

The second major change in the federal structure since Putin came to power is the introduction of a new law that affects the composition of the Federation Council. As noted above, each member of the federation has had two representatives on the Federation Council: the respective heads of the regional legislative and executive branches. By the start of 2002, however, the constituent units will be required to have "full-time" Senators, one appointed by the head of the executive branch and the other elected by the legislature. This arrangement is expected to make the Federation Council more efficient and effective.

In order to placate the regional heads who no longer have a seat in the federal Parliament as a result of the changes to the Federation Council, Putin has created two new federal consultative bodies: the State Council and its Presidium. The State Council includes all the Governors and Presidents of the constituent units and meets quarterly at the request of the Russian President to discuss particular issues. The Presidium is comprised of seven members of the State Council (determined on a rotating basis) and meets on a monthly basis. These new bodies give the regional leaders an opportunity to express their opinions on major initiatives undertaken by the federal government.

In addition to pursuing reforms at the federal level, the Putin government has also waged a bloody war to keep the Republic of Chechnya in the Russian Federation. For most of the post-Soviet period, the separatist-minded government of Chechnya, an ethnic republic in the Caucasus region of southern Russia, has sought independence from the Russian Federation. The first Chechen War (1994–1996) resulted in a fragile cease-fire and federal promises of a negotiated settlement. Violent raids into neighbouring republics by Chechen separatist guerrillas and a series of bombing incidents (which the Russian government blamed on Chechen terrorists) in 1999, however, once again brought conflict to this troubled region.

One of the greatest challenges facing Russia in the future is the task of redefining its position with its regional neighbours and the West. Through organizations such as the Commonwealth of Independent States (CIS) – a confederation of independent states that were formerly members of the Soviet Union – Russia has encouraged closer co-operation among the countries of the area. The recent political union with Belarus, and Russia's involvement in the Caspian region and Central Asia suggest that it will continue to play a dominant role as a regional power.

Russia's position on the world stage, however, has waned since the Soviet period. Its relationship with the West and, in particular the United States, is fraught with ambiguity. Russia depends on Western economic assistance for its financial wellbeing and is seeking to integrate itself into the Western financial system through organizations such as the Group of Eight (G8) and the World Trade Organization

(WTO). (It is not yet a member of the WTO.) At the same time, Russia wants to assert its political autonomy and authority in an increasingly monopolar world and has strongly opposed such Western initiatives as the 1999 NATO bombing of Yugoslavia and NATO's expansion into Eastern Europe.

4 SOURCES FOR FURTHER INFORMATION

Alexseev, Mikhail (ed.), *Centre-Periphery Conflict in Post-Soviet Russia: A Federation Imperiled*, New York, NY: St. Martin's Press, 1999.

Hanson, Philip and Michael Bradshaw (eds), *Regional Economic Change in Russia*, Cheltenham, UK: Edward Elgar, 2000.

Kelly, Donald R., *Politics in Russia and the Successor States*, Fort Worth, TX: Harcourt Brace College Publishers, 1999.

Nicholson, Martin, *Towards a Russia of the Regions*, London: International Institute for Strategic Studies – Adelphi Paper, 1999.

Remington, Thomas F., *Politics in Russia*, New York, NY: Longman, 1999.

Westlung, Hans, Alexander Granberg and Folke Snickars, *Regional Development in Russia: Past Policies and Future Prospects*, Cheltenham, UK: Edward Elgar, 2000.

http://www.gov.ru

http://www.government.gov.ru

http://www.regions.ru

Table I
Political and Geographic Indicators

Capital city	Moscow
Number and type of constituent units	89 constituent units: *21 Republics:* Adygeya, Altai, Bashkortostan, Buryatiya, Chechnya, Chuvash, Daghestan, Ingushetia, Kabardino-Balkarian, Kalmykia, Karachayevo-Cherkessian, Karelia, Khakassia, Komi, Mariy El, Mordovia, Sakha (Yakutia), North Ossetia-Alania, Tatarstan, Tyva, Udmurtian; *49 Oblasts (Provinces):* Amur, Arkhangelsk, Astrakhan, Belgorod, Bryansk, Chelyabinsk, Chita, Irkutsk, Ivanovo, Kaliningrad, Kaluga, Kamchatka, Kemerovo, Kirov, Kostroma, Kurgan, Kursk, Leningrad, Lipetsk, Magadan, Moscow, Murmansk, Nizhni Novgorod, Novgorod, Novosibirsk, Omsk, Orenburg, Oryol, Penza, Perm, Pskov, Rostov, Ryazan, Sakhalin, Samara, Saratov, Smolensk, Sverdlovsk, Tambov, Tomsk, Tula, Tver, Tyumen, Ulyanovsk, Vladimir, Volgograd, Vologda, Voronezh, Yaroslavl; *10 Autonomous Okrugs (Districts):* Aginsk Buryat, Chukotka, Evenk, Khanty-Mansi, Komi-Permyak, Koryak, Nenets, Taimyr (Dolgano-Nenets), Ust-Ordyn Buryat, Yamalo-Nenets; *6 Krays (Territories):* Altai, Khabarovsk, Krasnodar, Krasnoyarsk, Primorie, Stavropol; *2 Cities of Federal Significance:* Moscow, St. Petersburg; *1 Jewish Autonomous Oblast.* Note: Russia has also recently been divided into *11 Economic Regions (and the Kaliningrad Region)*: The Central-Chernozyem Economic Region, The Central Economic Region, The Eastern Siberian Economic Region, The Far East Economic Region, The Kaliningrad Region, The North Economic Region, The Northern Caucasus Economic Region, The North-Western Economic Region, The Povolzhye Economic Region, The Ural Economic Region, The Volga-Vyatka Economic Region, The Western Siberian Economic Region. However, these divisions are based on economic grouping only, and do not represent administrative constituent units.
Official language(s)	Russian
Area	17 075 400 km^2
Area – Largest constituent unit	Sakha (Yakutia) (3 103 200 km^2)
Area – Smallest constituent unit	St. Petersburg (600 km^2)
Total population	145 924 900

Table I (continued)

Population by constituent unit (% of total population)	Moscow (city) 5.8%, Moscow (oblast) 4.4%, Krasnodar 3.4%, St. Petersburg 3.2%, Sverdlovsk 3.2%, Rostov 3.0%, Bashkortostan 2.8%, Tartarstan 2.6%Nizhni Novgorod 2.5%, Chelyabinsk 2.5%, Samara 2.2%, Tyumen 2.2%, Krasnoyarsk 2.1%, Kemerovo 2.0%, Perm 2.0%, Irkutsk 1.9 %, Novosibirsk 1.9%, Saratov 1.8%, Volgograd 1.8%, Altai 1.8%, Stavropol 1.8%, Voronezh 1.7%, Orenburg 1.5%, Primorie 1.5%, Omsk 1.5%, Daghestan 1.4 %, Tula 1.2%, Leningrad 1.1%, Udmurtian 1.1%, Tver 1.1%, Vladimir 1.1%, Kirov 1.1%, Penza 1.1%, Khabarovsk 1.0%, Arkhangelsk 1.0%, Belgorod 1.0%, Ulyanovsk 1.0%, Bryansk 1.0%, Yaroslavl 1.0%, Khanty-Mansi 0.9%, Chuvash 0.9%, Vologda 0.9%, Kursk 0.9%, Ryazan 0.9%, Tambov 0.9%, Chita 0.9%, Lipetsk 0.8%, Ivanovo 0.8%, Komi 0.8%, Smolensk 0.8%, Kurgan 0.7%, Kaluga 0.7%, Tomsk 0.7%, Buryatiya 0.7%, Murmansk 0.7%, Astakhan 0.7%, Sakha 0.7%, Amur 0.7%, Mordovia 0.6%, Kaliningrad 0.6%, Oryol 0.6%, Chechnya 0.5%, Kostroma 0.5%, Kabardino-Balkarian 0.5%, Karelia 0.5%, Mariy El 0.5%, Novgorod 0.5%, Pskov 0.5%, North-Ossetia Alania 0.4%, Sakhalin 0.4%, Khakassia 0.4%, Yamalo-Nenets 0.3%, Adygeya 0.3 %, Karachayevo-Cherkessian 0.3%, Kamchatka 0.3%, Kalmykia 0.2%, Ingushetia 0.2%, Tyva 0.2%, Magadan 0.2%, Jewish Autonomous Oblast 0.1%, Altai 0.1%, Komi-Permyak 0.1%. Ust-Ordyn Buryat 0.1%, Chukotka 0.06%, Aginsk Buryat 0.05%, Nenets 0.03%, Taimyr (Dolgano-Nenets) 0.03%, Koryak 0.02%, Evenk 0.01%
Political system - federal	Federation – with characteristics of both the Parliamentary and Republic systems.
Head of state - federal	President Vladimir Putin (2000). Directly elected to serve a 4-year term. President appoints the Prime Minister and Cabinet, subject to the approval of Parliament.
Head of government - federal	Prime Minister (Chairman of the Government) Mikhail Kasyanov (2000) appointed by the President to serve a 4-year term. Both Prime Minister and Cabinet Ministers do not have to be elected members of Parliament, but they must have the confidence of Parliament.

Table I (continued)

Government structure - federal	Bicameral - Federalnoye Sobraniye (Federal Assembly): *Upper House* - Soviet Federatsii (Federation Council), 178 seats. 2 delegates come from each constituent unit. One of the members is the locally elected executive head. The other is the head of the regional legislature, elected by regional deputies. These seats are filled ex officio by the top executive and legislative officials in each of the 89 federal administrative units. The term of the members is not limited, but is dependent upon their terms at the local government level. Note: changes to the structure of the Federation Council are scheduled for 2002. *Lower House* - Gosudarstvennaya Duma (State Duma), 450 seats. Members are elected through 2 types of mandates: 225 seats are divided among those parties that have clear a 5% vote barrier and the other 225 are elected by a party-list vote, whereby the seats are distributed through single member constituencies on a "first-past-the-post" basis. All members are elected by direct popular vote to serve 4-year terms.
Number of representatives in lower house of federal government – State Duma	450 Seats: Kommunisticheskaya Partiya Rossiiskoi Federatsii - KPRF (Communist Party of the Russian Federation) 113, Mezhregional'noye Dvizhenie Yedinstvo - MEDVED (Inter-Regional Movement Unity) 72 *Otechestvo Vsya Rossiya (Fatherland All Russia):* Comprised of Otechestvo (Fatherland) and Vsya Rossiya (All Russia) (OVR) 66, Soyuz Pravikh Sil - SPS (Union of Right Forces) 29 *LDPR/Blok Zhirinovskogo (Zhironovsky Blok:* Comprised of the Electoral organization of the Liberalno-Demokraticheskaya Partiya Rossii – LDPR-BR (Liberal Democratic Party of Russia) 17 Yabloko (Apple) 21, Partiya Pensionerov - PP (Pensioners' Party) 1, Nash dom Rossiya - NDR (Our Home is Russia) 7, Kongress russkikh obshchin i Dvizhenie Y.Boldureva – KRO-DYB (Congress of Russian Communities and Movement of Y. Boldurev) 1, Obsherossiskoe Politcheskoye Dvizhenie v podderzhku armii - DPA (All-Russian Political Movement in Support of the Army) 2, Russkaya Sotsialisticheskaya Partiya - RSP (Russian Socialist Party) 1, non-partisans 106
Number of representatives in lower house of federal government for most populated constituent unit	Moscow (city): 15

Table I (continued)

Number of representatives in lower house of federal government for least populated constituent unit	Evenk: 2
Number of representatives in upper house of federal government – Federation Council	178 Seats: Kommunisticheskaya Partiya Rossiiskoi Federatsii – KPRF (Communist Party of the Russian Federation) 12, Russia's Choice 7, Independent 142, others 9
Distribution of representation in upper house of federal government – Federation Council	2 delegates come from each constituent unit. One of the members is the locally elected executive head. The other is the head of the regional legislature, elected by regional deputies.
Constitutional court (highest court dealing with constitutional matters)	Constitutional Court. Judges are nominated by the President and confirmed by the Federation Council.
Political system of constituent units	Unicameral - Legislative body can be called Duma, Legislative Assembly or State Council, depending upon the constituent unit. Most have presidential systems of power directly elected by the people. In the case of the Udmurtia Republic, a Parliament is the governing body. On average, the legislative bodies are elected for 2-5 year terms. The first elections were held in 1993, with the legislative bodies serving for 2-year terms. The Okrugy (districts) are each headed by a federally appointed presidential representative who is primarily responsible for overseeing the activities of the federal institutions and making sure that regional laws comply with their federal counterparts and the federal constitution.
Head of state and Head of government - constituent units	Governor, President or Chairman of the Government, directly elected for 4-5 year terms. The exception is Daghestan, where the supreme leader is elected by a special representative assembly.

Table II
Economic and Social Indicators

GDP	US$1.12 trillion
GDP per capita	US$7 700
Mechanisms for taxation	There is a single tax body, the State Tax Service, which collects all taxes and redistributes these revenues. • Personal Income Tax: The rates cover 3 brackets and range from 12-30%. A revision of the tax system will eventually lead to a flat income tax of 13% and the adoption of a Social Security tax. Central Government and Constituent Units share the VAT, Corporate Tax (approximately 30%), and excise taxes, with the rates being negotiated between each unit and the Central Government. Less than 10 constituent units are classified as "donor" or "have" regions in the Russian Federation.
National debt (external)	US$163 billion
National unemployment rate	10.5% (plus considerable underemployment)
Constituent unit with highest unemployment rate	N/A (Note: The regions with the highest recorded unemployment are in the Far East, Siberia, the North, and the Northern Caucasian regions.)
Constituent unit with lowest unemployment rate	N/A
Adult literacy rate	98%
National expenditures on education as a % of GDP	3.0%
Life expectancy in years	67.19
Doctors per population ratio (national)	421 doctors per 100,000 inhabitants
Doctors per population ratio in constituent units (highest)	N/A
Doctors per population ratio in constituent units (lowest)	N/A
National expenditures on health as a % of GDP	2.2%

Sources

Central Bank of Russian Federation. www.cbr.ru/english

Central Intelligence Agency (CIA), *World Fact Book 2000*. CIA, www.cia.gov/cia/publications/factbook/index.html

Curtis, Glenn E. "Russia, A Country Study." *The Area Handbook Study*. Washington, DC: Federal Research Division, Library of Congress, 1996.

Economist Intelligence Unit. "Country Commerce - Russia." *The Economist Intelligence Unit 2000*. New York: EIU, 2000.

Elazar, Daniel J. (ed.) *Federal Systems of the World: A Handbook of Federal, Confederal and Autonomy Arrangements.* 2nd Edition. Jerusalem Institute for Federal Studies. London: Longman Group/Westgate House, 1994.

International Monetary Fund (IMF). "Table 10. Russian Federation: Unemployment Rate by Regions (ILO methodology), 1993-1997" and "Table 36. Russian Federation: Main Characteristics of 10 Top and 10 Bottom to Regional GDP." *Russian Federation: Recent Economic Developments 1999.* IMF Staff Country Report No.99/1000 www.imf.org/external/country/RUS/index.html

Organization for Security and Co-operation in Europe (OSCE). *Russian Federation: Elections to the State Duma, 19 December 1999 - Final Report.* OSCE and the Office for Democratic Institutions and Human Rights, Warsaw. www.osce.org/odihr/

PRS Group, "Country Overview - Russian Federation," *Political Risk Yearbook Database,* ISSN: 1054-6243, Released November 1999.

Russian Federation Ministry of Finance Official Website. www.minfin.ru/

State Committee of the Russian Federation on Statistics. "Estimation of number de-facto and de-jure population on the Subjects of Russian Federation on January 1, 2000." www.gks.ru

State Committee of the Russian Federation on Statistics. *Current Statistical Survey - A Quarterly Issue.* www.gks.ru/eng/

UNESCO. *World Education Report 1998: Teachers and Teaching in a Changing World.* Paris: UNESCO, 1998.

United Nations. *Human Development Report, 2000.* UNDP and the Human Development Report Office (HDRO). www.undp.org/hdro/report.html

United Nations Statistics Division. "InfoNation." www.un.org/

Watts, Ronald L. *Comparing Federal Systems,* 2nd Edition. School of Policy Studies. Montreal/Kingston: McGill-Queen's University Press, 1999.

World Bank Country Office of the Russian Federation, "Characteristics of the Economic Regions of the Russian Federation." www.worldbank.org.ru/eng

World Bank. *World Development Report 2000/2001: Attacking Poverty.* www.worldbank.org/poverty/wdrpoverty/report/index.htm

World Health Organisation (WHO), *Highlights on Health in the Russian Federation,* Produced by the WHO Regional Office for Europe, Denmark, On-line source, www.who.dk

World Health Organisation (WHO). *World Health Report 2000,* Geneva, Switzerland, 2000. www-nt.who.int/whosis/statistics/menu.cfm.

Federation of St. Kitts and Nevis

Capital: Basseterre
Population: 39,000

Boundaries and place names are representative only and do not imply any official endorsement.

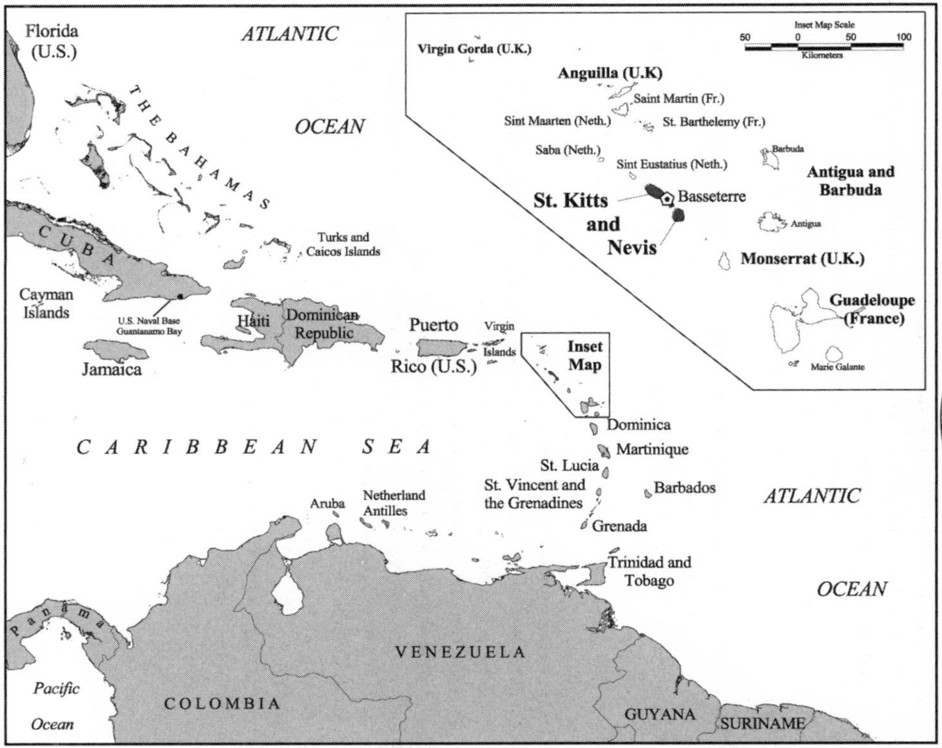

Sources: CIA World Factbook; ESRI Ltd.; Times Atlas of the Oceans; UN Cartographic Dept.

St. Kitts and Nevis
(*Federation of St. Kitts and Nevis*)

ANN L. GRIFFITHS

1 HISTORY AND DEVELOPMENT OF FEDERALISM

The islands of St. Kitts (168 km^2) and Nevis (93 km^2) are located in the Lesser Antilles chain of islands in the Eastern Caribbean. They are separated by a channel of just over three kilometres.

The islands were historically inhabited first by the Sibonay who arrived approximately 2,000 years ago from Central America. They were followed by the Arawak and then the Caribs who both came north from South America. The first European to record the presence of the islands was Christopher Columbus in November 1493. He named the islands San Cristobel (St. Christopher), after his patron saint, and Santa Maria de las Nieves (Nevis) because the island's mountains reminded him of the snow-capped peaks in Europe. Although the Spanish claimed the islands, they never settled on them, and in 1623 St. Christopher became the first British territory in the West Indies. Nevis was colonized by the British in 1628. French settlers arrived on the islands in the 1620s, and the two settler colonies made the native Caribs their common enemy, ensuring that the Caribs were either killed or fled the island.

Until the 1713 Treaty of Utrecht when the French gave up their claims to Saint Christophe, there was intermittent fighting between the British and French settlers on the islands. After the French left, the colony officially became St. Christopher (shortened to St. Kitts). The Treaty of Versailles (1783) made the islands wholly British.

Recognizing the importance of regional cooperation and unity, the British always favoured governing their island colonies jointly so there is a history of federal or cooperative arrangements in the eastern Caribbean. Beginning in 1671 St. Kitts and Nevis were joined with other islands in the area in the Leeward Caribbee Islands Government. In an attempt at federation, the Leeward Islands (consisting of Antigua, Montserrat and St. Kitts-Nevis-Anguilla) were made a single administrative unit in 1871 and St. Kitts-Nevis-Anguilla were joined as a unit in the Leeward Islands Federation in 1882. Under this arrangement the colonies shared a Governor and a Supreme Court (shared also with the Windward Islands), but had separate legislatures. This arrangement lasted until 1956 when St. Kitts-Nevis-Anguilla became a separate colony.

Britain continued to push for a larger federation of its colonies in the West Indies. In January 1958 the Federation of the West Indies came into existence after more than 10 years of talks. The federation consisted of 10 British colonies, each made up of a number of islands in the Caribbean. The 10 colonies were Barbados, Jamaica, the Leeward Islands (Antigua, Montserrat, St. Kitts-Nevis-Anguilla), Trinidad and Tobago, the Windward Islands (Dominica, Grenada, St. Lucia, St. Vincent). (The Cayman Islands and Turks and Caicos Islands became part of the federation somewhat later.) The federation was headed by a Governor-General who took office 3 January 1958. Federal elections were held in March 1958 and were won by the West Indies Federal Labour Party which formed the government, provisionally located in Port of Spain, Trinidad.

In 1959 a conference was held in London to discuss constitutional reform in the Leeward Islands. It was agreed that from 1 January 1960, the islands would become autonomous units within the Federation of the West Indies. The British government agreed to appoint an administrator in each territory as head of government and abolish the position of Governor of the Leeward Islands.

The federation quickly ran into conflict – indeed, it appeared unable to agree even on where the capital would be permanently located. Inter-governmental committees were established in 1960 to discuss problems relating to the establishment of a customs union, the federal power of taxation, and the basis for political representation in the federal government. Jamaica was increasingly unhappy with its membership in the federation – in particular with the proposals to establish a customs union and increase the federal government's power to levy taxes. As the largest unit of the federation, Jamaica feared losing control over its own development to the federal government.

A conference was held in London in May-June 1961 to outline the details of the constitution of the federation after its independence from Britain. Jamaica agreed to the details only after its concerns had been met. With an agreement in place, the British government agreed that it would grant independence to the Federation of the West Indies on 31 May 1962. In Jamaica, however, a referendum to decide on the colony's continued membership in the federation was held in September 1961. The result was a vote against remaining, and by the end of 1961 Jamaica had made plans to leave. Jamaica's departure made the constitutional arrangements negotiated in London unworkable. It was clear that terms would have to be re-negotiated. Any new arrangement would need the participation of Trinidad and Tobago – as the largest remaining colony – which, by the end of 1961, was not certain. The Federation of the West Indies was dissolved on 31 May 1962, the date Britain had planned to give it its independence. Eight members of the Federation – the Windward and Leeward Islands and Barbados – briefly flirted with the idea of forming another federation but did not negotiate such an arrangement.

St. Kitts-Nevis-Anguilla became a state in voluntary association with Britain in February 1967 as a first stage toward independence. Anguilla was resentful of the domination of St. Kitts and eventually left the arrangement. A constitutional conference was held in London in December 1982 to iron out the final details of the independence of St. Kitts and Nevis. Independence was achieved on 19 September 1983. Dr. Kennedy Simmonds of the People's Action Movement (PAM) was the first Prime Minister of the independent St. Kitts and Nevis.

2 CONSTITUTIONAL PROVISIONS RELATING TO FEDERALISM

The British colonial legacy is evident in the Westminster system of government adopted by St. Kitts and Nevis. The Federation of St. Kitts and Nevis is a parliamentary democracy within the British Commonwealth. Her Majesty Queen Elizabeth II is head of state, and is represented on the islands by a Governor-General. The constitution came into force on 23 June 1983. The provisions of the constitution that affect the parameters of federalism are as follows.

The constitution establishes a federal entity consisting of two constituent units – the island of St. Kitts and the island of Nevis. The federal system established by the constitution is asymmetrical in that only Nevis is endowed with its own government (the Nevis Island Assembly (NIA)) headed by the Nevis Island Administration led by a Premier and located in Charlestown (s. 102). St. Kitts does not have a government which represents only the interests of the island. This means that Nevis has a say in national affairs – and the affairs of St. Kitts – through its Representatives in Parliament, but the reverse is not true as St. Kitts does not have a say in affairs relating solely to Nevis.

The division of power between the federal government and the constituent unit (in this case only Nevis receives jurisdiction as a constituent unit) is weighted in favour of Nevis. Section 106(1) sets out matters falling into the exclusive jurisdiction of the Nevis Island Administration. The Administration has jurisdiction over the following *within the island of Nevis*: airports and seaports; education; extraction and processing of minerals; fisheries; health and welfare; labour; land and buildings appropriated to the use of the government; and licensing of imports and exports (s. 106(1)(a-h)). This power is somewhat limited by Section 106(2)(b) which states that the NIA cannot take any action that relates to issues of national concern without the concurrence of the Prime Minister, or take any action that "is inconsistent with the general policy of the Government as signified by the Prime Minister in a written communication to the Premier."

The only powers specified in the constitution that are exclusively in the jurisdiction of the federal government as they relate to Nevis are external affairs and defence (s. 37(4)). The federal government can, however, make laws relating to other matters with respect to Nevis, if the NIA has requested or consented to these provisions (s. 37(3)).

The federal Parliament, located in Basseterre in St. Kitts, is unicameral and consists of a National Assembly. Section 26(1)(a), in accordance with Section 50 which establishes the Constituency Boundaries Commission, sets out the rules regulating the number of Representatives elected to Parliament. As the Assembly stands, there are 11 elected Representatives – 8 for St. Kitts and 3 for Nevis. The constitution does not specify how these Representatives are to be elected, but by tradition the country utilizes the British first-past-the-post electoral system, rather than proportional representation.

Despite the fact that the Parliament is unicameral, the constitution makes provision for the existence of Senators in St. Kitts and Nevis. Section 26(2) states that there shall be "three or such greater number (not exceeding two-thirds of the number of Representatives) [of Senators] as may be prescribed by Parliament." Senators are appointed as specified by Section 26(1)(b) in accordance with Section 30, and they sit in the National Assembly. Unlike the tradition in many other federations, representation in the Senate is not based on geographic or regional representation (although this may sometimes occur). One-third of the Senators are appointed by the Governor-General on the advice of the Leader of the Opposition, and the others are appointed by the Governor-General on the advice of the Prime Minister (s. 30(1)(a-b)).

The constitution does not specifically outline federal financial arrangements, i.e., by what means the central government and NIA can raise revenue. In terms of the NIA, the constitution only states (in s. 108(1)) that "all revenues ... raised or received by the Administration ... shall be paid into and form a fund styled the Nevis Island Consolidated Fund." Section 108(2) states that the provisions relating to finance as applied to the national government also apply to the NIA.

Chapter VI, "Finance," specifies the process of expenditures of public funds and provisions for the auditing of public accounts. Section 110(1) states that the proceeds of all "takes" collected in St. Kitts and Nevis under any law are to be shared between the federal government and the Nevis Island Administration based on population. The share going to the NIA, however, is subject to deductions (s. 110(2)), such as the cost of common services and debt charges, as determined by the Governor-General (s. 110(3)) on the advice of the Prime Minister who can also take advice from the Premier of Nevis (s. 110(4)).

Like most other federations, the constitution of St. Kitts and Nevis contains procedures for the resolution of constitutional disputes. Section 97 states that any question as to the interpretation of the constitution can be referred by the lower courts to the High Court, and appeals can be made to the Court of Appeal or Her Majesty in Council. Section 112 states, however, that the High Court, to the exclusion of any other court, has "original jurisdiction in any dispute between the Administration and the Government."

There are a number of steps to be taken before the constitution can be amended. A bill to alter any of the provisions of the constitution must receive the support of at least two-thirds of all Representatives in the National Assembly (s. 38(2)). As well, there must be a period of at least 90 days between the first and second reading of the bill (s. 38(3)(a)). Finally, before any bill to amend the constitution can be signed by the Governor-General it must also be approved in a referendum by not less than two-thirds of all votes cast on the island of St. Kitts and two-thirds of the votes cast on the island of Nevis (s. 38(3)(b)).

The constitution of St. Kitts and Nevis includes a number of interesting provisions, including a section (s. 6) on protection from slavery or forced labour, and a long section (s. 8) on the protection from deprivation of property. In terms of federalism, however, there is one special provision which should be mentioned – the section that discusses the separation of Nevis from St. Kitts. Section 113(1) states that "the Nevis Island Legislature may provide that the island of Nevis shall cease to be federated with the island of Saint Christopher and accordingly that this Constitution shall no longer have affect in the island of Nevis." In effect, this is a provision for unilateral secession. A bill proposing to separate Nevis from the federation must be passed by at least two-thirds of the elected members of the Nevis Island Assembly (s. 113(2)). After a bill has been passed, it must be approved in a referendum on Nevis by two-thirds of all votes cast (s. 113(2)(b)). "A full and detailed proposal for the future constitution of the island of Nevis" must be presented to the Nevis Island Assembly at least six months before the referendum, and be made available to the public at least 90 days before the referendum (s. 113(2)(c)).

3 RECENT POLITICAL DYNAMICS

A general election was held in St. Kitts and Nevis on 6 March 2000. The Labour Party, led by Dr. Denzil Douglas, was re-elected with 64.2% of the votes cast, and on 7 March Dr. Douglas was sworn in as Prime Minister for his second consecutive term. The Labour Party increased its representation in Parliament by winning all eight seats in St. Kitts. In Nevis, the Concerned Citizens Movement retained the two seats it had held since 1995, and the Nevis Reformation Party retained its one seat. Both the Labour Party and the Concerned Citizens Movement campaigned on the basis of a promise of enhanced relations between Nevis and the national government, and resolved to pursue greater cooperation.

The threat of secession has been a persistent one in St. Kitts and Nevis, and secession has been a longstanding and divisive issue. Indeed, the inclusion of the provision for secession in the constitution caused the Labour Party (which was not in power at the time) to walk out of the constitutional discussions in London in 1982 and refuse to sign the final document.

The most recent chapter in the matter of the secession of Nevis occurred in 1998. On 10 August 1998, a referendum was held on Nevis on the question of secession. A majority of votes cast were in favour of secession – 61.7% – but this was less than the two-thirds necessary to secede. It is interesting to note, however, that only 58% of registered voters on the island of Nevis cast a ballot in the referendum.

The federal government has established several commissions and committees in an attempt to deal with the threat of secession. A Constitutional Review Commission (the Phillips Commission) was created in 1995. A Constitutional Task Force was given a mandate in 1999 to look at constitutional reform based on the 1998 Report of the Phillips Commission, and to carry out public consultations. Since the 1998 referendum the governing Labour Party has indicated its willingness to forge new arrangements in order to keep Nevis in the federation. On 18 April 2000, Prime Minister Douglas and Nevis Premier Vance

Amory met to discuss ways to improve the working relationship between the Nevis Island Administration and the national government. They now meet on a regular basis.

The Federation of St. Kitts and Nevis provides a clear example of a paradoxical global trend. Thus, at the same time that Nevis is threatening to secede and create an even smaller sovereign political unit, the federation is increasingly cooperating with other islands in the region in the recognition that the pressures of modern economics demand larger political and economic units. Thus, St. Kitts and Nevis is a member of the Caribbean Community (CARICOM), the Association of Caribbean States (ACS) and the Organization of Eastern Caribbean States (OECS). One of the main achievements of the OECS – which consists of Anguilla, Antigua and Barbuda, the British Virgin Islands, Dominica, Grenada, Montserrat, St. Kitts and Nevis, St. Lucia, and St. Vincent and the Grenadines – has been the establishment of a single monetary currency, the Eastern Caribbean dollar. The OECS and CARICOM have been establishing common institutions such as the Eastern Caribbean Central Bank (ECCB), the Eastern Caribbean Home Mortgage Bank, the Eastern Caribbean Institute of Bankers, the Eastern Caribbean Currency Authority, the Eastern Caribbean Securities Exchange (ECSE), the Caribbean Epidemiology Centre (CAREC), the Education Reform Unit, the Eastern Caribbean Supreme Court, and the Caribbean Telecommunications Authority (ECTEL). As well, the OECS has been considering proposals for passport-free travel among the members, harmonization of tax and fiscal systems, and the creation of a customs union.

The Federation of St. Kitts and Nevis shares the economic problems common to small island states. The economy was historically based on the cultivation and production of sugar, and it was labour shortages in this industry that justified the use of slaves brought from Africa (until Britain abolished slavery in 1833). The sugar industry is, however, currently in dire straits. The country's small size prevents large-scale cultivation of sugar and thus it cannot compete with larger Central or Latin American countries. As well, labour costs are high, it is too far from major markets (especially the United States) and its domestic market is too small. Another major hindrance to continued economic growth has been the destruction caused by several devastating hurricanes in recent years. The government has attempted to overcome the country's difficulties in the globalized economy by emphasizing the service sector – including finance, tourism and information technology. Nevis in particular has tried to sell itself as an international financial centre, although this has been hampered by the Organization of Economic Cooperation and Development (OECD) listing St. Kitts and Nevis as a country it considers to be practising "harmful" tax policies and as a "non-cooperative jurisdiction" in the prevention of money laundering. As is the case elsewhere, the economic success or failure of the country will have major repercussions on the continuation of St. Kitts and Nevis as a federation.

4 SOURCES FOR FURTHER INFORMATION

James Ferguson, *Eastern Caribbean: A Guide to People, Politics and Culture*, New York: Interlink Books, 1997.

http://www.stkittsnevis.net

http://website.llineone.net/;slstkittsnevis/nation.htm#English

http://www.fsd.gov.kn/main/general_summary.html

http://www.georgetown.edu/pdba/constitutions/kitts/stkitts-nevis.html

http://www.sknlabourparty.org/spokesman

http://cnn.ch/WORLD/election.watch/america.st.kitts.nevis.html

http://www.oneworld.org/euforic/courier/170e_kit.htm

http://ehmt.com/narticle.htm

Table I
Political and Geographic Indicators

Capital city	Basseterre
Number and type of constituent units	*2 Islands:* Nevis, Saint Kitts (Saint Christopher)
Official language(s)	English
Area	261 km^2
Area – Largest constituent unit	Saint Kitts (168 km^2)
Area – Smallest constituent unit	Nevis (93 km^2)
Total population	45 000
Population by constituent unit (% of total population)	Saint Kitts 75%, Nevis 25%
Political system – federal	Constitutional Monarchy – Parliamentary System
Head of state – federal	Queen Elizabeth II, represented by Governor-General Dr. Cuthbert Montraville Sebastian (1996)
Head of government – federal	Prime Minister Dr. Denzil Douglas (1995/2000), Saint Kitts-Nevis Labour Party (SKNLP). The leader of the directly elected majority party is appointed to the post of Prime Minister by the Governor-General, who also appoints the Cabinet, based on the Prime Minister's recommendations. Both PM and Cabinet serve for a maximum 5-year term. The Cabinet consists of 4 ministers and the Attorney General.
Government structure – federal	Unicameral – National Assembly: 14 seats. 11 members are popularly elected from single-member constituencies, to serve maximum 5-year terms. The remaining 3 seats are appointed, 1 by the Leader of the Opposition and 2 by the Prime Minister. The appointed members of the National Assembly are referred to as Senators.
Number of representatives in federal government	14 seats: Saint Kitts-Nevis Labour Party (SKLP) 8, Concerned Citizens' Movement (CCM) 2, Nevis Reformation Party NRP 1, and 3 appointed Senators
Number of representatives in federal government for most populated constituent unit	Saint Kitts: 8 representatives
Number of representatives in house of federal government for least populated constituent unit	Nevis: 3 representatives

Table I (continued)

Constitutional court (highest court dealing with constitutional matters)	High Court
Political system of constituent units	Nevis has a unicameral legislature – Nevis Island Assembly. It is composed of 9 members, one of whom is the Queen (represented by the Governor-General). Of the other 8 members, five are directly elected and 3 are appointed (1 by the Leader of the Opposition, and 2 by the Premier). All serve a 5-year term. Note: Saint Kitts does not have its own legislature.
Head of state – constituent units	Queen Elizabeth II, represented by Governor General Dr. Cuthbert Montraville Sebastian (1996).
Head of government – constituent units	Premier, elected member of the Legislature and leader of the majority party to serve a maximum 5-year term. The Premier is appointed by the Governor-General, who also appoints an additional 2 members to form the Cabinet of the Nevis Island Administration.

Table II
Economic and Social Indicators

GDP	US$274 million
GDP per capita	US$7 000
Mechanisms for taxation	There is no personal income tax in St. Kitts and Nevis. The Central Government levies: • Corporate Taxes (of around 38%) • Land and House Tax (based on 5% of annual rental values of property) • Social Service levy of 8% is deducted from wages. The Central Government also levies substantial Custom taxes. There are no consumption taxes, sales taxes, or turnover taxes. Note: The Nevis Island Assembly has significant power over the allocated taxes.
National debt (external)	US$115.1 million
National unemployment rate	4.5%
Constituent unit with highest unemployment rate	N/A
Constituent unit with lowest unemployment rate	N/A
Adult literacy rate	90%
National expenditures on education as a % of GDP	4.1%
Life expectancy in years	70.73
Doctors per population ratio (national)	117.1 doctors per 100 000 inhabitants
Doctors per population ratio in constituent units (highest)	N/A
Doctors per population ratio in constituent units (lowest)	N/A
National expenditures on health as a % of GDP	6.0%

Sources

Central Intelligence Agency (CIA), World Fact Book 2000. CIA, www.cia.gov/cia/publications/factbook/index.html

Eastern Caribbean Supreme Court. "About the ECSC." www.ecsupremecourts.org.lc

Economic Commission for Latin America and the Caribbean (ECLAC), *Statistical Yearbook for Latin America and the Caribbean 1999*. ECLAC, www.eclac.org/estaditicas

Elazar, Daniel J. (ed.) *Federal Systems of the World: A Handbook of Federal, Confederal and Autonomy Arrangements.* 2nd Edition. Jerusalem Institute for Federal Studies. London: Longman Group/Westgate House, 1994.

Federal Government of St. Kitts and Nevis. www.stkittsnevis.net/economy.html

Ministry of Finance for St. Kitts and Nevis. www.fsd.gov.kn

Nevis Island Administration. www.nevisweb.kn/frameset.html

Organisation of Eastern Caribbean States (OECS). "Country Profile." www.caribisles.org/index.cfm

Pan-American Health Organization (PAHO/WHO). "Profiles of the Health Services System" of respective countries. www.paho.org

United Nations Statistics Division. "InfoNation." www.un.org/

United Nations. *Human Development Report, 2000.* UNDP and the Human Development Report Office (HDRO). www.undp.org/hdro/report.html

World Bank. "Country Profiles." www.worldbank.org/data/countrydata/countrydata.html

World Bank. *World Development Report 2000/2001: Attacking Poverty.* www.worldbank.org/poverty/wdrpoverty/report/index.htm

World Health Organisation (WHO). "Estimates of Health Personnel." www-nt.who.int/whosis/statistics

World Health Organisation (WHO). "Annex Table 8, Selected national health accounts indicators for all Member States, estimates for 1997." *World Health Report 2000.* Geneva, 2000. www-nt.who.int/whosis/statistics/menu.cfm

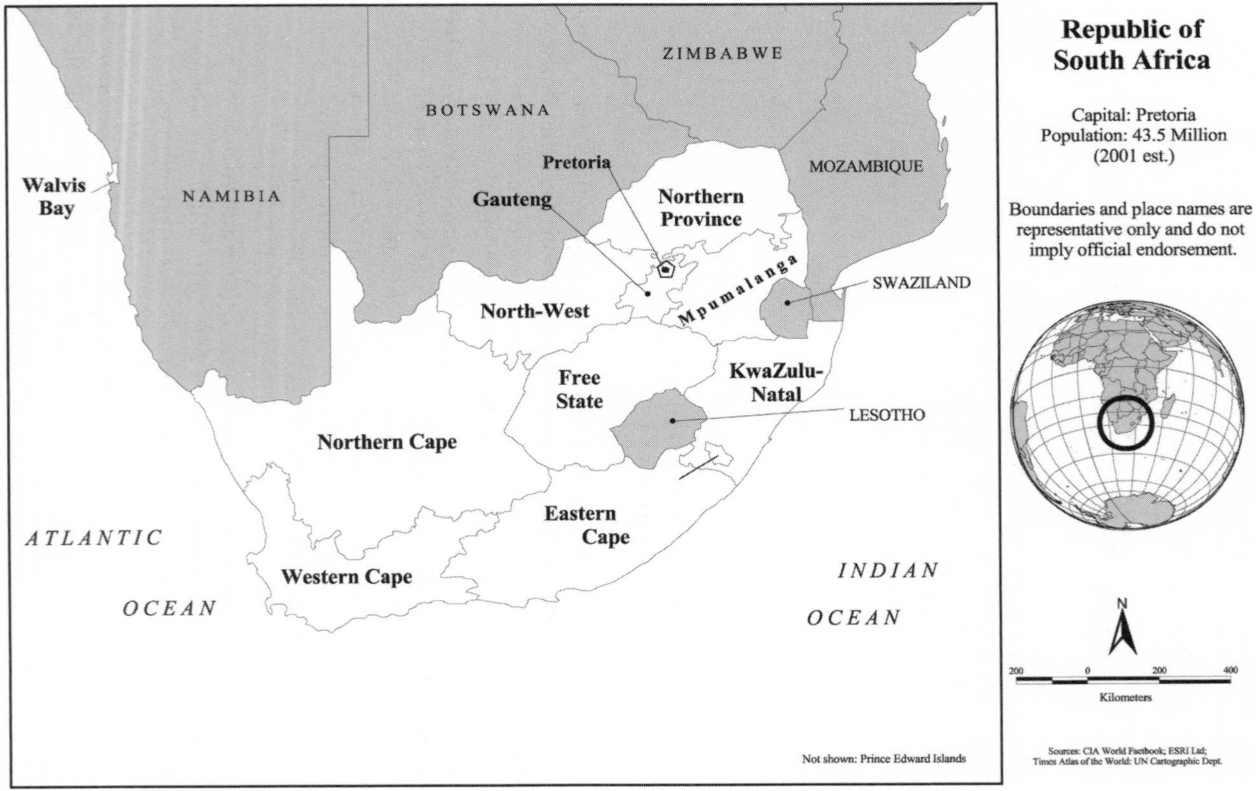

ZIMBABWE
BOTSWANA
NAMIBIA
MOZAMBIQUE
Walvis Bay
Pretoria
Gauteng
Northern Province
Mpumalanga
SWAZILAND
North-West
Free State
KwaZulu-Natal
LESOTHO
Northern Cape
Eastern Cape
Western Cape
ATLANTIC OCEAN
INDIAN OCEAN
Not shown: Prince Edward Islands

Republic of South Africa

Capital: Pretoria
Population: 43.5 Million
(2001 est.)

Boundaries and place names are representative only and do not imply official endorsement.

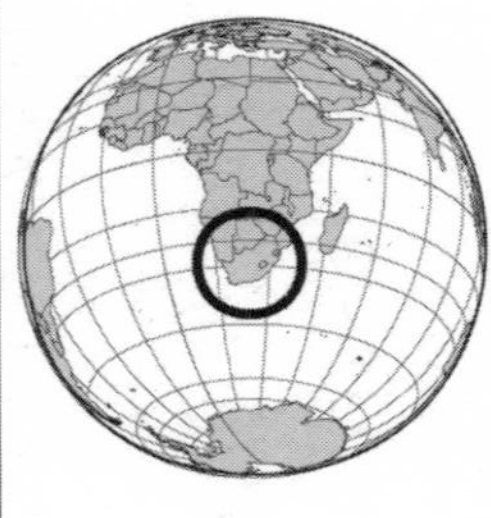

Sources: CIA World Factbook; ESRI Ltd; Times Atlas of the World: UN Cartographic Dept.

South Africa
(*Republic of South Africa*)

JANIS VAN DER WESTHUIZEN

1 HISTORY AND DEVELOPMENT OF FEDERALISM

South Africa is located at the very southern tip of the African continent and dominates the southern African region. Namibia, Botswana, Zimbabwe and Mozambique are its immediate neighbours, whilst South Africa entirely surrounds Swaziland and Lesotho. The country occupies 1,221,038 km^2, and is inhabited by approximately 43 million people. As of the 1990s, the population was approximately 75.2% black, 13.6% white, 8.6% coloured and 2.6% Indian. Federalism has had a marred and highly contested reception in South Africa and this continues to be so, given its historically deeply divided polity.

Four British territories – the Cape Colony and Natal (formerly under British control) and the Boer Republics of the Transvaal and the Orange Free State – were merged under the South Africa Act passed by the British Parliament in 1909. In May 1910 South Africa became a self-governing dominion within the British Commonwealth. The Union was a historic compromise: Afrikaners felt it meant greater independence and weakened British imperial influence, while the English saw the Union as consolidating British influence. Initially, the 1910 Union of South Africa explicitly rejected any federalist pretensions. At that time, the Union, celebrated as the reconciliation between Afrikaner and English interests, overshadowed white/black race relations. In fact, the process of creating the Union facilitated a protracted attack against the political rights of black and "coloured"

South Africans. Although the Union began reconciling Afrikaner and English interests, it failed to unite South Africa, given that the black majority was excluded from political participation – the issue which subsequently shaped South African history until the 1990s.

With the advent of the apartheid state in the 1950s, power was increasingly centralized with the four provinces of the Transvaal, Orange Free State, Natal and Cape existing as administrative units of (white) South Africa proper. The "bantustans," or ethnic homelands, were in effect treated as constitutional annexes or adjuncts consisting of four nominally "independent states" of Bophutswana, Venda, Ciskei and Transkei as well as six "self-governing territories." These entities stood at the heart of so-called "grand apartheid," for it was through these territories constituted along tribal lines that black South Africans were supposed to exercise their civil and voting rights. In effect, it meant that they enjoyed little more than "sojourner" status as *gastarbeiter* (guest workers) in 'white' South Africa. Hand-in-hand with grand apartheid, stood "petty apartheid" which was a vast network of state control through which virtually every conceivable aspect of daily life between South Africans of different races were segregated, including transport, residential areas, universities, shop entrances, public amenities, and even sex and marriage.

However, the sheer cost which such a massive attempt at social engineering imposed, together with the ruling regime's inability to provide "separate but equal" life opportunities to black South Africans, ultimately lead to apartheid's collapse. Urbanization continued unabated, making the notion of grand apartheid all but a fiction. And, as black South Africans became trapped in poverty, unemployment and frustrated aspirations, social protest throughout the 1960s, 1970s and 1980s triggered international condemnation, isolation and, ultimately, declining economic growth. Facing the vicious circle of international divestment, unemployment and social upheaval, F.W. de Klerk, the apartheid state's last President, lifted the ban on the African National Congress (ANC) and other popular political movements. This began a process that involved Nelson Mandela's release from prison, negotiations leading to an interim constitution and inter-party agreement on a quasi-federal constitution, democratic elections which resulted in a coalition government under the interim constitution, the operation of the democratically elected Parliament as a constitutional assembly to draft the new constitution, and the adoption of a new constitution in 1996.

Given that apartheid was justified, in part, on a federalist rationale, the federalist idea continued to be viewed with considerable scepticism – if not outright rejection – by many of the disenfranchised during South Africa's political transition in the early 1990s. Members of the ANC in particular saw proposals for strong regional government as a form of neo-apartheid, especially because the incumbent National Party became the most ardent champion of federalism with the onset of the transition. The ANC and its allies feared that a federal order with delegation of powers to the provinces would weaken and disperse authority considerably, thereby heavily restricting the central government's capacity to implement and consolidate mechanisms for reconstruction and development in the post-apartheid era.

The support for federalism came from a variety of quarters. Besides the National Party (NP), and the liberal democratic Democratic Party (DP), the Inkhata Freedom Party (IFP), which often projects itself as the sole custodian of Zulu political interests, also demanded a highly autonomous KwaZulu-Natal where Zulus remain the ethnic majority, and even claimed the right to self-determination. Similarly, a small group of radical, ultra-right Afrikaners clamoured for the creation of a *Volkstaat*, effectively a homeland exclusively for white Afrikaners. Indeed, the convergence – despite considerable ideological differences between these constituencies – due to their interest in autonomy resulted in a regular, informal, if odd coalition during the negotiations process to enhance the federalist features of the South African constitution. Most importantly, the NP – representing the majority of whites (and increasingly "coloureds") – saw federalism, and with it a Bill of Rights, as providing an important check on the excesses of power by a new majority government.

Strongly contested and often threatening to upstage the negotiations process altogether, the impasse was finally broken by a March 1993 proposal contained in a confidential *Report to Political Parties* commissioned by the Consultative Business Movement. The proposal suggested the "34 constitutional principles," which would have to be followed by the democratically elected Constitutional Assembly when it devised the final constitution. The most important of these included requiring each level of government (national and provincial) to have both exclusive and concurrent powers (Principle XIX) and, highlighting the principle of subsidiarity, that decisions should be taken at whatever level is most "responsible and accountable" (Principle XX).

Most analysts view the South African constitution as essentially a federal one, drawing especially upon the German model of integrated federalism with framework legislation implemented by the Länder and fairly tight integration between the central and provincial governments achieved through the Bundesrat. In other words, although the regions fully participate in policy formulation regarding the provinces, the central government has the final say.

2 CONSTITUTIONAL PROVISIONS RELATING TO FEDERALISM

The Republic of South Africa is a parliamentary democracy with the President acting both as head of government and head of state. South Africa's hybrid presidential-parliamentary system and constitution came into effect on 11 October 1996. The South African constitution and especially the Bill of Rights has been labelled as one of the most progressive in the world and makes special provisions for a number of commissions and offices (Chapter 9). These include: the Auditor-General (s. 188); the Public Protector (s. 182); the Human Rights Commission (s. 184); the Commission on Gender Equality (s. 187); the Independent Electoral Commission (s. 190); the Commission for the Promotion and Protection of the Rights of Cultural, Religious and Linguistic Communities (s. 185); and finally, the Independent Broadcasting Authority (s. 192).

The constitution establishes a federal entity of nine constituent units, namely the provinces of KwaZulu-Natal, Gauteng, Free State, Western Cape, Eastern Cape, North, North West and Mpumalanga (s. 103). Unlike most federations in deeply divided societies, the provincial boundaries are not designed to coincide with racial or tribal boundaries in recognition of the political need to escape similar past practices. The constitution recognizes three "spheres" of government – Chapter 3 of the constitution rejected the use of the term "level of government." The formal recognition of local government as a distinct constitutional sphere in South Africa contrasts with the practice in many federations where local governments fall under the jurisdiction of the constituent units.

The 1996 constitution is designed to promote a model of cooperative federalism rather than competitive federalism. The provincial governments are therefore required to operate in accordance with the letter and spirit of the principles of cooperative government as set out in chapter 3 of the constitution. A rigid separation of tasks and functions between the different "spheres" of government is absent – clearly suggested by the Council of Provinces with its confluence of national, provincial and local government interests. Nevertheless, the principle of cooperative government does not undermine provincial autonomy. For example, both the Western Cape and KwaZulu-Natal provinces have exercised the right to establish their own provincial constitutions (s. 104) with only that of the former securing approval by the Constitutional Court (s. 144). Yet, it must be acknowledged that the division of power privileges the central government, which sets national standards and norms and may over-ride provincial standards which threaten national unity or national standards. There is a very short list of "exclusive" provincial powers (i.e., abattoirs, provincial planning, roads, sport, cultural, and veterinary matters). In more critical issue areas, powers are concurrent and thus either sphere can legislate, although national law again prevails in matters which cannot be effectively managed by provinces or require uniformity to be effective.

South Africa has a bicameral Parliament consisting of the National Assembly (NA) and the National Council of Provinces (NCOP), both located in Cape Town (s. 42(6)). The National Assembly consists of 400 representatives elected on the basis of proportional representation and party list system (Chapter 4, ss. 60–72). As the democratically elected lower house, the National Assembly must ensure "government by the people under the Constitution." There is a strong possibility that Parliament will be relocated to the administrative capital of Pretoria in the near future in order to reduce the costs associated with split legislative and administrative capitals.

The upper house was called the Senate in the interim constitution, but in the 1996 constitution it is called the National Council of Provinces. This body consists of 90 members representing the particular interests of the nine provinces and ensures that those interests are not seriously abrogated by the central government (s. 42(4)). The 1996 constitution makes a decisive break with the British-inspired principle of parliamentary sovereignty in that Parliament is subject to limitations imposed by the constitution.

As far as fiscal arrangements are concerned, the provinces enjoy limited revenue-raising capabilities as well as very limited borrowing powers (s. 230). Basic rules are set in the constitution and the Intergovernmental Fiscal Relations Act, first implemented in the 1999 budget. Fiscal federalism is highly centralized with distribution taking such factors into account as the needs of national government, the effectiveness of provincial governments as well as the need to overcome income inequalities "within and among provinces" (s. 214(2)(g)). The Finance and Fiscal Commission has been created to make recommendations on the distribution of the budget (s. 220). Section 227 provides for each province to be allocated an equitable share of revenue raised nationally. Additional revenue raised by the provinces or municipalities may not be deducted from their share of revenue raised nationally or from other allocations made to them out of national government revenue (s. 227(2)).

The South African constitution has clear guidelines relating to the resolution of constitutional disputes (Chapter 8). In addition to the principle of cooperative government, all spheres of government need to exhaust "every reasonable effort to resolve any disputes through intergovernmental negotiation" (s. 41(3)) and employ every method before approaching the courts to resolve the matter. The courts can even refer such a dispute back to the different parts of government if they consider that substantial efforts have not been made in this regard (s. 41(4)). If a court of law is unable to resolve a dispute, national legislation prevails over provincial legislation or the provincial constitution in cases where conflict over the interpretation of legislation is concerned (s. 146(3) and s. 148). Nevertheless, the Constitutional Court has final say about issues involving central, provincial and local government (s. 167). The Constitutional Court is the highest court regarding constitutional matters. It consists of a President, Deputy-President, and nine other judges (s. 167(1)), and matters must be heard by at least eight judges. The Constitutional Court decides disputes between organs of the state, and on disputes relating to the constitutionality of any provincial or parliamentary bill or constitutional amendment (s. 167(4)). These matters can be brought directly to the Constitutional Court by any person, provided it is "in the interests of justice and with leave of the Constitutional Court" (s. 167(6)).

Special and rigid procedures have to be followed in order to make constitutional amendments (s. 74). Such amendments can be classified according to five categories, with different degrees of rigidity involved. Since not all these can be described in detail here, suffice it to indicate that amendments to the entrenched powers of the constitution itself may only be amended by a bill passed by at least 75 per cent of the Assembly *together* with the support of at least six of the provinces in the National Council of Provinces. The Bill of Rights – a category two amendment – may only be amended by a minimum two-thirds in the Assembly and with the support of at least six of the provinces in the NCOP (s.74(2)). Other amendments which (a) relate to matters affecting the NCOP or (b) alter provincial boundaries, functions or institutions or (c) amend a provision which specifically deals with a provincial matter, also require at least two-thirds support in the Assembly as well as the support of at least six of the provinces in the NCOP.

The recognition of the constitutional role of traditional leaders and the right to self-determination (s. 235) is an interesting feature of the South African constitution. The constitution recognizes that traditional authority predates the advent of European colonization of South Africa. To ameliorate the considerable tension which arises from the traditionalism of African indigenous law and its authoritarian patriarchal nature on the one hand, and the modernist, democratic and egalitarian ethos of the constitution on the other, a Council of Traditional Leaders has been established (s. 212). Members are appointed by the Provincial Houses of Traditional Leaders as provided in Section 212(2)(a) of the constitution and are eligible for re-nomination. At the provincial level, Houses of Traditional Leaders have also been created. Nevertheless it is clear that customary law and traditional leaders are empowered essentially to perform a symbolic and advisory role and traditional leadership remains subject to Chapter 12 of the constitution.

In relation to the highly sensitive and controversial right to self-determination – largely in reaction to the ultra rightwing Afrikaners and certain constituencies within the IFP – the constitution does not preclude "recognition of the right to self-determination of any community sharing a common cultural and language heritage, within a territorial entity in the Republic or in any other way, determined by legislation" (s. 235).

3 RECENT POLITICAL DYNAMICS

Since implementation of the constitution, no substantive movement has been made toward the creation of a *Volkstaat.* Local government elections in December 2000 brought new tensions between traditional leaders – known as the *amakhosi* – and newly created municipal structures to the fore. Traditional authorities often co-exist alongside modern institutions. For example, local chiefs would provide permission for the acquisition of residential sites by government. With the expansion of local government structures, however, the *amakhosi* fear that municipal powers and functions will erode their control over land and the administration of justice, ultimately leading to their own demise. Indeed, tensions between government and the *amakhosi* were so severe that the latter threatened to disrupt local government elections if their status was not secured. Such a bill is to be passed in Parliament in 2001.

In the local government elections of 5 December 2000, the ruling ANC garnered approximately 62 per cent of all votes cast nationally and the official opposition, the Democratic Alliance – which amalgamated with the remnants of the National Party shortly before the elections – attained approximately 22.5 per cent. This reflected an almost six percentage point increase on the 17 per cent vote which its constituent parties, the Democratic Party, the National Party and Federal Alliance, won in the general elections of June 1999.

Whereas only 48 per cent of ANC supporters voted, the Democratic Alliance was able to get 57 per cent of its voters to the polls. Many observers contend that the degree of apathy displayed by would-be ANC voters – and black African youth in particular – reflects a considerable degree of disillusionment with the lack of social delivery and development six years after South Africa's first and widely celebrated elections in 1994.

Indeed, these voting patterns are symptomatic of the profound challenges facing the ANC. Although South Africa's complex political transition was widely acclaimed, success in terms of reconstruction and development remains elusive. Rather than embarking upon a kind of Keynesian, demand-induced macro-economic program, on which the ANC rose to power, the pressures of globalization have forced a dramatic swing to a neo-liberal program. Although the government has succeeded in luring some foreign direct investment – especially from 1997 to 1999 – and has generally succeeded in gaining the respect of the world's capital markets, domestic political strains loom within the broader governing alliance of which the ANC is the dominant partner. The process of privatization, deregulation and liberalization has incurred the wrath of one of the ANC's most important constituents, namely labour, represented within the ruling alliance by the Congress of South African Trade Unions. How the ANC manages to consolidate the neo-liberal program on which it has embarked and yet prevent the ruling alliance, or even the party, from splitting will continue to be crucial in shaping the nature of the South and southern African political landscape.

At the provincial level, the ANC's control of all but two provinces – Western Cape, under the opposition DA, and KwaZulu-Natal, governed by the IFP – has stymied the overall process of the provinces gaining a greater degree of freedom from control by the centre. The most direct expression of central efforts to prevent the provinces getting more control has been the appointment of Premiers from ANC headquarters. Tensions between the central government and opposition-run provinces has meant that attempts by the latter to pursue autonomous initiatives relating to relatively 'technical' issues (for example, crime prevention strategies) have become highly politicized.

More immediate and specific challenges include, first, preventing and overcoming some of the highest rates of HIV/AIDS infection in the world. Second, the government must take measures to reduce the crime rate (which appears to have stabilized in many areas recently). Third, it is necessary to address issues relating to the fact that, although unemployment is high, there is a lack of skilled and semi-skilled labour, especially in management and information technology.

4 SOURCES FOR FURTHER INFORMATION

Abedian, Iraj, Tania Ajam and Laura Walker, *Promises, Plans and Priorities: South Africa's Emerging Fiscal Structures,* Institute for Democracy in South Africa, 1997.

Calland, Richard, *The First Five Years: A Review of South Africa's Democratic Parliament,* Institute for Democracy in South Africa, 1999.
Devenish George E., *A Commentary on the South African Constitution,* Durban: Butterworths, 1998.
Hailbronner, Kay and Christine Kreuzer, "Implementing Federalism in the Final Constitution of the Republic of South Africa," *Konrad Adenauer Foundation, Occasional Paper Series,* September 1995.
Ndlela, Lindiwe, *A Practical Guide to Local Government in South Africa,* Institute for Democracy in South Africa, 2001.
Robinson, Jenny, "Federalism and the Transformation of the South African State," in Grahan Smith (ed.) *Federalism: The Multiethnic Challenge,* New York & London: Longman, 1995, pp. 255–278.
Www.polity.org/za/govdocs/constitution/saconst.html
www.concourt.gov.za
www.washlaw.edu/farint/africa/soaf.html
www.idasa.org.za/democracy/constit.html
www.idasa.org.za/democracy/institut.html
www.h-net.msu.edu/;slsapsa/
www.constitution.org.za

Table I
Political and Geographic Indicators

Capital city	Pretoria Note: Cape Town is the legislative capital and Bloemfontein the judicial centre.
Number and type of constituent units	*9 Provinces:* Eastern Cape, Free State, Gauteng, KwaZulu-Natal, Mpumalanga, North-West, Northern Cape, Northern Province, Western Cape
Official language(s)	11 Official Languages: Afrikaans, English, isiNdebele, Sepedi, Sesotho, Siswati, Xitsonga, Setswana, Tshivenda, isiXhosa, isZulu
Area	1 219 912 km^2
Area – Largest constituent unit	Northern Cape (361 830 km^2)
Area – Smallest constituent unit	Gauteng (17 010 km^2)
Total population	43 586 097
Population by constituent unit (% of total population)	KwaZulu-Natal 20.3%, Gauteng 18.9%, Eastern Cape 15.5%, Northern Province 10.9%, Western Cape 10.9%, North West 8.0%, Mpumalanga 7.0%, Free State 6.5%, Northern Cape 2.0%
Political system – federal	Republic – Parliamentary System
Head of state – federal	President Thabo Mvuyelwa Mbeki (1999) African National Congress (ANC). Elected by the National Assembly to serve for a 5-year term.
Head of government – federal	President Thabo Mvuyelwa Mbeki. President appoints the Cabinet.
Government structure – federal	Bicameral – Parliament: *Upper/Second House* – National Council of Provinces (NCOP), 90 seats. 10 members each are elected by the Provincial Parliaments to serve for a 5-year term. *Lower House* – National Assembly, 400 seats. Representatives are elected on the basis of proportional representation and party list system (200 seats are elected from provincial lists, 200 from a national list) to serve a 5-year term.

Table I (continued)

Number of representatives in lower house of federal government – National Assembly	400 Seats: African National Congress (Includes South African Communist Party) (ANC) 266, Democratic Party (*DP) 38, Iqembu Lenatha Yenkululeko/Inkatha Freedom Party (IFP) 34, New National Party (*NNP) 28, United Democratic Movement (UDM) 14, African Christian Democratic Party (ACDP) 6, Vryheidsfront/Freedom Front (VF) 3, United Christian-Democratic Party (UCDP) 3, Pan African Congress of Azania (PAC) 3, Federal Alliance (*FA) 2, Minority Front (MF) 1, Afrikaner Eenheidsbeweging – AEB (Afrikaner Unity Movement) 1, Azanian People's Organisation (AZAPO) 1. *The FA joined the DP electoral lists, and the DP and the NNP merged into the Democratic Alliance.
Number of representatives in lower house of federal government for most populated constituent unit	Note: Due to election by proportional representation and the list system, representatives' constituent-unit origin is of much lesser importance.
Number of representatives in lower house of federal government for least populated constituent unit	See previous category.
Number of representatives in upper house of federal government – National Council of Provinces	90 members: African National Congress (ANC) 61, (New) National Party (NP) 17, Freedom Front (FF) 4, Inkatha Freedom Party (IFP) 5, and DP 3
Distribution of representation in upper house of federal government – National Council of Provinces	Each of the 9 provinces has 10 seats.
Constitutional court (highest court dealing with constitutional matters)	Constitutional Court. There are 11 justices: 9 men and 2 women. Justices serve for non-renewable 12-year terms, but must retire at the age of 70 years.
Political system of constituent units	Unicameral provincial legislatures elected by proportional representation. (Note: Houses of Traditional Leaders have also been created. Nevertheless, it is clear that traditional leaders essentially perform a symbolic and advisory role.)
Head of state – constituent units	A provincial constitution may provide for the institution, role, authority and status of a traditional monarch.
Head of government – constituent units	Premier, appointed by majority party according to the Westminster system.

Table II
Economic and Social Indicators

GDP	US$369 billion
GDP per capita	US$8 500
Mechanisms for taxation	Most taxation power is held by the central government. • Corporate Taxes: 30%, with some private companies facing a Secondary Tax on Companies (STC) on their dividends at a rate of 12.5%. • Personal Income Taxes: 6 tax brackets ranging from 19–42%. • Provinces are able to tax the gambling industries within their jurisdiction. • Value-added Tax (VAT): 14% with some basic necessities being exempt. • "Perks" taxes on luxury items.
National debt	US$25.6 billion
National unemployment rate	30%
Constituent unit with highest unemployment rate	Eastern Cape – 48.5%
Constituent unit with lowest unemployment rate	Western Cape – 17.9%
Adult literacy rate	81.8%
National expenditures on education as a % of GDP	7.9%
Life expectancy in years	48.09
Doctors per population ratio (national)	56.3 doctors per 100 000 inhabitants
Doctors per population ratio in constituent units (highest)	Gauteng – 128 doctors per 100 000 inhabitants
Doctors per population ratio in constituent units (lowest)	Northern Province – 11 per 100 000 Inhabitants
National expenditures on health as a % of GDP	7.1%

Sources

Central Intelligence Agency (CIA), *World Fact Book 2000*. CIA, www.cia.gov/cia/publications/factbook/index.html

Constitutional Court of South Africa. www.concourt.gov.za

Derbyshire, J. Denis. "South Africa." *Encyclopedia of World Political Systems.* Volumes I and II, New York: Sharpe Reference, M.E. Sharpe, Inc, 2000.

Economist Intelligence Unit, "Investing, Licensing and Trade in South Africa," Released February 2000, *The Economist Intelligence Unit Database 2000*, New York 2000. www.eiu.com

Elazar, Daniel J. (ed.) *Federal Systems of the World: A Handbook of Federal, Confederal and Autonomy Arrangements.* 2nd Edition. Jerusalem Institute for Federal Studies. London: Longman Group/Westgate House, 1994.

International Labour Office. "Indicators on Unemployment." www.un.org/Depts/unsd/social/unempl.htm

International Monetary Fund (IMF). *International Financial Statistics*, Vol. LIII, No. 12, December 2000. Washington, DC: the IMF Statistics Department, 2000.

UNESCO. *World Education Report 1998: Teachers and Teaching in a Changing World.* Paris: UNESCO, 1998.

United Nations Population Division. Department of Economic and Social Affairs. "Population in 1999 and 2000: All Countries," *World Population Prospects: The 1998 Revision, Vol. 1 Comprehensive Tables.* www.un.org/Depts

United Nations. *Human Development Report, 2000.* UNDP and the Human Development Report Office (HDRO). www.undp.org/hdro/report.html

United Nations Statistics Division. "InfoNation." www.un.org/

World Bank. *World Development Report 2000/2001: Attacking Poverty.* www.worldbank.org/poverty/wdrpoverty/report/index.htm

World Health Organisation (WHO). "Estimates of Health Personnel." www-nt.who.int/whosis/statistics

World Health Organisation (WHO). "Annex Table 8, Selected national health accounts indicators for all Member States, estimates for 1997." *World Health Report 2000.* Geneva, 2000. www-nt.who.int/whosis/statistics/menu.cfm.

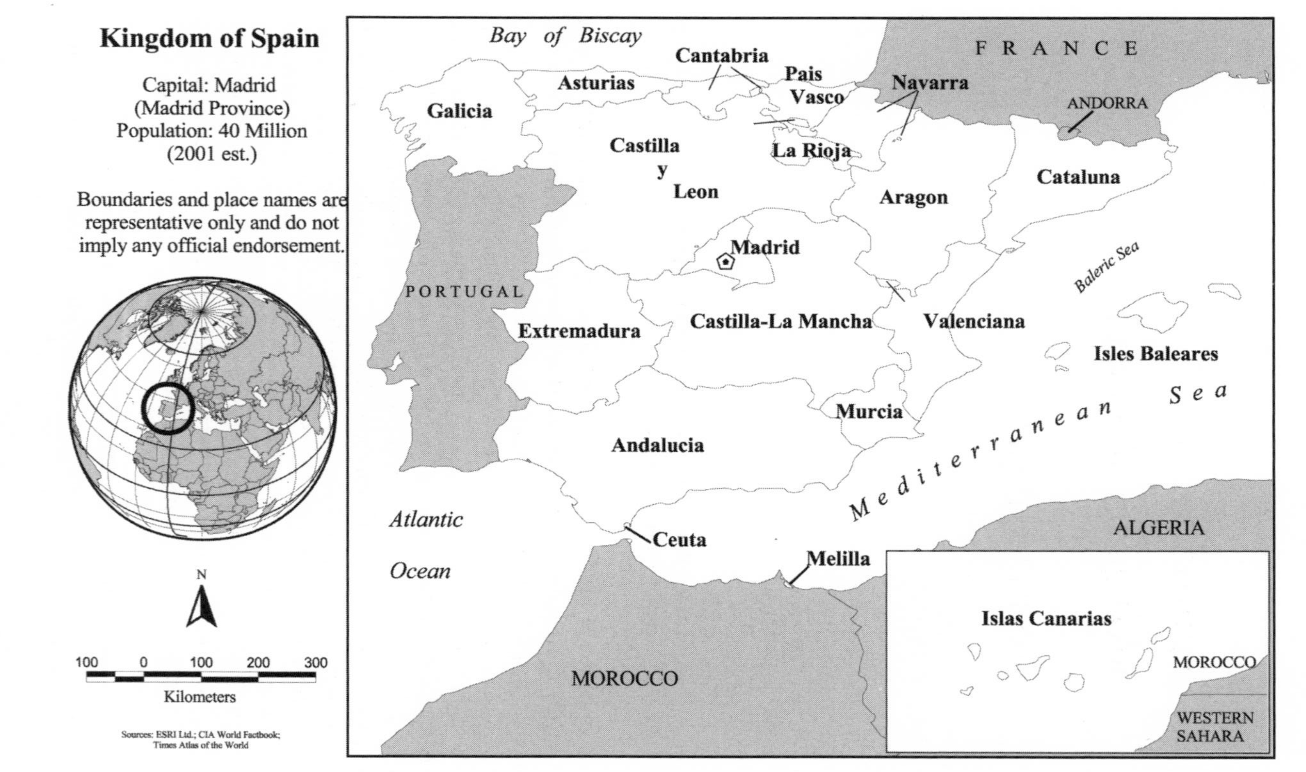
Kingdom of Spain
Capital: Madrid
(Madrid Province)
Population: 40 Million
(2001 est.)
Boundaries and place names are representative only and do not imply any official endorsement.
N
100 0 100 200 300
Kilometers
Sources: ESRI Ltd.; CIA World Factbook; Times Atlas of the World
Bay of Biscay
FRANCE
ANDORRA
Galicia
Asturias
Cantabria
Pais Vasco
Navarra
Castilla y Leon
La Rioja
Aragon
Cataluna
Madrid
PORTUGAL
Extremadura
Castilla-La Mancha
Valenciana
Baleric Sea
Isles Baleares
Mediterranean Sea
Murcia
Andalucia
Atlantic Ocean
Ceuta
Melilla
ALGERIA
MOROCCO
Islas Canarias
MOROCCO
WESTERN SAHARA

Spain*
(*Kingdom of Spain*)

SIOBHÁN HARTY

1 HISTORY AND DEVELOPMENT OF FEDERALISM

The Kingdom of Spain (504,750 km^2) is located in the southwestern part of the European continent, on the Iberian Peninsula. Its population for 1999 was just over 40 million. The country's current configuration dates back to 1492, when the last Muslim kingdom fell in Granada. From 711 until 1492, a period known as the *Reconquista*, Christian and Islamic forces were locked in a battle over control of the territory. During this period, Spain was a series of kingdoms, two of the most powerful of which, Castile and Aragón, were united in 1469 with the marriage of Ferdinand of Aragón and Isabella of Castile.

Until the eighteenth century, Spain was made up of various kingdoms on the Iberian peninsula. Each kingdom was treated as a distinct entity with its own laws and institutions. Spain's composite monarchy was a loose dynastic union that worked against the consolidation of a unified and coherent Spanish national identity, the consequences of which have been felt up until the present day. In the eighteenth century, a new Bourbon monarchy attempted to centralize state power along the French model most notably by eliminating Catalan political institutions following the War of Spanish Succession (1700–13).

* The author and the Forum of Federations would like to thank Ferran Requejo, Professor of Political Science, Pompeu Fabra University, Barcelona, for his helpful comments on this article.

In the nineteenth century several political and military challenges stretched the capacity of the Spanish crown to build a unified nation-state and remove the threat of rival nationalities in the peripheral regions, including the Napoleonic invasion, a succession of civil wars, and the loss of Spain's last colonies. The consequence of these events was a weak state that relied heavily on the military to maintain order. Added to these difficulties was a particular pattern of industrialization that was concentrated in Catalonia and later the Basque Country, bringing wealth and prosperity to these regions while Castile remained largely agricultural. The state's inability to achieve political and economic modernization was compounded by competing visions of the Spanish state and national identity, most notably state centralism, which did not preclude some political or administrative decentralization, and unitarism, which viewed the territorial state and the Spanish nation as one and indivisible.

Federalism was one possible response to the problem of state and nation building in Spain. Historically, federalism was a democratizing force in Spain, which meant that it was a political project pursued by many republicans. The failure of nineteenth and early twentieth century republicanism, then, necessarily meant the failure of federalism. There was, first, the radical experiment of the Federal Republic – also known as the First Republic – of 1873–74 which sought to introduce federalism *abajo-arriba* (from the bottom up). Due to political opposition, however, republican leaders failed to introduce and implement a federal territorial structure and division of power.

Under the Second Republic (1931–39) there was never an explicit commitment to creating a federation, although the "*Estado integral*" may have provided some similarities in terms of its emphasis on regions. During the Second Republic Madrid was controlled by centralist republicans, while in the regions, federal republicans worked towards self-government through Statutes of Autonomy. Catalonia led the way with a Statute that was passed by the Spanish Parliament in 1932. The Autonomy Statutes created a political controversy that contributed directly to the outbreak of the Civil War (1936–1939), which was won by the forces of General Francisco Franco.

The Civil War was, in part, about destroying regional autonomy and re-instating Spanish unity. During Franco's dictatorship (1939–1975), the regime severely repressed nationalism and regional culture in the Basque Country, Catalonia and Galicia. Towards the end of the dictatorship, the minority nations began campaigning for a return to autonomy. But the autonomy question and the idea of federalism would prove to be substantial obstacles to a peaceful transition to democracy following Franco's death (1975). Nevertheless, a commitment on the part of Spanish political elites (including the King) to reverse discrimination against minority nations opened up the path to constitutional innovations.

2 CONSTITUTIONAL PROVISIONS RELATING TO FEDERALISM

Spain is a parliamentary monarchy with King Juan Carlos I as its current head of state. The constitution of the Kingdom of Spain was passed by the Cortes Generales on 31 October 1978 and was ratified by the Spanish people in a referendum on 7 December 1978.

Spain is not a federation in name nor is it a state made up of "constituent units," as is the case with most federations, but it does share many of the institutional features of federal states. Nevertheless, there has been much debate in Spain over the precise nature of the constitutional relationship between Madrid and the regions, especially the historic nationalities of Catalonia, the Basque Country and Galicia. The debate is due to the ambiguity of Article 2 of the constitution, which states that "[t]he Constitution is based on the indissoluble unity of the Spanish Nation, the common and indivisible country of all Spaniards; it recognizes and guarantees the right to autonomy of the nationalities and regions of which it is composed, and solidarity amongst them all." Although this article promotes the idea that there is only one constituent nation (Spanish), there are constitutional provisions that promote aspects of federalism. Thus, according to Article 137, "[t]he State is organized territorially into municipalities, provinces and any Autonomous Communities that may be constituted. All these bodies shall enjoy self government for the management of their respective interests." Accession to autonomy is a voluntary right and the constitution specifies how this right can be exercised. Since there are three different ways in which a territory can acquire autonomy, Spain is often referred to as characterized by a form of asymmetrical federalism.

The first path to acquire autonomy is through Transitory Provision No. 2, which allowed the Basque Country, Catalonia and Galicia, as "territories which in the past have, by plebiscite, approved draft Statutes of Autonomy and which at the time of the promulgation of this Constitution, have provisional autonomous regimes," to proceed to autonomy immediately after the constitution was passed. (The Statutes of the Basque Country and Catalonia came into force in 1979 and that of Galicia in 1981.) This procedure, known as the "rapid route" to autonomy, recognized the status of these three communities as historic nationalities.

Second, according to Article 143, "bordering provinces with common historic, cultural and economic characteristics, island territories and provinces with historic regional status may accede to self-government and form Autonomous Communities." Generally referred to as the "slow route" to autonomy, Article 143 requires several complicated steps intended to prove popular support for autonomy before a community could acquire powers specified in Article 148. However, it produced a limited form of autonomy, since a newly-established community had to wait five years before expanding the range of its powers to include those allowed under Article 149.

Third, Article 151 (the "exceptional route") allowed non-historic communities to proceed to autonomy along a route that eliminated the five-year waiting period through a system of local initiatives and referenda. This process is even more complicated than that outlined in Article 143 as it requires more than one popular referendum. Andalucia is the only community that was allowed to proceed to autonomy along this path.

Spain's central government is bicameral. The Cortes Generales consists of the Congreso de Diputados (Congress of Deputies), the legislative body, and the Senado (Senate), the upper house. Article 64 of the constitution states that the Senate is a chamber of territorial representation for the Autonomous Communities. However, most Senators are elected from provinces[1] – only a minority is elected from among the members of the regional assemblies of the Autonomous Communities. In 1994, an inter-party working group was set up in the Senate to consider the possibility of a constitutional amendment that would transform the upper house into a chamber of the regions. Although there is support for such an amendment, its progress has been slow.

There are 17 Autonomous Communities in Spain, each having an Autonomy Statute that was approved by the Spanish *Cortes*. In this sense, the autonomy of each community ultimately depends on parliamentary authority. The Autonomy Statute sets out the constitutional division of powers, which is provided for in Articles 148, 149 and 150.

---

1 As noted above, Spain is divided into municipalities and provinces, as well as the Autonomous Communities. The provinces are territorial units that were established in the nineteenth century. Historically, each province was run by a *diputación*, a delegation from Madrid, and some of these bodies still exist.

Article 148 specifies the exclusive powers of the Autonomous Communities and includes: matters relating to the institutions and functioning of self-government; planning and public works; some transport; agriculture, forestry, fishing and the environment; tourism; museums, libraries and the promotion of culture; sports and leisure; health and hygiene; and social assistance.

Article 149 specifies the exclusive powers of the Spanish state. These powers include: international relations; the administration of justice and certain areas of the law (criminal, penitentiary and commercial); certain legislation (civil rights, labour, intellectual property); the armed forces; immigration and emigration; economic planning; customs and tariffs; foreign trade; taxation; promotion of scientific research; public safety; and promotion of Spanish culture.

Several Autonomous Communities have, over time, negotiated the transfer of the central state's exclusive powers through two mechanisms contained in Article 150. The first mechanism is the delegation of powers and the transfer of financial resources to fund these powers. This delegation in no way implies a ceding of sovereignty on the part of the central power. Second, some normally exclusive powers of the state (justice, fiscal affairs, public security and international affairs) have been acquired by the "rapid route" Autonomous Communities.

There is one important special constitutional provision related to the division of powers – Additional Provision No. 1. According to this, the constitution protects and respects the historic rights of the territories with "*fueros,*" which are the historic privileges of different Spanish regions. Most of these privileges were lost during the eighteenth and nineteenth centuries, although the Basque Country and Navarra retained some of theirs. The *fueros* are not merely residual powers that are largely irrelevant for the twenty-first century; Additional Provision No. 1 makes it clear that these privileges can be updated within the framework of the Autonomy Statutes. Indeed, the *fueros* have been central to current debates on increasing federalism in Spain (see Section 3, below).

The financing of the governance of the Autonomous Communities is provided for under several different constitutional articles. Article 156 recognizes the right of the Autonomous Communities to financial autonomy. Article 157 stipulates that "[t]he resources of the Autonomous Communities shall comprise: a) taxes wholly or partially made over to them by the State; surcharges on State taxes and other shares in State revenue; b) their own taxes, rates and special levies; c) transfers from an inter-territorial clearing fund and other allocations to be charged to the General State Budget; d) revenues accruing from their property and private law income; e) the yield from credit operations." In addition, Article 158 states that an allocation may be made to the Autonomous Communities in the General State Budget in proportion to the volume of state services and activities for which they have assumed responsibility.

The details of the financial arrangements and mechanisms to be applied to finance the Autonomous Communities were laid out in the Organic Law on the Funding of Autonomous Communities (*Ley Orgánica de Financiación de las Comunidades Autónomas*, LOFCA) in 1980. In addition to the law, various multi-year agreements have been negotiated between a state body set up by this law and the regional assemblies. Financing is also regulated by the principle of solidarity among the communities, which is designed to correct regional imbalances (Articles 2, 138, 156). The Inter-Regional Compensation Fund (Article 157.1) redistributes funds among regions according to criteria such as population density, relative income, level of unemployment, level of integration, population dispersal and insularity.

The central government has primary responsibility for raising taxes under Article 133.1, but Autonomous Communities and local governments may also raise some taxes (Article 133.2) where the state has delegated the power to do so. Very few Autonomous Communities do raise taxes, the exceptions being the Basque Country and Navarra, which have retained historic tax-raising powers through Additional Provision No. 1. The rates for some of these taxes (personal income tax, company tax and VAT) must be the same as those set by the state.

Given Spain's troubled constitutional history, the fathers of the current constitution were careful to create institutions and procedures for the resolution of disputes, and in particular this role falls to the Constitutional Court (Title IX (Articles 159–165)). According to Article 159, the Court consists of 12 members appointed for nine years. Members are nominated by Congress (4), the Senate (4), the government (2) and General Council of the Judiciary (2). The Court has jurisdiction over all Spanish territory and is empowered to hear appeals about the unconstitutionality of laws and regulations, individual appeals for protection against violation of rights and liberties, and conflicts of jurisdiction between the state and the Autonomous Communities or between the Autonomous Communities themselves (Article 161). The Spanish government is permitted to contest before the Constitutional Court rules and regulations adopted by the agencies of the Autonomous Communities (Article 161.2). This right can potentially cause divisions between Madrid and the Autonomous Communities since the decision to contest a provision causes its immediate suspension. The Court then has five months in which to ratify or lift the suspension.

The procedures for constitutional amendment are complicated and vary depending on which parts of the constitution are to be amended. The government, Congress or Senate, can propose an amendment (Article 166), which must then be approved by three-fifths of both Houses (Article 167.1). Once this has been achieved, the amendment is submitted to a popular referendum, if one-tenth of either House requests it within 15 days of its passage (Article 167.3). If, however, the three-fifths threshold is not reached in the two Houses, a Commission of Deputies and Senators is set up to redraft the bill. It is then resubmitted to the two Houses for voting (Article 167.2). If approval is not achieved in this way, but at least the majority of the Senate has passed the bill, then the Congress can pass the bill by a two-thirds vote in favour (Article 167.2).[2]

The amendment procedure is more complicated in the two following situations: (1) a total revision of the constitution is proposed or (2) a partial proposal is made that will affect the Preliminary Title (Articles 2–9), Chapter Two, Section 1 of Title I (Fundamental Rights and Liberties), or Title II (the Crown). In these cases, two-thirds of each House must approve the principle of amendment, at which point the *Cortes* is dissolved and general elections are held (Article 168.1). The newly-elected *Cortes* must approve the decision, proceed to an examination of the new constitutional text and ratify it through a two-thirds majority of both Houses (Article 168.2). Finally, the new constitution must be ratified in a popular referendum (Article 168.3).

3 RECENT POLITICAL DYNAMICS

Spain's transition to constitutional democracy is an achievement of which the population and its political leadership are justly proud. However, the constitution of 1978 is not without its critics. Some groups, such as the extreme Basque terrorist organization ETA (Euskadi Ta Askatasuna/Basque Land and Freedom), have never accepted its legitimacy. More moderate, nationalist groups in the Basque Country, Catalunya and Galicia have criticized the narrow interpretation of the

2 It appears from this that the role of the Autonomous Communities is limited in the amendment process – Article 87.2 states only that "the Assemblies of the Autonomous Communities may request the Government to pass a bill or refer a non-governmental bill to the Congressional Steering Committee and to delegate a maximum of three Assembly members to defend it."

federalizing capacity of the constitution by the ruling parties in Madrid. Since 1998, there have been new public debates on federalism and the constitution. Several factors explain the timing of these debates and suggest that they are unlikely to go away. There is, first, the fact that Spain is a member state of the European Union, where regionalism is an accepted and promoted feature of integration. Second, there is widespread agreement that Spain's democracy is now stable enough for a public debate on increasing federalism. Third, the twentieth anniversary of the constitution, in 1998, was viewed as an opportune moment for reflecting on the capacity of Spain's asymmetrical federalism to promote the self-government of its minority nations. Finally, the beginning of ETA's ceasefire on 18 September 1998 removed the threat of violence from the public sphere.

In the months leading up to the twentieth anniversary of Spain's constitution, the ruling nationalist parties in the Basque Country (Partido Nacionalista Vasco (PNV)), Catalonia (Convergència i Unió (CiU)) and Galicia (Bloque Nacionalista Galego (BNG)), joined forces in an effort to promote a re-reading of the constitution that would recognize what they termed the "plurinational" nature of the Spanish state. Their public agenda was made known through the "Declaration of Barcelona" (16 July 1998) and the "Santiago Agreement" (1 November 1998). The first of these called for a public debate on a new political culture that recognizes and supports the plurinational character of the Spanish state. The Santiago Agreement made clear that the three nationalist parties sought "a change in the centralist and non-autonomist interpretative criteria used by the state legislators and supported, in general terms, by the Constitutional Court, that has resulted ... in the negation of the exclusive competencies of the autonomous communities." Instead, they demanded an "enhanced re-reading of the Constitution that guarantees the juridico-political recognition of the national realities [of the Basque Country, Catalonia and Galicia] without excluding the possibility of reform."

For these three historic groups, a plurinational Spain is one in which all minority nations coexist equally with the Spanish nation. They argue that this perspective in no way challenges Article 2 of the constitution, which recognizes that Spain is a nation of nations. Plurinationalism also promotes the notion of shared sovereignty and exclusive competencies. Similarly, in their opinion, Spain could cede authority to the governing structures of the Autonomous Communities so that they could enjoy exclusive competencies in matters such as: public security; tax-regulating and tax-raising powers; language and culture; increased judicial competencies; local administration; natural resources;

and representation in international fora. They envision a federal structure that recognizes the sovereignty of each constituting nation. The coalition of nationalist parties has argued that increased federalism can be achieved through the constitution itself, using Additional Provision No. 1 (see Section 2, above).

There have been two types of response to the demands for increased federalism on the part of Spain's three historic minority nations. There was, first, the response by the leadership of the ruling Partido Popular – and echoed by the socialist opposition, Partido Socialista Obrero Español (PSOE) – that the constitution is not to be tampered with in any way. The Spanish Prime Minister, José María Aznar, dismissed the possibility of re-reading the constitution, and criticized nationalist parties for promoting irresponsible ideas that would affect Spain's fundamental institutions (*El País*, 4 November 2000).

Second, there has been a response from other Autonomous Communities anxious to avoid any move on the part of the Basque Country, Catalonia and Galicia to acquire further powers. For example, the Presidents of three Autonomous Communities (Andalucia, Castilla-La Mancha and Extremadura) signed the "Declaration of Mérida" (6 October 1998) in opposition to the pacts signed by the nationalist parties. Reaffirming their support for the constitution, the three Presidents underscored that there exists "no natural right, neither a priori nor a posteriori to the Constitution, that can be invoked to justify granting privileges to certain territories or creating inequalities among Spaniards."

The climate for public discussions on the constitution and plurinationalism changed dramatically on 3 December 1999, when ETA broke its ceasefire. Between December 1999 and December 2000, 23 people were killed by the terrorist organization and scores of others injured. Given the threat to public security posed by ETA, the Partido Popular government is not prepared to discuss any moves towards increased federalism in the Basque Country, Catalonia and Galicia, since many Spaniards would view this as a further destabilization of the state. According to an opinion poll published at the end of 2000, a vast majority of Spaniards stated that they considered terrorism to be one of the principal problems in Spain.

In 2000, the Spanish government came under severe criticism for its strategy of dealing with ETA. Its strategy is to refuse any negotiations not only with ETA and its political wing Euskal Herritarrok, but also with any Basque political party that has signed the "Pact of Lizarra-Garazi." This pact, signed by political parties and associations of the Basque Country on 12 September 1998, states that any peace negotiations between the

Basque Country and Madrid must be open-ended – that is, they must not stop short of Basque independence, if that is the most viable solution to the problem. Many politicians, political commentators and intellectuals across Spain have publicly called for dialogue as the only way to combat terrorism. Although the Spanish public is highly mobilized in its public demonstrations against ETA, it is felt that some more concrete action is required. Towards that end, the year 2000 concluded with the government attempting to regain public confidence by signing an anti-terrorism agreement (The Agreement for Liberties and against Terrorism) with the opposition party PSOE. Other parties and sectors, such as labour and business, are also considering signing the pact. However, despite requests, the ruling nationalist party in Catalonia, CiU, has refused to add its name.

4 SOURCES FOR FURTHER INFORMATION

Agranoff, Robert (ed.), *Accommodating Diversity: Asymmetry in Federal States*, Baden-Baden: Nomos, 1999.

Agranoff, Robert and Rafael Bañón I. Martine (eds), *El Estado de las Autonomias: Hacia un Nuevo Federalismo?*, Vitoria: Administración de la Communidad Autónoma de Euskadi, Instituto Vasco de Administración Pública, 1999.

Agranoff, Robert and Juan Antonio Ramos Gallarin, "Toward Federal Democracy in Spain: An Examination of Intergovernmental Relations," *Publius: The Journal of Federalism*, Vol. 27, No. 4 (1997).

Gibbons, John, *Spanish Politics Today*, Manchester: Manchester University Press, 1999.

Gillespie, Richard, Jonathan Story and Fernando Rodrigo, *Democratic Spain*, London and New York: Routledge, 1995.

Moreno, Luis. *The Federalization of Spain*, London: Frank Cass, 2001.

Newton, Michael T. (with Peter J. Donaghy), *Institutions of Modern Spain: A Political and Economic Guide*, Cambridge: Cambridge University Press, 1997.

Requejo, Ferran and E. Fossas (eds), *Asimetría federal y estado plurinacional. El debate sobre la acomodación de la diversidad en Canadá, Bélgica y España*, Madrid: Editorial Trotta, 1999.

Requejo, Ferran (ed.), *Pluralisme nacional i legitimitat democràtica*, Barcelona: Editorial Proa, 1999.

Requejo, Ferran and U. Preuss (eds), *European Citizenship, Multiculturalism and the State*, Baden-Baden: Nomos, 1998.

Requejo, Ferran, *Zoom Polític. Democràcia, Federalisme i Nacionalisme, des d'una Catalunya europea*, Barcelona: Editorial Proa, 1998.

– *Federalisme, per a què?*, Valencia: Editorial tres i quatre, 1998.
http://www.la-moncloa.es/ (in Spanish)
Spain in Figures, 1999. Available at: http://www.ine.es/espcif/espcifin/espcifin.htm
http://www.spainemb.org/information/constitucionin.htm
Partido Popular: http://www.pp.es/index.asp
Partido Socialista Obrero Española: http://www.psoe.es/Nuevas-Politicas-NuevosTiempos/home.htm
Partido Nacionalista Vasco: http://www.eaj-pnv.com/homecas.htm
Convergència Democràtica de Catalunya: http://www.convergencia.org
Unió Democràtica de Catalunya: http://www.unio.es
Bloque Nacionalista Galego: http://www.bng-galiza.org

Table I
Political and Geographic Indicators

Capital city	Madrid
Number and type of constituent units	*17 Autonomous Communities:* Andalucia, Aragon, Asturias, Balears (Balearic Islands), Canarias (Canary Islands), Cantabria, Castilla-La Mancha, Castilla y Leon, Cataluna, Communidad Valenciana, Extremadura, Galicia, La Rioja, Madrid, Murcia, Navarra, Pais Vasco (Basque Country) Note: There are five sovereign areas off the coast of Morocco: Ceuta and Melilla are administered as autonomous regions; Islas Chafarinas, Penon de Alhucemas, and Penon de Velez de la Gomera are under direct Spanish administration; Andora is a principality under the shared sovereignty of Spain and France.
Official language(s)	Castilian Spanish
Area	504 782 km^2
Area – Largest constituent unit	Castilla y Leon (94 224 km^2)
Area – Smallest constituent unit	Balears (4 992 km^2)
Total population	40 037 995
Population by constituent unit (% of total population)	Andalucia 18.2%, Cataluna 15.4%, Madrid 13%, Communidad Valencian 10%, Galicia 6.8%, Castilla y Leon 6.2%, Pais Vasco (Basque Country) 5.3%, Castilla-La Mancha 4.3%, Canarias (Canary Islands) 4.1%, Aragon 3%, Murcia 3%, Asturias 2.7%, Extremadura 2.7%, Baleares (Balearic Islands) 2%, Cantabria 1.3%, Navarra 1.3%, La Rioja 0.07% (Note: The remaining 0.3% of the population is in the 5 sovereign areas.)
Political system – federal	Constitutional Monarchy – Parliamentary System
Head of state – federal	King Juan Carlos I de Borbón y Borbón (1975)
Head of government – federal	President José María Aznar (1996/2000). President is elected by the National Assembly through the mechanism of investure (absolute majority if it is the first voting, and simple majority if it is the second voting). President appoints the Cabinet (Council of Ministers). Both serve for a 4-year term. (Note: There is also a Council of State that is the supreme consultative organ of the government.)

Table I (continued)

Government structure – federal	Bicameral: Las Cortes Generales (General Courts/ National Assembly) *Upper House* – Senado (Senate), 259 seats. 208 members are directly elected by popular vote. The remaining 51 are appointed by the regional legislatures to serve 4-year terms. *Lower House* – Congreso de Diputados (Congress of Deputies), 350 seats. Members are elected by popular vote on block lists by proportional representation to serve 4-year terms. Note: In both Houses, the term Grupos Parlamentarios (Parliamentary Groups) is used not political parties. Parliamentary Groups are produced by political or ideological affinities of the members elected through proportional representation. Similar to the practice with political parties, positions on committees are assigned in proportion to the number of seats claimed by the different Parliamentary Groups. A minimum of 15 members is required to form a Parliamentary Group, or 5 members if political parties on the list system have obtained 15% of the vote in a particular constituent unit, or 5% of the national vote. Members who do not voluntarily join a Parliamentary Group are incorporated into the Grupo Mixto (Mixed Group).
Number of representatives in lower house of federal government – Congress of Deputies	350 Seats: Grupo Parlamentario Popular (People's Parliamentary Group) 183, Grupo Parlamentario Socialista (Socialist Parliamentary Group) 125, Grupo Parlamentario Catalán (Convergència i Unió) (Catalonian Parliamentary Group (Convergence and Union)) 15, Grupo Parlamentario Federal de Izquierda Unida (United Left) 8, Grupo Parlamentario Vasco (EAJ-PNV) (Basque Parliamentary Group) 7, Grupo Parlamentario de Coalición Canaria (Canarian Coalition Parliamentary Group) 4, Grupo Parlamentario Mixto (Mixed Parliamentary Group) 8.
Number of representatives in lower house of federal government for most populated constituent unit	Andalucía: 62
Number of representatives in lower house of federal government for least populated constituent unit	La Rioja: 4

Table I (continued)

Number of representatives in upper house of federal government – Senate	259 Seats (208 elected + 51 appointed): Grupo Parlamentario Popular (People's Parliamentary Group) 150 (127 elected + 23 appointed), Grupo Parlamentario Socialista (Socialist Parliamentary Group) 69 (53 elected + 16 appointed), Grupo Parlamentario Catalán (Convergència i Unió) (Catalonian Parliamentary Group (Convergence and Union)) 11 (8 elected + 3 appointed), Grupo Parlamentario Catalana de Progrés (Catalonian Parliamentary Group for Progess) 11 (8 elected + 3 appointed), Grupo Parlamentario de Senadores de Nacionalistas Vascos (Nationalist Basque Senators Parliamentary Group) 8 (6 elected + 2 appointed), Grupo Parlamentario de Senadores de Coalición Canaria (Canarian Coalition Senators Parliamentary Group) 6 (5 elected + 1 appointed), Grupo Parlamentario Mixto (Mixed Parliamentary Group) 4 (1 elected + 3 appointed).
Distribution of representation in upper house of federal government – Senate	Distribution of 51 appointed seats in the Autonomous Communities: Andalucia 8, Aragón 2, Asturias 2, Balears 1, Canarias 2, Cantabria 1, Castilla-La Mancha 2, Castilla y Leon 3, Cataluna 7, Communidad Valenciana 5, Extremadura 2, Galicia 3, Madrid 6, Murcia 2, Navarra 1, Pais Vasco 3, Rioja 1. Distribution of 208 elected seats in the constituencies of the Autonomous Communities: 4 seats for each of the following constituencies: Álava, Albacete, Alicante, Almería, Asturias, Ávila, Badajoz, Barcelona, Burgos, Cáceres, Cádiz, Cantabria, Castellón, Ciudad Real, Córdoba, A Coruña, Cuenca, Girona, Granada, Guadalajara, Guipúzcoa, Huelva, Huesca, Jaén, León, Lleida, Lugo, Madrid, Málaga, Murcia, Navarra, Ourense, Palencia, Pontevedra, Rioja (La), Salamanca, Segovia, Sevilla, Soria, Tarragona, Teruel, Toledo, Valencia, Valladolid, Vizcaya, Zamora, Zaragoza; 3 seats for each of: Gran Canaria, Mallorca, Tenerife; 2 seats for: Melilla; 1 seat for each of: Fuerteventura, La Gomera, El Hierro, Ibiza-Formentera, Lanzarote, Balears, La Palma.
Constitutional court (highest court dealing with constitutional matters)	Constitutional Court. There are 12 members of the Constitutional Court of which 4 are nominated by a three-fifths majority in Congress, four are nominated by the Senate with the same majority, two are nominated by the government, and two by the General Council of the Judiciary. Justices are appointed for a nine-year term and one third of the membership is renewed every three years. Members cannot be re-appointed.

Table I (continued)

Political system of constituent units	Unicameral: The Legislative Assemblies of each of the autonomous communities are proportionally elected, with the specific composition being determined by the community.
Head of state – constituent units	President of the Governing Council
Head of government – constituent units	President of the Governing Council. The President is elected by the Legislative Assembly from among its own members and is then formally appointed by the Monarch.

Table II
Economic and Social Indicators

GDP	US$720.8 billion
GDP per capita	US$18 000
Mechanisms for taxation	Taxes are usually levied by the central government, but the autonomous communities also have the right to raise certain taxes. However, with the exception of the Basque Country and Navarra, this seldom happens. • Personal Income Tax: 6 tax brackets ranging from 18.0%–48.1%. • Value-added Tax (IVA): Three ranges, 16% on most goods and service, 7% as a reduced rate, and 4% for basic goods and services. • Corporate Taxes (average rate of 35%). • Real Estate Taxes (often levied by local authorities, ranging from 0.3% to 1.17%). • Excise taxes. Canary Island, Ceuta and Melilla are exempt from many of these taxes.
National debt (external)	US$90 billion
National unemployment rate	14%
Constituent unit with highest unemployment rate	Andalucia – 26.8%
Constituent unit with lowest unemployment rate	Balears – 7.92%
Adult literacy rate	97.4%
National expenditures on education as a % of GDP	5.8%
Life expectancy in years	78.79
Doctors per population ratio (national)	424 doctors per 100 000 inhabitants
Doctors per population ratio in constituent units (highest)	Aragón – 530 doctors per 100 000 inhabitants
Doctors per population ratio in constituent units (lowest)	Castilla-La Mancha – 310 doctors per 100 000 inhabitants
National expenditures on health as a % of GDP	7.1%

Sources

Behrens, Axel. "Regional Gross Domestic Product in the European Union 1998." *Statistics in Focus,* Theme 1–3/2001. www.europa.eu.int/comm/eurostat/

Behrens, Axel. "Unemployment in the Regions of the European Union 1999." *Statistics in Focus,* Theme 1–3/2000. www.europa.eu.int/comm/eurostat/

Central Intelligence Agency (CIA), *World Fact Book 2000,* CIA, Washington, DC, 2000, On-line source, www.cia.gov/cia/publications/factbook/index.html

Congress of Spain. www.congreso.es

Economist Intelligence Unit, "Country Commerce – Argentina," *The Economist Intelligence Unit 2000*. New York: EIU, 2000.

Elazar, Daniel J. (ed.) *Federal Systems of the World: A Handbook of Federal, Confederal and Autonomy Arrangements.* 2nd Edition. Jerusalem Institute for Federal Studies. London: Longman Group/Westgate House, 1994.

Eurostat. "Table IV.I Expenditures 1992" and "Table VII.I Health Personnel and Equipment." *Regions: Statistical Yearbook 1996*. Luxembourg: Office of Statistics for the European Community (Eurostat), 1996.

International Monetary Fund (IMF). *International Financial Statistics*, Vol. LIII, No. 12, December 2000. Washington, DC: the IMF Statistics Department, 2000.

INE (Instituto nacional estadística) (Spain's National Institute of Statistics). *Spain in Figures 1999*. www.ine.es

Organization for Economic Co-operation and Development (OECD). www.oecd.org/std/gdp.htm

Senate of Spain. "Composition of Senate." www.senado.es/home_i.html

Sí, Spain. "The Constitutional Court." Politics and Public Administration. www.sispain.org/english/politics

UNESCO. *World Education Report 1998: Teachers and Teaching in a Changing World.* Paris: UNESCO, 1998.

United Nations. *Human Development Report, 2000*. www.undp.org/hdro/report.html

World Bank. *World Development Report 2000/2001: Attacking Poverty*. www.worldbank.org/poverty/wdrpoverty/report/index.htm

World Health Organisation (WHO). "Estimates of Health Personnel." www-nt.who.int/whosis/statistics

World Health Organisation (WHO). "Annex Table 8, Selected national health accounts indicators for all Member States, estimates for 1997." *World Health Report 2000*. Geneva, 2000. www-nt.who.int/whosis/statistics/menu.cfm

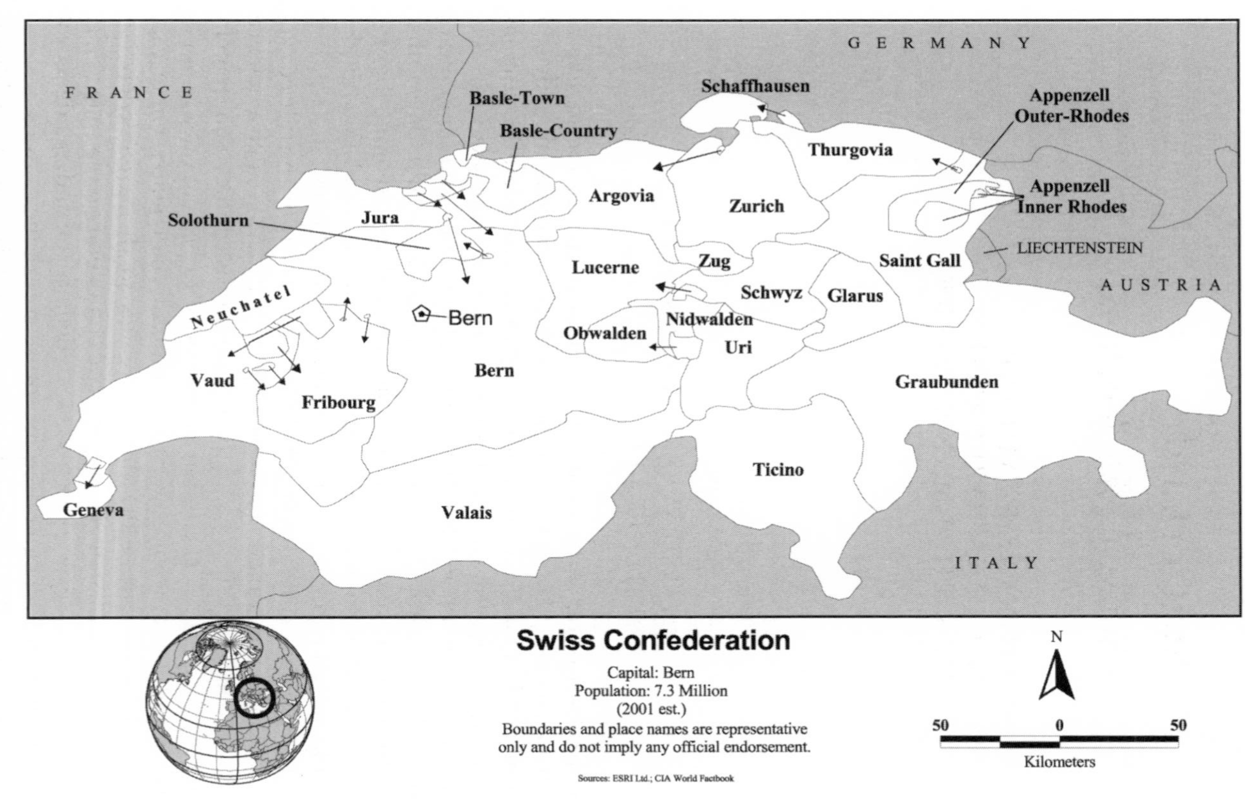
GERMANY
FRANCE
AUSTRIA
ITALY
LIECHTENSTEIN
Schaffhausen
Basle-Town
Basle-Country
Appenzell Outer-Rhodes
Appenzell Inner Rhodes
Thurgovia
Argovia
Zurich
Solothurn
Jura
Lucerne
Zug
Saint Gall
Schwyz
Glarus
Neuchatel
Bern
Obwalden
Nidwalden
Uri
Vaud
Fribourg
Graubunden
Ticino
Geneva
Valais
Swiss Confederation
Capital: Bern
Population: 7.3 Million
(2001 est.)
Boundaries and place names are representative
only and do not imply any official endorsement.
Sources: ESRI Ltd.; CIA World Factbook
N
50
0
50
Kilometers

Switzerland
(*Swiss Confederation*)

THOMAS STAUFFER,
NICOLE TÖPPERWIEN,
URS THALMANN-TORRES

1 HISTORY AND DEVELOPMENT OF FEDERALISM

Switzerland is a country of about 7 million people in the middle of Europe. Its neighbours are Germany, Austria, Liechtenstein, Italy and France. It has been a federation since 1848, and its federal institutions have meant that the country has been able to accommodate diversity politically. Historically, the 26 cantons and the about 3,000 communes were able to develop their own traditions and cultures so that Switzerland had and still has cultural, cantonal and communal diversity. Switzerland did not attempt to homogenize its population nor did it split according to linguistic, religious, or cultural lines.

The official starting point of Swiss history is 1291. In 1291 three cantons (at this time called *Orte*) concluded a treaty and created a defence union combined with a system of arbitration for conflict management among the cantons. The union was intended to prevent outside dominance and guarantee a power balance within the country. Other cantons joined by concluding further treaties so that a confederation based on a treaty system developed. The confederation was to facilitate as much cooperation as necessary to defend the independence of Switzerland while safeguarding the sovereignty of the cantons.

At the end of the eighteenth century modernization in neighbouring countries, industrialization and the professionalization of the army, combined with the ideas of the French Revolution, triggered demands for some centralization and modernization in Switzerland. In 1798 French forces led by Napoleon invaded and created a centralized state in accordance with the French example. The cantons were transformed into equal but purely administrative units. Switzerland, however, quickly proved to be ungovernable as a centralized state, and Napoleon brought back the cantonal system.

After Napoleon's defeat, Switzerland opted again for a loose confederation. In the Vienna Congress (1815) the borders and the neutrality of Switzerland were recognized. While many of the Protestant cantons adopted progressive democratic governments, in other predominantly Catholic cantons the old influential families re-introduced conservative power structures. The progressive cantons pressed for democratization and centralization of the union. In order to limit the pressure of the progressive (mostly Protestant) cantons, the conservative (predominantly Catholic) cantons formed a secret union (*Sonderbund*). This violated the treaty of confederation. When the union was revealed and the Catholic cantons refused to dissolve it, the Protestant cantons dissolved it by force. The year 1847 entered Swiss history as the year of civil war. After the civil war, the defeated Catholic cantons elected new democratic governments.

In 1848 the people and the cantons of Switzerland adopted a federal constitution. This constitution was a compromise between the winners and losers of the civil war. It introduced some centralization but it also guaranteed, through the institutional set-up and the limitation of competencies of the central government, respect for cantonal diversity.

With the 1848 constitution, Switzerland took an important step towards modernity. It became a federal country based on constitutionally-guaranteed shared rule and self-rule. The modernization did not aim at homogenization of the population but tried to create a Swiss nation by preserving the pre-existing diversity. The combination of shared rule and self-rule enabled the country to create diversity in unity.

While over the years the institutions and political processes have developed further, and there have been two total revisions of the constitution (1874, 1999), the over-all design has stayed the same. The federal constitution has provided the basis for the peaceful cohabitation of different cultural, linguistic and religious groups.

2 CONSTITUTIONAL PROVISIONS RELATING TO FEDERALISM

Switzerland is a federation composed of 26 cantons (Article 1), of which six are so-called "half cantons," arising out of the historic division of three cantons taking place before the foundation of the federation in 1848. These half cantons have the same independence as the other 20 cantons (Article 3), with the exception that they have only half the representation when the formal tools of shared rule are concerned. This means that they have only one representative in the Senate (Article 150), and only half of a cantonal vote when the majority of cantons is required for a referendum (Article 142).

According to the Swiss Federal Constitution of 1999, as well as earlier constitutions, cantons are "sovereign" as long and insofar as their sovereignty is not limited by the constitution (Article 3). Sovereign in this case means that they have the exclusive right to execute the legislative, executive and judicial powers within their territory in all domains that can be subject to state power. The Confederation is obliged to respect this exclusive sovereignty of the cantons. ("Confederation" refers to the official name of the Swiss federal state, Confederatio Helvetica or "Swiss Confederation" in English. Despite its traditional name, however, the modern Swiss political structure does not fit the modern concept of a confederation, but is rather a federation.)

This sovereignty is not absolute, however. The 1999 constitution places limitations on the sovereignty of the cantons in several different ways. For example, it guarantees fundamental rights to all people living in Switzerland (Articles 7–36) and provides judicial review by the Swiss Federal Supreme Court, which watches over the observance of fundamental rights by cantonal authorities. Even more clearly, the limitations to the sovereignty of the cantons come out of the legislative and executive competencies of the Confederation.

However, there are still important subjects over which the Confederation has no, or very little, competence. As a consequence, these matters remain within cantonal jurisdiction. Listed below are some examples of major importance to cantonal self-determination and cultural identification.

State constitutions. The drafting of state constitutions is purely cantonal. The cantons define their own political system.

Municipalities. The territorial division of the cantons into municipalities has a very long tradition. Each canton grants different powers to its municipalities, but once these powers are laid down in the law, they are guaranteed and protected by the Swiss Federal Court in much the same way as it protects the fundamental rights of individuals.

Education. Education on all levels is an almost purely cantonal matter. Cantons themselves define the curriculum, and appoint, employ or elect the teaching staff, etc.

Public order. In peace-time, public order is a purely cantonal matter. A federal police force does not exist.

Direct taxes. Cantons raise their own taxes on income.

There are no issue-areas that are in the domain neither of the Confederation nor of the cantons. Each new issue that is not mentioned in the constitution automatically falls within cantonal power (Article 3). So, theoretically speaking, there can never be lacunae in the division of powers.

A further observation concerns the power to distribute the competencies. As the revision of the 1999 constitution is a federal matter (Articles 192–195), and the distribution of competencies arises exclusively from the constitution, the revision of powers is a federal competence. However, this power is limited by the cantonal role in the decision-making process at the federal level.

Several institutions and practices give the cantons an important influence in decision making at the federal level (shared rule). First, the federal law-drafting authorities are obliged to inform the cantons directly about their intentions and in most cases the law gives the cantons the right to be consulted. Thus, the cantons have influence on the process even before a proposition comes to the Parliament (Articles 45, 55). This is important as in this stage cantons can still have an important influence on the formulation of legislation, whereas afterwards their influence would be reduced to saying "yes" or "no."

Second, the Swiss federal Parliament, the Swiss Federal Assembly, is divided into two chambers, the National Council representing the people, and the Council of States representing the cantons. In the Council of States each canton has the same number of votes. Each chamber has exactly the same powers, and no federal statute can be enacted without the agreement of both of the chambers (Articles 148, 156, 163). The influence of the cantons through the Council of States has declined, however, due to the fact that cantons are not allowed to instruct their representatives (Article 161). The only external influence on Members of Parliament is their need to be re-elected. In elections to the Federal Assembly the cantons form the constituencies (Article 149) and the cantonal sections of the parties select the candidates. In Switzerland political parties are strongest at the cantonal level, and therefore the deputies of both chambers try to adapt their political actions to the interests of the cantonal section of their respective party. This is a very important element of shared rule in Switzerland and provides one of the most significant counter-weights to the centralizing force of the federal government.

Third, statutes and constitutional amendments are always subject to a popular referendum (Articles 140–142). Two different types of referendum must be distinguished. For ordinary legislation – a federal statute, for example – the referendum is optional and will only take place when 50,000 citizens have requested it. A proposition is approved if a majority of voters in the country as a whole agree. For the more important decisions – such as revisions of the constitution and the entry into international organizations for collective security, or organizations with supranational powers – a referendum is mandatory, and no collection of signatures has to take place. In this case, approval requires a majority of *cantons* in addition to a majority of voters. This means that a majority of the voters must approve in more than half of the cantons. Considering the large difference in terms of population between large cantons and small cantons, a proposal to revise the constitution can theoretically be rejected although 90 per cent of the population approved it, when the rejecting 10 per cent is evenly distributed in the smallest cantons. In other words, when it comes to the requirement of receiving approval in a majority of cantons, a voter of the (smallest) canton of Appenzell Innerhoden outweighs 40 citizens of Zurich.

And finally, the composition of the executive branch of the federal government, the Federal Council (Articles 174–179), is a very important factor of shared rule, mainly because the Federal Council and its administration draft almost all law-making propositions, and they negotiate whenever an international treaty is discussed. The Federal Council is one of the best examples to show the particularly Swiss way of conducting politics – what is called consensus-driven democracy. It is composed of seven Federal Councillors, elected by both chambers of the federal Parliament, each of whom is head of a ministry, and together they are the Swiss Executive. For government decisions, all members of the Federal Council have equal votes, which means that the federal President is only *primus inter pares.* As much as possible, all major groups are given representation in the Council. This means essentially that the important political parties are represented as well as the language groups, the cantons and both genders. This representation is not the result of a legal provision and is not even mentioned in the federal constitution. Nevertheless a German-speaking parliamentarian of the Radical Party would vote for a French-speaking socialist when it is the latter's turn to replace one of the Council representatives. The reason for this lies particularly in Switzerland's tradition of direct democracy; a legislative proposal would have little chance of being accepted by the people if one (or more) major group did not support it. Since a strong opposition would be able to block most legislative activity, it is in the interest of every party to have the other groups involved for all important proposals.

Since the revision of 1999, the constitution states that the Confederation will only assume the tasks that require uniform regulation (Article 42(2)). This rule binds the Confederation to the principle of subsidiarity in terms of the division of powers between the cantons and the central government. In this sense, the Confederation should only get jurisdiction if a uniform regulation is expected to be more efficient than regulation by the cantons.

The principle of subsidiarity also applies to the application of law. The Confederation does not itself implement a great deal of federal law enacted within its constitutional competencies; it is the cantons which are in charge of carrying out most federal law. This gives the cantons much space to manoeuvre and take cantonal particularities into account. According to the principle of subsidiarity, the Confederation is required to leave the application of its law to the cantons as far as possible, regulating only what is absolutely necessary.

Another unique characteristic of Swiss federalism is the lack of judicial review on the federal level. This means that, unlike in other federations, the Federal Supreme Court has no direct influence on the balance of powers between the cantons and the federation, even though it is "the highest federal judicial authority" (Article 188). The usual explanation of this unique constitutional provision is both historical mistrust of the population towards the power of judges, and an extremely strong belief in democracy. This led the constitution-makers to the decision that judges should not be able to abolish what has been decided democratically. In practice, the trust the constitution-makers had in the democratic institutions has mostly been justified. In general, federal law-makers obey the rules to which they are bound. Only in very few cases, has the federal Parliament enacted statutes where its competence to do so has been questioned.

The federal and referendum-based system – especially the requirement for majority cantonal approval in important decisions, and the lack of harmonization within cantonal domains – is sometimes criticized for its tendency to slow down the political process in Switzerland. Progressive politicians in particular see major problems, notably because most of the small cantons are conservative in their voting behaviour, and can, due to their power in referenda and their strong representation in the Senate, block many progressive propositions. This is one of the reasons why Swiss politics are slower than politics in other comparable countries. But on the other hand, this system forces policy-makers to think their ideas over and has probably prevented Switzerland from many rash decisions. In this sense, the system might be one of the factors that has helped maintain the political stability that has lasted since the foundation of the Confederation in 1848 – a remarkable feat given that it was a poor, rural country, which had just experienced a civil war that reflected a series of major political changes, social troubles and religious differences.

3 RECENT POLITICAL DYNAMICS

On 1 January 2000 a new federal constitution came into force replacing the constitution of 1874. This marked not the end of but a decisive step in a process initiated by the federal Parliament in 1965. The general feeling at that time was that the Swiss political system was not fit to cope with the far-reaching changes occurring in the post-World War II era. While not changing the meaning of the existing constitutional norms, the new constitution formulates them using modern language and re-structures their order. However, some new content was introduced as well, especially with respect to cooperative federalism (see the discussion on foreign policy below). Major institutional reforms of the judicial system and direct democracy were postponed. (Since then a proposal relating to judicial reform has been approved in a referendum but has not yet been implemented.)

Most of the recent trends in Swiss federalism can be traced to the phenomenon of increasing and accelerating integration. Whereas at the global level integration is still mainly restricted to the economy, it has become a powerful political project at the European level. This has been changing the political landscape in Switzerland in recent years by providing a platform for the growth of the populist and nationalist-conservative Swiss People's Party which is opposed to political integration at both the European and global levels. Until now this has not threatened the coalition government in place since 1959, but it has strained Swiss unity because it has created a cleavage between the French cantons which are in favour of political integration and the German-speaking ones which oppose it. For the time being it is still the policy of the Federal Council to join the European Union (EU), but *after* the implementation of bilateral treaties on air, road and rail traffic, free movement of persons, public procurement and technical barriers to trade, as well as agricultural products and research. The question remains how Swiss federalism can adapt to these developments without having to sacrifice its past accomplishments with respect to internal peace, political participation and welfare.

This trend toward integration has implications for the following three policy fields: (1) the role of the cantons in foreign policy; (2) reform of fiscal equalization; and (3) reform of the political and administrative institutions and processes.

Historically the Swiss cantons were full subjects under international law, but by the end of World War I they had given up even the very restricted powers in foreign affairs left to them by the federal constitution. Equally restricted was their participation in the foreign policy of the federal state. These restrictions were offset by their exceptionally high degree of independence within Switzerland (self-rule). Since the end of World War II this arrangement has come under strain because the international treaties signed by the federal government increasingly trench on the competencies of the cantons. The gradual but steady integration of Switzerland into Europe is making it necessary to find new solutions based on increased shared-rule in foreign policy to compensate for the loss of self-rule. A step in this direction has been made by the 1999 constitution, which enshrines the right of the cantons to participate in the making of foreign policy decisions. As well, in cases pertaining to their exclusive powers the cantons can participate in international negotiations. Furthermore there is a trend for the cantons and their associations to take full advantage of the existing possibilities for international cooperation (e.g., through membership in the Assembly of European Regions).

The second trend relates to the reform of fiscal equalization. The Swiss fiscal system is marked by comparatively strong decentralization both of expenditures and revenues. Formal fiscal equalization at the federal level was introduced only in 1959, when the federal government was constitutionally given the mission to provide for fiscal equalization among the cantons. The fiscal equalization law has the objective of providing all cantons with the means necessary to carry out their functions and provide their citizens with a basic (but not equal) level of services. The main instrument to attain these objectives is the disbursement of federal grants and cantonal contributions to the funding of federal tasks according to a formula based on an index of financial capacities. The same index is used in revenue sharing and in determining cantonal contributions to social security.

This system combines little actual equalization with lack of transparency regarding financial flows and decision making. It is being challenged because of its inefficiency and because of the shift in the relative capacity and burden of the cantons. Global integration is not only favouring those cantons with strong industrial and especially service-based economies, but is also affecting them through immigration and competitive pressure. European integration is weakening the autonomy of the cantons which are already heavily dependent on federal grants-in-aid.

Thus, a joint working group has been formed to study the issue. It proposes to: (a) disentangle the respective responsibilities; (b) invigorate cooperation among the cantons with a institutionalized system of burden-sharing; (c) create new ways of cooperating in the areas of joint responsibility; and (d) create a new system of direct fiscal equalization. This system will on the one hand provide every canton with a minimal endowment through unconditional horizontal transfers between the cantons, complemented by federal transfers where necessary. On the other hand, it includes horizontal compensations for spill-overs and vertical support for extraordinary burdens (geographic, topographic or socio-demographic). Despite substantial criticism from various groups, among others the municipal governments, the joint working group plans to submit a bill to the government by autumn 2001.

The third trend relates to the reform of political and administrative institutions and processes. The increased competitive pressure experienced by the cantons, but also by Switzerland as a whole, has led in many cases to the demand that the institutions developed over the decades be (radically) changed. First steps in this direction have been made through the introduction of elements of competition, outcome-orientation and flexibility into public management at all levels, and through the corporatization and privatization of public enterprises. From the perspective of Swiss federalism, however, potentially much more significant are the plans to merge cantons. The most advanced plan is the initiative to merge the Cantons of Geneva and Vaud which might be submitted to a popular vote simultaneously in both cantons in 2002.

4 SOURCES FOR FURTHER INFORMATION

Auer, Andreas, Giorgio Malinverni and Michel Hottelier, *Droit constitutionnel suisse*, Berne: Staempfli, 2000.

Basta-Fleiner, Lidija R. and Thomas Fleiner (eds), *Federalism and Multiethnic States – The Case of Switzerland*, 2nd ed., Basel, Geneva, Munich: Helbing & Lichterhahn (Publications of the Institute of Federalism, Fribourg Switzerland PIFF, Vol. 16), 2000.

Linder, Wolf, *Swiss Democracy – Possible Solutions to Conflict in Multicultural Societies*, 2nd ed., Hampshire and London: Macmillan Press Ltd., 1998

Steinberg, Jonathan, *Why Switzerland?* 2nd ed., Cambridge, UK: Cambridge University Press, 1996.

Institute of Federalism: http://www.federalism.ch/

Table I
Political and Geographic Indicators

Capital city	Bern
Number and type of constituent units	*26 Cantons* (6 are half-cantons): Aargau, Appenzell (Ausserrhoden and Innerrhoden), Basel (Basel-Landschaft and Basel-Stadt), Bern, Fribourg, Genève, Glarus, Graubünden, Jura, Luzern, Neuchâtel, Unterwalden (Nidwalden and Obwalden), St. Gallen, Schaffhausen, Schwyz, Solothurn, Thurgau, Ticino, Uri, Valais, Vaud, Zug, Zürich
Official language(s)	German, French, Italian, Romansch
Area	41 290 km^2
Area – Largest constituent unit	Graubünden (7 105 km^2)
Area – Smallest constituent unit	Basel-Stadt (37.2 km^2)
Total population	7 209 924
Population by constituent unit (% of total population)	Zürich 17%, Bern 13%, Vaud 8.6%, Aargau 7.5%, St. Gallen 6.2%, Genève 5.6%, Luzern 5.0%, Ticino 4.3%, Valais 3.8%, Basel-Landschaft 3.6%, Solothurn 3.4%, Fribourg 3.3%, Thurgau 3.2%, Basel-Stad 2.6%, Graubünden 2.6%, Neuchâtel 2.3%, Schwyz 2.0%, Zug 1.3%, Schaffhausen 1.0%, Jura 0.1%, Appenzell Ausserrhoden 0.08%, Glarus 0.05%, Nidwalden 0.05%, Obwalden 0.05%, Uri 0.05%, Appenzell Innerrhoden 0.02%
Political system – federal	Federal Republic
Head of state – federal	Technically, the head of state in Switzerland is the Federal Council (Bundesrat) *in corpore*, which serves also as the Chief Executive Authority. Moreover, a President (Chair) is appointed to serve a 1-year term and chairs the Cabinet or Federal Council, which is comprised of 7 representatives serving 4-year terms. Both the President and the Council are elected by the Federal Assembly.
Head of government – federal	President Moritz Leuenberger (2001), Kaspar Villiger (2002). The power and duties of the Head of Government are shared among the 7 members of the Federal Council. (Note: The President acts as "primus inter pares," but does not have the wide-ranging power commonly assigned to a President.)

Table I (continued)

Government structure – federal	Bicameral – Swiss Federal Assembly: *Second Chamber* – Ständerat (Council of States), 46 seats. 2 members come from each of the 20 full cantons and one from each of the 6 half-cantons. Electoral procedure is determined by cantonal law and can vary from canton to canton. *First Chamber* – Nationalrat (National Council), 200 seats. Members are directly elected for 4-year terms, in proportion to the population of each canton (each of which must have at least 1 representative).
Number of representatives in lower house of federal government – Council of States	200 Seats: Sozialdemokratische Fraktion (Social-Democratic Group) 53, Freisinnig-demokratische Fraktion (Radical-Democratic Group) 42, Christlich-Demokratische (Christian Democratic Group) 35, Fraktion der Schweizerischen Volkspartei (Swiss People's Group) 45, Grüne Fraktion (Green Group) 10, Liberale Fraktion (Liberal Group) 6, Evangelische und Unabhängige Fraktion (Evangelicals, Independents and Federal Democratic Union) 5, Fraktionslos (Factionless Group) 4.
Number of representatives in lower house of federal government for most populated constituent unit	Zürich: 34 seats
Number of representatives in lower house of federal government for least populated constituent unit	Uri, Obwalden, Nidwalden, Glarus, and Appenzell Innerrhoden: 1 seat each.
Number of representatives in upper house of federal government – National Council	46 Seats: Freisinnig-Demokratische Fraktion (Radical-Democratic Group) 18, Christlich-Demokratische Fraktion (Christian Democratic Fraktion) 15, Fraktion der Schweizerischen Volkspartei (Swiss People's Group) 7, Sozialdemokratische Fraktion (Social-Democratic Group) 6
Distribution of representation in upper house of federal government – National Council	Each canton has 2 seats, and each half-canton has one seat.
Constitutional court (highest court dealing with constitutional matters)	Federal Supreme Court. This is the highest court but it does *not* have the power of judicial review.

Table I (continued)

Political system of constituent units	Unicameral: Parliament (Kantonsrat, Grosser Rat or Grand Conseil), is directly elected. In the cases of the cantons of Appenzell Innerrhoden and Glarus, there is also a Landsgemeinde, or an "open-air assembly" of all voters (which does not replace the Parliament). (Note: the political systems used among the different cantons vary greatly.)
Head of state – constituent units	Chairperson: Chair of the Executive Council (structure differs among Cantons). The Executive Council and Chair are directly elected with the Chair serving for 1 or 2 year(s).
Head of government – constituent units	Chairperson and Executive Council

Table II
Economic and Social Indicators

GDP	US$207 billion
GDP per capita	US$28 600
Mechanisms for taxation	Income Taxes are levied at the Federal level, but mostly at the Cantonal and Municipal levels. The Federal rate covers 13 brackets, with rates ranging from 1–13%; Cantonal and Municipal Income Tax rates vary from each constituency and range in rate from 2–13%. Value-added Tax (VAT): Levied at the Federal level, the rate averages 7.6% and is on all goods and services; Corporate taxes, Stamp taxes, excise taxes and real estate taxes are all levied at the federal and cantonal level.
National debt (external)	N/A
National unemployment rate	1.9%
Constituent unit with highest unemployment rate	Geneva: 4.4%
Constituent unit with lowest unemployment rate	Appenzell Innerrhoden: 0.3%
Adult literacy rate	99%
National expenditures on education as a % of GDP	5.4%
Life expectancy in years	79.5
Doctors per population ratio (national)	323 doctors per 100 000 inhabitants
Doctors per population ratio in constituent units (highest)	Basel-Stadt: 343 doctors per 100 000 inhabitants
Doctors per population ratio in constituent units (lowest)	Appenzell Innerrhoden: 90 doctors per 100 000 inhabitants
National expenditures on health as a % of GDP	10.4%

Sources

Central Intelligence Agency (CIA), *World Fact Book 2000*. CIA, www.cia.gov/cia/publications/factbook/index.html

Economist Intelligence Unit. "Country Commerce." *The Economist Intelligence Unit Database 2000*. New York, 2000. www.eiu.com

Elazar, Daniel J. (ed.) *Federal Systems of the World: A Handbook of Federal, Confederal and Autonomy Arrangements*. 2nd Edition. Jerusalem Institute for Federal Studies. London: Longman Group/Westgate House, 1994.

Federal Supreme Court of Switzerland. "Judges and Personnel." www.supreme-court.ch

International Labour Office. "Indicators on Unemployment." www.un.org/Depts/unsd/social/unempl.htm

International Monetary Fund (IMF). *International Financial Statistics*, Vol. LIII, No. 12, December 2000. Washington, DC: the IMF Statistics Department, 2000.

Organization for Economic Co-operation and Development (OECD) 2000. www.oecd.org/std/gdp.htm

Statistisches Jahrbuch der Schweiz 2001/Annuaire statistique de la Suisse 2001. Office fédéral de la statistique. Zürich: Verlag Neue Zürcher Zeitung, 2001.

Swiss Federal Statistical Office (SFSO). www.statistik.admin.ch

Swiss Confederation Parliamentary Website. www.parlement.ch

UNESCO. *World Education Report 1998: Teachers and Teaching in a Changing World.* Paris: UNESCO, 1998.

United Nations. "Human Development Index." *Human Development Report 2000.* www.undp.org/hdro/report.html

Watts, Ronald L. *Comparing Federal Systems.* 2nd Edition. School of Policy Studies. Montreal/Kingston: McGill-Queen's University Press, 1999.

World Bank. *World Development Report 2000/2001: Attacking Poverty*. www.worldbank.org/poverty/wdrpoverty/report/index.htm

World Health Organisation (WHO). "Estimates of Health Personnel." www-nt.who.int/whosis/statistics

World Health Organisation (WHO). "Annex Table 8, Selected national health accounts indicators for all Member States, estimates for 1997." *World Health Report 2000.* Geneva, 2000. www-nt.who.int/whosis/statistics/menu.cfm

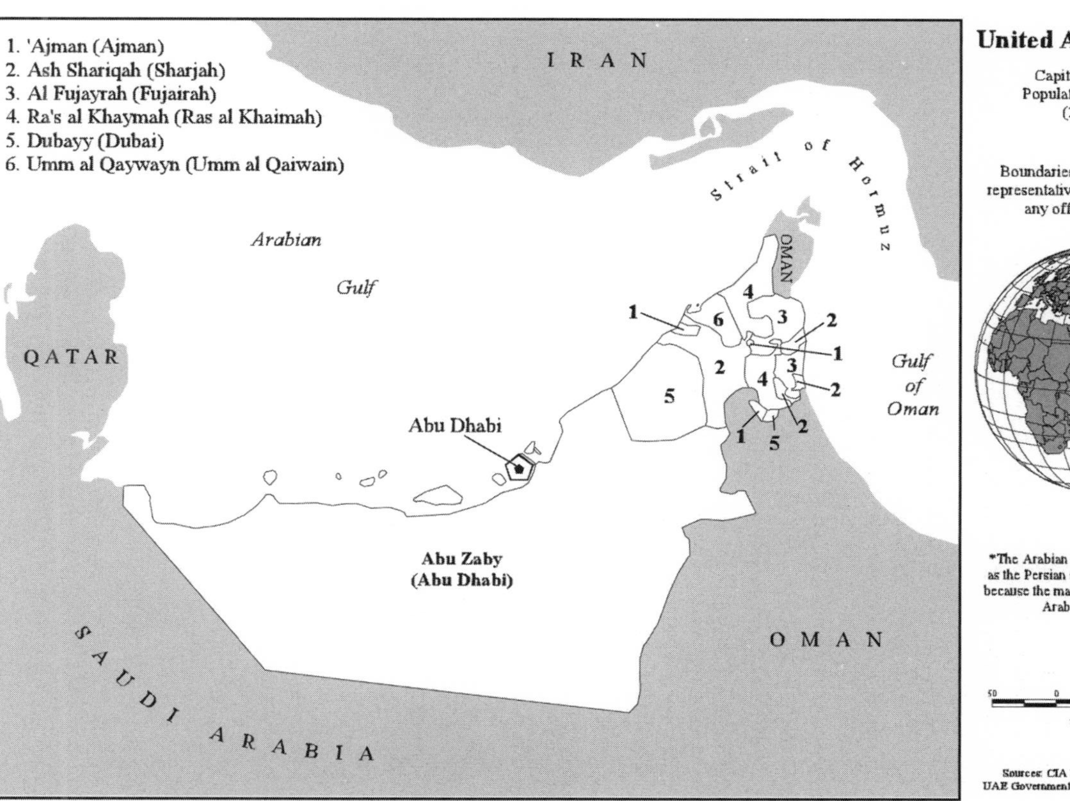

1. 'Ajman (Ajman)
2. Ash Shariqah (Sharjah)
3. Al Fujayrah (Fujairah)
4. Ra's al Khaymah (Ras al Khaimah)
5. Dubayy (Dubai)
6. Umm al Qaywayn (Umm al Qaiwain)
IRAN
Strait of Hormuz
Arabian
Gulf
QATAR
OMAN
Gulf of Oman
Abu Dhabi
Abu Zaby (Abu Dhabi)
SAUDI ARABIA
OMAN
United Arab Emirates
Capital: Abu Dhabi
Population: 2.4 Million
(2001 Est.)
Boundaries and place names are representative only and do not imply any official endorsement.
*The Arabian Gulf is also recognized as the Persian Gulf. Arabian is chosen because the map shown emphasizes the Arabian Pennisula.
50 0 50 100
Kilometers
Sources: CIA World Factbook; ESRI Ltd
UAE Government; UN Cartographic Department.

The United Arab Emirates

JULIE M. SIMMONS

1 HISTORY AND DEVELOPMENT OF FEDERALISM

The United Arab Emirates (83,600 km²) is situated on the eastern tip of the Arabian Peninsula. The country is bordered by Oman, Saudi Arabia, Qatar and the Persian (Arabian) Gulf, and its territory includes 200 islands.

It is unclear when this area was first inhabited. Archaeological discoveries suggest that settlements may have been established as early as the fifth millennium BC. Arab migration along the South Arabian coast in the first centuries AD and subsequent movement from the north brought a mix of Arab tribes to the area.

In the early sixteenth century Portuguese traders represented the first European challenge for control of the region. In the seventeenth and eighteenth centuries the Dutch and British competed in the area for access to the sea trade routes and to local traders. The "maritime warfare" of the local traders or "piracy" (according to the British) frustrated British attempts to achieve dominance in the region, and by the late 1700s the French threatened British aspirations. In the early 1800s the Qawasim (or *Qasimi*) controlled parts of the Gulf coast, and present-day rulers of the emirates of Sharjah and Ras al-Khaimah can trace their lineage to the Qawasim. Beginning with the 1820 General Treaty of Peace, the British signed a series of agreements with various rulers (sheikhs) which were designed to guarantee peace between Britain and the tribes and end the practice of piracy. Following the signing of the 1853 Perpetual Maritime Truce the sheikhdoms became known as "The Trucial States" or "Trucial Oman." With the 1892 "Exclusive Agreement" Britain accepted responsibility for the foreign affairs and defence of the sheikdoms.

The British favoured greater cooperation among the Trucial States and in 1952 the seven sheikhdoms – Abu Dhabi, Dubai, Ajman, Fujairah, Ras al-Khaimah, Sharjah and Umm al-Qaiwain – formed the Trucial States Council which provided a forum for the discussion of issues of mutual concern and coordination. Over the years the Council grew in formality and administrative structure. By 1964 it included sub-committees for agriculture, education and public health, and a development office for infrastructure projects. A committee, comprised of two representatives from each of the emirates, helped develop Council agendas and priorities.

The British Labour government issued a White Paper in 1967 reflecting its desire to reduce the cost of military bases east of Suez. In 1968 a proposal calling for British withdrawal from the Gulf by 1971 was announced in Parliament. In 1968 Bahrain and Qatar joined with the Trucial States and agreed to establish the Federation of the Arab Emirates, which was to be an independent state. The nine leaders formed the Supreme Council, which met several times. However they were unable to reach agreement on the parameters of a constitution and this union disbanded after 18 months. Bahrain and Qatar, which were not part of the Trucial Council, became independent states in 1971. In July of 1971, the seven Trucial States met again to discuss forming a union. After eight days of discussions, all but Ras al-Khaimah reached agreement on a provisional constitution. The rulers elected from among themselves Sheikh Zayed bin Sultan al-Nuhayan of Abu Dhabi as the President and Sheikh Maktoum bin Rashid al-Maktoum of Dubai as Vice-President. Both formally assumed their positions on 2 December 1971 when the treaties with Britain ended and the United Arab Emirates became an independent state. On 10 February 1972, Ras as-Khaimah joined the federation, without modification of the provisional constitution.

Petroleum was first discovered in 1958 off the coast of Abu Dhabi. Onshore deposits were found shortly thereafter in Abu Dhabi and Dubai. This industry accounts in part for the UAE's high GNP per capita incomes ($17,870 US in 1998 according to the World Bank). However, the wealth of the emirates varies significantly. Abu Dhabi (over 85% of the total geographical area) and Dubai (about 5% of total area) are the most affluent and together account for more than three-quarters of the country's Gross Domestic Product (GDP). Consistent efforts to diversify the economy, particularly in Dubai but also in

Sharjah and Abu Dhabi, have made trade, tourism and manufacturing into alternatives to gas and oil as revenue generators – thus, according to the Emirates Industrial Bank, revenues from crude represented just 38% of GDP in 2000.

The UAE's abundant oil wealth fuelled the development of a modern welfare state in the last 30 years. The country has been transformed from a state with few schools, hospitals, airports, proper housing or safe drinking water to a state with a network of social services including education and health services. The UAE is ranked 45th in the United Nation's Human Development Index of 174 countries in 2000, based on life expectancy (74 years), education and standard of living (derived from GDP per capita). According to the World Bank, however, the illiteracy rate is still 25%. The country's population has increased rapidly in the past 20 years, to over 2 million (World Bank estimates) – of which almost 40% are located in Abu Dhabi and almost 30% are in Dubai – and 96% of the population is Muslim. It is interesting to note that less than 50% of the population are UAE citizens. Nonnationals are primarily South Asian, Arab and Iranian.

2 CONSTITUTIONAL PROVISIONS RELATING TO FEDERALISM

The provisional constitution of the United Arab Emirates (UAE), which was made permanent in 1996, states that the country is a federation of seven constituent emirates: Abu Dhabi, Dubai, Ajman, Fujairah, Ras al-Khaimah, Sharjah and Umm al-Qaiwain. It is a federation that mixes aspects of traditional and modern rule. The constitution reflects a compromise between emirates in favour of a more centralized or integrated federation and those that preferred preserving the autonomy of the individual emirates. Sheikh Zayed of Abu Dhabi has always been an advocate of the former, while Sheikh Rashid of Dubai traditionally supported the latter.

The Supreme Council of Rulers is the highest federal authority, and has both legislative and executive powers. The emirate rulers, who are the traditional monarchs in their respective jurisdictions rather than elected representatives, form the Supreme Council. They derive their legitimacy from their status within their emirates, rather than from the Supreme Council itself, giving this body a confederal character.

The constitution distributes power asymmetrically among the emirates in that Abu Dhabi and Dubai effectively have a veto within the Supreme Council. All decisions on "substantive matters" require the consent of a majority of five of its members and this majority must include Abu Dhabi and Dubai (Article 49). The head of state is the

President who, like the Vice-President, is elected for a five-year term by the Supreme Council from among its members. The Supreme Council generally meets four times per year.

The constitution describes the Council of Ministers or Cabinet as "the Executive Organ of the Union." It is responsible for "all the internal and external matters within the competence of the Union" (Article 60). The President chooses the Prime Minister to head the Council of Ministers, and appoints its members. The more populated emirates traditionally have greater representation in Cabinet. According to the constitution, the Council of Ministers can propose draft federal laws and supervise the implementation of federal court judgements, and federal laws, decrees, decisions and regulations (Article 60). However, it is the responsibility of the Supreme Council to formulate the general policy of the federation.

The legislature is the unicameral 40 member Federal National Council (FNC). The constitution specifies that Abu Dhabi and Dubai have eight seats each, Sharjah and Ras al-Khaimah have six seats each and Ajman, Fujairah and Umm al-Qaiwain have four seats each (Article 68). Rulers of the constituent emirates appoint members to the seats allocated to their jurisdiction for two-year (renewable) terms (Article 72). The method of appointment is at each ruler's discretion (Article 69). The Federal National Council is a consultative body only, with legislative authority actually residing with the Supreme Council and Council of Ministers. Article 89 of the constitution stipulates that federal draft laws – including financial drafts – are brought before the FNC by the Council of Ministers. However, amendments put forward by the FNC may not be taken into account by the Council of Ministers before presentation to the Supreme Council (Article 92). If the FNC's suggested amendments are not acceptable to the President or the Supreme Council, he may promulgate any law after it is ratified by the Supreme Council (Article 110).

Almost invariably federalism is associated with democratic procedures. In the UAE, however, other than the election of the President and Vice-President by the rulers of the emirates, there are no elections. There are also no political parties. Male subjects can communicate with emirate leaders through the longstanding tradition of *majlises* or councils held by ruling families, but women do not directly participate in political institutions. The UAE Women's Federation provides services specifically for women such as education, health and literacy programs.

The division of powers between the federal government and the emirates is as follows. Articles 120 and 121 specify subjects for which the federal government has jurisdiction. The areas of federal jurisdiction outlined in Article 120 include foreign affairs, defence and security matters, postal, telephone and other communication services, air traffic control and aircraft licences, education, public health and currency. Labour relations and social security, delimitation of territorial waters, extradition of criminals, banking, and printing and publishing are among the areas listed in Article 121. According to Articles 138 and 146, the formation of unified armed forces and declaration of marital law are also under the jurisdiction of the federation.

Despite the apparently broad array of federal powers, the constitution provides for a loosely bound federation in practice. While the constitution states that "the Union shall exercise sovereignty in matters assigned to it in accordance with this Constitution over all territory and territorial waters lying within the international boundaries of the member Emirates" (Article 2), it also emphasizes that the member emirates "exercise sovereignty over their own territories and territorial waters in all matters not within the jurisdiction of the Union" (Article 3). Thus residual powers remain with the member emirates (Articles 116 and 122). Perhaps most significantly, the "natural resources and wealth" in each emirate are considered to be the public property of the emirate rather than the federation (Article 23). Individual emirates are also permitted to promulgate legislation in the areas of jurisdiction allocated to the federation in Article 121 (Article 149).

The development of local governmental institutions has affected the balance the federation. Local governments vary in size, structure and degree of autonomy from central institutions according to a number of factors including population and the level of economic and social development of each emirate. Mature local government systems were not in place in 1971 when the constitutional arrangements were made which means that the relationship between federal institutions and local governments has evolved, taking different forms according to the capacity of the local government institutions. In some cases this has led to integrated arrangements, with some emirates merging some of their departments with their federal counterparts. However, regardless of these arrangements, as a member of the Supreme Council, the ruler of each emirate has a significant role in determining the nature and extent of local government activities.

The constitution does not clearly specify what the financial arrangements are to be in the federation, or what proportion of funds each emirate is required to make available for supporting the federal budget. Clearly, with their retention of "natural resources and wealth," the emirates must contribute to the federal budget. Article 127 states that member emirates "shall contribute a specified proportion of their annual revenues to cover the annual general budget expenditure of the

Union." This leaves the capacity to implement federal laws contingent on the funds provided by the individual emirates. Abu Dhabi, the wealthiest of the emirates, and whose ruler has supported a more integrated federation, has historically contributed much of the financial resources.

The federal judiciary is comprised of the Supreme Court and the Courts of First Instance (Article 95). Although there are also local judicial authorities, in most emirates these authorities have now been transferred to the federal system. Most criminal cases are now heard in Shari'a courts (Islamic law courts). The constitution identifies the five-member Supreme Court, appointed by the President (Article 96), as the body responsible for the resolution of constitutional disputes. Whenever "any one of the interested parities" so requests, the Supreme Court will adjudicate disputes between member emirates or between one or more emirates and the federal government (Article 99). The ambiguity of the constitution could provide for flexible interpretation of the division of powers. All interpretations or judgments are binding on all parties (Article 101).

The procedure for amending the constitution is the same as the procedure for approving laws (Article 144.2(b)) – i.e., the Council of Ministers prepares a law and submits it to the Federal National Council after which the Supreme Council can ratify the law, accepting or rejecting any suggestions of either the Council of Ministers or the National Council. The constitution stipulates that FNC approval for draft constitutional amendments "shall require the agreement of two-thirds majority of the votes of members present" (Article 144.2(c)). However, substantive decisions require the consent of the leaders of Abu Dhabi and Dubai, who have historically shared contrasting views on the issue of a more centralized federation, making major constitutional change difficult. The constitution remained provisional until 1996 in large part because of the alternative visions of "unionists" and "federalists."

The constitution of the UAE contains a number of special provisions. Despite historical tribal rivalries, the common tribal and Arab Muslim heritage of the emirates is thought to contribute to cohesion among them. These characteristics are emphasized in several articles in the constitution. The first article states that "any other independent Arab country may join the Union, provided that the Supreme Council agrees unanimously to this." Article 6 states that "the Union shall be part of the Great Arab Nation," bound by "ties of religion, language, history and common destiny," and Article 7 states that "Islam shall be the official religion of the union" and that "[t]he Islamic Shari'ah shall be a principal source of legislation in the Union."

The constitution contains a section entitled "The Fundamental Social and Economic Bases of the Union," which declares that the basis of community shall be "equality, social justice ... and equality of opportunity for all citizens" (Article 14), and that "education shall be a primary means of social development ... compulsory in its primary stage and free at all stages within the Union" (Article 17). This section also declares that "medical protection ... shall be guaranteed by society for all citizens" (Article 19). These provisions recognize that even at the time of the formation of the UAE, the emirates varied in economic potential and development. The commitment of Abu Dhabi in particular to share its financial resources across the emirates is thought to have strengthened the federal system.

3 RECENT POLITICAL DYNAMICS

Although the UAE is a decentralized federation in practice, this decentralization has not negatively affected the country which has enjoyed a significant degree of stability throughout its 30 years of independence. The leading federal figures in the UAE have changed very little since independence. The current President, Sheikh Zayed of Abu Dhabi, was elected as the country's first President in 1971, and has been re-elected every five years since (the last election for President and Vice-President was in October 1996 – the next election is in 2001), and the last major Cabinet changes were made in 1997. Sheikh Maktoum bin Rashid al-Maktoum, ruler of Dubai, is currently Vice-President and Prime Minister and has held both posts since 1990. His father, Sheikh Rashid bin Said al-Maktoum of Dubai was elected by Supreme Council members as the first Vice-President and held this post until his death in 1990. (The leader of Dubai took on the post of Prime Minister for the first time in 1979, signalling his support for the federation.) It is thought that both the current President and the Vice-President have the unanimous support of the other members of the Supreme Council.

The wealth of the country is key to the strength of the federal system. But since the wealth is not distributed evenly, as noted in Section 1, it is important that Abu Dhabi in particular continues to be committed to the federal system and continues to contribute disproportionately to the federal finances. Continuing high prices in the oil industry mean that the country's wealth is not in jeopardy. According to the Emirates Industrial Bank, the UAE's GDP grew 14 per cent in 2000 largely as a result of increases in the prices of oil. This increase is the result of reduced production agreed to by OPEC member states (of which the UAE is one) in 1998 and 1999. Prior to these price increases, the federal government made financial commitments to further infrastructure development and job creation, and began exploring participation of the private sector in utilities. Given its continuing oil wealth, the federal arrangements in the UAE have not been tested, as they have been in other federations, by the tensions inherent in budget cuts and government retrenchment.

The UAE and the other members of the Arab Gulf Cooperation Council (AGCC) – Saudi Arabia, Kuwait, Oman, Qatar and Bahrain – have made significant efforts to create a trading bloc. Since foreign policy is primarily federal jurisdiction, any such agreement may affect the balance of power between central and local governing institutions within UAE in the future. As well, at the last meeting of the AGCC in December of 2000, the six member states signed a mutual defence pact calling for defence resources to be shared, took steps to issue a common currency, and approved measures to allow citizens of all AGCC states to practice "all economic activities and professions [with a few exceptions] in other member states." Since defence, security and currency are also matters that fall into federal jurisdiction, it will be interesting to see how this affects the balance of the country's political arrangements.

The emirates are generally united in their views on foreign policy which provides some cohesion to federal actions. Thus, the UAE has been united in its commitment to resolving a longstanding dispute over three islands – Abu Musa and the Greater and Lesser Tunbs – located in the Arabian Gulf near important shipping routes. Abu Musa had been jointly administered by Iran and Sharjah (one of the UAE's seven emirates), and in 1992 the UAE argued that, in restricting access to Abu Musa, Iran was in breach of the terms of the Memorandum of Understanding between Sharjah and Iran. Particularly since 1992 the UAE has garnered support from other states for its diplomatic measures, especially among AGCC states.

A question confronting the UAE is how the federation will change when Sheikh Zayed, now over 80 years old, is no longer President. His well-known pragmatic approach to the careful balancing of traditional and modern rule, and to resolving unionist/federalist debates has been a source of stability in the country. The longevity of his tenure is noteworthy. Some observers have suggested that any future leader is unlikely to enjoy Zayed's status among the people. This means that his successor will confront a set of new challenges, and may benefit from stronger central institutions. The UAE's experience of becoming a modern welfare state in the last 30 years reveals that it can successfully undergo dramatic transition in terms of adopting new governing institutions.

4 SOURCES FOR FURTHER INFORMATION

Ghareeb, Edmund and Ibrahim Al Abed (eds), *Perspectives on the United Arab Emirates,* London: Trident Press, 1997.

Peck, Malcolm C., *The United Arab Emirates: A Venture into Unity,* Boulder, CO: Westview Press, 1986.

United States Central Intelligence Agency, *The World Factbook 2000,* "United Arab Emirates," http://www.odci.gov/cia/publications/factbook/geos/tc.html

The Europa World Year Book 2000, Vol. 2, "United Arab Emirates," London: Europa Publications Ltd., 2000.

http://www.uae.gov.ae

http://www.emirates.org

http://www.uae.org.ae

http://www.uaeinteract.com

http://www.gulfnews.com

Table I
Political and Geographic Indicators

Capital city	Abu Dhabi
Number and type of constituent units	*7 Emirates (Imarah)*: Abu Dhabi, Ajman, Al Fujairah, Ash Shariqah (Sharjah), Dubai, Ra's al Khaimah, Umm al Qaiwain
Official language(s)	Arabic
Area	82 880 km^2
Area – Largest constituent unit	Umm al Qaiwain (77,700 km^2)
Area – Smallest constituent unit	Ajman (250 km^2)
Total population	2 407 460 (Note: includes 1 576 472 resident non-nationals)
Population by constituent unit (% of total population)	Abu Dhabi 41.3%, Dubai 26%, Ash Shariqah (Sharjah) 17%, Ra's al Khaimah 7.2%, Ajman 4%, Al Fujairah 3.4%, Umm al Qaiwain 1.8%
Political system – federal	Federation – Parliamentary
Head of state – federal	President (Emir) Shaykh Zayed ibn Sultan Al Nuhayyan, ruler of Abu Dhabi (1971), elected for a 5-year term by the Supreme Council of Rulers. The Supreme Council is the highest federal authority and is comprised of the Emirs of the 7 emirates. Abu Dhabi and Dubai effectively have veto power within the Supreme Council.
Head of government – federal	Prime Minister: Shaykh Maktum ibn Rashid Al Maktum of Dubayy (1990), ruler of Dubai. The President chooses the Prime Minister to head the Council of Ministers, which is also appointed by the President.
Government structure – federal	Unicameral – Parliament: Majlis Watani Ittihad (Federal National Council), 40 seats. Members are appointed by the Emirs to serve 2-year terms. The method of appointment is left to the Emirs' discretion. Members are representatives of the Emirates but function in an advisory capacity only. No political parties are allowed.
Distribution of representatives in house of federal government – Federal National Council	40 seats: Abu Dhabi and Dubai – 8 seats each, Ash Shariqah (Sharjah) and Ra's al Khaimah – 6 seats each, Ajman, Al Fujairah and Umm al Qaiwain – 4 seats each.
Constitutional court (highest court dealing with constitutional matters)	Supreme Court. 5 judges are appointed by the President and Supreme Council of Rulers.
Political system of constituent units	Emirates are effectively ruled by an absolute monarch (Emir) who may have an appointed advisory council, often composed of family relations.
Head of state – constituent units	Emir (Monarch), hereditary title
Head of government – constituent units	Emir (Monarch), hereditary title

Table II
Economic and Social Indicators

GDP	US$54 billion
GDP per capita	US$22 800
Mechanisms for taxation	The federal government of the United Arab Emirates imposes no taxes. Corporate tax decrees have been issued by the individual emirates, but, *de facto*, taxes have been imposed only on oil and gas producing companies and petrochemical companies at rates determined in their government concession agreements, and on branches of foreign banks at rates determined in agreement with the Rulers of the Emirates in which the branches operate. There are no withholding taxes.
National debt (external)	US$12.6 billion
National unemployment rate	Note: Unemployment statistics are difficult to obtain due to the fact that the workforce is largely composed of non-nationals, regarding whom statistics are not kept.
Constituent unit with highest unemployment rate	N/A
Constituent unit with lowest unemployment rate	N/A
Adult literacy rate	74.6%
National expenditures on education as a % of GDP	1.7%
Life expectancy in years	74.06
Doctors per population ratio (national)	181 doctors per 100 000 inhabitants
Doctors per population ratio in constituent units (highest)	N/A
Doctors per population ratio in constituent units (lowest)	N/A
National expenditures on health as a % of GDP	4.2%

Sources

Central Intelligence Agency (CIA), *World Fact Book 2000*. CIA, www.cia.gov/cia/publications/factbook/index.html

Derbyshire, J. Denis. "United Arab Emirates." *Encyclopedia of World Political Systems*. Volumes I and II, New York: Sharpe Reference, M.E. Sharpe, Inc, 2000.

Ernst and Young. EY Passport Countries. "United Arab Emirates." *The Worldwide Corporate Tax Guide*. www.ey.com/GLOBAL/gcr.nsf/EYPassport/United_Arab_Emirates-EYPassport#2

Elazar, Daniel J. (ed.) *Federal Systems of the World: A Handbook of Federal, Confederal and Autonomy Arrangements*. 2nd Edition. Jerusalem Institute for Federal Studies. London: Longman Group/Westgate House, 1994.

UNESCO. *World Education Report 1998: Teachers and Teaching in a Changing World.* Paris: UNESCO, 1998.

United Nations Population Division. Department of Economic and Social Affairs. "Population in 1999 and 2000: All Countries." *World Population Prospects: 1998 Revision, Vol. 1 comprehensive tables.* www.un.org/Depts.htm

United Nations. *Human Development Report, 2000.* www.undp.org/hdro/report.html

United Nations Statistics Division. "InfoNation." United Nations Statistical Database, 2000. www.un.org/cgi-bin/pubs/infonatn.html

World Bank. *World Development Report 2000/2001: Attacking Poverty.* www.worldbank.org/poverty/wdrpoverty/report/index.htm

World Health Organisation (WHO). *World Health Report 2000.* Geneva, Switzerland, 2000. www-nt.who.int/whosis/statistics/menu.cfm

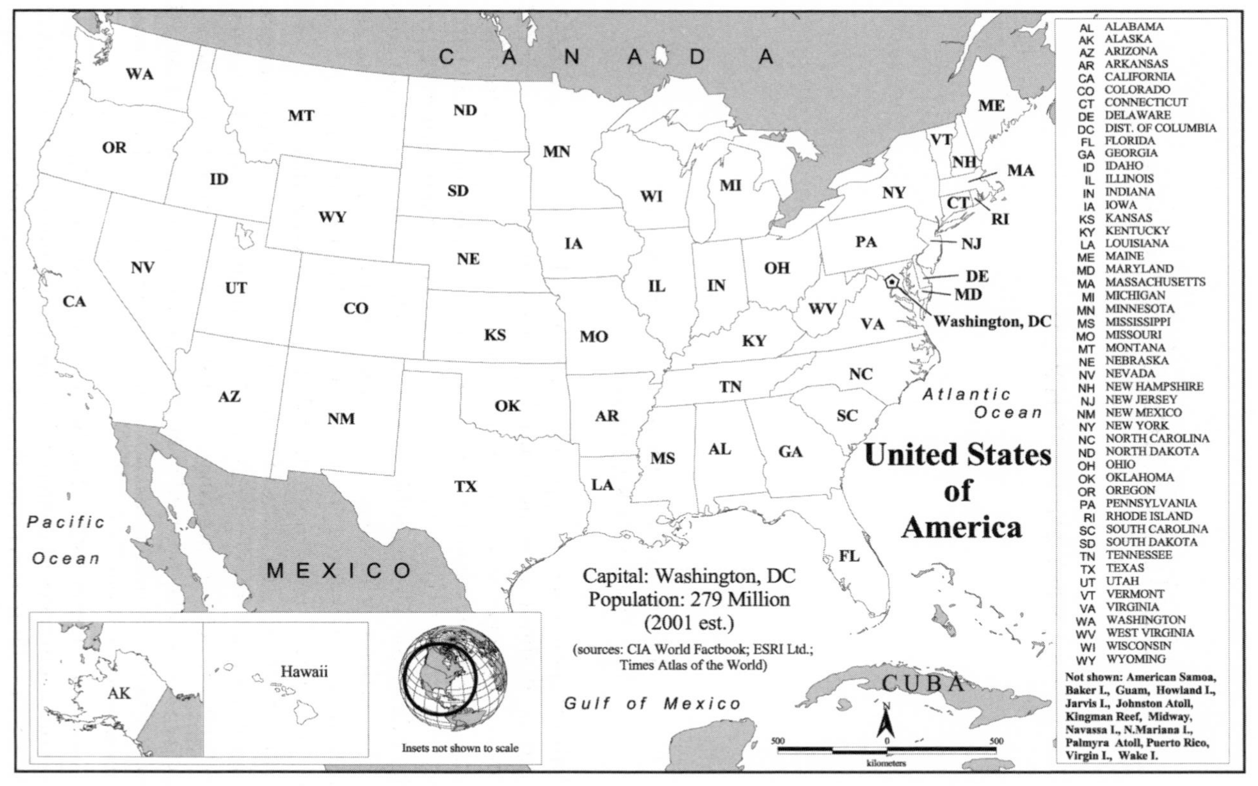
CANADA
WA
OR
CA
NV
ID
MT
WY
UT
CO
AZ
NM
ND
SD
NE
KS
OK
TX
MN
IA
MO
AR
LA
WI
IL
MI
IN
OH
KY
TN
MS
AL
GA
FL
SC
NC
VA
WV
PA
NY
VT
NH
ME
MA
CT
RI
NJ
DE
MD
Washington, DC
Pacific Ocean
Atlantic Ocean
MEXICO
Gulf of Mexico
CUBA
United States of America
Capital: Washington, DC
Population: 279 Million
(2001 est.)
(sources: CIA World Factbook; ESRI Ltd.; Times Atlas of the World)
AK
Hawaii
Insets not shown to scale
N
500
0
500
kilometers
AL ALABAMA
AK ALASKA
AZ ARIZONA
AR ARKANSAS
CA CALIFORNIA
CO COLORADO
CT CONNECTICUT
DE DELAWARE
DC DIST. OF COLUMBIA
FL FLORIDA
GA GEORGIA
ID IDAHO
IL ILLINOIS
IN INDIANA
IA IOWA
KS KANSAS
KY KENTUCKY
LA LOUISIANA
ME MAINE
MD MARYLAND
MA MASSACHUSETTS
MI MICHIGAN
MN MINNESOTA
MS MISSISSIPPI
MO MISSOURI
MT MONTANA
NE NEBRASKA
NV NEVADA
NH NEW HAMPSHIRE
NJ NEW JERSEY
NM NEW MEXICO
NY NEW YORK
NC NORTH CAROLINA
ND NORTH DAKOTA
OH OHIO
OK OKLAHOMA
OR OREGON
PA PENNSYLVANIA
RI RHODE ISLAND
SC SOUTH CAROLINA
SD SOUTH DAKOTA
TN TENNESSEE
TX TEXAS
UT UTAH
VT VERMONT
VA VIRGINIA
WA WASHINGTON
WV WEST VIRGINIA
WI WISCONSIN
WY WYOMING
Not shown: American Samoa, Baker I., Guam, Howland I., Jarvis I., Johnston Atoll, Kingman Reef, Midway, Navassa I., N.Mariana I., Palmyra Atoll, Puerto Rico, Virgin I., Wake I.

United States of America

SANFORD F. SCHRAM

1 HISTORY AND DEVELOPMENT OF FEDERALISM

With independence in 1776 the American colonies formed a confederation. Without a strong central government, however, centrifugal forces soon began to pull the states apart. Instead of working together, some states began coining their own money and erecting trade barriers, and the state governments were too weak on their own to ensure the rule of law. These problems seemed to be a result of shortcomings in the Articles of Confederation and Perpetual Union. It was to address these issues that a convention was held in Philadelphia in 1787. The result was a new constitution that has survived to this day.

In 1789 the United States of America adopted what was at that time an entirely unique form of governance. The government created by the new constitution became, arguably, the first structured according to principles of what is today referred to as federalism. Confederalism had existed for centuries; federalism had not. While confederalism called for a loose union of states, federalism called for a two-tier system of governance and it was a revolutionary idea. The Swiss canton system of the Middle Ages and other instances of confederalism were built upon by the framers of the US Constitution to create this new form of governance.

The constitution that emerged from Philadelphia sought to build a national government on top of the states to create a "more perfect union" that could ensure liberty while enforcing law and order. The constitution was, however, less than a systematically planned blueprint for the development of a federal system. It was to emerge out of a series of compromises during the days of deliberation in Philadelphia. One major compromise of particular significance for the new federal system was the specification of a bicameral Congress with the Senate providing equal representation to each state in the form of two Senators, and a House of Representatives providing representation of the people by districts based on population. In this way, less populous states could agree to the development of a new national government because they were accorded better representation in it than would be the case if representatives were apportioned strictly on the basis of population.

Even with such compromises, the constitution was not without its opponents. The battle over its ratification pitted Federalists and Anti-Federalists against each other largely over the question of whether the new national government would become an all-powerful source that would threaten the liberty of the common people. This battle threatened to doom the constitution until a compromise was reached. According to this compromise, the first Congress under the new constitution would put a bill of rights before the states for ratification. The result was the first 10 amendments to the constitution which guaranteed such rights as the freedom of speech, press and religion, the right to jury trials, protection against unwarranted searches and seizures, the right to bear arms, and even an amendment that suggested there were other unspecified rights beyond those listed in the constitution.

James Madison was in many ways one of the most important thinkers behind the idea of a new federation. He reasoned that an "expanded republic" would actually increase the protection of liberty, by introducing diversity and cancelling out the power of a tyrannous minority or even a tyrannous majority. And the United States did indeed become an expanded republic with the Louisiana Purchase in 1803 in particular massively increasing the territory and creating the basis for the westward expansion and the gradual growth of the country from 13 to 50 states.

Sectionalism, however, was always a threat to the viability of the expanded republic. In particular the issue of slavery increasingly divided the country along a north-south axis in the first half of the nineteenth century and eventually led to the Civil War (1861–1865). The Civil War was to have a critical impact upon the shape of US federalism, leading as it did to the national government asserting its responsibility for upholding the Union as inviolable. The national government's imposition of a period of reconstruction on the South from 1865–1876 solidified its role as the keeper of the Union and gave new meaning to the constitution's statement that the laws of the national government were supreme.

After reconstruction, the power of the national government was not asserted to a similar degree, but rapid industrialization of the country created forces of nationalization that would lay the basis for the growth of federal power. In the twentieth century, two world wars, and the emergence of the United States as a world power would further redefine the character of US federalism. The national government, particularly the office of the President would assume increased significance and authority. Today, the national government is far stronger than it was when it was first established. All three branches of the national government – not just the presidency, but also the Congress and the Supreme Court – have assumed greater power in the federal system than they had in the early years of the republic.

Nonetheless, for more than 200 years the US Constitution has resisted giving answers as to the definitive shape and scope of American federalism. Instead, all questions regarding it have remained subject to contestation, from its origins, to its purposes, to, most commonly and critically, its distribution of powers between the national government and the states. The division over the origin of the federal system is critical to understanding it. If the "compact" theory – which argues that the two-tier federal system of governance is the product of a compact between the different states – holds, then the states, and their people as citizens of separate states, are the fundamental units of the federal system. If the "national democracy" theory – which argues that the federal system was a creature of the American people as a democratic polity unto itself – holds, then both the states and the national government are creatures of that collective will and are subservient to it. James Madison seems to have tried to have it both ways, trying to resolve the conflict so as to ensure both the sovereignty of the states *and* supremacy of the new national government, thereby hoping to ensure it would not become a mere creature of the states.

For over two centuries this debate has persistently arisen, even as the issues changed, thus, for example, undermining national law, as with the National Bank under President Andrew Jackson, and taking the country into civil war, as with the battle over slavery. The compact theory was reintroduced by Ronald Reagan in his inaugural address in 1981 when he stated that he was committed to reducing the power of the national government so as to "restore the balance between the levels of government."[1] He justified this at the time on the grounds that the federal government had improperly come to exercise too much control over the states. He then famously noted: "The federal government did not create the states; the states created the federal government."

For Reagan, the compact theory was unassailable and unquestioned. Yet this is not the case for many others. Today, President George W.

1 Samuel H. Beer, *To Make a Nation: The Rediscovery of American Federalism* (Cambridge, MA: The Belknap Press of Harvard University Press, 1993), p. 2.

Bush develops his domestic agenda to turn back power to the states. He faces opposition from Democrats in Congress, however, who see constitutional justification for the national government to assert its role in influencing the states on matters of national importance concerning issues as diverse as education and the environment, welfare and discrimination, economic development and crime.

2 CONSTITUTIONAL PROVISIONS RELATING TO FEDERALISM

The national government has three branches – the bicameral Congress (made up of the House of Representatives and the Senate) serving as the legislative branch, the independently elected President heading the executive branch, and the Supreme Court heading the judicial branch. The relationship of each of these branches to the states has changed since the federation was created. With the rise in power of the presidency along with the increasing responsibility of that office for the national economy, Presidents have become the national political figures they were originally intended to be. The Supreme Court – made up of nine Justices appointed by the President, but ratified by the Senate, and removable only by impeachment – has come a long way from first asserting in *Marbury v. Madison* (1803) the right of judicial review to serve as the final arbiter as to the constitutional questions.

Article I, Section 3(1) of the constitution specifies that states are to be represented in the national government by two Senators from each state. With 50 states, there are 100 Senators, each serving a six-year term and one-third of whom are up for election every two years. The Seventeenth Amendment (1913) switched the election of Senators to popular vote from election by the legislature in each state. While this undoubtedly has led Senators to become more independent of state legislatures, they continue to be a source of federalism in the national government, often focusing on representing the interests of their states more so than the interests of the country as a whole.

The division of powers between the national government and the states is specified in the constitution. Article VI of the constitution includes the "supremacy clause" that makes the constitution and the laws of the national government supreme. The "enumerated powers" of the Congress are listed in Article I, Section 8, and authorize Congress to:

1 lay and collect taxes;
2 pay the debts;
3 provide for the common defence;
4 promote the general welfare of the United States;

5 borrow money on the credit of the United States;
6 regulate commerce with inter-state commerce;
7 establish uniform rules for naturalization;
8 establish uniform rules for bankruptcies;
9 coin money and regulate its value;
10 fix the standard of weights and measures;
11 establish a Post Office and post roads;
12 issue patents and copyrights;
13 constitute tribunals inferior to the Supreme Court;
14 define and punish felonies committed on the high seas, and offences against the "law of nations;"
15 raise and support an army and a navy; and
16 declare war.

Article I, Section 8, ends by stating that Congress shall also have the power to make all laws which shall be "necessary and proper for carrying into execution the foregoing powers, and all other powers vested by the Constitution in the Government of the United States." This clause has been referred to as the "elastic clause" because it has allowed over time for a great expansion of the powers of the national government especially to regulate inter-state commerce and promote the general welfare. It is also important to note that the Fourteenth Amendment, ratified after the Civil War, specifies that the national government must ensure that state actions do not deny citizens due process, privileges and immunities and rights to equal protection of the laws.

Despite the "enumerated powers" listed above, the division of power between the national government and the states is not outlined in explicit terms by the constitution. It is possible that this is because the framers intended there to be overlapping or concurrent powers, including, inter alia, the power to tax, the power to regulate forms of commerce, and the power to initiate social policies. The supremacy clause, however, has at times been invoked to preempt state concurrent powers, for instance in recent years regarding the regulation of air and water pollution. The area of concurrent powers suggests that the debates about the allocation of power in the US federal system are unavoidable.

Article IV, Section 4, guarantees all states a "republican form of government." The Tenth Amendment reserves all power not granted to the national government to the "states or the people." While the early years of the constitution saw the growth of a national government, for much of its history especially after the Civil War, the Tenth Amendment has served to create a great reservoir of residual powers for the states. This changed with the Great Depression which spurred President Franklin Delano Roosevelt to initiate the "New Deal" with its great expansion of federal powers. In the post–World War II era, the

Tenth Amendment lost much of its power, but in recent years to some degree the Supreme Court has renewed it as a constraint on the growth of federal power.

The procedure for amending the constitution is specified in Article V which in part reads: "The Congress, whenever two thirds of both Houses shall deem it necessary, shall propose Amendments to this Constitution, or, on the Application of the Legislatures of two thirds of the several States, shall call a Convention for proposing Amendments." Three-fourths of the states must approve an amendment for it to be ratified as part of the constitution.

Yet, formal revision of the constitution has not been the primary means by which power has been re-allocated in the system. While the Fourteenth Amendment did significantly revise the division of powers between the national government and the states, most of the shift has been accomplished by means other than formal amendment of the constitution – decisions of the Supreme Court in particular. The Supreme Court has performed a critical constitutional role, at times reining in federal power over the states, and at times allowing for the growth of federal power. The variations in American federalism have been regulated by the Court which over time built on its assertion of judicial review to establish itself as an independent arbiter between the states and the federal government on constitutional issues.

In its early years, the Court, particularly under the leadership of Chief Justice John Marshall, was a nationalist court that asserted the supremacy of the national government. Starting after Marshall and until the New Deal, however, the Court limited the ability of Congress to expand its powers at the expense of the states. At first the Court struck down key New Deal legislation in the mid-1930s as violating principles of federalism, but under intense political pressure from Roosevelt, a new majority emerged on the Court and it began to uphold expansion of national power in ways that would continue into the 1970s. The Court, thus, became a strong supporter of the growth of national power, especially in the areas of regulating inter-state commerce, expanding social policy initiatives, and enforcing the Fourteenth Amendment to ensure civil rights. In recent years, however, the Court has changed again. A slim 5–4 states' rights majority on the Court under the leadership of Chief Justice William Rehnquist has worked to strike down national legislation as undercutting the constitutional autonomy of the states. In particular, the Court has resurrected the idea that the national government cannot legislate away the "sovereign immunity" of states, thereby reducing the extent to which citizens can sue states for failure to uphold federal laws.

The conceptualization of national-state government relations has changed over time as well. A contrast has historically been between the theories of dual and cooperative federalism. Dual federalism emphasized the separateness of the tiers and the need to limit the national government so that it did not undermine the sovereignty of each state as vouchsafed by the constitution. Others noted that the framers' vague wording in the constitution intended a more nuanced system of overlapping powers necessitating a more cooperative federalism of sharing powers and supporting each other as the national government helped states fulfill basic functions and states helped the national government fulfill national objectives. Still others have noted that since the presidency of Richard Nixon, but especially since Reagan, there has been an effort to have a "new federalism" that insists on turning power "back" to the states.

The status of the fundamental constitutional rights of citizens has been significantly affected by the shifts in federalism over time. The Civil War brought a major assertion of national power and resulted in the ratification of three constitutional amendments that still have supreme importance in the system. The Thirteenth Amendment barred slavery (and all involuntary servitude except for punishment of a crime), the Fourteenth Amendment prohibited all states from denying any citizens equal protection of the laws and guaranteed due process of the laws and privileges and immunities, and the Fifteenth Amendment extended that guarantee to all black citizens including former slaves. While slavery is not likely to return, these amendments remain significant in their creation of national power. With these amendments, the national government assumed ultimate responsibility for ensuring that states did not deny citizens their civil rights under the constitution. The Supreme Court, however, at times leaned towards allowing states substantial latitude and, thus, in *Plessy v. Ferguson* (1896) infamously upheld the racially exclusionary "separate but equal" Jim Crow laws in the South. The "separate but equal" doctrine would hold until the 1954 decision of *Brown v. Board of Education* at which time a new era of national intervention in the states commenced in order to enforce civil rights. The Rehnquist Court has in recent years stopped further extensions of federal power in this area.

The fiscal arrangements of the federal system have changed dramatically. Article I, Section 8(1), gave Congress the power to raise taxes and impose duties. The national government levied an income tax during the Civil War but did not implement a graduated income tax until the early twentieth century. With the Supreme Court questioning the constitutionality of such a tax, it could only finally be established as a constitutionally legitimate power of the national government with the ratification of the Sixteenth Amendment in 1913. With this power to levy taxes on incomes, the federal government increasingly became the primary source of revenue in the federal system. The federal government increasingly relied on this power to gain leverage on the states, enticing them to enlist in national programs by offering them conditional grants-in-aid. This leverage was maximized during the Johnson Administration's "Great Society" during the 1960s. The high-water mark in federal grants-in-aid was the 1970s. With the budget cuts adopted by the Reagan Administration in the early 1980s, federal aid began a long decline. Once President Bill Clinton proposed, and Congress enacted, a balanced federal budget in the late 1990s, the downward trend had been set. In addition, since 1994 Congress has moved toward turning more power back to the states. This has prompted interest in shifting away from narrow categorical grants with matching-fund requirements for the states toward removal or relaxation of conditions-of-aid and the conversion of categorical grants into block grants.

Even with reforms, the power of the "federal fisc" remains strong and grants-in-aid are still a potent source of federal leverage over the states. The relatively new idea of "performance partnership" grants suggests a trend toward giving states substantial discretion in using grant funds while making allocations in part contingent upon performance effectiveness in achieving nationally specified goals.

3 RECENT POLITICAL DYNAMICS

Even before he was elected in late 2000, the presidency of Republican George W. Bush quickly demonstrated the persistence of old issues of federalism in the new millennium. Most controversially, Bush gained office even as he got fewer popular votes than his main opponent, Democrat Al Gore, Bill Clinton's Vice-President. Bush narrowly won a majority of the Electoral College votes, only after a prolonged battle contesting the outcome of voting in the state of Florida. This historic battle dramatically reminded the world just how decentralized the system of voting is in the United States and how significant principles of federalism are in the system of electing a President. Yet, the end result, with the states' rights majority (5–4) on the Supreme Court intervening to overturn the decision of the Supreme of Court of Florida, caused some to worry that a highly politicized process had made a mockery of important principles of federalism and in a way that made them less viable for the future.

The presidential election of 2000 powerfully underscored how federalism is even built into the only truly nationally elected office in the land. Citizens only vote indirectly for the President because the votes are used to determine the allocation of electors from each state who then vote accordingly as an "Electoral College" to choose the President (and the designated Vice-President). The process therefore makes the election a question of garnering enough support in enough states in order to achieve a majority in the Electoral College. In addition, all states but Maine and Nebraska give *all* their electors to the candidate who gets the most popular votes. Also, small states are overrepresented in the Electoral College because the number of electors is based on the number of Senators (each state has two) and the number of members of the House of Representatives (each state has a delegation which is based on the population of the state, but small states have at least one representative). All of these factors make the national election very much a federal one, where candidates must develop a strategy to build support, not necessarily nationwide, but in a number of selected states in order to garner a majority of electoral votes. The Electoral College works against the idea that a simple national majority, concentrated or dispersed, can be relied upon to win even the one nationally elected office of the system.

Therefore, even though Bush lost the national popular vote, he could still win the presidency as three other Presidents had before him. All he needed in the end was to carry Florida. Yet, Florida was to highlight another dimension of the federalism of presidential elections. Each state gets to run its election largely on its own terms as long as it is consistent with the constitution and federal law. And Florida, like most states, allows local election boards to vary their practices within state law. The result was that in Florida, as in most other states, different counties used different mechanisms for recording votes, with poorer areas in particular more likely to use outdated machinery that is subject to error. The Florida election proved to be extremely close, with Bush ahead by fewer than 2,000 votes. Gore subsequently asked for hand recounts of the ballots and eventually won a decision from the Florida Supreme Court to hand recount all ballots in the state for which machines did not record a vote for President. Bush appealed to the Supreme Court in spite of his having campaigned as a candidate who promoted states' rights and discouraged federal, particularly judicial, intervention in the affairs of states. And even more dramatically, the slim 5–4 states' rights majority on the Supreme Court surprised many when it took the case and ruled in *Bush v. Gore* (2000) that the hand recounts violated federal standards of equal protection under the Fourteenth Amendment. Many accused the Court of allowing partisanship to affect its decision, thereby handing the presidency to Bush at the expense of preserving important principles of federalism.

Bush as President faces not only questions of legitimacy but a Senate evenly divided between Democrats and Republicans at 50–50, and a closely divided House. The spectre of gridlock which has haunted the national government in recent years is poised to linger longer. Nonetheless, Bush continues to push for more of the "new federalism" that had been touted by his Republican predecessors. His efforts include the turning of welfare programs over to local community agencies, including faith-based organizations, so as to reduce the power of the federal government further and thereby create even greater opportunities not only for states but communities to exercise more discretion in the use of federal funds. Yet, such actions could also further weaken national commitments to provide service, enforce rights and protect values across a gamut of policy areas. Supporters emphasize that Bush is seeking to enable states and local governments to act independently of federal regulation. Opponents stress that he is threatening to eviscerate federal commitments in key areas of social policy and the environment in particular.

If all the turmoil of the presidential election clouded the picture, one historic reality remains persistently clear – federalism lies at the centre of the system and disputes about almost any policy issue inevitably raise issues of federalism. In spite of all that happened in the presidential election, the federal nature of the system is not about to go away.

4 SOURCES FOR FURTHER INFORMATION

Beer, Samuel H., *To Make a Nation: The Rediscovery of American Federalism*, Cambridge, MA: The Belknap Press of Harvard University Press, 1993.

Donahue, John D., *Disunited States: What's at Stake as Washington Fades and the States Take the Lead*, New York, NY: Basic Books, 1997.

Elazar, Daniel J., *American Federalism: A View from the States*, New York, NY: Thomas Y. Crowell Co., 1966.

Kincaid, John, "The International Competence of U.S. States and Their Local Governments," *Regional and Federal Studies*, Vol. 9 (Spring 1999), pp. 108–130.

Peterson, Paul E., Barry G. Rabe and Kenneth K. Wong, *When Federalism Works*, Washington DC: The Brookings Institution, 1986.

Zimmerman, Joseph F., "National-state Relations: Cooperative Federalism in the Twentieth Century," *Publius: The Journal of Federalism*, Vol. 31, No. 2 (Spring 2001, forthcoming).

www.senate.gov

www.census.gov/populatio/cen2000

www.house.gov

www.publicdebt.treas.gov

Table I
Political and Geographic Indicators

Capital city	Washington, District of Columbia
Number and type of constituent units	*50 States:* Alabama, Alaska, Arizona, Arkansas, California, Colorado, Connecticut, Delaware, Florida, Georgia, Hawaii, Idaho, Illinois, Indiana, Iowa, Kansas, Kentucky, Louisiana, Maine, Maryland, Massachusetts, Michigan, Minnesota, Mississippi, Missouri, Montana, Nebraska, Nevada, New Hampshire, New Jersey, New Mexico, New York, North Carolina, North Dakota, Ohio, Oklahoma, Oregon, Pennsylvania, Rhode Island, South Carolina, South Dakota, Tennessee, Texas, Utah, Vermont, Virginia, Washington, West Virginia, Wisconsin, Wyoming; *1 Federal District*: Washington, District of Columbia. Note: The United States of America also claims administrative relations with: *2 Federacies:* Puerto Rico, Northern Marianas*; 3 Associated States:* Republic of Palau, Federated States of Micronesia, Republic of the Marshall Islands; 3 *Local Home-Rule Territories*; *3 Unincorporated Territories*; and *130 Native American Domestic Dependent Nations.*
Area	9 629 091 km²
Area – Largest constituent unit	Alaska (1 530 700 km²)
Area – Smallest constituent unit	District of Columbia (178 km²)
Official language(s)	The USA does not declare an official language. *De facto*, the language of the state for all governing and judicial bodies is English.
Total population	285 230 516

Table I (continued)

Population by constituent unit (% of total population)	California 11.9%, Texas 7.3%, New York 6.6%, Florida 5.6%, Illinois 4.3%, Pennsylvania 4.2%, Ohio 4.0%, Michigan 3.5%, New Jersey 3.1%, Georgia 3.0%, North Carolina 2.8%, Virginia 2.5%, Massachusetts 2.3%, Indiana 2.2%, Washington 2.1%, Tennessee 2.0%, Missouri 1.93%, Wisconsin 1.91%, Maryland 1.83%, Arizona 1.81%, Minnesota 1.7%, Louisiana 1.62%, Alabama 1.6%, Colorado 1.5%, Kentucky 1.41%, South Carolina 1.4%, Oklahoma 1.22%, Oregon 1.21%, Connecticut 1.2%, Iowa 1.0%, Arkansas 0.9%, Mississippi 0.1%, Kansas 0.1%, Utah 0.09%, Nevada 0.07%, New Mexico 0.063%, West Virginia 0.062%, Nebraska 0.061%, Idaho 0.052%, Maine 0.051%, New Hampshire 0.043%, Hawaii 0.042%, Rhode Island 0.041%, Montana 0.033%, Delaware 0.032%, South Dakota 0.031%, Alaska 0.023%, North Dakota 0.022%, Vermont 0.021%, Wyoming 0.020%, District of Columbia 0.021%
Political system – federal	Federal Republic
Head of state – federal	President George W. Bush (2000), Republican Party. President and Vice-President are elected on the same ticket by an Electoral College composed of electors from each state equal to the total number of Senators and Congress representatives, plus three from the District of Columbia. The members of the Electoral College are chosen by party slates by popular vote within each state. In theory, they are free to choose any presidential candidate, but by convention, the electors are bound to support the candidates to whom they are pledged. The President can serve no more than two 4-year terms.
Head of government – federal	President George W. Bush. The President appoints Cabinet, but Cabinet members must be approved by the Senate.
Government structure - federal	Bicameral: Congress: *Upper House* - Senate, 100 seats. Senators are popularly elected to serve 6-year terms, with one-third elected every two years. *Lower House* - House of Representatives, 435 seats. Representatives are directly elected to serve 2-year terms. Each state is guaranteed at least one representative.
Number of representatives in lower house of federal government – House of Representatives	435 seats: Republicans 221, Democrats 211, independents 2, Vacancies 1.

Table I (continued)

Number of representatives in lower house of federal government for most populated constituent unit	California: 52
Number of representatives in lower house of federal government for least populated constituent unit	Alaska, Delaware, South Dakota, North Dakota, Montana, Vermont, Wyoming: 1 representative each
Number of representatives in upper house of federal government – Senate	100 seats: 50 Democrats, 49 Republicans, 1 independent
Distribution of representation in upper house of federal government – Senate	Each of the 50 states has two representatives in the Senate.
Constitutional court (highest court dealing with constitutional matters)	Supreme Court. Nine justices are appointed for life by the President with confirmation by the Senate.
Political system of constituent units	Bicameral (except Nebraska). State Senates and Houses of Representatives are directly elected with the duration of the terms varying from state to state.
Head of state - constituent units	Governor - Popularly elected with the term in office varying from 2 years (2 states) to 4 years (48 states), depending upon the state.
Head of government - constituent units	Governor

Table II
Economic and Social Indicators

GDP	US$9.963 trillion
GDP per capita	US$36 200
Mechanisms for taxation	Income Tax jurisdiction is divided between the federal and state governments. Some municipalities levy an income tax but this is only because their state has granted them permission to do so. Personal Income Tax covers five brackets (15-39%). In addition, state and municipal governments impose various taxes on such things as capital gains and property/real estate, as well as corporate taxes.
National debt (external)	US$862 billion
National unemployment rate	4.0%
Constituent unit with highest unemployment rate	Washington, DC: 6.1%
Constituent unit with lowest unemployment rate	Connecticut: 2.0%
Adult literacy rate	99 %
National expenditures on education as a % of GDP	4.7%
Life expectancy in years	77.12
Doctors per population ratio (national)	279 doctors per 100 000 inhabitants
Doctors per population ratio in constituent units (highest)	Washington DC - 737 doctors per 100 000 inhabitants
Doctors per population ratio in constituent units (lowest)	Idaho - 154 doctors per 100,000 inhabitants
National expenditures on health as a % of GDP	12.9%

Sources

Central Intelligence Agency (CIA), *World Fact Book 2000*. CIA, www.cia.gov/cia/publications/factbook/index.html

Economist Intelligence Unit, "Country Commerce - Argentina," *The Economist Intelligence Unit 2000*. New York: EIU, 2000.

Elazar, Daniel J. (ed.) *Federal Systems of the World: A Handbook of Federal, Confederal and Autonomy Arrangements*. 2nd Edition. Jerusalem Institute for Federal Studies. London: Longman Group/Westgate House, 1994.

International Monetary Fund (IMF). *International Financial Statistics*, Vol. LIII, No. 12, December 2000. Washington, DC: the IMF Statistics Department, 2000.

National Center for Education Statistics. "Education Indicators: An International Perspective." www.nces.ed.gov/pubsearch

The PRS Group. "USA - A Country Report 1999." *Political Risk Yearbook On line Database*. www.prsgroup.com

UNESCO. *World Education Report 1998: Teachers and Teaching in a Changing World*, Paris: UNESCO, 1998.

United Nations. *Human Development Report, 2000.* www.undp.org/hdro/report.html

United Nations Statistics Division. "InfoNation." United Nations Statistical Database, 2000. www.un.org/cgi-bin/pubs/infonatn.html

United States Bureau of Labor Statistics. "Unemployment Rates, December 2000." www.stats.bls.gov/eag/eag.us.htm

United States Census Bureau. *Census 2000.* www.census.gov

United States Census Bureau. "State Government Finances." *State Rankings 1998.* www.census.gov/govs/www/state98.html

United States Census Bureau. *Statistical Abstract of the United States 2000.* www.census.gov/prod/2001pubs.html

United States Census Bureau. "Table 11 - States Ranked According to Per Pupil Elementary-Secondary Public School System Finance Amounts: 1996-1997 (in dollars)." *Public Education Finances: 1997 Census of Governments.* Volume 4. www.census.gov

United States House of Representatives Website. www.house.gov

United States Senate Website. www.senate.gov

Watts, Ronald L., *Comparing Federal Systems.* 2nd Edition, School of Policy Studies. Montreal/Kingston: McGill-Queen's University Press, 1999.

World Bank. *World Development Report 2000/2001: Attacking Poverty.* www.worldbank.org/poverty/wdrpoverty/report/index.htm

World Health Organisation (WHO). "Estimates of Health Personnel." www-nt.who.int/whosis/statistics

World Health Organisation (WHO). "Annex Table 8, Selected national health accounts indicators for all Member States, estimates for 1997." *World Health Report 2000.* Geneva, 2000. www-nt.who.int/whosis/statistics/menu.cfm.

Aruba (Neth.)
Netherland Antilles (Neth.)
Dependencias Federales
Grenada
Distrito Federal
Nueva Esparta
CARACAS
TRINIDAD and TOBAGO
COLOMBIA
Falcon
Yaracuy
Zulia
Lara
Miranda
Aragua
Sucre
Trujillo
Cojedes
Garabobo
Portuguesa
Anzoategui
Monagas
Delta
Merida
Barinas
Guarico
Amacuro
Tachria
Apure
Bolivar
GUYANA
COLOMBIA
Amazonas
BRAZIL

Republic of Venezuela

Capital: Caracas
(in Distrito Federal)

Population: 24 Million
(2001 est.)

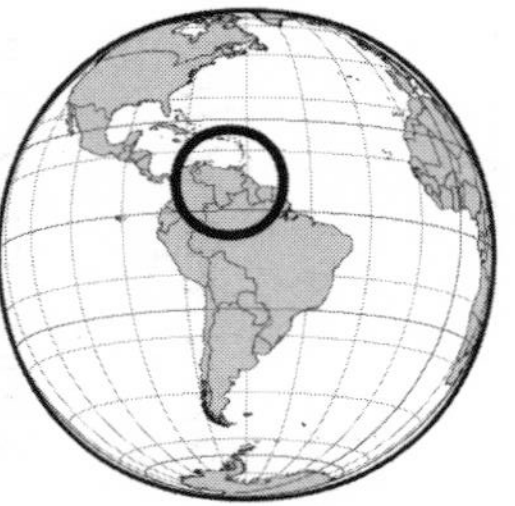

Boundaries and place names are representative only and do not imply any official endorsement.

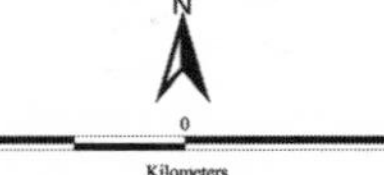

Sources: CIA World Factbook; ESRI Ltd.; Time Atlas of the World

Venezuela
(*Bolivarian Republic of Venezuela*)

ALLAN R. BREWER-CARÍAS

1 HISTORY AND DEVELOPMENT OF FEDERALISM

The Republic of Venezuela is located in the northernmost section of South America. It is the seventh largest country in Latin America, with an area of 912,000 km^2 and 24 million inhabitants. The territory is divided into states, a Capital District that covers part of Caracas, and Federal Dependencies comprised of a number of islands located in the Caribbean Sea. Its economy has been greatly influenced by the presence of oil.[1]

In 1777, after three centuries of Spanish colonization, the seven provinces that later comprised Venezuelan territory were grouped into the General Captaincy of Venezuela. In April 1810, these provinces, beginning with the province of Caracas, one by one declared their independence from Spain, and even drew up their own constitutions. Thus, Venezuela became the first Latin American country to gain independence from the Spanish Crown. In 1810, their elected representatives formed the first General Congress of the Provinces of Venezuela. This Congress enacted the first of the constitutions of an independent

1 In 1928 Venezuela was the world's leading oil exporter, and the country was instrumental in the creation of the Organization of Petroleum Exporting Countries (OPEC) in 1960. In 1975 the oil industry was nationalized.

Latin American country, the Federal Constitution for the States of Venezuela, on 21 December 1811.

This constitution was directly influenced by the constitutional principles that had been conceived of and established in the constitutions arising from the US War of Independence and the French Revolution. Although democracy was not forthcoming for some years, the Venezuelan Constitution of 1811 contained all the principles of modern constitutionalism: state sovereignty and republicanism; supremacy of the constitution as a product of the will of the people; organic separation of powers; territorial distribution of power; declaration of the rights of the country and citizens; and constitutional control to ensure constitutional supremacy.

The 1811 constitution adopted a federal form of government which means that, following the United States, Venezuela was the second country to adopt federalism. Venezuela's adoption of federalism doubtlessly occurred under the influence of the US Constitution, and had territorial justification similar to that which gave rise to the federal form of government in the north – in particular, the existence in the territory occupied by the former General Captaincy of Venezuela of seven provinces isolated one from the other, and socially and politically configured in different ways.

A federal constitutional system enabled the establishment of an independent state which could unite what had never before been united. Consequently, federalism is an important part of Venezuelan constitutionalism and discussions about centralism-federalism have occurred throughout the country's history. Indeed, the Liberator, Simón Bolivar, attributed the demise of the First Republic in 1812 to the federal form of government which unleashed a war of independence that lasted more than a decade. Under Bolivar's influence, centralism was introduced, as evidenced by the constitutional reorganization of Venezuela in 1819 and in its disappearance and integration into the Republic of Colombia in 1821.

Among other factors, it was the centrifugal forces that developed in the Venezuelan provinces which contributed to the failure of the "Gran Colombia" project, and led, in 1830, to the re-establishment of Venezuela with a centralized but federal form of government. Struggles between the central region and provincial forces began in 1830, and ended with a five-year war that was known as the Federal War (1858–1863). The triumph of the federal forces led to the establishment of the United States of Venezuela (1864). From that moment the form of government in Venezuela has always been federal.

During the second half of the nineteenth century the country was riven by civil war. The federal system of government was kept, even following a revolution, but it remained limited by the centralizing elements that historically characterized the system. The marked centralism (military, administrative, tax and legislative) continued during the first decades of the twentieth century under the autocratic regime of Juan Vicente Gómez which ended in 1935. By that time the territorial distribution of power and territorial autonomy had almost disappeared, even though the government continued to maintain its federal form.

Democratization of the country began in the 1930s, but the process was interrupted by the 1945 October Revolution and a decade of control by the military (1948–1958), led by Marcos Pérez Jiménez, who was overthrown by other military officers in 1958. It was under this junta that the move to democracy was reinstated. Elections held in 1959 were won by Rómulo Betancourt, who served as President until 1964.

According to the 1961 constitution, the democratic government continued to be federal in form, but with highly centralized powers at the national level. A political decentralization process was begun in 1989 and included transferring competencies and powers of the national government to the states. Also in 1989, for the first time since the nineteenth century, state Governors were elected by universal, direct and secret votes, and regional political life began to play an important role in the country.

A crisis in the party system gave rise to the 1999 Constituent Assembly process and to a radical change in the political players nationwide. This Constituent Assembly was the tool that the newly elected (1998) President, Hugo Chávez Frías – a former Lieutenant-Colonel who led an attempted coup d'état in 1992 – used to provoke a democratic takeover of all the powers of government. The Assembly was elected in July 1999 and was made up of 131 members, 125 of whom were blind supporters of the President. Only a few dissident voices were heard during the six months it functioned – a very precarious "opposition." In December 1999, a new constitution was sanctioned by the National Assembly and approved by referendum on 15 December 1999. The new constitution of 1999 did not, however, undertake the changes that were needed most – namely the effective political decentralization of the federation and the reinforcement of state and municipal political powers. The constitution of 1999 actually continued with the same centralized foundation and in some cases, centralized certain aspects even more.

2 CONSTITUTIONAL PROVISIONS RELATING TO FEDERALISM

According to Article 4 of the constitution in effect as of 30 December 1999, the Republic of Venezuela "is a decentralized Federal State under the terms set out in the Constitution and is governed by the principles of territorial integrity, solidarity, concurrence and co-responsibility." The standard, thus, is precise: it is a *decentralized federal state* according to "the terms set out in the Constitution," although these terms are without a doubt centralizing. Venezuela has incorporated elements of federalism since 1811, but it has also been a "centralized federation," and continues as such despite the affirmation to the contrary in Article 4.

Article 136 of the constitution states that "[p]ublic power is distributed among the municipal, state and national entities." This article thus establishes three levels of political autonomy in the territory: national power exercised by the republic (federal level); state power, exercised by the 24 states; and municipal power, exercised by the 338 existing municipalities. On each of the three levels, the constitution states that government must always be "democratic, participatory, elected, decentralized, alternative, responsible, plural and with revocable mandates" (Article 6).

The organization of institutions on each territorial level is characterized by the principle of the organic separation of powers. On the national level, national public power is split among the "Legislative, Executive, Judicial, Citizen and Electoral" divisions (Article 136). The 1999 constitution thus surpasses the classic tripartite division of power by adding Citizen Power (Public Ministry, General Comptrollership of the Republic and the Public Defender), as well as Electoral Power (National Electoral Council).

National executive power is exercised by the President of the Republic whose decisions often must be adopted in a Cabinet Meeting (Articles 236, 242). All Cabinet members are accountable to the National Assembly (Articles 242, 244), where the ministers are entitled to voice their opinions and may also be questioned (Article 245). The President is aided by an Executive Vice-President exclusively designated by the President (Article 238).

The constitution of 1999 established a one-chamber National Assembly thus eliminating the country's traditional bicameralism and specifically eliminating the Senate which had played a role as the egalitarian chamber of representatives of the states. The constitution simply established that the states "are politically equal" (Article 159). Consequently, Venezuela has become a federal state without a federal chamber in which the states can be equal. The constitution specifies that "the delegates [to the National Assembly] jointly are representatives of the people and the states and are not subject to mandates, nor instructions, but only to the dictates of their conscience" (Article 201), which effectively eliminates all vestiges of territorial representation.

Representatives are elected based on a number calculated according to a basis of population equivalent to 1.1 per cent. Thus in 2000, as the estimated population of the country was 24 million, the population basis was 264,000 (24 million x 1.1% = 264,000). Each state, including the District Capital, is elected through the principle of proportional representation (Article 182), with one representative per each 264,000 inhabitants.

Each state has a Governor who is elected by universal, direct and secret vote (Article 160), and a State Legislative Council which is comprised of representatives elected according to proportional representation (Article 162). It is the responsibility of the Legislative Councils to enact the constitution of each state, in order to organize public powers along the guidelines of the Venezuelan Constitution which guarantees the autonomy of the states (Article 159). This, however, is seriously limited in the 1999 constitution which states that the organization and functioning of the State Legislative Chambers must be regulated by *national* law (Article 162) – a manifestation of centralism heretofore unforeseen in the history of Venezuelan federalism. It is true that the state Legislative Councils have the jurisdiction to legislate with respect to matters that are in the state's competency (Article 162), but the problem is that the matters that are in their competency depend on national decisions and regulations, which in effect means that the legislative competency of the states is very limited, as it has always been in the past. The effectiveness of all federations lies in the territorial distribution of jurisdictional competencies – Governors and Legislative Councils in the states are of little use if they do not have specific competencies to exercise. This is the case of Venezuela where the 1999 constitution did little to ease the centralizing tendencies in the country, and indeed, contributed to intensifying that centralization.

As to the municipalities, their autonomy is provided for in the constitution. This autonomy does not, however, have any constitutional guarantees, because it can be limited by national law (Article 168). The separation of power at the municipal level is maintained between the executive, represented by Mayors who are elected by universal, direct and secret vote (Article 174), and Municipal Councils, whose members are elected on the basis of proportional representation (Article 175).

The constitution enumerates a number of issues for which competency is attributed to the bodies representing the National Power (Article 156) and Municipal Power (Article 178). According to Article 156, the National Power has competency in, for example, international relations, security and defence, nationality and alien status, national police, economic regulations, mining and oil industries, national policies and regulations on education, health, the environment, land use, transportation, industrial and agricultural production, and post and telecommunications. The administration of justice also falls within the exclusive jurisdiction of the national government (Article 156.31), except with regard to justices of the peace who are regulated by municipalities (Articles 178.7 and 285).

Article 178 outlines that Municipal Powers have competency in, for example, urban land use, housing, urban roads and transport, advertising regulations, urban environment, urban utilities, electricity, water supply, garbage collection and disposal, basic health and education services, and municipal police. Some of these powers are of an exclusive nature but most of them are concurrent.

As to State Power, the constitution fails to enumerate substantive, exclusive competencies and rather concentrates on formal and procedural ones. Furthermore, the limited number of those that it establishes are concurrent in nature – for example, municipal organization, non-metallic mineral exploitation, police, state roads, administration of national roads, and commercial airports and ports (Article 164). The constitution has limited the concurrent competencies – which traditionally have provided a broad field for possible action by state bodies – by subjecting their exercise to what the National Assembly establishes by means of "fundamental laws" that may subsequently be developed by the state Legislative Councils (Article 165). The legislation referring to concurrent competencies must adhere to the principles of interdependence, coordination, cooperation, co-responsibility and subsidiarity (Article 165).

Except in the constitution of 1953 (1953–1961) which regulated in favour of the central government, residual power favouring the states has been a constitutional tradition in Venezuela. In the 1999 constitution, however, this residual competency of the states has been limited by expressly attributing to the national government a parallel and prevalent residual competency in taxes not expressly attributed to the states or municipalities (Article 156.12).

It is important to note that although the constitution of 1999 is characterized by pronounced centralism, it did, however, preserve and re-affirm some decentralizing principles. Consequently, it repeated the standard of the 1961 constitution which allowed the National Assembly to transfer specific matters that are of national competency to the municipalities and states in order to promote decentralization (Article 157). It likewise expanded the decentralizing principle regarding the states to include the municipalities (Article 165), and with respect to both territorial levels, the constitution went one step further to include communities and organized neighbourhood groups as well

(Article 184). Therefore, there is a pronounced tendency in the constitution to favour decentralization, which is even defined as "national policy" that "must strengthen democracy by bringing power closer to the people" (Article 158).

Mention should be made of the sections in the constitution that discuss the financing of the federation. Virtually everything concerning the taxation system is more centralized than in the 1961 constitution, and the competency of the states in tax matters has been basically eliminated. Not only does the constitution list the competencies of the national government with respect to basic taxes (income tax, inheritance and donation taxes, taxes on capital, production, value added, taxes on hydrocarbon resources and mines, taxes on the import and export of goods and services, and taxes on the consumption of liquor, alcohol, cigarettes and tobacco) (Article 156.12), and expressly attribute to the municipalities taxation competencies with respect to local taxes (Article 179), but it also, as was earlier stated, gives the national government residual competencies in tax matters (Article 156.12).

The constitution, thus, does not grant the states competency in terms of taxation, except with respect to official stationery and revenue stamps (Article 164,7). States can only collect taxes when the national government expressly transfers to them, by law, specific taxation competencies (Article 167.5). Lacking therefore their own resources from taxation, state financing is accomplished basically by the transfer of national financial resources through three different channels. First, it is done by means of the so-called "Constitutional Contribution by the Federal Government," which is an annual item in the National Budget Law that is equivalent to a minimum of 15% and a maximum of 20% of total ordinary national income, estimated annually (Article 167.4). Second, a national law has established a system of special economic allotments for the benefit of those states in the territories of which mining and hydrocarbon projects are being developed. According to this law these benefits that have also been extended to include other states (Article 156,16). And third, financing for states and municipalities comes from national funds, such as the Intergovernmental Fund for Decentralization, created in 1993, or the Interstate Compensation Fund which is foreseen in the constitution (Article 167.6).

3 RECENT POLITICAL DYNAMICS

The democratic system established in 1958 developed over the past four decades as a democracy of parties, or a nation of parties, in which traditional political parties that were formed in the 1940s monopolized representation and political participation by controlling all the levels of power. Although during the first two decades of democracy this system ensured the implementation of democracy in one of the Latin American countries with the least democratic tradition, in recent decades that same system has had a perverse effect on democracy and on the functioning of the political system. Political parties and the institutions themselves progressively lost democratic legitimacy and the capacity to evolve and adopt the reforms that democracy needed. Those few reforms that were undertaken, such as political decentralization of the federation, did not make much headway.

This led to a crisis in the political system and a serious power void as a result of the lack of leadership among the political parties. In 1998, that power void led to the collapse of the parties and to the ascent, by popular vote, of a military and grassroots leader (Hugo Chávez Frías). Chávez gave impetus to what was inevitable – change in the system. This is why a new constitution was drafted by a Constituent Assembly in 1999.

As stated earlier, the constitution of 1999 consolidated the "Centralized Federation" that Venezuela has had for more than a century by centralizing power even more. In addition, it accentuated presidentialism by allowing unlimited legislative delegation by the President of the Republic (Articles 207, 237.8) whose term was extended to six years. Moreover, the constitution is characterized by a markedly military style that obscures the principle of the subjugation of military power to civil power with broad and obsolete regulations no longer used in the contemporary democratic world. As well, it contains detailed provisions regarding national security and defence that are reminiscent of the national security doctrine so in vogue in the Southern Cone Latin American countries of the 1970s.

The blend of centralism, presidentialism and militarism gives Venezuela a constitution with a marked authoritarian inclination. This can be seen as the outcome of the crisis in the democratic system of parties whose leadership did not know how to introduce, in time, the changes needed to perfect democracy by making it less focused on parties and the state.

4 SOURCES FOR FURTHER INFORMATION

Brewer Carías, Allan R., *La Constitución de 1999*, Caracas, 2000.
– *Las Constituciones de Venezuela*, Caracas, 1997.
– *Federalismo y Municipalismo en la Constitución de 1999 (Una reforma insufuciente y regresiva)*, Caracas, 2001.
– «Los problemas de la federación centralizada en Venezuela» en

Revista Ius et Praxis, Facultad de Derecho y Ciencias Políticas, Perú: Universidad de Lima, N 12, diciembre 1988, pp. 49–96.

Brewer-Carías, Allan R., et al., *Leyes y Reglamentos para la descentralización política de la Federación,* Caracas, 1994.

Combellas, Ricardo, *Derecho Constitucional. Una introducción al Estudio de la Constitución de la República Bolivariana de Venezuela,* Caracas, 2000.

Delfino, María de los Angeles, *La Descentralización en Venezuela,* Caracas: Parámetros Legales y Constitucionales, PNUD, COPRE, 1996.

Rondón de Sansó, Hildegard, *Comentarios a la Constitución de 1999,* Caracas, 2000.

Villalba, Gustavo León, *Descentralización en Venezuela,* Caracas: FIDES, 1996.

Table I
Political and Geographic Indicators

Capital city	Caracas
Number and type of constituent units	*23 States (Estados)*: Amazonas, Anzoátegui, Apure, Aragua, Barinas, Bolívar, Carabobo, Cojedes, Delta Amacuro, Falcón, Guárico, Lara, Mérida, Miranda, Monagas, Nueva Esparta, Portuguesa, Sucre, Táchira, Trujillo, Vargas, Yaracuy, Zulia; *1 Federal District* (Distrito Federal): Caracas; *1 Federal Dependency* (Dependencia Federal): consists of 72 islands.
Official language(s)	Spanish
Area	912 050 km^2
Area – Largest constituent unit	Bolívar (238 000 km^2)
Area – Smallest constituent unit	Federal District – Caracas (1 930 km^2)
Total population	23 706 000
Population by constituent unit (% of total population)	Zulia 12.97%, Miranda 10.55%, Carabobo 8.53%, Federal District – Caracas 7.41%, Lara 6.37%, Aragua 5.97%, Bolivar 5.29%, Anzoategui 4.30%, Táchira 4.15%, Portuguesa 3.36%, Sucre 3.29%, Mérida 3.0%, Falcón 2.99%, Guárico 2.57%, Monagas 2.41%, Barinas 2.36%, Trujilllo 2.34%, Yaracuy 2.09%, Apure 1.88%, Nueva Esparta 1.53%, Vargas 1.53%, Cojedes 1.06%, Delta Amacuro 0.56%, Amazonas 0.40%
Political system – federal	Federal Republic
Head of state – federal	President Hugo Rafael Chávez Fríaz (1999/2000), Movimiento Quinta República (MVR). Directly elected for a 6-year term. The President may serve only 2 consecutive terms.
Head of government – federal	President Hugo Rafael Chávez Fríaz (1999/2000), Movimiento Quinta República – MVR (Movement for the Fifth Republic). President appoints Cabinet (Council of Ministers).
Government structure – federal	Unicameral: Under the 1999 Constitution, the bicameral Congress of the Republic was replaced by a unicameral Asamblea Nacional (National Assembly). There are currently 165 seats in the Chamber of Deputies, the only chamber in the National Assembly. Members are directly elected through proportional representation (a combination of party list and single-member constituencies) to serve 5-year terms (three seats are reserved for the indigenous peoples of Venezuela).

Table I (continued)

Number of representatives in house of federal government – Chamber of Deputies	165 seats: Movimiento V República – MVR (Movement for the Fifth Republic) 76, Acción Democrática – AD (Democratic Action) 33, Movimiento al Socialismo – MAS (Movement Toward Socialism) 20, Proyecto Venezuela – PROVEN (Project Venezuela) 6, Partido Social Cristiano de Venezuela – COPEI (Social Christian Party of Venezuela) 5, Primero Justicia (Justice First) 5, LAPY 3, La Causa Radical – CR (The Radical Cause) 3, Nuevo Tiempo (New Times) 3, Consejo Nacional Indio de Venezuela – CONIVE (National Indian Council of Venezuela) 3, others 8.
Number of representatives in house of federal government for most populated constituent unit	Zulia: 15
Number of representatives in house of federal government for least populated constituent unit	Amazonas: 3
Constitutional court (highest court dealing with constitutional matters)	Supreme Tribunal of Justice (Tribuna Suprema de Justicia). Magistrates are elected by the National Assembly for a 9-year term. Elections take place for one third of the tribunal every three years. Magistrates are eligible for reelection.
Political system of constituent units	Unicameral – Legislative Council. Members are directly elected through proportional representation for a 5-year term.
Head of state – constituent units	Governor – Directly elected for a 5-year term.
Head of government – constituent units	Governor

Table II
Economic and Social Indicators

GDP	US$146.2 billion
GDP per capita	US$6 200
Mechanisms for taxation	Forms of taxation: The 1999 constitution centralized the powers of taxation. • Income Tax: Imposed by the central government in 8 tax brackets ranging from 6%–34%. • Value-Added Tax (VAT): Imposed by the central government. 14.5% tax on sale of tangible goods, services and import of goods and services. (Note: Nueva Esparata is exempt from VAT.) • Excise taxes on liquor, tobacco, cigarettes and petroleum products. Imposed by the central government. • Municipal License Tax: Imposed by municipal governments. Annual levy for doing business in a district. Rate is based on sales. Constituent units have the right to tax with respect to official stationery and revenue stamps, and when the national government expressly transfers tax power.
National debt (external)	US$34 billion
National unemployment rate	13.7%
Constituent unit with highest unemployment rate	N/A
Constituent unit with lowest unemployment rate	N/A
Adult literacy rate	92%
National expenditures on education as a % of GDP	5%
Life expectancy in years	73.07
Doctors per population ratio (national)	263.3 doctors per 100 000 population
Doctors per population ratio in constituent units (highest)	N/A
Doctors per population ratio in constituent units (lowest)	N/A
National expenditures on health as a % of GDP	3.9%

Sources

Asamblea nacional de Venezuela (National Assembly of Venezuela). www.asambleanacional.gov.ve

Central Intelligence Agency (CIA), *World Fact Book 2000*. CIA, www.cia.gov/cia/publications/factbook/index.html

Economic Commission for Latin America and the Caribbean (ECLAC), *Statistical Yearbook for Latin America and the Caribbean 1999*. ECLAC, www.eclac.org/estaditicas

Economist Intelligence Unit (EIU). "Country Commerce – Venezuela: Released October 2000." *The Economist Intelligence Unit Database.* New York: The Economist June 2000. www.eiu.com

Elazar, Daniel J. (ed.) *Federal Systems of the World: A Handbook of Federal, Confederal and Autonomy Arrangements.* 2nd Edition. Jerusalem Institute for Federal Studies. London: Longman Group/Westgate House, 1994.

International Labour Office. "Indicators on Unemployment." www.un.org/Depts/unsd/social/unempl.htm

International Monetary Fund (IMF). *International Financial Statistics, Vol. LIII, No. 12,* December 2000. Washington, DC: the IMF Statistics Department, 2000.

Latin-Focus: The Leading Source for Latin American Economies. www.latin-focus.com/index.html

Pan-American Health Organization (PAHO/WHO). "Profiles of the Health Services System" of respective countries. www.paho.org

Tribunal Supremo de Justicia de Venezuela. www.tsj.gov.ve

United Nations. "Human Development Index," "Gender-Related Development Index," *Human Development Report, 2000.* Human Development Report Office. www.undp.org/hdro/report.html

World Bank. *World Development Report 2000/2001: Attacking Poverty.* www.worldbank.org/poverty/wdrpoverty/report/index.htm

World Health Organisation (WHO). *World Health Report 2000.* Geneva, Switzerland, 2000. www-nt.who.int/whosis/statistics/menu.cfm

Federal Republic of Yugoslavia

Capital: Beograd (Belgrade)
Population: 10.5 Million
(2000 est.)

* Vojvodina and Kosovo are Autonomous Provinces; Serbia and Montenegro are the first-order Republics making up Yugoslavia.

Boundaries and place names are representative only and do not imply official endorsement.

N

75 0 75

kilometers

Sources: CIA World FActbook;
ESRI Ltd.; UN Cartography Department.

Yugoslavia
(*Federal Republic of Yugoslavia*)

MIHAILO CRNOBRNJA

1 HISTORY AND DEVELOPMENT OF FEDERALISM

Although not an old country by any standard, the Federal Republic of Yugoslavia (FRY) has had a very dynamic and turbulent history. The country has survived long dominance by foreign powers and, in the twentieth century, it passed four constitutions and two sets of major constitutional amendments in less than 75 years. The country called Yugoslavia has also changed names, its size and the number of federal units which comprise it. It even disappeared off the map during World War II.

The peoples of the area were ruled by foreign powers from the mid-1400s until the collapse of the Austro-Hungarian Empire after World War I. Austria controlled Slovenia, Hungary controlled Croatia, Venetians controlled parts of the coastal regions of what is now Croatia, and Serbia (which included what are now Macedonia and Montenegro) and Bosnia were under the control of the Ottoman Empire. At the Congress of Berlin in 1878, which followed a war by Serbia, Montenegro and Russia against Turkey, Serbia gained independence from the Ottoman Empire, and Montenegro's independence was recognized. At the outbreak of war in 1914 Montenegro decided to join Serbia in the war effort, and in November 1918 a national assembly voted for union with Serbia.

Yugoslavia became a country after the end of World War I. On 1 December 1918, Bosnia, Croatia and Slovenia (the latter two were formerly part of the Austro-Hungarian Empire which had collapsed by 1918) decided to join Serbia and Montenegro and Macedonia in forming a new, multi-ethnic country. Initially the country was called the Kingdom of the Serbs, Croats and Slovenes but King Alexander changed its name to Yugoslavia in 1929. This "First Yugoslavia" was a constitutional monarchy with a Parliament and the Serbian dynasty Karadjordjevic as sovereigns. Although multi-ethnic, and composed of distinct ethnic regions with individual histories, the country was centralized. The regions and ethnic groups had no autonomy in political affairs, or in cultural affairs. This was the cause of many tensions particularly among the Serbs and Croats.

During World War II Yugoslavia was partitioned. Parts of the country were annexed to the German Reich, the coast was given to Italy, most of Macedonia was annexed by Bulgaria, Kosovo was given to Albania (then an Italian puppet state), and small parts in the north went under Hungarian jurisdiction. Two "independent" states were created – Croatia and Serbia – both effectively run by the German occupying forces. During the war two major resistance movements emerged. One group – the Chetnics – were royalists and fought for the restoration of the monarchy and "First Yugoslavia." They operated exclusively in the Serb-populated areas. The other group – known as Partizans and led by Marshal Josip Broz Tito – operated across all territories that had been part of Yugoslavia. They fought for a new, different Yugoslavia. Recognizing that the previously highly centralized state was ill-suited to the diversity of the ethnic groups that comprised it, the Partizans declared as early as 1943 their intention to organize a future Yugoslavia as a federal state.

Tito's Partizans eventually gained international recognition which strengthened them internally. With minimal assistance from Allied troops they managed to liberate all the territories of former Yugoslavia. They then set out to create the new, "Second Yugoslavia." On 29 November 1945 the country became the Federal People's Republic of Yugoslavia, and the constitution of 1946 organized Yugoslavia as a federal state. The new federal Yugoslavia was made up of six republics: Bosnia-Herzegovina, Croatia, Macedonia, Montenegro, Serbia and Slovenia. Two autonomous provinces were created within Serbia in recognition of the large minorities living there (Hungarians in Vojvodina and Albanians in Kosovo).

Although nominally a federation, Yugoslavia was in fact a highly centralized state. Since the core of the Partizan movement was made up of Communists, it was no surprise that the political system soon became a replica of that in the Soviet Union. Although each republic had a constitution, an assembly, a flag and other symbols of sovereignty, most if not all political decision making took place in the Central Committee and the Politburo of the Yugoslav Communist Party. There was, however, considerable cultural and linguistic autonomy, which was some improvement over the pre-war situation.

In 1948 Yugoslavia was expelled from the Soviet bloc for being too independent-minded. From that point on, the history of the Yugoslav state is basically one of gradual democratization and decentralization of state power from the centre to the federal republics. In 1963 a new constitution was adopted. Other than changing the name of the country to the Socialist Federal Republic of Yugoslavia (SFRY), to underline and emphasize the ideological core of the country's politics, the new constitution relegated considerable decision-making power to the republics. Thus, the fields of education, health and social policy were now primarily the responsibility of the republics. The judiciary and the law enforcement system were also changed to increase the power of the republics and decrease the responsibilities of the federal state.

The state structure was changed yet again by the constitution of 1974 which gave the republics even more prerogatives. The new head of state, that would eventually replace Tito, was to be a collective presidency with a yearly rotating chairman. While Tito was alive this collective body was only symbolic but it did, in effect, take over when he died in 1980.

In the constitution of 1974 the republics gained a right to secede, but the mechanism according to which this could be undertaken was not specified, leading to major disagreements when the country dissolved in 1991–92. The republics also developed military structures, a kind of national guard and a supplementary component to the Yugoslav standing army. Finally, republics were allowed limited international relations and ministries of foreign affairs appeared in all of them.

But the most controversial aspect of the constitution of 1974 was the treatment of the autonomous provinces in Serbia. While still nominally parts of Serbia, Kosovo and Vojvodina were at the same time federal units and had direct representation at the federal level where they were treated as almost equal to Serbia, which was one of the republics of the federation. The only difference was in the number of representatives that Serbia and Vojvodina/Kosovo respectively sent to the two chambers of the federal Parliament. This situation irritated Serbs enormously but they could do nothing while Tito was alive. After his death, the tension caused by such a constitutional arrangement helped a great deal in fomenting Serbian nationalism and the rise of Slobodan Milosevic to power.

The period between Tito's death and the definite disappearance of the Second Yugoslavia in 1992 was a period of gradual but steady atrophy of the federation. It became ever more dysfunctional and easy prey to mounting aspirations of leaders in the republics. From 1987 on, the rise of ethnic nationalism made the debate on the future of Yugoslavia even more passionate and heated. Every ethnic group claimed that it was dissatisfied with the existing arrangement and that another ethnic group (or groups) was getting a better deal. While Tito's reign was symbolized by an *inclusive* agenda, one favouring centripetal forces, after his death the new elites in the republics favoured *exclusive* agendas which were divisive and strongly centrifugal.

Since the constitution did not provide a clear mechanism for the dissolution of the federation, each side interpreted the process in the way best suited to it. Agreement was impossible and republics left Yugoslavia by unilateral decisions. The first to do so were Slovenia and Croatia, followed by Macedonia and finally Bosnia-Herzegovina. Unilateral declarations of independence were followed by wars in Slovenia, Croatia and Bosnia-Herzegovina. Only Macedonia left the federation without firing a shot. Serbs first tried to keep Yugoslavia together by using military force in Slovenia. When that failed, they tried to create a greater Serbia which would include territories of Croatia and Bosnia inhabited by Serbs. This led to bloody ethnic wars which lasted almost four years.

2 CONSTITUTIONAL PROVISIONS RELATING TO FEDERALISM

Today the Federal Republic of Yugoslavia (FRY) is a federation of two units: the Republic of Montenegro and the Republic of Serbia. The capital is Belgrade. In terms of culture, religion and ethnic origins there is no difference between the populations of the two republics – these are two states of the same ethnic people. Serbia is six times larger in terms of territory, 16 times in terms of population and roughly 20 times in terms of economic power. Creating a federation of such disproportionate partners was not easy. Running it has been even more of a problem.

The current constitution of FRY came into force on 27 April 1992. The Preamble states that the two republics freely joined to make a new federation which is to continue as the sole legal successor of the previous state. The constitution declares the equality of all people as well as the equality of the two federal units of FRY (Article 1). It also provides the possibility of other states joining the FRY if they so desire, and if they accept the conditions specified by the constitution (Article 2). According to Article 3, the borders between the two republics can be changed only if an agreement between them to that effect has been reached.

The constitution resolves the issue of the division of power by stating explicitly the functions that the joint state is expected to perform. All other issues are by implication the prerogative and responsibility of the constituent units (Article 6). Section 4 of the constitution deals with the functions of the state to be performed at the federal level. They are listed in Article 77 as:

1 the adoption of a common civil code and due process of law, and the necessary instruments, organizations and institutions for its implementation;
2 the creation of the institutions of a common market, monetary policy, the banking system, foreign-exchange system, customs, financial relations with third parties and the basis of a fiscal system;
3 the implementation of a common development policy designed to overcome the differences and disparities between regions and the two federal units;
4 the maintenance and development of a common physical infrastructure and communication systems, protection of the environment and regulation of the use of rivers and the sea;
5 the provision of physical and financial security for individuals and organizations;
6 the conduct of foreign policy and the administration of border crossings and status of aliens;
7 the security and defence of FRY;
8 the protection of the health of the population from epidemics, ionized radiation, the manufacture and sale of medicaments, control of the production, distribution and transportation of firearms, hazardous and radioactive materials; protection of animals and plants from disease;
9 the financing of the competencies of the FRY;
10 the organization and work of the organs of the FRY; and
11 the establishment of national holidays and the orders of merit to be issued by the federal state.

To perform these functions, the organs and institutions of the federal state have autonomous sources of revenue which include revenues from customs, duties and international tariffs, a portion of the general turnover tax, and other sources specified by federal law.

The highest federal decision-making and law-making body is the Federal Assembly (Article 78). According to Section V, Article 78, the Federal Assembly's powers include, among other things, the ability to decide on the admission of other states in the FRY, make decisions on any alterations to the borders of the country, and adopt and enact the federal budget. As well, according to Amendment II (which replaced Article 78(7) of the constitution), the Federal Assembly has the power to choose and dismiss the President of the Federal Government (also referred to as the Prime Minister), members of the federal government, judges of the Federal Constitution Court, judges of the Federal Court, the Federal Prosecutor, the Governor of the National Bank and other federal officials. The Federal Assembly may also dismiss the President of the Republic when the Federal Constitutional Court confirms that the President has violated the constitution. At least two-thirds of the representatives of both Chambers of the Federal Assembly must accept a proposal for dismissal (Amendment VII, supplementing Section V, Paragraph 2 of the constitution).

The Federal Assembly is bicameral (Article 80) and consists of the Council of Citizens and the Council of the Republics. Members of Parliament are elected to the Council of Citizens by universal, direct and secret ballot, for a period of four years, each of them representing a constituency of 65,000. Member republics are guaranteed at least 30 members of the Council of Citizens (Article 80). The Council of Republics consists of 20 representatives from each republic (Article 80, and see Amendment III of the constitution). Both of these provisions in Article 80 benefit Montenegro because of its smaller population. The election of members of the Council of Citizens is regulated by federal law while the election of members of the Council of Republics is regulated by laws in the respective republics. Article 86 of the constitution states explicitly that members of the Chamber of Citizens represent the citizens of the FRY, while members of Chamber of Republics "represent the member republics from which they were elected." Both Chambers decide concurrently on matters in the jurisdiction of the Federal Assembly (Article 90).

The federal government of Yugoslavia is led by a Prime Minister (or President of the Federal Republic) who is selected by a majority vote during a secret ballot held in both Chambers of the Federal Assembly (Amendment VIII, which replaced Articles 101(3), 102(2), 103(1), 104(1, 3, 4), 105(1)). The government must account for its actions to the Federal Assembly and can be dismissed on the grounds of non-confidence based on a majority vote of representatives in both Chambers of the Federal Assembly.

According to Amendment V (which replaced Article 97 of the constitution), elections for the President of the Republic are to be held every four years, and the President is now directly elected by the population via secret ballot (according to the defunct Article 97 the President was elected by the Federal Assembly). The President's duties include, *inter alia,* representing the country abroad, promulgating federal laws, ratifying international treaties, nominating a candidate for Prime Minister (after hearing opinions from groups in the Federal Assembly) and calling elections for the Federal Assembly (Article 96). It is important to note that Amendment V also states that "according to the rules," the President of the Republic and the President of the Federal Government (also referred to as the Prime Minister) cannot be from the same member republic.

The constitution makes provision for a Federal Court (Articles 108–110) and a Federal Constitutional Court (Articles 124–132). Justices are appointed for a nine-year term. The Federal Court acts as a court of highest instance, and is responsible for hearing appeals coming from the republic's courts. It also rules on conflicts of jurisdiction between courts, and "lays down the principles governing the uniform enforcement of federal statutes, other federal laws and general enactments by the courts." The Federal Constitutional Court rules on the conformity of the republics' constitutions to the federal constitution, the conformity of FRY laws to international treaties, the conformity of the republics' statutes to federal law, conflicts of jurisdiction between the republics or between a republic and the federal government, and violations of electoral law.

Acts of constitutional amendment can be made only if approved by two-thirds of members in both chambers of the Federal Assembly (Article 139). An amendment of the FRY constitution "shall be deemed to be accepted" when the assemblies of both member republics have approved and adopted it (Article 141, paragraph 2). As noted in this section, there have been a number of important amendments made to the constitution since 1992.

It is important to note that there are no provisions in the constitution for the dissolution of the federation, i.e., for a case in which one of the constituent units decides to leave.

3 RECENT POLITICAL DYNAMICS

The Federal Republic of Yugoslavia, which has recently been re-admitted to the UN, the Organization for Security and Cooperation in Europe (OSCE), the Stability Pact, and the International Monetary Fund (IMF), is once again shaking from within. For some time now, the government of Montenegro has been openly advocating a major reconstruction of the country. In fact, according to the latest suggestion coming from Montenegro, the federation would be dissolved and a union of two independent, internationally recognized states would take its place.

This policy of distancing itself from Serbia, its federal partner, was initiated by Montenegro in 1997 when Slobodan Milosevic became the

President of FRY. He chose as his Prime Minister a political leader from the opposition in Montenegro rather than from the ruling coalition. In effect, he chose a partner by loyalty and not by the spirit of the constitution. Since that time the ruling coalition in Montenegro has gradually but surely distanced itself from the federal authorities, declaring them illegal and illegitimate. Until recently, the West supported such political dynamics in Montenegro, offering moral, political and financial assistance to what was seen as a major irritant to Milosevic's authoritarian rule and a bridgehead for the development of democracy in FRY.

Initially, Montenegro maintained that it wanted to be a federal partner but that Milosevic was standing in the way with his authoritarian and heavy-handed rule which all but ignored the existence of Montenegro. But distancing from Milosevic's policies in effect became a process of distancing from the federation. During the year 2000, for example, Montenegro replaced the Yugoslav *dinar* with the German *deutsche mark* as the currency in circulation, a violation of the federal constitution.

The momentum toward Montenegro's independence did not stop when Milosevic's rule came to an end in October 2000. Milosevic continued to be an irritant in Yugoslav relations even after his removal, and indeed the federal government collapsed in a dispute over Milosevic's extradition to the International Criminal Tribunal for the Former Yugoslavia in the Hague.

The democratically-elected President of Yugoslavia, Vojislav Kostunica, and the democratically-elected government of Serbia offered immediate talks on the amendment of the existing constitution or the drafting of a new one based on federal principles. So far, Montenegro insists on, at best, an association or union of independent states.

It will be up to Montenegro to decide the future of the federation, if any. But that will not be simple. Since Milosevic's removal from power, the West has changed its position on Montenegrin independence and in fact is now suggesting that Montenegro should remain part of Yugoslavia. Perhaps more importantly, within Montenegro itself, the majority in support of independence is very slim at this time – approximately 55 per cent – and the issue is very divisive. The main opposition party in Montenegro is flatly against independence, as is a junior coalition partner. Not only is the issue divisive, but it is also very emotional. Both sides of the debate about independence are very passionate about their respective positions so that violent confrontations and territorial division cannot be ruled out. Future constitutional talks will be necessary in order to find a mutually acceptable constitutional arrangement within the federal framework.

It is not just Montenegro, however, which is agitating for change to the borders of Yugoslavia. No discussion of Yugoslavia would be complete without mention of the status of Kosovo within the federation. Since 1999 Kosovo, a formerly "autonomous region" within Serbia, has been de facto an international protectorate, run by UNMIK (The UN Mission in Kosovo). In 2001 elections were held to elect the local parliament and President of Kosovo, increasing self-rule within the region. The final status of Kosovo, within or without Yugoslavia and Serbia, is still a long way from being decided. UN Security Council Resolution 1244 states that the solution must be found within the framework of Yugoslavia. So far, the international community has kept to both the spirit and the letter of the Resolution, fearing a new wave of disintegration within the Balkans if Kosovo gains independence. The Serbs, of course, are also in favour of a "Kosovo within Yugoslavia" while the Albanians of Kosovo strongly reject the idea. The gap between the two positions is very wide and it will take a long time, and a lot of hard work on the ground, to find a suitable bridge.

4 SOURCES FOR FURTHER INFORMATION

Crnobrnja, Mihailo, *The Yugoslav Drama,* 2nd ed., Montreal: McGill-Queen's University Press, 1997.

Lampe, John, *Yugoslavia as History,* New York: Cambridge University Press, 1996.

Ramet, Sabrina Petra, *Nationalism and Federalism in Yugoslavia,* 2nd ed., Bloomington, IN: Indiana University Press, 1992.

http://lcweb2.loc.gov/frd/es/yutoc.html (Library of Congress)

http://www.gov.yu (Official web-site of the Yugoslav government)

http://centraleurope.com/yugoslaviatoday/

http://www.ssees.ac.uk/prospectprogramb.htm

http://www.crisisweb.org

Table I
Political and Geographic Indicators

Capital city	Belgrade
Number and type of constituent units	*2 Republics (Republika)*: Montenegro and Serbia; Note: *Two nominally autonomous provinces:* Kosovo and Vojvodina
Official language(s)	Serbian, Albanian
Area	102 350 km^2
Area – Largest constituent unit	Serbia (88 412 km^2)
Area – Smallest constituent unit	Montenegro (13 938 km^2)
Total population	10 393 177 (Note: The exact population is difficult to estimate due to large displacement of persons during the war in 1999)
Population by constituent unit (% of total population)	Serbia 94%, Montenegro 6%
Political system – federal	Federal Republic
Head of state – federal	Federal President (President of the Republic) Vojislav Koštunica (2000): Demokratska Opozicija Srbije (Democratic Opposition of Serbia)/Demokratska Stranka Srbije – DOS-DDS (Democratic Party of Serbia). Directly elected by the population for 4-year term.
Head of government – federal	Federal Prime Minister (also called President of the Federal Republic) Dragisa Pesic (2001) Socijalisticka narodna partija Crne Gore (Socialist People's Party of Montenegro (SNP)). PM is nominated by the President and then elected by the Federal Assembly to serve a 4-year term. The current federal government is formed by Demokratska Opozicija Srbije (Democratic Opposition of Serbia (DOS)) and Socijalisticka Narodna Partija Crne Gore – SNP (Serbian People's Party of Montenegro). The Cabinet is also appointed by the President. The constitution states that the President and Prime Minister must come from different republics.

Table I (continued)

Government structure – federal	Bicameral: Savezna Skupstina (Federal Assembly): *Second Chamber* – Vece Republika (Council of the Republics), 40 seats. Members serve 4-year terms, with 20 members selected by each of the two republican parliaments. *First Chamber* – Vece Građjana (Council of Citizens), 138 seats. Members serve a 4-year term. 108 members are directly elected from the republic of Serbia and 30 from the republic of Montenegro. Half of the Serbian seats are elected by single-member constituencies through a system of majority, and half by party lists. 6 of the Montenegro seats are elected from single-member constituencies and the remaining seats are elected through party lists.
Number of representatives in lower house of federal government – Council of Citizens	138 Seats: *Demokratska Opozicija Srbije (Democratic Opposition of Serbia (DOS)) comprised of:* Demokratska Stranka (Democratic Party), Demokratska Stranka Srbije – DSS (Democratic Party of Serbia), Građanski Savez Srbije – GSS (Civic Alliance of Serbia), Demokratski Centar (Democratic Centre), Demokratska Alternativa (Democratic Alternative), Nova Demokratija – ND (New Democracy), Demohriščanska Stranka Srbije (Christian-Democratic Party of Serbia), Socijaldemokratska Unija (Social-Democratic Union), Liga socijaldemokrata Vojvodine (Social-Democratic League of Vojvodina), Savez Vojvodanskih Madara, Reformska Demokratska Stranka Vojvodine (Reform Democratic Party of Vojvodina), Socijaldemokratija (Social Democracy), Koalicija Vojvodina (Vojvodina Coalition), Pokret za Demokratsku Srbiju (Movement for a Democratic Serbia), Nova Srbija (New Serbia), Asocijacija Slobodnih i Nezavisnih Sindikata – DOS (Association of Free and Democratic Trade Unions) 58, Socialisticka Partija Srbije – SPS (Serb Socialist Party) and Jugoslovenska Levica – JUL (Yugoslav United Left) 44, Socijalisticka narodna partija Crne Gore – SNP (Socialist People's Party of Montenegro) 28, Srpska Radikalna Stranka – SRS (Serb Radical Party) 5, Serbian People's Party of Montenegro (SNSCG) 2, Vajdasági Magyar Szövetsége/Savez Vojvodjanskih Mađara – VMSZ (Vojvodina's Hungarian Union) 1.
Number of representatives in lower house of federal government for most populated constituent unit	Serbia – 108 representatives

Table I (continued)

Number of representatives in lower house of federal government for least populated constituent unit	Montenegro – 30 representatives
Number of representatives in upper house of federal government – Council of the Republics	40 Seats: Socijalisticka Narodna Partija Crne Gore – SNP (Socialist People's Party of Montenegro) 19, Demokratska Opozicija Srbije – DOS (Democratic Opposition of Serbia) 10, Socialisticka Partija Srbije Jugoslovenska Levica – SPS-JUL (Serb Socialist Party/ Yugoslav United Left) 7, Srpska Radikalna Stranka – SRS (Serb Radical Party) 2, Serbian People's Party of Montenegro – SNSCG 1, Srpski Pokret Obnove – SPO 1.
Distribution of representation in upper house of federal government – Council of the Republics	Each republic has 20 seats in the Council of the Republics.
Constitutional court (highest court dealing with constitutional matters)	Constitutional Court. Judges are appointed by the Federal Assembly for nine-year terms.
Political system of constituent units	Each republic has its own directly appointed national assembly, with Serbia having a 250-member assembly and Montenegro having a 78-member assembly. In 1990, the government of Serbia dissolved the Kosovo National Assembly.
Head of state – constituent units	President, directly elected
Head of government – constituent units	President and Executive Council

Table II
Economic and Social Indicators

GDP	US$24.2 billion
GDP per capita	US$2 300
Mechanisms for taxation	There is no federal tax authority in Yugoslavia. The republics of Serbia and Montenegro levy and distribute taxes and revenues; however, no details of taxation mechanisms currently in place are available. (Note: A significant number of strategic plans with objectives for reform are being made available by several international financial and taxation aid agencies.)
National debt (external)	US$14.1 billion
National unemployment rate	30%
Constituent unit with highest unemployment rate	Serbia: 30%
Constituent unit with lowest unemployment rate	Montenegro: 23%
Adult literacy rate	93%
National expenditures on education as a % of GDP	N/A
Life expectancy in years	73.5
Doctors per population ratio (national)	82.4 doctors per 100 000 inhabitants
Doctors per population ratio in constituent units (highest)	N/A
Doctors per population ratio in constituent units (lowest)	N/A
National expenditures on health as a % of GDP	N/A

Sources

Central Intelligence Agency (CIA), *World Fact Book 2000*. CIA, www.cia.gov/cia/publications/factbook/index.html

Derbyshire, J. Denis. "Yugoslavia." *Encyclopedia of World Political Systems*. Volumes I and II, New York: Sharpe Reference, M.E. Sharpe, Inc, 2000.

Ernst & Young. "EY Passport Countries, Federal Republic of Yugoslavia." Worldwide Corporate Tax Guide. www.ey.com/GLOBAL/gcr.nsf/EYPassport/Yugoslavia-EYPassport

Federal Statistics Office of Yugoslavia, "Yugoslavia in Figures," on-line database, www.szs.sv.gov.yu/homee.html

International Monetary Fund (IMF). *Federal Republic of Yugoslavia: Membership and Request for Emergency Post Conflict Assistance*. IMF Staff Report and Press Release on the Executive Board Discussion, January 2001. Country report No. 01/07. www.imf.org

United Nations/ECE. *Trends in Europe and North America 1999: Country Profiles from the UN/ECE Statistical Yearbook*. UN/ECE Statistical Division. www.unece.org/stats/trend/trend_h.html

United States Department of State. "Federal Republic of Yugoslavia Country Report on Human Rights Practices." Bureau of Democracy, Human Rights and Labour www.state.gov/www/global/human_rights/

World Health Organisation (WHO). "Estimates of Health Personnel." www-nt.who.int/whosis/statistics

World Health Organisation (WHO). "Annex Table 8, Selected national health accounts indicators for all Member States, estimates for 1997." *World Health Report 2000*. Geneva, 2000. www-nt.who.int/whosis/statistics/menu.cfm.

Yugoslav Chamber of Commerce and Industry Website. www.pkj.co.yu

PART TWO

Comparative Articles

Federalism and Foreign Policy: Comparative Answers to Globalization[1]

NELSON MICHAUD

INTRODUCTION

In the early 1990s, literature about federalism was greatly influenced by the collapse of both the USSR and the former Yugoslavia and, given these examples, the prognosis for the future of federalism seemed grim. The mid- to late 1990s and the early 2000s present a significantly different portrait. The literature of this period seems to indicate that if federalism is still challenged, it is not as much from the inside as it is from external sources associated with globalization. Nevertheless, research published in the mid-1990s was still pessimistic. It perceived "classical" federalism as obsolete, and some authors even forecast the end of the nation-state, of national territory, and of federalism. The literature appeared to conclude that federalism was not compatible with globalization since it did not favour the emergence of solutions to increasing pressures. International values and challenges were seen as having reached people's daily life and constituent units, which are generally closer to their citizens, seemed to be in a better position to answer the needs of their population than central governments. Thus, globalization was jeopardizing central governments much more than it was their constituent governments by eroding federal powers and jurisdictions. However, after a decade of reflection there is no convincing evidence to support the apocalyptic conclusions of earlier studies. Against all odds, federations are alive and well and, more importantly, some unitary states have adopted for themselves some characteristics usually associated with federalism. Thus, for example, Tony Blair's government in the United Kingdom has implemented a policy of devolution, and China has established autonomous regions. The new international context and the survival of federalism as a way to organize governance suggest that questions linking both need to be re-evaluated.

The future of federalism has been debated over the last decade and within the debate it has been acknowledged that the international context, including the increasing role of multinational corporations and civil society, has changed dramatically. The state is no longer the sole actor on the international scene. It is interesting that most research about federalism can be found in the fields of political theory, constitutional studies, or public administration. Until recently, very little research has been conducted in the realm of international relations. The novelty of the topic and the ongoing debate about the subject in part explains this rarity. As well, differences that exist among federal states and local concerns make the conduct of a comparative study challenging. These factors, however, do not prevent the conduct of an analysis that could help better understand the new relationship between federalism and foreign policy; a topic in need of new evaluation.

Moreover, from a practitioner's standpoint, the evolving international and national contexts introduce several issues in need of examination. In particular, given the fact that sub-national governments have more irons in the fire of globalization, the challenges of globalization increasingly affect their fields of jurisdiction as well as the jurisdiction of the central government. Decision-makers, from both the national and sub-national levels, therefore, have to define their respective interventions and levels of action. Their task is made more complex by the lack of compiled and comparative parameters outlining common practices (or lack thereof) in such circumstances.

This chapter aims to bridge these gaps, from the perspective of both academics and practitioners. It will be interesting to see how federal states manage the new challenges posed by globalization in formulating the aspects of their foreign policy that relate to their constituent units. In order to address this subject, this chapter will first provide a concise review of the theoretical framework upon which I will rely to conduct my analysis. The review will outline two elements: the rationale for the choice of the countries included in this survey; and the choice of indicators that will be used. It will then proceed with an overview of five federal countries – Australia, Belgium, Brazil, Canada and Germany – in order to compare their reaction to globalization in the realm of foreign policy and to identify if there is a general trend or a behavioural pattern.

EXPLORING THE FOREIGN POLICIES OF FEDERAL STATES

The selection of a country for a comparative analysis on federalism and foreign policy should rely on criteria that take into consideration factors related to the international reaction of both the federal state and its constituent units to the stimuli of globalization. How each level of government reacts to international conditions in specific fields of activity will therefore constitute an interesting benchmark from which comparison will be possible.

In order to undertake this examination, the first step is to identify which countries will be part of our sample. To help us in this task we could rely on Herperger who has established a threefold typology that encompasses the types of federations examined in most comparative studies.[2] He identifies the following groups of federations: (1) those that exist in developed industrialized countries such as the United States, Switzerland, Germany, Australia and Canada; (2) Commonwealth federations in developing countries that emerged after 1945, which include India, Pakistan, Malaysia and Nigeria; and (3) recent instances of federal states such as Brazil, Spain and Belgium.

This typology offers an interesting grouping from which we can start our analysis. However, although this categorization reflects important elements of comparison among countries, a few elements still need to be refined. This is due in large part to how the typology has been used; it has proved useful for analysing public and fiscal policies, but it has not yet been rigorously applied to foreign policy analysis and, thus foreign policy factors such as the international role of states have been neglected. But it is the heterogeneous nature of Herperger's first group that makes it difficult to use as is in this study. Including, for example, a superpower like the United States, a neutral country, Switzerland, a major power, Germany, and several countries that claim the role of middle powers[3] could prove to be a major stumbling block when trying to compare the foreign policy response of federal countries to the challenges posed by globalization. Moreover, despite their more recent experience with federalism, Brazil and Belgium exhibit other characteristics that allow comparison with many countries of the first category. We will therefore keep in mind the general idea behind Herperger's typology, but we will add to it in this analysis.

In order to make a useful comparison, we need countries that illustrate similarities in terms of both their federal nature and their foreign policy. In this regard, this study will examine three countries from the first of Herperger's categories – Australia, Canada and Germany –

which meet our criteria of possessing a federal nature. Moreover, Australia and Canada are two middle powers that are often paired for analytical purposes. Germany might pose a threat to the uniformity of the subject countries due to its status as a great power rather than a middle power, but the fact that it is not a permanent member of the United Nations Security Council[4] means that its foreign policy behaviour can be seen as much closer to that of Canada and Australia than it is to that of the United States or Russia. With the exception of some transitory financial measures, the distribution of powers in the new Germany (i.e., including the five Länder added after re-unification) has not changed much, and the Länder exhibit several similarities with the Canadian provinces.

To these three we have added Brazil and Belgium, two countries that exhibit characteristics that allow comparison with many countries of Herperger's first category. From a foreign policy perspective, Brazil – as is the case for Canada and Australia – can also be considered a middle power that plays an influential role in its region. And, although Belgium is a smaller power, it is a federal country which exhibits many of the foreign policy characteristics of the other countries. Moreover, Belgium offers several similarities with Canada when one considers the mechanisms developed for the governance of a bilingual and multicultural society. Thus, as can be seen from this discussion, from both an organizational and a foreign policy perspective, these countries offer enough ground to make comparison interesting and useful.

Other countries might have been considered as well. Russia is one of them. Russia is a federal entity by name, however – despite the fact that some regional leaders have usurped a great deal of power and resist control from Moscow – the federal government acts and behaves much as a unitary state. This is why it was rejected for this study. Austria was also considered, but the nature of Austrian federalism prohibits its easy inclusion in this comparative study. Spain would also appear to be a candidate for inclusion and yet it is not included here. The Spanish constitution allows for the establishment of "autonomous communities," an intermediate level between central and local governments. Although it was at first thought that only a few autonomist/nationalist regions would take advantage of it (Catalonia, Basque Country and Galicia), there are now 17 of these communities. Some have their identity established on common culture, language and history, but only a few. Therefore, it is not surprising that there are significant divergences that make comparison difficult.

Having established the list of countries that will be compared, the next step consists of identifying indicators with which to compare them. This study aims at examining how these five federal states manage the new challenges posed by globalization in formulating the elements of their foreign policy that relate to their constituent units. To assess this, we must first postulate that there is indeed a role or at least some potential for influence in the establishment of foreign policy for the units in a federation. In other words, unless we first determine that such a role exists we cannot determine if globalization has influenced it – globalization could be the source of problems in the fields of jurisdiction of the units, a challenge to which they respond by trying to influence the international stance to be defended by their federal state.

The contextual differences specific to each country require the establishment of a common ground from which to start. Keating has identified three motivations that characterize the interests of the constituent units in a federation: economic, political and cultural.[5] These characteristics become significant factors in a foreign policy context marked by globalization. The constituent units look abroad for investments and markets for their products, technologies and services; they experience political motivations that vary from international recognition from within their federation to pure independence; and they look for international support for policies aimed at enhancing the protection of their cultural identity. All this results in paradiplomatic efforts, a phenomenon that tends to be accentuated in parallel with the growth of globalization. In fact, we find here a foreign policy rationale in agreement with the argument that the constituent units in a federation are in a better position than the central government to meet challenges to the interests of their populations.

These paradiplomatic activities have sometimes been perceived as mere opportunism and as almost random attempts at gathering international attention. However, from these origins they soon evolved into a more institutionalized exercise. Unfortunately, there have been few comparative studies of the foreign policy stances of the constituent units of federal countries. It is therefore difficult to rely on a set of indicators that has already been used. To complement Keating's classification, one of the few issue areas where some kind of comparative assessments exists is the environment – in this both Australia and Brazil have inspired some research.[6] This can be explained by the importance of biodiversity in these countries as well as the front-line role played by the constituent units. Moreover, environment is seen by some as a key sector for the domestic inter-governmental coordination of policies that are discussed and managed at the international level. For instance, referring to the American case, Kraft and Scheberle concluded that "the old paradigms of federally dominant command-and-control regulated world have to be changed,"[7] leaving room for more input from the states.

It is hard to state that these four indicators – economy, politics, culture and the environment – are sufficient to encompass the whole spectrum of fields of intervention where the federal nature of a country might influence its foreign policy and, in fact, they are not. Issues relating to social security, workers' rights, or health programs might well be the next areas of jurisdiction to be challenged by globalization and brought to the table. However, not only are these issues more domestic in nature – although undeniably increasingly influenced by international pressures – but the phenomena, despite their rapid emergence, do not yet offer enough elements for analysis. And while it is obvious that there are other aspects that could be examined, we are confident that these four elements will provide at least a broad enough reading to allow the drawing of some interesting conclusions. We will therefore concentrate our efforts on them.

In order to see how these factors are at play, we will rely on some key indicators. Hence, the economic factor will be evaluated to the light of the level of autonomy the constituent units exercise in promoting their economic self-interests compared to what is done at the federal level. The political aspect will be measured by the role played by the units at the international level – in particular their level of activity, their representation abroad, and the level of cooperation with their central government. Cultural dimension will be explored through the level of interest manifested by the units and the level of coordination with their central government. Finally, the environmental questions will be studied by examining the integration of policies defended on the international scene.

AUSTRALIA

The Commonwealth of Australia has been conceived of as a decentralized federation comprised of six states and two territories. Such decentralization results in a wide network of inter-governmental arrangements and the level of cooperation among constituent units and the central government could be expected to be generally high. The importance of this is acknowledged in the 1997 White Paper on Australian foreign policy which states:

> Achieving Australia's foreign and trade policy goals over the next fifteen years will require communication and consultation on policies and priorities among Commonwealth, State and Territory governments, the private sector and NGOs. As globalization blurs the dividing line between domestic and international issues, consultation and communication with State and Territory governments will become more important.[8]

We can therefore hypothesize a high degree of integration of the concerns of the states and territories in Australian foreign policy.

The constitution indeed specifies that the federal Parliament can make laws with respect to external affairs (s. 51(xxix)), but it also authorizes a state Parliament to "make laws on all kinds of matters" with only a few exceptions (matters of exclusive federal jurisdiction, matters taken away from the states, matters in offence of some federal prohibition), whereas the federal Parliament can make laws only on specific matters.[9] Moreover, the Australia Acts 1986 "enhance the powers of a State Parliament to the extent that it can now make the kind of law the United Kingdom used to make for the peace, order and good government of that State."[10] As well, the powers of disallowance do not apply and some bills no longer have to be reserved for the Queen's pleasure.

Both from a political and from an administrative point of view, Australia's foreign policy underwent a major re-organization in 1987, which was part of "the most extensive re-organization of the public sector in Australian history."[11] In this re-organization, trade was amalgamated into the Department of Foreign Affairs, thus encouraging a centralization of the foreign policy-making process.

Economic incentives such as investments, technological transfers, tourism and exports are the main motivations behind this move towards integration, and these are the key sectors where both state and Commonwealth interests merge. However, all Australian states do not display the same level of interest in international affairs and are consequently not involved to the same degree. Queensland and Western Australia exercise a clear leadership in economic matters. For instance, Western Australia's Department of Trade and Commerce has established international contacts through both the Australian embassies and its own parallel network. It has trade offices in Europe, Japan, South Korea, China, Indonesia, India, Philippines, Taiwan and Thailand. These International Trade Offices are mainly involved in market studies and provide support to foreign investors. They also organize trade missions and play a role of political brokerage. The department also has an International Trade Relations Team that is involved in promotional activities abroad, such as workshops, seminars, publications, and support to trade missions. Other states have also played an international economic role. Thus, for example, the state of Victoria exercised economic pressures in protest against French nuclear tests in 1995 and New South Wales has worked towards enhancing its trade relationship with China.

This is not to say that the central government leaves the states on their own. In fact, Australia practices a collective commercial approach that could be compared to the concept of the Team Canada trade missions utilized by Canada. Moreover, since 1991, Australia has developed a National Trade Strategy Consultative Process (NTSCP) under the aegis of the Department of Foreign Affairs and Trade. The main objective of the NTSCP is to coordinate trade strategies and activities among the Commonwealth, the states, and the private sector. It organizes an annual forum and publishes an annual report. Such practices lead to the conclusion that Australian federalism, while accommodating the autonomy of pro-active state actors, facilitates the orchestration of joint Commonwealth-wide efforts under the leadership of the federal government.

When looking at political factors, one cannot ignore this economic strategy since it is articulated and institutionalized through the political will of the participant states. However, it must be noted that these efforts are not part of a state/territorial self-defined and self-administered "foreign policy." In fact, no Australian state has within its government a department or an organization that would take care of the coordination of a self-proclaimed foreign policy. This can be explained in large part by the single-issue agenda – that is, the economy – that the most autonomous states possess. In this regard, it is particularly interesting to note that, by contrast, there are no cultural motivations behind the international activities of Australian states. Despite what appears as a seamless integration of interests with the Commonwealth of Australia, one cannot neglect the fact that most Australian states are active in nurturing international representation. Thus, in terms of offices abroad, Western Australia has 14, Queensland 8, South Australia 7, Victoria 7, Northern Territory 2, and New South Wales 2; only Tasmania has none.

Finally, the fourth indicator, the environment, also reveals a keen interest and a front-line role played by the constituent units. These efforts are channelled through a well-integrated, decentralized series of consultative mechanisms that help take the points of view and the priorities of the Australian states into account in defining national environmental policy. These consultative mechanisms include the Resource Assessment Commission, the Intergovernmental Agreement on the Environment, the National Environment Protection Council and the Commonwealth Environmental Protection Agency. Moreover, jurisprudence has clearly indicated that there is a role to be played by the state governments in environmental matters relating, for example, to the territorial sea and submerged land.

All these elements are characteristics of a *de jure* flexible form of federalism. Since *de facto* tensions and divergent points of view between Commonwealth and state governments occasionally surface, these are discussed and settled through institutionalized consultative mechanisms and result in better harmonized policies that are defended by the central government, which has the final say in defining national interests and strategies to implement Australian foreign policy. Within this context, globalization does not pose a challenge to federalism. As well, globalization seems to have affected the conception of Australian foreign policy more than its elaboration. Because Australian federalism is decentralized, the input of the constituent units in international political debates comes as a natural process. In fact, the Australian case reveals an example of how globalization has accelerated reflection on the place Australia should occupy in the post–Cold War world and the re-evaluation of the country's historic dependence on the United States and Great Britain.

BELGIUM

Federalism in Belgium is influenced by the desire of the Flemish population to obtain cultural autonomy and of the French-speaking Walloons to acquire economic self-sufficiency. This duality nurtured the evolution of Belgium from a unitary state (from 1830), to a regionalized state (constitutional revisions from 1967 to 1971), to a federal state (since the late 1980s). The three regions of this newly emerged federal state (Flanders, Wallonia, and the Brussels-capital region) have jurisdiction in the fields of regional development, environment, agriculture, water, housing, economy, energy, transportation, public works and scientific research. The three communities (French, Flemish, and German-speaking) have responsibilities in matters of culture, education, and language. Moreover, the 1993 constitutional reform clarified the role of the federal government in a specific chapter. The King kept responsibility for international relations "without prejudice to the jurisdiction of the communities and the regions" (s. 167). The latter have powers to conclude "treaties bearing on matters of their Council's jurisdiction." A concertation process is also outlined to avoid or settle jurisdictional conflicts. Consequently, there is no doubt that Belgian federalism influences this country's foreign policy. To understand how, it is important to look at the international role played by its two main constituent units.

Wallonia has experienced an impressive institutional evolution over the last decade. It started with an approach some have described as the policy of the "non-stated" – i.e., in matters of external relations, all that is not explicitly forbidden is considered to be authorized. In a 1992 declaration, the executive of Wallonia made its intention more explicit. It established that Wallonia would look for an optimal extension of all its jurisdictions at the international level, including trade and foreign aid. In 1993, the government adopted a bill that outlined the type of action to be taken by the region in commercial matters, including: providing export, import, and investment risks guarantees; implementing an international cooperation policy; implementing a trade policy and organizing trade missions; and offering lines of credit. This being said, it is important to note that there are also efforts being made to integrate trade programs and missions with those of the Belgian Department of Trade. Hence, Wallonia takes an active part in trade and economic missions organized by the Office belge du commerce extérieur.

Wallonia's main concern remains its capacity to count on an efficient and effective network of representation abroad. This was not an easy task and the region had to rely on a memorandum of agreement signed in July 1988 between the ministers responsible for international relations for the central government, the region, and the French-speaking community to settle the issue. According to this agreement, the region and/or the community may identify representatives who will act on its behalf abroad. These individuals are part of the Belgian diplomatic mission and are under the authority of the post's highest ranking official. Notwithstanding this line of authority, their chain of command comes from somewhere else since they receive their instructions from the government they represent, whether it is the region or the community. This allows representatives to be posted on all five continents and in international organization such as la Francophonie. It provides the region opportunities to play a political role for the defence of interests related to both economic and cultural realities.

The competition that exists between the two Belgian regions for international recognition would lead one to think that a pattern similar to Wallonia's is found in Flanders. For both, cultural and political prestige is paramount. It is therefore not surprising to note that Flanders has issued a five year foreign policy plan.[12] Similarly to Wallonia, it states that within the limits of federal loyalty, the Flemish government will ensure that its autonomy in matters of foreign policy is respected and will exercise its full jurisdiction regarding these matters. And in order to carry out this mandate, it has chosen to ask specific ministers to be responsible for the different aspects of the Flemish foreign policy. Hence, the Minister-President is also Foreign and European Affairs Minister and in this capacity, he coordinates Flemish foreign policy. The Minister of Culture carries his or her mandate to the international scene, and there is a Minister for Cooperation and Development, a new initiative.

This political apparatus is supported abroad through an important network of over 90 representatives posted on all continents. Their mission is to work for a better Europe with specific concerns for an international policy based on sustainable economic and ecological development, social justice North and South, democracy, and human rights. This means that efforts are made to ensure that Flanders will have its say within the European Union (EU) – in fact, its concerns with European integration are similar to that of the German Länder – and in other multilateral fora such as UNESCO, the Organization of Economic Cooperation and Development (OECD), the World Trade Organization (WTO), and so on. Moreover, the Flemish government's international representatives work to sustain the economic health of Flanders and towards reducing the disparity between Western and developing countries. Its bilateral relations are foremost with the Netherlands, France, Germany and the UK.

It can therefore be said that Belgium also provides a much decentralized setting that allows its regions and communities to answer directly the challenges of globalization in the fields of economy, culture and the environment. It can also be said that such action is supported by political willingness that is translated into some paradiplomatic tools such as foreign policy statements and a network of offices and representatives abroad. Since this decentralization offers the regions a key role in the process, Belgian federalism is not directly attacked by the values associated with globalization.

BRAZIL

Brazil offers a much different image from the countries that have been discussed above. Although its federal status is recent, as is the case with Belgium, the similarities end there. The 26 federated states and five regions have not yet succeeded in displacing the central government in many fields of policy. As Roeet argues: "The states have had meaning in Brazil only insofar as the political objectives of the national government have required it,"[13] to which Schneider adds that "the state apparatus is still marked by a closed style, low transparency, very limited accountability, strong clientelism ties, and a low capacity for implementation and enforcement."[14] Corruption plays a role, but the heavy bureaucratic structure is a major factor not to be neglected.[15]

The new Brazilian constitution also offers contrasts with the other countries discussed here. Although it outlines some sharing of power with the constituent units, allocates some important but ill-defined powers to their executives and, theoretically, lays out the possibility for the states to intervene in questions such as ecology, urban development and soil management, it leaves foreign policy in the hands of the central government. Only a few matters (among them trade) allow some input from the state actors. Thus, most policies, strategies and foreign policy decisions are orchestrated at the Itamaraty, the Brazilian Department of Foreign Affairs.

In order to respond to the challenges of globalization, this department has developed new directorates, divisions, programs and services that have received a clear mandate to this end. Hence, the promotion of exports, economic integration, human rights, and other "global issues" fall under the department's responsibility. The Itamaraty can also count on the International Relations Research Institute (Instituto das Pesquisas das Relaçoes Internacionais), a foreign policy think-tank created by the department. This means that the political dimension is very centralized and that the states rarely act by themselves on the diplomatic scene.

On the economic front, the situation is closer to what we have found in Australia, that is, much discrepancy according to the state at which you look. As Roeet outlines:

> The economic development of each [of the five regions] has contrasted markedly with that of others. Each region, and the states it encompasses, illustrates the tremendous diversity of the Brazilian federation and helps to explain the calculated use of the federalism by the national state in its effort to dominate and control the nation.[16]

This means that the richest states might exercise some degree of autonomy, but it is fair to say that most of the states have at most a very limited involvement in trade policy making and implementation.

The cultural policy sector presents a very different portrait. In this domain, the states have much more power. However, the conflicts with the central government are almost non-existent – which contrasts with other fields of mixed jurisdiction and shared powers – and examples of efficient cooperation are easy to find. This phenomenon can be explained in large part by the homogeneity of Brazilian culture. Moreover, the cultural sector is well financed – one of the positive effects of the efficient cooperation and the involvement of the private sector[17] – and Brazilian culture exercises an important attraction pole for the rest of Latin America. Most Brazilians speak Portuguese which constitutes a powerful homogenizing factor, and the country exports its cultural productions while importing relatively few (not even from Portugal). The challenge represented by the English language imperialism associated with globalization is therefore met with a common front of well-integrated efforts.

In contrast to the harmonious efforts with regard to culture, the management of environmental questions is much more confrontational. The Amazonian rain forest is located in Brazil, and there is no need to expand here on the role of this forest, and its exceptional biodiversity, on the planet's delicate ecological balance. Quite naturally, it has become one of the major stakes of Brazilian foreign policy. The federal government created the Brazilian Institute for the Environment and Renewable Resources in 1989 and, in 1992, a fully-fledged Environment Ministry to which the Institute responds. Two years later, the coordination of environmental policies related to Amazonia was exercised by the federal department.

Although the 1988 constitution permits the states to have wide powers in environmental matters, agriculture remains mainly under federal leadership, and decentralization in matters related to environment is not much observed in fact. The states primarily defend their own local economic interests, which often clash with sustainable development policies and although the environmental and natural resources policies of Brazil are widely considered among the most advanced legislative frameworks in the world, it has been difficult to implement them due to weak inter-governmental coordination and blurred jurisdictions. In this sense, global economic actors benefit from a huge advantage – they go to the weaker regulation implementation level and play actors against each other.

An important conclusion to be drawn about the Brazilian federation's response to globalization reflects its own nature. Brazil is characterized first by an asymmetric federalism dominated in many regards by the central government and, second, by partners showing unequal power in matters of economic or political issues. Moreover, powers are not well defined in the constitution. All of these factors result in a response to the challenges of globalization that is different according to the sector at which we look, and that ranges from a strong integrated answer as in the case of culture to a disorganized and weak response in questions related to the environment. Finally, it can be said that the implementation of federal mechanisms and values seems to have a direct influence on the response to global issues.

CANADA

From its beginnings as a sovereign state in 1867, Canada has been a federation, but an odd one. The founding fathers had two models from which to take their inspiration: a federation personified in their southern neighbour, which was torn apart by a civil war; and a unitary government in the metropolis, England, which was at the head of an Empire over which "the sun never set." John A. Macdonald, one of Canada's founding fathers, looked to the latter image, and he had many supporters to agree with him. For Georges-Étienne Cartier, another founding father, things were quite different. For him there was a need to recognize the differences that characterized what would become the province of Québec; after all, even the British conqueror had done so with the Québec Act of 1784. The compromise used to bridge the gap between these opposite views – that is, a federation with the distribution of power leading in fact to the implementation of a strong central government – was at the heart of the Canadian constitution in 1867, and remained a prominent feature of the 1982 Canada Act. For all intents and purposes, jurisdiction over foreign matters is, however, forgotten in the constitution.[18] If it were not for Québec's demands, Canada would probably never have been a federation and since there is no well-defined jurisdiction in foreign policy matters, the same need for recognition might surface for international questions as it has done domestically. In fact, the importance of this factor is such that it is reflected in all aspects we have selected to study.

However, it would be an exaggeration to state that Québec is the only Canadian province to conduct some sort of foreign policy.[19] Québec's unique characteristics of language and culture, values, legal system and economic identity[20] contribute to making its actions to have its voice heard over its boundaries more salient. In fact, this could be dated back to pre-Confederation years when Lower Canada opened an agency in London as early as 1816. Québec also opened an office headed by an *agent général* in Paris in 1881, and an "economic bureau" in New York in 1941. However, the Duplessis government in the 1940s and 1950s represented an interruption of this trend, and what could be seen as the true launch of Québec's foreign policy is the 1965 Gérin-Lajoie doctrine that stated that Québec would extend abroad operations related to its domestic fields of jurisdiction.[21] This type of behaviour ruffled some feathers in Ottawa and most federal governments have tried to minimize the role Québec plays on the international scene.[22] This is done in large part in the name of the federation, that is, to counter initiatives that are perceived as attempts to enhance the separatist aspirations of some Quebeckers by giving Québec international recognition before "the fact."

From a political point of view, the Canadian provinces rely on a constitutional provision (Section 92.4) that has allowed a long history of offices abroad. Even when economic hardship forced restraint, many provinces would keep a reduced number of officials in offices rented from Canadian embassies. In this sense, Québec is therefore not unique. However, what characterizes Québec is its network of *délégations* and offices around the globe, the political role they often play, and the fact that it has a Ministry of Foreign Relations that publishes White Paper-type policy statements,[23] while the "foreign affairs" bureaucracies of other provinces range from a handful of officials in central agencies to modest coordinating agencies reporting to a department. For some in Ottawa, this is a real thorn in the side. The 2001 Summit of the Americas hosted by Canada in Québec City provided several examples of how difficult it could be for the two levels of government to harmonize their actions.

From an economic standpoint, the situation is not much clearer. For instance, the provinces do not hesitate to lobby foreign governments on economic issues. Many recent examples can be provided: British Columbia has lobbied in Washington about the dispute over softwood lumber; the Premier of Ontario has gone to Washington to defend the Auto Pact; and the Premier of Alberta recently travelled to Washington to discuss Alberta's provision of energy to the United States. And although there is some harmonization through the concept of Team Canada, which is essentially an economic mission led by the Prime Minister and Premiers, Team Canada and Team Québec – for Québec also has its own trade missions – compete for the same piece of pie. However, since business people are at the heart of these missions, politics is often relegated to the back stage, which is not the case with cultural issues.

Although there are significant regional differences in Canadian culture outside of Québec, most of them face the same challenge: not being American. The same language, in some regards a similar way of life, and the hegemony of the American cultural industries are factors that contribute to the necessity of defining Canadian culture in comparison with that of the United States. In Québec's case, the sharp contrasts we previously outlined add to this differentiation. Concretely, this translates to the fact that all Québec governments since 1960 have, to a greater or a lesser degree, mistrusted the federal government to defend Québec's interests in matters of culture. This lack of confidence in the federal government's efforts comes from its prime mandate, that is, to defend Canadian culture, of which Québec is only a part. No matter if this evaluation is well-founded or not – in fact other provinces voice the same complaint on other issues as well – the fact remains that Québec governments are much more active to export the culture of Québec than the other Canadian provinces which tend to concentrate their efforts on economic issues.

Environmental questions pose a slightly different problem. It is difficult to identify where the division of powers falls since the constitution is silent on this subject. Historically, the responsibility fell into the laps of the provinces. The rationale for this is related to several factors. First, environmental issues are closer to the people and such issues are usually recognized in the constitution to be under provincial jurisdiction. Second, environmental infractions are perceived as closer to questions considered under civil law, which are also under the responsibility of the provinces. Most provinces are acting according to this principle on issues such as forest preservation in British Columbia, fishing resources in Newfoundland, or energy in Québec and Alberta. On the other hand, the federal government is taking interest in many fields that were at one time considered of relevance to the provinces. Thus, this argument cites the example of pollution which falls under federal jurisdiction because it is related to trade and commerce, and claims that for the same reasons the environment should too. Moreover, since the environment falls under no constitutional provisions and residual powers are assigned to the federal government for the sake of the "peace, order, and good government" of the country, then environment should be administered by Ottawa. Finally, since matters relating to the environment often involve international negotiations and treaties, this belongs to the recognized state at the international table – that is, Canada. Both sides argue their points and there is no final answer as yet. The possibility of duplication and counter efforts is therefore high, and the only way to avoid it is through administrative cooperation, a route that has generally succeeded.

Since environmental concerns are rarely specific to a level of government, it is easier, but by no means automatic, to put aside politicking and take the administrative route, which leads to better harmonization, and addresses the challenges of globalization. In other sectors, it seems much more difficult to find common ground, especially for the federal government and the government of Québec. Hence, globalization presents a much higher degree of risk both for the actors in the area of concern and for the federation per se. The more divergent or antagonistic the central government's position is when compared with that of Québec and vice versa, the more the advocates of the rupture of the federation will have arguments in their favour. This is what Québec Premier Bernard Landry and his Minister for International Relations, Louise Beaudoin, have advocated concerning cultural protection in the negotiation of the Free Trade Area of the Americas (FTAA). According to their position, if the federal government does not address issues of concern for Québec on the international scene, Québec will have no other choice but to defend itself its stance over these issues. It therefore seems that a strategy coined for the protection of federalism might indeed work the reverse way.

GERMANY

According to Arthur Benz:

From a comparative point of view, German federalism is a case in itself. One reason for this can be found in the Constitution. It assigns legislative power mainly to the federal government, whereas the Länder are, in most cases, responsible for implementing the law. Moreover, the federal system in embedded in a society with centralized organizations of interest in a highly developed welfare state, in a increasingly Europeanized economy, and in a political culture that emphasizes national unity and uniform living conditions in all regions.[24]

He adds that "co-operative federalism in Germany is much more flexible and open to institutional adaptation and policy change than is often assumed ... The German federal state has to be acknowledged as a dynamic system."[25] Such dynamism finds its source in the dual organization of law making in Berlin and law implementation at the Länder level. These ingredients could be the source of problems with both levels competing on the basis of divergent economic priorities, important cultural differences, and so on. However, a relatively small territory, and a homogenous culture and society shelter Germany from these problems.[26]

In foreign policy matters, responsibility constitutionally belongs to the central government, but, as is the case with other policy fields, there is the possibility of some joint responsibility to be exercised. Problems related to the management of foreign policy lie in its complexity and difficult implementation rather than Länder contesting the central government's authority over the question. In fact, Länder may conclude, with the agreement of the central government, treaties with foreign states. As a result, almost all Länder have signed partnership agreements with American cities and states and in 1988 three of them established relationships with Jiang-Su, a Chinese province, and others have relations with Russia at a sub-national level. Bavaria nurtures a continuous relationship with Austrian states, provinces in northern Italy and South Africa, departments in southern France, and the government of Québec, and since 1990 support to Central and Eastern European states constitutes an important dimension of its foreign relations.

How Länder manage their own foreign representations varies from Land to Land. There is no single model. Gress and Lehne state that "each Land acts within the framework of its own political and legal capabilities and thus enhances its unique political profile."[27] In this, German Länder behave the same way as some Australian states, Belgian regions and some Canadian provinces.

European integration is an object of interest and, in some cases, of major concern to the German Länder, a phenomenon we also observed with the Belgian regions. In this regard, acting on their concern that their influence was eroding, as expressed by Bavaria in particular, the Länder obtained – with the assistance of the central government – the right to participate formally and directly in decision making at the EU. In addition to this right, the central government has a tradition of taking into account the points of view of the Länder when negotiating questions related to their jurisdiction at the international level.

Such coordination might explain that, although Länder are very active politically on the international scene, they do not rely on an extensive network of offices abroad. In fact, it is quite the contrary. Länder organize "punctual" offices to answer specific, temporary needs. This practice is reinforced by official visits abroad of Ministers-Presidents.

The cultural foreign policy of the German Länder provides another good example of the complexity that characterizes Germany's federalism. Despite a keen interest and an active role in official exchanges with international counterparts, international activity is in some regards, timid, to say the least. Responsibility in matters of culture mainly lies with the Länder, which would lead one to expect a strong involvement and indeed, they maintain important international cultural relations. But even if they *may* sign international agreements in this field, they often do not. This is in part because the Länder prefer to resort to "shared statements" to avoid the cumbersome task of getting the central government's authorization for a formal agreement, a process that illustrates well the complexity of German federalism. Moreover, Merkel notes that, due to a troubled history of state-sponsored culture, Länder governments prefer to leave the administration of cultural policies to autonomous organizations.[28] This is not because they do not have competent personnel in matters of culture or education – in fact, their resources are reported to be better than what the federation can count on – but they refer easily to five organizations that are at the forefront of the German culture: the Goethe Institüt, the Deutscher Akadenmischer Austauschdienst, the Alexander von Humboldt Foundation, Inter Nationes, and the Institute for Foreign Relations. The financing of these organizations comes mainly from federal budgets and Foreign Affairs officials have a seat on their Boards of Directors, but it is rare that the central government will object to their projects. This means that Länder refer issues of their jurisdiction to autonomous bodies that are federally sponsored. And if all this was not complex enough, the federation often selects Länder representatives as delegates for meetings of the EU Ministers of Culture.

Environmental policies also offer an interesting context that takes into account both ideological and institutional factors. First, it is recognized by most analysts that Germany is a leader in environmental questions. To give but a few examples, in the first half of the 1990s, emissions of carbon dioxide (CO_2) have dropped by 12 per cent, both methane and nitrogen dioxide (NO_2) by 16 per cent, and sulphur dioxide (SO_2) by 43 per cent in four years.[29] The success and the ensuing parliamentary if not governmental presence of the Green

Party is a factor to be taken into account while at the same time it reveals the ideological sensitivity German society manifests towards ecological issues. The institutional side of this brings us back to the importance of a rigid constitution in policy making. As Weale argues, "a programmatic statement of general principles is seen as an essential prologue to legislation and policy development, a tendency that is probably reinforced by the practice of coalition government in which political parties of different political persuasions have to come to some agreement on the running of the government."[30]

Since environmental problems have no boundaries, any level of government might feel it is appropriate to intervene. In fact, Länder are very active on environmental issues. They have instituted 5,300 nature reservations, 6,000 protected sites, and 12 parks that cover one-quarter of the national territory. Moreover, economic activities are banned on 15 per cent of the land, which constitutes a unique ecological network.[31] Notwithstanding such interest and involvement, the aims and areas of environmental policy have been developed and established at the federal level. As noticed by Busch, "the predominance of Federal Law is due to the fact that ... by an amendment to the Basic Law[32] in 1972, legislative powers were granted to the Bund [federal government] in specific environmental fields: control of air pollution, waste management, and noise control."[33] The principle of subsidiarity, meaning that the level of government closer to the people – that is, in the German context, the national level[34] – should take charge of a given problem, is prominent at the European level and therefore contributes to enhancing the central government's role and responsibilities.

This does not prevent Germany from exercising its leadership through international channels, primarily at the European level where, for instance, Germany strongly advocated Resolutions 3626/82 (against commercialization of endangered species) and 2078/92 (agricultural products). However, its international actions do not seem to compete with the priorities of the Länder. It could therefore be said that due to its leadership role supported by ideological and institutional frameworks, Germany is in good position to deal with the challenges of globalization in matters of the environment.

This conclusion can largely be extended to all the domains we have explored. The legal-rational framework that prevails in almost all policy fields offers the country a shield that diffuses attacks from the exterior while strengthening the domestic inter-governmental policy stances. Culture might be an exception since the main responsibility lies with the Länder, but, as we have seen, there is still national coordination that is involved through the independent cultural institutions that bear, *mutati mutandis*, the same final result.

CONCLUSION

This study aims at a better understanding of the new relationship between federalism and foreign policy by seeing how federal states manage the new challenges posed by globalization in formulating aspects of their foreign policy that relate to their constituent units. In order to do so, five countries were selected and compared along four factors: politics, economics, culture and environment. Moreover, we introduced characteristics such as the level of power and the age of the federation in order to complete our review. The results appear in Table 1.

The first conclusion that we can reach is that, contrary to what some might have expected, there is no uniform pattern across the countries we studied and the differences we have observed do not match the age of the federation nor the international rank (i.e., middle or great power status) of the country. At most, two tendencies are identifiable. First, the level of economic activities of the constituent units is generally high and it is often matched with a certain degree of autonomy. Second, the level of interest in defending cultural issues is generally high, but when considering the efforts related to such defence, the level of coordination with the central government varies a great deal. These two tendencies correspond to the elements that define the constituent units in a federation – i.e., a country adopts federalism in part because the constituent units differ in terms of economic activity or culture – and therefore could be expected in a federal state where the political system allows, by its nature, the recognition and expression of differences.

An interesting aspect that also clearly comes out is the importance of coordinating political efforts within a federation in order to constrain the challenges posed by globalization. For instance, on environmental issues Brazil seems weak due to the discrepancies and the lack of harmonized interests of the two levels of government. In the case of Canada, it seems that globalization is a challenge not only for the issues at stake, but for the federation as a whole since proponents of separatism use these questions to enhance their agenda by pointing to the lack of protection the federal regime offers. This underscores the need for a set of policies that takes into account both the demands made on states as international actors and the nature of their constituent units. Nossal portrayed this delicate act of balance very well when he stated that "Federalism cannot work unless sovereignty is divided. The assumed indivisibility of sovereignty in the international system and the necessary divisibility of domestic sovereignty converge in a federal state's external policy."[35]

This is indeed what this study has found, and it is its main conclusion. Where there are mechanisms within the federal state to manage this duality, the challenges of globalization can be met more effectively. However, in the absence of such mechanisms, the federation lacking them could become easy prey for the forces of global uniformity. We should therefore nuance the commonly accepted evaluation, to which I referred at the beginning of this chapter, by stating that from a federal point of view globalization should be seen as providing a catalyst to challenges coming from within the state as much as a threat coming from abroad.

Table I
Comparing Federal States:
Globalization and the Role of Federated States in Foreign Policy Making

Indicators	*Australia*	*Belgium*	*Brazil*	*Canada*	*Germany*
POWER	Middle	Smaller	Middle	Middle	Major
AGE OF FEDERATION	Elder	Recent	Recent	Elder	Elder
POLITICS:					
Level of activity	Low	High: policy statements	Low	High for some provinces: Québec has issued foreign relations statements	High: official visits abroad of ministers-presidents
Offices abroad	Most have	Very well developed network	None	Several have	Yes, but most are "punctual"/ temporary
Coordination with central government	High: central government has the final say in defining national interests and strategies to implement foreign policy	Through constitutional jurisdictions and agreements	Low: since highly centralized; on some issues opposition	Varies: in Québec's case, low, often due to political reasons	High: but not often used due to bureaucratic burden; in fact, highly centralized
ECONOMY:					
Level of activity	High	High	Varies: limited powers; only richest states show some level of autonomy	High	High
Offices/missions	Joint/some autonomous	Autonomous/joint	None	Most have	Autonomous

Indicators	*Australia*	*Belgium*	*Brazil*	*Canada*	*Germany*
Coordination with central government	Some states are more autonomous; joint efforts co-ordinated by central government	In this field, regions have jurisdiction; some joint efforts with central government	Central government dominates, with few exceptions that clash with other priorities	Exists through Team Canada efforts; some provincial initiatives	High centralization, but with input from the Länder
CULTURE:					
Level of interest	Low	High	High	High, especially in Québec	High
Coordination with central government	N/A	Of regional/ community jurisdiction	High	Federal Department of Heritage; with Québec: low for demographic and political reasons	Low, but independent national organizations do this work; Länder representatives as delegates to EU meetings
ENVIRONMENT:					
Coordination with central government	High: several co-ordinating mechanisms	Of regional jurisdiction	Of regional jurisdiction; federal interventions; clashes with economic interests	Jurisdiction not clearly defined; through administrative cooperation	Ideologically and institutionally supported; de facto, then de jure federal responsibility; high input from Länder;
General influence of globalization	Not a challenge to federalism, but it seems to have affected the Australian foreign policy conception more than its elaboration	New constitution allows answers being provided by regions within the federal framework	High in sectors with lack of co-ordination	Can jeopardize not only sectors affected, but to a certain extent give ammunition to advocates of the rupture of the federation	German constitution shelters from exterior attacks while strengthening the domestic intergovernmental policy stances

NOTES

1 This paper was written with the collaboration of Manon Tessier. Nelson Michaud is substitute professor, École nationale d'administration publique, Université du Québec, chercheur-membre of the Institut québécois des hautes études internationales, and Research Fellow at the Centre for Foreign Policy Studies, Dalhousie University. He can be contacted at nelson_michaud@enap.uquebec.ca. He wishes to thank the SSHRC Federalism and Federations Program that helped fund part of this research. At the time of the research, Manon Tessier was associate researcher at the Groupe d'études et de recherche sur la sécurité internationale (GERSI) and is now senior research officer at the International Security Research and Outreach Programme, Department of Foreign Affairs and International Trade Canada.

2 Dwight Herperger, *Répartition des pouvoirs et fonctions dans les régimes fédéraux* (Ottawa: Approvisionnements et Services Canada, 1991).

3 On the role of middle powers, see: Louis Bélanger and Nelson Michaud "Looking for New Voices Opportunities: Canada and International Security Institutions after the Cold War" in Onnig Beylerian and Jacques Lévesque (eds), *Major Powers and International Security Institutions* (Kingston and Montreal: McGill-Queen's University Press); Andrew F. Cooper, "Niche Diplomacy: A Conceptual Overview" in Andrew F. Cooper (ed.), *Niche Diplomacy: Middle Powers After the Cold War* (London: Macmillan, 1997); Andrew F. Cooper, Richard A. Higgott and Kim R. Nossal, *Relocating Middle Powers: Australia and Canada in a Changing World Order* (Vancouver: UBC Press, 1993).

4 On this, see Philippew Hébert and Paul Létourneau, "L'institutionalisme dans la politique extérieure allemande: ajustements et continuité," *Études internationales*, Vol. 30, No. 2 (1999), pp. 325–348.

5 Michael Keating, and J. Loughlin (eds), *The Political Economy of Regionalism* (London: Frank Cass, 1997), p. 2.

6 Stephen Randall and Roger Gibbins (eds), *Federalism and the New World Order* (Calgary: University of Calgary Press, 1994); Peter May (ed.), *Natural Resources Valuation and Policy in Brazil: Methods and Cases* (New York, NY: Columbia University Press, 1999).

7 Michael Kraft and Denise Scheberle, "Environmental Federalism at Decade's End: New Approaches and Strategies," *Publius: The Journal of Federalism*, Vol. 28, No. 1 (1998), p. 134.

8 Government of Australia, *White Paper on Foreign Policy*,1997, paragraph 192.

9 P.H. Lane, *An Introduction to the Australian Constitution* (Sydney: The Law Book Company, 1994), pp. 208–11.

10 Ibid.

11 Andrew F. Cooper, Richard A. Higgott and Kim Richard Nossal, *Relocating Middle Powers: Australia and Canada in a Changing World Order* (Vancouver, BC: UBC Press, 1993), p. 42.

12 http://www.flanders.be/public/authority/government/policy/noteorientation.html
13 Riordan Roeet, *Brazil: Politics in a Patrimonial Society* (4th ed., Westport, CN: Praeger, 1993), p. 6.
14 Ronald Schneider, *Brazil: Culture and Politics in a New Industrial Powerhouse* (Boulder, CO: Westview Press, 1996), p. 132.
15 Howard Wiarda and Harvey Kline, *Latin American Politics and Development* (3rd ed., Boulder, CO: Westview Press, 1990), p. 192.
16 Roeet, *Brazil: Politics in a Patrimonial Society*, p. 11.
17 For instance, see Véronique Mortaigne, "Sao Paolo, capitale culturelle sur fonds privés" in *Le Monde*, 29 October 1999, p. 29.
18 Section 132 of the Canada Act 1867 gives to the Parliament of Canada powers "necessary or proper for performing the obligations of Canada or of any Province thereof, as Part of the British Empire, towards foreign countries, arising under Treaties between the Empire and such foreign countries." Obviously, this provision is now obsolete. Moreover, it does not pertain to the jurisdictional attributions as much as it deals with the obligation for the government of Canada to meet international obligations contracted in its name by the Empire. In a 1937 judgement, the Judicial Committee of the Privy Council ruled that the provinces are not bound by treaties affecting their jurisdictions, a severe limit imposed to the meaning of s. 132. In other words, the constitution defines no jurisdictional attribution in matters of Canadian foreign policy, the issue being the responsibility of the Empire at the time the Constitution Act 1867 was written.
19 For an historical perspective, see Ronald G. Atkey, "The Role of Provinces in International Affairs," *International Journal*, Vol. 26, No. 1 (1971), pp. 249–273; for a more recent perspective, see Kim Richard Nossal, "The Provinces as International Actors" in Nossal (ed.), *The Politics of Foreign Policy* (Scarborough, ON: Prentice-Hall, 1997); or for an instance of a specific case study, see Nossal, "'Micro-diplomacy': the case of Ontario and Economic sanctions against South Africa," in William M. Chandler and Christian W. Zöllner (eds), *Challenges to Federalism: Policy-Making in Canada and Germany* (Kingston, ON: Queen's University Institute of Intergovernmental Relations, 1989).
20 After decades of control by the English speaking minority, Québec's economy radically changed during the years of the Quiet Revolution, with the emergence of a French speaking economic elite, original institutions, and an economic credo (support for free trade being a prime example) that differentiated it further from other parts of the country.
21 Facing an urgent need to structure its emerging public service in fields such as education, Québec had to find administrative cooperation arrangements with other departments of education such as France's. In order to do so, it had to sign an international agreement, but did not want Ottawa

to do it on its behalf, since the question is exclusively of provincial jurisdiction. Hence, this April 1965 declaration of Paul Gérin-Lajoie, Minister of Education in the Lesage government, in which he referred to the extension at the international level of fields of provincial jurisdiction. On the origins of Québec foreign relations, see Claude Morin, *L'art de l'impossible: la diplomatie québécoise depuis 1960* (Montréal, PQ: Boréal, 1987); Jean-Marc Léger, *Le temps dissipé: souvenirs* (Montréal, PQ: Hurtubise HMH, 1999); Paul Gérin-Lajoie, *Combats d'un révolutionnaire tranquille* (Montréal, PQ: Centre éducatif et culturel, 1989).

22 The exception being the Mulroney Conservative government, which was much more accommodative as demonstrated by Luc Bernier, "Mulroney's International « Beau Risque »: The Golden Age of Québec's Foreign Policy" in Nelson Michaud and Kim Richard Nossal (eds), *Diplomatic Departures. The Conservative Era in Canadian Foreign Policy, 1984–1993* (Vancouver, BC: UBC Press, 2001). About the evolution of Québec foreign policy for the first thirty years, see Louis Balthazar, Louis Bélanger, Gordon Mace et al., *Trente ans de politique extérieure québécoise* (Québec, PQ: Centre québécois des relations internations et Septentrion, 1993); on the dilemma of Québec's foreign policy priorities, Luc Bernier, *De Paris à Washington: La politique internationale du Québec* (Québec, PQ: Les Presses de l'Université du Québec, 1996).

23 The latest being *Le Québec dans un ensemble international* (Québec, PQ: Ministère des relations internationales, 2001).

24 Arthur Benz, "From Unitary to Asymmetric Federalism in Germany: Taking Stock after 50 years," *Publius: The Journal of Federalism*, Vol. 29, No. 4 (1999), p. 55.

25 Ibid., p. 56.

26 East Germany could have brought some discrepancies that faded with time. On aspects of the German reunification see Philip Zelikow and Condoleeza Rice, *Germany Unified and Europe Transformed* (Cambridge, MA: Harvard University Press, 1995).

27 Franz Gress and Richard Lehne, "Governance in a Global Era: The Case of Hess," *Publius: The Journal of Federalism*, Vol. 29, No. 4 (1999), p. 88.

28 Christoph Merkel, "Politique culturelle extérieure de la République fédérale d'Allemagne au niveau de l'État fédéral, des Länder et des organisations médiatrices" in Marc Uyttendaele (ed.), *Fédéralisme et relations internationales* (Bruxelles: Bruylant, 1998), p. 47.

29 Numbers quoted by Pierre Frois, *Développement durable dans l'Union européenne* (Paris: L'Harmattan, 1998).

30 Albert Weale, *The New Politics of Pollution* (Manchester: Manchester University Press, 1992), pp. 81–82.

31 Frois, *Développement durable dans l'Union européenne*, p. 86.

32 Literal translation of *Grundgesetz*, the constitution.

33 Jost-Dietrich Busch, "German environmental Policy" in Chandler and Zöllner (eds), *Challenges to Federalism*, p. 253.

34 This could appear as a contradiction with what we have said about Canada. However, it has to be noted that in Germany, in contrast to Canada (where the environment is not constitutionally attributed to either level of government and thus is dealt with by both), the responsibility for environmental matters is constitutionally given to the federal government and therefore, in the German case, the federal government is the government to which the population will turn in matters relating to the environment. Therefore, the same principle applies although it results in the involvement of a different level of government.

35 Nossal, *The Politics of Canadian Foreign Policy*, p. 294.

Federal Political Systems and the Accommodation of National Minorities[1]

JOHN McGARRY

There is a debate among experts on federalism about what constitutes a federal political system. The traditional position is to define federalism narrowly, emphasizing distinctions between federal and other forms of political autonomy.[2] A more recent perspective, embraced by Daniel Elazar and others, is more inclusive. It insists that federalism is a "broad genus … embracing a variety of species," of which the classic federal state (or federation) is merely one.[3]

For the purposes of this chapter, I will adopt this second approach, describing as a "federal political system" any state that is divided into territorial units that enjoy a substantial degree of political autonomy. Federal systems thus include federations as well as decentralized states in which substantial autonomy has been bestowed on regional institutions, and what Elazar called "federacies," where central authorities enter into a bilateral (entrenched) agreement with a part of their state's territory.[4] In homage to the traditional position, however, I will underline that the distinctions between these different types of federal system are important, and that minorities are often crucially interested in these distinctions.

Federal systems can be used to accommodate national minorities. Such minorities are not primarily defined by a distinct culture, language or set of values, as is sometimes claimed, but by a common desire for collective self-government.[5] It is often thought that this desire for self-government conflicts with the territorial integrity of existing states. This criticism is raised by majority groups who emphasize the potentially destabilizing character of accommodating national minorities.

The criticism is accepted by hard-line minority nationalists who insist on independent statehood, and intellectuals, such as Ernest Gellner, who believe that the main goal of nationalism is to make nation and state congruent.[6] A federal system, however, presents itself as a possible solution to the tension between the desire to maintain the territorial integrity of existing states and the desire of national minorities for self-government. It has the potential to allow national minorities some measure of self-government within the contours of existing states.

The establishment of federal systems as a way of accommodating national minorities goes back to the creation of the Swiss and Canadian federations in the nineteenth century. However, it has become particularly fashionable, at least in the West, in recent decades.[7] Within the past quarter-century, several Western states, including Belgium, the United Kingdom and Spain, have transformed themselves from unitary states into states in which national minorities exercise considerable autonomy. Even France, the home of the Jacobin model of centralized government, has recently established a regional assembly for the Corsicans, and is currently examining ways to expand this autonomy.[8] Canada, which since its inception in 1867 has accommodated Quebec francophones through its federal system, has more recently begun to experiment with new forms of self-government for its indigenous peoples.

However, not everyone endorses *multi*-national federal arrangements, and authorities in Eastern Europe and most of Africa and Asia are strongly resistant to them. Their main concern, which is shared by some Western intellectuals, including socialists, liberals and conservatives, is that multi-national federalism promotes instability and threatens state unity.

This chapter is divided into three parts. The first distinguishes between three different types of federal political systems that can be used to accommodate national minorities: devolved (or decentralized) political systems, federations and federacies. It also discusses two difficulties that are faced by those who seek to accommodate national minorities through federal arrangements: what can be done for minorities who are left outside the unit that is controlled by their group (or who do not have a federal unit that they control); and what can be done about national minorities who aspire to political links with co-nationals in neighbouring states, i.e., who will not be satisfied with mere self-government within the state in which they reside. The second part explains that federal political systems can be used to control and assimilate national minorities, as distinct from accommodating them. The final part considers the arguments against accommodating national minorities through federal systems. The paper suggests that these arguments are often substantially weaker than their proponents think.

FEDERAL SYSTEMS AND THE ACCOMMODATION OF NATIONAL MINORITIES: DEVOLVED (OR DECENTRALIZED) STATES, FEDERATIONS AND FEDERACIES

Even centralized states can make provision for national minorities, by giving them privileges within the central government and by recognizing the importance of local traditions. Prior to devolution in the late 1990s, the unitary United Kingdom had a number of complex arrangements for accommodating its national minorities, particularly the Scots. The latter had their own cabinet minister and a sizable bureaucracy located in Edinburgh, while Scottish MPs played a special, though not decisive, role when Scottish legislation was being debated at Westminster. The Scottish legal, local government, and education systems were also kept intact, despite the legislative union of 1707. Unitary Spain, at least before Franco, recognized the importance of the *fueros* (local privileges) of the Basque region. Before Belgium became a federation, its Walloon minority was protected by a range of consociational provisions at the level of the central government in Brussels. Francophones in the province of Canada (1841–1867) were similarly protected.

While such measures go some way towards meeting the needs of national minorities, they do not satisfy their basic desire for collective self-government. States that want to respond to this desire, without permitting secession, have three options, which are discussed here as ideal types: they can "devolve" or decentralize power to regional governments and legislatures; they can establish a federation, in which the entire state is divided into autonomous units and there is a constitutionally entrenched division of powers; or they can establish a "federacy," that is, enter into a bilateral and guaranteed autonomy agreement with a part of the state's territory.

Devolution (or Decentralization)

Devolution is a term that is used in the United Kingdom to describe the decentralization of power. State authorities can devolve or decentralize power to a region or number of regions. They can devolve different amounts of power to each region, a flexibility that allows them to respond to asymmetrical demands for self-government. A fundamental feature of devolution is that the central government retains sovereignty and can alter the terms of devolution or rescind it altogether. From the centre's perspective, this has the advantage of allowing it to change or end an experiment that has failed. In the United Kingdom, where there is no written constitution, such steps merely require the passage of legislation at Westminster. Elsewhere, it may involve constitutional change, which is usually more difficult than repealing legislation. If the constitutional clause granting autonomy can be changed by the central legislature alone (or by majority vote in a referendum), it amounts to what is described here as devolution or decentralization. While minorities in devolved states have their own governments, they generally do not have representation, as units, in the central legislature. In all of these respects, as will be discussed later, devolution is distinct from federation.

The United Kingdom established a devolved Parliament at Stormont in Northern Ireland between 1921 and 1972. In the late 1990s, it established a Parliament in Scotland, an assembly in Wales and an assembly in Northern Ireland. Support for devolution was much stronger in Scotland and Northern Ireland than in Wales, so Scotland and Northern Ireland were given extensive law-making powers, while the Welsh Assembly was restricted to passing secondary legislation within a framework established by Westminster. England, and regions within England, were not given their own regional legislatures, because there was no demand for them. In the case of Canada, in 1999, an act of the federal Parliament partitioned one of Canada's two "territories," creating a third territory of Nunavut. The decision was taken to give autonomy to the Inuit majority in the region.

While it might be thought unlikely that a democratic central government would rescind a grant of autonomy, particularly when, as in the United Kingdom, these grants have been ratified by popular referenda, it can happen. Westminster abolished Northern Ireland's Parliament in 1972, because the government of Northern Ireland had become patently incapable of maintaining stability and upholding human rights.[9] It also abrogated a number of elected regional councils in the 1980s, including the country's largest, the Greater London Council, ostensibly for reasons of efficiency but more likely because these councils, which were leftist-controlled, were opposed to the Thatcher government's ideological project. In a more recent case, in February 2000, the British government suspended Northern Ireland's current devolution arrangements because of a disagreement between the parties sharing power in the executive over what should be done with paramilitary weapons. The institutions were restarted in May 2000. Westminster's decision to suspend devolution was taken against the wishes of Northern Ireland's large nationalist minority and the Irish government. It was taken despite the fact that the agreement on which the institutions were based was the subject of an international pact between the United Kingdom and Ireland and had been ratified by large majorities in referenda in both parts of Ireland. The suspension was a forceful display of Westminster's view that it retained ultimate sovereignty even in these circumstances.[10]

It is sometimes claimed that minorities should prefer devolution over federation because of its flexibility. The centre, it is said, can respond quickly and pragmatically to minority needs by a majority vote in the central legislature or (with more difficulty) by changing its constitution, whereas changes to federal constitutions normally require complex amending procedures involving both levels of government. This claim, however, requires a rather benign view of majoritarianism, one that minorities seldom hold. Rather than seeing devolution as flexible, minorities are likely to prefer forms of self-government that cannot be revoked or altered by majority fiat. After Westminster suspended the Stormont Parliament in 1972, Northern Ireland's unionists, who had dominated it, sought to have it restored and made suspension-proof. While Irish nationalists welcomed the abolition of the Stormont Parliament in 1972, it was this group, ironically, which bitterly condemned the British government's decision in 2000 to suspend Northern Ireland's new autonomous institutions, and which is seeking to entrench these to prevent future suspensions.[11] Aboriginal minorities in Canada (and elsewhere) are also very wary of accepting any form of self-government that is in the majority's gift. This is one of the reasons they insist on their "inherent right" to self-government: an inherent right is one that they already possess and that cannot be taken away. Aboriginal leaders have generally demanded that any grant of self-government be constitutionally entrenched so that it cannot be altered without their community's consent.

These concerns of national minorities are not simply a reflection of their desire to secure the powers of self-government. There is also a fundamental issue of national status involved. If a political body controlled by a majority nation can simply abolish a minority nation's government, it indicates that the latter is subordinate to the former. Irish nationalists were upset not simply because the British government suspended the Northern Ireland Assembly in 2000, but because this suspension was clearly at odds with the right of the Irish people to national self-determination, a right that Westminster had appeared to recognize in the agreement that established the Assembly. Concerns like this also lie at the heart of the opposition of Canada's natives to mere delegated powers from the federal government.[12]

Federation

These concerns help to explain why minorities generally prefer federations over devolved or decentralized political systems. In a federation, sovereignty is divided between a central government and the constituent units (provinces, states,[13] länder, cantons, entities, etc.).[14] Each level of government has exclusive responsibility for certain functions, with the division of powers entrenched in a written constitution. Neither the federal government nor the constituent units can change the constitution unilaterally – there is an amending formula that involves the assent of both. As well, constitutional disputes are decided by an impartial judicial tribunal. Elazar emphasized the distinction between federation and devolution by referring to the former as involving "non-centralization" rather than decentralization.[15]

Federations also imply bicameral legislatures at the national level. In the federal as opposed to the popular chamber, the smallest component units are usually disproportionately represented, i.e., over-represented. In addition to entrenching minority self-government, therefore, federations normally provide for a minority role in the decisions of the centre. In federations, unlike many decentralized states, autonomous units usually cover the entire state's territory, with exceptions sometimes made for capital city regions. There is also greater pressure in federations than in decentralized states to ensure that the autonomous units are symmetrical in powers and status. This pressure is generally resented by national minorities who normally prefer an elevated status for their unit over single units belonging to the majority population. The degree of self-government enjoyed by minorities in federations varies: some are less "non-centralized" than others. Ironically, while federations offer more secure autonomy to minorities than devolved polities, they do not necessarily offer more autonomy. Northern Ireland, a devolved region of the United Kingdom between 1921 and 1972, had powers that were at least as wide-ranging as those enjoyed by the constituent units of the United States.

Federation has been used as a method for accommodating minorities in several states. Switzerland is the oldest multi-ethnic federation. It was established in 1848 and is divided into cantons that are German-, French- and Italian-speaking. Canada has been a multinational federation since 1867. Many anglophones wanted a unitary state, but francophones in Quebec successfully resisted this. Both India and Nigeria became multi-national federations after decolonization. The communist states of the Soviet Union, Yugoslavia and Czechoslovakia established federal institutions to accommodate their distinct national communities, and the Russian Republic, one of the constituent units of the Soviet Union, was itself organized along federal lines. These communist states did not in practice, however, bestow genuine democratic self-government on the minorities involved.

More recently, Belgium has evolved into a federation, and many academic specialists think Spain has too. Some believe that this is also the direction in which the United Kingdom is moving. While the three communist federations of Eastern Europe fell apart in the early 1990s, Yugoslavia still hangs together (barely) as a dyadic federation incorporating Serbia and Montenegro, and Bosnia was transformed into a federation by the internationally enforced Dayton Peace Agreement of 1995. Russia has been transforming itself into a democratic federation since 1991, although the quality of its democracy remains open to question. Both Euro-optimists and pessimists think that the European Union (EU) is developing into a federation. In addition, federations are being proposed as solutions for a number of long-running conflicts, including in Georgia (to accommodate the Abkhazians) and in Cyprus.

As these examples indicate, a federation can develop from previously independent states (including from a confederation of independent states) or separate ex-colonies deciding to join together. This was the route followed in the case of Switzerland and the United States. It is the route upon which many think the European Union is embarked. A federation can also develop out of a unitary state, however, as has happened in the case of Spain and Belgium, and may happen in the case of the United Kingdom. Canada's birth was a hybrid of these two processes – on the one hand, it involved the joining together of a number of previously separate British North American colonies, while on the other hand, it involved the division of the unitary colony of the "Two Canadas" into the separate federal units of Ontario and Quebec. Most recent federations have involved unitary states transforming themselves into federations, and one leading academic believes that it is much more difficult to form a federation from states that have previously enjoyed an independent existence (an observation that should please Euroskeptics).[16] Stepan has noted a third type of federation, one that has been "forced" together, and he cites the Soviet Union, which was established by Red Army troops rather than by voluntary consent, as an example.[17] While many Bosniacs (Bosnian Muslims) would consider their federation as springing from a unitary state, many Bosnian Serbs and Croats (as well as outsiders) would see it as another example of a federation that was forced together, in this case by the international community.[18] The prospects for such federations, under conditions of democracy, are not good.

A federation is distinct from a confederation, although the two are sometimes confused.[19] The former is a state with citizenship and a single international personality while the latter is a union or alliance of (independent) states, established usually for a limited set of purposes such as defence or economic cooperation. Federal governments have a direct role in the lives of their citizens, while confederations normally interact with the citizens of their member-states indirectly through the governments and bureaucracies of these states. As confederations are much looser unions than federations, they are more likely to have decision-making rules based on unanimity. It is also (formally) easier to leave a confederation than a federation.

The distinction between federation and confederation, however, is not as clear as it once was. Some federations allow their constituent units a role in international relations. Both Canada and Belgium permit constituent units with French-speaking populations to sit in La Francophonie, the league of French-speaking states.[20] As a result of a recent ruling by Canada's Supreme Court, each of its provinces now has a constitutional right to secede, providing certain procedures are followed.[21] From the other direction, the European Union, which originated as a confederation, has been developing federal characteristics. Since the Maastricht Treaty, there has been EU citizenship, and the "Eurocracy" in Brussels is increasingly having an impact on the lives of these citizens. The EU's dominant decision-making rule is shifting from unanimity to majority rule, a process that will be hastened if the recent Treaty of Nice is ratified.

The opening up of a grey area between federation and confederation has the potential to help manage a number of thorny conflicts. Thus, for example, the long-running dispute in Cyprus is largely over a Greek-Cypriot insistence on a "bi-zonal bi-communal" federation, whereas Turkish-Cypriots insist on a confederation. And, while Ottawa wants to keep Quebec within the Canadian federal system, Quebec separatists demand "sovereignty-association," by which they mean confederation. The compromise position in both cases lies in the middle ground between federation and confederation ideal-types. This is also the way forward, incidentally, for the European Union, many of whose member-states want a closer union than a confederal one, but others of which, primarily the United Kingdom, are hostile to the idea of a European federation.[22] If it is accepted that there is a continuum between federation and confederation, and that the two are not water-tight compartments, it would facilitate agreement in all these cases. Getting such an acceptance may not be easy, however, as the stalemate in Cyprus shows.[23]

Federacy

When a national minority seeks guaranteed autonomy, but there is no general desire among the majority group for a federation, the state can establish what Elazar called a "federacy," that is, it can enter into a bilateral arrangement in which secured autonomy is offered to a part of the state only. The primary difference between federacy and federation is that the former involves selective and asymmetrical self-government. The primary difference between federacy and devolution is that the grant of self-government cannot be revoked by the centre unilaterally. In addition, the units that are given autonomy in federacies are generally islands, and are not considered by the state's majority group to be an integral part of the state's territory.

The relationship between the Åland Islands, whose inhabitants are Swedish-speaking, and the rest of Finland, is that of a federacy. Its autonomy is guaranteed by an international agreement between Sweden and Finland. Other examples, according to Elazar, include the relationship between the Azores and Portugal, and between Greenland and Denmark.[24] The fact that the autonomous units are islands, with relatively small populations, makes such asymmetrical arrangements less problematic than if they were integral and well-populated parts of their state. Northern Ireland's nationalists, and a leading expert on the Northern Ireland conflict, think that the Good Friday Agreement of 1998 converted Northern Ireland's relationship with the rest of the United Kingdom into that of a federacy.[25] Nationalists thought they had negotiated institutional arrangements that could not be changed without their consent. Their interpretation of the agreement, however, ran up against the doctrine of British parliamentary sovereignty.

In the examples that have been listed, the state functions in most of its territory as a unitary state. Elazar also listed Puerto Rico's relationship with the US federation as that of a federacy. In this case, the relationship exists not because Puerto Rico wants *guaranteed* autonomy, which it could have as a state of the United States, but that it also wants *greater* autonomy than any of the states (the relationship also exists, of course, because the United States has been reluctant to grant statehood).

Generally, federacies, unlike federations, do not entail bicameral arrangements in which the units are represented at the centre. In fact, federacies can be marked by under-representation of the autonomous unit at the centre, and even virtually no representation, as in the case of Puerto Rico. This under-representation is justified as a *quid pro quo* for the fact that the unit enjoys powers and status that are not enjoyed by the rest of the country.

The Problem of National Minorities Without Their Own Federal Units

Federalism works to accommodate national minorities by giving them a degree of territorially-based autonomy. However, in several multinational federal systems, some minorities lack their own unit of self-government or significant proportions of the minority live outside the unit that is controlled by their group. These minorities are in the unenviable position of being "double" minorities, that is, they are both minorities in the state as a whole and minorities within its self-governing units. One response to this problem, in keeping with the spirit of multi-national federalism, is to redraw the initial internal boundaries of the federal system so that minority and constituent unit coincide better.[26] This option has been employed in Nigeria, India and Switzerland. In the last case, a new canton of Jura (largely French and Catholic) was carved out of the mostly German-speaking canton of Berne in 1979.

An additional possibility is to engage in what is sometimes called corporate federalism (or corporate autonomy), that is, to extend autonomy to a minority community as distinct from a territorial community. Corporate federalism might be considered particularly attractive where boundary revisions are not feasible, either because of ethnic inter-mixing or because the authorities are unwilling to establish autonomous territorial units. It was proposed by the Austro-Marxists, Karl Renner and Otto Bauer, as a way to accommodate the territorially interspersed minorities of the Austro-Hungarian empire.[27] The "millet" system, employed by the Ottoman Empire to accommodate its non-Muslim minorities, can also be seen as a form of corporate federalism. Federal systems that possess elements of corporate federalism include Belgium, Canada and the United Kingdom. Belgium's Flemish- and French-speaking Communities (communal authorities) have responsibility for Flemish- and French-speakers, respectively, in the capital region of Brussels. In Canada, French-speaking minorities outside Quebec enjoy the right, as a result of a court decision, to control their own school boards. In the United Kingdom, the Catholics of Northern Ireland also have an autonomous education system.

Beyond redrawing boundaries or allowing minorities a measure of corporate autonomy, federal (central) and, less commonly, constituent unit governments can opt to promote the group rights of minority communities in a number of ways. Since the 1960s, the Canadian federal government has passed legislation extending a number of privileges to francophone minorities outside Quebec, including funding for minority-language schools, a bilingual federal public service, and publicly subsidized television and radio transmissions in the minority language. It also helps to finance the efforts of these groups to extract services from their provincial governments. The provincial government of New Brunswick provides a bilingual provincial public service to accommodate its substantial francophone minority, and Ontario offers a range of bilingual services in designated parts of the province. Since 1982, many of the measures promoted by the federal government and the government of New Brunswick have been entrenched in the Canadian Charter of Rights.

Some federalists stretch the term federalism to include these various non-territorial forms of conflict regulation (as the phrase "corporate federalism" suggests). From this perspective, federalism is equivalent to the institutional toleration of diversity, whatever form it takes. National minorities, however, make an important distinction: territorial autonomy, particularly if the autonomy is extensive, is almost always preferred to non-territorial accommodation. National minorities seek *autonomy* because their central aspiration is to be collectively self-governing. This is why they are unlikely to be satisfied with the state's provision of services in their language. They also seek to be collectively self-governing on their national *territory*, which is why corporate autonomy is less than ideal.

The Problem of Minorities with Co-nationals and National Territory in Neighbouring States

Another serious challenge arises when some of the nation and the national territory with which the minority identifies is in a neighbouring state, i.e., across an international frontier. A multi-national federal system cannot easily accommodate such minorities in the same way that it can accommodate those that are fully included within the state. Devolution in the United Kingdom, to take one case, cannot satisfy the aspiration of Northern Irish nationalists for collective self-government in the same way it can that of Scottish nationalists, because part of the Irish nation and its national territory lie outside the United Kingdom. There are numerous cases of national minorities with co-nationals across state frontiers, including not just Northern Irish nationalists but also the Hungarian minorities of Slovakia and Romania, the Serbs of Bosnia, the Basques, and the Albanians of Macedonia and Kosovo.

One way to accommodate such minorities is to establish trans-border institutions that allow cooperation between the two parts of the national community. Within these areas of cooperation, the nation can be said to be collectively self-governing, if only in a limited fashion. Most states, however, are still wedded to the traditional "Westphalian" system of discrete sovereign states, and are reluctant to consider such institutions. The fear is that these will encourage national minorities to seek (re)unification with their co-nationals and encourage irredentism among the latter.

However, at least within the European Union, where relations between states are friendly and where traditional notions of state sovereignty are weakening, such institutions are becoming possible. The most far-reaching example stems from Northern Ireland's Good Friday Agreement of 1998. In addition to the devolution of power from Westminster to the Northern Ireland Assembly, the agreement provides for a number of political institutions linking Northern Ireland (part of the United Kingdom) with the Republic of Ireland. The most important of these is a North-South Ministerial Council (NSMC), a body comprised of the Republic of Ireland's government and the Northern Ireland Executive.[28] In addition, the agreement led to the establishment of six all-Ireland "implementation" bodies, which were given the task of cooperating to develop joint policies over inland waterways, food safety, trade and business development, special EU programs, the Irish and Ulster Scots languages, and aquaculture and marine matters.[29] The driving force behind Ireland's trans-border institutions was the fact that mere devolution, the establishment of a regional assembly in Northern Ireland, would not have satisfied the aspirations of Irish nationalists.

In addition to Ireland's institutions, various other regions of the European Union have been permitted to cooperate with neighbouring regions in other states to develop common policies, and sometimes, as in the case of Italy's South Tyrol and neighbouring parts of Austria, this has involved cooperation between a minority in one state and its co-nationals in another. The signatories to the Council of Europe's 1980 Madrid Outline Convention on Transfrontier Cooperation between Territorial Communities or Authorities agreed to promote such cross-border cooperation, and to allow regional authorities to make agreements with neigbouring regions in other countries within their fields of competence. There are also cases in Europe, besides the Irish one, of a region of one country being permitted to cooperate with another state (as distinct from a region on the other side of the frontier), for example, the Netherlands-Flanders Language Union Treaty of 1982.[30]

Such forms of cooperation offer a useful way to address the desire of national minorities to forge links with co-nationals and national territory in neighbouring countries. They have obvious relevance for several parts of the world, including Eastern Europe, the former Soviet Union, India (Kashmir), and the Kurdish region of the Middle East.

FEDERAL SYSTEMS THAT DO NOT ACCOMMODATE NATIONAL MINORITIES

If states do not want to accommodate minorities, the most common practice is to maintain centralized political structures. This was the approach of Spain, France and the United Kingdom until relatively recently, and remains the practice in other European states such as Turkey, Greece, Estonia, Poland and Slovakia. It is also the case throughout much of Africa and Asia, where several states are centralized, often under the control of military strongmen or dominant ethnic communities. It would be a mistake, however, to regard all federal systems as minority-friendly in nature. Some are consistent with policies of assimilation and control rather than accommodation. In this section, the paper discusses two broad ways in which federal systems have been employed towards such ends.

National Federalism

Some federal systems are aimed at the construction of a nation-state rather than a multi-national state. This is the case with the Brazilian, Australian, German, Mexican and American federations. In each of these cases, the decision was taken to establish or retain federations rather than unitary states for reasons that had nothing to do with accommodating national minorities, for example: to provide for accessible government in a large country (Brazil, Australia and the United States); to coax previously independent units into joining a union without extinguishing their identity/existence (the United States and English Canada); and to protect against the concentration and abuse of power (Germany and the United States).

In the case of these national federations, steps were taken, where necessary, to ensure that national minorities did not become self-governing. As the United States, to take the most prominent case, expanded southwestward from its original homogeneous (except for black slaves) 13 colonies, it was decided that no territory would receive statehood unless minorities were outnumbered by White Anglo-Saxon Protestants (WASPS).[31] Sometimes, the technique employed was to gerrymander state boundaries to ensure that Indians or Hispanics were outnumbered, as in Florida. At other times, as in Hawaii and the southwest, statehood was delayed until the region's long-standing residents could be swamped with enough WASP settlers. The American authorities were even sceptical of immigrant groups concentrating in particular locations lest this lead to ethnically-based demands for self-government, and grants of public land were denied to ethnic groups in order to promote their dispersal.[32] In line with nation-building aims, minorities were required to conform to the culture and identity of the Anglo-Saxon core. However, in the case of blacks in the southern states until the 1960s (i.e., until nearly a century after slavery was abolished), American federalism facilitated control rather than assimilation. Blacks, ironically, would probably have been better served by centralized political structures than they were by federalism. Control was largely dismantled as a result of the combined intervention, starting in the 1950s, of the federal (central) judicial, executive and legislative branches of government.

American history, including a disastrous civil war over secession, and anti-black discrimination in the Deep South, has helped to make most American intellectuals wary about using federalism to accommodate distinct cultural communities.[33] Eric Nordlinger, one of the first American political scientists to take an interest in ethnic conflict regulation, rejected the use of federalism as an instrument for accommodating minorities as he feared it would lead to state break-up and to the abuse of power by ethnocentric minorities.[34] Other American authorities on conflict regulation and federalism, including Seymour Martin Lipset, Daniel Elazar and Donald Horowitz, have argued that the boundaries of federal units should intersect, rather than coincide with, the boundaries of ethnic minorities. Federalism, in this argument, produces "cross-cutting cleavages" (or overarching identities) because it encourages inter-ethnic bonds to develop along lines of shared regional interest.[35] Rogers Brubaker, a leading American specialist on nationalism, argues that giving minorities federal autonomy promotes divisive identities, and implies that (at least some of) these identities would not exist in the absence of such autonomy.[36] When American intellectuals recommend federalism for diverse societies abroad, it is the American brand of national federalism they usually have in mind, and not the Canadian or Spanish multi-national variety.[37]

Pseudo-federalism

A second possibility, distinct from the American or German model, is pseudo-federalism. This is where minorities are given their own federal units but these units are not genuinely autonomous. Pseudo-federalism occurs when federal units are not self-*governing* – i.e., the constitutional division of powers/rule of law is ignored in practice – or when the federal units are not *self*-governing – i.e., there is no democracy (freedom of expression, freedom of organization, regular competitive elections). In either scenario, it is impossible to describe the institutional arrangements as genuinely accommodating of national minorities. If these two conditions are borne in mind, it can be seen that a significant number of so-called multi-national federations are of the pseudo-variety. They include the communist federations of the Soviet Union, Yugoslavia and Czechoslovakia, as well as Nigeria during its several bouts of military rule.

While the United States can be seen as the paradigmatic example of national federalism, the Soviet Union is the most prominent case of pseudo-federalism. While its state structure was federated from the beginning, real power lay in the tightly centralized Communist Party (the CPSU), which operated according to the principle of "democratic centralism."[38] The Union Republics were therefore not autonomous in any meaningful way. Moreover, their legislatures (the Soviets), although in theory elected by local populations, were in fact rubber-stamp bodies nominated by the CPSU. Key institutions, including the army and police, were controlled by Moscow. As well, no effective judicial review existed to decide on the division of rights and functional spheres between the centre and the republics.

While the Yugoslav federation was, at times, less centralized than its Soviet or Czech counterparts, it was no less undemocratic or hostile to minority nationalism. There was no opportunity, therefore, for genuine multi-national political accommodation, or even for the open expression of nationalist goals. When democratization did occur, in the late 1980s/early 1990s, the federal structures of the communist federations were used as platforms by minority politicians to stake and win claims to independence. The experiences of these states, however, tells us little about the durability of genuine (democratic) federalism.

Ironically, Canada, which is now one of the most non-centralized federations in the world, may have been intended by its Anglophone founders to be pseudo-federal in character. Important provisions in the British North America Act (1867), gave the most important powers (of the day) to the federal government, while allowing it to strike down provincial legislation and to take over any provincial area of jurisdiction. Canada developed into a genuine federation because powers allotted to the provincial governments (including health care, education and natural resources) gradually became important areas of government activity, and because the federal government's disallowance and takeover powers fell into abeyance.

ARE MULTI-NATIONAL FEDERAL SYSTEMS A GOOD IDEA?

Accommodating national minorities through federal political systems is an attractive method of conflict regulation and preferable to many of the alternatives.[39] In this final section I defend this practice through a negative argument, that is, by showing the problems with the main criticisms of it. The most important criticisms are that multi-national federal systems promote illiberalism; are not necessary (as support for them is superficial); and that they institutionalize and exacerbate conflict, leading, in many cases, to the break-up of the state. These criticisms are associated with majority opinion. In addition, minority hard-liners claim that multi-national federal systems are unworkable and insufficient, and demand an independent state.

Multi-national Federal Systems Promote Illiberalism

During the French Revolution, the Jacobins famously argued that federalism was a refuge for illiberal reaction, and this view has had an important impact on the institutional development of the French polity (and many of France's former colonies) until today. American intellectuals put an important qualification on Jacobin sentiment – according to them, it is *multi-national* federal systems, which give control of federal units to national minorities, that are likely to be illiberal. This latter view is connected to a general belief that minority nationalism is backward and ethnocentric, a "revolt against modernity" as S.M. Lipset describes it.[40]

Much of this can be dismissed as metropolitan prejudice. Several contemporary national minorities, including the Catalans, Québecois and Scots, espouse civic rather than ethnic versions of nationalism, and appear reasonably tolerant of minorities in their midst.[41] Others, such as the Flemish, do give uncomfortable levels of support to far-right parties, but in this respect, they are little different from several national majorities, including the Austrians, Germans and French. Nothing general can be said about the propensity of minorities to abuse human rights, just as nothing general can be said about the propensity of majority groups to promote them. Put differently, all territorial units are capable of promoting or undermining human rights, regardless of whether they are minority- or majority-controlled.

There are other grounds, however, for thinking that multi-national federal systems are *more* consistent with the promotion of individual liberties than national federal systems or unitary states. As Will Kymlicka has shown, a proper understanding of liberal individual rights requires respect for the culture of individuals, and this respect requires allowing minorities the power to protect and promote their culture.[42] In addition, the (American) liberal argument that federalism provides a defence against the spread of authoritarianism, because it diffuses power, has even more force in multi-national (multi-linguistic and multi-cultural) federal systems than in national (mono-linguistic and mono-cultural) federal systems. Cultural diversity acts as an additional barrier to the rapid expansion of authoritarian ideas and political parties.[43]

Rather than denying autonomy to minorities, liberals who are concerned about illiberal abuses have to ensure that federal arrangements are consistent with the protection of basic liberal individual rights. One way to do so is to ensure that the federal arrangements exist within an overarching (national and international) regime of human rights.

Multi-national Federal Systems Are Inappropriate: Support for Self-Government among Minorities Is Exaggerated

A second criticism, implicitly or explicitly promoted by majority politicians and intellectuals, is that support for self-government among minorities is superficial and should not be taken seriously. This is in line with leftist and liberal thinking that the only authentic divisions are based on class or individuals, and that support for nationalism among minorities is exaggerated by their elites for self-interested purposes. From this perspective, it is thought that people from "minority" groups will be happy with centralized political systems, provided they are treated as equal citizens. This thinking was central to the arguments of British integrationists in Northern Ireland during the 1970s and 1980s, particularly under the leadership of Enoch Powell.[44] It is a mainstay of French republican discourse and that of the Turkish regime in Ankara. Similar arguments are used by Canadians who oppose autonomy for Canada's indigenous peoples, and/or who oppose extending Quebec's autonomy.[45]

The proper response to this argument is that determining whether support for autonomy exists or not should be based on support for political parties that advocate it, providing elections are free and competitive. It is profoundly undemocratic and insulting to voters to argue that support for an autonomy-seeking party, under these conditions, represents a form of false consciousness. It also begs the question of why parties that reject autonomy in favour of cross-cutting appeals are not as good at "manipulating" voters as those who advocate it.

Nonetheless, it should be noted that some minorities, those that are not "national" minorities, are not interested in territorially-based autonomy. This includes recent immigrants in Western democracies, as well as groups that have been resident in their countries for substantial periods, including American blacks, the various south Asian communities that live (or lived) in east Africa or Fiji, and several African (black) communities.[46] All of these groups are interested in what Gurr calls "access" and Hirschmann calls "voice," rather than autonomy.[47] They aspire at a minimum to be free from discrimination on the basis of their race or ethnicity. They may also support affirmative action for their group, particularly if their economic position is weak, and they seek respect for their culture (that is, multi-cultural integration rather than republican assimilation). Non-territorial minorities may also be interested in corporate federalism, the establishment of non-territorial forms of self-government,[48] and they may seek representation in governmental institutions along group (consociational) lines rather than territorial lines.

Multi-national Federal Systems Are Unworkable

I: They Promote Instability and Endanger State Unity. The most powerful and pervasive argument against multi-national federal systems, one that is endorsed by socialists, liberals, conservatives, and (political) unionists alike, is that they deepen divisions by institutionalizing them.[49] Socialist critics believe that multi-national federal systems obstruct the construction of the type of state-wide social solidarity that is needed to support class politics and redistributive programs,[50] liberals that they promote group identities at the expense of the individual, conservatives that they cause instability and conflict, and unionists that they facilitate the break-up of the state.

Such criticisms appear to rest on reasonably strong foundations. The creation of a territorially autonomous unit creates a need for elections that are limited to and focussed on the unit. This can facilitate the growth of parties that take a parochial view at the expense of state-wide parties that stress cross-cutting (integrating) issues such as class. Electors may vote for a minority nationalist party in regional elections, where it has a reasonable chance of forming a government and where its policies appear more relevant, but not do so in a state-wide election where a vote for a minority party may seem wasted. In the 1999 elections to the Scottish Parliament and the Welsh Assembly, to take two cases, nationalist parties took a significantly higher share of the popular vote than they had achieved in the immediately preceding national election to the Westminster Parliament – their share of the vote rising from 9.9% to 28.5% in Wales and from 22.1% to 28.7% in Scotland.

Federal systems also lend material and symbolic support to the development of minority identities. On the one hand, they provide for legislatures and executives, and thereby resources, that are controlled by minorities. Such minorities will often have their own nation-building agendas, which rival state-wide nation-building efforts. On the other hand, the identification of the minority with its region may be strengthened by the existence of its own "national" government, legislature, and flag, and by the "map image" provided by its unit's territorial boundaries.

Even federal systems that are not multi-national produce intergovernmental conflict over a range of issues. Constituents units can be expected to seek to expand their autonomy at the expense of the centre, to haggle over the allocation of resources, and to blame problems, including economic downturns, on the central government's policies. One can expect these conflicts to be magnified when the two levels of government are controlled by different national communities.

In addition, multi-national federal systems can expect a particular kind of divisive conflict – over the question of whether the state's different territorial units should be organized symmetrically or asymmetrically.[51] National minorities tend to defend a principle of equality of nations, where their nation enjoys parity with the state's dominant nation (or other nations). This principle requires that the minority's territorial unit enjoys a higher status and more powers than any single unit belonging to the majority. Politicians from the majority's units, however, tend to resent any suggestion that they should enjoy second class status and they respond with an opposing principle of equality of units. They are often supported by central elites concerned that special status for a minority will undermine its allegiance to the centre, which would have less responsibility for the minority than for the rest of the state's population.

This is the source of a serious dispute between Québec and the rest of Canada. Québec nationalists resent the fact that Canada is divided into 10 provinces that enjoy essentially equal powers and status. Their view is that Canada is a compact between two founding peoples (English and French) and they have sought for decades to elevate Québec's status to reflect this duality. The English-speaking majority, taking its cue from the symmetrical structure of the US federation, appears unwilling to concede such a status to Québec, with some English-speakers fearing that this would be a halfway house to secession.[52] Similar issues have arisen in the Spanish and Russian federations where national minorities have sought to promote asymmetry while elements in the majority population insist on symmetry.[53]

Disputes over symmetry/asymmetry may be particularly difficult to resolve. Even if agreement can be reached on giving a minority's self-governing unit more powers and prestige than individual units belonging to the majority, the question then arises of what to do with the minority's representatives in the central legislature. Should these representatives be allowed to vote on issues that are under the jurisdiction of their (minority) legislature but that in the rest of the country are the responsibility of the central legislature? This issue has given rise to a minor conflict in the United Kingdom where the opposition Conservatives have threatened to exclude Scottish members of the Westminster Parliament from votes on issues that have been devolved to Scotland.[54]

Critics of multi-national federal systems can also point to the presence of significant secessionist movements in Québec, Scotland, the Basque Country and Chechnya despite the existence of territorial autonomy. In the case of Canada, the fact that it is one of the most decentralized states in the world did not prevent Québec's separatists from coming within one percentage point of winning a referendum on sovereignty in 1995.[55] In addition, virtually all of the new states created as a result of secession in the post-World War II period – including the states that succeeded pre-1971 Pakistan, the West Indies Federation, the Soviet Union, pre-1991 Yugoslavia, and Czechoslovakia – were previously federal units.

The fear that autonomy for minorities is a one-way path to conflict and state break-up is so strong that political elites in Eastern Europe, most of Africa and much of Asia, will not consider it. Many of them consider federalism their "f" word. Indeed, several Eastern European states have been moving in the opposite direction in recent years, replacing multi-national federations with what Brubaker calls "nationalizing" states, that is, states that are tightly centralized and controlled by, and in the interests of, their dominant national community.[56] While fears about secession are less widespread in the West, they are present there also. Significant numbers of politicians in the United Kingdom, Spain and France warn that federal systems are inconsistent with state unity, and they are often supported by intellectuals, including some who are sympathetic to minorities.[57]

While plausible, however, the argument that autonomy for minorities undermines solidarity and individualism while promoting conflict and endangering state unity rests on a seriously flawed assumption. This assumption is that solidarity, individualism, stability and unity will exist in multi-national societies in the absence of autonomy (or existed before autonomy was granted). There is little basis for this view. Conflict and instability often pre-date concessions of autonomy, and they are frequently a reaction to a lack of autonomy in minority regions or to a process of centralization (i.e., a move by the centre to tighten its control of minority regions). The eruption of violent Basque nationalism in the 1950s and 1960s was a response to the centralizing policies of the Franco dictatorship. The mobilization of indigenous minorities in Canada occurred in reaction to the Canadian government's assimilation policies, and in particular, to Ottawa's proposal in 1969 to erode the reserve system. The Tamil rebellion in Sri Lanka, which began in the early 1980s, occurred in a tightly centralized state. Scottish and Welsh nationalism received a boost from the centralizing Conservative government of Margaret Thatcher.[58] Centralization also played a role in promoting rebellions by Kurds in Turkey, Abkhazians in Georgia, Trans-Dniestrians in Moldova, Uighurs in Xinjiang province (China), and Kosovars in what is left of the former Yugoslavia. The latter owes its origins to the decision of Slobodan Milosevic to suspend the autonomy of Kosovo in 1989.

While centralization does not eliminate conflict, neither does it guarantee unity. Most of Ireland seceded from the unitary United Kingdom in 1921 after a war of independence. In recent years, East Timor and

Eritrea have broken away from the centralized states of Indonesia and Ethiopia, respectively. In fact, the entire decolonization process which led to the establishment of numerous new states in Asia and Africa (and, earlier, to the establishment of the United States) makes it clear that nationalist mobilization and successful bids for independence do not require groups to be already self-governing, as colonies lack genuine self-government by definition. Even the "evidence" from the communist federations (the Soviet Union, Czechoslovakia and Yugoslavia) suggests that it is centralism and a lack of democracy rather than federalism that promotes secession, because these states were highly centralized and, before the late 1980s, undemocratic. If this is so, the post-communist centralizing elites of Eastern Europe may be reading the wrong lessons from the break-up of the communist federations.

Centralization in multi-national states was more compatible with stability half a century ago than today. Before the 1960s, it was routine for one people to govern another, but we now live in a world in which self-determination is a widespread and accepted norm. It is this understanding that centralism can no longer deliver stability (or justice) that has led Western elites in recent decades to consider autonomy for minorities as an alternative form of conflict regulation, including in Canada, the United Kingdom, Spain and France. There is also some evidence that the revised strategy has worked. Thus, the Basque Country may still have a violent separatist movement, but the concession of autonomy in the 1970s has done much to ostracize this to the margins of Basque society. It is also probable that more substantive autonomy, including a formula that recognizes the Basques' right to self-determination, would put considerable pressure on ETA to end its campaign of violence. The devolution package included in the Good Friday Agreement has helped consolidate peace in Northern Ireland, which had experienced serious conflict during a quarter-century of ultra-centralist "direct rule" from London. One of Ted Gurr's main findings, after a massive world-wide study of ethnic hot-spots, is that federal systems have been an effective remedy for conflict in a significant number of cases.[59] This is also Michael Hechter's conclusion in his important new book.[60]

It is clear from this that one cannot accept in the abstract the argument that multi-national federal systems exacerbate divisions by institutionalizing them. Rather, the evidence suggests that such institutional arrangements are sometimes a *response* to conflict rather than the *cause* of it, and that they sometimes, although not always, play a role in alleviating conflict. What political scientists must determine, then, is if there are particular conditions in which federal systems are more likely to succeed, and if there are particular institutional structures that are more likely to promote harmony than others.

One condition that greatly improves the long-term survival prospects of federal systems is the existence of "nested" identities among the minority group, i.e., some sense of allegiance to the whole state as well as to their minority homeland.[61] This condition is only likely to exist if the majority community also accepts that its state is a multinational state, and that the survival of the minority national community should be supported.[62] If these conditions are absent, or cannot be nurtured, a federal system cannot last.

The importance of reasonably harmonious minority-majority relations makes the timing of the creation of federal systems relevant. It is much better for such institutions to be put in place before antagonisms have become intense. While a generous grant of autonomy to Kosovo may have helped to maintain the unity of Yugoslavia in 1989–91, it is less likely that it will work today.[63] One problem here is what Tim Sisk calls the "timing paradox": while early accommodation is more likely to work, central elites may not recognize the need for concessions until conflict has heightened and it is too late.[64] As the creation of federal systems in the United Kingdom and elsewhere in western Europe appears to indicate, however, central elites are sometimes capable of engaging in self-denying prophecies.

In the same vein, institutional arrangements should be designed not simply to provide autonomy to minorities but, equally importantly, to ensure that they have adequate influence in central (federal) institutions. Such arrangements help to prevent the exercise of majoritarianism at the centre, and make it more likely that minorities have a stake in state unity. Protecting the minority at the level of the centre is crucial to the survival of multi-national federalism, and is too frequently ignored or downplayed in academic accounts.

Various consociational mechanisms are available – central governments, legislatures, courts and bureaucracies can be made representative of the state's different communities, and minorities can be given vetoes over acts of the central legislature and over constitutional change. Such provision for minorities within central institutions may be entrenched in laws or constitutional documents, or, less attractively from the minority's perspective, they may be informal, the result of political conventions or of general election results (that leave minorities holding the balance of power in central legislatures).[65] Inclusive central government institutions have played an important role in keeping the Canadian, Swiss and Belgium federations together.[66] Conversely, the undermining of such arrangements can have centrifugal effects. One reason for the strains in the relationship between the Québécois and English-Canadians was the removal of Québec's (informal) veto by the 1982 Constitution Act.[67]

While institutions should reflect and accommodate national differences within a state, as reflected in democratic elections, they should avoid exaggerating these. Single-member plurality (SMP) electoral systems often do exactly this, turning what is merely a plurality of opinion within a particular constituency into the only opinion. Canada's recent federal elections, which are conducted under single-member plurality, illustrate the problem: they exaggerate radical nationalist support in Québec and anti-Québec support in western Canada while punishing more moderate parties. SMP electoral systems can also distort elections for the assemblies of constituent units by exaggerating support for secessionists. Québec's current separatist Parti Québécois government, which almost won a referendum on secession in 1995, achieved office in the last provincial election without even winning a plurality of votes. It had fewer votes than the federalist Liberal Party, which became the opposition.[68] Scotland's new electoral system is, by contrast, more proportional in nature. This helps to ensure that Scotland's separatists, the Scottish Nationalist Party, will only be able to form a government, and call a referendum on secession, if the party first wins the confidence of a majority of the Scottish electorate (or persuades another party to enter into coalition with it). One way to reduce the prospects of secession then, without repressing differences, is to ensure that the state's electoral institutions deliver results that are representative of the electorate's wishes.[69]

•

II: Independence Is Needed. While critics from majority groups worry that federal systems promote conflict because they institutionalize national differences that would otherwise be unimportant, minority nationalist hard-liners argue that differences are so profound that there is no point in trying to manage them through federal systems: only independence will do. Both sets of critics share the same basic view that multi-national states are undesirable and unworkable, and that nation and state should be congruent, although they differ over where the boundaries of the nation-state should be. A number of minority political parties in Western states consider federal systems to be unworkable, including the Parti Québécois (and its sister party, the Bloc Québécois), the Scottish Nationalist Party, Euskal Herritarok and Sinn Féin. This is also the dominant position among minority nationalist communities in Kosovo, Chechnya and Israel/Palestine. Secessionists may accept a federal system as preferable to a centralized one, but they see it as at best a transitional step, as bestowing, to cite Michael Collins, the "freedom to win freedom."[70]

In certain cases, secession is the best alternative. Sometimes, relations between national communities have become so antagonistic, and their identities defined in opposition to each other, that nothing will work short of the establishment of separate states. This is clearly the case between Chechens and Russians, Israelis and Palestinians, and Kosovars and Serbs. It was also the case between the British and Irish in 1921, and between the East Timorese and Indonesians more recently. However, if inter-national relations have not polarized, and particularly where much of the minority population holds nested identities (they identify with the minority's region *and* with the state as a whole), the prospects for an enduring federal system are reasonable. This is what the examples of Switzerland and Canada suggest. It is also what is suggested by the experience of Spain, Belgium and the United Kingdom, although their experiments with federal systems are of more recent vintage.

A profound problem with secessionists' arguments relates to their view that national identities are discrete and that their new state will be a nation-state, i.e., nationally homogeneous.[71] Both premises are often wrong. First, particularly in multi-national federal systems, where minorities have enjoyed extensive political accommodation, one can expect the existence of nested identities among the minority group. This is clearly the case with the Québécois, Scots and Catalans. Second, it is extremely difficult to draw international frontiers in ways that clearly separates national communities (just as it is difficult to draw internal federal boundaries in such a way). As a consequence, any new state, created as a result of secession, is as likely to be as nationally heterogeneous as the state from which it seceded. The number of people involved will be different, but not necessarily the degree of national diversity.

Where national communities cannot be separated, seceding from a multi-national federal system in order to construct a nation-state is extremely problematic. A multi-national federal system is, by definition, more capable of accommodating diverse national identities (including nested identities) than a nation-state. The only way to make the new state as accommodating of its minorities as the one it left is, ironically, to convert it into a multi-national federal system too. The governors of breakaway states are usually unwilling to do this, however. If they have seceded from a multi-national federal system, they will understandably consider such arrangements to be unstable and fragile.

CONCLUSION

In this paper I have argued that multi-national states that want to bestow territorial autonomy on national minorities have three ideal models from which to pick. They may devolve or decentralize powers to a region or regions controlled by minorities; they may establish a federation; or they may construct a federacy. Each of these models has been applied in a variety of places, and each has particular advantages.

A decision to establish a multi-national federal political system involves the rejection of assimilation or repression (control) as methods of conflict regulation. Recent history appears to indicate that both these methods are difficult to sustain in any case, at least in the West. With self-determination an increasingly important international norm, assimilation and control are more likely to promote minority mobilization than political and social stability.

Multi-national federalism is also a way to accommodate the aspirations of national minorities without breaking up the state, with all the problematic consequences associated with the latter. It has the potential to satisfy a minority nation's need for self-determination, and its record of success in a number of Western democracies directly contradicts Ernest Gellner's famous argument that nationalism requires making the state and nation congruent. While there are serious concerns that federalism is a transitional step towards the break-up of the state, virtually all failed "federations" have been pseudo-federal systems and not the genuine variety.

This does not mean that multi-national federalism will succeed in all contexts. If inter-national relations are polarized, as they are in several parts of Eastern Europe and elsewhere, it is unlikely that mere federal autonomy will satisfy minorities. However, the status quo in these countries is not working either.

NOTES

1 The author would like to thank Walker Connor, Margaret Moore and Ron Watts for comments on this paper. The Social Sciences and Humanities Research Council of Canada and the Carnegie Corporation of New York assisted with funding.

2 For examples of approaches that highlight the differences between federal and other arrangements, see B. Burrows and G. Denton, *Devolution or Federalism: Options for a United Kingdom* (London: The Macmillan Press, 1980); and C. Palley, "Towards a Federal or a Confederal Irish State?," in J. McGarry and B. O'Leary (eds), *The Future of Northern Ireland* (Oxford: Oxford University Press, 1990), pp. 69–99.

3 D. Elazar, *Exploring Federalism* (Tuscaloosa, AL: University of Alabama Press, 1987). Also see R. Watts, *Comparing Federal Systems* (Kingston, ON: Institute of Intergovernmental Relations, 1999), pp. 6–7. The quotation is from R. Watts, "Federalism in Fragmented and Segmented Societies," in J. Kramer and H-P. Schneider (eds), *Federalism and Civil Societies* (Baden-Baden: Nomos Verlagsgesellschaft, 1999), p. 146.

4 Elazar and Watts include confederation as a type of federal political system. In this paper, however, I prefer to focus on cases of territorial autonomy *within* states, and not on forms of cooperation *between* states. Confederations belong in the second category, although, as I will point out, the line between confederations and intra-state forms of territorial autonomy is becoming blurred.

5 For a discussion of the fallacy of "shared values" in discussing national groups, see Wayne Norman, "The Ideology of Shared Values" in Joe Carens (ed.), *Is Quebec Nationalism Just?* (Montreal: McGill-Queens University Press, 1995). For a discussion of nationalist mobilization, see Margaret Moore, *The Ethics of Nationalism* (Oxford: Oxford University Press, 2001), Chapter 1.

6 Ernest Gellner, *Nations and Nationalism* (Ithaca, NY: Cornell University Press, 1983).

7 See T. Gurr, *People versus States* (Washington DC: United States Institute of Peace, 2000); R. Lapidoth, *Autonomy: Flexible Solutions to Ethnic Conflict* (Washington DC: United States Institute of Peace, 1996); M. Hechter, *Containing Nationalism* (Oxford: Oxford University Press, 2000); W. Kymlicka, *Politics in the Vernacular: Nationalism, Multiculturalism and Ethnicity* (Oxford: Oxford University Press, 2001), Chapter 5.

8 F. Daftary, "The Matignon Process and Insular Autonomy as a Response to Self-determination Claims in Corsica," paper presented at the Association for the Study of Nationalities (ASN) Convention, New York, April 2001.

9 See B. O'Leary and J. McGarry, *The Politics of Antagonism: Understanding Northern Ireland* (London: Athlone Press, 1996), Chapter 4.

10 See B. O'Leary, "Comparative Political Science and the British-Irish Agreement" in J. McGarry (ed.), *Northern Ireland and the Divided World* (Oxford: Oxford University Press, 2001). An earlier example of a government abolishing a legislature that had been established to accommodate a national minority occurred in Lower Canada (the populated region of modern day Quebec) in 1841. The colony of Québec had been divided into Upper and Lower Canada in 1791, largely to separate French- and English-speakers. This experiment was ended in 1841, when the two colonies were re-united.

11 "SF targets UK right to suspend institutions," *Irish Times*, 25 June 2001. Nationalists support the new institutions because they are consociational (or power-sharing) in nature, whereas the old Stormont Parliament operated like a mini-Westminster on majoritarian principles. Nationalists are also concerned that Westminster's decision to suspend is at odds with central aspects of the agreement that established the institutions, in which the British government recognizes the right of the Irish people to self-determination.

12 See P. Macklem, *Indigenous Difference and the Constitution of Canada* (Toronto, ON: University of Toronto Press, 2001), pp. 174–80.

13 Here "state" means one of the constituent units of the United States, e.g. the "state" of New York. Except when I am discussing one of the states of

the United States, the use of the term "state" in this paper refers to an independent state.

14 Federal units are sovereign only within those areas of jurisdiction assigned exclusively to them in federal constitutions. They are not sovereign states with international personalities in the way that members of a confederation are. At a recent conference I attended in Cyprus, one of the Greek Cypriot speakers from the communist party, AKEL, insisted that federal units did not possess any form of sovereignty. He was concerned that if it was recognized that federal units had any type of sovereignty, Turkish Cypriots would use this to secede from a future Cypriot federation. See T. Tsielepis, "Federation or Confederation," paper presented at the Roundtable on Cyprus: Sharing the Canadian Experience of Living Together, 15–17 June 2001, Larnaka, Cyprus.

15 D. Elazar *Federalism and the Way to Peace* (Kingston, ON: Institute of Intergovernmental Relations, 1994), p. 9.

16 J. Linz, "Democracy, Multinationalism, and Federalism," paper presented to the Juan March Institute, Spain, June 1997 (working paper 1997/103).

17 A. Stepan, "Federalism and Democracy: Beyond the U.S. Model," *Journal of Democracy*, Vol. 10, No. 4 (1999), pp. 19–34. Stepan and Linz describe federations that emerge from previously independent units as "coming together" federations and those that emerge from unitary states as "holding together" federations.

18 Whether a federation has been 'forced' together or not will usually be contested. Many Quebec nationalists view the Canadian federation as having being forced together, because the colony of Québec was conquered by Britain in 1759, and because there was considerable pressure on Québec's leaders to accept the federation package between 1864 and 1867. One could also argue that the ex-colonial federations of India and Nigeria were forced together, as they were artificial units of the British Empire.

19 The confusion arises because the term *confederation* is used sometimes to describe a *federation* that emerges from the coming together of previously separate units. Thus, the federation of Canada, which started at least partly in this way (Ontario and Québec were separated from each other but joined New Brunswick and Nova Scotia) is routinely referred to as a confederation. The Swiss Constitution of 1848 describes itself as the "The Federal Constitution of the Swiss Confederation."

20 For a discussion of the role of federal constituent units in international relations, see also U. Leonardy, "Treaty-Making Powers and Foreign Relations of Federated Entities" in B. Coppieters, D. Darchiashvili and N. Akaba (eds), *Federal Practice: Exploring Alternatives for Georgia and Abkhazia* (Brussels: VUB University Press, 2000), pp. 151–68.

21 Canada is not the first federation to allow these "confederal" characteristics. The Soviet Union happily allowed Ukraine and Belarus to take seats at

the United Nations, and the Soviet constitution entrenched the right of each union republic to secede. As I will argue later, however, the Soviet Union was not a genuine democratic poly-centric federation.

22 European leaders understand that the solution lies in this middle ground. Lionel Jospin, the French Prime Minister, searching for a compromise between confederation and federation, suggested recently that the EU should become a "federation of nation-states." *Economist*, 2 June 2001, p. 3.

23 Both Greek and Turkish Cypriots appear to believe that there are federations and confederations, with nothing in between. See Tsielepis, "Federation or Confederation."

24 Elazar, *Exploring Federalism*, pp. 35–36.

25 See O'Leary, "Comparative Political Science and the British-Irish Agreement."

26 In Nigeria, central elites created new states not merely to give self-government to small minorities that had previously been denied this, but also to spread each of the state's dominant groups (Ibo, Hausa, Yoruba) across a number of different units.

27 For a discussion of corporate federalism, including the work of Renner and Bauer, see J. Coakley, "Approaches to the Resolution of Ethnic Conflict: The Strategy of Non-territorial Autonomy," *International Political Science Review*, Vol. 15, No. 3 (1994), pp. 297–314.

28 The NSMC was intended to function much like the Council of Ministers in the European Union, with ministers having considerable discretion to reach decisions, but remaining ultimately accountable to their respective legislatures. It is to meet in plenary format twice a year, and in smaller groups to discuss specific sectors (say, agriculture, or education) on a "regular and frequent basis."

29 The agreement committed both parts of Ireland to a further six functional areas of cooperation – including some aspects of transport, agriculture, education, health, the environment and tourism.

30 See A. Alcock, "From Conflict to Agreement in Northern Ireland: Lessons in Europe" in J. McGarry (ed.), *Northern Ireland and the Divided World* (Oxford: Oxford University Press, 2001), p. 168.

31 See W. Kymlicka, "Federalism and Secession: At Home and Abroad," *The Canadian Journal of Law and Jurisprudence* Vol. XIII, No. 2 (2000), pp. 210–11. This paragraph borrows heavily from Kymlicka's account.

32 See M. Gordon, *Assimilation in American Life* (New York, NY: Oxford University Press, 1964), p. 133. William Penn dissuaded Welsh immigrants from setting up their own self-governing barony in Pennsylvania, Gordon, *Assimilation in American Life*, p. 133.

33 Elazar, *Federalism and the Way to Peace*, pp. 128–9 and 163–4.

34 E. Nordlinger, *Conflict Regulation in Divided Societies* (Cambridge, MA: Harvard Center for International Affairs, 1972), pp. 31–32.

35 S.M. Lipset, *Political Man* (New York, NY: Anchor Books, 1963), p. 81; D. Horowitz, *A Democratic South Africa* (Berkeley, CA: University of California Press, 1991), pp. 214–16; Elazar, *Federalism and the Way to Peace*, p. 168.

36 R. Brubaker, *Nationalism Reframed* (Cambridge: Cambridge University Press, 1996), chapter 2.

37 S. Mozzafar and J. Scarritt, "Why Territorial Autonomy is not a Viable Option for Managing Ethnic Conflict in African Plural Societies" in W. Safran and R. Maiz (eds), *Identity and Territorial Autonomy in Plural Societies* (London: Frank Cass, 2000), pp. 246–47.

38 D. Lieven and J. McGarry, "Ethnic Conflict in the Soviet Union and its Successor States" in J. McGarry and B. O'Leary (eds), *The Politics of Ethnic Conflict Regulation* (London: Routledge, 1993), pp. 62–83.

39 See McGarry and O'Leary, "The Political Regulation of National and Ethnic Conflicts."

40 S.M. Lipset, "The Revolt against Modernity," in S.M. Lipset, *Consensus and Conflict: Essays in Political Sociology* (New Brunswick, NJ: Transaction, 1985). For a recent example of such thinking, see "Corsica: The Perils of Devolution," *Economist*, 7 July 2001, p. 49.

41 M. Keating, *Nations Against the State: The New Politics of Nationalism in Quebec, Catalonia and Scotland* (London: Macmillan Press, 1996).

42 Kymlicka, *Multicultural Citizenship.*

43 See T. Homer Dixon, "We Need a Forest of Tongues," *Globe and Mail*, 7 July 2001, p. A13.

44 For a critique of this view, see J. McGarry and B. O'Leary, "Five Fallacies: Northern Ireland and the Liabilities of Liberalism," *Ethnic and Racial Studies*, Vol. 18, No. 4 (1995), pp. 837–61.

45 Particularly in the 1960s, liberal Canadian political elites, influenced by the integrationist message of the American Martin Luther King Jr., appeared to believe that natives were like US blacks, i.e., they wanted integration rather than separation. It is not unusual, even now, for critics of self-government for indigenous peoples to attribute appeals for it to the interests of "grasping" leaders eager to distribute the spoils among their family members and cronies.

46 Mozzafar and Scaritt, "Why Territorial Autonomy is Not a Viable Option." Ironically, while many states deny territorial autonomy to minorities who seek it, South Africa's apartheid state imposed it on black ethnic communities who (for the most part) did not want it. Pretoria's "Homelands" policy was part of a divide and conquer strategy.

47 Gurr, *Peoples versus States*, p. 151; A. Hirschman, *Exit, Voice and Loyalty* (Cambridge, MA: Harvard University Press, 1970).

48 See Coakley, "Approaches to the Resolution of Ethnic Conflict."

49 See Brubaker, *Nationalism Reframed*, chapter 2.

50 See D. Miller, *On Nationality* (Oxford: Oxford University Press, 1995). Such concerns were pivotal in the defeat of devolution for Scotland and Wales in the 1970s. It was not so much the Conservative opposition that derailed the Labour government's devolution plans, as the fact that leading members of the Labour Party in Scotland and Wales strongly opposed it, including Tam Dalyell and Neil Kinnock. A leading Canadian academic's main concern with the extension of aboriginal self-government is that it will encourage Canada's wealthy majority to abdicate its responsibility for impoverished aboriginals. See Alan Cairns, *Citizens Plus: Aboriginal Peoples and the Canadian State* (Vancouver, BC: University of British Columbia Press, 2000).

51 See Kymlicka, *Politics in the Vernacular,* chapter 5.

52 It is not just English-speakers who have such concerns. The fear that "distinct society" status for Québec would undermine relations between Quebecers and the government of Canada, thereby facilitating secession, was at the heart of Pierre Trudeau's opposition to it.

53 For a comparative treatment of asymmetry in federations, see R. Agranoff (ed.), *Accommodating Diversity: Asymmetry in Federal States* (Baden-Baden: Nomos, 1999).

54 "Hague: 'Defending the Union also means giving England a fair say' ", *Daily Telegraph,* 29 March 2000. One reason why Britain's dispute over asymmetry is less serious than Canada's may be because the latter is a federation, where symmetry is a more central value than in devolved systems.

55 The 'Yes' side gained 49.4% of the vote, the 'No' side 50.6%.

56 Brubaker was writing in the mid-1990s. Subsequent election results in Croatia, Slovakia and Serbia have eased the position of minorities, but not dramatically. There is still little movement in this region towards meaningful territorial autonomy for minorities.

57 See N. Davies, *The Isles: A History* (Oxford: Oxford University Press, 1999). For an account of such thinking in Canada, Britain, Spain and Belgium, see R. Simeon and D. Conway, "Federalism and the Management of Conflict in Multinational Societies" in A. Gagnon and J. Tully (eds), *Struggles for Recognition in Divided* Societies (Cambridge: Cambridge University Press, 2001).

58 As Charlotte Davies argues, the Welsh nationalist movement emerged initially in reaction to an earlier bout of centralization, the establishment of the British welfare state. See her *Welsh Nationalism in the Twentieth Century* (London: Praeger, 1989).
Before this, the Conservatives, formerly the Conservative and Unionist Party, had performed a brokerage role that helped to preserve UK unity. Their reluctance to decentralize, however, helped to cost them every parliamentary seat they held in Scotland and Wales in the 1997 election (the party won one seat throughout Scotland and Wales in the 2001 general election). Ironically, for a party that cherishes the Union, the Conservatives

have now become an English party, whose current attitudes towards Scotland and Wales may be as much a threat to the unity of the UK as those of Scottish and Welsh separatists.

59 Gurr, *Peoples Versus States*, p. 208.

60 Hechter, *Containing Nationalism*. Another author, Tim Sisk, who is aware of the problems associated with federal systems, notes that "without federalism ... India might well have disintegrated long ago." T. Sisk, *Power Sharing and International Mediation in Ethnic Conflicts* (Washington, DC: United States Institute of Peace Press, 1996), p. 52.

61 If this is present, it may provide a base for state-wide brokerage parties. Some academics call for such integrationist political parties to organize as if they are capable of promoting overarching identities as a matter of will. The construction of such unifying identities is more complicated than that, and is linked to the presence of traditions of accommodation. Paradoxically, the establishment of overarching identities may best be facilitated by the recognition and accommodation of divided identities.

62 Canada's difficulty in recent years can be explained not simply by the fact that many Québécois think of only one national community (based on Québec), but by the fact that many English-Canadians think of only one national community (based on Canada). These monistic views feed off each other, producing a polarizing dynamic that may well destroy the country.

63 Unfortunately, centralist elites in much of Eastern Europe are probably correct to think that giving territorial autonomy to their minorities at this point would promote secession.

64 Sisk was referring to the issue of international intervention in ethnic conflict, but his insight also applies to decisions to create federal systems. Sisk, *Power Sharing and International Mediation in Ethnic Conflicts*, p. 111.

65 Prior to the recent general election in Spain, the ruling Conservatives governed with the support of Catalan nationalists. As a result of the election, it now governs alone. *Ceteris paribus*, one can expect the former situation to be more helpful for state unity than the latter.

66 In the case of the Belgium and Swiss federations, provisions for the main linguistic groups within the central executive are entrenched in law. In Canada, the French-speaking minority is proportionately included in the federal Cabinet as a result of convention, though it is proportionately represented in the Canadian Supreme Court as a matter of law.

67 The federal parliament, which has a constitutional veto, resolved in the late 1990s that it would not amend the constitution without the approval of Québec's provincial legislature. This restoration of Québec's veto may have gone some way towards placating Québec nationalists, but their veto remains dependent on the federal Parliament.

68 One might argue that it does not matter if separatists get elected on plurality votes as long as they need to win majority support in a referendum

before secession takes place. Winning elections, however, gives a separatist party resources to promote its goal, and it gives it the ability to shape the question that is put before the electorate.

69 The more conventional view is to argue that proportional electoral systems facilitate the emergence of separatist parties. There is some truth in this. The Scottish Nationalist Party has usually been penalized by the single member plurality system that is used for elections to the Westminster Parliament, and it did much better under the hybrid (mixture of single-member plurality and proportional) system used for elections to the Scottish Parliament in 1999. As the example of Québec shows, however, electoral systems based exclusively on single-member plurality can lead to separatists being over-represented as well as under-represented.

70 Collins is widely regarded as the father of the Irish Free State, created as a result of the Anglo-Irish Treaty of 1921. Not every Irish separatist accepted his logic. He was assassinated a year later because he had not gained full independence and because he had agreed to the partition of Ireland.

71 See John McGarry, "Orphans of Secession: The Problem of National Pluralism in Secessionist Regions and Post-Secession States" in Margaret Moore (ed.), *National Self-Determination and Secession* (Oxford: Clarendon Press, 1998), pp. 215–32.

The Distribution of Powers, Responsibilities and Resources in Federations

RONALD L. WATTS

INTRODUCTION

The essential characteristic of federations is that they are composed of two (or more) orders of government and operate within a constitutional structure that combines *shared rule* through common institutions for certain specified purposes, and regional *self-rule* through the governments of the constituent territorial units for certain specified purposes.

More specifically, the generally common structural characteristics of federations as a form of political organization have in practice been the following:

- two (or more) orders of government each acting directly on their citizens;
- a formal constitutional distribution of legislative and executive authority, and allocation of revenue resources between the orders of government ensuring some areas of genuine autonomy for each order;
- provision for the designated representation of distinct regional views within the federal policy-making institutions, usually provided by the particular form of the federal second legislative chamber;
- a supreme written constitution amendable only with the consent of a significant proportion of the constituent units;
- an umpire (in the form of courts or provision for referendums) to rule on disputes between governments; and

- processes and institutions to facilitate inter-governmental collaboration for those areas where governmental responsibilities are shared or inevitably overlap.

The distribution of powers, responsibilities and financial resources, thus, represents a fundamental aspect in the design and operation of federations.[1] In considering this topic, there are several introductory points to note. First, while a constitutional distribution of legislative and executive powers and financial resources is a fundamental feature of federations, there is enormous variation among federations in the form and scope of distribution of authority, responsibilities and financial resources. This chapter will therefore devote considerable attention to the variety of arrangements within federations.

Second, account also needs to be taken of differences within federations between constitutional form and operational reality. In many federations political practice has transformed the way the constitution operates. Consequently, to understand the distribution of powers and resources in federations it is necessary to examine not only their constitutional law but also their politics and how these interact with each other. This means that not only the structural features but the nature of the political processes within a federation are important to understanding the distribution of powers and resources.

THE DISTRIBUTION OF LEGISLATIVE AND EXECUTIVE AUTHORITY

The Issue of Balancing Unity and Diversity

A common feature in federations has been the simultaneous existence of powerful motives to be united for certain purposes and of deep-rooted motives to ensure autonomous regional governments for other purposes. This has expressed itself in the design of federations by the distribution of powers between the federal government for the purposes shared in common and the regional units of government for the purposes related to the expression of regional identity and interests.

The specific form and allocation of the distribution of powers has varied according to the underlying common interests and diversity within the society of the particular federation in question. Different geographical, historical, economic, ecological, security, linguistic, cultural, intellectual, demographic and international factors, and the inter-relation of these have been significant in contributing to the strength of the motives for union and for regional identity, and therefore have affected the particular distribution of powers in different federations. Generally the more homogeneity within a society, the greater the powers that have been allocated to the federal government, and the more diversity, the greater the powers that have been assigned to the constituent units of government. Even in the latter case it has often been considered desirable, however, that the federal government should have at least sufficient powers to resist tendencies to balkanization.

In addition to expressing a balance between unity and diversity, the design of federations has also required a balance between the independence and interdependence of the federal and regional governments in relation to each other. The classic view of federation, as enunciated by K.C. Wheare, considered the ideal distribution of powers between governments in a federation to be one in which each government was able to act independently within its own watertight sphere of responsibility.[2] In practice federations have found it impossible to avoid overlaps in the responsibilities of governments and a measure of interdependence is typical of all federations. An example of this in its most extreme form is the interlocking relationship between governments in the German federation which has developed because most federal legislation is administered by the states. Such a strong emphasis upon coordination through joint decision making may carry its own price in terms of the reduction in opportunities for flexibility and variety of policy through autonomous decision making by different governments. There is, therefore, a need to find a balance between the independence and interdependence of governments within a federation.

The process by which a federation is established may affect the character of the distribution of powers. Where the process of establishment has involved the aggregation of previously distinct units giving up some of their sovereignty to establish a new federal government, the emphasis has usually been upon specifying the new limited set of exclusive and concurrent federal powers with the residual (usually unspecified) powers remaining with the constituent units. The United States, Switzerland and Australia provide classic examples. Austria and Germany followed this traditional pattern, although their reconstruction during the post-World War II period did involve some devolution by comparison with the preceding autocratic regimes. By contrast, where the creation of a federation has involved a process of devolution from a formerly unitary state, the reverse has usually been the case: the new powers of the regional units have been specified and the residual authority has remained with the federal government. Belgium and Spain provide examples. Some federations like Canada, India and Malaysia have involved a combination of these processes of aggregation and devolution, and they have typically listed specific exclusive federal, exclusive

provincial, and concurrent powers and the residual authority. Thus, the residual authority in Canada and India (and the earlier Malayan Federation), but not the Malaysian Federation, was assigned to the federal government. As well, in those instances where there have been previous periods of military or authoritarian rule, such as in Argentina, Brazil, Mexico, Nigeria and Venezuela, this has significantly affected the degree of centralization within the federation.

The Relationship between Distributions of Legislative and Executive Authority

In some federations, particularly those in the Anglo-Saxon tradition, each order of government has generally been assigned executive responsibility in the same fields for which it has legislative authority. Classical examples are the United States, Canada and Australia. There are several reasons for favouring such an arrangement. First it reinforces the autonomy of the legislative bodies. Second, it assures that each government has the authority to implement its own legislation which might otherwise prove meaningless. Third, in such cases as Canada and Australia where the principle of parliamentary executives responsible to their legislatures has been adopted, it is only if legislative and executive jurisdiction coincide that the legislature can exercise control over the body executing its laws.

In European federations – particularly Switzerland, Austria and Germany – administrative responsibility has commonly not coincided with legislative authority. Administration for many areas of federal legislative authority has been assigned by the constitution to the governments of the constituent units. This enables the federal legislature to lay down uniform legislation while leaving this to be applied by regional governments in ways that take account of varying regional circumstances. Such an arrangement, however, in practice requires extensive collaboration between the levels of government.

In practice the contrast between these two approaches is not quite as sharp as the constitutional provisions might suggest. Even in the Anglo-Saxon federations federal governments have delegated considerable responsibilities for federal programs to constituent governments, often by providing financial assistance through grant-in-aid programs. Furthermore, in Canada the constitution itself provides an exception to the general pattern by providing for federal legislation and provincial administration in the sphere of criminal law. New federations such as India and Malaysia have also provided in their constitutions for state administration of federal laws made in areas of shared concurrent jurisdiction. Belgium contrasts with the other European

federations, since the allocation of executive powers there is closely tied to the allocation of legislative powers. And, the current Russian constitution stipulates that the federal and unit executive bodies constitute a single system of executive authority within the federation.

Variations in the Form of the Distribution of Legislative Authority

Exclusive Legislative Powers. In most federations some areas of responsibility have been assigned exclusively to one level of government or the other. Indeed, in Canada, originally in Switzerland (but somewhat less so under the new 1999 constitution) and more recently in Belgium, most areas of responsibility were assigned exclusively to either the federal or the constituent unit governments.

By contrast to these three federations, in the United States and Australia the powers assigned exclusively to the federal government were much more limited, and most federal powers were identified as shared concurrent powers. In Austria, Germany, India, Malaysia, Argentina, Brazil and Venezuela there are fairly extensive categories of both exclusive and concurrent powers constitutionally specified.

The advantages of assigning a responsibility exclusively to one government or the other are two-fold. It reinforces the autonomy of that government and it makes clear which government is accountable for policy in that area. In practice, however, even where most powers have been assigned exclusively to one level of government or the other, experience, such as that of Switzerland and Canada, has indicated that jurisdictional overlap is unavoidable because it is virtually impossible to define watertight compartments.

Concurrent Legislative Powers. The recognition of the inevitability of overlap in many fields has led to extensive areas of concurrent legislative jurisdiction being allocated in the constitutions of the USA, Australia, Germany, India, Malaysia, Argentina, Brazil and Venezuela. By contrast in Canada the only constitutionally specified areas of concurrent jurisdiction are agriculture, immigration, old age pensions and benefits, and export of non-renewable natural resources, forest products and electrical energy.

Concurrency has a number of advantages. It has provided an element of flexibility in the distribution of powers, enabling federal governments to postpone the exercise of potential authority in a particular field until it becomes a matter of federal importance. The constituent governments can thus be left in the meantime to pursue their own initiatives. The federal government may use concurrent jurisdiction to legislate federation-wide standards while giving regional

governments room to legislate the details and to deliver the services in a manner sensitive to local circumstances. Indeed, in Austria and Germany there is a special constitutional category of jurisdiction specifying a federal power to enact "framework legislation" in certain fields leaving the Länder to fill out these areas with more detailed laws. In addition, in Germany a constitutional amendment in 1969 added a category of "joint tasks" in relation to higher education, improvement of regional economic structures, and agrarian improvement and coastal preservation in which the federal government would participate in the discharge of Länder responsibilities.

Concurrent lists of legislative power avoid the necessity of enumerating complicated minute sub-divisions of individual functions to be assigned exclusively to one area of government or the other, and reduce the likelihood that changing circumstances will make such subdivisions become obsolete over time.

Normally where concurrent jurisdiction is specified, the constitution has also specified that in cases of conflict between federal law and unit law the federal law prevails. One notable exception occurs in Canada where old age pensions are an area of concurrent jurisdiction but in cases of conflict provincial law prevails over federal law. This has enabled the province of Quebec to preserve its own pension system and other provinces to accept a uniform federal pension jurisdiction.

Residual Powers. The residual authority consists of the assignment by the constitution of jurisdiction over those matters not otherwise listed in the constitution. In most federations, especially those created by a process of aggregating previously separate units, the residual power has remained with the unit governments. Examples of this are the United States, Switzerland, Australia, Austria, Germany and Malaysia. The residual authority is also assigned to the states in Argentina, Brazil, Mexico and Venezuela, although in these countries the full exploitation by federal governments of their designated jurisdiction has in many instances seriously reduced the scope of the residual authority. In some federations, however, usually where devolution from a more centralized unitary regime has been an element in the process of formation, the residual powers were left instead with the federal government. Examples have been Canada, India and Belgium, although in the case of Belgium it has been agreed (but yet to be implemented) to reformulate the constitutional distribution of powers so that the residual power lies with the unit governments.

The significance of the residual authority is related to the number and comprehensiveness of the enumerated lists of legislative powers. The greater the enumeration of specific powers the less significant the residual power. Thus in federations like India and Malaysia and to a lesser extent Canada (where the constitutions set out comprehensive lists of exclusive federal, exclusive provincial and concurrent legislative powers), the residual power has been relatively less significant than in federations like the USA, Australia and Germany where the state powers were not enumerated but simply covered by a substantial unspecified residual authority. In these latter federations the assignment of a significant residual authority to the states was intended to underline their autonomy and the limited nature of powers transferred to the federal government. It is important to note, however, that in practice there has been a tendency in these federations for the courts to read the maximum "implied powers" into the specified federal authority at the expense of the scope of the unspecified residual state powers, thus producing over time the progressive centralization of government powers. Paradoxically, in such federations as Canada, India and Malaysia where the centralist founders enumerated what were intended to be limited specific provincial powers, the courts have tended to read those powers broadly thus limiting the expansion of federal authority.

In a few federations the constitution provides the federal government with specific over-ride or emergency powers to invade or curtail in certain conditions what would otherwise normally be provincial constitutional powers. These reflect the fears of their founders about the prospects of potential balkanization or disintegration. The most extensive examples of such quasi-unitary powers are found in the Indian, Malaysian, Argentinian and Venezuelan constitutions. The Canadian constitution also includes some such powers (e.g., the federal powers of reservation and disallowance; the declaratory power; and the peace order and good government clause as interpreted by the courts) but these have fallen into disuse over the past half century.

The Scope of Legislative Powers Allocated

Apart from the form that the constitutional distribution of powers has taken, the particular powers assigned to each order of government have also varied from federation to federation according to the particular circumstances and balance of interests within each federation.

Generally speaking, in most federations international relations, defence, the functioning of the economic and monetary union, major taxing powers and inter-regional transportation have been assigned to the jurisdiction of the federal government. Social affairs (including education, health services, social welfare and labour services), maintenance of law and security, and local government have usually been assigned to the regional governments, although parts of these areas, especially relating to social services, are often shared as have been the areas of agriculture and natural resources. Nevertheless, there is considerable variation in the specific allocations within different federations.

Some subject matters have proved particularly troublesome. One of these is that of foreign affairs where, in many federations, federal jurisdiction may be used to over-ride jurisdiction that would otherwise belong to the regional governments. In a few federations, however, the federal treaty power has been limited by the requirement that where treaties affect the jurisdiction of regional governments consultation must occur or their consent must be obtained. In the case of Canada, as a result of judicial interpretation, implementing provincial legislation is required where treaties relate to fields in the exclusive jurisdiction of the provinces. In the case of Germany such treaties require the endorsement of a majority in the Bundesrat which is composed of delegates of the Land governments.

Coordinating public debt has also sometimes been a problem because a constituent unit government may by its borrowing affect the credit-worthiness of other governments within the federation. This led in Australia to provision for the coordination of public borrowing by an inter-governmental Loan Council with power to make decisions binding on both levels of government. In some other federations such concerns have led to federal control of public borrowing, particularly foreign borrowing, by constituent unit governments.

Two areas where in practice there has tended to be extensive activity by *both* levels of government are economic policy and social affairs. In the former, regional units of government have been concerned to ensure the economic welfare of their own citizens and to develop policies related to their own particular economic interests. This has sometimes extended to the establishment of trade offices in foreign countries to encourage both trade and investment, a pattern found in such federations as the United States, Canada, Australia and Germany. In the area of social affairs, including health, education and social services, regional governments have usually had primary constitutional responsibility, but often extensive federal financial assistance has been necessary because of program costs and because of the pressures for federation-wide standards of service to citizens.

The Distribution of Administrative Responsibilities

As already noted, in a number of federations, especially those in the Anglo-Saxon tradition (e.g., the United States, Canada and Australia), the distribution of administrative responsibilities in most matters corresponds with the distribution of legislative authority. However, in some federations, there are constitutionally mandated and entrenched provisions for splitting legislative and administrative jurisdiction in an area between different orders of government. These permanent and constitutionalized arrangements are to be distinguished from temporary delegations of legislative and executive authority that also occur in many federations. Examples of extensive constitutionalized allocation of executive and administrative responsibilities differing from the allocation of legislative jurisdiction occur in Switzerland, Austria, Germany, India and Malaysia. In all five, autonomous canton and state governments are constitutionally responsible for the implementation and administration of a wide range of federal legislation. In India and Malaysia all federal legislation enacted in the area of concurrent jurisdiction is specified by the constitution as resting with the states for its administration. Thus, while these federations are relatively centralized legislatively, they are much more decentralized administratively. These federations have shown that benefits can flow from the administrative decentralization of federal legislation particularly in adapting it to the different circumstances and sensitivities of the various regions.

THE DISTRIBUTION OF FINANCES

Importance of the Allocation of Financial Resources

The allocation of financial resources to each order of government within a federation is important for two main reasons: first, these resources enable or constrain governments in the exercise of their constitutionally assigned legislative and executive responsibilities; and second, taxing powers and expenditure are themselves important instruments for affecting and regulating the economy.

The Distribution of Revenue Sources

Most federations specify in their constitutions (or in the case of Belgium in special legislation) the revenue-raising powers of the two orders of government. The major taxing powers usually identified are customs and excise, corporate taxes, personal income taxes, and various sales and consumption taxes. Customs and excise taxes have almost always been placed under federal jurisdiction in the interests of ensuring an effective internal customs and economic union. Corporate income taxes have also most often come under federal jurisdiction because corporations in earning their income tend to cross the boundaries of the internal regional units and the location of their headquarters does not necessarily reflect the geographical sources of their income. Nevertheless, in some federations this taxation may be shared and, if so, usually under concurrent jurisdiction. Personal income taxes may be more directly attributed to location of residence and therefore are often shared by federal and regional governments although in some federations these taxes have been exclusively federal (e.g., Austria and India). Sales and consumption taxes are revenue sources which in most federations both federal and regional governments share although there are some exceptions to this pattern.

A common characteristic of the allocation of fiscal powers in nearly all federations is that the majority of major revenue sources have been assigned to the federal governments. Even where some tax fields are shared or placed under concurrent jurisdiction, the federal governments tend to predominate because of the federal power to preempt a field of concurrent jurisdiction and because of provisions limiting the range of tax sources, both direct and indirect, that regional governments have been assigned. Two factors have been particularly influential in creating this general pattern. The first factor is that the concentration of resources in the federal government is necessary if it is to perform the redistributive role usually expected of it. The other is the influence of Keynesian theories concerning policies for economic stability and development prevalent at the time that many of the current federal fiscal arrangements were developed.

In addition to taxation there are two other important sources for governmental raising of funds. The first is public borrowing, a source open to both orders of government in most federations, although foreign borrowing in some cases (most notably Austria, India and Malaysia) is placed under exclusive federal jurisdiction. As mentioned earlier, in the case of Australia all major public borrowing by both orders of government is coordinated through the operation of the inter-governmental Loan Council. The second source is the operation of public corporations and enterprises, the profits of which may serve as a source of governmental income. In most federations this latter is a source open to both orders of government.

The Allocation of Expenditure Powers

Broadly speaking the distribution of expenditure powers in each federation corresponds to the combined scope of the legislative and administrative responsibilities assigned to each government within the federation. But three points should be noted. First, where the administration of a substantial portion of federal legislation is constitutionally assigned to the governments of the constituent units – as in Switzerland, Austria, Germany, India and Malaysia – the constitutional expenditure responsibilities of the regional governments are significantly broader than would be indicated by the distribution of legislative authority taken alone. In these federations, substantial federal transfers, either as portions of federal tax proceeds or in the form of unconditional and conditional grants, therefore, are a typical feature.

Second, the expenditure requirements of different areas of responsibilities may vary. For instance, in relative terms health, education and social services are high cost functions compared to those relating more to regulation than the provision of services.

Third, in most federations the spending power of each order of government has not been limited strictly to the enumerated legislative and administrative jurisdiction. Governments have usually been taken to possess a *general* spending power. Thus, federal governments have used their general spending power to pursue certain objectives in areas of state jurisdiction by providing grants to regional governments that otherwise could not afford to provide the services being demanded of them. For their part, constituent unit governments have in a number of federations used their general spending power to establish trade and promotion offices outside the federation even where there was no constitutional jurisdiction in external affairs specified.

The Issue of Vertical and Horizontal Imbalances

Virtually every federation has found the need to correct two kinds of financial imbalances, referred to here as vertical and horizontal imbalances. Vertical imbalances occur when constitutionally assigned federal and unit government revenues do not match their constitutionally assigned expenditure responsibilities. These imbalances occur generally for two reasons. First, it has usually been found desirable to allocate the major taxing powers to the federal government because these are closely related to the development of the customs union and more broadly to an effective economic union, while some of the most expensive expenditure responsibilities such as health, education and social services have usually been considered best administered on a regional basis where particular regional circumstances can be taken into account. A second reason for vertical imbalances is that no matter how carefully the original designers of the federation may attempt to match the revenue resources and expenditure responsibilities of each order of government, over time the significance of different taxes (such as income taxes and consumption taxes) changes and the costs of expenditures vary in unforeseen ways. Consequently, there is a need to build in processes whereby these imbalances can be adjusted regularly from time to time.

Horizontal imbalances represent a second problem that requires correction. Horizontal imbalances occur when the revenue capacities of different constituent units within a federation vary so that they are not able to provide their citizens with services at the same level on the basis of comparable tax levels. In addition to horizontal revenue imbalances, there can also be inter-provincial imbalances on the expenditure side due to differences in the "expenditure needs" of different constituent units because of variations in the socio-demographic characteristics of their populations. These variations can include population dispersion, urbanization, social composition and age structure, and the cost of providing services affected by such factors as the scale of public administration and the physical and economic environment.

The Role of Financial Transfers

In order to correct these imbalances most federations have found it necessary to make arrangements for financial transfers from one level of government to another. Because federal governments generally have controlled the major tax sources, adjustments have usually taken the form of transfers from the federal to the regional units of government. Their purpose has been both to remove vertical imbalances by transfers in the form of tax-shares, unconditional block grants or specific-purpose conditional grants, and to remove horizontal imbalances by grants to assist poorer units. Inter-governmental transfers as a percentage of provincial or state revenues have ranged in the mid-1990s from 75.6% in Spain to 17.9% in Malaysia. Some further examples are: 40.7% in Australia, 39.4% in India, 29.6% in the United States, 18.9% in Canada, 18.9% in Switzerland, and 18.3% in Germany.[3]

Conditional or Unconditional Transfers

The degree of provincial or state dependence or autonomy is affected not only by the proportion that federal transfers represent in their revenues but even more by whether these transfers are conditional or unconditional in character. Federal transfers to regional units of government may have conditions attached to them in order to influence how they are spent. This "golden lead," as it is referred to in Germany, may undermine the autonomy of the regional units of government especially if conditional transfers constitute a high proportion of the transfers and hence a significant portion of total unit revenues. To avoid this, transfers may take the form of unconditional transfers (either set percentages of certain federal tax proceeds as occurs in many of the newer federations, or unconditional block grants).

There is considerable variation among federations in the proportion of conditional and unconditional transfers. The proportion of conditional transfers to the constituent units appears to have been highest in the United States and the European Union (at 100%) ranging down to 53% in Australia, 38% in India, and 23.5% for the most autonomous of the Autonomous Communities in Spain. The almost wholly unconditional character of the Canadian Health and Social transfers (CHST) means that among federations, Canada has the lowest proportion of conditional transfers, only 4.3%.[4]

The proportion of total constituent unit revenue made up by federal conditional transfers provides one significant measure of the constraints upon state or provincial autonomy. In most federations conditional transfers constitute between 10% and 30% of total unit revenues but in Canada they are substantially less.

Arguments have been advanced in support of both forms of transfer. In support of conditional grants has been an argument based on the principle of financial responsibility and accountability – i.e., that since the federal government has the nasty task of raising the funds by taxation it should, in the interests of accountability to the tax-payer, control and set the conditions for the use of these funds by the state governments. This is an argument which has particularly tended to dominate discussion of the subject in the United States. Consequently, in recent decades, conditional grants have predominated in the federal transfers in the United States.

Countering this, however, is the concern in other federations that conditional grants are likely to undermine the autonomy of the regional units of government by inducing them to undertake expenditures not necessarily in tune with their own priorities. Furthermore, in those federations where the regional units of government have parliamentary executives responsible to their own legislatures, it has been argued that these governments can be held responsible for the use of unconditional transfers through their accountability to their own legislatures and hence electorates. These arguments have led in the case of most parliamentary federations to a significantly lower reliance upon conditional transfers and a higher proportion of unconditional transfers than in the United States.

Equalization Transfers

The importance of "equalization" transfers lies in the view that all citizens within a federation should be entitled to comparable services without having to be subject to excessively different tax rates. The need for such transfers has arisen in most federations from a recognition that disparities in wealth among regions within a federation are likely to have a corrosive effect on cohesion within a federation. Indeed, it is for this reason that in most European federations equalization transfers have been labelled "solidarity" transfers.

Several points on this subject are especially noteworthy. First, the extent of the equalization transfers has varied considerably from federation to federation. Most federations, with the exception of the United States, have some formal equalization scheme but the scope of such transfers has been greater in some (Germany, Canada and Australia) than in others (Switzerland).

Second, in all but the German case, equalization has been achieved by redistribution among the regional units of government effected by federal transfers to the poorer regional units of government. Germany is unique in providing constitutionally for inter-state transfers to cover a substantial portion of the adjustments for horizontal imbalances.

Third, in Canada, the effort to correct horizontal imbalances through federal equalization payments has focussed primarily on adjusting for differences in the revenue capacities of the provinces. While this approach is typical of many federations, in some and most notably in Australia, there has been considerable effort in equalizing to account as well for expenditure imbalances.

Fourth, the formula for equalization transfers to regional units of government varies. There are transfers that are based on an agreed formula – e.g., Switzerland, Canada, Germany, Austria, Malaysia, Belgium, Spain and Brazil – although in some of these cases the federal government dominates the process of arriving at an agreement. In others – notably Australia and India – the allocations have been based largely on the recommendation of standing or periodic independent commissions (which may themselves use a variety of formulae to arrive at their recommendations).

Fifth, in some circumstances there may be a relationship between the degree of decentralization in a federation and the need for equalization arrangements. The more fiscally decentralized a federation is and the greater the inter-state disparities in revenue capacity and expenditure need, the greater is likely to be the need for equalizing mechanisms to promote horizontal balance. Brazil would appear to be a relevant example.

Sixth, it would appear that different federations vary in terms of the tolerance of their citizens for horizontal imbalances. For example, egalitarian Australia, which is blessed with relatively modest inter-state disparities in revenue capacity, goes to great lengths to equalize fully on both the revenue and expenditure aspects. Germany also provides nearly full equalization, at least on the revenue side. The United

States, with relatively large inter-state disparities but no formal equalization system at all, appears to have a much greater tolerance for horizontal imbalances. Canada lies somewhere between these two extremes. It has a substantial equalization program that, because of the particularly large revenue capacity disparities among the provinces, only delivers partial equalization. One factor affecting variations in the tolerance for horizontal imbalances in different federations is the relative value placed upon inter-provincial equity as opposed to provincial autonomy and non-centralization.

Processes and Institutions for Adjusting Financial Arrangements

Because, as has already been noted, the values of revenue resources and the costs of expenditure responsibilities change over time, federations have found it necessary to establish processes and institutions to facilitate dealing periodically with vertical and horizontal imbalances.

In terms of the processes for adjusting federal finance, four distinct patterns can be identified. In Australia and India, although in different form, expert commissions established by the federal government have been entrusted with the primary task of determining distributive formulae. In Australia, for example, there is a standing commission while in India by constitutional requirement a Finance Commission is appointed every five years to recommend the appropriate allocations for the next five-year period. These commissions hear representations from the state governments and report to the federal government, which normally follows their recommendations. A second pattern is the constitutional provision for an inter-governmental council composed of federal and state representatives – the Malaysian National Finance Council is an example of this arrangement. A third pattern is exemplified by Germany, Austria, Switzerland, Belgium and the United States where grants to the states are determined by the federal government, but the federal legislature contains state representatives who are involved in approving them. A fourth pattern is that found in Canada where the determination of an equalization formula, other tax transfer programs and tax agreements is under the control of the federal government the legislature of which contains no provision for the formal representation of provincial governments or legislatures. Nevertheless, because of the importance of these issues, federal-provincial financial relations in Canada have been a matter for extended discussion in innumerable committees of federal and provincial officials, and the source of much public polemics between federal and provincial governments.

In virtually all federations, but most notably Australia, India, Malaysia, Germany and Canada, a variety of inter-governmental councils, commissions and committees have been developed to facilitate adaptation of the financial arrangements. Australia has gone furthest in developing such institutions with three inter-governmental institutions worth noting here: the Premiers Council, composed of the Commonwealth Prime Minister and the state Premiers, plays a key role in deliberations on financial transfers; the Loan Council, composed of Commonwealth and state representatives and with a formal voting rule, coordinates federal and state government borrowing; and the Commonwealth Grants Commission, a standing body of experts that, since 1933, has advised the Australian federal government on equalization transfers and relativities among states in the vertical transfers. In Germany, because of the unique character of the federal second legislative chamber which is composed of the delegates of the Land executives, the Bundesrat and its committees have played a key role in inter-governmental deliberations relating to the adjustment of financial arrangements. In other federations, including Switzerland and Belgium, periodic commissions have from time to time advised governments on the adjustment of inter-governmental financial arrangements.

SOME SIGNIFICANT ISSUES

Constitutional Symmetry and Asymmetry within Federations

The issue here is whether the constitutional distribution of powers and resources within a federation should apply uniformly – i.e., symmetrically – to all the constituent units, or whether there should be variations – i.e., asymmetry – to take account of the different circumstances or requirements of the constituent units within the federation.

In many federations, most notably the United States, Switzerland, Australia and Germany, the formal constitutional distribution of legislative and executive jurisdiction has applied symmetrically to all the full-fledged member states.[5] In some other federations, however, significant variations among the full-fledged constituent units, related to different intensities in the regional pressures for autonomy and sharp variations in social and cultural composition, economic situation or geographic size and population, have led to the provision of constitutional asymmetry in the jurisdiction assigned to full-fledged constituent units.[6]

There have been basically five approaches to establishing constitutional asymmetry in the distribution of powers within federal systems. One has been to increase from the norm the federal authority in particular member states for certain specified functions. Such arrangements have existed in India and in the short-lived Federation of Rhodesia and Nyasaland (1953–63).

A second approach has been to increase from the norm the jurisdiction of particular member states. Examples are the differentiated powers for Sabah and Sarawak within the Malaysian federation, and in India in relation to the state of Jammu and Kashmir and to some of the newer smaller states that contain distinct ethnic groups. Canada from the beginning has had a measure of constitutional asymmetry principally related to the use of French in the legislatures and the courts, the civil law, and provisions for education for intra-provincial minorities. Among unitary states the asymmetrical devolution in the United Kingdom represents a radical example of this approach.

A third approach has been to exempt the full application of central authority in specific areas. An example has been the European Union's exemptions in the application of the Maastricht Treaty to Britain and Denmark.

The fourth approach is for the constitution to give formally symmetrical jurisdiction to all member states, but to include provisions that permit any state in certain circumstance to "opt in" or "opt out" of these assignments. Such arrangements retain the formal symmetry of the distribution of jurisdiction, but provide specific means for accommodating within this framework a *de facto* asymmetry in the exercise of these powers. This approach has been applied in a variety of ways in Canada, extensively in Russia by separate inter-governmental treaties, and in Spain by granting each Autonomous Community its own Statute of Autonomy tailored to its particular circumstances.

A fifth approach is that found in the complex example of Belgium where constitutional asymmetry exists not only in the differences in jurisdiction of the three territorial constituent Regions and of the three non-territorial Communities, but also in the inter-relation between Regional Councils and Community Councils.

An important factor influencing the powers and autonomy that member states in a federation are able to exercise is the constitutional allocation of financial resources. The extensive literature on fiscal federalism has invariably noted that where there has been a symmetrical constitutional allocation of taxing powers and financial resources within a federation, sharp variations in the wealth and fiscal capacities of their member states have led to significant disparities in the services they are able to provide to their citizens. Consequently, most federations have attempted to reduce the corrosive impact on federal unity of such disparities by schemes for redistribution and equalization of resources among member states, as discussed above. Thus, paradoxically, redistributive asymmetrical financial inter-governmental transfers have been employed to make the fiscal capacities of the member states more symmetrical.

Clearly where there is constitutional asymmetry in the powers and resources assigned to regional units within a federation, this has introduced greater complexity. Nevertheless, some federations have found that the only way to accommodate sharply varying intensities in the pressures in different regional units for political autonomy has been to incorporate asymmetry in the constitutional distribution of powers. The most notable cases have been the Borneo states in Malaysia, Quebec in Canada, the northeastern states and Jammu and Kashmir in India, and the Flemish region and Brussels in Belgium. In some other cases, asymmetry has proved useful as a transitional arrangement accommodating regions at different stages of political development. Examples are the arrangements within Spain for the various Autonomous Communities and the concept of a European Union with a "variable geometry" proceeding at "varying speeds." In some cases, pressures for asymmetry have induced contentious counter-pressures for greater symmetry, for example in Canada, Spain and Russia. These suggest that there may be limits to constitutional asymmetry beyond which extreme asymmetry may become dysfunctional. Nevertheless, in a number of federations, it would appear that on balance the recognition of constitutional asymmetry has provided the only effective way of accommodating major differences among constituent units in the relative intensity of their pressures for regional autonomy.

Degrees of Decentralization and Non-centralization

Given the variety in the forms and scope of the distribution of powers, responsibilities and financial resources among federations outlined in the previous sections, a question naturally arises about the extent to which federations have differed in degrees of decentralization or non-centralization. While in ordinary language we may loosely compare differing degrees of decentralization within federations, the comparative measurement of decentralization or non-centralization is actually a complex issue.[7]

To begin with we need to distinguish between "decentralization" and "non-centralization." Some authors have suggested that since decentralization implies a hierarchy with power flowing from the top or centre downwards, "non-centralization" is a more appropriate term for federations because it infers a constitutionally structured dispersion of power between orders of governments and, therefore, represents better the character of a federation.[8]

A major problem in any comparative assessment of the degree of non-centralization (or centralization) of the distribution of powers and resources is that no single quantifiable index can adequately measure the scope of effective jurisdictional centralization or non-centralization and the degree of autonomy of decision making of the different governments within a political system. Among the multiple indicators, although not all of equal weight, that need to be considered in any such assessment are the form and scope of legislative and executive authority allocated to each government, the allocation of financial resources and the degree of dependence upon transfers and particularly conditional transfers, the existence and extent of unilateral powers by which particular governments may over-ride the constitutional distribution of powers, and the degree to which constituent unit governments are given the opportunity to participate effectively in federal decision making that affects them.

Although no precise measurement of relative degrees of non-centralization is possible because of the variety of different indicators that have to be taken into account and the difficulty of weighing in quantitative terms their relative importance, it is possible to make two broad sets of generalizations. First, the particular areas of jurisdiction that are centralized or non-centralized have varied from federation to federation to meet the particular political, economic, demographic and social conditions of each federation. Thus, to take just one specific example, Canada is more centralized than the United States regarding banking and criminal law, but more non-centralized in a large number of other areas. Numerous such variations in allocations of specific functions can be found among federations.

Second, while it is, therefore, difficult to arrive at a precise quantifiable ranking of federations in terms of overall centralization or non-centralization because of the different indices that have to be taken into account, nevertheless, it is possible to arrive at some tentative general assessments.

A comparison of federal-state-local expenditures (after transfers) gives a general indication of the relative costs of the functions performed by each government in various federations. For example, a comparison of a representative group of federations in terms of federal expenditures as a percentage of total federal-state-local expenditures (after transfers) in the mid-1990s indicates that these would range in descending order of decentralization from Malaysia (85.6%), Austria (68.8%), Spain (68.5%), United States (61.2%), India (54.8%), Australia (53.0%), Germany (41.2%) and Canada (40.6%), to Switzerland (36.7%).[9] This ranking has to be moderated, however, when a number of other factors are considered. Germany, for instance, ranks where it does because of the high level of administrative decentralization which affects the expenditure levels, but this does not reflect sufficiently the high degree of legislative centralization.

Furthermore, if one examines the distribution of federal-state-local revenues (before transfers), it is clear that in terms of taxing powers, as contrasted with expenditures, federal governments are somewhat more dominant in comparative terms in Australia, the United States, India and Germany.[10] Furthermore, the differing degrees to which constituent units are dependent upon transfers from their federal governments and particularly upon conditional transfers (as outlined above) give some indication of the degree of the relative financial dependence or autonomy of the constituent unit governments in different federations.

When all these financial figures are taken into account, together with further adjustments for the various other non-financial indices referred to earlier, we may in general terms rank a representative group of contemporary federations broadly in descending order of centralization as follows: Malaysia, Austria, Spain, Germany, United States, Australia, India, Belgium, Canada and Switzerland. Among the Latin American federations, both Venezuela and Mexico would rank as even more centralized than Malaysia because of the predominant political party domination, although in Mexico with the recent election of Vicente Fox that is beginning to change. Argentina would probably rank next to Malaysia in degree of centralization and Brazil next to Spain.

The preceding analysis has indicated an enormous variation among federations in terms of the relative degrees of centralization or noncentralization regarding both particular functions and overall. This raises the question of whether experience suggests that there is a minimum list of federal powers required for a federation to be effective over the long term.

Although there have been many variations among federations in terms of the precise distribution of powers, responsibilities and financial resources, nevertheless, as a broad pattern it has usually been found necessary to assign to the federal government the major responsibility for defence, international relations, currency, debt, and equalization, and the primary (although not exclusive) responsibility for management of the economy and the economic union. On the other hand, provinces or states have usually been given exclusive or primary responsibility for education, health, social policy and municipal affairs. Areas such as agriculture, environment, immigration, language and culture have often been shared through some form of concurrency, legislative delegation or inter-governmental agreements. However, in some multicultural or multilingual federations, such as Switzerland and Belgium, the governments of the constituent units have been given a primary responsibility for their own language policy and culture.

Interdependence and Inter-governmental Collaboration

The inevitability within federations of overlap and interdependence in the exercise by governments of their powers and responsibilities has generally required the different orders of government to treat each other as partners. This has in practice required extensive consultation, cooperation and coordination between governments within federations.

The institutions and processes for inter-governmental collaboration serve two important functions: conflict resolution; and a means of adapting to changing circumstances.

These inter-governmental relations have two important dimensions: relations between the federal and unit governments; and inter-unit relations. Typically, in federations both kinds of inter-governmental relations have been important. Within each of these two dimensions, relations may commonly involve all of the constituent units within the federation, regional groupings of units or bilateral relations (i.e., between the federal government and one regional unit or between just two regional units).

One important element of inter-governmental relations that occurs within federations is the variety of *informal* direct communications (e.g., by letter, telephone etc.), between ministers, officials and representatives of different governments with each other. These are extensive in most federations.

In addition to these there are in most federations a range of more *formal* institutions to facilitate inter-governmental relations, such as those we have already noted above relating to financial relations. These have usually taken the form of a variety of standing and ad hoc meetings involving ministers, legislators, officials and agencies of different governments. A noteworthy feature in parliamentary federations, where first ministers and Cabinet ministers responsible to their legislatures tend to predominate within both orders of government, is the prevalence of "executive federalism" – i.e., the predominant role of governmental executives (ministers and their officials) – in inter-governmental relations. Where executive federalism has prevailed inter-governmental relations have been dominated by negotiations between both the ministers and their officials of each order of government. The institutions and processes of executive federalism have usually developed pragmatically rather than by constitutional requirement, but in such federations as Canada, Australia, Germany, India and Malaysia they range extensively from meetings of officials to councils of ministers and to first ministers' meetings. Within some federations there have been well over 500 such committee, council and conference meetings a year. These meetings have provided institutional processes for consultation, negotiation, cooperation and, on occasion, joint projects. On occasion, however, these meetings have also been the arena for inter-governmental confrontation and conflict.

Not uncommonly, where executive federalism has been the characteristic mode of inter-governmental relations, governments have each established their own internal specialized intra-governmental organizations to coordinate their relations with other governments within the federation.

An interesting development in Australia was the establishment in 1992 of the Council of Australian Governments to oversee the collaborative processes and in particular to make the operation of the Australian economic union more effective, but after an active period in its first few years it seems to have experienced something of a demise. Among contemporary federations executive federalism in inter-governmental relations is probably the most extensively developed in Australia and Germany, with the Bundesrat serving as the central focal point in the latter.

Where there has been a separation of legislative and executive powers within each government of a federation, as in the United States and Switzerland, channels for inter-governmental relations have been more dispersed. These have involved a variety of channels between executives, administrators and legislators in different governments often in crisscrossing patterns. A notable feature has been the extensive lobbying of federal legislatures by various state and cantonal representatives. Nevertheless, the new (1999) Swiss constitution includes provisions recognizing that even there inter-governmental executive relations have been taking on increasing importance.

The need for extensive inter-governmental relations has been further accentuated in those federations such as Austria, German and Switzerland where there are constitutional requirements that a considerable portion of federal legislation must be administered by the governments of the regional units. In Germany, for instance, this has been a major factor contributing to the "interlocking federalism" for which that federation is noted.

In virtually every federation, inter-governmental relations have had both vertical and horizontal dimensions. In addition to relations between federal and constituent unit governments, inter-unit relations have usually been extensive. The latter often deal with cross-boundary issues affecting neighbouring states or provinces, for example jointly shared rivers, transportation routes or environmental issues. In addition, there have often been efforts by regional groupings to cooperate on issues of regional concern. Sometimes inter-unit efforts at cooperation have been extended even more broadly to encompass all the states or provinces within a federation to deal with issues of wider scope without resort to the centralizing impact of relying on federal government action.

The prevalence of interdependence and the need for inter-governmental institutions and processes to deal with this has led to an emphasis on "cooperative federalism" within most federations. But equally significant is the concept of "competitive federalism." Analysis indicates that there are benefits and costs associated with each approach.

"Cooperative federalism" contributes to the reduction of conflict and enables coordination but when it becomes "interlocking federalism" to the extent experienced for example in Germany, it may lead to what has been called the "joint decision trap" which reduces the autonomy and freedom of action of governments at both levels and leads to general policy inertia.[11] Furthermore, where "executive federalism" predominates, it may limit the role of legislatures. Nevertheless, virtually every federation has found that it is impossible to isolate the activities of the different levels of government in a federation into watertight compartments. Given the unavoidability of overlaps of jurisdiction, cooperative federalism in the form of inter-governmental collaboration has in practice proved necessary in all federations. The question remains, however, to what degree such inter-governmental cooperation may, if excessive, limit or undermine the opportunity for flexible and autonomous action by each order of government.

Advocates of "competitive federalism" argue that competition between governments in a federation may actually produce beneficial results for citizens. For example, Albert Breton in his supplementary note to the MacDonald Commission Report in Canada, argues that just as in the economic realm competition produces superior benefits compared to monopolies or oligopolies, so competition between governments serving the same citizens is likely to provide citizens with better service.[12] He equates "cooperative federalism" with collusion directed at serving the interests of governments rather than of citizens. But it must be noted that "competitive federalism" to excess can lead to inter-governmental conflict and acrimony and have a divisive impact within a federation.

As with all partnerships, it would appear that in federations, given the inevitable interdependence of the different orders of government, a blend of both cooperation and competition is likely in the long run to be the most fruitful.

NOTES

1 For a fuller discussion including detailed comparative tables see R.L. Watts, *Comparing Federal Systems* (2nd ed., Montreal and Kingston: McGill-Queen's

University Press, 1999), pp. 6–18, 35–41, 44–55, 57–61, 67–68, 71–81, 125–130.

2 K.C. Wheare, *Federal Government* (4th ed., London: Oxford University Press, 1963), p. 14.

3 Watts, *Comparing Federal Systems*, Table 9, p. 48.

4 Ibid., Table 10, p. 49.

5 In some of these federations, federal territories or peripheral associated states and federacies are, however, treated differently.

6 R. Agranoff (ed.), *Accommodating Diversity: Asymmetry in Federal States* (Baden-Baden: Nomos Verlagsgesllshaft, 1999).

7 Watts, *Comparing Federal Systems*, pp. 71–77.

8 D.J. Elazar, *Exploring Federalism* (Tuscaloosa, AL: University of Alabama Press, 1987), pp. 34–6.

9 Watts, *Comparing Federal Systems*, Table 8, p. 47.

10 Ibid., Table 7, p. 46.

11 F. Scharpf, "The Joint Decision Trap: Lessons from German Federalism and European Integration," *Public Administration*, Vol. 66 (Autumn 1988), pp. 238–78.

12 A. Breton, "Supplementary Statement" in Royal Commission on the Economic Union and Development Prospects for Canada, *Report*, Vol. 3 (Ottawa: Supply and Services Canada, 1985), pp. 486–526.

Asymmetric Federalism as a Comprehensive Framework of Regional Autonomy

PETER PERNTHALER

INTRODUCTION: THE FUNCTIONAL APPROACH TO FEDERALISM AND REGIONALISM

From a traditional constitutional perspective, constituent states within federal systems and regional autonomous systems within decentralized unitary states are thought to incorporate fundamentally different types of autonomy. In this paper, however, both systems will be classed under the term of "functional federalism" if an autonomous system complies with certain minimum criteria regarding legal and political self-determination.[1] Thus, autonomy has to be embodied in constitutional or international law and, furthermore, it has to permit public functions to be fulfilled within the autonomous sphere of competencies. As well, in order to exercise state functions such as legislation, administration and perhaps jurisdiction, the autonomous system must have financial means at its disposal. And, finally, it must have a democratic system of its own. On this basis, an autonomous system must not only be able independently to define and control its own political aims in order to realize its general welfare, but also to participate in cooperative systems at the regional, central, even perhaps the transnational, level.[2]

Such a system of regional autonomy – no matter how its legal structure may be in detail – today corresponds to a common European "federalistic standard."[3] Thus, it can be compared to other European regions with regard to their functions and enter into cooperative relations with them, thereby co-sharing and co-developing the complex system of European regionalism. The concept of functional federalism overlaps systems insofar as it includes not only various national systems but, also, European and international law may serve as a basis for establishing or guaranteeing self-government within a nation-state. In the following article, however, the different dimensions of national, European and international argumentation shall be differentiated as much as possible, since they are still subject to different legal systems and legal methods, although they are increasingly getting closer to each other.

THE PRINCIPLE OF SUBSIDIARITY AS THE REASON FOR HOMOGENEITY AND ASYMMETRY IN FEDERALISM

The Difference between Homogeneous and Asymmetric Federalism

The term "homogeneous federalism" generally focusses on the equality of autonomous sub-systems (constituent states, regions, but also member states within confederations). Formally at least, international law grants states equality through sovereignty (cf. Article 2, para. 1 of the UN Charter)[4] and, with few exceptions, the ruling constitutional doctrine also regards equality as the regular structure of constituent states.[5]

Particularly in the European context, however, the non-homogeneity of regions with regard to their competencies and functions is the dominant structure which applies to regionalism. Within the framework of individual constitutional systems of decentralization, distinctions and asymmetries among the autonomous sub-systems (regions or local administrative units) can frequently be found. In this context, one particularly thinks of the Spanish and Italian regions and provinces which have a special status, or, regarding the United Kingdom, of the fundamentally different autonomies of Northern Ireland, Scotland, Wales and Greater London. However, regional autonomy is granted in a completely distinct way by international law. Even if regional autonomy is founded on an international treaty, it is shaped individually and can at best be compared to similar institutions – for instance, in terms of minority protection.

Federal systems can differ according to the legal position of the units as well as according to the functions of individual autonomous sub-systems. These differences can be justified by the following:

1 geographical position (particularly islands, for instance the autonomies of the Canary Islands,[6] the Azores and Madeira,[7] and of the Åland Islands,[8] but also other geographically peripheral areas);

2 specific politico-social structure (for instance, the establishment of the Swiss "Half-cantons" Appenzell Außerrhoden and Appenzell Innerrhoden as well as Basel-Stadt and Basel-Landschaft, which originated in religious differences within the populations of these cantons); or
3 national (ethnic) criteria (for instance, the special status of Quebec in Canada or the combination between the national federalism of the Flemish and the Walloons and the regional autonomy granted in order to protect the German minority in Belgium; similar examples of asymmetries can particularly be found in Russian federalism, but also in Spanish as well as UK regionalism or, as it is frequently called, "quasi-federalism").

Systems incorporating such differences are generally referred to as asymmetric federations.[9] It should be pointed out that asymmetric federal systems are based on homogeneous federal systems which, however, are combined with elements of differentiation, such as mentioned above.

The Principle of Subsidiarity as a Triple Standard

The principle of subsidiarity is the organizational foundation of each kind of functional federalism.[10] Its meaning sounds very abstract and depends on the socio-philosophical context in which it is conceived and interpreted. If applied to concrete legal or political systems, however, the principle of subsidiarity gets a much clearer meaning, since it is intended to operate in three different dimensions and can be defined accordingly.[11]

The first dimension can be referred to as the "Principle of Subsidiarity as a Subjective Principle of Justice." Catholic social doctrine has particularly moulded this aspect of the principle of subsidiarity.[12] According to this principle, it is regarded as "unjust" if a small social unit – at the smallest, an individual human being – is deprived of functions which it can easily (i.e., without any help) perform itself. It is unjust as well that a smaller unit is not helped by a larger unit if it cannot or must not perform a function itself because of its quality or its overlapping dimensions. According to Catholic social doctrine, *government authority* – the then supreme social order – clearly originates in the principle of subsidiarity.[13] Today one can truly say that the European Union (EU), in particular the European Community (EC), has taken over the former functions of government authority – again, however, on account of the principle of subsidiarity.[14] Because of its subjective structure, this dimension of the principle of subsidiarity is highly controversial. Nonetheless, one should be aware that it has gained much political importance and influence.

The second dimension can be referred to as the "Principle of Subsidiarity as a Rationalizing Principle of Efficiency." Under this dimension, the principle of subsidiarity is understood as a rule to optimize the performance of functions at specific levels. Thus, each level should assume those public functions for which – depending on its own size and capacity as well as the quality of the function – it is best suited. The allocation of public functions at specific levels is facilitated by a couple of standards and criteria which were developed by the theory of economic federalism.

Despite the attempts to objectify the allocation of public functions, it has proven to be impossible to exclude any (political) subjective judgements, since the allocation of space or functions depends on more elements than just objective and technocratic criteria. Political preferences and the historic development of the respective systems obviously play an important role (politico-economic criteria).

The third dimension can be called "The Principle of Subsidiarity as a Procedural Rule for the Allocation of Functions." Since the concretization of the principle of subsidiarity by no means prevents subjective judgements, everything depends on the question of who judges in which procedure. If the principle of subsidiarity is understood as a procedural rule,[15] it will signify that the judgement cannot be taken solely at the higher nor at the lower level, as neither of these levels possesses sufficient information required for the allocation of functions in a federal system. The fact that – lacking the participation of the lower level – the higher level does not possess sufficient information regarding the question of which public tasks may be fulfilled in the interest of the lower level or due to its capacity, is called the "dilemma of federalism" or the "circular reasoning of federalism." In such a case, the higher level is forced to distribute public tasks according to its own notions which is repugnant to the principle of federalism.

Instead, the allocation of functions within an interlocking federal system ought to be decided only in a coordinated process, which would enable lower units to participate sufficiently in the decision-making process concerning their own tasks and functions. In this way the autonomous sphere of South Tyrol ("Package"), for instance, was formulated by joint commissions in accordance with Article 2 of the Treaty of Paris (1946) "with the participation of the local German-speaking population."

In this context, the Spanish example is worth mentioning. Thus, according to Article 148 of the Spanish constitution the Autonomous Communities (Communidades autonomas) *may* – but need not –

assume competencies within the framework of a select list of competencies. Under Article 147(2) of the Spanish constitution the statutes of autonomy have to list those competencies that were assumed. After five years have elapsed and through the reform of their statutes, the Autonomous Communities may then expand their competencies within the framework established in Article 149 (exclusive competencies of the state). However, a reform of statutes would require the approval of the National Parliament (Cortes Generales) by means of an organic law (Article 147(3) of the Spanish constitution). Despite the fact that, if they want to assume competencies, they are obliged to choose them from a limited list, the Autonomous Communities are in principle entitled to participate in a cooperative process of formulating their competencies.

In this context, one might also think of specific cooperative proceedings required for the amendment of the distribution of competencies. Article 140(1) of the Swiss federal constitution of 1999, for instance, provides that revisions of the constitution, including the distribution of competencies, have to be submitted to the vote of the people and the cantons (as did revisions prior to the 1999 constitution). According to Article 142(2) of the Swiss constitution revisions will be accepted if the majority of those voting and the majority of the cantons approve of them.

Article V of the US constitution serves as another example. In the US case amendments to the constitution need to be ratified by the legislatures of three-fourths of the states, or by conventions (on the application of the legislatures of two-thirds of the states) in three-fourths thereof. This procedural rule applies to the Tenth Amendment (Rights Reserved to States (1791)), and it has also become part of the constitution in the described way.

The Principle of Subsidiarity as a Basis of the Homogeneity and Asymmetry of Autonomies

If the principle of subsidiarity is such a triple standard, it does not permit a uniform solution with regard to the homogeneity or asymmetry of autonomous systems in a federal or a regional state.[16] In the EU, too, one can perceive a mixture between homogeneity and asymmetry with regard to the spheres of competence of the Union and the member states according to the new principle of "flexibility" of integration (Article 40 EU Treaty).[17]

Which public tasks (competencies) are performed by the sub-system depends on the quality of a federal sub-system, its capacity, its demands and, last but not least, how it phrases its own political interests and identity. The nature of the sub-system also determines which kind of state functions and how the self-determined phrasing of public functions must be balanced against the general welfare of the federal system as a whole, which has to be formulated politically as well. This should be done according to the principles of adequacy, expediency of competition, and tolerance towards minorities, which may be regarded as the basis of the political and cultural principle of pluralism and which – as well as the principles of competition and pluralism – belongs to the essential principles of federalism.

Thus, one will attain very different kinds of autonomy depending upon which foundation the self-determination of each sub-system is based, and which aims it is supposed to serve. Autonomy, which is understood as a political way of life of a specific people, of a language group or an ethnic group, needs competencies different from those needed by a historically or politico-geographically separate island or by a Land within a nationally homogeneous federal system, such as Germany or Austria.[18]

One can proceed from the assumption that federal homogeneity must apply to the principal democratic and legal structure of political sub-systems[19] and their participation in interlocking federal systems.[20] However, the example of the Austrian federal system shows that there may be a difference between political participatory rights according to the size (population) of constituent states which, according to the early terminology of Plato,[21] is called "geometric" equality. Thus, in Austria, the Land with the largest number of citizens delegates 12 representatives to the Federal Council (Bundesrat), every other Land delegates as many as the ratio in which its citizens stand to those in the largest Land, with remainders which exceed half the coefficient counting as full. At any rate, every Land is entitled to representation of at least three members. According to Article 34 of the Austrian Federal Constitutional Act, the number of members to be delegated by each Land is laid down after every general census by the federal President.

The phrasing of public tasks and the functions of sub-systems are rather more open to differentiation since they have to consider peculiar features such as ethnic origin, language, economy, society, or religion, which form the democratic foundation of a respective autonomous unit. Asymmetry therefore is a particularly frequent structure of federalism if it serves the organization of multinational states (particularly Belgium, Canada, Russia and the Federation of Bosnia-Herzegovina[22]) or protects ethnic, religious, or language minorities. Under the principle of equality a specific legal status may be required as well. Minority rights are considered to be "protection guarantees," which means that they are particular provisions designed to protect and privilege minorities which originate in a "value judgement in favour of a minority" and which should compensate for the structural discrimination minorities suffer in a majority democracy.[23] To a much higher extent, however, a specific legal status is required by the principle of (internal) self-determination, on which the regional autonomy of ethnic groups is based.

INSTITUTIONS AND PROCEDURES OF ASYMMETRIC FEDERALISM

The Mixture between Different Organizational Structures and Functions of Autonomies

The most evident form of asymmetric federalism is the connection of very different legal structures of autonomy, thereby creating a uniform system. This is only possible under the premise of functional federalism, which does not regard formal constitutional or international criteria of self-determination as being decisive, but rather establishes the structure and connection required by the principle of subsidiarity in order to perform public functions within an interlocking system consisting of different levels, as the proper organizational purpose and standard. The most important examples of such mixed systems of federalism are the following types.

The Mixture between a Federal State and Regional Autonomy. Whereas the connection between a federal state and a local autonomous unit fits with the system of federalism and is very common since local autonomy is regarded as a sub-structure of a constituent state (see, for instance, Article 116 of the Austrian Federal Constitutional Act or Article 28 of the Bonner *Grundgesetz*), the connection between a federal state and a regional autonomous unit exceeds the scope of the system. In this case, the classical federal system of "dual government," which implies that the central state and the constituent states clearly stand opposite each other, gets connected with a structurally very different system that consists of the central state and a regional autonomous unit.

The reasons for the specific treatment of an autonomous system in contrast to the constituent states may be:

1 a geographically peripheral area. For instance, Alaska and Hawaii before they were transformed into states, the Northern Territories of Canada (Northwest Territories, Yukon Territory, Nunavut) or the Northern Territories on the Australian continent which lack the population required to establish them as genuine constituent states;

2 a specific politico-historic development. For instance, the islands around Australia (Ashmore and Cartier Islands, Christmas Island, Cocos (Keeling) Islands, Coral Sea Islands, Jervis Bay, Norfolk Island), which are territories outside the continent and which are granted different types of autonomy by federal law in accordance with Article 122 of the Australian constitution. Regarding the USA, one could mention the Unincorporated Territories – i.e., American Samoa, Guam and the Virgin Islands – and the Incorporated Territories – i.e., the Commonwealth of Northern Marianas and the Commonwealth of Puerto Rico; or

3 ethnic differences within the population of a certain area. A striking example is the autonomy of the German-speaking population in Belgium. This contrasts with the situation in Austria where attempts to establish an autonomous organization of the ethnic group of Carinthian Slovenes have had no success yet. In Canada, the Nunavut Territory which was claimed by the Inuit of Nunavut came into existence in 1999. In November 2000, three new states (Chhatisgarh, Jharkhand and Uttaranchal) were created in India according to Articles 3 and 4 of the Indian constitution. In striking contrast to the previous process of territorial re-organization in India, the reasons for the recent creation of states may not be found in language differences, but rather a specific regional economic situation combined with traditional factors of ethnic identity.

The territory of the federation's capital is frequently given regional autonomy (see, for instance, USA, Brazil, Nigeria). Even if the capital or other cities are established as constituent states within a federal system (see, for instance, Austria[24] or Germany[25]), this is a case of asymmetric federalism, because these cities are thereby brought out of the regular structure of local government in a federal state and thereby the structure of constituent states is shaped asymmetrically as well. A most impressive example of a mixture between extremely different legal structures of autonomous systems was the former USSR, from which the Russian Federation inherited a wide range of federal and regional sub-systems featuring very different legal structures. The Russian Federation now consists of 89 federated units which formally are on an equal level – i.e., the Republics (21), the Regions (49), the Territories (6), the Autonomous Areas (10), the cities with special status (2) and the Jewish Autonomous Region.[26]

The connection between former colonies and their motherland appears to be a particular constitutional problem if the motherland is a unitary state. The examples of France and England show that not only all kinds of autonomy, but also federal and even confederal structures of "self-government" have been connected with totally different structures featured by their respective motherland. The French Départements d'outre-mer (French Guiana, Guadeloupe, Martinique, Réunion) are considered to belong to the motherland, whereas the Territoires d'outre-mer (i.e., the overseas territories French Polynesia, New Caledonia, Wallis and Futuna) are granted a limited form of self-government. In contrast, the forms of self-government of the British Dependent Territories are completely different. Anguilla, Bermuda, the Cayman Islands, Montserrat and the Turks and Caicos Islands have been granted "internal autonomy," and all Dependent Territories were given constitutions and parliaments.

The Mixture between Different Regional and Local Autonomies. Italy,[27] Spain[28] and the United Kingdom[29] are the most striking examples of states incorporating very different types of regions the specific competencies and functions of which arise from a certain politico-historic development, ethnic or national particularities and different political aims of the respective communities – in fact, from the concretization of the subsidiarity principle in its triple meaning, to which this paper has already referred.

With regard to Italy, the specific autonomies of Sardinia, Sicily, Trentino-Alto Adige, Friuli-Venezia Giulia and Valle d'Aosta are worth mentioning. In the United Kingdom, "devolution" is the key word used for describing the recent process of decentralization, which has been realized by the Labour government after a long historic process. One should be aware, however, that the strengthening of regional identity has only applied to certain parts of the United Kingdom (Scotland, Wales, Northern Ireland and Greater London). Moreover, it has not been applied in a uniform, but rather a thoroughly asymmetric way. Scotland may be seen as the region which has gained most from devolution, although the Scotland Act 1998 lacks many elements deemed to be essential for establishing federal or "quasi-federal" systems.

A similar diversity and asymmetry of autonomies can also be found in states featuring strong local government, such as, in particular, the Scandinavian states. In Sweden, for example, the *primärkommuner* (289) and the *läns/landstingkommuner* (21) form two different layers of local government.[30] The 21 *läns* have a strange dual organizational structure. Institutionally, they are separated into an administrative-national level (*länsstyrelse*, national administrative authorities in the *läns*) and a political-municipal level (*landsting*, a directly elected provincial parliament), each of them with its own competencies, which increasingly rival each other.[31] In the United Kingdom, too, completely different types of autonomous (sub)units – i.e., counties (47), metropolitan counties (7), districts (26), regions (9) and islands areas (3) – belong to "local government." Moreover, the number, type and structure of these units are different depending on to which part of the United Kingdom (England, Scotland, Wales and Northern Ireland) they belong. In the Netherlands, both the *Waterschappen* (66) and the *Gemeenten* (633) play an essential role at the sub-national level, whereas the *Provincies* (12) are of comparatively little political and administrative importance. Local government is also split into two levels in Germany (*Gemeinde-Kreis*), France (*commune-département*), Italy (*municipio-provincia*) and many other states of the world.

In these states one can see not only different levels of local government as a regular structure, but also a special status of larger cities and agglomerations which may be of a differentiated, complex or homogeneous nature. Greater London may serve as an example since it was granted special status by the Greater London Authority Act 1999.

All these different types of regional and local autonomy regularly form cooperative institutions between each other. These institutions are particularly intended to secure representation of interests and participation in joint projects as well as in interlocking tasks shared between them and the national state.

The Differentiated (Asymmetric) Federal State. In contrast to the ruling constitutional doctrine[32] the difference between individual constituent states regarding their competencies or functions within a federal system is not at all unusual but – just as the special status of regions – frequently arises from a specific national, ethnic or politico-historic development of certain constituent states. According to the principle of subsidiarity, their legal status has to be differentiated adequately. In this context, the special status of the province of Québec in Canada,[33] of the constituent states of Sabah and Sarawak in Malaysia[34] and of the constituent state of Jammu and Kashmir in India[35] is worth mentioning. Even in such a centralized and unitary federal system as Austria one cannot fail to realize a strong constitutional disposition to asymmetry which, however, is hardly being used presently, since the homogeneity of the system is politically much more favoured.

The Differentiation and Dynamics of the Distribution of Competencies

If the procedure of distributing competencies in a federal system meets with the criteria of subsidiarity, which have been mentioned already, the allocation of functions at the central or at the autonomous levels can much better comply with the actual and political particularities of individual sub-systems and become much more flexible than the traditional structure of tiers possessing uniform, inflexible competencies. If, on the contrary, participatory rights and objectified value judgements (material criteria) are combined in order to distribute autonomous competencies, a fair balance between individual and collective interests will be observed in each case and the system as a whole will be adjusted according to the principles of interlocking functions ("functional federalism") rather than according to the model of a strictly separated multi-tier governance. Nevertheless, even within a system of functional federalism one must not abandon the principle of performing functions independently, since the nature and the specific capacity of a system featuring autonomous structures are based on it, thereby providing a prerequisite of the principle of "competitive federalism."

The differentiation and dynamics of the distribution of competencies in an asymmetric federal system are based on the following elements, which will be described in the following pages[36]:

1 the combination between a relatively homogeneous basic structure and specific competencies;
2 devolution or delegation of specific competencies;
3 the combination between regional and supra-regional competencies regarding the same public task; and
4 opting out of joint tasks.

The Combination between a Relatively Homogeneous Basic Structure and Specific Competencies. Within a federal system featuring a variety of autonomous sub-systems, uniform allocation of basic competencies will be required regularly, not only for reasons of clarity and efficiency, but also because functions should be performed in a citizen-oriented way. Only on such a uniform basis should individual regions or constituent states be differentiated according to their particularities.

Devolution or Delegation of Specific Competencies. The flexibility of the distribution of competencies is formally granted by the possibility to transfer and re-transfer competencies between the central and the autonomous unit. In conformity with the principle of subsidiarity a competence must be transferred if a unit claims it and if the other units consent. Furthermore, such a transfer must meet the criteria of adequacy and capacity of the various units.

The Combination between Regional and Supra-regional Competencies Regarding the Same Public Task. Although autonomous regional competencies should usually comprise self-contained public functions and not only parts of a function, the principle of allocating competencies separately at different levels cannot be realized completely because of the complexity of many of today's public functions. In Europe, the same administrative matter frequently involves regional, national and European – often also international – competencies. In this case, the principle of subsidiarity on the one hand demands participatory rights for the lower tiers; on the other hand, legislation and planning at the higher levels should primarily be given the form of final directives so that scope may be left for autonomous regional implementation and concretization.

Opting Out of Joint Tasks. Modern federalism can be characterized not only as a system of interlocking functions, but also by a strong cooperative component to be applied if tasks are performed jointly according to overlapping programs and organizations. Asymmetric federalism therefore signifies that individual autonomies may choose to carry out a respective competence autonomously instead of performing it jointly, if it is their wish and if the same standards of performance are granted.

Regional Clusters as Performers of Tasks

For various reasons, individual regions (constituent states) may perform autonomous competencies jointly, something which is called horizontal "cooperative federalism." Such cooperation is often founded on specific economic reasons – such as the saving of expenses – or it may be citizen-oriented, since a joint performance standardizes services and legal rules. As is the case with the autonomous Italian provinces of South Tyrol/Alto Adige and Trentino, there may also be historic and/or politico-geographic reasons for the cooperation of neighbouring regions. On the other hand, one can observe rather frequently that historically fixed borderlines do not correspond to today's functional and economic networks within the border area. Thus, new trans-border planning units ("regions" in a technical sense) become necessary. With regard to Austria, one could mention the so-called "Planungsgemeinschaft Ost" ("Planning Group East") which was founded by the Länder Burgenland, Lower Austria and Vienna in 1978,[37] and also several agreements between the Länder which were concluded in order to allow cooperative spatial planning in border areas.[38] Moreover, a joint performance of regional tasks may be also suitable because of the small size of autonomous units. Within homogeneous federal systems, such inter-regional cooperation regularly requires formal agreements and auxiliary bodies (see Article

15(a) of the Austrian Federal Constitutional Act which entitles the federation and the Länder to conclude agreements among themselves about matters within their respective sphere of competence), since there must not be a new "third level" which possesses sovereignty (i.e., inter-regional cooperative bodies must not be sovereign since this would create a third level of government between the central authorities and the autonomous units). This applies both to the national sphere and, increasingly, to trans-border regional cooperation. Article 16 of the Austrian Federal Constitutional Act, for example, entitles the Länder to conclude treaties with states, or their constituent states, bordering on Austria, in matters within their own sphere of competence, but not to transfer "sovereign rights" as the federation is entitled to do under Article 9 of the Austrian Federal Constitutional Act. The same applies to the (delegated) power to conclude international treaties which the Italian border regions are granted according to the Madrid Framework Convention and its implementing regulations.

Asymmetric federalism, on the contrary, forms the basis of a possible "third level" consisting of integrated regional autonomous units between the state and the regions, if such a level is required on account of a particular politico-geographical situation or because of the region's intention to enhance the integration of its autonomous power ("pooling").[39] In particular, such a concept could serve the joint performance of European programs and planning by neighbouring regions that co-operate through joint bodies ("*Europaregionen*"). The "Treaty of Karlsruhe" which was concluded in 1996–1997 between France, Germany, Luxembourg and Switzerland (the latter on behalf of the cantons Solothurn, Basel-Stadt, Basel-Landschaft, Aargau and Jura), for instance, sets an example of how to institutionalize trans-border cooperation between territorial entities and public authorities. Moreover, several bilateral "Frontier Treaties" have been concluded so far – for instance, the Treaty of Isselburg-Anholt regarding the German-Dutch Border in 1991–1993, the Treaty of Rome regarding the French-Italian border in 1993–1995, the Treaty of Bayonne regarding the Spanish-French Border in 1995–1997 and the Treaty of Mainz regarding the German-Belgian border in 1996–1997.

Specific Systems of Cooperation between Central States and Autonomous Units

Whereas general cooperation between a central state and all of its autonomous sub-systems is a characteristic feature of each type of federalism, the specific cooperation between the central unit and an individual autonomous unit creates asymmetries. Their adequacy and effects on the remaining non-participating sub-systems have to be strictly balanced against each other.

Such "special compacts" within federal systems may be adequate, though, if they accrue from the ethnic particularities of a respective region, from a specific politico-geographical position, from the historic development, but also from economic necessities that demand an equalization of the weaknesses or disadvantages of regional capacities. The so-called "particular federal law"[40] or exceptions from the general legal system of a state, particularities of the educational system or social administration may be legally provided for in certain regions without changing the general distribution of competencies between the state and its autonomous sub-systems. All kinds of asymmetric autonomy, however, presuppose an agreement between the central state and the respective region as well as a reason for a special treatment. If these preconditions change, the specific legal status or the special economic program which the state grants the region falls away.

Constitutional Differentiation

An essential characteristic of a federal state is the constitutional autonomy of the constituent states, which means that the states are free to give themselves constitutions of their own as long as they do not violate federal constitutional law. Within the wide borders of federal constitutional homogeneity, however, constituent states may use their constitutional autonomy in order to establish their own electoral and governmental systems, their fundamental aims and programs, the administrative organization, fundamental rights, and the internal structure of (local or functional) autonomous units, the shape of which may differ in accordance with their own traditions and political ideas.

Regions regularly do not have constitutional autonomy, but are entirely institutionalized by the constitution. The more a constitution (or "statute") considers the particularities and political ideas of the regional population – such as, for instance, Article 2 of the Treaty of Paris which grants autonomy to the Italian Province of South Tyrol/ Alto Adige – the more regional autonomy approaches the model of asymmetric federalism and the constitutional differentiation between autonomous units typical thereof. The constitutions of the Spanish Autonomous Communities feature a similar differentiation, which corresponds to their own political intentions. The pronounced constitutional differentiation of UK regional autonomies could be pointed out as well, although the particularities of British constitutional law do not allow one to speak of "constitutional autonomy."

A Differentiating Fiscal System

There is no uniform model of a federal fiscal system. In both federal and regional systems there is a wide range of models concerning the adjustment of taxes, the self-determined power to tax, and outside financing by the central state. A fiscal system that offers sub-systems different financial models, which consider their specific capacity, financial demands and efficiency with regard to the fulfilment of tasks, is typical of asymmetric federalism. If an autonomous unit is basically funded from outside means, at least the regional tax yield will have to be considered, since this is the only way to consider the connection between the economic capacity and the financial means of a region. Several systems leave the autonomous units at least a limited choice between their participation in the interlocking system and autonomous tax raising.[41] At any rate, the constitutional rules governing public finances in an asymmetric federal system must grant that differences between the competencies of different sub-systems and between their participation in the performance of joint tasks are taken into account by differentiating adequately between them with regard to the financial means with which they are endowed.

ASYMMETRIC FEDERALISM AS A EUROPEAN AND INTERNATIONAL PRINCIPLE OF ORDER

Asymmetry as a Basic Structure of European Regionalism

European regionalism is a feature not to be overlooked within the infrastructure of European integration.[42] Only since the Treaty of Maastricht (1993) have regions been considered within the organization of the European Union. This has been done through the Committee of the Regions which was established by the Treaty of Maastricht (Article 263 EC Treaty), and through the fact that member states have been entitled to delegate state representatives of ministerial rank to participate in the Council (Article 203 EC Treaty).[43] Moreover, regions have become increasingly important for the practical implementation and execution of programs and legal rules of the EU or the European Council. Transborder cooperation between the regions is promoted by the European Council and the EC. Frequently, the specific democratic legitimacy which accrues from the basis of a region and its participation in the integration process is emphasized.

A basic problem of European regionalism is the different structure of regions and their position within EU member states. Apart from constituent states and regions that have the power to legislate, there are regions which may be characterized as self-governing bodies or planning units. Many member states lack regions at all, and in these cases higher-level local government which performs functions similar to those of the regions is a rather frequent structure. The consequence is that regions and municipalities of very different character are represented within the joint organs of European organizations, and the particular quality of regions featuring legislative functions is not considered correspondingly. Federal sub-systems often do not have the power to act at the European level, since they are bound by different internal rules,[44] and the central states must represent the regional competencies and interests in the decision-making process of European organs, which are only vested with participatory rights themselves.

This strange incongruity between the functions and the organizational position of higher-levelled regions within European integration can be expected to change if the principle of subsidiarity is extended from European law to the regional and local level, and if asymmetric federalism is simultaneously brought to fruition as a structural principle of the establishment and the participatory rights of European regions. Since a thorough homogeneity of competencies and structures of European regions is neither within reach nor desirable, their organizational incorporation within the institutions and procedures of the European Union and the European Council must be asymmetric, depending on their different structures and functions.[45]

At any rate, regions that have the power to legislate and whose competencies correspond to the "federalistic standard," should obtain the power to act at the European level as far as their scope is concerned and should get full authority with regard to regional trans-border co-operation as well – in particular, this would apply to the implementation of European programs and directives. Since the internal position of many European regions has been strengthened, it seems logical that they should get more power at the European level, particularly considering that the principle of constitutional homogeneity which is applicable to the relationship between national constitutions and the (future) European constitution would also require homogeneous treatment of the regions. In today's Europe, the democratic principle is not solely the centralistic model of the classical French concept of the nation-state, but – in many states – a highly structured and differentiated model of democracy conforming to the concept of asymmetric federalism. A democratic legitimization of the European Union through a future European constitution must consider these federal structures of European democracy, in order to stop the process of centralization and the tendency of alienating citizens from the process of integration.

FEDERALISM AND REGIONALISM AS AN INTERNATIONAL MINORITY PROTECTION SYSTEM

Collective minority rights and, in particular, a minority's claim to self-government within its autochthonous territory are alien to universal international law. However, in the nineteenth and twentieth centuries a system of protection through international treaties was developed, including agreements that are concluded in order to grant federal or regional autonomy. The latter may be regarded as the most highly developed form of collective minority protection.[46] Very different rules apply to the detailed provisions concerning institutions and competencies of autonomous political systems. They have in common, however, a normative connection between international and national law which makes federalistic structures *sui generis*. By including third states into the international guarantee system or through constitutional agreements between the constituent ethnic groups, very complex connections between federal and confederal elements of a political system may develop which cannot easily be registered among the traditional categories of national law. A most striking example of legal complexity is the constitutional framework of Bosnia-Herzegovina.[47]

The question of whether minority protection through regional autonomy (if it meets a "federalistic standard") or multinational federalism corresponds to a people's right to self-determination is controversial.[48] In my opinion, minority protection through regional autonomy is acceptable if an ethnic group is allowed to participate in establishing the autonomy.

THE REGIONS AS THE COMPONENTS OF GLOBALIZATION

Classical international law regarded only states as international subjects, excluding federal sub-systems from direct international relationships. Today this basic structure of international relations has become much more relative. Due to the process of globalization, the monopoly national states had with regard to legal relations with foreign states has lost importance since other legal subjects – including international organizations, multinational enterprises, but also individual human beings – increasingly link directly across borders.

Regions, too, are included in these new transnational networks of legal and economic relations and thus have to adapt their politics to their changed situation. On the one hand, they have to consider the direct effects international organizations and their legislation have on their autonomous competencies and political scopes, while on the other hand, trans-border and international regional activities gain increasing importance with regard to the success or failure of regional policy regarding national and international competition. If federal sub-systems themselves have the power to enact constitutions and to legislate, they will increasingly be bound by the growing network of international rules concerning human rights and environmental protection, social welfare and the protection of cultural heritage.

The discrepancy between the legal involvement of regions and their almost complete lack of power to act at the international level continues to grow. This gives rise to one of the most important aims of constitutional reform which federal and more highly developed regional systems want to achieve. Thus, only if the regional structures have been adequately considered by international law, will asymmetric federalism develop an up-to-date organizational framework of regional autonomy.

NOTES

The author would like to thank Dr. Anna Gamper, for her assistance in preparing this chapter.

1 The term self-determined (*selbständig*) is used in Article 2 and Article 15 paragraph 1 of the Austrian Federal Constitutional Act. It indicates the statehood of the Länder in contrast to local autonomy which is granted in Article 118 of the Austrian Federal Constitutional Act ("non-delegated sphere of competencies"); see P. Pernthaler, "Die Stellung der Länder in der Bundesverfassung", in *Österreichische Parlamentarische Gesellschaft* (ed.), 75 Jahre Bundesverfassung, Wien: Verlag Österreich, 1995, 659 et seq. (659 et seq. and 666 et seq.). Similarly, the Swiss Federal Constitution of 1999 designates the cantons as "sovereign" (Article 3 of the Swiss Federal Constitution of 1999); see P. Saladin, *Art 3 BV 1874*, in J.-F. Aubert, K. Eichenberger, J.P. Müller, R.A. Rhinow, D. Schindler (eds), *Kommentar zur Bundesverfassung der Schweizerischen Eidgenossenschaft vom 29.* Mai 1874, Basel: Helbing & Lichtenhahn/Schulthess/Stämpfli, 1986, paragraph 42 et seq.; and U. Häfelin, W. Haller, *Schweizerisches Bundesstaatsrecht*, Zürich: Schulthess, 1998, 4th ed., para 168.

2 See the definition of "European regionalism" given by the European Parliament in its "Community Charter of Regionalisation," *Official Journal* 1988, C 326; P. Häberle, *Der Regionalismus als werdendes Strukturprinzip des Verfassungsstaates und als europarechtliche Maxime*, in *AÖR*, 1993, 1 et seq. (16 et seq.).

3 The definition and criteria were developed by P. Pernthaler, I. Kathrein, K. Weber, *Der Föderalismus im Alpenraum*, Wien: Braumüller, 1982, 33 et seq.

4 See H. Neuhold, "Abgrenzungen, Strukturmerkmale und Besonderheiten der Völkerrechtsordnung", in H. Neuhold, W. Hummer, C. Schreuer (eds),

Österreichisches Handbuch des Völkerrechts, Wien: Manz, 1997, 3rd ed., 8 et seq.; I. Seidl-Hohenveldern, *Die Staaten,* ibidem, 134 et seq. (144 et seq.).

5 D. Schindler, "Differenzierter Föderalismus", in W. Haller, A. Kölz, G. Müller, D. Thürer (eds), FS U. Häfelin, Zürich: Schulthess, 1989, 371 et seq.; H. Huber, *Die Gleichheit der Gliedstaaten im Bundesstaat,* in *ÖZÖR* 18, 1968, 247 et seq. See also the opposed position of P. Pernthaler, *Der differenzierte Bundesstaat,* Wien: Braumüller, 1992.

6 See their Statute of Autonomy, i.e., the *Ley Orgánica 10/1982,* based on Article 143 of the Spanish constitution, and the *Ley Orgánica 11/1982,* based on Article 150 of the Spanish constitution which grants a specific delegation of certain competencies.

7 Cf. chapter 7 (Articles 225–234) of the Portuguese constitution and the respective Statutes of Autonomy based on Article 226 of the Portuguese constitution.

8 See section 120 of the Finnish constitution and the Statute of Self-Government for Åland; in detail see L. Hannikainen, *Cultural, Linguistic and Educational Rights in the Åland Islands,* Helsinki: 1992.

9 Regarding the term asymmetric federalism, see the references given by P. Pernthaler, "(Kon)Föderalismus und Regionalismus als Bewegungsgesetze der europäischen Integration", in *JRP,* 1999, 48 et seq. (62[note 104]).

10 See Ch. Millon-Delsol, *L'état subsidiaire,* Paris: Presses Université de France, 1992; A. Riklin/G. Batliner (eds), *Subsidiarität: Ein interdisziplinäres Symposium,* Vaduz: Verlag der Liechtensteinischen Akademischen Gesellschaft, 1994; A. Waschkuhn, *Was ist Subsidiarität?,* Opladen: Westdeutscher Verlag, 1995; K.W. Nörr and Th. Oppermann (eds), *Subsidiarität: Idee und Wirklichkeit,* Tübingen: J.C.B. Mohr (Paul Siebeck), 1997 and P. Pernthaler, "(Kon-)Föderalismus".

11 These three dimensions were developed by P. Pernthaler, "(Kon-)Föderalismus", cit., 56 et seq.; cf. also idem, *Bundesstaat,* cit., 18 et seq.

12 "*Quadragesimo Anno,*" Pius XI., 1931, section 5, para 79 and 80 (Acta Apostolicae Sedis 23, 1931, 203); cf. H. Stadler, *Subsidiaritätsprinzip und Föderalismus,* Freiburg: Universitäts-Buchhandlung, 1951; A. F. Utz, *Formen und Grenzen des Subsidiaritätsprinzips,* Heidelberg: Kerle, 1956; A. Klose, W. Mantl, V. Zsifkovits (eds), *Katholisches Soziallexikon,* Innsbruck: Tyrolia/Styria, 1980, 2nd ed., 2994 et seq.; P. Pernthaler, "(Kon-)Föderalismus", cit., 57.

13 See "*Quadragesimo anno,*" section 5, paragraph 80 and ibid.

14 See Article 2 EU Treaty, Article 5 EC Treaty and the Protocol (No. 30) on the Application of the Principles of Subsidiarity and Proportionality, *Official Journal* 1997, C 340/105, and the ruling doctrine.

15 The meaning of the principle of subsidiarity as a procedural rule is particularly emphasized, without, however, attempting to concretize it as is done here, by M. Frenkel, *Föderalismus und Bundesstaat,* II, Bern: Lang, 1986, No. 957 et seq.; and P. Pernthaler, *Kompetenzverteilung in der Krise,* Wien: Braumüller, 1989, 143 et seq.

16 See P. Pernthaler, *Bundesstaat*, cit., 22.

17 There are plans to intensify this principle in order to develop the constitution to a "centre of gravitation" of the (enlarged) EU; see J. Fischer, "Vom Staatenbund zur Föderation – Gedanken über die Finalität der europäischen Integration", in *Integration*, 2000, 149 et seq.; H. Schneider, *Alternativen der Verfassungsfinalität: Föderation, Konföderation – oder was sonst?*, ibidem, 171 et seq.; B. Kohler-Koch, *Ziele und Zukunft der Europäischen Union: Eine Frage der Perspektive*, ibidem, 185 et seq.; and Ch. Busse, "Braucht Europa einen Kern?", in *Aus Politik und Zeitgeschichte* B 47/2000, 2000, 3 et seq.

18 See P. Pernthaler, "(Kon-)Föderalismus", cit., 62.

19 The democratic and legal homogeneity of constitutional systems primarily is a typical organizational category of federal states. Regarding Austria cf. K. Weber, "Wirtschaftseinheit und Bundesstaat", in I. Seidl-Hohenveldern (ed.), *Österreich als einheitliches Wirtschaftsgebiet und die europäische Gemeinschaft*, FS H. Klinghoffer, Wien/New York: Springer, 1988, 141 et seq. (152 et seq.) and P. Pernthaler, K. Weber, "Landeskompetenzen und bundesstaatliches Homogenitätsprinzip", in O. Martinek, G. Wachter (eds), *Arbeitsleben und Rechtsordnung*, FS G. Schnorr, Wien: Manz, 1988, 557 et seq.; regarding Germany cf. K. Stern, *Das Staatsrecht der Bundesrepublik Deutschland*, I, München: C.H. Beck, 1984, 2nd ed., 704 et seq.; from a comparative perspective see M. Frenkel, *Föderalismus und Bundesstaat*, 23 et seq. However, homogeneity as an organizational category can be found in confederations as well (e.g., in a particularly pronounced way in the "Deutscher Bund" of 1815) and has been expressly embodied as "horizontal and vertical" constitutional homogeneity of the European Union and EU member states by Article 6 EU Treaty; see P. Pernthaler, P. Hilpold, "Sanktionen als Instrument der Politikkontrolle – der Fall Österreich", in *Integration*, 2000, 105 et seq.; and F. Schorkopf, *Homogenität in der Europäischen Union – Ausgestaltung und Gewährleistung durch Art. 6 Abs. 1 und Art. 7 EUV*, Berlin: Duncker & Humblot, 2000.

20 The equality of participatory rights of all (different) autonomies ("political equality") is urged by Schindler, *Differenzierter Föderalismus*, 372.

21 Plato, *Gorgias*, and idem, *Nomoi*.

22 Whether the qualification "multination state" applies to Spain, is controversial; with regard to the United Kingdom it may be assumed to be the reason for the Northern Irish, perhaps also the Scottish autonomy.

23 See P. Pernthaler, *Allgemeine Staatslehre und Verfassungslehre*, Wien: Springer, 1996, 2nd ed., 64 et seq.; and P. Hilpold, *Minderheitenschutz in Österreich und in Italien* (forthcoming).

24 See the status of Vienna (Articles 108–112 of the Austrian Federal Constitutional Act).

25 The city-states of Hamburg, Bremen and Berlin were explicitly termed Länder in Article 23 of the Bonner *Grundgesetz* (unamended version)

before the Treaty of Union (BGBl. II S. 889). Since then the Preamble of the Bonner *Grundgesetz* has enumerated them explicitly; see A. Dittmann, "Föderalismus in Gesamtdeutschland", in J. Isensee, P. Kirchhof (eds), *Handbuch des Staatsrechts*, Heidelberg: C.F. Müller, 1997, 229 (234).

26 See Article 5 and Article 65 et seq. of the Russian constitution. It must be noted, however, that many of the Russian constituent units have negotiated specific treaties with Moscow relating to their particular powers.

27 See generally Articles 114 et seq. of the Italian constitution and the Constitutional Acts regarding the specific autonomies, based on Article 116 of the Italian constitution.

28 See Articles 143 et seq. of the Spanish constitution; see D. Nohlen, J.J.G. Encinar (eds), *Der Staat der Autonomen Gemeinschaften in Spanien*, Opladen: Leske & Budrich, 1992; T. Wiedmann, *Die Erfindung des Autonomiestaates*, in *ZaöRV*, 1997, 363 et seq.; K. Wendland, *Spanien auf dem Weg zum Bundesstaat?*, Baden-Baden: Nomos, 1998.

29 Devolution has been embodied in the Scotland Act 1998, the Government of Wales Act 1998, the Northern Ireland Act 1998 and the Greater London Authority Act 1999. See, for example, V. Bogdanor, *Devolution in the United Kingdom*, Oxford: Oxford University Press, 2001.

30 See chapter 1, Article 7 of the Swedish constitution.

31 Regarding this conflict as well as the attempts to reform the "regional chaos" see L. Weihe-Lindeborg, "Schweden – Von rigorosem Unitarismus zu modellhafter Regionalisierung", in *Europäisches Zentrum für Föderalismus-Forschung*, Tübingen (ed.), 266 et seq.

32 D. Schindler, "Differenzierter Föderalismus", in W. Haller, et al (eds), 1989.

33 See for example, Articles 93, 98 and 133 of the Canadian Constitution Act 1867.

34 See Article 95(b-e) of the Malaysian constitution.

35 See Article 370 of the Indian constitution and the Constitution [Application to Jammu and Kashmir] Order 1954.

36 The following systematics of a dynamic and differentiated distribution of competencies was developed first by P. Pernthaler, *Bundesstaat*, cit., 23 et seq.; the autonomous competencies of the special autonomy of the Italian province of South Tyrol (Alto Adige) were mainly fixed in accordance with this system.

37 *Vereinbarung über die Errichtung einer Planungsgemeinschaft zwischen den Ländern Burgenland, Niederösterreich und Wien* (e.g. Burgenland LGBl 1978/20).

38 For example, between Salzburg and Upper Austria in 1978 ("*Vereinbarung der Länder Oberösterreich und Salzburg über die Zusammenarbeit in Angelegenheiten der Raumordnung im gemeinsamen Grenzgebiet*," e.g. Salzburg LGBl 1978/86, which was amended by LGBl 1993/89).

39 See P. Pernthaler, *Bundesstaat*, 31 and 36; and D. Schindler, "Differenzierter Föderalismus", 386 regarding the established practice of "pooling"

the legislations in Austria and Canada. See also the novel draft about the interactive "second level region" Trentino-South Tyrol by G. Andreatta, P. Pernthaler, R. Toniatti, *Prime riflessioni sulla necessità giuridico-politica e sui fondamenti costituzionali di uno speciale ente comune comprendente l'Alto Adige-Südtirol e il Trentino, nel caso di una riforma in senso federale dello stato,* n.d.

40 Regarding the legal figure of "particular federal law" see P. Pernthaler, *Bundesstaat,* 63 et seq.

41 See the examples of highly differentiated federalistic fiscal systems given by D. Schindler, "Differenzierter Foderalismus", 383 et seq.

42 See the references given by P. Pernthaler, "(Kon-)Föderalismus", cit. 59 et seq.; P. Häberle, op. cit., 1 et seq.; O. Audéoud (ed.), *Les Régions dans L'Europe – L'Europe des Régions,* Baden-Baden: Nomos, 1999; B. Kohler-Koch (ed.), *Interaktive Politik in Europa,* Opladen: Leske und Budrich, 1998; A. Benz, *Regionalisierung,* Opladen, Leske und Budrich, 1999.

43 See T. Wiedmann, "Der Ausschuss der Regionen nach dem Vertrag von Amsterdam", in *EuR,* 1999, 49, et seq.; V.M. Hackel, "Subnationale Strukturen im supranationalen Europa", in W. Graf Vitzthum (ed.), *Europäischer Föderalismus,* Berlin: Duncker & Humblot, 2000, 57 et seq. (76 et seq.); R. Hrbek, "Der Ansschuss der Regionen – Eine Zwischenbilanz zur Entwicklung der jüngsten EU-Institution und ihrer Arbeit" in *Euopäisches Zentrum für Föderalismus-Forschung,* Tübingen (ed.), op. cit., 461 et seq.

44 Regarding Germany see Article 23 paragraphs 4–7 of the Bonner *Grundgesetz;* regarding Austria see Article 23(d) paragraphs 1, 2 and 4 of the Federal Constitutional Act.

45 See the model shown by P. Pernthaler, "(Kon-)Föderalismus", 62 et seq.; see also the political institutionalization of the "*Konferenz der Präsidenten der regionalen gesetzgebenden Parlamente*" (cf. Institut für Föderalismus [ed.], *24. Bericht über die Lage des Föderalismus in Österreich [1999],* Wien: Braumüller, 2000, 71 et seq.).

46 Regarding the historic development of European minority law see F. Ermacora, *Menschenrechte in der sich wandelnden Welt,* I, Wien: Verlag der Österreichischen Akademie der Wissenschaften, 1974, 234 et seq., 352 et seq. and F. Pan, *Der Minderheitenschutz im Neuen Europa und seine historische Entwicklung,* Wien: Braumüller, 1999.

47 See W. Graf Vitzthum, M. Mack, "Multiethnischer Föderalismus in Bosnien-Herzegowina", in W. Graf Vitzthum (ed.), op. cit., 81 et seq.

48 See F. Ermacora, *Autonomie;* H-J. Heintze, *Selbstbestimmungsrecht und Minderheitenrechte im Völkerrecht,* Baden-Baden: Nomos, 1994; S. Simon, *Autonomie im Völkerrecht. Ein Versuch zum Selbstbestimmungsrecht der Völker,* Baden-Baden, Nomos, 2000; P. Hilpold, *Der Osttimor-Fall. Eine Standortbestimmung zum Selbstbestimmungsrecht der Völker,* Frankfurt: Lang, 1996; M. Mohr, *Abgrenzung von Selbstbestimmungsrecht und Minderheitenschutz,* 1997.

About the Contributors

DIRK ANTHONY BALLENDORF Dr. Ballendorf received a Master's Degree in History from Howard University in Washington, DC, and his Doctorate from Harvard University. In 1977 he was appointed President of the College of Micronesia at Pohnpei in the Eastern Caroline Islands. In 1979 he joined the faculty of the University of Guam's Micronesian Area Research Center. Since 1997, Professor Ballendorf has also been a member of the faculty at the American Military University (AMU) in Manassas Park, Virginia.

Professor Ballendorf has written 10 books, more than 200 articles in academic and professional journals, and some 150 book reviews on Micronesian history, culture and politics. He has been a Fulbright Senior Fellow at Macquarie University in Australia, a Visiting Professor at Hannover University in Germany, a Visiting Professor at Wollongong University in Australia, and a Visiting Professor at the Macmillan Brown Center for Pacific Studies, University of Canterbury in New Zealand.

KAISER BENGALI Kaiser Bengali holds a PhD in Economics from the University of Karachi, Pakistan and a Masters in Economics from Boston University, USA. He is currently the Deputy Managing Director and Acting Managing Director of the Social Policy and Development Centre, Karachi, Pakistan and has earlier held research and teaching positions in Pakistan at the Sustainable Policy Development Institute, the Applied Economics Research Centre, University of Karachi, Pakistan Institute of Labour Education and Research, and abroad at the Institute of Development Studies, University of Sussex in the UK, the Institut Universitaire d'Études du Développement, University of Geneva in Switzerland, and the Consulting Centre for Finance and Investment in Saudi Arabia.

His research interests include estimation of regional accounts, urban and regional development, local governance, industrialization and employment, and a number of public policy issues. In addition to several research and conference papers, he is the author of a book titled *Why Unemployment?* and editor of a book titled *The Political Economy of Managing Water.* He is currently President of the Social Democratic Movement, a political reform movement to promote economic justice and federal democracy.

ALLAN R. BREWER-CARÍAS Allan R. Brewer-Carías obtained his law degree (1962) at the Central University of Venezuela, where he also obtained his doctorate in law (1964). He took post-graduate courses on administrative law at the University of Paris (1962–63). He is Professor Emeritus in the Faculty of Law at Central University of Venezuela, where since 1963 he has taught administrative and constitutional law. Since 1960 he has also worked at the Public Law Institute of the same university, and was its Director between 1978 to 1987. He was Visiting Scholar at the University of Cambridge, UK (1972–74), and was Simon Bolivar Professor in the Faculty of Law at Cambridge (LLM Courses) in 1985–86. He has also been Professor at the University of Paris II (1989–90) and at the University of Paris X (2000). He has also been Professor in the University of Rosario, Bogotá. He is Honorary Doctor of the University of Granada, Spain and of the University Carlos III of Madrid.

He is Vice-President of the International Academy of Comparative Law, Member of the Executive Board of the Interamerican Institute of Human Rights, Member of the Venezuelan Academy of Social and Political Sciences. He has been Senator for the Federal District, Minister of State for Decentralization, and was a Member of the National Constituent Assembly that approved the 1999 constitution. He has received the National Sciences Award of Venezuela (1981). He has written more than 100 books on public law, constitutional history and political sciences, and more than 700 articles on the same subjects in journals and edited volumes.

DAVID R. CAMERON Dr. Cameron received his MSc and his PhD from the London School of Economics. From 1968–80 he was at Trent University. He has taught in the Department of Political Science at the University of Toronto since 1985. He currently also serves as advisor to the government of Ontario on inter-governmental relations, national unity and Quebec. From 1990 to 1995 he was Special Constitutional

Advisor to the Premier of Ontario. He also served as Deputy Minister, Ministry of Intergovernmental Affairs, government of Ontario from 1987–89, and with the federal government of Canada in the Department of the Secretary of State (1982–85) and the Federal-Provincial Relations Office (1980–82).

He has written or edited a number of articles and books. Recent publications include: Editor, *The Referendum Papers: Essays on Secession and National Unity* (Toronto: University of Toronto Press, 1999); with Janice Stein and Richard Simeon, *Citizen Engagement in Conflict Resolution: Are There Lessons for Canada in International Experience?* (Toronto: C.D. Howe Institute, 1997); "National Unity and Paradigm Shifts," *Queen's Institute of Intergovernmental Relations Working Papers*, Vol. 7 (1998); "Does Ottawa Know It Is Part of the Problem?" in John Trent, Robert Young and Guy Lachapelle (eds), *Quebec-Canada: What is the Path Ahead?* (Ottawa: University of Ottawa Press, 1996); "Faltering Scapegoat: Canadian Federalism and its Prospects," in Paul Fox and Graham White (eds), *Politics: Canada* (Toronto: McGraw Hill, 1995); "Half-eaten Carrot, Bent Stick: Decentralization in an Era of Fiscal Restraint," *Canadian Public Administration*, Vol. 37, No. 3 (Fall 1994).

VALERIANO MENDES FERREIRA COSTA Professor Costa has been an Associate Professor in the Department of Political Science at the State University of Campinas, São Paulo, since 1998. Formerly he worked as an Associate Researcher in the Center of Contemporary Cultural Studies (CEDEC) in the City of São Paulo, where he took part in several research projects about the Brazilian transition to democracy, consolidation of political institutions at the state and municipal levels of government, decentralization of public policies, and reform of public administration at the federal level of government. He is co-author, with Fernando Abrucio (FGV-SP) of *Reforma do Estado e o Contexto Federativo Brasileiro* (*Reform of the State in the Brazilian Federative Context*).

MIHAILO CRNOBRNJA Dr. Crnobrnja received his MA in Economics from the University of Maryland and his PhD in Economics from the University of Belgrade. From 1974 to 1989 he was Professor of Political Economy at the Faculty of Political Science, University of Belgrade. Also during this time he was Chief Economist of the largest Yugoslav bank, a member of the Presidium of the City of Belgrade and Minister of Economic Planning in the Republic of Serbia. He ended his Yugoslav career as Ambassador of Yugoslavia to the European Union. Since moving to Canada he has taught economics, political science and business as an Adjunct Professor at McGill, Concordia and Carleton Universities and at the College of William and Mary in the United States.

He is the author or co-author of seven books and over 140 essays and articles and reviews in professional journals. His books in English include: *The Yugoslav Drama* (3rd ed., Montreal: McGill-Queen's University Press, 2002); and with Zarko Papic, *The Economic Price of War* (Zug, Switzerland: The Foundation for Peace and Crisis Management, 1996).

AISHA GHAUS-PASHA Dr. Aisha Ghaus-Pasha has about 15 years experience in teaching and undertaking research and consulting assignments in public finance, social sector economics, and urban and regional economics. She has a PhD from the University of Leeds, United Kingdom. She is currently Senior Technical Advisor at the Social Policy Development Centre, Karachi, Pakistan. Previously, she managed this research institute as Deputy/Acting Managing Director since 1995. Prior to that she was associated in various capacities with the Applied Economics Research Centre at the University of Karachi.

Dr. Ghaus-Pasha has been a member of several Task Forces, Committees and Commissions constituted by various governments in Pakistan on public finance, social sectors, poverty alleviation and institutional reforms. She has undertaken consultations for a number of international, multilateral and bilateral agencies like UNICEF, UNDP, the World Bank, the Asian Development Bank and the Canadian International Development Agency (CIDA). Dr. Ghaus-Pasha has published over 75 books, journal articles and reports.

ANN GRIFFITHS Dr. Ann Griffiths received her MA from the University of Calgary and her PhD from Dalhousie University. She is currently Assistant Professor in the Department of Political Science at Dalhousie University, and Publications Manager for the Centre for Foreign Policy Studies at Dalhousie. Her research interests include federalism, peacebuilding and democratization. She was formerly Managing Editor of *The Canadian Journal of Law and Society/Revue canadienne de droit et société*, and Editor of *International Insights: A Journal of International Affairs*. She is currently on the Editorial Board of the Pearson Peacekeeping Press.

Recent publications include: with Peter T. Haydon and Richard H. Gimblett (eds), *Canadian Gunboat Diplomacy: The Canadian Navy and Foreign Policy* (Fall 2000); "Introduction," in A. L. Griffiths (ed.), *Ethnicity and Conflict in the Former Yugoslavia* (December 1999); with Frank P. Harvey (eds), *Foreign and Security Policy in the Information Age* (September 1999); with Peter T. Haydon (eds), *Canada's Pacific Naval Presence: Purposeful or Peripheral?* (1999); with R.H. Thomas and Peter T. Haydon (eds), *The Changing Strategic Importance of International Shipping* (November 1998); "Introduction," in A.L. Griffiths (ed.), *Building Peace and Democracy in Post-Conflict Societies* (July 1998).

SIOBHÁN HARTY Dr. Siobhán Harty is Lecturer in Comparative European Politics in the Department of International Politics at the University of Wales, Aberystwyth. She received her PhD from McGill University and her MA from St. John's College, Oxford University, where she was a Rhodes Scholar. She specializes in the fields of nationalism, liberalism and multiculturalism. In 1996–1997 she served as Research Associate at the Instituto de Estudios Sociales Avanzados (Barcelona and Madrid) of the Consejo Superior de Investigaciones Científicas.

She has published articles that examine aspects of nationalism in Spain in the *Canadian Journal of Political Science*, *Comparative Politics* and *Law and History Review*. Recent publications include: "The Nation as a Communal Good: A Nationalist Response to the Liberal View of Community," *Canadian Journal of Political Science*, Vol. 32, No. 4 (December 1999); "The Institutional Foundations of Substate National Movements," *Comparative Politics*, Vol. 33, No. 2 (January 2001); "Restoring Order: Ethnic Conflict, Political Institutions and Peace," in Ann L. Griffiths (ed.), *Ethnicity and Conflict in the Former Yugoslavia* (Halifax: Centre for Foreign Policy Studies, 1999); "The Social Bases of a Catalan Nationalist Party: The Lliga Regionalista, 1901–1923" (under review); "Codification and State-Building in Nineteenth-Century Spain: The Failure of Civil Law Reform and the Emergence of Catalan Nationalism" (under review); *Constitutional Innovation, National Identities and Democratic Inclusiveness: The United Kingdom in Comparative Review* (work in progress).

RUDOLF HRBEK Professor Hrbek is Professor of Political Science at Tuebingen University. His main fields of interest are European integration and issues relating to the European Union, and problems of federalism. His more than 150 publications concentrate on these issues. He is Speaker of the European Center for Research on Federalism at Tuebingen University and Chairperson of the German European Community Studies Association. He has been Visiting Professor at the College of Europe (Bruges, Belgium) and at universities in the United States, Italy, Switzerland and Thailand.

JOHN KINCAID John Kincaid earned a PhD in Political Science at Temple University, Philadelphia, Pennsylvania, in 1981 and an MA in Urban Affairs at the University of Wisconsin, Milwaukee, in 1968. Dr. Kincaid is currently the Robert B. and Helen S. Meyner Professor of Government and Public Service and Director of the Meyner Center for the Study of State and Local Government at Lafayette College, Easton, Pennsylvania. He has also served as Acting Head of the Department of

Government and Law at Lafayette College (1997–98); as Kestnbaum Fellow (1994–95), Executive Director (1988–94), and Director of Research (1986–88) of the US Advisory Commission on Intergovernmental Relations, Washington, DC; and as Assistant and then Associate Professor of Political Science at the University of North Texas (1979–94). Professor Kincaid has lectured and consulted on issues of constitutionalism, federalism, inter-governmental relations, and regional and local governance throughout the United States as well as in Australia, Belgium, Brazil, Canada, Cyprus, the Czech Republic, Germany, India, Japan, Mexico, Nigeria, Russia, South Africa, Spain, Switzerland, Turkey, Ukraine, and the United Kingdom.

He is editor of *Publius: The Journal of Federalism*; editor of a 50-book series on the *Governments and Politics of the American States* being published by the University of Nebraska Press; elected fellow of the National Academy of Public Administration; member of the Editorial Board of the *African Journal of Federal Studies* and of the *State Constitutional Law Bulletin*; 2001 recipient of the Distinguished Federalism Scholar Award of the Section on Federalism and Intergovernmental Relations of the American Political Science Association. He is editor of *Political Culture, Public Policy and the American States* (1981); *Competition among States and Local Governments: Efficiency and Equity in American Federalism* (1991), co-editor of *The Covenant Connection: From Federal Theology to Modern Federalism* (2000), and author of various works on federalism and intergovernmental relations. He has also served as President of the International Association of Centers for Federal Studies (1998–2001) and as President of the Southwestern Political Science Association (1993–94).

ANDRÉ LECOURS André Lecours received his PhD from Carleton University. He is currently teaching in the Department of Political Science at Concordia University in Montreal. His research interests are nationalism, regionalism, institutional change and the foreign policy/international relations of regional governments, with an area of specialization on Western Europe and a particular focus on Belgium and Spain. He has published articles on nationalism and identity politics in *Nationalism and Ethnic Politics* and *The Canadian Journal of Political Science.* He has forthcoming articles on Belgium in *The Canadian Review of Studies in Nationalism* and *National Identities.*

GEORGE MATHEW Born in Kerala, Dr. George Mathew took his PhD in Sociology from the Jawaharlal Nehru University, New Delhi. He is the Founding Director, and still serves as Director, of the Institute of Social Sciences in New Delhi.

Some of the important academic positions he has held are: Visiting Fellow of the University of Chicago South Asian Studies Center (1981–82) and Visiting Professor, University of Padova (1988). He was awarded the Fulbright Fellowship in Summer 1991 for working at the University of Chicago. Dr. Mathew is a member of several committees of the federal government and is on the Board of Governors of national and international organizations. He has participated and presented papers in international conferences on political process, democracy, federalism, human rights, religion and society. His current specialization is local government systems, decentralization and gender equity. His major works include *Communal Road to a Secular Kerala* and *Panchayati Raj from Legislation to Movement.* He has edited the following works: *Shift in Indian Politics*; *Dignity for All: Essays in Socialism and Democracy*; *Panchayati Raj in Karnataka Today: Its National Dimensions*; *Panchayati Raj in Jammu and Kashmir*; *Status of Panchayati Raj in States of India 1994*; and *Status of Panchayati Raj in the States and Union Territories of India 2000.* He is a regular contributor to *The Hindu*, a national daily of India, and has contributed research articles and papers to national and international academic and research journals and books.

JOHN MCGARRY John McGarry was born in Belfast, Northern Ireland in 1957. He grew up in Ballymena, Co. Antrim and was educated at St. McNissi's College, Garron Tower, County Antrim, Trinity College Dublin and at the University of Western Ontario. He was a Professor of Political Science at the University of Western Ontario from 1989 to 1998, and is now Professor of Political Science at the University of Waterloo, Canada. He is a specialist in national and ethnic conflict regulation, and a regular contributor to public media. He is the editor of *Northern Ireland and the Divided World* (Oxford University Press, 2001); co-editor of *The Future of Northern Ireland* (Oxford University Press, 1990), *The Politics of Ethnic Conflict Regulation* (Routledge,1993), *State of Truce: Northern Ireland after Twenty-Five Years of War* (1995) and *Minority Nationalism and the Changing International Order* (Oxford University Press, 2001); and co-author of *The Politics of Antagonism: Understanding Northern Ireland* (Athlone Press, 1993 and 1996), and *Explaining Northern Ireland: Broken Images* (1995). His latest (co-authored) book is *Policing Northern Ireland: Proposals for a New Start* (1999). In addition he has written several articles on conflict regulation (specifically on consociationalism, secession, and state-directed population movements) in a variety of edited collections and in such journals as *Ethnic and Racial Studies*, *Nationalism and Ethnic Politics*, *Political Studies*, *Parliamentary Affairs*, *Journal of Conflict Studies*, and the *Journal of Commonwealth and Comparative Politics.*

GORDON P. MEANS Gordon P. Means is Professor Emeritus of Political Science at McMaster University in Hamilton, Ontario. He received his BA from Reed College and his MA and PhD in Political Science from the University of Washington. He was an Associate Professor at the University of Washington, 1966–67 before he moved to McMaster University and taught there from 1973 to 1992.

He has held 17 foreign research grants or academic exchanges to universities and research institutes in Malaysia, Singapore, Indonesia, India and China. He is the author and/or editor of seven books and a contributor to 16 books and numerous scholarly journal articles. His research and writing has concentrated on the states of Malaysia, Singapore and Indonesia with a primary focus on public policy issues relating to ethnicity, religion and politics, aboriginal peoples, development policies and the impact of globalization. After his retirement he held research and teaching positions with Brock University, the Shastri Indo-Canadian Institute and the University of Minnesota. He continues to remain engaged in research and writing on topics relating to Southeast Asia and South Asia.

NELSON MICHAUD Nelson Michaud (PhD, Laval) is a Professor at the École nationale d'administration publique, Researcher-Member of the Institut Québécois des Hautes Études Internationales, and Research Fellow at the Centre for Foreign Policy Studies (Dalhousie University). He has taught at Dalhousie and Laval Universities. Prior to his academic career, Dr. Michaud worked for nine years with the federal government mainly as policy analyst, including in the office of the President of the Privy Council. His current research interests are decision making, particularly in Canadian foreign policy, media and foreign policy, the impact of bureaucratic politics on policy formulation, and political/administrative institutions.

His research has been published in refereed journals including the *Canadian Journal of Political Science, Études internationales, Australian Journal of International Affairs*, the *Journal of Legislative Studies*, and the *British Review of Canadian Studies.* His work has also been published as chapters in collective works, and as articles in an encyclopedic dictionary. He has also authored several books, and with Dr. Kim Richard Nossal, he co-edited *Diplomatic Departures? Canadian Foreign Policy in the Mulroney Era* (UBC Press). He has appeared as an analyst/commentator on radio and TV (Radio-Canada, RDI, CBC, Global) and in dailies such as *Le Devoir, The Halifax Chronicle Herald*, and *The Mail Star.*

YEMILE MIZRAHI Dr. Mizrahi received her PhD in Political Science from the University of California, Berkeley (1994). She worked at the

Centro de Investigación y Docencia Económicas in México City from 1991 to spring 2001. Her fields of research are political parties, state and local government, decentralization, and federalism. Currently, she is a Public Policy Scholar at the Woodrow Wilson Center for International Scholars in Washington, DC, where she is working on the same research topics mentioned above as well as collaborating in the Center's newly launched "Mexico Project."

Some of her recent publications include: "Los Determinantes del Voto en Chihuahua: Evaluación del Gobierno, Identidad Partidista y Candidatos," Documento de Trabajo N. 106, CIDE, División de Estudios Políticos, 2000; "Las Elecciones en Puebla: La Continuidad de la Dominación Priista," Documento de Trabajo N.106, CIDE, División de Estudios Políticos, 2000; "Voto Retrospectivo y Desempeño Gubernamental: Las Elecciones de 1998 en Chihuahua," Documento de Trabajo N. 100, CIDE, División de Estudios Políticos, 1999; "La Alternancia Política en Chihuahua: El Regreso del PRI," in Víctor Alejandro Espinoza Valle (ed.), *Gobiernos de Oposición en México,* México: Grijalbo, 2000; "Dilemmas of the Opposition in Government: Chihuahua and Baja California," *Mexican Studies,* Vol. 14, No. 1 (Winter 1998); "The Costs of Electoral Success: The Partido Acción Nacional in México" in Mónica Serrano (ed.), *Governing Mexico: Political Parties and Elections,* The Institute of Latin American Studies, University of London, 1998; "Pressuring the Center: Opposition Governments and Federalism in Mexico," Documento de Trabajo No. 71, División de Estudios Políticos del CIDE, 1997. She recently finished a book about the Partido Acción Nacional (PAN) in Mexico.

FAÏSSOILI BEN MOHADJI M. Mohadji is currently Directeur Régional adjoint du Développement Rural et Chef de Service Régional Environnement Mohéli in the capital city of the Comoros, Moroni. He is also a national consultant for le Projet Biodiversité et Développement Durable. His areas of interest are rural development, the integration of women into development programs, the environment, community development, marine tortoises. He has written a number of reports and articles relating to development and the environment in the Comoros.

FESTUS NZE Since the beginning of 2001 Festus C. Nze has been Professor of Public Administration in the Department of Political Science and Administrative Studies at the University of Swaziland. He received his BA (Honours) degree in Public Administration from Ahmadu Bello University, Zaria, Nigeria in 1971. In 1981, he received an MA from the University of Minnesota (Hubert Humphrey Institute of Public Affairs). Until 1999, he taught at the Institute of

Administration, Ahmadu Bello University Zaria. From 1999 to 2000, he was a Visiting Professor in the Department of Political Science and Administrative Studies, National University of Lesotho, Southern Africa. He has published many articles in Nigerian and international scholarly journals in Public Administration. He co-edited: *Perspectives in Human Resource Development and Utilization in Nigeria.* His *Project 2010 AD: Development and Public Policy in Nigeria: Futuristic Scenarios,* has gone to publishers in the USA.

VIVIANA PATRONI Dr. Patroni received her MA and PhD from York University. She is currently Director, Centre for Research on Latin American and the Caribbean at York University in Toronto, and Associate Professor, Division of Social Sciences at York University. She has also taught at Wilfrid Laurier University (1995–2000) and Brock University (1994–95). From 1998 to 2001 she was Secretary Treasurer, Canadian Association of Latin American and Caribbean Studies (CALACS), and in July 1997 she served as an International Observer for the Mexican Congressional Elections (invited by Alianza Cívica).

Her recent publications include: "Democracy and Organized Labour in Argentina: Challenges and New Alternatives?" in Remonda Bensabat-Kleinberg and Janine Clark (eds), *Economic Liberalization, Democratization and Civil Society in the Developing World* (London and New York: Macmillan Press, 2000); with Jim Gronau, "Canadian Foreign Aid as Support for Human Rights and Democratization in Guatemala," in Liisa North and Alan Simmons (eds), *Journeys of Fear: Refugee Return and National Transformation in Guatemala* (Montreal and Kingston: McGill-Queen's University Press, 1999); "The Decline and Fall of Corporatism? Labour Legislation Reform in Mexico and Argentina in the 1990s," *Canadian Journal of Political Science* (forthcoming); "A Discourse of Love and Hate: Eva Perón and the Labour Movement (1940s-1950s)," *Canadian Journal of Latin American Studies,* Vol 24, No. 48 (December 1999); "Estado, empresarios y restructuración: Argentina y México durante los ochenta" ("State, private sector and restructuring: Argentina and Mexico during the 1980s"), *Acta Científica Venezolana* Vol. 50, No. 2 (1999), "The Politics of Labour Legislation Reform in Mexico," *Capital and Class,* Vol. 65 (Summer 1998); "Los Empresarios al Comienzo de los Gobiernos de Salinas y Menem: Cambios Económicos y Nuevos Consensos Políticos" ("The Private Sector at the Beginning of the Salinas and Menem Administrations: Economic Change and New Political Consensus"), *Historia y Grafía,* No. 3, (August 1994).

TOM PÄTZ Since August 1998 Tom Pätz has been Government Advisor in Ethiopia to the Office of the Prime Minister on behalf of the Deutsche Gesellschaft für Technische Zusammenarbeit (GTZ). He works on state reform in extremely fragile societies and exceptionally underdeveloped political-administrative systems. He studied Political Science, Economics and Business Studies at the University of Hamburg and at the Postgraduate School of Administrative Science in Speyer Public Administrative Science, both in Germany. Since 1980 he has worked for different development organizations in various functions and served in 12 developing countries mainly in the field of state-reform. He spent four years as a part-time lecturer at German universities.

PETER PERNTHALER Dr. Peter Pernthaler gained professorship at the University of Innsbruck in 1963 and subsequently worked as an academic advisor at the Office of the Federal Chancellor (Constitutional Department). From 1966 until 1968 he held a chair at the Hochschule für Bodenkulture in Vienna and since 1968 he has held a chair at the University of Innsbruck. In addition to a series of special investigations, his work includes monographs on important aspects of constitutional and administrative law as well as on political science and general theories of the state. Professor Pernthaler was Director of the Institut für Föderalismusforschung – an Institute founded by the Austrian Länder Tyrol, Vorarlberg and Salzburg – from 1975 to 2000. He is currently at Institut für öffentliches Recht, Finanzrecht und Politikwissenschaft (Institute of Public Law, Financial Law and Political Science) at the University of Innsbruck During the academic years 1979–1980 and 1980–81, Professor Pernthaler was Dean of the Faculty of Law at the University of Innsbruck. He was Visiting Professor in Australia and Canada in 1982 and 1983. Since 1996 he has been a full member of the Österreichische Akademie der Wissenschaften (Austrian Academy of Sciences).

CHERYL SAUNDERS Cheryl Saunders is Associate Dean Graduate Studies and a Director of the Melbourne JD (Juris Doctor) at the University of Melbourne. She is also Director of the Institute for Comparative and International Law and of the Centre for Comparative Constitutional Studies. She has held a personal chair in the Faculty since 1989 and is a Fellow of the Academy of Social Sciences in Australia. She has special interests in constitutional law and comparative constitutional law, including federalism and inter-governmental relations, constitutional design and change, and constitutional theory. Other positions presently held by Cheryl Saunders include Vice-President of the International Association of Constitutional Law, of the International Association of Centres for Federal Studies and the Australian Association of Constitutional Law. She is an editor of the

Public Law Review and of the constitutional title of the Laws of Australia, and a member of the editorial boards of a range of Australian and international journals, including *I.Con* and *Publius.* In 1994, Cheryl Saunders was made an Officer of the Order of Australia for services to the law and public administration.

SANFORD F. SCHRAM Dr. Schram received his MA and PhD in Political Science from SUNY/Albany. He has taught at the School of Social Work, University of Hawai'i at Manoa, the Department of Political Science, University of Hawai'i, (1996–97), Department of Political Science, Macalester College (1991–96), Department of Political Science, SUNY/Potsdam (1978–1991). Since 1997, he has been Visiting Professor at the Graduate School of Social Work and Social Research at Bryn Mawr College in Bryn Mawr, Pennsylvania. He is Co-Editor, Annual Review for *Publius: The Journal of Federalism,* 1995–2000.

Some of his recent publications include: *Words of Welfare: The Poverty of Social Science and the Social Science of Poverty* (Minneapolis, MN: University of Minnesota Press, 1995; Winner of the Michael Harrington Book Award for 1996 from American Political Science Association); co-edited with Philip T. Neisser, *Tales of the State: Narrative in U.S. Politics and Public Policy* (Lanham, MD: Rowman & Littlefield, 1997); co-edited with Samuel H. Beer, *Welfare Reform: A Race to the Bottom?* (Baltimore, MD: Johns Hopkins University Press, 1999); *After Welfare: The Culture of Postindustrial Social Policy* (New York, NY: New York University Press, 2000); with Carol Weissert, "Federalism 1995–1996: An Overview," *Publius,* Vol. 26, No. 3 (Fall 1996); with Carol Weissert, "Federalism 1996–1997: An Overview," *Publius,* Vol. 27, No. 2 (Spring 1997); with Carol Weissert, "Federalism 1997–1998: An Overview," *Publius,* Vol. 28, No. 2 (Spring 1998); with Carol Weissert, "The State of U.S. Federalism: 1998–1999," *Publius,* Vol. 29, No. 2 (Spring 1999); "In the Clinic: The Medicalization of Welfare," *Social Text,* 62, 18, 1 (Spring 2000); with Carol Weissert, "The State of U.S. Federalism: 1999–2000," *Publius,* Vol. 30, No. 1–2 (Winter/Spring 2000).

JULIE SIMMONS Julie Simmons received her MA from the University of Toronto. She is currently working on her PhD at the University of Toronto. Her research interests include federalism, and public policy in Canada. In particular, she is interested in federal-provincial relations, theories of political participation and the politics of process. Her current work examines the role of non-governmental interests and identities in the negotiation of recent inter-governmental agreements. She has worked as a Policy Researcher for the Ontario Ministry of Intergovernmental Affairs.

Her publications include: "Approaches to Democratic Innovation in Ministerial Council Decision Making," in Paul Thomas (ed.), *The Changing Nature of Democracy and Federalism* (Winnipeg, Manitoba: University of Manitoba Press, forthcoming); and "Recent Intergovernmental Agreements in Retrospect" and "First Ministers Conferences in Canada" are being considered for publication in Harvey Lazar, Peter Meekison and Hamish Telford (eds), *Canada: The State of the Federation, 2001–2002* (Kingston, Ontario: Institute of Intergovernmental Relations, forthcoming).

THOMAS STAUFFER Dr. Thomas Stauffer is a Senior Research Fellow at the Institute of Federalism of the University of Fribourg in Switzerland. The main activities of the Institute are consultancy and documentation in the field of Swiss federalism, research in the field of comparative constitutionalism and human rights, as well as consultancy for constitution-writing and decentralization in developing countries. Dr. Stauffer has earned a PhD in Political Science and holds a JD. He works on questions of inter-governmental fiscal relations and fiscal federalism. His publications deal mostly with issues of public finance and public management in a interdisciplinary perspective. In the article about federalism in Switzerland contained in this volume, he wrote Section 3, "Recent Political Dynamics."

ROLAND STURM Dr. Roland Sturm was educated in Political Science, History, English Language and Literature at the Free University of Berlin, University of Sheffield (England), University of Heidelberg and Stanford University. He received his PhD from the University of Heidelberg in 1981. In 1988–89 he was Professor of Public Administration at the University of the Bundeswehr in Hamburg; from 1991–96 he was Professor of Political Science at the University of Tubingen; in 1992 he was Visiting Professor at the University of Washington (Seattle); and since 1996 he has been the Chair of Political Science at the University of Erlangen, Nuremberg. He has written 21 books and numerous articles in the fields of federalism and regional policies; politics of European integration; German politics, comparative politics and comparative public policy, and economic politics. Recent publications include *The Information Society and the Regions in Europe: A British-German Comparison*, edited with Georg Weinmann (Baden-Baden: Nomos, 2000), and *Foderalismus in Deutschland* (Opladen: Leske & Budrich, 2001).

URS THALMANN-TORRES Urs Thalmann-Torres is Research Fellow at the International Research and Consulting Center of the Institute of Federalism of the University of Fribourg in Switzerland. The main activities of the Institute are consultancy and documentation in the field of Swiss federalism, research in the field of comparative constitutionalism and human rights, as well as consultancy for constitution-writing and decentralization in developing countries. Mr. Thalmann-Torres is presently writing his doctoral dissertation in the field of Swiss and comparative federalism. Further publications and conference papers of his concern Swiss constitutionalism, and comparative federalism and decentralization. In the article on federalism in Switzerland contained in this volume, he wrote Section 2, "Constitutional Provisions Relating to Federalism."

NICOLE TÖPPERWIEN Nicole Töpperwien is a Research Fellow at the Institute of Federalism of the University of Fribourg in Switzerland. The main activities of the Institute are consultancy and documentation in the field of Swiss federalism, research in the field of comparative constitutionalism and human rights, as well as consultancy for constitution-writing and decentralization in developing countries. At the moment Ms. Töpperwien is writing her PhD dissertation which is entitled "Nation-State and Normative Diversity." Her publications predominately deal with Swiss federalism and comparative constitutional law. In the article about federalism in Switzerland contained in this volume, she wrote Section 1, "History and Development of Federalism."

JANIS VAN DER WESTHUIZEN Dr. Westhuizen received his BA (Law) and BA (Hons) from Rand Afrikaans University, his MA in Political Science from University of Stellenbosch, and his PhD from Dalhousie University in Halifax, Nova Scotia. He is currently teaching in the Political Science Programme, Faculty of Human Sciences, University of Natal (Durban). His research interests include International Relations, International Political Economy, Comparative Politics (Southern Africa and Southeast Asia).

Some of his current publications include: with Philip Nel and Ian Taylor: "Multilateralism in South Africa's Foreign Policy: In Search of a Critical Rationale," *Global Governance*, Vol. 6 (2000); "South Africa's Emergence as a Middle Power," *Third World Quarterly*, Vol. 19, No. 3 (1998); "A Forum on South African Foreign Policy? Drawing on the Canadian Experience," *The South African Journal of International Affairs*, Vol. 5, No. 2 (Winter 1998); "Can the Giant be Gentle? Peacemaking as South African Foreign Policy," *Politikon: South African Journal of Political Science*, December 1995; with Timothy M. Shaw, "Towards a Political Economy of Trade in Africa: States, Companies and Civil Societies" in Brian Hocking and Steven McGuire (eds), *Trade Politics: Actors, Issues and Processes* (New York & London: Routledge, 1999);

"Comparative Responses to the Challenges of Governance and Globalization: Malaysia and South Africa," in Tim Shaw, Sandra Maclean and Fahim Quadir (eds), *Ethnicities and Crises of Governance in Asia and Africa* (London: Macmillan, 2000); "Marketing the Rainbow Nation: The Power of the Sport, Film and Music Industry in South Africa," in Kevin Dunn (ed.), *Africa's Challenge to International Relations Theory* (London: Macmillan, 2000); with Ian Taylor and Philip Nel, "Launching a "Democratic" Foreign Policy: Post-Apartheid South Africa's Multilateral Behaviour," in Neil Macfarlane and Jens Meierhenrich (eds), *Democracy and Foreign Policy: Post-Apartheid South Africa in the International System* (Oxford: Oxford University Press, 1999); "Selling South Africa Successfully: Marketing as Foreign Policy," *Global Dialogue: An International Affairs Review Published by the Institute for Global Dialogue,* Vol. 5, No.1 (August 2000); co-edited with Philip Nel and Ian Taylor, *South Africa's Multilateral Diplomacy and Global Change* (Aldershot: Ashgate, forthcoming); Co-editor with Philip Nel, *Democratising Foreign Policy: Lessons from South Africa,* forthcoming.

RONALD L. WATTS Dr. Ronald L. Watts, is Principal Emeritus and Professor Emeritus of Political Studies at Queen's University where he has been a member of the academic staff since 1955 and was Principal and Vice-Chancellor 1974–84. He is a Fellow and former Director of the Institute of Intergovernmental Relations at Queen's University. He was President of the International Association of Centres for Federal Studies 1991–98, and is currently a member of the Board of the international Forum of Federations. On several occasions he has been a consultant to the Government of Canada during constitutional deliberations, most notably 1980–81 and 1991–92, and has been a constitutional advisor to governments in several other countries. As a political scientist he has worked for over 40 years on the comparative study of federal systems and on Canadian federalism, and has written or edited over 20 books, monographs and reports and over 60 articles and chapters in books. His most recent book is *Comparing Federal Systems* of which the second edition was published in 1999. He has received five honourary degrees. He became an Officer of the Order of Canada in 1979 and was promoted to Companion of the Order of Canada in 2000.

GARY WILSON Dr. Gary N. Wilson is an Associate at the University of Toronto's Centre for Russian and East European Studies. He holds a BA from Carleton University, and an MA and PhD from the University of Toronto. Dr. Wilson specializes in Russian federalism, with a particular focus on inter-governmental relations in the Russian natural resource sector. He will begin teaching at the University of Northern British

Columbia (UNBC) in fall 2001. He has presented numerous papers on comparative federalism and Russian politics at conferences in Canada and the United States. His most recent publication, "Reconceptualizing Intergovernmental Relations in Post-Soviet Russia: "Matreshka Federalism" and the Case of the Khanty Mansiysk Autonomous Okrug," will be published in *Post-Soviet Affairs* in 2001.

MARIE-JOELLE ZAHAR Dr. Zahar received her PhD from McGill University in Montreal. She is a Fellow at the Munk Centre for International Studies at the University of Toronto. In 1998–2000 she was a Visiting Fellow at the Center for International Security and Cooperation at Stanford University. Her most recent publication is "Proteges, Clients, Cannon Fodder: Civilians in the Calculus of Militias," in *Managing Armed Conflicts in the Twenty-First Century*, a special issue of *International Peacekeeping* (forthcoming 2001). She has contributed chapters to a number of edited volumes including, *Ethnicity and Conflict in the Former Yugoslavia* (Halifax: Centre for Foreign Policy Studies, 1999).

List of Liaison Partners of the Forum of Federations

AUSTRALIA

Centre for Comparative Constitutional Studies (Melbourne)
Prof. Cheryl Saunders, Director
Faculty of Law
723 Swanston Street (2nd Floor)
The University of Melbourne
Victoria 3010
Tel: +61-3-8344-0801
Fax: +61-3-8344-9374
e-mail: cccs@law.unimelb.edu.au

BRAZIL

Fundaçao do Desenvolvimiento Administrativo – FUNDAP *(São Paulo)*
Dr. Rui de Britto Affonso
Fundaçao do Desenvolvimiento Administrativo
428 Cristiano Viana Street
São Paulo, Brazil
Telephone: (011)-55-11-3061-1768
Fax: (011)-55-11-3061-5306
Email: raffonso@fundap.sp.gov.br

GERMANY

European Centre for Comparative Government and Public Policy (Berlin)
Dr. Joachim Jens Hesse
Rheinbabenallee 49

D-14199 Berlin
Germany
Tel: +49–30–841–7510
Fax: +49–30–841–751–11
eurozent@zedat.fu-berlin.de (jdhesse@zedat.fu-berlin.de)

INDIA
Institute of Social Sciences (New Delhi)
Dr. George Matthew
Institute of Social Sciences
8, Nelson Mandela Road, New Delhi – 110 070
IndiaPhone: (91) 11–612 1902, 612 1909, 689 5370
Fax: (91) 11–613 7027
E-mail: iss@nda.vsnl.net.in

NIGERIA
Institute for Governance and Social research – IGSR (Jos)
Prof. Isawa Elaigwu, Ph.D
Institute of Governance and Social Research
Plot No A76, Liberty Boulevard
Liberty Dam layout, P.M.B. 2156
Jos, Plateau State
Nigeria
Phone: (073) 46 17 27
Fax: (073) 46 08 94
E-mail: igsr@infoweb.abs.net

RUSSIA
Foundation for the Development of Parliamentarism in Russia (Moscow)
Alexey S. Avtonomov
Deputy President on Legal Issues
Foundation for the Development of Parliamentarism in Russia
121808, Moscow, Novyi Arbat, 21.
Russia
ph.: (095) 291–37–30, fax: (095) 202–79–63
E-mail: postmaster@legislature.ru;
Web: http: //www.legislature.ru/fund/eng/found.htm
Personal E-mail: avtonomov@legislature.ru;
Business: (095) 291–3781; Home: (095) 275–6252

SOUTH AFRICA
Community Law Centre (Bellville)
Prof. Nico Steytler, Director

Community Law Centre
University of the Western Cape
Private Bag X17
Bellville 7535
South Africa
Phone: (+ 27 21) 959-2950/1
Fax: (+ 27 21) 959-2411
E-mail: nsteyt@law1.uwc.ac.za

SWITZERLAND

Institute of Federalism (Freiburg)

Dr. Thomas Fleiner, Director
University of Freiburg
Route Englisberg 7
CH-1763 Granges-Paccot
Freiburg
Switzerland
Tel: +41-26-300-8125
Fax: +41-26-300-9724
federalism@unifr.ch

UNITED STATES

The Council of State Governments (Lexington, KY)

Dan Sprague, Executive Director
3660 Iron Works Pike
P.O. Box 11910
Lexington
KY 40578-1910

The Meyner Center for the Study of State and Local Government (Easton, PA)

Prof. John Kincaid, Director
002 Kirby Hall of Civil Rights
Lafayette College
Easton
PA 18042-1785
meynerc@lafayette.edu